Advances in Digital Marketing in the Era of Artificial Intelligence

This book highlights the technological advances that are transforming the future of digital marketing and covers important areas of research in this field. The book demonstrates advances in digital marketing as well as tools, techniques, methods and strategies based on artificial intelligence. It also identifies gaps in research into effective digital marketing tools, techniques and methods, and it bridges the interaction between digital marketing strategies and organisations' business plans, on the one hand, and customer relations, on the other, in the age of artificial intelligence.

This book presents the concepts and applications of digital marketing in the age of artificial intelligence to readers in a comprehensive manner. The book highlights the major breakthroughs and technologies in digital marketing for effective interaction, analysis, prediction and design to formulate the best strategy for a business by using artificial intelligence solutions. This enables specialists to apply advances in digital marketing in the age of artificial intelligence in the right way to serve customers and solve business problems in this competitive age.

Covering the intersection of marketing and artificial intelligence, this book is a first-rate reference and an indispensable resource for business leaders, academics, salespeople, marketing professionals, managers, business owners, researchers, practitioners, instructors, college and university libraries, students, consultants, businesspeople, computer scientists, and customer-focused institutions.

Advances in Digital Marketing in the Era of Artificial Intelligence

Case Studies and Data Analysis for Business Problem Solving

Edited by

Moez Ltifi

CRC Press
Taylor & Francis Group
Boca Raton London New York

CRC Press is an imprint of the
Taylor & Francis Group, an **informa** business

Designed cover image: © Shutterstock

First edition published 2025
by CRC Press
2385 NW Executive Center Drive, Suite 320, Boca Raton FL 33431

and by CRC Press
4 Park Square, Milton Park, Abingdon, Oxon, OX14 4RN

CRC Press is an imprint of Taylor & Francis Group, LLC

ISBN: 978-1-032-58511-6 (hbk)
ISBN: 978-1-032-58512-3 (pbk)
ISBN: 978-1-003-45044-3 (ebk)

DOI: 10.1201/9781003450443

Typeset in Times
by MPS Limited, Dehradun

Contents

Contributors

Kapil Ahlawat
Department of Management Studies
Graphic Era (Deemed to be University)
Dehradun, India

Komal Ahuja
MM Institute of Management
Maharishi Markandeshwar (Deemed to be University)
Ambala, India

Mansoor Alghamdi
Applied College
University of Tabuk
Tabuk, Saudi Arabia

Malek Alrashidi
Applied College
University of Tabuk
Tabuk, Saudi Arabia

Habiba Ben Ameur
Faculty of Economics and Management
Business Analytics and Decision Making Laboratory (BADEM)
University of Tunis
Tunis, Tunisia

Nadia Arous
Business Analytics and Decision Making Laboratory (BADEM)
Tunis Business School
University of Tunis
Tunis, Tunisia

Raneem Bennani
Higher Institute of Management
Sousse, Tunisia

Alia BesbesSahli
Higher Institute of Management
Sousse, Tunisia

Suyash Bhardwaj
Department of Computer Science and Engineering
Faculty of Engineering and Technology
Gurukula Kangri (Deemed to be University)
Haridwar, India

Khem Chand
Mittal School of Business
Lovely Professional University
Phagwara, India

Sachin Chaudhary
School of Computer Science and Applications
IIMT University
Meerut, India

Yaricsa Vilca Coaquera
Jorge Basadre Grohmann National University
Tacna, Peru

Pedro Pablo Chambi Condori
Department of Commercial Engineering
Jorge Basadre Grohmann National University
Tacna, Peru

Sachin Ghai
Department of Management Studies
Graphic Era (Deemed to be University)
Dehradun, India

Jamel-Eddine Gharbi
Laboratory for the Enhancement of Natural and Cultural Heritage
Faculty of Legal, Economic, and Management Sciences
University of Jendouba
Jendouba, Tunisia

Karima Ghzaiel
Department of Management Sciences
Faculty of Economics and Management
Monastir University
Monastir, Tunisia
and
LRM Marketing Research Laboratory
Faculty of Economics and Management
University of Sfax
Sfax, Tunisia

Mausmi Goel
School of Graduate Studies
Quantum University
Roorkee, India

Manel Hassairi
Department of Management Sciences
Higher Institute of Management of Sousse
Sousse University
Sousse, Tunisia
and
Applied Research in Business Relationships and Economics
ARBRE Laboratory
Higher Institute of Management
Tunis University
Tunis, Tunisia

Ahmad Hassanat
Computer Science Department
Mutah University
Karak, Jordan

Thouraya Hmidi
Department of Business Administration
College of Science and Humanities
Shaqra University
Shaqraa, Saudi Arabia

S. V. Annlin Jeba
Department of Computer Science and Engineering
Sree Buddha College of Engineering
Kerala, India

Manel Khadraoui
Business Analytics and Decision Making Laboratory (BADEM)
Tunis Business School
University of Tunis
Tunis, Tunisia

Bhupendra Kumar
School of Computer Science and Applications
IIMT University
Meerut, India

Parvathy S Kurup
Department of Computer Science and Engineering
Sree Buddha College of Engineering
Kerala, India

Moez Ltifi
College of Science and Humanities
Shaqra University
Shaqraa, Saudi Arabia
and
Higher School of Commerce
University of Sfax
Sfax, Tunisia

Sami Mnasri
Applied College
University of Tabuk
Tabuk, Saudi Arabia
and
CNRS-IRIT Laboratory
University of Toulouse II
Toulouse, France

Arvind Mohan
Department of Management Studies
Graphic Era (Deemed to be University)
Dehradun, India

Amrita Baid More
Department of Marketing
Prestige Institute of Management and Research
Indore, India

Rajneesh Panwar
School of Computer Science and Applications
IIMT University
Meerut, India

Kaouther Saied Ben Rached
Faculty of Economics and Management
University of Tunis
Tunis, Tunisia

Kewal Krishan Sharma
School of Computer Science and Applications
IIMT University
Meerut, India

Kirti Sharma
UITHM – Management Cluster
Chandigarh University
Ajitgarh, India

Nirmesh Sharma
Department of Management Studies
Quantum University
Roorkee, India

Pooja Sharma
IIMT University
Meerut, India

M. P. Singh
Department of Management Studies
Graphic Era (Deemed to be University)
Dehradun, India

Lilia Smida
Laboratory for the Enhancement of Natural and Cultural Heritage
Faculty of Legal, Economic, and Management Sciences
University of Jendouba
Jendouba, Tunisia

Rajesh Tiwari
Department of Management Studies
Graphic Era (Deemed to be University)
Dehradun, India

Thierry Val
CNRS-IRIT Laboratory
University of Toulouse II
Toulouse, France

Vandana
Department of Computer Application
Sir Chhotu Ram Institute of Engineering and Technology
CCS University
Meerut, India

Tarun Kumar Vashishth
School of Computer Science and Applications
IIMT University
Meerut, India

Sangeet Vashishtha
IIMT University
Meerut, India

Vineeta Verma
Department of Basic Science
College of Agriculture
Sardar Vallabhbhai Patel University of Agriculture and Technology
Meerut, India

Vikas
School of Computer Science and Applications
IIMT University
Meerut, India

Suchita Vishwakarma
IILM Academy of Higher Learning
Lucknow, India

Aicha Zaidi
University of Monastir
Mahdia, Tunisia

Preface

There is no doubt that today we are on the path of technologies that will perform many tasks that require, for now, the human brain to accomplish. We are experimenting with artificial intelligence (AI) in the commercial sector.

The "Le Robert" dictionary defines artificial intelligence *as "the set of theories and techniques for developing complex computer programs capable of simulating certain traits of human intelligence (reasoning, learning, etc.)".* We are therefore talking about systems capable of learning and making decisions.

Marketing is undoubtedly a field where it is crucial to follow technological developments in order to adapt. Artificial intelligence is the fact that a machine or a program performs tasks by imitating human cognitive functions. The fields of application of artificial intelligence are constantly expanding into ever wider areas. Today, many companies see artificial intelligence (AI) as the future of marketing strategy.

With its extraordinary ability to collect and analyze customer data, AI can have a huge impact on marketing strategy. It is increasingly being used by companies to meet marketing needs, such as directing e-mail campaigns, social media strategies, conversing with customers (chatbots), etc.

However, 61% of marketers say that artificial intelligence is the most important aspect of their data strategy. Still, 15% of companies expect to invest more in artificial intelligence in 2022.

Global spending on artificial intelligence (AI) is $77.6 billion in 2022, while its business value is $3.9 trillion. In addition, the McKinsey State of Artificial Intelligence survey shows that 50% of the companies surveyed have adopted artificial intelligence in at least one business function, mainly in service operations, product or service development, marketing and sales. In fact, 17% of those using AI are deploying the technology for customer service analysis and 14% for customer segmentation.

Finally, more than two-thirds of respondents who said they had adopted it in these areas said that its use had increased their revenue. Among these functions, the majority of respondents say they have increased their turnover for stock and parts optimization, pricing and promotion, customer service analysis and sales and demand forecasting.

Artificial intelligence technology not only increases revenue, but also improves conversion rates and customer experiences when shopping online. According to a study by "Evergage", when asked about the benefits of personalization through artificial intelligence, 63% of respondents mentioned increased conversion rates, while 61% confirmed improved customer experience.

Artificial intelligence is revolutionizing digital marketing. The evolution of digital and society is pushing developers to optimize and develop their algorithms by integrating artificial intelligence in order to perform and stay ahead of the curve. As people become increasingly impatient, curious and demanding of the information available on the internet, there is a need to find solutions to enhance their customer experience.

However, current research efforts lack explanations of the smart relationship between companies and customers based on artificial intelligence. Therefore, this book highlights the importance of studying technological solutions and advances in digital marketing in the age of artificial intelligence.

Keywords: artificial intelligence, machine learning, automated content creation, programmatic ads, chatbot, image recognition, blockchain, project automation

This edited book highlights the technological advancement that is transforming the future of digital marketing and covers important research areas in this field. This book demonstrates advances in digital marketing and artificial intelligence-based tools, techniques, methods and strategies. It identifies gaps in the research of effective digital marketing tools, techniques and methods and bridges the interaction between digital marketing strategies and business plan of organizations on the one hand and the relationship with customers on the other hand in the age of artificial intelligence.

This book presents the concepts and applications of digital marketing in the age of artificial intelligence to the readers in a comprehensive manner. It highlights the major breakthroughs and technologies in digital marketing for effective interaction, analysis, prediction and design to formulate the best strategy for a business by using artificial intelligence solutions. This enables specialists to apply the advances in digital marketing in the age of artificial intelligence in a way that is appropriate to serve customers in this competitive era.

The objective of this book is to study the advances of digital marketing in the smart relationship between companies and customers based on artificial intelligence by providing new scientific research avenues covering many application areas.

Moez Ltifi
Shaqra University, Saudi Arabia
University of Sfax, Tunisia

Editor

Moez Ltifi holds a doctorate in business administration, a research master's degree in marketing, a professional master's degree in negotiation and sales, a master's degree in marketing and a bachelor's degree in marketing. He is currently Associate Professor (HDR) in Marketing at Shaqra University in Saudi Arabia and at Sfax University in Tunisia. He has relevant academic and research experience in the field of digital marketing.

His research interests include consumer behavior, online shopping, attitude, satisfaction, trust, e-loyalty, acceptance of new technologies, retailing, banking marketing, mobile marketing, tourism marketing, governance, performance, branding, digital marketing, chatbot, blockchain technology and artificial intelligence.

Dr Ltifi is the author and co-author of several indexed, classified and impacted books and scientific articles. He has contributed to several conference proceedings. He is a reviewer for various international academic journals.

His most recent articles have been published in international peer-reviewed journals such as *International Journal of Bank Marketing, Management Decision, Management and Prospective, Journal of Global Marketing, International Journal of Law and Management,* Corporate Governance: *The International Journal of Business in Society, Journal of Knowledge Management, Journal of Air Transport Management* and *Future Business Journal.*

1 AI and Advertising

Unraveling the Dynamics of Consumer Behavior and Brand Engagement

Komal Ahuja
Maharishi Markandeshwar (Deemed to be University), Ambala, India

1.1 INTRODUCTION

Artificial intelligence has witnessed remarkable advancements in recent years, thanks to advances in machine learning techniques, natural language processing, computer vision, and big data analytics. AI has enormous implications in business, revolutionizing how organizations function, make decisions, and connect with customers. Businesses may improve operational efficiency, improve decision-making, personalize experiences, and remain at the forefront of their industries in the quickly expanding digital landscape by embracing AI technologies.

Artificial intelligence has become a game changer in the realm of advertising due to its ability to revolutionize the advertising industry and give better outcomes for advertisers. Marketers will definitely discover new and innovative methods to employ AI into their brand-building and advertising activities as technology evolves. AI has been a vital component for the success of the advertising industry, whether in ad-tech, CTV advertising, or personalization. Advertisers may increase the effectiveness and efficiency of their campaigns by leveraging the power of AI. Advertisers may offer more relevant and powerful commercials to the correct audience by employing AI, resulting in higher advertising effectiveness and a better return on investment.

The goal of this chapter is to investigate the impact of artificial intelligence (AI) on consumer behavior and brand engagement, as well as to examine how AI technologies are impacting consumer behavior and redefining brand engagement methods in the context of advertising. The purpose of this chapter is to provide marketers and advertisers with practical insights and advice on how to use AI to better understand customer behavior and increase brand engagement. It delves into best practices, difficulties, and opportunities for incorporating AI technologies into advertising strategies, with a focus on creating meaningful connections with customers and generating business outcomes.

1.2 SIGNIFICANCE OF AI IN ADVERTISING

AI is an exciting and advanced technology that complements a company's existing content strategy. From its previous depiction in science fiction, artificial intelligence has emerged as a tangible presence in our daily lives, transforming the way we shop, communicate, and engage with brands. With AI-powered technologies becoming increasingly prevalent, businesses must recognize its impact and adapt their strategies accordingly to meet the changing needs and expectations of consumers.

DOI: 10.1201/9781003450443-1

AI incorporates various technologies like natural language processing, machine learning (ML), deep learning, computer vision, and more. ML has a significant impact on the digital marketing landscape as it can analyze data and provide valuable analytical insights. This helps marketing teams conduct data-driven analyses based on customer needs. By utilizing AI tools, businesses can save time and allocate resources to other aspects of digital marketing. AI is an ever-evolving technology with wide-ranging implications, making it crucial for businesses to embrace it in their digital marketing efforts. By doing so, they can create meaningful connections with their target audience, foster innovation, improve productivity, and stay ahead in the rapidly evolving digital landscape.

It holds immense significance in the business world, revolutionizing how organizations operate, make decisions, and interact with customers. With its advanced algorithms and data processing capabilities, AI enables businesses to unlock valuable insights, improve operational efficiency, and deliver enhanced customer experiences. AI-powered analytics can analyze vast amounts of data in real time, uncovering patterns and trends that help businesses make informed decisions and identify growth opportunities. Machine learning algorithms enable businesses to automate repetitive tasks, optimize processes, and streamline operations, leading to increased productivity and cost savings. AI also plays a vital role in customer service, powering chatbots and virtual assistants that provide personalized and efficient support, improving customer satisfaction and engagement. Additionally, AI enables targeted marketing campaigns by analyzing consumer behavior, preferences, and demographics, allowing businesses to deliver tailored and relevant messages to their target audience.

By leveraging AI technologies, advertisers can deliver more relevant and personalized messages, improve customer experiences, optimize campaigns, and achieve better results. Embracing AI in advertising enables companies to stay ahead of the curve, adapt to evolving consumer behaviors, and ultimately drive business growth in a highly competitive market.

1.3 ROLE OF AI IN CONSUMER BEHAVIOR ANALYSIS

Consumer behavior encompasses the entirety of consumer decision-making, encompassing the choices individuals make regarding the purchase, consumption, and disposal of products and services. It extends beyond mere patterns of product and service purchases and influences various aspects of life, including decisions related to voting during elections. With the emergence of AI technologies, there is a remarkable capability to process data, analyze information, and offer valuable insights or knowledge-based solutions that serve the interests of organizations while enhancing consumer satisfaction. These AI-driven advancements have the potential to revolutionize how businesses understand and cater to consumer needs, ultimately leading to more effective decision-making and improved customer experiences.

The role of AI in consumer behavior analysis is instrumental in understanding and decoding the complex patterns of consumer decision-making. AI technologies provide powerful tools for collecting, analyzing, and interpreting vast amounts of consumer data. Machine learning enables teams to decode vast amounts of accumulated data, allowing them to extract valuable insights that aid in identifying target audiences, understanding customer preferences, conducting trend analysis, and crafting user-focused sales funnels. By leveraging machine learning algorithms, businesses can streamline their processes, saving valuable time and resources, while also optimizing their conversion rates. The ability to decode and analyze data through machine learning empowers teams to make data-driven decisions that enhance customer experiences and improve the likelihood of converting prospects into customers.

AI-powered predictive analytics further enhances consumer behavior analysis by forecasting future trends, enabling businesses to anticipate and meet evolving consumer needs. Predictive analytics is the process of using data to forecast future outcomes. This technique utilizes data analysis, machine learning, and statistical models to find patterns that could possibly anticipate future behavior. Organizations can use historic and current data to forecast trends and behaviors into the future with a great deal of precision. This includes analyzing historical customer data, including purchase history, browsing behavior, demographics, another relevant variables to identify patterns and correlations. For example, an AI model can discover that customers who have previously purchased certain products are more likely to make similar purchases in the future. With this information, marketers can actively target these customers with personalized recommendations or promotions for related products, increasing the likelihood of repeat purchases and maximizing customer lifetime value.

Additionally, AI facilitates sentiment analysis, allowing marketers to measure brand perception and sentiments in real time, assisting in effective brand management. For this, the AI algorithms are specifically designed and trained to comprehend and interpret human language, empowering them to accurately recognize emotions, context, and subtle nuances within customer feedback. By leveraging a combination of natural language processing techniques and machine learning algorithms, these AI systems can efficiently process and analyze vast amounts of textual data. As a result, businesses gain access to valuable real-time insights, enabling them to stay informed about customer sentiments and perceptions. For example, I algorithms can analyze social media posts, comments, and mentions to gauge the sentiments associated with a brand or campaign. By using natural language processing techniques, AI can classify social media content as positive, negative, or neutral, providing real-time insights into how consumers perceive the brand. Similarly, AI-driven chatbots and virtual assistants can employ sentiment analysis to understand customer emotions and sentiments during interactions. By analyzing the sentiments, marketers can identify frustrated or dissatisfied customers in real time and take appropriate actions to resolve their issues promptly. This innovation in technology transforms how businesses respond to client input, resulting in better decision-making, improved customer experiences, and more successful brand management tactics.

1.4 MAPPING THE CUSTOMER JOURNEY AND TOUCH POINTS

Tracing the path of consumer journeys and touch points: Tracing the path of consumer journeys involves mapping the stages a customer goes through while engaging with a brand or product. It initiates with the initial point of awareness and progresses through various stages until a desired action, such as a purchase, is taken. The customer journey typically consists of touch points, which are points of interaction between the consumer and the brand. These touch points can be online (website visits, social media engagement) or offline (physical store visits, customer service calls). By mapping this journey and identifying touch points, businesses gain a holistic view of how customers navigate their relationship with the brand. This insight is invaluable for tailoring marketing strategies, improving customer experiences, and optimizing interactions to guide customers seamlessly through the journey.

Examining patterns in consumer interactions and behaviors: Examining patterns in consumer interactions and behaviors involves analyzing the recurrent ways in which customers engage with a brand. This analysis extends to identifying common sequences of touch points, the frequency of interactions, and the type of content or products that seek the most attention. By investigating these patterns, businesses can reveal insights into consumer preferences, pain points, and the decision-making processes. For instance, if customers frequently visit a product page after engaging with a certain type of content, it suggests a significant association between content and product interest. Understanding these patterns firms may modify their marketing strategies to correspond with consumer behaviors, providing content and experiences that appeal to customers and lead them to make a purchase.

Recognizing pivotal instances for effective brand engagement: The term "pivotal instances" refers to critical moments within the customer journey where brand engagement can significantly influence buying behavior. These moments are frequently instances of decision or change, such as when a consumer is considering a purchase or evaluating options. It is essential to recognize these situations because they create golden opportunities for businesses to deliver relevant and powerful content. Businesses can recognize these occasions based on previous data and consumer behaviors by utilizing AI and data analysis. For instance, if consumers tend to abandon carts during the checkout process, businesses can intervene with personalized incentives to encourage completion. Recognizing pivotal instances enables businesses to optimize engagement strategies, delivering the right message at the right time, ultimately driving higher conversion rates and fostering positive brand experiences.

1.5 ETHICAL IMPLICATIONS AND CHALLENGES

Ethical implications and challenges in the context of AI integration present a complex and significant aspect of technological advancement. Advertising is only one area where artificial intelligence is becoming increasingly pervasive, raising serious questions about transparency, fairness, privacy, and the possibility of unforeseen effects. This interaction between AI's capabilities and ethical issues highlights the necessity for a careful analysis of the moral issues surrounding its application, especially in sensitive industries like advertising where consumer trust and societal influence are crucial.

Ethical implications and challenges arising from the integration of AI into advertising are critical considerations in today's digital landscape. These challenges include:

1.5.1 Transparency, Accountability, and Bias

Due to the opaque nature of AI algorithms employed in advertising systems, it can raise concerns about transparency and accountability. Advertisers must make sure that consumer-facing AI-driven judgments are clear and explicable. Additionally, careful control is necessary to prevent algorithmic bias, which could result in unfair targeting or discriminatory consequences, and to uphold ethical ad practices.

Legal and regulatory compliance: Due to the complexity of the laws and regulations governing privacy and data protection, it is important to be vigilant. The collection, processing, and use of customer data must be done in accordance with legislation like the General Data Protection Regulation (GDPR), which advertisers must abide with. Secure user consent, open data utilization, and respect for privacy rights are requirements for ethical Abuse.

Fairness and non-discrimination: AI-powered ad targeting and personalization, while enhancing engagement, can inadvertently reinforce stereotypes or discriminate against certain groups. Ensuring fairness is imperative to avoid perpetuating biases in advertising content. Striking a balance between personalization and safeguarding against discrimination requires careful consideration and algorithmic adjustments.

1.5.2 Impact on Vulnerable Consumers

The use of AI in advertising may have a negative effect on vulnerable or susceptible consumers. Advertisers must use caution to avoid exploitative or manipulative tactics that can sway consumer behavior against their best interests.

1.5.3 Sensitivity to Cultural and Contextual Differences

AI-powered advertisements may be sensitive to cultural and contextual differences. To prevent misunderstanding or offense, it is crucial to ensure that advertising content is sensitive to cultural differences and suitable for a wide range of audiences.

1.5.4 Data Privacy and Security

These are major concerns for AI-driven advertising. The primary ethical responsibility of marketers is to safeguard this data against breaches and to make sure that it is only used for legal purposes.

1.6 CONCLUSION

The integration of artificial intelligence (AI) into advertising represents a significant change in how brands engage with consumers and understand their behavior. This chapter has explored the multifaceted dynamics of consumer behavior and brand engagement in the context of AI-driven advertising. The rapid breakthroughs in AI technology have led to a new era where marketers can leverage data-driven insights, personalization, and real-time decision-making to create more meaningful and effective advertising experiences

AI's role in consumer behavior analysis, from data collection and predictive analytics to personalization and sentiment analysis, has been thoroughly examined. These AI-driven capabilities empower marketers to decode complex patterns in consumer decision-making, predict future trends, and deliver personalized content that aligns with individual preferences. Additionally, recognizing pivotal instances in the customer journey enables precise and effective brand engagement.

However, significant technical developments often bring with them ethical issues and challenges. This chapter has also highlighted the importance of addressing transparency, accountability, and bias in AI-driven advertising systems. Ensuring fairness and non-discrimination, complying with legal and regulatory frameworks, and safeguarding vulnerable consumers are essential ethical imperatives. Moreover, sensitivity to cultural and contextual differences and data privacy and security must be prioritized in AI-powered advertising.

1.7 RECOMMENDATIONS

1.7.1 Enhancing Transparency and Accountability

Advertisers and AI developers should prioritize transparency in AI-driven advertising systems consumers should be given concise explanations of the decision-making processes by AI algorithms. Furthermore, advertisers should establish accountability mechanisms to monitor and address potential biases or errors in the AI systems.

1.7.2 Ethics Education

Businesses that use AI for advertising should provide ethics education to their teams. Data privacy, ethical AI practices, and regulatory compliance should all be included in this training.

1.7.3 Regular Auditing and Evaluation

In order to detect and reduce biases and discriminatory effects, regular audits and reviews of AI algorithms should be carried out. Independent evaluations can offer important insights into the fairness of the system.

Consumer education: Advertisers should educate consumers about the advantages and limitations of AI-driven advertising. Consumer decision-making can be aided by transparent communication, which can also increase consumer trust.

Constant monitoring and adaptation: AI systems in advertising should be continually monitored and adapted to changing consumer behaviors and preferences. Regular updates and improvements are essential to maintaining effectiveness and ethical standards.

In conclusion, the amalgamation of AI and advertising has enormous potential for delivering highly personalized and engaging experiences to consumers. However, it also brings along with it profound ethical responsibilities. By embracing ethical AI practices, promoting transparency, and prioritizing consumer privacy and fairness, the advertising industry can harness the power of AI to build stronger relationships with consumers and drive long-term success while maintaining trust and credibility.

REFERENCES

Dawar N., and Bendle N. (2018). Marketing in the age of Alexa. Harvard Business Review, 96(3), 81–86

Dimitrieska S., Stankovska A., and Efremova T. (2018). Artificial intelligence and marketing. Entrepreneurship, 6 (2), 298–304

Haenlein M., and Kaplan A. (2019). A brief history of artificial intelligence: On the past, present, and future of artificial intelligence. California Management Review, 61 (4), 5–14

Kaplan A., and Haenlein M. (2019). Rulers of the world, unite! The challenges and opportunities of artificial intelligence. Business Horizons, 63(1).

Kumar V., Rajan B., Venkatesan R., and Lecinski J. (2019). Understanding the role of artificial intelligence in personalized engagement marketing. California Management Review 61 (4), 135–155.

Mugrauer A., and Pers J. (2019). Marketing managers in the age of AI: A multiple-case study of B2C firms. Master's thesis in Business Administration. UMEA University.

Qin X., and Jiang Z. The impact of AI on the advertising process: The Chinese experience. Journal of Advertising, 48(4), 338–346.

Scherer, M. U. (2015). Regulating artificial intelligence systems: Risks, challenges, competencies, and strategies. Harvard Journal of Law & Technology, 29, 353.

Wang, L., and Wenyang C. (2018). Online advertising programmatic buying: Technical thinking and process reengineering. Today's Mass Media, 26 (12), 100–102.

https://www.datatobiz.com/blog/artificial-intelligence-in-advertising.

https://www.sciencedirect.com/science/article/pii/S2666603022000136

https://www.sciencedirect.com/science/article/abs/pii/S0148296323004836

https://www.linkedin.com/pulse/unleashing-power-artificial-intelligence-digital-turning-oyejobi

https://linchpinseo.com/how-to-accelerate-your-advertising-with-artificial-intelligence/

https://ieeexplore.ieee.org/abstract/document/9455055

https://www.datasciencecentral.com/how-artificial-intelligence-has-influenced-consumer-behavior/

2 Enhancing Customer Experience through AI-Enabled Content Personalization in E-Commerce Marketing

Tarun Kumar Vashishth, Vikas, Kewal Krishan Sharma, Bhupendra Kumar, Sachin Chaudhary, and Rajneesh Panwar
IIMT University, Meerut, India

2.1 INTRODUCTION

In the digital age, where technological advancements are continuously reshaping the landscape of commerce, one prevailing truth remains: the customer experience is paramount. The realm of e-commerce, in particular, has witnessed an unprecedented evolution, revolutionizing the way businesses engage with consumers. Within this context, the fusion of artificial intelligence (AI) and content personalization has emerged as a transformative force, redefining the dynamics of e-commerce marketing and propelling customer experiences to new heights. This book chapter embarks on a comprehensive exploration of the multifaceted journey of enhancing customer experience through the revolutionary lens of AI-enabled content personalization in e-commerce marketing. The progression of customer experience has been a hallmark of the modern business landscape, shaped by the rapid advancement of technology, the expansion of digital platforms, and the changing behaviors of consumers. The traditional notion of shopping has metamorphosed into a complex web of online interactions, necessitating an intricate understanding of customer expectations. As consumers become more informed, empowered, and digitally connected, their demands for personalized, seamless experiences have intensified. The transition from mere transactions to experiential journeys has propelled businesses to seek innovative strategies that bridge the gap between customer desires and brand offerings.

2.1.1 The Essence of Personalization

In the ever-evolving landscape of modern marketing, the concept of personalization has emerged as a pivotal strategy, fundamentally transforming the way businesses connect with their customers. At its core, personalization revolves around the idea of establishing a deep and resonant connection with individuals, acknowledging their unique characteristics, preferences, and needs. This shift represents a departure from traditional marketing methods that often relied on generalized demographic categorizations, ushering in a new era where technology, specifically AI, plays a pivotal role in understanding and engaging customers.

DOI: 10.1201/9781003450443-2

Personalization, in its essence, seeks to create meaningful interactions that resonate with customers on a personal level. This approach recognizes the inherent diversity among customers and strives to cater to their distinct preferences and requirements. Unlike the traditional approach of categorizing customers solely based on demographic factors such as age, gender, and location, modern personalization harnesses the power of AI-enabled content personalization to delve much deeper into understanding individual behaviors and preferences. At the heart of AI-enabled personalization is the meticulous analysis of customers' digital footprints. These footprints comprise the vast trail of data left behind as customers interact with various digital platforms, products, and services. This includes their online search patterns, browsing habits, social media interactions, purchase history, and more. The beauty of AI lies in its ability to discern intricate patterns within this data that are often imperceptible to human marketers. By leveraging machine learning algorithms, AI can predict behaviors and preferences with an astonishing level of accuracy.

The predictive prowess of AI transforms the way businesses tailor their strategies. Instead of merely reacting to customer actions, AI empowers businesses to anticipate those actions. For instance, by analyzing a customer's consistent search and purchase history for outdoor adventure gear, AI can predict their interest in related products or experiences, enabling businesses to offer relevant recommendations even before the customer expresses their need. This proactive approach not only enhances customer satisfaction but also bolsters the likelihood of conversions. The ultimate goal of AI-driven personalization is to craft experiences that transcend mere transactions, forging deeper connections between businesses and customers. Armed with insights from AI analysis, businesses can tailor marketing messages, product recommendations, and user interfaces to align with each customer's unique preferences. This level of customization creates a more immersive and individualized journey for the customer, fostering a sense of connection and relevance (Figure 2.1).

2.1.1.1 The Convergence of AI and Content Personalization

This chapter delves into a groundbreaking convergence: the fusion of AI with content personalization, a union that holds immense promise for transforming personalized interactions within the realm of e-commerce marketing. AI, which draws its strength from vast datasets and sophisticated machine learning algorithms, has transcended its conventional role as a mere tool and risen to become a strategic catalyst. Through its prowess, it navigates the intricate landscape of customer behavior, deciphering complex patterns, and orchestrating customized experiences that resonate on both emotional and functional levels. This partnership transcends superficial personalization, aiming to not just meet but also anticipate customer desires, thereby amplifying engagement and nurturing brand loyalty. Picture an e-commerce platform that doesn't merely derive customer preferences from past transactions but also from their browsing history, social media engagements, and even their habitual time of day for online interactions. Powered by AI, this platform dynamically tailors its content, recommendations, and interactions to seamlessly align with the customer's distinct context. Whether through meticulously curated product suggestions, precisely targeted email campaigns, or instantaneous interactions facilitated by AI-driven chatbots, the landscape of AI-enabled content personalization orchestrates a harmonious symphony of engagement (Figure 2.2).

This symphony ensnares customers in an experiential journey that is expertly and exclusively crafted for them. The transformative impact of this amalgamation cannot be understated. AI's ability to discern underlying behavioral trends within a sea of data elevates personalization from a mere transactional interaction to an emotionally resonant experience. With AI as its backbone, e-commerce marketing morphs into a dynamic process of not only responding to customer cues but also predicting their needs before they surface. By analyzing a diverse spectrum of data points, AI can intuitively gauge a customer's preferences and inclinations, enabling marketers to tailor their approaches with a level of precision that was hitherto unimaginable.

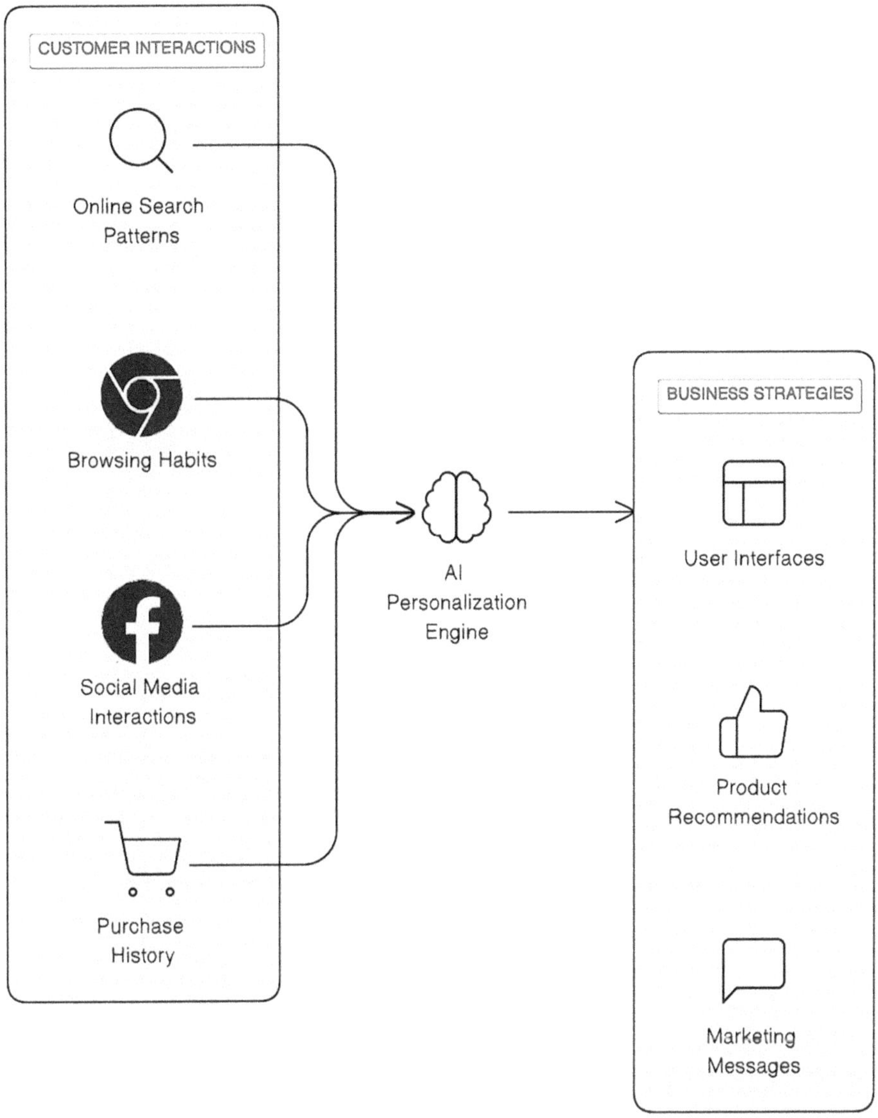

FIGURE 2.1 Artificial intelligence (AI), in understanding and engaging customers.

In the contemporary e-commerce landscape, the intersection of AI and content personalization augments the customer journey in profound ways. It transforms once-static touchpoints into interactive nodes that adapt and evolve in sync with the customer's preferences and habits. As this synergy continues to evolve, the potential for creating immersive, deeply personalized experiences expands, setting a new standard for customer engagement and loyalty in the e-commerce realm.

2.1.2 The Promise and Uncharted Territories

AI-enabled content personalization presents a multifaceted promise within the realm of e-commerce marketing, carrying the potential to revolutionize customer engagement and drive business success. This transformative approach not only enables businesses to differentiate themselves in a competitive digital landscape but also lays the foundation for building lasting customer relationships and achieving measurable returns on investment. Yet, the realization

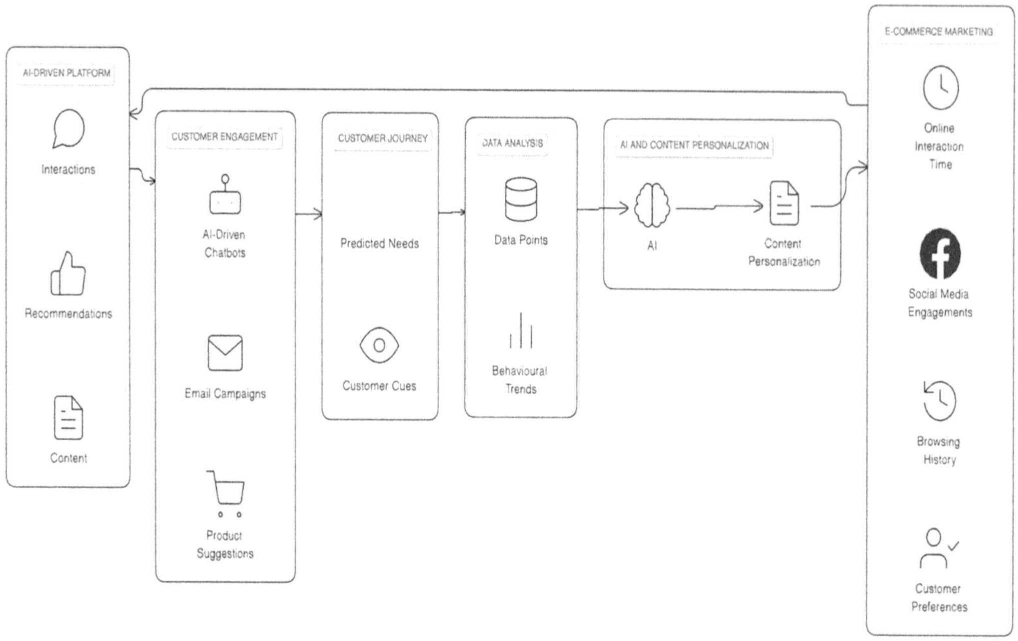

FIGURE 2.2 Fusion of artificial intelligence (AI) with content personalization.

of these opportunities necessitates a comprehensive exploration of various dimensions, taking into account ethical considerations, data privacy issues, and the delicate equilibrium between personalization and potential intrusion. At its core, AI-powered content personalization offers a means for businesses to truly connect with customers on an individual level. By analyzing diverse data sources ranging from online behavior to purchasing history, AI can decipher intricate patterns that reveal customer preferences and intentions. Armed with this insight, businesses can curate tailored experiences that resonate deeply with customers, transcending generic marketing approaches and driving higher levels of engagement.

However, while the potential benefits are compelling, ethical considerations must guide the deployment of AI-enabled personalization. Striking a balance between offering relevant content and safeguarding customer privacy is paramount. Transparency in data collection and usage, along with the ability for customers to control their data, becomes essential to ensure that personalization efforts are founded on mutual trust and respect. Moreover, the line between personalization and intrusion is delicate. AI's predictive capabilities can sometimes appear intrusive if not executed thoughtfully. Businesses must be vigilant in respecting boundaries, avoiding situations where customers feel their privacy is compromised or that their every move is being tracked. Striving for personalization that enhances user experience without making customers uncomfortable is a key challenge that marketers must navigate. Data security is another critical concern. As AI relies heavily on data analysis, businesses need to implement robust security measures to protect customer data from breaches or misuse. Ensuring compliance with data protection regulations is not just a legal necessity but also a fundamental ethical responsibility.

2.2 ENHANCED CUSTOMER SATISFACTION

Customer satisfaction is at the heart of any successful business, and in the context of e-commerce, it holds even more significance due to the absence of face-to-face interactions. Online shoppers often base their decisions on the quality of their digital experiences, making it imperative for e-commerce businesses to not only meet but exceed customer expectations. This is where AI-enabled content personalization emerges as a game-changer in the pursuit of enhancing customer satisfaction.

2.2.1 Understanding Customer Frustration and the Paradox of Choice

Imagine stepping into a massive department store with an overwhelming variety of products – clothing, electronics, home goods, and more. It's an exciting place, but it can also be bewildering. You may find yourself faced with numerous options, all differing in features, styles, and prices. While this variety is meant to cater to diverse preferences, it can often lead to decision fatigue and dissatisfaction. This phenomenon is known as the "paradox of choice," where having too many options can actually make customers less satisfied with their final decision. Now, transpose this scenario to the digital realm of e-commerce. Online shoppers encounter a similar conundrum – scrolling through pages upon pages of products, each vying for attention. The result is often similar – frustration, confusion, and sometimes abandonment of the shopping process altogether. This frustration stems from the difficulty of finding exactly what the customer needs amidst the vast sea of choices.

2.2.1.1 AI-Enabled Personalization: A Solution to Frustration

AI-enabled content personalization addresses this challenge by tailoring the shopping experience to the individual preferences and needs of each customer. By analyzing data gathered from a customer's previous interactions, browsing behavior, purchase history, and demographic information, AI algorithms can gain insights into their preferences, style, size, budget, and more.

Let's consider a practical example. A customer looking for a smartphone might have a preference for larger screens, an interest in photography, and a specific budget range. AI-enabled personalization takes these factors into account, presenting the customer with a curated list of smartphones that match their preferences. This saves the customer the time and frustration of scrolling through countless devices that do not meet their criteria (see Figure 2.3).

2.2.1.2 The Impact on Customer Satisfaction

The impact of AI-enabled personalization on customer satisfaction is multifaceted:

Relevance: By presenting products that align with a customer's preferences, personalization eliminates the frustration of irrelevant choices. This increases the likelihood of finding something that truly resonates with the customer's needs and desires.

Efficiency: Personalization streamlines the shopping process, helping customers find what they are looking for faster. This efficiency enhances the overall user experience and reduces the time spent searching.

Engagement: When customers encounter tailored content and recommendations, they are more likely to engage with the platform. This increased engagement leads to a deeper connection and a sense that the platform understands their needs.

Confidence: Personalization instils confidence in customers that the platform can cater to their preferences. This confidence fosters a positive shopping experience and encourages repeat visits.

Retention: Satisfied customers are more likely to return for future purchases and become loyal patrons. The personalized experience becomes a unique selling proposition that sets the platform apart.

2.2.2 Personalization as a Solution to Guide Customers to Relevant Products

In the digital age of e-commerce, the concept of personalization has emerged as a powerful tool to navigate the vast landscape of products and services. Personalization involves tailoring the shopping

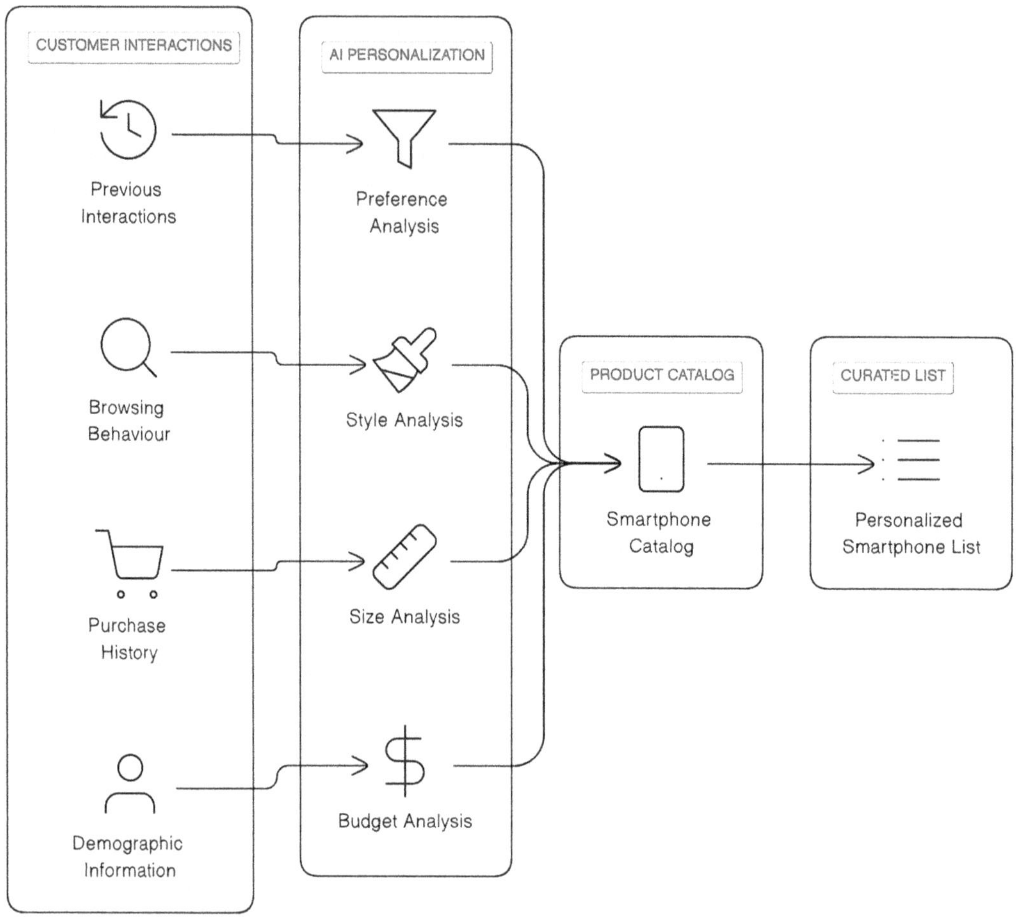

FIGURE 2.3 AI-enabled content personalization in the shopping experience to the individual preferences.

experience to match the unique preferences, behaviors, and needs of individual customers. It goes beyond the one-size-fits-all approach and seeks to provide customers with a curated journey that leads them to the products most relevant to their interests.The sheer volume of choices available to consumers in the online marketplace can often be overwhelming. This is where personalization steps in as a solution. By leveraging technologies such as AI and machine learning, businesses can analyze various data points, including past purchases, browsing history, demographic information, and even real-time interactions. This data-driven approach enables them to understand each customer on a granular level and make tailored recommendations. For instance, consider a customer who frequently shops for athletic wear. Through personalization, an e-commerce platform can showcase products like running shoes, workout clothing, and fitness accessories prominently in the customer's browsing interface. This not only streamlines the customer's shopping experience by eliminating the need to sift through irrelevant products but also increases the likelihood of a conversion (Figure 2.4).

In addition to product recommendations, personalization can extend to pricing, promotions, and even the layout of the website. A returning customer might be greeted with personalized discounts based on their previous purchases, enhancing their loyalty, and encouraging repeat business. Moreover, the layout of the website itself can adapt to suit individual preferences, displaying categories and products that align with the customer's demonstrated interests.

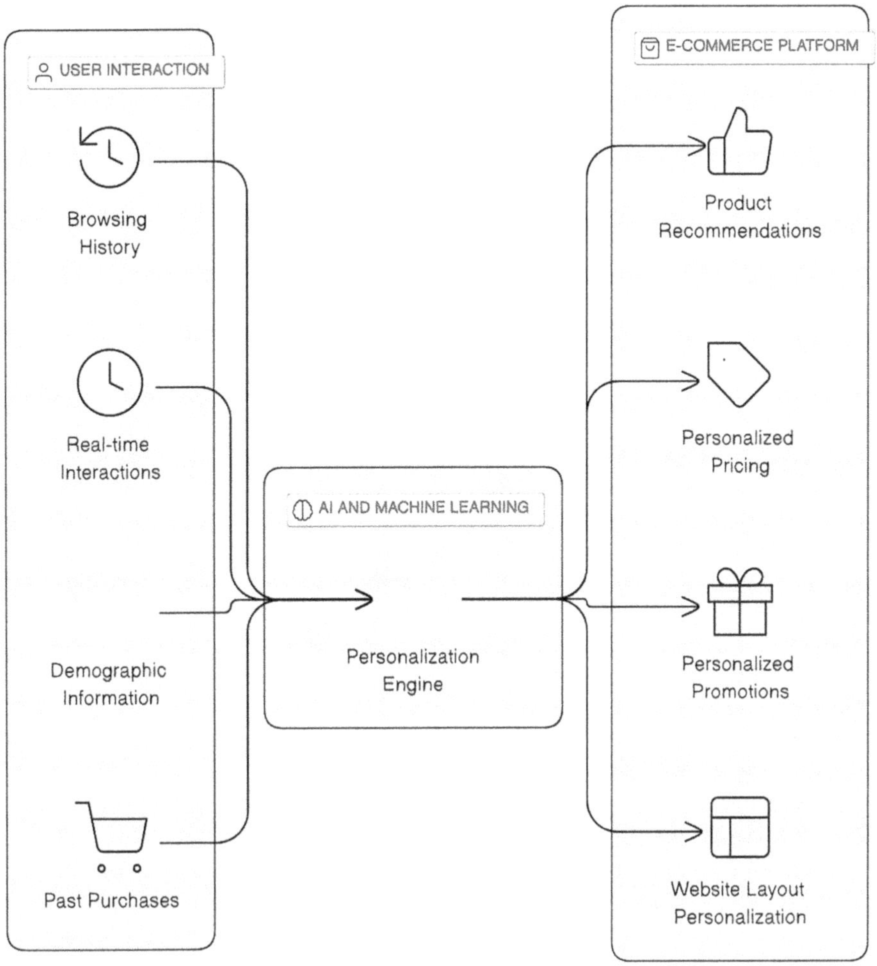

FIGURE 2.4 Leveraging technologies such as artificial intelligence (AI) and machine learning, businesses.

2.2.3 Customer Testimonials and Examples of Satisfaction-Driven Conversions

Customer testimonials and success stories play a pivotal role in building trust and credibility in the realm of e-commerce. These testimonials are real-life accounts of customers who have experienced a product or service firsthand and have found value, satisfaction, and positive outcomes. When potential customers are exploring a product, they often seek validation from others who have already made similar purchases. Customer testimonials provide social proof that the product delivers on its promises and meets customers' expectations. These testimonials can be in the form of written reviews, star ratings, video testimonials, or even before-and-after images. For instance, if a customer is considering purchasing a skincare product, reading testimonials from individuals who have achieved noticeable improvements in their skin texture and appearance can be persuasive. These stories offer relatable experiences that resonate with potential buyers and help them visualize the benefits of the product. Satisfaction-driven conversions, demonstrated through examples and testimonials, have a psychological impact on potential customers. They tap into the emotions of trust, validation, and the aspiration for positive outcomes. By showcasing how a product has solved real-world problems or fulfilled desires, businesses can create a sense of connection between the customer's needs and the product's potential to fulfill those needs.

2.3 LITERATURE REVIEW

In [1], Thandekkattu and Kalaiarasi delve into the realm of AI, spanning from its application in gaming to its integration into web applications. The study encompasses various facets of AI, including vision, predictive analysis, strategic implementation, and addressing uncertainties within AI models.

In [2], Fatima and Deepika present a CAPE model (Captivating Consumers by Using Chatbots for Interaction, Augmented AI Advertising, Personalized Content and Offerings, Engaging Consumers based on AI Data Insights), offering strategies for Indian e-commerce businesses and marketers to elevate customer engagement post-pandemic.

In [3], Verma et al. emphasize the significance of AI in marketing and outline potential directions for future research in the field.

In [4], Perez-Vega et al. present a conceptual framework that elucidates how firms and customers can improve the results of online customer engagement, both solicited and unsolicited, by employing AI-enabled information processing systems.

In [5], Song et al. provide an overview of the current status and future prospects of AI technology in e-commerce. The study delves into AI's applications in areas such as AI assistants, intelligent logistics, recommendation engines, and optimal pricing, using the case study of Baidu take-away for insight. The chapter explores the significant and impactful role of AI on the development of e-commerce.

In [6], Nimbalkar and Berad discuss the primary applications of AI in e-commerce, including the utilization of chatbots or virtual assistants, intelligent product recommendations, personalization, and inventory management.

In [7], Pallathadka et al. explore the applications of machine learning and AI in the realms of e-commerce, corporate management, and finance.

In [8], Wirth defines various forms of AI, including narrow AI, hybrid AI, and strong AI, and concludes by advocating the adoption of AI-based marketing insights solutions.

In [9], Cheng et al. contribute to an enhanced comprehension of organizational and customer behavior toward AI, encompassing privacy concerns, perceived benefits, and risks of AI-driven innovations in e-commerce, and the establishment of enduring trust relationships between users and AI.

In [10], Mahapatra et al. delve into the extent to which AI contributes to the success of customer consciousness intention to purchase and the customer journey in cognitive marketing.

In [11], Lari et al. aim to identify key applications of AI in E-commerce through a comprehensive review of research articles. The study concludes that AI significantly enhances the efficiency of E-commerce companies, driving increased investments to foster business growth and development in recent years.

In [12], Raj et al. delve into the essence of e-commerce and AI, elucidating their advantages and assessing the significance of AI's utilization in the e-commerce context based on existing research.

2.4 INCREASED CONVERSION RATES

Conversion rates are a fundamental metric in e-commerce, measuring the proportion of website visitors who take a desired action, such as making a purchase, signing up for a newsletter, or filling out a contact form. Enhanced customer experience through AI-enabled content personalization has been shown to significantly impact these conversion rates in a positive way. Here's how:

Relevance and Engagement: AI-enabled content personalization allows e-commerce platforms to present tailored content, product recommendations, and offers to each individual visitor. When visitors encounter content that aligns with their preferences and needs, they are more likely to engage with the website and explore further. This heightened engagement translates to a higher likelihood of converting, as visitors are more invested in the content that resonates with them.

Reduced Decision Fatigue: In a vast e-commerce landscape, visitors often face decision fatigue when presented with numerous options. AI-enabled personalization streamlines the decision-making process by presenting visitors with products that are highly relevant to their past behavior and preferences. This reduces the cognitive load on visitors, making it easier for them to make purchase decisions, which in turn leads to higher conversion rates.

Improved User Journey: A seamless and personalized user journey is a cornerstone of a positive customer experience. With AI-enabled personalization, visitors are guided through a journey that caters to their preferences and behaviors. This might involve showcasing products related to their previous purchases, displaying items frequently browsed, or even suggesting complementary products. This intuitive journey nudges visitors toward conversion by presenting them with options that align with their interests.

Dynamic Pricing and Offers: AI can analyze various factors, such as visitor behavior, purchasing history, and market trends, to dynamically adjust pricing and offer personalized discounts or promotions. Visitors who perceive value through personalized pricing are more likely to convert, as they feel they are receiving a deal tailored to their needs.

Abandoned Cart Recovery: Abandoned carts are a common challenge in e-commerce. AI-enabled content personalization allows businesses to send personalized reminders and incentives to visitors who abandon their carts. These reminders can include images of the abandoned products, personalized discounts, or even free shipping offers. By re-engaging with visitors who showed a clear intent to purchase, businesses can recover potentially lost sales and boost conversion rates.

Enhanced Trust and Loyalty: Personalized experiences foster a sense of connection and trust between customers and brands. When visitors perceive that a brand understands their preferences and needs, they are more likely to trust the recommendations and offers presented to them. This trust can lead to increased loyalty and repeat purchases, driving up the overall conversion rate of the e-commerce platform (Figure 2.5).

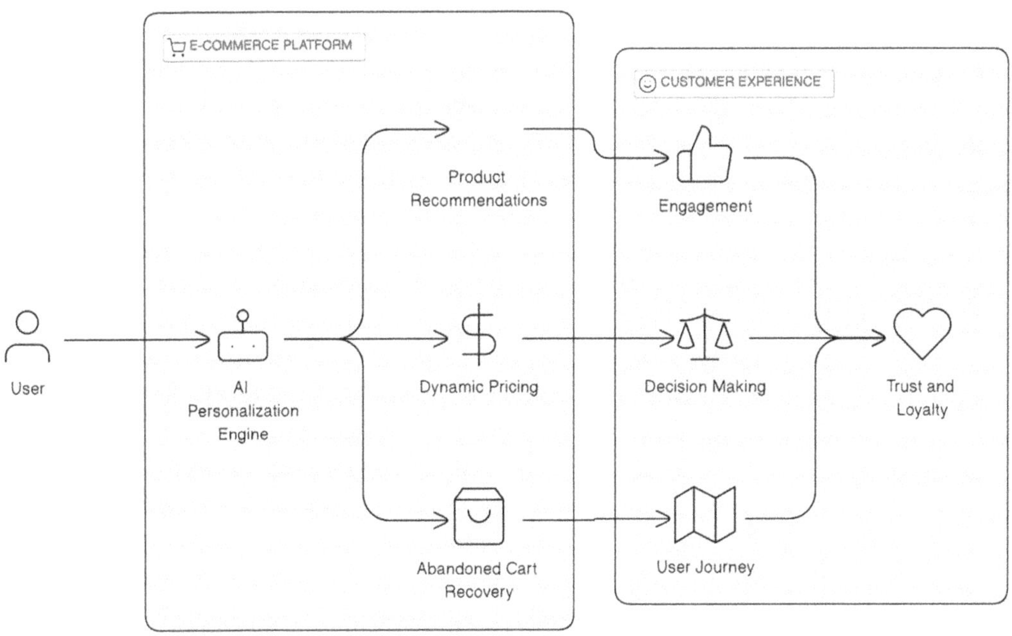

FIGURE 2.5 Enhanced customer experience and conversion rates through AI-enabled content.

2.4.1 Conversion as the Ultimate Goal of E-commerce Marketing

In the realm of e-commerce marketing, the ultimate goal is conversion. Conversion signifies the transformation of a visitor from a passive browser into an engaged customer by taking a desired action, typically making a purchase. The convergence of enhancing customer experience through AI-enabled content personalization amplifies the significance of conversion as the pivotal outcome in e-commerce marketing. Here's how this synergy is achieved.

Tailored Engagement: AI-enabled content personalization empowers e-commerce platforms to deliver highly tailored and relevant experiences to each visitor. By analyzing an individual's preferences, past behavior, and demographic information, the platform can present products, recommendations, and content that resonate with that specific visitor. This tailored engagement significantly increases the likelihood of capturing the visitor's interest, drawing them deeper into the purchasing journey.

Alignment with Customer Needs: Enhancing customer experience through personalization ensures that the content and products presented align with the customer's needs and desires. Visitors are more likely to convert when they encounter products that cater to their specific preferences and solve their unique problems. This alignment creates a sense of relevance and value, motivating visitors to take the desired action of making a purchase.

Emotional Connection: Effective e-commerce marketing does not solely focus on product features; it also aims to create an emotional connection between the customer and the brand. AI-enabled personalization allows businesses to understand customers at a granular level, enabling them to evoke emotions that resonate with each individual. This emotional connection fosters a sense of trust and affinity, influencing visitors to make the transition from passive observers to loyal customers.

Reducing Friction and Uncertainty: The e-commerce landscape is inundated with options, which can lead to decision fatigue and uncertainty among visitors. AI-driven personalization simplifies the decision-making process by presenting options that align with the visitor's preferences. This reduction in friction, combined with relevant content and recommendations, instils confidence in visitors' purchasing decisions, driving them toward conversion.

Creating a Seamless Journey: A well-crafted customer journey is a cornerstone of successful e-commerce marketing. AI-driven personalization ensures that visitors are guided through a seamless journey that caters to their unique preferences and behaviors. This cohesive experience minimizes distractions and hurdles, leading visitors along a path that culminates in conversion.

Higher Customer Lifetime Value: Conversion is not merely about the first purchase; it sets the stage for a lasting relationship between the customer and the brand. A positive initial experience, facilitated by AI-enabled personalization, increases the likelihood of repeat purchases and ongoing engagement. This subsequently elevates the customer's lifetime value, contributing to the long-term success of the e-commerce business.

2.4.2 How AI-Driven Recommendations Directly Impact Conversion Rates

AI-driven recommendations play a pivotal role in shaping the success of e-commerce businesses by directly influencing conversion rates. These recommendations leverage sophisticated algorithms and data analysis to suggest products and content tailored to individual customer preferences. Here's how AI-driven recommendations impact conversion rates within the context of enhancing customer experience through AI-enabled content personalization in e-commerce marketing:

Personalized Product Discovery: Traditional e-commerce experiences often involve customers sifting through numerous products to find what they are looking for. AI-driven recommendations analyze a customer's browsing history, purchase behavior, and preferences to present a curated selection of products that are highly relevant to them. This personalized approach eliminates the need for extensive searching, accelerating the discovery of products customers are likely to be interested in. As customers find products aligned with their preferences more quickly, the likelihood of converting increases.

Increased Relevance and Engagement: When customers encounter product recommendations that align with their preferences and needs, they are more likely to engage with the content. Engaged customers spend more time on the website, explore a greater range of products, and are more likely to proceed to the checkout page. AI-driven recommendations enhance relevance by considering a customer's entire digital footprint, leading to higher engagement rates and, consequently, improved conversion rates.

Cross-Selling and Upselling Opportunities: AI-powered recommendations not only suggest products related to a customer's current interests but also offer opportunities for cross-selling and upselling. By analyzing purchase patterns and complementary products, AI can recommend additional items that enhance the customer's purchase. This technique capitalizes on the customer's existing intent to buy and persuades them to consider related items, thereby increasing the average order value and boosting conversion rates.

Combating Decision Fatigue: A vast array of product choices can overwhelm customers and lead to decision fatigue, resulting in abandoned carts. AI-driven recommendations address this challenge by presenting customers with a manageable selection of products most likely to resonate with them. This tailored approach minimizes decision-making complexities, making it easier for customers to select products and proceed to checkout, positively impacting conversion rates.

Personalized Email Campaigns: AI-driven recommendations extend beyond the e-commerce platform to email marketing. Dynamic email content based on customer behavior and preferences enhances the effectiveness of email campaigns. Personalized product suggestions within emails increase the chances of customers revisiting the website and making a purchase. This continuity in personalized recommendations fosters a cohesive customer journey, leading to higher conversion rates.

Real-Time Adaptability: AI-driven recommendations continuously learn and adapt based on customer interactions. As customers engage with the recommendations and make purchases, the AI system refines its understanding of their preferences. This real-time adaptability ensures that recommendations become increasingly accurate and appealing over time, further improving conversion rates by providing more relevant suggestions.

2.4.3 Statistical Evidence of Conversion Rate Improvements with Personalization

The integration of personalization through AI-enabled content personalization has demonstrated substantial improvements in conversion rates within the realm of e-commerce marketing. Statistical evidence supports the transformative impact of personalized experiences on customer behavior and the subsequent conversion rates. Here's how statistical data showcases the effectiveness of personalization in enhancing conversion rates:

A/B Testing: A/B testing, also known as split testing, is a method used to compare two versions of a webpage or marketing campaign to determine which performs better. By implementing personalization in one version and omitting it in the other, e-commerce businesses can measure the conversion rates of each variant. Statistical analysis of the results can highlight the extent to which personalization positively impacts conversion rates. For instance, if the personalized version generates a significantly higher conversion rate, it offers concrete evidence of the effectiveness of personalization (Figure 2.6).

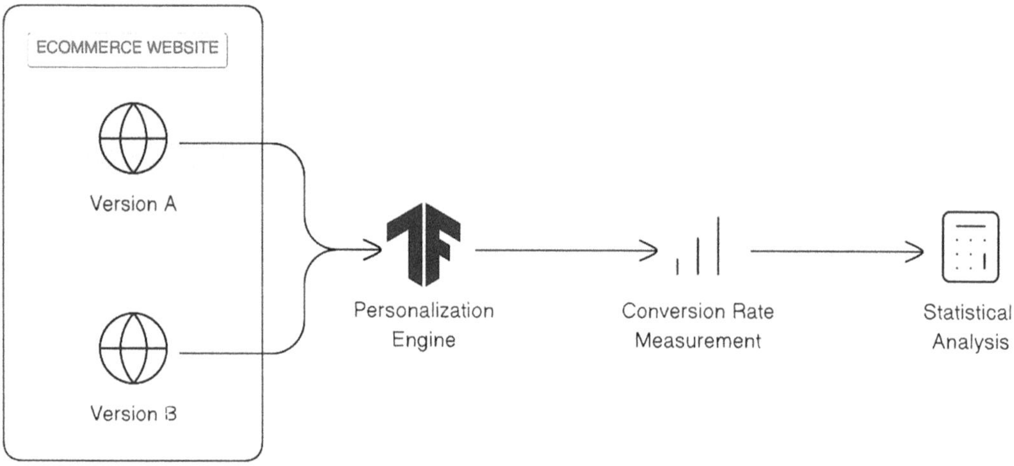

FIGURE 2.6 A/B Testing for concrete evidence of the effectiveness of personalization.

Case Studies and Industry Reports: Case studies and industry reports often provide quantitative data on the impact of personalization on conversion rates. These studies involve real-world examples where businesses have implemented AI-enabled personalization and subsequently observed improvements in their conversion rates. Sharing concrete numerical data and percentages showcases the degree of improvement and lends credibility to the effectiveness of personalization strategies.

Customer Segmentation Analysis: Personalization often involves segmenting customers based on various factors such as demographics, browsing behavior, and purchase history. By analyzing conversion rates within these segments before and after implementing personalization, businesses can determine the specific segments that experienced the most significant improvement. Statistical data that highlights increased conversion rates in targeted segments provides valuable insights into the effectiveness of personalization strategies.

Historical Data Analysis: Comparing conversion rates before and after the implementation of AI-enabled content personalization can provide compelling statistical evidence of its impact. By analyzing historical data, businesses can discern patterns and trends in conversion rates that coincide with the introduction of personalization. If a noticeable upward trend in conversion rates aligns with the implementation of personalization efforts, it establishes a causal link between the two.

Customer Surveys and Feedback: Surveys and feedback mechanisms can gauge customer perceptions of personalized experiences and their impact on conversion rates. By asking customers directly about their likelihood to convert due to personalized recommendations or content, businesses can gather quantitative data on the influence of personalization on conversion decisions. Analyzing survey responses statistically can provide insights into the correlation between personalization and improved conversion rates.

Comparative Benchmarks: Industry benchmarks provide context by comparing a business's performance to that of its competitors or the broader industry. Businesses that have effectively implemented personalization can outperform those that have not. Statistical analysis of such benchmarks can demonstrate the competitive advantage gained through personalization in terms of conversion rates.

2.5 BUILDING CUSTOMER LOYALTY

In the realm of e-commerce marketing, building customer loyalty is not just about making a sale; it's about establishing a lasting emotional connection between customers and brands. In this context, AI-enabled content personalization emerges as a powerful tool that not only enhances the shopping experience but also nurtures these vital emotional connections.

2.5.1 Nurturing Emotional Connections between Customers and Brands

Emotional connections go beyond transactional relationships. They stem from a sense of understanding, resonance, and alignment between customers' values and the brand's identity. AI-enabled content personalization contributes to this connection by creating experiences that feel tailored to each customer's preferences and needs.

When customers experience personalization in their interactions with an e-commerce platform, they perceive that the brand is taking the time to understand them. This perception cultivates a sense of care and consideration, forging an emotional bond. For instance, a customer who frequently shops for eco-friendly products might appreciate a platform that recommends sustainable options, demonstrating a shared commitment to values.

2.5.2 The Role of Personalized Experiences in Cultivating Brand Advocates

Personalization does not just enhance the shopping journey; it transforms customers into advocates. Advocacy involves more than making a purchase; it's about actively promoting the brand to friends, family, and peers. AI-driven personalization plays a pivotal role in this transformation.

When customers receive personalized recommendations that accurately reflect their tastes, they are more likely to share their positive experiences. They might post about their new finds on social media, write positive reviews, or recommend the platform to others. These actions not only serve as endorsements but also establish the customer as a trusted source of information for their network.

2.5.3 Real-World Instances of Brand Loyalty Driven by Content Personalization

Real-world examples showcase the tangible impact of AI-enabled content personalization in cultivating brand loyalty. Consider an e-commerce platform that specializes in skincare products. A customer who has a history of purchasing products for sensitive skin might receive tailored recommendations for hypoallergenic products. Over time, as this customer repeatedly receives spot-on suggestions, they build a sense of loyalty toward the platform. This loyalty extends beyond convenience; it's a loyalty grounded in the platform's ability to understand and cater to their specific needs (Figure 2.7).

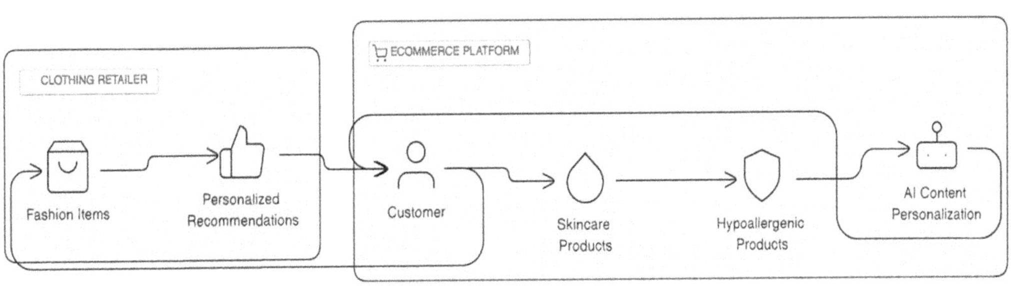

FIGURE 2.7 AI-enabled content personalization in cultivating brand loyalty.

Similarly, another scenario could involve a clothing retailer. A customer who consistently receives personalized recommendations for fashion items that resonate with their style preferences and size builds a strong affinity for the brand. This affinity translates into repeat purchases, an increased likelihood of exploring other product categories within the platform, and a willingness to engage with the brand beyond transactions.

2.6 OPTIMIZING MARKETING STRATEGIES

In the dynamic landscape of e-commerce, where competition is fierce and consumer behaviors are constantly evolving, optimizing marketing strategies is essential to stay ahead. AI-enabled content personalization serves as a powerful ally in this pursuit, offering insights and tools that enhance the effectiveness of marketing efforts.

2.6.1 Utilizing AI Insights for Refining Marketing Tactics

AI-driven personalization generates a wealth of data insights about customer preferences, behaviors, and interactions. These insights are invaluable for refining marketing tactics. By analyzing this data, businesses can understand what types of content, products, and messages resonate most with different customer segments.

For instance, an e-commerce platform selling fitness equipment might use AI insights to identify that a particular segment of customers is highly interested in home workout equipment. Armed with this knowledge, the platform can tailor its marketing campaigns to highlight relevant products, create targeted advertisements, and even craft personalized email content focused on home fitness solutions. As a result, marketing efforts become more impactful and engaging, directly speaking to the interests of specific customer groups.

2.6.2 Targeting Specific Customer Segments Effectively through Personalization

Gone are the days of the one-size-fits-all marketing approach. Consumers today expect messaging and offer that align with their unique preferences. AI-enabled content personalization enables businesses to segment their audience more precisely and target each segment with tailored content.

Continuing with the fitness equipment example, the platform could identify different customer segments such as beginners, fitness enthusiasts, and professional athletes. For each segment, personalized content could be created, showcasing relevant products, workout plans, and success stories. This personalized approach not only resonates with each customer group but also enhances the likelihood of conversion since the content directly addresses their interests and needs.

2.6.3 Maximizing Resource Allocation Based on Data-Driven Strategies

Resources are finite, and allocating them optimally is crucial for success. AI insights derived from content personalization can guide businesses in allocating their resources effectively. By analyzing which products or categories are most popular among different customer segments, businesses can make informed decisions about where to focus their marketing efforts and investments.Returning to our fitness equipment platform, if AI insights reveal that high-intensity interval training (HIIT) equipment is gaining traction among a particular customer group, the platform can allocate more resources to promote and develop HIIT-related products. This targeted approach maximizes the impact of marketing efforts, directing resources toward areas that are likely to yield the highest returns.

2.7 CHALLENGES AND ETHICAL CONSIDERATIONS

2.7.1 Data Privacy and Ethics

In the realm of AI-enabled content personalization, where data is the driving force behind creating tailored experiences, the significance of responsible data collection and usage cannot be overstated. This aspect extends beyond mere legal compliance – it delves into the ethical considerations that underpin customer trust and the integrity of e-commerce businesses.

2.7.1.1 The Importance of Responsible Data Collection and Usage

Data serves as the cornerstone of personalization, allowing businesses to gain insights into customer preferences, behaviors, and purchasing patterns. However, the collection and utilization of this data come with a responsibility to ensure that it is obtained with consent, used judiciously, and safeguarded against misuse. Imagine a scenario where an online retailer captures extensive customer data, including browsing history, location, and purchase records, without proper authorization. If this information is then exploited for targeted marketing campaigns without the customer's knowledge, it can erode trust and damage the brand's reputation. Responsible data collection emphasizes the necessity of obtaining explicit consent from customers, informing them about how their data will be used, and allowing them the option to control the information they share.

2.7.1.2 Adhering to Privacy Regulations and Maintaining Transparency

In an era of heightened privacy concerns, numerous regulations have been introduced to protect customer data. Examples include the European Union's General Data Protection Regulation (GDPR) and the California Consumer Privacy Act (CCPA). Adhering to these regulations is not just a legal obligation; it's a demonstration of a commitment to respecting customer privacy.

To ensure compliance, e-commerce businesses need to be transparent about their data collection practices. This transparency involves providing clear privacy policies that detail the types of data collected, the purpose of collection, how the data is processed, and the rights customers have over their information. It also includes obtaining affirmative consent for data collection and offering mechanisms for customers to access, modify, or delete their data (Figure 2.8).

2.7.1.3 Ensuring Ethical Handling of Customer Data in Personalization Efforts

The ethical dimension of data handling goes beyond compliance and extends to how data is used to shape customer experiences. AI-enabled content personalization has the power to influence purchasing decisions, and with great power comes great responsibility. Businesses must ensure that the use of customer data aligns with ethical principles and respects customer autonomy.

For instance, while personalization aims to offer recommendations that customers are likely to find appealing, it's essential not to manipulate their choices. By using AI insights to genuinely enhance the customer's shopping experience and provide relevant options, e-commerce businesses can maintain the integrity of personalization efforts.

2.7.2 Algorithmic Bias

As AI becomes increasingly integral to content personalization in e-commerce marketing, the issue of algorithmic bias comes to the forefront. Algorithmic bias refers to the unintentional favoritism or discrimination that can arise in AI models due to the data they are trained on. Understanding, monitoring, and mitigating algorithmic bias are critical to ensuring that AI-driven personalization remains fair, equitable, and unbiased.

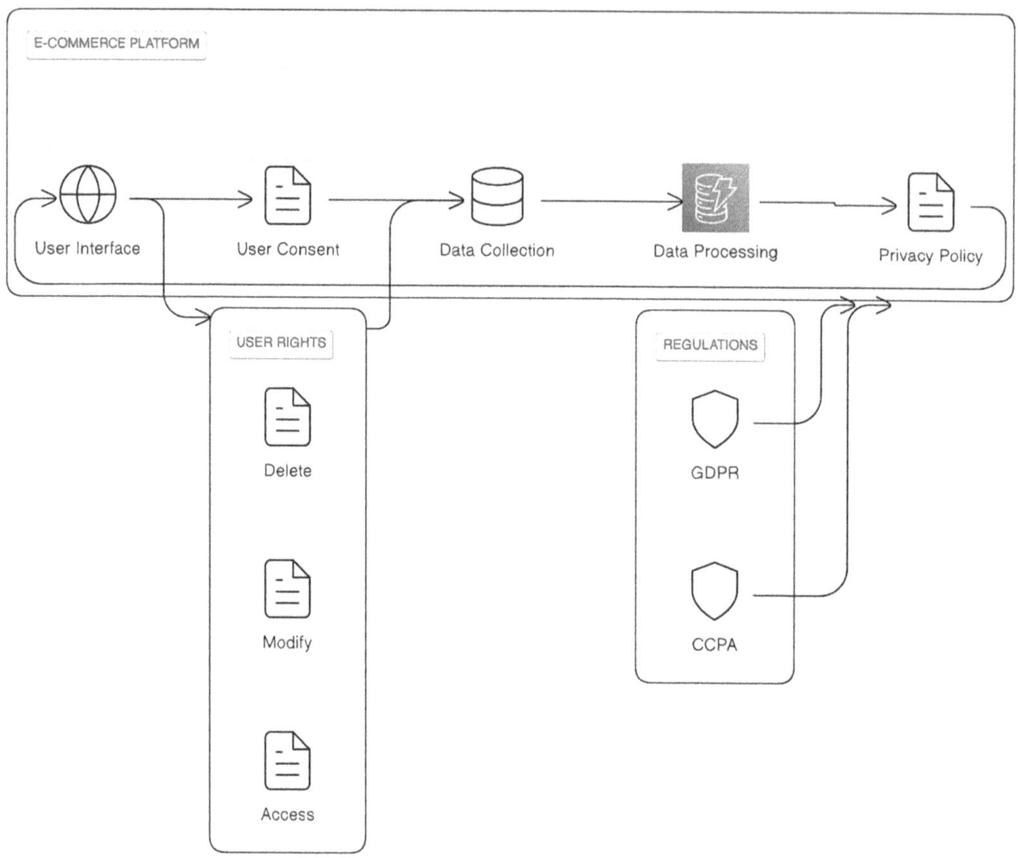

FIGURE 2.8 Regulations for demonstration of the commitment for respecting customer privacy.

2.7.2.1 Understanding the Potential for Bias in AI Models

AI models learn patterns and make predictions based on historical data. If this data contains biases or reflects societal inequalities, the AI model can inadvertently perpetuate those biases. For instance, if a training dataset for a fashion recommendation system predominantly includes images of people from a specific demographic, the AI model might struggle to accurately recommend fashion items for people from other demographics.

Algorithmic bias can lead to unfair treatment of certain customer segments, reinforcing existing disparities and potentially alienating customers. It is essential to acknowledge that bias is not always intentional but can emerge as a result of the data's inherent biases.

2.7.2.2 Monitoring and Addressing Algorithmic Bias in Content Recommendations

To tackle algorithmic bias, e-commerce businesses must be proactive in monitoring their AI models. Regularly analyzing the outcomes of personalized recommendations across different demographic groups can help identify patterns of bias. If certain segments consistently receive less relevant or less favorable recommendations, it's a sign that the AI model might be biased. Addressing algorithmic bias requires a combination of human oversight and technological interventions. This might involve revisiting the training data to ensure it is diverse and representative, creating more balanced datasets to train AI models, and implementing fairness-aware algorithms that actively counteract biases during the recommendation process.

2.7.2.3 Strategies to Mitigate Bias and Ensure Fairness in Personalization

Diverse and Representative Data: To mitigate bias, ensure that your training data is diverse and representative of your customer base. Include data from various demographics, geographic regions, and preferences to prevent the overrepresentation of one group.

Regular Auditing and Testing: Continuously audit and test your AI models for bias. Use metrics that measure fairness across different demographic groups and identify instances where recommendations might deviate from equitable outcomes.

Fairness-Aware Algorithms: Implement algorithms that actively counteract bias. These algorithms can adjust recommendations to ensure that no particular group is consistently disadvantaged.

Human Oversight: Incorporate human review into the recommendation process. Human reviewers can identify potential bias and ensure that recommendations align with ethical and fairness standards.

Transparency and Explainability: Make your AI systems transparent and explainable. Customers should have a clear understanding of how recommendations are generated, and they should be able to provide feedback on whether the recommendations align with their preferences.

2.7.3 Striking the Balance

In the pursuit of enhancing customer experience through AI-enabled content personalization, one of the critical challenges is finding the delicate equilibrium between automation and maintaining a human touch. Achieving this balance is paramount to ensure that while AI streamlines processes, it does not compromise the essential element of human empathy.

2.7.3.1 Balancing Automation with Maintaining a Human Touch

Automation, driven by AI algorithms, is invaluable for processing vast amounts of data, generating recommendations, and adapting to dynamic customer behaviors. However, customers still crave authentic interactions and human connections. Striking the right balance means leveraging the efficiency of AI while infusing the human touch to create a personalized and emotionally resonant experience. For instance, an e-commerce platform may use AI to suggest products based on a customer's browsing history and preferences. However, combining this with personalized messages from a customer support representative, offering assistance and genuine recommendations, can enhance the overall experience by making it feel more personable.

2.7.3.2 The Role of AI in Streamlining Processes While Preserving Empathy

AI is adept at handling repetitive tasks, sorting through vast datasets, and making rapid calculations. This capability allows it to free up human resources for tasks that require emotional intelligence and personalization. However, the challenge lies in ensuring that the efficiency of automation does not come at the cost of emotional resonance. AI can handle routine tasks like analyzing browsing behaviors to provide product recommendations. Meanwhile, humans can focus on addressing unique customer concerns, understanding individual preferences, and building rapport. This combination allows AI to enhance the efficiency of processes, while humans contribute their ability to connect on a deeper level.

2.7.3.3 Examples of Successful Human-AI Collaboration in Personalization

Virtual Stylists in Fashion E-commerce: Many fashion e-commerce platforms use AI to analyze a customer's style preferences, previous purchases, and fashion trends. While AI suggests outfits, a human stylist can step in to provide personalized advice, answer questions, and adjust recommendations based on the customer's emotional response.

Conversational AI in Customer Support: Chatbots powered by AI can handle routine customer inquiries, providing quick responses. However, if a complex or emotionally sensitive issue arises, a human customer support agent can seamlessly take over the conversation, offering empathy and tailored solutions.

Personalized Content Curation: Media streaming services often employ AI algorithms to recommend movies or songs based on user history. These recommendations can be enhanced by human curators who craft personalized playlists or collections that reflect the user's mood or special occasions.

2.7.4 Adapting to Changing Preferences

In the ever-evolving landscape of e-commerce, consumer preferences are not static; they shift and change over time due to trends, seasons, personal growth, and new experiences. Adapting to these changing preferences is a challenge that AI-enabled content personalization addresses, ensuring that recommendations remain accurate, relevant, and appealing to customers.

2.7.4.1 Acknowledging the Dynamic Nature of Consumer Preferences

Consumer preferences are influenced by a multitude of factors, including fashion trends, technological advancements, societal shifts, and individual experiences. What a customer loves today might not resonate with them tomorrow. Acknowledging this dynamism is crucial for maintaining engagement and relevance in an e-commerce environment. Consider a customer who frequently shops for tech gadgets. Their preferences might evolve as new technologies emerge or as their needs change. Without an adaptable approach, the e-commerce platform might continue recommending products that align with their past preferences but not with their current interests. This is where the ability to adapt becomes essential.

2.7.4.2 How AI Models Can Continuously Learn and Adapt to Evolving Tastes

AI models are designed to learn from data patterns, and this capacity for learning provides the foundation for adapting to changing preferences. Through machine learning techniques, AI models can identify shifts in customer behavior, track emerging trends, and adjust recommendations accordingly.In the context of the tech gadget shopper, the AI model can analyze their recent browsing and purchasing behavior to identify a shift toward a new category of products, such as smart home devices. By recognizing this change, the model can start tailoring recommendations to reflect the customer's evolving interests.

2.7.4.3 Ensuring Accuracy and Relevance of Recommendations over Time

The challenge is not just to adapt but to adapt accurately. AI models must ensure that they do not overreact to short-term fluctuations and that they accurately capture the customer's genuine preferences. This is where a balance between recognizing trends and understanding long-term shifts comes into play. To address this, AI models utilize techniques like reinforcement learning, which enables them to continuously fine-tune recommendations based on customer interactions and feedback. By leveraging historical data, the AI model can differentiate between passing fads and lasting preferences, ensuring that the recommendations provided remain valuable and relevant over time.

2.8 IMPLEMENTING AI-ENABLED CONTENT PERSONALIZATION

Implementing AI-enabled content personalization involves leveraging advanced technologies and data analysis to tailor digital experiences for individual users. This process harnesses the power of AI and machine learning to understand user behaviors, preferences, and patterns, thereby creating customized interactions that resonate on a personal level. Here's an in-depth explanation of how this implementation takes place:

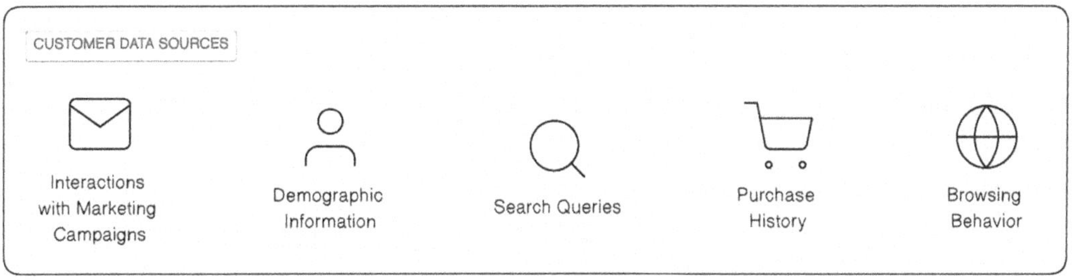

FIGURE 2.9 Identifying the various touchpoints where customer data is generated.

2.8.1 Holistic Data Collection

Holistic data collection is the process of gathering a comprehensive range of customer data from various sources to create a complete and accurate picture of individual preferences, behaviors, and interactions. This foundational step is essential for effective AI-enabled content personalization in e-commerce marketing.

2.8.1.1 Identifying and Collecting Relevant Customer Data Sources

The first step in holistic data collection is identifying the various touchpoints where customer data is generated. These touchpoints can include:

Browsing Behavior: Tracking the products customers view, the pages they visit, and the duration of their visits.

Purchase History: Recording past purchases to understand product preferences and buying patterns.

Search Queries: Analyzing the terms customers search for to identify their specific interests.

Demographic Information: Gathering data such as age, gender, location, and other relevant details.

Interactions with Marketing Campaigns: Tracking how customers engage with emails, ads, and promotions (Figure 2.9).

2.8.1.1.1 The Significance of Comprehensive Data for Accurate Personalization

The more comprehensive and diverse the data, the more accurately AI algorithms can predict customer preferences and behaviors. Imagine an e-commerce platform that only collects purchase history data but overlooks browsing behavior or demographic information. Such a limited dataset would hinder the platform's ability to understand the nuances of customer preferences and tailor recommendations accordingly. Comprehensive data allows AI models to recognize subtle patterns, identify emerging trends, and differentiate between short-term interests and long-term preferences. It enables the creation of detailed customer profiles that go beyond basic segmentation and provide insights into individual tastes.

2.8.1.2 Techniques for Data Aggregation and Organization

Managing and organizing the collected data is as crucial as gathering it. Techniques for data aggregation and organization include:

Data Warehousing: Storing data in centralized repositories, making it easily accessible for analysis.

Data Cleaning: Removing inaccuracies, duplicates, and irrelevant information to ensure data quality.

Data Integration: Combining data from different sources to create a unified view of customer interactions.

Segmentation: Dividing customers into groups based on shared characteristics for more targeted personalization.

Temporal Analysis: Analyzing how customer preferences change over time to adapt recommendations.

2.8.2 Algorithm Selection and Training

Algorithm selection and training lie at the core of AI-enabled content personalization in e-commerce marketing. The process involves choosing the right algorithms and machine learning models, tailoring them to specific objectives, and training them using historical data to predict and deliver personalized customer experiences.

2.8.2.1 Choosing Appropriate AI Algorithms and Machine Learning Models

Selecting the appropriate AI algorithms and models is a pivotal decision that directly impacts the effectiveness of personalization efforts. Various algorithms, ranging from collaborative filtering to content-based recommendations, offer distinct advantages based on the nature of the data and the desired outcomes. For instance, collaborative filtering algorithms analyze customer interactions to identify patterns and suggest products that similar users have enjoyed. Content-based algorithms, on the other hand, consider the attributes of products and match them to individual preferences. Hybrid approaches combine multiple algorithms to leverage the strengths of each. The choice depends on factors such as available data, customer behavior complexity, and the level of personalization desired.

2.8.2.2 Importance of Tailored Algorithms for Specific E-commerce Objectives

E-commerce businesses often have diverse objectives for personalization, ranging from increasing conversion rates to boosting average order values. The algorithms chosen must align with these objectives. A platform aiming to upsell might employ algorithms that analyze customer purchase history to recommend complementary products, while a platform focused on user engagement might leverage algorithms that curate personalized content.

Personalization algorithms should be adaptable to the business's goals and the evolving nature of customer behavior. This adaptability ensures that the AI models can continuously refine their predictions and recommendations based on new data.

2.8.2.3 Training Models Using Historical Data to Predict Customer Preferences

The training process is where AI models learn from historical data to make accurate predictions. Historical data includes information about customer interactions, behaviors, purchases, and preferences. This data is used to train machine learning models to recognize patterns and correlations that inform the generation of personalized recommendations. For example, a model can analyze a customer's past purchases, their browsing history, and the preferences of similar customers to generate recommendations. Over time, as new data is collected, the model refines its understanding, adapting to changes in customer tastes and preferences.

2.8.3 Real-Time Personalization

Real-time personalization is a dynamic approach to AI-enabled content personalization that involves delivering tailored recommendations to customers in the moment they engage with an e-commerce platform. This strategy requires implementing systems that process data on-the-fly, adapt to customer behavior, and enhance the overall user experience through instant and relevant content.

2.8.3.1 Implementing Systems for Delivering Real-Time Recommendations

Real-time personalization necessitates the integration of advanced AI algorithms and robust data processing systems. As customers interact with the platform – whether they are browsing products, adding items to their cart, or viewing recommendations – the AI system analyzes their actions and adjusts its recommendations instantaneously.

To achieve this, the platform must have a streamlined data processing infrastructure that can handle large amounts of data in real time. This involves efficient data pipelines, quick data retrieval mechanisms, and algorithms that can process and generate recommendations within milliseconds.

2.8.3.2 How Real-Time Personalization Enhances User Experience

The essence of real-time personalization lies in its ability to provide customers with instant gratification. As users engage with the platform, they receive recommendations that align with their current behavior and preferences. This eliminates the need for customers to search through extensive product listings, resulting in a more efficient and engaging shopping experience.

Imagine a scenario where a customer is exploring sneakers on an e-commerce platform. With real-time personalization, as they click on different sneaker models, the platform's AI system instantly updates the recommendations to showcase sneakers that are similar in **style or within** the customer's preferred price range. This immediate responsiveness not only saves time but also captures the customer's interest while it's still high.

2.8.3.3 Adapting Recommendations On-the-Fly Based on Customer Behavior

The real-time aspect of personalization extends beyond mere responsiveness. It involves continuously adapting recommendations as customers interact with the platform. This means that if a customer's preferences shift during their session, the recommendations shift accordingly.

For instance, if a customer initially explores camping gear but then starts looking at hiking equipment, the real-time personalization system should seamlessly adjust its recommendations to reflect the customer's evolving interests. This adaptability ensures that customers are presented with options that accurately match their current intentions, creating a fluid and intuitive shopping journey.

2.8.4 Continuous Testing and Enhancement

In the realm of AI-enabled content personalization, the journey does not end after implementing initial algorithms. Continuous testing and enhancement form a crucial iterative process that ensures personalization strategies remain effective, relevant, and aligned with evolving customer preferences.

2.8.4.1 The Iterative Process of Refining Personalization Algorithms

Personalization algorithms are not static entities; they evolve alongside customer behaviors and preferences. Continuous testing and enhancement involve a cycle of monitoring, analyzing, and refining algorithms based on the insights gained from customer interactions.

At the core of this process is the understanding that customer preferences are dynamic. What works effectively today might not resonate tomorrow. By frequently reassessing algorithms and adapting them to changing patterns, e-commerce businesses can ensure that their recommendations remain valuable.

2.8.4.2 A/B Testing and Its Role in Optimizing Personalization Strategies

A/B testing, a powerful technique in the arsenal of data-driven marketers, plays a pivotal role in optimizing personalization strategies. It involves comparing two versions of a webpage, recommendation system, or marketing campaign to determine which performs better.

For instance, an e-commerce platform might A/B test two versions of its homepage, each with a different layout of recommended products. By observing which version generates higher engagement, clicks, or conversions, the platform gains insights into which personalization approach is more effective.

2.8.4.3 Strategies for Analyzing Results and Making Data-Driven Improvements

Analyzing A/B test results and other data-driven insights is the linchpin of continuous enhancement. Here's a strategic approach:

- **Define Clear Metrics:** Establish metrics that align with your personalization goals, such as conversion rates, click-through rates, or revenue per user.
- **Collect Data:** Gather data from A/B tests and user interactions to measure the impact of different personalization strategies.
- **Analyze Results:** Examine the data to determine which version of a strategy yields better results. This involves statistical analysis to identify significant differences.
- **Iterate and Refine:** Based on the results, make informed adjustments to your algorithms. This could involve modifying recommendation algorithms, changing content placement, or adjusting messaging.
- **Monitor and Repeat:** Continuously monitor the impact of your refinements and repeat the process. Personalization is an ongoing journey, and frequent iterations are key to staying relevant (Figure 2.10).

2.8.4.3.1 Incorporating Customer Feedback

Customer feedback is a valuable resource that holds the potential to refine and elevate AI-enabled content personalization in e-commerce marketing. By actively listening to customer opinions, preferences, and suggestions, businesses can fine-tune their recommendations, foster deeper engagement, and align their strategies with customer expectations.

2.8.4.4 Leveraging Customer Feedback to Enhance Personalization

Customer feedback provides a direct window into their experiences, likes, dislikes, and aspirations. This information is a goldmine for refining AI-driven personalization. When customers share their thoughts on the products they have purchased, their satisfaction with recommendations, and the overall shopping journey, businesses gain insights that can guide improvements. For example, if a customer leaves a review praising a particular product recommendation that resonated with their needs, this feedback can serve as a positive affirmation that the recommendation algorithms are on the right track. On the other hand, if a customer expresses dissatisfaction with recommendations that did not align with their preferences, this feedback highlights areas for improvement.

2.8.4.5 Integrating Customer Suggestions into the Recommendation Process

Customer suggestions hold the potential to shape the direction of AI-driven personalization. Businesses can actively solicit suggestions from customers regarding their preferences, desired features, and the types of products they would like to see. By incorporating these suggestions into the recommendation process, businesses demonstrate responsiveness and create a more customer-centric experience.For instance, if customers express an interest in seeing more sustainable products within a specific category, the e-commerce platform can adjust its recommendation algorithms to prioritize these products. This not only aligns with customer values but also fosters a sense of involvement and partnership between customers and the platform.

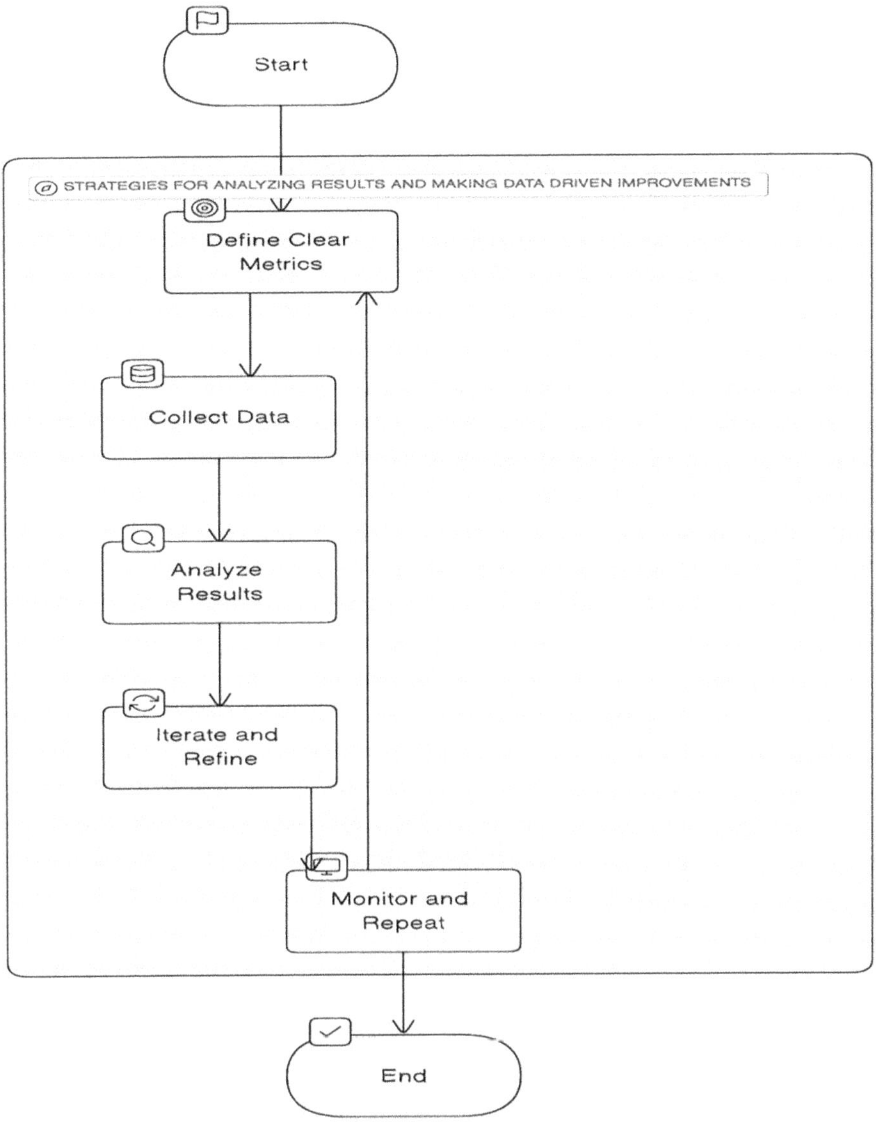

FIGURE 2.10 Data-driven insights are the linchpin of continuous enhancement.

2.8.4.6 Using Feedback to Align Recommendations with Customer Expectations

Customer feedback provides a reality check, allowing businesses to assess whether AI-driven recommendations align with customer expectations. When recommendations miss the mark, it's an opportunity to iterate and fine-tune the algorithms. By addressing these gaps, businesses can enhance the accuracy and relevance of recommendations. Consider a scenario where an e-commerce platform suggests unrelated products to a customer who frequently shops for home decor items. If the customer offers feedback indicating that the recommendations felt off-target, the platform can analyze this feedback to identify patterns and adjust its algorithms to deliver more pertinent suggestions in the future.

2.9 FUTURE ASPECTS IN AI-ENABLED CONTENT PERSONALIZATION IN E-COMMERCE MARKETING

As technology evolves and consumer behaviors continue to shift, the landscape of AI-enabled content personalization in e-commerce marketing is poised for exciting advancements. Here are some future aspects that hold promise for shaping the trajectory of personalized customer experiences:

Hyper-Personalization: The future of AI-enabled personalization lies in going beyond traditional segments and offering hyper-personalized experiences. AI will be able to analyze granular customer data to understand individual preferences and behaviors, leading to recommendations that are truly tailored to each customer's unique tastes.

Contextual Personalization: AI will be able to consider not only a customer's historical data but also their current context. This could include factors like location, weather, time of day, and even the customer's emotional state. This contextual awareness will result in recommendations that are not only relevant but also timely and situation-appropriate.

Multi-Modal Personalization: With the rise of voice assistants, virtual reality, and augmented reality, the future of personalization will likely encompass multiple modalities. AI will be able to provide personalized recommendations through different channels, adapting to the preferences and devices that customers use.

Ethical AI and Fairness: As awareness about algorithmic bias and ethical concerns grows, the future will see a heightened focus on building AI models that are inherently fair and unbiased. Ensuring that personalization efforts respect diversity and avoid discriminatory outcomes will become a top priority.

Predictive Personalization: AI will evolve to not only provide recommendations based on historical data but also predict future preferences and behaviors. This predictive element will enable businesses to proactively cater to customers' evolving needs, enhancing their shopping experiences.

Real-Time Adaptability: AI models will become more agile and capable of real-time learning. This means that recommendations can be adjusted on-the-fly as customers interact with the platform, ensuring that the personalization remains accurate and up-to-date.

Privacy-Preserving Personalization: As privacy concerns continue to grow, AI will need to find innovative ways to provide personalized experiences without compromising customer data. Techniques like federated learning, which trains AI models on decentralized data, will become more prominent.

Augmented Creativity: AI will work in tandem with human creativity, assisting in content creation and suggesting ways to enhance marketing campaigns. This collaboration will result in more innovative and effective personalized content.

Emotionally Intelligent Personalization: AI will advance to the point where it can gauge and respond to customers' emotional states. This will enable platforms to offer recommendations that resonate with customers' moods and emotional needs.

Integrated Shopping Experiences: AI will seamlessly integrate personalized experiences across various touchpoints, from online platforms to physical stores. This will result in a cohesive and immersive shopping journey for customers (Figure 2.11).

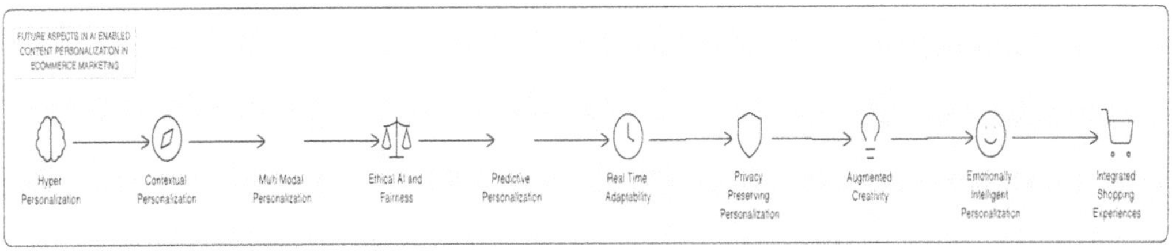

FIGURE 2.11 Future aspects that hold promise for shaping the trajectory of personalized customer experiences,

2.10 CONCLUSION

In the dynamic realm of e-commerce marketing, where customer preferences, behaviors, and expectations evolve at an astonishing pace, AI-enabled content personalization emerges as a transformative force. This synergy of AI and personalized experiences has reshaped the way businesses interact with customers, fostering connections that are both meaningful and efficient. Through this journey, several key themes have emerged.AI-enabled content personalization empowers businesses to transcend the boundaries of traditional marketing strategies. It bridges the gap between customers' desires and the products or services they seek, enabling tailored recommendations that resonate on a personal level. The ability to anticipate customer needs and curate offerings accordingly positions e-commerce platforms at the forefront of convenience and customer-centricity.

As data becomes the currency of the digital age, the ethical and responsible handling of customer information gains prominence. The safeguarding of privacy and adherence to regulations underscore the commitment to transparency and customer trust. Algorithms, while powerful, must not foster biases or manipulate decisions. Instead, they should reflect the values of fairness, diversity, and inclusion, ensuring that personalization transcends mere transactions to become a conduit for building lasting relationships. The journey does not end with technology; it embraces the human touch. The marriage of automation and empathy distinguishes exceptional e-commerce experiences. Customers seek authenticity and resonance – aspects that AI, in collaboration with human insights, can deliver. The future beckons with promises of hyper-personalization, contextual awareness, and predictive precision, signaling a path where AI evolves into an ever-attuned ally. In essence, AI-enabled content personalization is more than a marketing strategy; it's a philosophy that centers on the customer's journey. It's about not just meeting but surpassing expectations. It's about not just selling but forging relationships. As e-commerce continues its transformative journey, personalization stands as the beacon guiding the way – a beacon fueled by data, empowered by AI, and enlivened by the humanity that ultimately makes every interaction a remarkable experience.

REFERENCES

[1] Thandekkattu, Salu George, and M. Kalaiarasi. "Customer-Centric E-commerce Implementing Artificial Intelligence for Better Sales and Service." In Proceedings of Second International Conference on Advances in Computer Engineering and Communication Systems: ICACECS 2021, pp. 141–152. Singapore: Springer Nature Singapore, 2022.

[2] Vapiwala, Fatima, and Deepika Pandita. "Analyzing the Application of Artificial Intelligence for E-Commerce Customer Engagement." In 2022 International Conference on Data Analytics for Business and Industry (ICDABI), pp. 423–427. IEEE, 2022. 10.1109/ICDABI56818.2022.10041655

[3] Verma, Sanjeev, Rohit Sharma, Subhamay Deb, and Debojit Maitra. "Artificial intelligence in marketing: Systematic review and future research direction." International Journal of Information Management Data Insights 1, no. 1 (2021): 100002. 10.1016/j.jjimei.2020.100002

[4] Perez-Vega, Rodrigo, Valtteri Kaartemo, Cristiana R. Lages, Niloofar Borghei Razavi, and Jaakko Männistö. "Reshaping the contexts of online customer engagement behavior via artificial intelligence: A conceptual framework." Journal of Business Research 129 (2021): 902–910. 10.1016/j.jbusres.2020.11.002
[5] Song, Xia, Shiqi Yang, Ziqing Huang, and Tao Huang. "The application of artificial intelligence in electronic commerce." Journal of Physics: Conference Series 1302, no. 3 (2019): 032030. IOP Publishing. 10.1088/1742-6596/1302/3/032030
[6] Nimbalkar, A. A., and A. T. Berad. "The increasing importance of AI applications In E-commerce." Vidyabharati International Interdisciplinary Research Journal 13, no. 1 (2021): 388–391.
[7] Pallathadka, Harikumar, Edwin Hernan Ramirez-Asis, Telmo Pablo Loli-Poma, Karthikeyan Kaliyaperumal, Randy Joy Magno Ventayen, and Mohd Naved. "Applications of artificial intelligence in business management, e-commerce and finance." Materials Today: Proceedings 80 (2023): 2610–2613.
[8] Wirth, Norbert. "Hello marketing, what can artificial intelligence help you with?." International Journal of Market Research 60, no. 5(2018): 435–438.
[9] Cheng, Xusen, Jason Cohen, and Jian Mou. "AI-enabled technology innovation in e-commerce." Journal of Electronic Commerce Research 24, no. 1 (2023): 1–6.
[10] Mahapatra, Durga Madhab, Soumendra Kumar Patra, and Sukanta Kumar Baral. "Unleashing the Potential of Artificial Intelligence (AI) in Customer Journey of Cognitive Marketing and Consciousness Intention in E-Commerce Websites." In 2nd International Conference on Sustainability and Equity (ICSE-2021), pp. 44–51. Atlantis Press, 2022.
[11] Lari, Halima Afroz, Kuhu Vaishnava, and K. S. Manu. "Artifical intelligence in E-commerce: Applications, implications and challenges." Asian Journal of Management 13, no. 3 (2022): 235–244.
[12] Raj, S. S., Onyx Nathanael Nirmal, A. Kalaivani, Kismat Kaur, CGC CBSA, Punjab Author Mohali, Taranjit Singh Vij, and Y. Suryanarayana Murthy. "Artificial Intelligence in E-Commerce: A Literature Review." Artificial Intelligence 21, no. 01 (2023).

3 Redefining Marketing Strategies for Higher Education through AI Applications

A Critical Review

Suchita Vishwakarma and Sheetal Sharma
IILM Academy of Higher Learning, Lucknow, India

3.1 INTRODUCTION

The Higher Education (HE) industry is now operating as an open economy where the market is very competitive. The HE industry is referred to as a tertiary level of education, intending to provide multi-disciplinary and a variety of competitive courses. The HE industry has undergone radical changes over the last twenty years through technological disruptions (Caner, 2012). The AI interventions have transformed the Higher education sector. Marketing strategies related to student enrollment, student academic service and support, and student satisfaction management are being redefined with the help of AI based tools. Universities are compelled to market their services and products well to attract prospective students for enrollment and take care of the students' satisfaction.

The term AI was coined by John McCarthy who used the term artificial intelligence for the first time in 1956 (Russel & Norvig, 2010, p. 17). AI, according to Baker and Smith (2019), is "technology that accomplishes multiple tasks requiring decision making and analytical thinking akin to human minds" (p. 10). According to (Bates et al., 2020; DeMartini & Benussi, 2017) unlike any other sector, higher education (HE) will experience a significant and long-term impact of AI.

According to the Grand View research report published in 2022, the market size of AI was estimated to be US$ 119.78 billion globally and is expected to hit US$ 1,591.03 billion by 2030 with a registered CAGR of 38.1% from 2022 to 2030. The rising popularity of AI has been in all spheres of life, including the fields of medicine, automobiles, space and research, banking, manufacturing, daily use gadgets, and even gamification. During the last two decades, AI and adaptive learning technologies have been able to carve their position even in the field of education. The market for artificial intelligence in education is anticipated to reach US$ 32.27 billion by 2030, growing at a compound annual growth rate of 36.0% between 2022 and 2030 (Balderson Keelan, 2023).

In 2021, the market for AI in education was dominated by the higher education sector, which accounted for roughly 42.7% of global revenue. The high percentage of growth can be ascribed to rising academic standards and a shift in emphasis toward students' problem-solving skills, capacity for critical thought, and readiness for further education as well as career success (Figure 3.1).

DOI: 10.1201/9781003450443-3

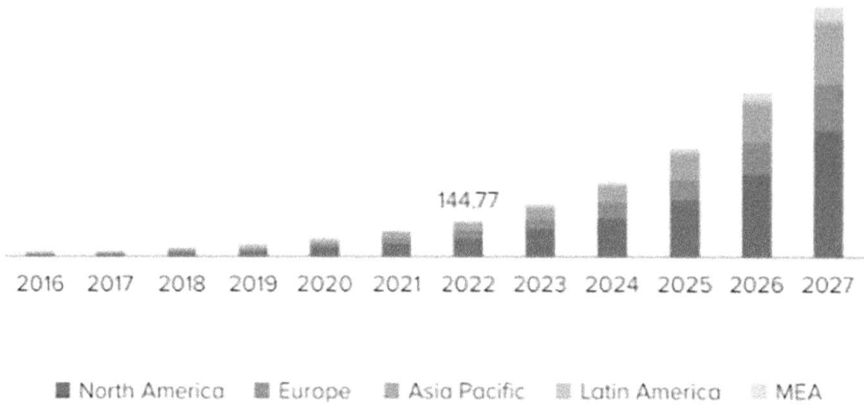

FIGURE 3.1 Region wise, Global AI market, 2016–2027 (USD Million).

Source: https://appinventiv.com/blog/10-ways-artificial-intelligence-transforming-the-education-industry/

UNESCO's Education Agenda 2030 aiming to provide fundamental values of equity and inclusion to all across the world, also seems to be possible only by harnessing the potential of AI technologies.

According to a research organization Tracxn, out of the approximately 300 Indian startups that are currently using AI in their core working and invention-related activities, around 11% of organizations lie in the category of Edtech industry (tracxn.com). According to Business Today, the Indian government is taking major initiatives in collaboration with NASSCOM to infuse AI into the Indian education system. The report states that by 2024, 47% of learning management tools adopted in the Indian education system will become AI-enabled and expects AI in the education industry to grow by a CAGR of 40.3% between 2019 and 2025 (IndiaAI Report, 2022).

This itself is a representation of the conviction on the power of AI in transforming HE ecosystem. The use of AI in higher education is primarily believed to be addressing educational inequality and ineffective assessments (Zawacki et al., 2019).

3.2 LANDSCAPE OF HIGHER EDUCATION IN INDIA

The All India Survey on Higher Education 2020–2021 released by the Indian Ministry of Education shows that the overall number of students enrolled in higher education climbed from 3.85 crore in 2019–20 to about 4.14 crore in 2020–21. NEP 2020 has set a target of raising the existing higher education GER from 27% to 50% by 2035. The data shows a progression of gross enrollment ratio (GER) of 7.5% from 2019–2020, to approximately 72 lakh (21%) during 2014–15. In the last few decades, the trend of education shows that India has played a role of leading sending country in the global education landscape. But in recent years this curve has slowed down. The stature of Indian education is now emerging as a destination for international students (Figures 3.2 and 3.3).

According to the recent educational reforms, the objective of prioritizing the higher education system can be broken down into a few overlapping objectives.

- The first is to increase access to higher education for all students within the nation, followed by retaining talented Indian students at Indian schools.
- The second objective is to attract students from overseas.

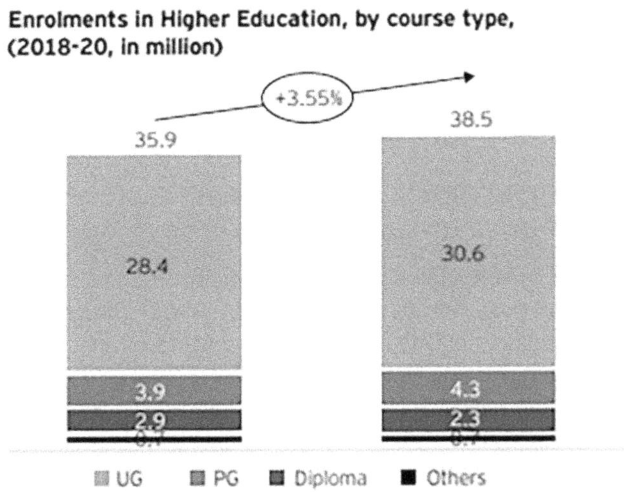

FIGURE 3.2 Enrollment in HE by course type.

Source: FICCI report on Higher Education in India: Vision 2047 by EY-Parthenon India Education Partner.

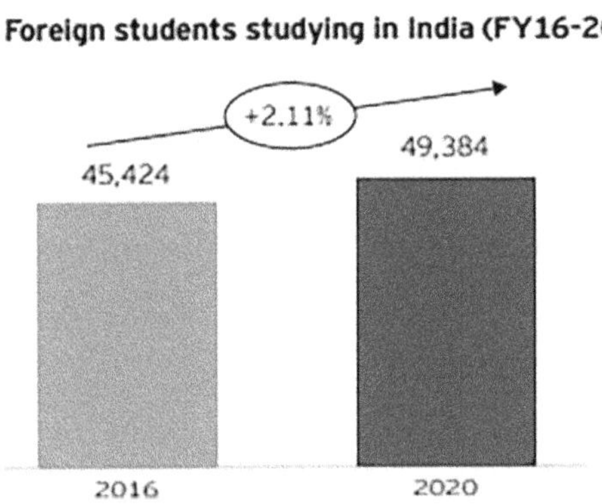

FIGURE 3.3 Foreign students studying in India.

Source: FICCI report on Higher Education in India: Vision 2047 by EY-Parthenon India Education Partner.

Higher education in India is characterized by both advancement and difficulties. Its reach is enormous, making it one of the largest higher education sectors in the world with 1,113 universities, 43,796 colleges, and 11,296 Standalone Institutions (AISHE report, 2023). Despite this, recent studies, reports, and feedback from businesses have raised concerns about the caliber of Indian graduates' talents. Bridging the gap between graduates and jobs is an additional challenge. According to the Indian Skills Report 2022, that was produced as a consequence of a recent study by Wheelbox, Taggd, and the Confederation of Indian Industry, graduates from Indian higher education institutions have employability skills below 50%.

The coronavirus outbreak at the beginning of 2020 further aggravated the challenge of equitable access to higher education in India. During the Covid period, the fast-worsening global health emergency negatively affected the students' educational plans. Universities were in a difficult situation that compelled them to change their projected enrollment projections right once and adopt more compatible teaching strategies. But at the same time, distance and MOOC education emerged as a solution to many of the problems. According to a report published by NAFSA in 2022, distance learning accounts for around 10% of the total enrollment in higher education in India. Thus, HE ecosystem in India needs to answer the following two questions to achieve the set targets under NEP:

1. What are some specific ways that can be used to improve the students' enrollment in higher education?
2. What are the various avenues which can be used in HE to improve the efficiency and outcome of higher education?

3.3 FINDING SOLUTION THROUGH THE MARKETING APPROACH FOR HE ECOSYSTEM

Education is a service being offered in the HE ecosystem. To remain competitive in today's dynamic environment, educational institutions must manage their marketing initiatives carefully. This would assist in persuading students, who are the customers, that the educational services offered by academic institutions are pertinent to their requirements. In order to impose the demand and desire, education providers must therefore consider the special qualities and advantages of their institutions and employ cutting-edge techniques to position themselves strongly. Marketing for education is thus designed as an innovation tool to help institutions build and consolidate their identity in the educational market (Mogaji & Yoon, 2019). Furthermore, educational marketing strategies aim to create and facilitate opportunities for customers-consumers, in this case students, to engage in democratic experiences of getting information, learning, and interaction (Khoshtaria et al., 2020).

Thus, the new age marketing strategies for higher education must be able to address the challenges and opportunities of this era in the two major goals of marketing:

i. Customer acquisition, in this case being student acquisition with the aim to increase the GER and
ii. Customer service and satisfaction, which in the case of education sector can be referred as students' engagement through the process of teaching, learning, participation, assessment, and skill development leading to enhanced employability opportunities for the student (Figure 3.4).

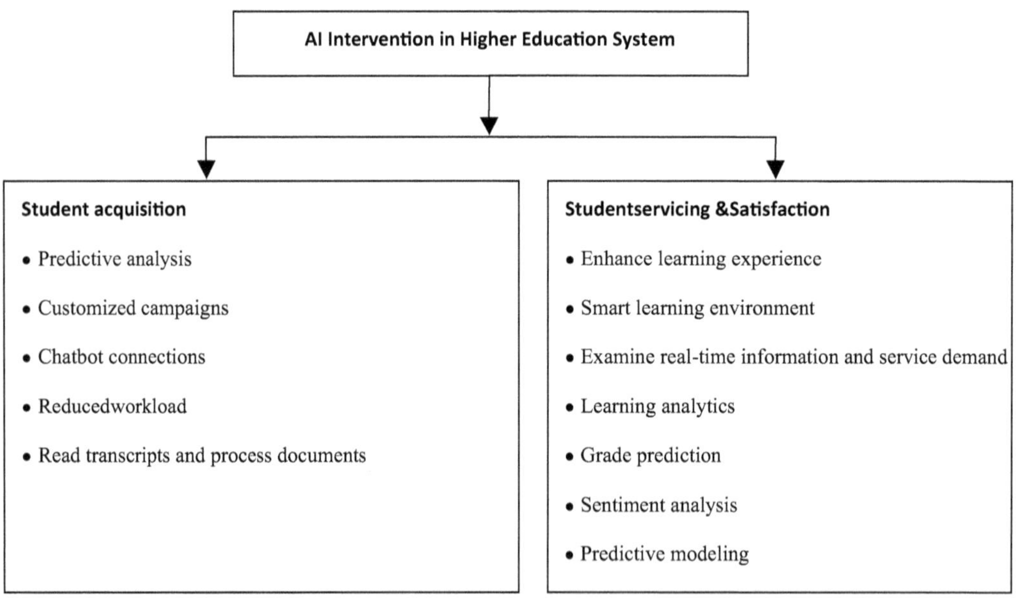

FIGURE 3.4 Conceptual model of AI intervention in HE (author's contribution).

3.4 LEVERAGING AI FOR STUDENT ACQUISITION

Acquiring customer is key to any business and so is for education. Organizations utilize AI to comprehend their consumers' requirements, tastes, and behaviors by using data and machine learning algorithms. This data can then be utilized further to develop customized marketing campaigns and sales experiences for each individual customer. So is the case in education too. AI is now increasingly being adopted by institutions to transform their marketing approach by allowing them to tailor campaigns, make data-driven decisions, and improve the entire student experience (Griol, 2014).

According to a recent IBM survey, more than 60% of Gen Z students prefer communicating with chatbots than dealing with human representatives. Chatbots have emerged as a vital service connection in the sector of education.

The University of Murcia in Spain reportedly deployed an AI-powered chatbot to facilitate regarding enrollment concerns and found that the chatbot displayed a high degree of expertise, answering over 38,708 questions correctly more than 91% of the time.

The process of admission and enrollment requires repetitive tasks to be administered. In this area application of AI can not only reduce the workload but also improve efficiency to a substantial level.

Many universities across the world have started using AI like the Georgia State University (GSU), which employs a chatbot called "Pounce" to help with admissions, financial aid, class registration, campus resources, and other tasks (gsu.edu). Berkeley Chatbot, an AI-powered chatbot at the University of California, Berkeley, is assisting students' enquiries. Other institutions following the same path include Deakin University and Staffordshire University.

Maryville University in Missouri has recently contracted to begin examining candidates' transcripts using Sia (a program from the business One Origin). The initial use of Sia would be the automation of reading the transcript, which would save a significant amount of time and allow the institution to focus on decision-making. According to Stephen W. Harmon, executive director of Georgia Institute of Technology's Center for 21st Century Universities, institutions are still experimenting with ways to harness AI (Globaladmissions).

The University of Denver is also using DUBot, a chatbot software tool that simulates a human, and assists in answering questions promptly. It provides instant help to the applicants by providing in-depth knowledge specific to the department. The university is also in the process to utlize AI in the next phase of implementation in its other academic and admin-related areas that includes parking, study abroad, ISSS, and University Libraries (du.edu).

3.5 INTEGRATING AI FOR IMPROVING SERVICE AND SATISFACTION IN EDUCATION INDUSTRY

Customer service is what a company does for the satisfaction of its customers, leading to higher profitability (Paul & Pradhan, 2019). According to Bovee and Thill, product quality and customer services are two important dimensions that project strong barriers against competition, and ensure customer loyalty, differentiate products, decrease marketing costs, and increase company's profit.

With the increased network of higher education ecosystems in India, competition has become intense. Thus, it is extremely critical for institutions of higher learning to enhance their customer service approaches. As per the marketing terminologies, all that a business does to ensure that its clients are satisfied is referred to as customer services.

Like any other industry, customer service in education entails supplying information (or assistance) while considering how to make the student's life easier (Harms, 2013), which would lead to student satisfaction. In the area of higher education, the student is the key to the entire value chain process. Student satisfaction in higher education (HE) is thus crucial for the performance of institutions as well as that of individual students, especially in the contemporary global environment (Butt, & Rehman, 2010).

Several studies were conducted in the past confirmed the existence of relationship between students' performance, learning process, and interaction with their satisfaction level (van Rooij et al., 2018).

Artificial intelligence (AI) has become a powerful tool in the age of technology, employed in a wide range of businesses to serve and meet the diverse needs of clients. AI has the potential to employs technology to examine real-time information and service demands by students across the world, utilizing data from all sources to offer customized solutions to students' inquiries or problems, even in case of exceptionally byzantine requirements.

The white paper of NITI Aayog's titled "Responsible AI" (2021) has brought the attention toward education as one of the sectors where AI has a high capability for solving societal needs. AI could enhance the learning experience of students through customized learning and assistance in analyzing the need for interventions for decreasing the dropout rate (Kasinathan, 2019). The use of AI in education has increased the accessibility to information and education across all students. It is considered a blessing for students who are residing in remote areas and for those students who are unable to attend physical classes due to any illness or injury. It overcomes the geographical barriers to learning and empowers students to learn from the best teachers in the world while sitting at home. It helps educators to identify gaps in the content and delivery (Lapina & Muursepp, 2016).

AI technologies are increasingly being used in educational institutions at all levels, from instruction to evaluation. Many educational institutions welcomed AI applications such as pedagogical agents, intelligent tutoring systems (ITS), smart learning environments, learning analytics, intelligent learning management systems (ILMS), and adaptive learning systems.

Many academic institutions in India too have started adopting AI in the entire process of education and not merely as one of the course offerings. According to *Indian Journal of Technical Education*, some institutions include IIT Kharagpur, the Centre for AI and Robotics connected with DRDO, the Robert Bosch Centre for Data Science and AI in IIT Madras, AI Group at IISC Bangalore and the Department of AI at IIT Hyderabad. The adoption of AI in education by Indian educational institutions is presently at a nascent stage and hence the implications and benefits are yet to be evident.

However, studies conducted in the west identified over 34,700 pupils who were expected to secure low grades were able to be managed and secured better grades owing to the AI grade prediction technology (Google Edu). Another incidence reported at Ivy Tech Community College in Indiana in 2016 using this technology observed that 98% of students who received support for intervention based on AI predictions earned a C or higher grades, while 80% of those who were not reached eventually failed as was expected.

AI can be customized to each student's unique requirements and talents. Knewton, an adaptive learning company that develops courses for higher education in the stream of STEM, has incorporated adaptive learning techniques to offer education content to tailor personalized lesson plans for students. In research conducted by Knewton, involving 10,000 pupils, it was found that the test scores increased by 62% because of AI.

Though not much work is available in this area to measure the actual impact, however, such studies do present that AI has the potential to measure and improve the learning outcome of students, especially in one-to-one settings (Dewan et al., 2018; McLeay & Yusoff, 2017).

3.6 CONCLUSION

The chapter aimed to provide a solution to the two major challenges faced by the Indian higher education ecosystem. The first being the opportunity to increase GER. In this perspective, it is important to understand that the potential of AI is huge in terms of processing information and offering customized solutions to students across the world. AI can also save time and be much more efficient, thereby providing the opportunity for educators to get involved into more creative decision-making to offer educational services which are more valued than the traditional ones.

The second objective of the chapter was to explore the avenues through which students servicing, engagement, and satisfaction can be improved. In this endeavor too, the HE institutions are required to benchmark its global competitors. Indian higher education ecosystem is currently at a very nascent stage of adoption of technology. With the current plan and policies regarding the transformation of education in India through implementation of NEP 2020, the fundamental requirement is to educate the stakeholders regarding application and benefits of AI. Apart from India, even at a global level, the adoption of AI, be it for teaching and learning or other administrative processes, is limited to a niche segment of institutes. The other few are still in the process of exploring the usage in limited functional areas.

However, this gives an opportunity for the countries and educational institutions to benchmark the ones which have started using AI as a tool to market their service (education) to students across the world and achieve better educational outcomes in terms of students' satisfaction and skill development. Admission is the critical success factor for any educational organization. The quantity and quality of enrollment decides the engagement and satisfaction level of students who are the key stakeholders. Wrong handling of the admission and post-admission process impacts the retention and satisfaction of existing students which in turn will impact the decision of the potential students and overall financial viability of institutions. Thus, careful consideration of AI in all its possible capacities may enhance the engagement of students across all levels of academic journey.

REFERENCES

AISHE Report (2023). Retrieved from https://aishe.gov.in/aishe/gotoAisheReports

Artificial Intelligence Market Size, Share & Trends Analysis Report By Solution, By Technology (Deep Learning, Machine Learning), By End-use, By Region, And Segment Forecasts, 2023–2030. https://www.grandviewresearch.com/industry-analysis/artificial-intelligence-ai-market. Last accessed online on June 1, 2023.

Baker, T., Smith, L., & Anissa, N. (2019). Educ-AI-tion rebooted? Exploring the future of artificial intelligence in schools and colleges. Last accessed on June 9, 2023.

Balderson Keelan (2023). 27 AI In Education Statistics You Should Know. Retrieved from mspoweruser.com (https://mspoweruser.com/ai-in-education-statistics).

Bates, T., Cobo, C., Mariño, O., & Wheeler, S. (2020). Can artificial intelligence transform higher education? International Journal of Educational Technology in Higher Education, 17(1), 1–12. Last accessed on June 7, 2023.

Butt, B. Z., & Ur Rehman, K. (2010). A study examining the students satisfaction in higher education. Procedia-Social and Behavioral Sciences, 2(2), 5446–5450.

Caner, M. (2012). The definition of blended learning in higher education. Blended Learning Environments for Adults: Evaluations and Frameworks, pp. 19–34.

Demartini, C., & Benussi, L. (2017). Do web 4.0 and industry 4.0 imply education X. 0? It Professional, 19(3), 4–7.

Dewan, M. A. A., Lin, F., Wen, D., Murshed, M., & Uddin, Z. (2018, October). A deep learning approach to detecting engagement of online learners. In 2018 IEEE SmartWorld, Ubiquitous Intelligence & Computing, Advanced & Trusted Computing, Scalable Computing & Communications, Cloud & Big Data Computing, Internet of People and Smart City Innovation (SmartWorld/SCALCOM/UIC/ATC/CBDCom/IOP/SCI) (pp. 1895–1902). IEEE.

Griol, D., Molina, J. M., & De Miguel, A. S. (2014). Developing multimodal conversational agents for an enhanced e-learning experience. ADCAIJ: Advances in Distributed Computing and Artificial Intelligence Journal, 3(1), 13–26.

Harms, B. (2013). Customer service in higher education: Adult-focused student services. Converge Consulting: A Higher Education Magazine. Available from www.academicimpression.comUSA

IndiaAI Report (2022). Retrieved from https://www2.ed.gov/documents/ai-report/ai-report.pdf

Kasinathan, G. (2019). Making AI Work for Indian Education. IT for Change. Retrieved from https://itforchange.net/sites/default/files/ 1 6 6 4 / Making -AI - Work - for - Indian - Education.pdf

Khoshtaria, T., Datuashvili, D., & Matin, A. (2020). The impact of brand equity dimensions on university reputation: An empirical study of Georgian higher education. Journal of Marketing for Higher Education, 30(2), 239–255.

Lapina, I., Roga, R., & Müürsepp, P. (2016). Quality of higher education: International students' satisfaction and learning experience. International Journal of Quality and Service Sciences, 8(3), 263–278.

McLeay, F., Robson, A., & Yusoff, M. (2017). New applications for importance-performance analysis (IPA) in higher education. Journal of Management Development, 36(6), 780–800. 10.1108/JMD-10-2016-018

Mogaji, E., & Yoon, H. (2019). Thematic analysis of marketing messages in UK universities' prospectuses. International Journal of Educational Management, 33(7), 1561–1581.

Paul, R., & Pradhan, S. (2019). Achieving student satisfaction and student loyalty in higher education: A focus on service value dimensions. Services Marketing Quarterly, 40(3), 245–268. 10.1080/15332969.2019.1630177

Report on 43 Examples of Artificial Intelligence in Education. University of San Diego. Retrieved from https://onlinedegrees.sandiego.edu/artificial-intelligence-education/

Russell, S. J. (2010). Artificial intelligence: A modern approach. Pearson Education, Inc.

Tracxn Report. Retrieved from https://tracxn.com/d/explore/ai-in-education-startups-in-india

UNESCO. Artificial intelligence in education. Retrieved from https://en.unesco.org/artificial-intelligence/education.

UNFPA Report (2023). Retrieved from https://www.unfpa.org/swp2023

University of Denver. Retrieved from https://www.du.edu/it/services/dubot

Van Rooij, E. C., Jansen, E. P., & van de Grift, W. J. (2018). First-year university students' academic success: The importance of academic adjustment. European Journal of Psychology of Education, 33, 749–767.

Zawacki-Richter, O., Marín, V. I., Bond, M., & Gouverneur, F. (2019). Systematic review of research on artificial intelligence applications in higher education–Where are the educators? International Journal of Educational Technology in Higher Education, 16(1), 1–27.

https://news.gsu.edu/2022/03/21/classroom-chatbot-improves-student-performance-study-says/

https://www.nafsa.org/ie-magazine/2022/4/12/indias-higher-education-landscape

4 Enhancing Customer Targeting in E-Commerce and Digital Marketing through AI-Driven Personalization Strategies

Suyash Bhardwaj
Gurukula Kangri (Deemed to be University), Haridwar, India

Nirmesh Sharma and Mausmi Goel
Quantum University, Roorkee, India

Vandana
CCS University, Meerut, India

Kirti Sharma
Chandigarh University, Ajitgarh, India

Vineeta Verma
Sardar Vallabhbhai Patel University of Agriculture and Technology, Meerut, India

4.1 INTRODUCTION

Artificial intelligence (AI) has emerged as a disruptive force in today's quickly expanding digital economy, where online firms are always exploring novel tactics to engage and keep clients. Among its numerous uses, AI-driven customization tactics stand out, altering how e-commerce and digital marketing interact with customers [1].

The integration of e-commerce and digital marketing has become critical to the success of companies seeking to develop a worldwide presence. The capacity to properly target and engage clients has become a strategic priority in this symbiosis. Consumers are overloaded with options, and businesses confront the difficult job of differentiating themselves while effectively engaging their audience. AI-driven personalization techniques serve as a guiding light for organizations navigating this challenging landscape. AI-driven customization tactics, which are based on machine learning and data analytics concepts, cover a wide range of methodologies. These methods use AI algorithms to examine massive information, deconstruct client behaviors, and determine individual preferences with unrivaled precision. AI-driven customization is the foundation of modern digital marketing tactics, from proposing personalized items and personalizing marketing messages to anticipating customer attrition and optimizing marketing campaigns [2].

DOI: 10.1201/9781003450443-4

This research work investigates various aspects of this paradigm shift ranging from the mechanics of recommender systems and the prowess of natural language processing (NLP) in content personalization to the insights gained through machine learning and predictive analytics [3]. AI-powered customization methods emphasize its place as a cornerstone of modern digital marketing. The tremendous impact of AI on improving consumer targeting demonstrates technology's transformational potential in determining the future of e-commerce and digital marketing [4].

In this chapter, we embark on a comprehensive exploration of AI-driven personalization strategies in the domains of e-commerce and digital marketing. We commence with an introduction, investigating the evolution of digital marketing and outlining the chapter's objectives. Following this foundation, we explore into the core theme of customer targeting in e-commerce and digital marketing, emphasizing its pivotal importance and the challenges that businesses encounter. The subsequent section focuses on AI-driven personalization techniques, including recommender systems, natural language processing (NLP), machine learning, and chatbots, elucidating their profound impact on customer engagement. We scrutinize the opportunities and challenges that arise from the integration of AI in digital marketing and e-commerce. In the next part, the chapter proceeds to explore the tangible impact of AI on product sales, encompassing enhanced conversion rates, reduced cart abandonment, and heightened customer loyalty. Subsequently, a thorough literature review offers insights into personalized recommendations, predictive analytics, NLP for content personalization, testing and optimization, and customer churn prediction. Ethical considerations take center stage, covering transparency, data privacy, informed consent, bias mitigation, user control, algorithmic accountability, and long-term customer value. Finally, we conclude by summarizing key takeaways and emphasizing the evolving landscape of AI-driven personalization in the digital age.

4.1.1 Evolution of Digital Marketing

The growth of digital marketing has been a revolutionary journey propelled by technology advancements and changes in customer behavior. It all started with the internet, which significantly altered marketing practises. According to [5], the internet signaled the change from traditional marketing to a digital-centric strategy. This development paved the way for firms to communicate with their target customers via websites and email marketing. The digital marketing scene, on the other hand, has continued to change. The expansion of internet channels, social media platforms, and the pervasiveness of mobile devices expanded the field's scope. In a research conducted by [6], on the influence of social media advertising, focusing on its function in engaging customers and fostering brand loyalty, it is observed that digital marketing has a great impact on product sales. Similarly, [1] investigate the importance of mobile marketing in reaching on-the-go customers.

Data-driven marketing has emerged as yet another milestone in the growth of digital marketing. In a work presented by [7], the authors have discussed how the availability of big data and advanced analytics technologies enabled firms to make educated decisions and offer highly personalized content to their target consumers. The evolution of digital marketing, as underlined by [5,6], [1], and [7], emphasizes the need for continual adaptation in this dynamic industry. From the internet's inception to the era of social media, mobile marketing, and data-driven strategies, digital marketing has evolved into a multifaceted discipline that demands ongoing innovation and a deep understanding of consumer preferences and behaviors.

4.1.1.1 Objectives

The primary objectives of this chapter are as follows:

- To understand the importance of customer targeting in e-commerce and digital marketing.
- To explore the various AI-driven personalization techniques available.

- To analyze the impact of AI-driven personalization on product sales.
- To assess the effectiveness of AI-driven personalization in digital marketing campaigns.

4.2 CUSTOMER TARGETING IN E-COMMERCE AND DIGITAL MARKETING

Customer targeting is a tactical approach used in e-commerce and digital marketing with the goal of locating and interacting with particular consumer categories most likely to become consumers. It entails a variety of methods and tools, including data analysis, machine learning algorithms, and the distribution of personalized content, to customize marketing initiatives to the particular tastes, behaviors, and requirements of certain clients. In the fiercely competitive online market, optimizing marketing efforts, improving customer experiences, and ultimately generating more conversions and revenue all depend on effective consumer targeting.

4.2.1 The Importance of Customer Targeting

E-commerce and digital marketing success is built on effective client targeting. Understanding individual consumers' tastes, behaviors, and demands that helps organizations to provide personalized experiences and achieve higher conversions.

Effective client targeting is the foundation of effective e-commerce and digital marketing campaigns. Gaining a thorough knowledge of individual consumers' tastes, behaviors, and demands enables organizations to create bespoke and personalized experiences, eventually leading to improved conversion rates. According to [8], consumer profile and segmentation are important in digital marketing since they improve the precision of targeting methods. Furthermore, the researchers in [3], investigate the influence of personalized recommendations on online purchasing behavior, revealing a significant rise in conversion rates when buyers are given personally appropriate product choices. These findings highlight the critical importance of consumer awareness and customization in optimizing the efficacy of e-commerce and digital marketing initiatives, providing a competitive advantage in the digital marketplace.

4.2.2 Challenges in Customer Targeting

In the continuously changing field of e-commerce and digital marketing, traditional approaches to client targeting frequently fall short. When confronted with the exponential expansion of data and the changing nature of customer preferences, the limits of these traditional techniques become clear. Businesses encounter several hurdles as they try for successful client targeting. This section attempts to shed light on these challenges by utilizing findings from credible research studies.

Enormous Data: The sheer volume of data created in the digital age is one of the key difficulties. The amount and complexity of this data might overwhelm standard consumer targeting approaches, making useful insights difficult to extract. According to a study conducted by [9], the era of big data brings both possibilities and difficulties for enterprises. While a plethora of data provides useful insights, it also needs the use of advanced analytics tools and methodologies to efficiently handle and exploit this information.

Changing Customer Preferences: The ever-changing environment of customer preferences is a huge challenge. A study by [10], emphasizes the dynamic nature of customer behavior, emphasizing the significance of continual adaptation in marketing tactics. Traditional techniques of client targeting frequently fail to keep up with these changing tastes, demanding agile and data-driven alternatives.

The limits of old methodologies, the deluge of data, and the changing nature of consumer preferences highlight the issues that organizations confront in customer targeting. The authors in [9] and [10] presented insightful perspectives on these issues, calling for the use of sophisticated analytics and adaptive tactics to negotiate the intricacies of successful consumer targeting in the digital era.

4.3 AI-DRIVEN PERSONALIZATION TECHNIQUES

The field of AI-driven personalization approaches is a dynamic and ever-changing environment that provides organizations with novel solutions to improve consumer engagement and happiness. These methods make use of the capability of Artificial Intelligence (AI) to provide personalized and relevant experiences to individual clients. Here are some of the ideas from various research works in the realm of AI-driven personalization to go deeper into this issue.

Recommender systems are one of the core approaches that has received a lot of attention. These systems, which are thoroughly explored in [11], use AI algorithms to analyze user behavior and preferences, eventually offering personalized suggestions. The research focuses on the various techniques and algorithms used in recommender systems, offering insight into their significance in improving user experience and generating conversions.

Natural Language Processing (NLP) is another popular AI-driven personalization tool. This method analyzes textual data, such as customer reviews and social media interactions, to acquire useful insights about customer sentiment and preferences. A study by [12], present a thorough introduction of NLP methods, focusing on their applications in sentiment analysis and content personalization.

AI-driven customization relies heavily on machine learning and predictive analytics. Businesses may use these strategies to forecast client behavior and modify marketing efforts appropriately. The study on elements of statistical learning by [13] is not specifically concerned with customization strategies; it provides a vital grasp of the statistical concepts that underlie many AI algorithms used in customized suggestions, predictive analytics, and consumer segmentation. Understanding the inner workings of AI-driven customization strategies used in modern digital marketing and e-commerce requires a fundamental understanding of this information. Various authors have explored the complexities of machine learning in their study, providing insights into its applications in predictive modeling and consumer segmentation. Chatbots and virtual assistants are AI-powered personalization solutions that interact with consumers in real time. A research conducted by [14], on the potential of conversational AI, sheds light on its function in improving customer service and offering personalized suggestions.

AI-driven personalization tactics comprise a wide range of strategies that use AI's capabilities to produce personalized experiences. Overviewing the works of [11–13], and [14] provides useful insights into the processes, uses, and implications of these strategies in the context of e-commerce and digital marketing. In the next part, the detailed discussion of various AI-powered personalization techniques is presented. (Figure 4.1)

4.3.1 Recommender Systems

Recommender systems, which are an important part of the digital environment, utilize advanced AI algorithms to analyze user behavior and preferences, resulting in personalized product suggestions.

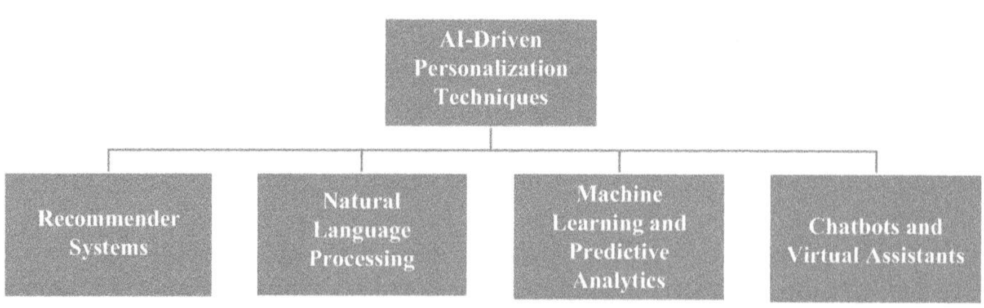

FIGURE 4.1 AI-Driven personalization techniques.

This section seeks to improve our understanding of recommender systems by relying on authoritative research in the fields of AI-driven customization and e-commerce.

Collaborative filtering has emerged as a key approach in the field of recommender systems. Authors in [15], conducted research that gives thorough insights on collaborative filtering, offering light on its principles and uses. Collaborative filtering uses user-item interaction data to find trends and offer products based on comparable users' tastes, increasing user engagement and conversion rates.

Another critical strategy in recommender systems is content-based filtering. A study by [16], investigate the mechanics of content-based filtering, emphasizing its potential to propose things by analyzing the traits and characteristics of objects that fit with a user's interests. This technique goes beyond collaborative filtering to provide personalized suggestion, which is especially effective when user-item interaction data is minimal.

Hybrid recommender systems that combine collaborative and content-based filtering provide a more comprehensive approach to personalized suggestions. The researchers in [17], investigates the notion of hybrid recommender systems, emphasizing their ability to overcome the limits of individual methodologies and give consumers with more accurate and diversified product choices.

Recommender systems have had a substantial influence on consumer engagement and conversion rates in the setting of e-commerce. The paper published in the "Recommender Systems Handbook" by [11] provides insights into the practical uses of recommender systems in e-commerce environments, emphasizing their importance in improving the entire buying experience.

Recommender systems powered by AI algorithms play an important role in e-commerce by personalizing product recommendations to particular user tastes. The reviews presented in [15–17], and [11] broadens our understanding of the mechanics, methodologies, and real-world applications of recommender systems in the digital commerce arena.

4.3.2 Natural Language Processing (NLP)

Natural language processing (NLP) approaches have proven to be important tools for firms wanting to analyze large volumes of unstructured data, such as customer reviews, feedback, and social media interactions. These strategies enable businesses to get valuable insights into client sentiment, preferences, and behaviors, boosting their capacity to personalize marketing material. This section provides a deeper insight into the many uses of NLP in customer-centric strategies, drawing on credible research in the fields of NLP and marketing.

According to [18], NLP plays an important role in sentiment analysis by understanding consumer sentiment from textual data. Businesses may use sentiment analysis tools to evaluate consumer views and emotions, offering useful input for product enhancements and marketing plan optimization. We obtain a better knowledge of the physics of sentiment analysis and its practical implications for personalized marketing material by referring to this study.

In addition to sentiment analysis, NLP techniques can be harnessed to craft personalized marketing content. A study conducted by [19], presents a comprehensive survey on sentiment analysis and opinion mining, shedding light on the vast possibilities of NLP in understanding customer sentiment and preferences. In their study, [20] conducted a comprehensive analysis to investigate the impact of online reviews on product sales. They employed a joint sentiment-topic analysis approach to gain insights into how online reviews influence consumer behavior and product sales. This research sheds light on the significant role that online reviews play in shaping purchasing decisions and provides valuable insights for businesses seeking to leverage customer feedback to enhance their marketing strategies and drive sales.

Beyond sentiment analysis, NLP may be used to create prsonalised marketing material. A study by [21], investigate the application of NLP approaches in producing personalized product suggestions based on customer evaluations and textual data in their study. This study demonstrates how NLP may be used to develop customized marketing material that connects with certain clients.

NLP approaches are critical in determining consumer sentiment, extracting insights from comments, and personalizing marketing material. The researches published by [18–20] and [21] give useful insights into the practical uses of NLP in identifying client preferences and optimizing marketing tactics in the digital era.

4.3.3 Machine Learning and Predictive Analytics

Machine learning models have the ability to anticipate client behavior, allowing firms to adjust marketing campaigns and product suggestions. This section digs into the practical uses of machine learning in consumer targeting, drawing on authoritative research in the domains of machine learning and marketing analytics.

Machine learning, a cornerstone of current data-driven decision-making, provides organizations with the capacity to effectively forecast client behavior. This predictive capability enables businesses to create highly personalized marketing campaigns and product suggestions, hence improving their consumer targeting methods. The work done by [22], exemplifies machine learning's ability to anticipate client behavior. Their study looks into the use of machine learning models in customer churn prediction, showing the potential of these approaches to detect consumers who are about to leave a business.

Furthermore, a study by [23], explain, predictive analytics as a strong facet of machine learning. Predictive analytics foresee future outcomes based on previous data, helping firms to anticipate client preferences and behaviors. The researchers have obtained insights into how predictive analytics might guide marketing strategy and improve consumer targeting for better sales. Machine learning is useful in providing personalized product suggestions in the context of e-commerce. Deep reinforcement learning is used in the context of online advertising impressions in recommender systems in the research by [24]. This study provides insight into how machine learning approaches are developing, notably deep reinforcement learning, and its prospective effects on AI-driven customization strategies in digital marketing. This work enhances personalized suggestions and consumer targeting by optimizing advertising impressions, highlighting the value of cutting-edge machine learning in enhancing recommender system performance.

Machine learning and predictive analytics enable firms to accurately forecast and comprehend client behavior. The overall discussion in the works of [22,23], and [24] broadens our understanding of machine learning applications in client targeting, emphasizing its potential to transform marketing tactics in the digital era.

4.3.4 Chatbots and Virtual Assistants

Chatbots and virtual assistants employ artificial intelligence to give real-time client service and personalized recommendations. Chatbots and virtual assistants, powered by artificial intelligence, have become essential components of today's digital world. Their capacity to provide real-time customer care and personalized suggestions has transformed the way businesses connect with their consumers. This section provides a detailed discussion of the complex function of chatbots and virtual assistants in improving the customer experience, drawing on authoritative research in the disciplines of artificial intelligence and customer service.

The research work conducted by [14], investigate the possibilities of conversational AI, focusing on its function in offering personalized suggestions and engaging customers in meaningful conversations. The authors presented a better knowledge of how chatbots and virtual assistants use natural language processing (NLP) to grasp client enquiries and personalize replies, ultimately improving the overall customer experience.

Chatbots and virtual assistants have also proven useful in offering real-time customer service. The study by [25], analyze features in smart tourism technologies, particularly in destination chatbots, and their impact on visitor happiness. In the tourism sector, where AI-driven technologies are rapidly being employed to improve the travel experience, this research examines the changing role of chatbots. Despite the fact that the study's primary focus is on visitor satisfaction, it also highlights the broader applications of AI-driven chatbots in the tourism industry, emphasizing their potential to offer individualized recommendations and support, ultimately enhancing customer targeting and engagement in the context of digital marketing and e-commerce within the travel industry.

As proved by [14] and [25], chatbots and virtual assistants play critical roles in improving the consumer experience. These AI-powered entities have altered the way organizations deal with their consumers in the digital age through personalized suggestions, engaging interactions, and efficient customer service.

4.3.5 Opportunities and Challenges of AI-Driven Personalization in Digital Marketing and E-Commerce

AI-powered customization approaches have revolutionized digital marketing and e-commerce by providing new ways to engage customers. They do, however, raise issues that must be addressed in order for them to be implemented successfully. This section, presents an overview of the benefits and drawbacks of AI-driven personalization strategies.

4.3.5.1 Opportunities

Enhanced Customer Engagement: AI-powered customization helps businesses to provide highly personalized and relevant information and suggestions for individual customers, resulting in higher engagement and longer user sessions [26].

Improved Conversion Rates: Personalized experiences frequently result in improved conversion rates since customers are provided with items and information that correspond to their tastes, resulting in increased sales [3].

Customer Loyalty is Increased: Personalized interactions increase customer loyalty, leading to repeat purchases and long-term partnerships [27].

Efficient Marketing Cost: AI can optimize marketing cost by precisely targeting the proper audience and minimizing resource waste [28].

Data-Driven Insights: Artificial intelligence (AI) offers significant data insights from consumer behavior that can be used to influence future marketing strategies and product development [29]. (Figure 4.2)

4.3.5.2 Challenges

Data Privacy and Security: The collecting and use of huge volumes of consumer data raises privacy and data security problems, needing strict safeguards [30].

Openness and Fairness: Achieving ethical AI-driven personalization requires ensuring openness in AI algorithms as well as preventing prejudice and discrimination [31].

Algorithmic Accountability: Businesses must develop systems to hold AI algorithms responsible for their actions, particularly when those decisions affect [32].

Personalization:it may present ethical quandaries, such as the manipulation of user preferences or the usage of personal data without informed consent [33].

Algorithmic Complexity: Implementing and maintaining complex AI algorithms can be challenging, requiring specialized skills and resources [34].

Navigation: Navigating these potential and obstacles properly is crucial for firms that want to use the power of AI-driven personalization while maintaining ethical standards and customer confidence. (Figure 4.3)

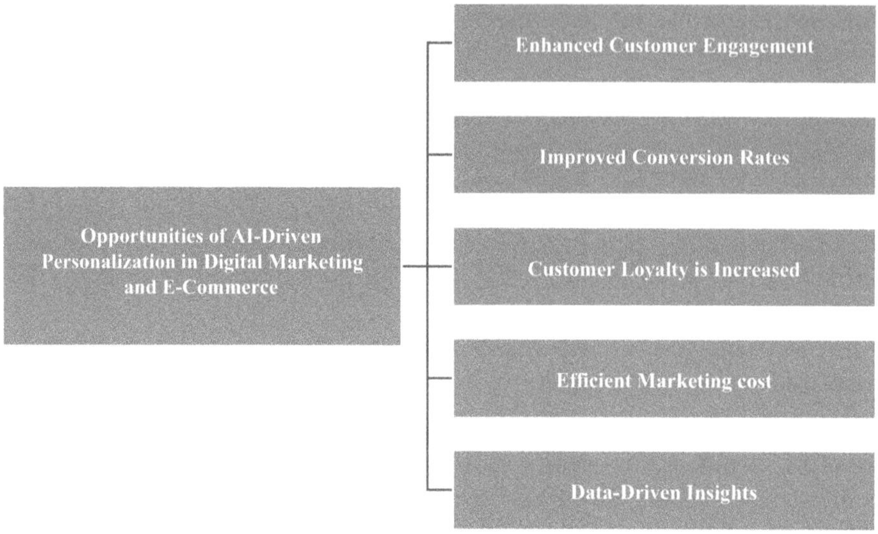

FIGURE 4.2 Opportunities of AI-driven personalization in digital marketing and e-commerce.

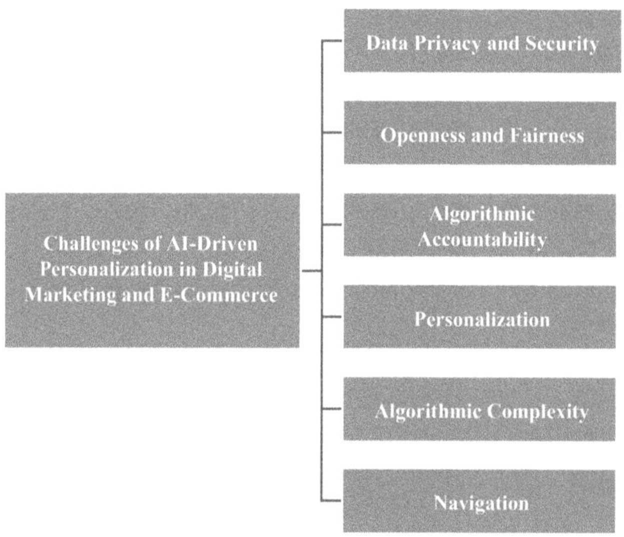

FIGURE 4.3 Challenges of AI-driven personalization in digital marketing and e-commerce.

4.4 IMPACT ON PRODUCT SALES

One of the most important aspects of digital marketing is how artificial intelligence (AI) affects product sales, and recent research has shown both the challenges and prospects in this area. The increasing role of AI in marketing is highlighted by [35], who emphasize the necessity to avoid possible pitfalls while taking use of the benefits it brings. The authors in [36] evaluate the dynamic environment of AI in marketing, highlighting its ever-evolving nature, and add to this understanding. According to [37], personalization's importance in the context of product sales increases, by customizing suggestions to specific client tastes. AI-driven customization approaches, ranging from recommender systems to predictive analytics, have the potential to drastically affect product sales. These developments promote client engagement while also improving conversion rates, decreasing cart abandonment, and fostering stronger customer loyalty. To ensure that the pursuit of sales growth is consistent with transparency, fairness, and long-term customer value, organizations must be aware of the ethical issues and potential biases related to AI-driven personalization.

4.4.1 Increased Conversion Rates

Personalized product suggestions and marketing material enhance conversion rates, which leads to greater sales. Personalized product suggestions and personalized marketing material have developed as a powerful method for increasing conversion rates in e-commerce and digital marketing. The researchers in [3], found that personalized recommendations have a significant influence on online buying behavior, with significant improvements in conversion rates when customers are given with personally appropriate product options. This research presents actual proof of a direct relationship between personalization efforts and increased conversion rates, illustrating the practical importance of customization in increasing sales.

Furthermore, in the research by [38] the insights of field of content recommendation, a key element of AI-driven customization methods are presented. Although the study focuses on content suggestion, it is consistent with more general AI-driven tactics employed in digital marketing and e-commerce. The study investigates the use of topic modeling, a crucial AI method, to improve content recommendation systems. By doing this, it advances knowledge of how AI-driven customization, a key component of contemporary digital marketing and e-commerce practises, may enhance client targeting by presenting information that is in line with specific interests and preferences.

4.4.2 Reduced Cart Abandonment

Artificial intelligence-driven personalization strategies can address common causes of cart abandonment by offering customized rewards and reminders. AI-powered personalization strategies have proven effective in e-commerce's persistent problem of cart abandonment. A thorough study and research program on online shopping cart abandonment were undertaken by [39], which clarified the numerous causes and tactics at play. They emphasize the opportunity for personalized AI-driven incentives and reminders to reduce cart abandonment rates. The researchers in [40], also explore why certain customers still choose in-person purchasing over online alternatives. Their investigation on online shopping cart abandonment patterns deepens understanding of the difficulties and possibilities brought about by AI-driven personalization in e-commerce. Collectively, these studies highlight the value of personalization in enhancing client retention and income while optimizing the e-commerce conversion funnel.

4.4.3 Enhanced Customer Loyalty

Customer loyalty is increased via personalized experiences, which leads to repeat purchases and long-term connections. Customer loyalty may be fostered through personalized experiences, according to considerable research in the fields of e-commerce and digital marketing. The authors in [41] conducted research on the link between personalized interactions and customer loyalty, emphasizing that customized experiences lead to higher customer retention, repeat purchases, and the formation of long-term relationships. This reference emphasizes the empirical evidence that personalization is a significant driver of increased consumer loyalty in the digital era.

In addition, the authors in [42] investigate the influence of personalized product suggestions on consumer loyalty in the context of online shopping. AI-driven customization techniques may give product ideas that connect with individual requirements by analyzing consumer behavior and preferences, generating a sense of value and loyalty among customers. This research gives insights into the practical applications of customization strategies in the development and maintenance of client loyalty.

Furthermore, as demonstrated by [41] and [42], greater consumer loyalty is a concrete result of personalized experiences in e-commerce and digital marketing. Businesses may develop long-lasting connections with their consumers by adapting interactions, suggestions, and content to individual interests.

4.5 LITERATURE REVIEW

Improving client targeting has arisen as a strategic necessity for organizations in the rapidly changing world of e-commerce and digital marketing. AI-driven personalization tactics have been important in this endeavor, employing deep learning and a range of AI approaches to improve client engagement. In this section, the review of the literature is presented on the most recent research and insights interested in the use of AI-driven personalization in digital marketing and e-commerce, with a focus on personalized recommendations, predictive analytics for customer segmentation, natural language processing (NLP) for content personalization, testing, and optimization, and customer churn prediction and retention strategies.

4.5.1 Personalized Recommendations

Personalized suggestions have become an essential component of current e-commerce and digital marketing tactics. AI-powered algorithms, particularly deep learning models, have transformed the way organizations analyze user behavior and preferences in order to provide highly personalized product recommendations. The researchers in [43] performed a thorough examination of deep learning approaches used in personalized suggestions. They investigated sophisticated strategies for improving recommendation systems, emphasizing the need for granular awareness of user preferences. This study emphasizes the ongoing attempts to increase the sophistication of recommendation algorithms in order to better serve consumers.

The use of neural collaborative filtering is one of the most notable advances in personalized suggestions. The authors in [44] pioneered neural collaborative filtering as an innovative method that outperforms standard approaches. Neural collaborative filtering excels in capturing nuanced user-item interactions by utilizing deep learning techniques, resulting in suggestions that are more closely aligned with individual tastes.

In addition, recent advances in recommendation systems[45] have investigated hybrid techniques that integrate collaborative and content-based filtering, resulting in more accurate and diversified suggestions. These hybrid models employ deep learning to combine numerous data sources, improving user personalization of information and goods.

The subject of client targeting in digital marketing through personalized suggestions is quickly evolving. Recent research [44,45] shows a strong trend towards using deep learning techniques and hybrid models to increase suggestion quality, hence improving the user experience and boosting company success. These developments emphasize the crucial role that AI-driven personalization initiatives play in today's highly competitive digital market.

4.5.2 Predictive Analytics for Customer Segmentation

Predictive analytics powered by AI has emerged as a significant tool in the domain of digital marketing. It enables organizations to successfully segment their consumer base by taking into account a variety of criteria such as behavior, demographics, and purchasing history. A study by [46], explored the use of AI technology in the contemporary digital marketing environment in their study. The revolutionary potential of AI to revolutionize digital marketing practises is acknowledged in this study. Recommendation systems and predictive analytics are just two examples of AI-driven personalization techniques that have become indispensable tools for companies looking to improve consumer targeting and engagement. By utilizing AI, marketers can optimize marketing efforts as well as customize product and content suggestions based on the interests of specific customers. These developments are essential for enhancing marketing efficiency, expanding product sales, and cultivating long-lasting client relationships. The work of researchers in [46], advances the knowledge of how AI is changing the landscape of digital marketing and provides insightful advice for companies hoping to succeed in this fast-changing setting.

The researchers in [3], also investigated the transition from multi-channel to omni-channel commerce, emphasizing the importance of predictive analytics in consumer segmentation. Businesses may more successfully adjust marketing tactics for distinct client groups by utilizing AI-driven segmentation methodologies, optimizing their marketing efforts across multiple digital platforms.Recent breakthroughs in predictive analytics have also emphasized the possibility of automated machine learning (AutoML) for consumer segmentation. AutoML technologies make predictive model development easier, democratizing access to sophisticated analytics capabilities [47]. This enables companies of all sizes to leverage the power of predictive analytics for better consumer targeting.

Predictive analytics powered by AI and powerful machine learning techniques is revolutionizing client targeting in digital marketing. With a growing body of evidence to back it up, predictive analytics provides organizations with the ability to build more accurate and personalized marketing efforts, resulting in increased consumer engagement and overall marketing performance. In the ever-changing field of digital marketing and client segmentation, this technology has the potential to be a game changer.

4.5.3 Natural Language Processing (NLP) for Content Personalization

Natural Language Processing (NLP) has undeniably changed the landscape of content personalization in digital marketing, allowing firms to glean useful insights from consumer reviews, feedback, and social media data. Recent research has shed light on the extraordinary uses of deep learning models, particularly transformer-based architectures, in sentiment analysis and content recommendation [48].

In their study, [49] focuses on the application of BERT, a cutting-edge natural language processing (NLP) model, in sentiment analysis. Sentiment analysis is a pivotal aspect of content personalization in digital marketing, as it enables businesses to gain profound insights into customer sentiment and preferences. By leveraging BERT, this study contributes to the advancement of NLP techniques, enhancing their effectiveness in tailoring marketing content to align with customer emotions and opinions, thereby fostering improved engagement and personalized experiences in the digital marketing landscape.

Furthermore, [50] investigated sophisticated algorithms for effective text categorization, which is essential in content personalization. Their study demonstrated the ability of deep learning models to automate the categorization of user-generated information such as reviews and comments. This efficiency enables firms to quickly find useful insights and create marketing material that connects with specific customers.NLP approaches, in addition to sentiment analysis, have proved useful in the creation of content recommendation systems. Recent study [51] has highlighted the importance of attention processes, which are an important component of transformer-based models, in improving content recommendation accuracy. These technologies enable organizations to produce content that is more closely aligned with their consumers' tastes and interests.

NLP approaches are redefining content personalization in digital marketing. Businesses can now produce marketing material that not only connects with individual customers but also stimulates increased engagement and brand loyalty with the help of deep learning models like BERT and revolutionary research in efficient text categorization and content suggestion. The influence of natural language processing on client targeting is unquestionably important, and it is primed for additional breakthroughs in the expanding digital marketing landscape.

4.5.4 Testing and Optimization

Tools for A/B testing and optimization powered by AI have proven to be useful resources for businesses looking to improve their real-time marketing initiatives. These deep learning-powered systems provide a dynamic method for improving customer targeting and marketing campaign optimization. The promise of AI-powered optimization tactics for improving consumer targeting and raising conversion rates is demonstrated by a remarkable work by [52] on budget-constrained bidding by model-free reinforcement learning in display advertising. Furthermore, the use of deep learning in automated testing and optimization is gaining traction. Recently, [53] investigated the application of convolutional neural networks (CNNs) in analyzing consumer interaction data for campaign optimization. Businesses may use this strategy to find trends in client interactions and modify their marketing efforts accordingly.

Additionally, the use of reinforcement learning techniques in automated optimization and testing has been growing. Deep reinforcement learning's potential for improving click-through rates was studied by [54]. These strategies boost click-through rates, conversion rates, and overall campaign effectiveness.

AI-driven A/B testing and optimization powered by deep learning algorithms provide a dynamic approach to consumer targeting in digital marketing. Recent studies [53,54] shows that deep reinforcement learning and the use of convolutional neural networks may be used to improve campaign success. These technological improvements enable organizations to fine-tune their marketing efforts in real-time, resulting in higher conversion rates, click-through rates, and overall campaign efficacy. Testing and optimization technologies continue to be key components of modern digital marketing strategies, growing in response to the needs of a dynamic digital marketplace.

4.5.5 Customer Churn Prediction and Retention Strategies

AI-powered machine learning models have shown to be crucial in anticipating customer attrition and developing successful retention tactics, making them important tools in customer targeting for digital marketing. Recent study has shed light on many facets of these tactics, emphasizing creative approaches and their influence on customer attrition and lifetime value.

In their study, [55] focus on customer churn prediction and marketing retention strategies, particularly within the context of B2B e-commerce. They employ support vector machines and emphasize the importance of the AUC parameter-selection technique in achieving accurate predictions. This research sheds light on the significance of predictive analytics and machine learning in identifying potential customer churn, offering valuable insights that can aid businesses in devising effective retention strategies for their B2B e-commerce endeavors.

In another research work by [56], a novel approach to customer churn prediction in the telecom industry using a Swish RNN model is presented. Their study not only focuses on predictive accuracy but also introduces a unique feature selection strategy, enhancing the effectiveness of churn prediction. This research contributes to the ongoing efforts to address customer retention challenges within the telecom sector by leveraging advanced machine learning techniques and innovative feature selection methods, offering valuable insights for businesses seeking to reduce churn and enhance customer relationships. Furthermore, the use of convolutional neural networks (CNNs) in customer churn prediction has grown in popularity. As investigated by [57], the use of CNNs for analyzing consumer behavior data. This method enables organizations to uncover patterns and trends that may suggest possible churn, allowing them to take proactive steps to retain important clients.

Additionally, the application of machine learning has resulted in considerable breakthroughs in retention tactics. The research conducted by [58], on the creation of personalized retention tactics based on consumer segmentation. This method uses machine learning models to personalize retention efforts to specific customer demands and preferences, resulting in more successful client retention techniques. AI-driven machine learning models, such as deep learning neural networks, continue to drive innovation in digital marketing by forecasting client attrition and adopting effective retention measures. Recurrent neural networks (RNNs), convolutional neural networks (CNNs), and personalized retention methods have been shown in studies to reduce customer turnover and increase customer lifetime value. In the ever-changing digital market, these improvements enable firms to proactively handle customer churn, resulting in enhanced consumer targeting and long-term client relationships.

The use of deep learning and AI approaches in consumer targeting for e-commerce and digital marketing has created new opportunities for personalized interaction. The subject, however, is still evolving, with continuous research focusing on enhancing the accuracy, efficiency, and ethical issues of AI-driven personalization tactics. These developments offer great potential for firms looking to improve client targeting and marketing effectiveness in the digital age.

4.6 ETHICAL CONSIDERATIONS

The ethical implications of using AI in digital marketing span a wide range of crucial problems. Concerns concerning privacy and data security, openness in algorithmic decision-making, fairness in targeting, and accountability for AI-driven decisions are particularly significant. The study by [59], emphasizes the ethical issues raised by AI in marketing, underlining the significance of responsible AI governance and ethical norms. Similarly, [33]examine the ethical implications of AI and machine learning in a variety of disciplines, underlining the need of anticipating ethical issues. These studies give an academic foundation for the ethical problems that businesses and marketers must address when employing AI in digital marketing, hence ensuring proper AI technology integration.

Ethical concerns in client targeting in the fields of e-commerce and digital marketing have grown in importance as businesses capitalize on the promise of artificial intelligence to improve customer experiences and enhance revenues. In this next section we present the various ethical considerations for the implementation of AI based personalization methods in digital marketing and e-commerce. (Figure 4.4)

4.6.1 Transparency and Fairness

To develop confidence and assure ethical practises in the field of AI-driven personalization, AI systems must be transparent and unbiased. Transparency indicates that customers understand how their data is being used to customize their experiences. The transparency of the inner workings of AI algorithms demystifies the customization process and provides clients with insights into the decision-making mechanisms underlying product suggestions and content curation.

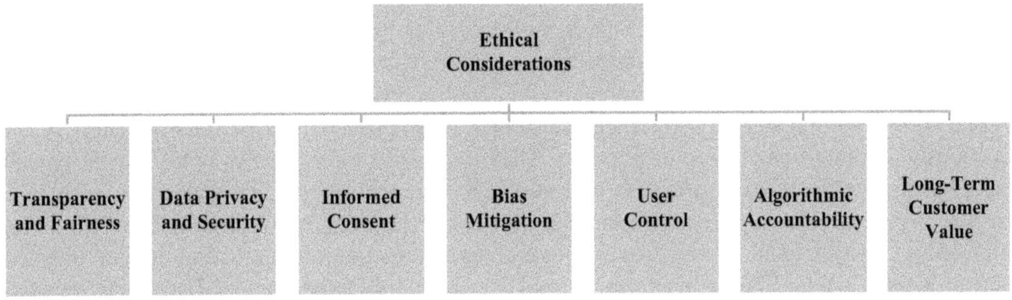

FIGURE 4.4 Ethical considerations.

Furthermore, fairness inside AI systems is critical to avoiding prejudice or discrimination. Maintaining ethical standards requires ensuring that the artificial intelligence system does not favor or discriminate against certain demographic groups. Fairness protects against situations in which certain consumers receive uneven treatment or opportunity based on variables such as ethnicity, gender, or socioeconomic status.

This dedication to openness and fairness not only adheres to ethical values but also plays an important role in the building of customer trust. Customers are more willing to deal with companies who are transparent about their data practises and fair in their interactions. Businesses that follow these principles may lay a firm foundation of trust, which is essential for long-term consumer relationships [60].

4.6.2 Data Privacy and Security

In an era of increased privacy awareness, people are becoming increasingly concerned about how their data which is gathered and utilized. As a result, it is critical for firms to manage this situation responsibly and transparently. One of the most important ethical issues is the safeguarding of client data. This includes protecting sensitive data, such as personal information, purchase history, and surfing habits, against unauthorized access or harmful use. Businesses are entrusted with this information, and it is their ethical responsibility to keep it secure. This obligation stems not just from ethical concerns, but is also strengthened by legislative frameworks such as Europe's General Data Protection Regulation (GDPR)[61]. Compliance with such restrictions is not just a legal need but also a moral one.

Failure to secure consumer data can have serious ethical and legal ramifications. Unauthorized access or data breaches can endanger sensitive client information, potentially causing injury, identity theft, or financial losses. Such accidents diminish consumer trust and can harm a company's brand and credibility for a long time. As a result, organizations are not only morally obligated but also financially encouraged to invest in comprehensive data security measures such as encryption, access limits, and frequent security audits. In doing so, they not only meet their ethical requirements but also foster a trusting atmosphere in which consumers can be certain that their data is being treated with care and respect [62].

4.6.3 Informed Consent

In the age of data-driven personalization, gaining informed permission is a fundamental pillar of ethical practise. Businesses must prioritize openness and respect for individual liberty in their goal of exploiting consumer data for personalization. Customers who provide informed consent are more than just passive data subjects; they are active players in the data-sharing process. To do this, businesses must guarantee that their consumers have a clear and thorough understanding of how their data will be used. This understanding includes not just the goals for which data will be used but also the amount to which it will be analyzed, shared, and preserved. It is critical to present this information in a simple and intelligible manner; jargon and complex terminology should be avoided to allow true comprehension.

The issue of willingness is also critical. Customers must provide their permission willingly and voluntarily, without compulsion or pressure. They must have the option to opt in or out of data gathering and customization practises without fear of repercussions. This aspect of choice is necessary to guarantee that consent is really informed and not influenced unduly. Obtaining informed permission entails more than just legal compliance; it represents a commitment to ethical data processing. It enables consumers to make educated decisions about how their personal information is used, fostering a sense of agency and ownership over their data. As a result, trust grows and the customer-business connection improves.

Furthermore, because data privacy legislation such as the GDPR[61] emphasize the need for informed permission, companies that prioritize this ethical concept not only comply with legal obligations but also position themselves as guardians of consumer trust. Businesses that practise informed consent not only respect individual privacy rights but also contribute to a more open and ethical digital environment [63].

4.6.4 Bias Mitigation

In the realms of data-driven personalization and AI-driven decision-making, bias mitigation inside AI algorithms is a fundamental need. Bias, whether caused by skewed training data or algorithmic biases, has the potential to bring unfairness into AI systems, resulting in unbalanced recommendations and even discriminating consequences. As a result, removing prejudice is both a technological difficulty and an ethical imperative. The data used for training is one of the key sources of bias in AI algorithms. If the training data reflects past prejudices, inequities, or imbalances, the AI system's recommendations may accidentally perpetuate and magnify these biases. For example, if previous purchase data reveals gender preferences, the AI may accidentally offer things based on gender preconceptions, propagating gender prejudice [64].

Researchers and practitioners are currently investigating strategies like as debiasing and fairness-aware machine learning to combat these biases. These techniques seek to detect and correct bias in AI models and algorithms. Pre-processing the training data to minimize or eliminate existing biases ensures that the AI system does not learn discriminating tendencies. In contrast, fairness-aware machine learning adds fairness restrictions into the model's optimization process, aiming to give equal outputs for all user groups.

This continuing study demonstrates the company's commitment to advancing justice and equity in AI-powered personalization. The objective is to construct AI systems that are not just precise and efficient but also morally sound and unbiased, by constantly improving and developing these methodologies. Furthermore, as fairness and transparency become increasingly important in data privacy rules and consumer expectations, organizations that actively address prejudice are better positioned to acquire customer trust and demonstrate a commitment to ethical AI [65].

4.6.5 User Control

Giving users discretion over the level of personalization they receive is an ethical tenet in the field of AI-driven personalization. Recognizing that people have varied levels of comfort and preferences when it comes to data usage, organizations must prioritize user agency and privacy. This means providing consumers with a range of alternatives for tailoring their customization experience to their own wants and concerns. The notion of user permission and customization is central to this approach. Users should be able to make educated decisions about their customization settings and understand how these choices will impact their interactions with digital platforms. Businesses must provide transparent and user-friendly interfaces that explain the ramifications of each privacy option.

Users' options should include the opportunity to modify privacy settings to their comfort levels. Users, for example, may choose to submit relatively minimum information in order to obtain basic suggestions, or they may pick a more complete sharing method in order to receive highly personalized experiences. Most importantly, these options should be easily reversible, allowing users to change their selections as their needs change. Furthermore, the opportunity to opt out of personalized recommendations should be simple and straightforward. This opt-out tool protects the privacy of consumers who may be concerned about data-driven personalization. It guarantees that people may continue to access and use digital services without feeling obliged to engage in customization practises.

The work carried out by [66], emphasizes the relevance of user control as an ethical concept. Their findings show that giving people agency and customization choices not only adheres to ethical principles but also fosters trust and great user experiences. Businesses demonstrate a commitment to respecting individual choices and promoting a responsible and ethical digital environment by putting consumers in control of their personalized journey.

4.6.6 Algorithmic Accountability

In the age of AI-driven personalization, enterprises must accept full responsibility for the actions and results of their AI systems. This obligation encompasses a wide range of scenarios, including not just accomplishments but also failures, biases, and unexpected effects that may result from automated decision-making procedures. Such a commitment to responsibility is not just an ethical need but also a necessary component of fostering trust and assuring the ethical use of AI. To begin, firms must keep a close eye on the functioning of their AI algorithms. Continuous review and assessment are required to discover and correct any flaws or biases that may arise during the execution of the algorithm. This proactive strategy reduces the possibility of making suggestions or conclusions that are erroneous, discriminatory, or unjust.

Furthermore, when problems or unforeseen repercussions develop, firms should act quickly and transparently. This involves swiftly admitting and correcting errors, as well as addressing any biases that may have formed. Besides, organizations should communicate honestly with impacted users, detailing the nature of the problem, how it was resolved, and what efforts were made to avoid such occurrences in the future. Accountability also includes adhering to appropriate legislation and ethical standards. Businesses must guarantee that their AI algorithms follow legal and ethical criteria, such as those governing data protection and justice. When violations occur, firms should bear responsibility for correcting the situation and putting in place steps to prevent future violations.

The study by [31], emphasizes the necessity of this commitment to accountability, emphasizing that organizations must approach AI algorithms as instruments that demand responsible monitoring rather than as black boxes. Businesses not only achieve their ethical commitments in this manner, but they also position themselves as trustworthy and responsible stewards of AI technology.

4.6.7 Long-Term Customer Value

The ethical issues facing AI-driven personalization go beyond short-term sales and quick advantages. While organizations surely want to increase short-term income through personalized methods, they must also prioritize the creation and maintenance of long-term client relationships. This includes refraining from exploitative practises that prioritize short-term profits over consumer well-being and happiness, as [67] emphasized in their research. In this framework, one of the most important ethical concepts is sustainability. AI-powered personalization should not be regarded as a one-time transactional endeavor but rather as a long-term strategy geared at fostering long-term client loyalty. Businesses must recognize that client pleasure and loyalty are inextricably linked to their success. As a result, it is critical to prioritize methods that not only generate immediate revenue but also establish the groundwork for long-term client connections.

This ethical viewpoint emphasizes the significance of offering value to clients at every stage of their journey. Businesses should focus on creating meaningful and relevant experiences rather than hammering clients with endless advertising or personalized offers that may not fit with their actual requirements or preferences. This includes suggestions that truly benefit consumers, educational and entertaining material, and personalized interactions that establish a sense of connection and trust. Furthermore, ethical issues include transparency and honesty. Customers should be fully informed about how their data is handled and the benefits that personalization may provide.

Misleading or dishonest practises weaken trust and can have long-term negative consequences for the reputation of a brand.

Ethical AI-driven personalization seeks to achieve a compromise between short-term benefits and long-term client happiness. Businesses that adhere to ethical standards and prioritize customer well-being over quick profits not only promote trust and loyalty but also contribute to a sustainable and responsible digital marketing environment. Ethical issues in consumer targeting via AI-driven customization are critical for establishing trust, maintaining fairness, and adhering to legislation. These issues are critical in striking a delicate balance between personalization and privacy, which will eventually shape the ethical landscape of digital marketing and e-commerce. As AI-driven personalization tactics improve and become increasingly integrated into businesses' operations, businesses must constantly review and handle these ethical problems.

4.7 CONCLUSION

Customer targeting in e-commerce and digital marketing has been revolutionized by AI-driven customization, significantly altering how businesses interact with their clients. It increases overall marketing efficacy as well as product sales. However, building trust requires a priority on ethical issues. AI will play a bigger part in customer targeting as technology develops quickly. Companies must face these difficulties with integrity. This change in customer targeting highlights the transition from exploitative, short-term partnerships to long-term, mutually beneficial ones. Businesses must put long-term client satisfaction and loyalty ahead of short-term revenue. Organizations must continue to be flexible, inventive, and socially responsible in their pursuit of success as AI's role in consumer targeting expands.

In this study, we have given a succinct summary of customer targeting utilizing cutting-edge AI algorithms, along with its moral implications for client retention in the commercial market. In-depth explanations of the techniques' ethical applications are provided in this research work in addition to the techniques themselves. This study includes a thorough evaluation of the literature, establishing it as a pioneering effort in the subject that will surely help future scholars.

REFERENCES

[1] A. N. Smith, E. Fischer, and C. Yongjian, "How does brand-related user-generated content differ across YouTube, Facebook, and Twitter?," *Journal of Interactive Marketing*, vol. 26, no. 2, pp. 102–113, May 2012, doi: 10.1016/j.intmar.2012.01.002.

[2] T. H. Baek, J. Kim, and J. H. Yu, "The differential roles of brand credibility and brand prestige in consumer brand choice," *Psychol. Mark.*, vol. 27, no. 7, pp. 662–678, Jun. 2010, doi: 10.1002/mar.20350.

[3] P. C. Verhoef, P. K. Kannan, and J. J. Inman, "From multi-channel retailing to omni-channel retailing," *Journal of Retailing*, vol. 91, no. 2, pp. 174–181, Jun. 2015, doi: 10.1016/j.jretai.2015.02.005.

[4] H. (Alice) Li and P. K. Kannan, "Attributing conversions in a multichannel online marketing environment: An empirical model and a field experiment," *Journal of Marketing Research*, vol. 51, no. 1, pp. 40–56, Feb. 2014, doi: 10.1509/jmr.13.0050.

[5] D. Chaffey and P. R. Smith, *Digital marketing excellence: Planning, optimizing and integrating online marketing*, Sixth edition. Milton Park, Abingdon, Oxon: Routledge, 2023.

[6] H. Ha, J. John, S. Janda, and S. Muthaly, "The effects of advertising spending on brand loyalty in services," *European Journal of Marketing*, vol. 45, no. 4, pp. 673–691, Apr. 2011, doi: 10.1108/03090561111111389.

[7] B. Marr, *Big data in practice: how 45 successful companies used big data analytics to deliver extraordinary results*. Chichester, West Sussex: Wiley, 2016.

[8] J. Järvinen and H. Karjaluoto, "The use of web analytics for digital marketing performance measurement," *Industrial Marketing Management*, vol. 50, pp. 117–127, Oct. 2015, doi: 10.1016/j.indmarman.2015.04.009.

[9] B. McAfee, A. E., T. H. Davenport, D. J. Patil, & D. Barton, "Big data: The management revolution".
[10] M.-H. Hsu, C.-M. Chang, and L.-W. Chuang, "Understanding the determinants of online repeat purchase intention and moderating role of habit: The case of online group-buying in Taiwan," *International Journal of Information Management*, vol. 35, no. 1, pp. 45–56, Feb. 2015, doi: 10.1016/j.ijinfomgt.2014.09.002.
[11] F. Ricci, L. Rokach, and B. Shapira, "Introduction to recommender systems handbook," in *Recommender Systems Handbook*, F. Ricci, L. Rokach, B. Shapira, and P. B. Kantor, Eds., Boston, MA: Springer US, 2011, pp. 1–35. doi: 10.1007/978-0-387-85820-3_1.
[12] C. D. Manning, P. Raghavan, and H. Schütze, *Introduction to information retrieval*, 1st ed. Cambridge University Press, 2008. doi: 10.1017/CBO9780511809071.
[13] E. R. Ziegel, "The elements of statistical learning," *Technometrics*, vol. 45, no. 3, pp. 267–268, Aug. 2003, doi: 10.1198/tech.2003.s770.
[14] I. Serban *et al.*, "A hierarchical latent variable encoder-decoder model for generating dialogues," *AAAI*, vol. 31, no. 1, Feb. 2017, doi: 10.1609/aaai.v31i1.10983.
[15] Y. Koren, R. Bell, and C. Volinsky, "Matrix factorization techniques for recommender systems," *Computer*, vol. 42, no. 8, pp. 30–37, Aug. 2009, doi: 10.1109/MC.2009.263.
[16] M. J. Pazzani and D. Billsus, "Content-based recommendation systems," in *The Adaptive Web*, vol. 4321, P. Brusilovsky, A. Kobsa, and W. Nejdl, Eds., in Lecture Notes in Computer Science, vol. 4321., Berlin, Heidelberg: Springer Berlin Heidelberg, 2007, pp. 325–341. doi: 10.1007/978-3-540-72079-9_10.
[17] R. Burke, "Hybrid recommender systems: Survey and experiments," *User Modeling and User-Adapted Interaction*, vol. 12, no. 4, pp. 331–370, 2002, doi: 10.1023/A:1021240730564.
[18] B. Pang and L. Lee, "Opinion mining and sentiment analysis," *FNT in Information Retrieval*, vol. 2, no. 1–2, pp. 1–135, 2008, doi: 10.1561/1500000011.
[19] C. Vinodhini, G R. M., "Sentiment analysis and opinion mining: A survey".
[20] X. Li, C. Wu, and F. Mai, "The effect of online reviews on product sales: A joint sentiment-topic analysis," *Information & Management*, vol. 56, no. 2, pp. 172–184, Mar. 2019, doi: 10.1016/j.im.2018.04.007.
[21] X. Zheng, S. Zhu, and Z. Lin, "Capturing the essence of word-of-mouth for social commerce: Assessing the quality of online e-commerce reviews by a semi-supervised approach," *Decision Support Systems*, vol. 56, pp. 211–222, Dec. 2013, doi: 10.1016/j.dss.2013.06.002.
[22] K. Coussement and D. Van Den Poel, "Churn prediction in subscription services: An application of support vector machines while comparing two parameter-selection techniques," *Expert Systems with Applications*, vol. 34, no. 1, pp. 313–327, Jan. 2008, doi: 10.1016/j.eswa.2006.09.038.
[23] T. H. Davenport and J. G. Harris, *Competing on analytics: the new science of winning*, Updated, with A new introduction. Boston, Massachusetts: Harvard Business Review Press, 2017.
[24] X. Zhao *et al.*, "DEAR: Deep reinforcement learning for online advertising impression in recommender systems," *AAAI*, vol. 35, no. 1, pp. 750–758, May 2021, doi: 10.1609/aaai.v35i1.16156.
[25] M. Orden-Mejía and A. Huertas, "Analysis of the attributes of smart tourism technologies in destination chatbots that influence tourist satisfaction," *Current Issues in Tourism*, vol. 25, no. 17, pp. 2854–2869, Sep. 2022, doi: 10.1080/13683500.2021.1997942.
[26] P. Kireyev, K. Pauwels, and S. Gupta, "Do display ads influence search? Attribution and dynamics in online advertising," *International Journal of Research in Marketing*, vol. 33, no. 3, pp. 475–490, Sep. 2016, doi: 10.1016/j.ijresmar.2015.09.007.
[27] Xiao and Benbasat, "E-commerce product recommendation agents: Use, characteristics, and impact," *MIS Quarterly*, vol. 31, no. 1, p. 137, 2007, doi: 10.2307/25148784.
[28] E. A. Hogan, "The attention economy: Understanding the new currency of business By Davenport, Thomas H. and Beck, John C. Boston: Harvard Business School Press, 2001. 256 pages, hardcover, $29.95.," *AMP*, vol. 15, no. 4, pp. 145–147, Nov. 2001, doi: 10.5465/ame.2001.5898765.
[29] K. Kuang, M. Jiang, P. Cui, H. Luo, and S. Yang, "Effective promotional strategies selection in social media: A data-driven approach," *IEEE Trans. Big Data*, vol. 4, no. 4, pp. 487–501, Dec. 2018, doi: 10.1109/TBDATA.2017.2734102.
[30] S. D. Warren and L. D. Brandeis, "The right to privacy," *Harvard Law Review*, vol. 4, no. 5, p. 193, Dec. 1890, doi: 10.2307/1321160.
[31] N. Diakopoulos, "Accountability in algorithmic decision making," *Commun. ACM*, vol. 59, no. 2, pp. 56–62, Jan. 2016, doi: 10.1145/2844110.

[32] D. Gunning, E. Vorm, Y. Wang, and M. Turek, "DARPA's explainable AI (XAI) program: A retrospective," Preprints, preprint, Nov. 2021. doi: 10.22541/au.163699841.19031727/v1.
[33] M. Taddeo and L. Floridi, "How AI can be a force for good," *Science*, vol. 361, no. 6404, pp. 751–752, Aug. 2018, doi: 10.1126/science.aat5991.
[34] S. Khanra, A. Dhir, A. K. M. N. Islam, and M. Mäntymäki, "Big data analytics in healthcare: A systematic literature review," *Enterprise Information Systems*, vol. 14, no. 7, pp. 878–912, Aug. 2020, doi: 10.1080/17517575.2020.1812005.
[35] A. De Bruyn, V. Viswanathan, Y. S. Beh, J. K.-U. Brock, and F. Von Wangenheim, "Artificial intelligence and marketing: Pitfalls and opportunities," *Journal of Interactive Marketing*, vol. 51, pp. 91–105, Aug. 2020, doi: 10.1016/j.intmar.2020.04.007.
[36] B. Vlačić, L. Corbo, S. Costa E Silva, and M. Dabić, "The evolving role of artificial intelligence in marketing: A review and research agenda," *Journal of Business Research*, vol. 128, pp. 187–203, May 2021, doi: 10.1016/j.jbusres.2021.01.055.
[37] G. Adomavicius and A. Tuzhilin, "Toward the next generation of recommender systems: A survey of the state-of-the-art and possible extensions," *IEEE Trans. Knowl. Data Eng.*, vol. 17, no. 6, pp. 734–749, Jun. 2005, doi: 10.1109/TKDE.2005.99.
[38] S. Papneja, K. Sharma, and N. Khilwani, "Content recommendation based on topic modeling," in *Computational Methods and Data Engineering*, vol. 1227, V. Singh, V. K. Asari, S. Kumar, and R. B. Patel, Eds., in Advances in Intelligent Systems and Computing, vol. 1227., Singapore: Springer Singapore, 2021, pp. 1–10. doi: 10.1007/978-981-15-6876-3_1.
[39] S. Wang, J. Cheah, and X. Lim, "Online shopping cart abandonment: A review and research agenda," *Int J Consumer Studies*, vol. 47, no. 2, pp. 453–473, Mar. 2023, doi: 10.1111/ijcs.12876.
[40] S. Wang, Y. Ye, B. Ning, J.-H. Cheah, and X.-J. Lim, "Why do some consumers still prefer in-store shopping? An exploration of online shopping cart abandonment behavior," *Front. Psychol.*, vol. 12, p. 829696, Jan. 2022, doi: 10.3389/fpsyg.2021.829696.
[41] V. Kumar and W. Reinartz, "Creating enduring customer value," *Journal of Marketing*, vol. 80, no. 6, pp. 36–68, Nov. 2016, doi: 10.1509/jm.15.0414.
[42] W. Sung-Shun and L. Mei-Ju, "Personalized product recommendation in e-commerce," in *IEEE International Conference on e-Technology, e-Commerce and e-Service, 2004. EEE '04. 2004*, Taipei, Taiwan: IEEE, 2004, pp. 413–420. doi: 10.1109/EEE.2004.1287340.
[43] Y. Guan, Q. Wei, and G. Chen, "Deep learning based personalized recommendation with multi-view information integration," *Decision Support Systems*, vol. 118, pp. 58–69, Mar. 2019, doi: 10.1016/j.dss.2019.01.003.
[44] X. He, L. Liao, H. Zhang, L. Nie, X. Hu, and T.-S. Chua, "Neural collaborative filtering," in *Proceedings of the 26th International Conference on World Wide Web*, Perth Australia: International World Wide Web Conferences Steering Committee, Apr. 2017, pp. 173–182. doi: 10.1145/3038912.3052569.
[45] S. Zhang, L. Yao, A. Sun, and Y. Tay, "Deep learning based recommender system: A survey and new perspectives," *ACM Comput. Surv.*, vol. 52, no. 1, pp. 1–38, Jan. 2020, doi: 10.1145/3285029.
[46] K. Nair and R. Gupta, "Application of AI technology in modern digital marketing environment," *WJEMSD*, vol. ahead-of-print, no. ahead-of-print, Jan. 2021, doi: 10.1108/WJEMSD-08-2020-0099.
[47] M. Feurer, A. Klein, K. Eggensperger, J. Springenberg, M. Blum, and F. Hutter, "Efficient and robust automated machine learning," in *Advances in Neural Information Processing Systems*, Curran Associates, Inc., 2015. Accessed: Sep. 24, 2023. [Online]. Available: https://proceedings.neurips.cc/paper_files/paper/2015/hash/11d0e6287202fced83f79975ec59a3a6-Abstract.html
[48] D. Khurana, A. Koli, K. Khatter, and S. Singh, "Natural language processing: State of the art, current trends and challenges," *Multimed Tools Appl*, vol. 82, no. 3, pp. 3713–3744, Jan. 2023, doi: 10.1007/s11042-022-13428-4.
[49] S. Alaparthi and M. Mishra, "Bidirectional encoder representations from Transformers (BERT): A sentiment analysis odyssey," 2020, doi: 10.48550/ARXIV.2007.01127.
[50] A. Joulin, E. Grave, P. Bojanowski, and T. Mikolov, "Bag of tricks for efficient text classification," 2016, doi: 10.48550/ARXIV.1607.01759.
[51] R. Gozalo-Brizuela and E. C. Garrido-Merchan, "ChatGPT is not all you need. A state of the art review of large generative AI models," 2023, doi: 10.48550/ARXIV.2301.04655.
[52] D. Wu *et al.*, "Budget constrained bidding by model-free reinforcement learning in display advertising," in *Proceedings of the 27th ACM International Conference on Information and Knowledge Management*, Torino Italy: ACM, Oct. 2018, pp. 1443–1451. doi: 10.1145/3269206.3271748.

[53] Q. Liu, F. Yu, S. Wu, and L. Wang, "A convolutional click prediction model," in *Proceedings of the 24th ACM International on Conference on Information and Knowledge Management*, Melbourne Australia: ACM, Oct. 2015, pp. 1743–1746. doi: 10.1145/2806416.2806603.

[54] M. Liu, S. Cai, Z. Lai, L. Qiu, Z. Hu, and Y. Ding, "A joint learning model for click-through prediction in display advertising," *Neurocomputing*, vol. 445, pp. 206–219, Jul. 2021, doi: 10.1016/j.neucom.2021.02.036.

[55] N. Gordini and V. Veglio, "Customers churn prediction and marketing retention strategies. An application of support vector machines based on the AUC parameter-selection technique in B2B e-commerce industry," *Industrial Marketing Management*, vol. 62, pp. 100–107, Apr. 2017, doi: 10.1016/j.indmarman.2016.08.003.

[56] R. Sudharsan and E. N. Ganesh, "A Swish RNN based customer churn prediction for the telecom industry with a novel feature selection strategy," *Connection Science*, vol. 34, no. 1, pp. 1855–1876, Dec. 2022, doi: 10.1080/09540091.2022.2083584.

[57] H. Pan and H. Zhou, "Study on convolutional neural network and its application in data mining and sales forecasting for E-commerce," *Electron Commer Res*, vol. 20, no. 2, pp. 297–320, Jun. 2020, doi: 10.1007/s10660-020-09409-0.

[58] W. Verbeke, K. Dejaeger, D. Martens, J. Hur, and B. Baesens, "New insights into churn prediction in the telecommunication sector: A profit driven data mining approach," *European Journal of Operational Research*, vol. 218, no. 1, pp. 211–229, Apr. 2012, doi: 10.1016/j.ejor.2011.09.031.

[59] V. Dignum, *Responsible artificial intelligence: How to develop and use AI in a responsible way.* in Artificial Intelligence: Foundations, Theory, and Algorithms. Cham: Springer International Publishing, 2019. doi: 10.1007/978-3-030-30371-6.

[60] F. Doshi-Velez and B. Kim, "Towards A rigorous science of interpretable machine learning," 2017, doi: 10.48550/ARXIV.1702.08608.

[61] L. Carmi, M. Zohar, and G. M. Riva, "The European General Data Protection Regulation (GDPR) in mHealth: Theoretical and practical aspects for practitioners' use," *Med Sci Law*, vol. 63, no. 1, pp. 61–68, Jan. 2023, doi: 10.1177/00258024221118411.

[62] A. Acquisti, C. Taylor, and L. Wagman, "The economics of privacy," *Journal of Economic Literature*, vol. 54, no. 2, pp. 442–492, Jun. 2016, doi: 10.1257/jel.54.2.442.

[63] S. M. Mohammad and P. D. Turney, "Croud Sourcing a word – Emotion association lexicon," *Computational Intelligence*, vol. 29, no. 3, pp. 436–465, Aug. 2013, doi: 10.1111/j.1467-8640.2012.00460.x.

[64] Dr V. P. S., "How can we manage biases in artificial intelligence systems – A systematic literature review," *International Journal of Information Management Data Insights*, vol. 3, no. 1, p. 100165, Apr. 2023, doi: 10.1016/j.jjimei.2023.100165.

[65] M. Hardt, E. Price, E. Price, and N. Srebro, "Equality of opportunity in supervised learning," in *Advances in Neural Information Processing Systems*, Curran Associates, Inc., 2016. Accessed: Sep. 24, 2023. [Online]. Available: https://proceedings.neurips.cc/paper_files/paper/2016/hash/9d2682367c3935defcb1f9e247a97c0d-Abstract.html

[66] P. A. Norberg, D. R. Horne, and D. A. Horne, "The privacy paradox: Personal information disclosure intentions versus behaviors," *Journal of Consumer Affairs*, vol. 41, no. 1, pp. 100–126, Jun. 2007, doi: 10.1111/j.1745-6606.2006.00070.x.

[67] J. Van Doorn *et al.*, "Customer engagement behavior: Theoretical foundations and research directions," *Journal of Service Research*, vol. 13, no. 3, pp. 253–266, Aug. 2010, doi: 10.1177/1094670510375599.

5 Current Advances on the Application of Blockchain Solutions in Digital Marketing

Opportunities and Threats

Sami Mnasri
University of Tabuk, Tabuk, Saudi Arabia
University of Toulouse II, Toulouse, France

Ahmad Hassanat
Mutah University, Karak, Jordan

Mansoor Alghamdi and Malek Alrashidi
University of Tabuk, Tabuk, Saudi Arabia

Thierry Val
University of Toulouse II, Toulouse, France

5.1 MARKETING APPLICATIONS OF BLOCKCHAIN

Improving data recording, market connections, measuring intangible assets, and marketing for enhanced business performance.

5.1.1 Branding and Blockchain

Blockchain technology can enhance brand transparency and authenticity by creating a secure and immutable record of product information and transactions. Blockchain technology can enhance brand transparency and authenticity by creating a secure and immutable record of product information and transactions (Zhu et al, 2023).

The application of Blockchain in branding focuses in general on enhancing transparency, authenticity, and trust in numerous aspects of brand management and consumer interaction. Some potential applications of blockchain solutions in the field of branding are detailed in what follows:

- **Brand and Intellectual Property Control:** Blockchain technology may be used to safely manage patents, copyrights, and brands, prohibiting unlawful use, and safeguarding the intellectual property of the company.
- **Counterfeit Product Prevention:** Reputational harm and financial losses can result from the sale of counterfeit goods. Blockchain technology can assist in establishing a tamper-proof trail of each product's travels, making it more challenging for counterfeiters to reproduce.

DOI: 10.1201/9781003450443-5

- **Sustainable/Green Branding:** Companies that care about the environment and the future of the planet may use blockchain to demonstrate their commitment to sustainability and to demonstrate the openness of their supply chains.
- **Digital Identity and Authentication:** Blockchain may be used to provide things with a trustworthy and unchangeable digital identity. This can aid customers in determining the legitimacy of products and stop the selling of illicit goods.
- **Loyalty Programs:** By establishing transparent and traceable incentive systems, blockchain may improve loyalty programs. Customers can be sure that the recording and use of their reward points are accurate.
- **Product Details and Storytelling:** Businesses may utilize blockchain to share comprehensive details about the path their products take from conception to distribution. Information about sourcing, production techniques, and sustainability initiatives may be included.
- **Customer Participation:** Tokens or assets based on blockchain may be used to reward customer participation, such as doing surveys, giving feedback, or posting material about brands on social media.
- **Collaboration and Partnerships between Brands:** Blockchain can support safe and open brand collaborations, guaranteeing that joint projects are publicly and correctly documented.

To appropriately integrate the Blockchain technology with the existing branding systems, the steps in Figure 5.1 can be followed.

Indeed, first, pinpoint the functions of your brand where blockchain might provide value. Supply chain transparency, counterfeit prevention, product provenance, digital identification, and consumer involvement are typical use cases. Identify the areas of your brand where more openness and trust would be most beneficial.

Then, the goals you want to accomplish with blockchain integration should be made very clear. Do you wish to increase consumer trust, stop fraud, or improve supply chain operations, for instance? Your Blockchain implementation plan will be guided by setting clear goals.

Afterwards, select a distributed ledger system that fits the requirements of your brand. Decentralization is offered by public Blockchains like *Binance* or *Ethereum* Smart Chain, although scalability concerns may arise. Although less decentralized than public blockchains, private or consortium blockchains offer greater oversight on participants and data. Consider elements such as scalability and compatibility with existing systems.

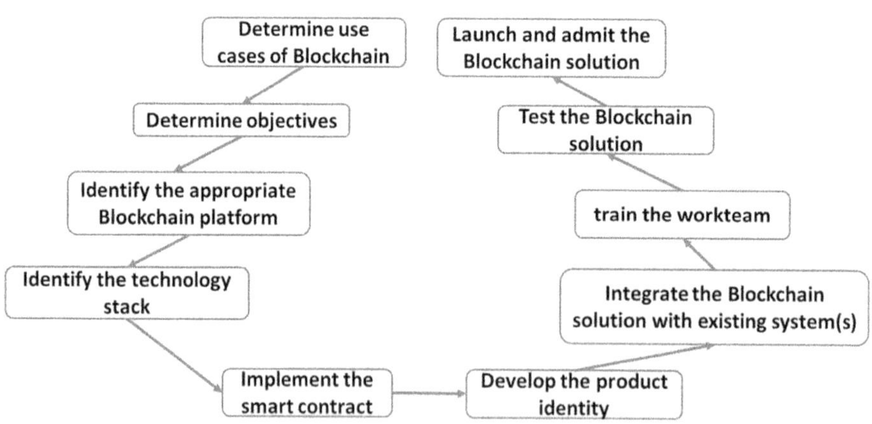

FIGURE 5.1 Incorporate Blockchain into brand management.

Besides, choose the technological stack your Blockchain solution will require. This entails deciding on coding languages, software platforms, and tools for creating decentralized apps and smart contracts.

Moreover, develop DApps and smart contracts. For instance, you might create a DApp that enables users to trace the whole supply chain or a smart contract to confirm the legitimacy of your items.

After that, create a mechanism for producing, storing, and validating these identities if you're utilizing Blockchain to create product IDs or digital credentials. This might entail designing distinctive tokens for your items.

Also, connect your Blockchain solution to your current databases and systems. This guarantees smooth data transfer across your company's infrastructure's Blockchain and non-Blockchain components.

Furthermore, inform your employees, your business partners, and your clients on the advantages of Blockchain technology and how to use the new capabilities you are adding. This will facilitate a smoother adoption by making the changes and their advantages clearer to everyone.

Additionally, before making your Blockchain solution available to the public, thoroughly test it in a controlled setting. Address any problems or weaknesses found during testing.

Finally, launch your Blockchain solution to your intended audience as soon as it is complete. Market the Blockchain-enabled functionalities to your stakeholders and consumers, emphasizing the improved advantages and experiences they may anticipate.

Despite this significant potential of application of Blockchain solutions in branding, it still relevant to note that Blockchain adoption in branding is still relatively nascent, and challenges such as regulatory compliance, scalability, or user adoption need to be addressed for widespread implementation. Besides, use cases of use of Blockchain in branding vary depending on the industry and the objectives of each brand.

5.1.2 Online Advertising and Blockchain

Blockchain can provide transparency and security in online advertising by ensuring ad views and clicks are legitimate. Hence, by using Blockchain, advertisers and publishers can increase efficiency and improve targeting for a more effective ad campaign. Blockchain's decentralized network records transactions, improving accountability and preventing fraudulent behavior in online advertising. Indeed, decentralized advert exchange ecosystem governs online ads in Blockchain exchanges, enhancing media supply chain's transparency and immutability (Zheng et al, 2018).

Hence, why do we need Blockchain technology in the realm of digital advertising? When online information expansion leads to inconsistency, the Blockchain platforms become a necessity. Publishers then started looking for a better solution for transparency. Since the previous decade, advertising networks like Facebook and Google Ads have benefited from the dominant infrastructure in the digital advertising sector. These advertising demons oversaw the data and information to generate enormous net profits. Due to its many possibilities, Blockchain is now being included into advertising systems.

Blockchain applications in digital advertising includes avoiding intermediaries while buying and selling, ensuring supply chain transparency, concentrating on the correct crowd (audience), information management, personalized advertising, social media advertising campaigns, security of data, promotion examination, and promotion automated processes.

5.1.3 Pricing and Blockchain

Blockchain offers security in pricing by enabling a decentralized, tamper-proof record of transactions. Blockchain's ability to automate price negotiation and enforce smart contracts can simplify and expedite pricing processes for businesses. Moreover, using Blockchain for pricing helps prevent fraud, collusion, and misinformation, and can enable dynamic and automated pricing strategies.

In a world where customers are becoming more participatory in their interactions with brands due to the introduction of information technology and channels that facilitate this interaction, there appears to be a significant shift in how firms include their customers in management decisions, including pricing techniques and sales models. The shift reflects a shift away from previous pricing procedures that were largely centralized inside the company and toward a more interactive and customized approach driven by feedback from customers. Managers must know that individuals with the greatest readiness to pay (WTP) have two key dimensions: dishonest clients who have a motivation to get cheaper pricing and their incapacity to measure value.

This is mostly due to information asymmetry difficulties. Because of the arbitrary nature of their valuation, customers set a value on a thing that is a perceived value but not the actual worth of the product itself. This is where Blockchain solution, a decentralized transactional and documentation-based technique that eliminates intermediaries between companies, might play a significant role in transforming revenue stream models and consumer interactions.

For more details about the use of Blockchain for pricing, the study in (Wang et al, 2022) gives an introduction of how companies might assess perceived standards and WTP, as well as a quick explanation of potential pricing techniques that firms could employ and the significance of trustworthiness. The study will investigate potential real-world uses of Blockchain technology in peer-to-peer, B2B, and B2C business models, as well as how customers might directly monetize their interactions with enterprises. Lastly, this article addresses how Blockchain technologies might affect managerial decisions about pricing and income stream models, as well as the limits of this technology.

In (Tao et al, 2023), the authors discuss the influence of the Blockchain system on the best pricing and quality decisions made by the supply chains discovers that when consumer adoption of Blockchain is low, the goods using Blockchain possess not only a high quality but also a low price among the two products in a single platform. Conversely, in the scenario of the two competing platforms, while Blockchain will allow the ecosystem that leverages this technology to supply high-quality, low-cost items, the benefits are not evident. Nonetheless, when customer adoption is strong, both competing platforms tend to deliver high-quality, low-cost items, independently from the use of Blockchain technology.

Our findings show that, while Blockchain will help customers as well as suppliers, in some situations, the supplier may have a temptation to reduce the quality level of the items using Blockchain model, that will ultimately adversely affect consumers.

5.1.4 Privacy and Blockchain

Blockchain can help protect customer privacy by providing a secure and transparent way to store and share personal data. Besides, by leveraging blockchain, companies can enable customers to have greater control over their personal information and build trust with them.

The Blockchain technology is a wonderful example of how privacy and security are unrelated. While it is feasible to create an inviolable, resistant to tamp transaction. This transaction is visible to all nodes on the network. zk-SNARKs, which are carried out by zCash on Ethereum, are presently the most intriguing studies on privacy for Blockchain technology. The integration of the two technologies allows for the implementation of anonymous payments, the blind auctions as well, and systems for voting.

The use of both public and private keys is a crucial component of privacy in Blockchains. Blockchain systems safeguard user transactions using symmetric cryptography (Archana et al, 2018). Each user in these systems has a public and a private key. These keys are connected to cryptography and consist of random numbers. A user cannot, theoretically, infer a different user's private key from his public key. Users are shielded from hackers and security is improved as a result. Since public key scans do not divulge any personal information, they might be shared with other network users. Utilizing a hash function, each user's address is created from the public key. On the Blockchain, these addresses are used to transfer and receive assets like cryptocurrency.

Users can check previous transactions and prior Blockchain activity since Blockchain networks are accessible by all members.

The following section discusses the most relevant cryptographic Blockchain based techniques used for privacy preservation.

- Zero-knowledge proofs: A zero-knowledge proof (ZKP) is an encryption technique that allows one party named "prover" to demonstrate a different party named "verifier" that a particular statement is true without imparting any information other than the reality that the statement is true. The "prover" provides no details about the transaction in question. To strengthen Blockchain privacy, such proofs are often integrated into systems utilizing ZK-SNARKs (Yunsen et al, 2018).
- Ring signatures which are another means of obscuring the sequence of transactional operations on the public Blockchain.
- Mixing: Even with a pseudo anonymous cryptocurrency, bitcoin tumblers can be utilized to boost privacy. Furthermore, rather than employing mixers as an extension service, the mixing of publicly accessible addresses, like in Dash, may be built-in as a technique in the Blockchain system (Corin et al, 2022).

However, some challenges arise in this context. Blockchain technology is a wonderful example of how and when privacy-enhancing technologies are used. However, because metadata is still produced, even if the data is encrypted, statistical analysis will expose "some" information, allowing the execution of pattern detection processes for example. In addition, scaling is a developing issue, as the consensus procedure is now prohibitively costly. A substantially faster transaction speed is required for trading money or any other value on a Blockchain-based application. Ethereum presently has a transaction rate of 2.8 transactions per second, while bitcoin has a transaction rate of roughly 3.2 transactions per second. It takes so long because each transaction requires a complicated consensus process Consensus specs(2023), Satoshi(2008). Blockchain technology is a wonderful example of how privacy and another assault to be aware of is the 51%-attack, also known as the "Majority Hash Rate Attack." If a person or company controls 51% of the hash control, the attacker can reverse transactions he made, block transactions from receiving confirmations, and prohibit other participants from mining (Meni et al., 2014).

5.2 POSSIBLE IMPLICATIONS OF BLOCKCHAIN IN MARKETING

Product origin and supply chain can be investigated by blockchain technology, which enables fast and secure transactions for price, improve distribution in place, and enhance targeted promotion. This facilitates the traceability and proof of ownership for luxury goods or collectibles and prevents counterfeit products. Hence the focus here will be on the relationship between blockchain from one side and Product, Price, place, and promotion from the other side.

Blockchain technology has a transformative impact on the field of marketing, reshaping various practices and offering novel opportunities (Gleim et al, 2021). One of the foremost impacts is the heightened transparency and accountability it brings to marketing operations. Blockchain's decentralized ledger records every transaction, interaction, and data exchange, ensuring that information is temper-proof and accessible to all relevant parties. This newfound transparency cultivates trust between businesses and consumers, as brands can provide verified information about their products, supply chains, and marketing claims, thereby enhancing their reputation.

A pivotal change that Blockchain ushers in is the enhancement of data security and privacy. Through its encryption and distributed storage, Blockchain mitigates the risk of data breaches and unauthorized access, safeguarding sensitive customer information. In an era where data privacy is a paramount concern, this innovation resonates deeply with both marketers and consumers.

Furthermore, Blockchain technology offers a formidable solution to combat the persisting issue of ad fraud. The transparency and immutability of Blockchain make it exceedingly difficult for fraudulent activities, such as click fraud or impression fraud (Roriz et al, 2019), to manipulate advertising metrics.

This empowers advertisers with accurate data, ensuring that their investments yield legitimate results.

Supply chain transparency is another area significantly impacted by blockchain in marketing. Industries reliant on complex supply chains, like the food and luxury goods sectors, can leverage Blockchain to provide end-to-end visibility. By tracing each step of a product's journey, marketers can authenticate claims of authenticity, ethical sourcing, and product quality, reinforcing consumer confidence.

Decentralized advertising networks represent a notable evolution facilitated by Blockchain. This innovation facilitates direct peer-to-peer interactions between advertisers and publishers, bypassing intermediaries. This decentralization fosters equitable revenue distribution, precise targeting, and reduced fees, thereby reshaping the dynamics of the advertising industry.

Customer engagement takes on new dimensions with Blockchain-powered loyalty programs. By employing Blockchain-based tokens, brands can create loyalty rewards that customers can earn and utilize across diverse businesses. This approach not only strengthens customer loyalty but also encourages active engagement.

Smart contract automation is another substantial impact. These self-executing contracts codify terms directly into code, streamlining various marketing agreements. Processes such as influencer collaborations, affiliate marketing, and royalty payments can be automated, minimizing administrative overhead and reducing the potential for disputes.

Content authenticity is also addressed through Blockchain. Brands can validate the originality of digital content, ensuring that their marketing materials remain credible and free from plagiarism.

Moreover, Blockchain grants consumers ownership over their data, enabling them to decide when and how their information is used. This shift to consumer-controlled data sharing fosters a more respectful and transparent relationship between marketers and consumers.

In essence, Blockchain's influence on marketing is comprehensive. It redefines trust, data security, and engagement, while also introducing novel concepts like token-based advertising, digital asset ownership, and more ethical marketing practices. However, challenges such as scalability, integration, and regulatory considerations must be navigated for Blockchain to reach its full potential in the marketing realm.

5.3 PRACTICAL USES OF BLOCKCHAIN IN MARKETING

The use of Blockchain in marketing fields can be in the following practical contexts:

- **Fraud Prevention:** Blockchain can enhance the fraud prevention in marketing by leveraging its unique features. Blockchain offers a secure way to track and verify data, preventing fraud and enhancing transparency in marketing operations. Marketers can use Blockchain for identity verification, ad tracking, and personalization while protecting consumer privacy and data security from any potential fraud.
- **Immutable and Transparent Ledger:** Blockchain's core feature is its immutable and transparent ledger. If the information is saved on the Blockchain, it becomes unchangeable without consensus from the network participants. This prevents fraudsters

from manipulating data, such as inflating click counts or creating fake conversions in digital advertising.

- **Traceable Supply Chains:** In cases where marketing involves physical products, Blockchain can ensure the authenticity of products along the supply chain. This prevents fraud related to counterfeit goods, as each step of the product's journey is recorded and verified on the Blockchain.
- **Decentralization:** Blockchain's decentralized nature removes the need for a central authority, reducing the risk of a single point of failure. This can make fraudulent activities that rely on central vulnerabilities more challenging to execute.
- **Secure Identity Verification:** Blockchain can enhance user identity verification by securely storing and verifying user information. This helps prevent fraudulent account creation and ensures that only genuine users participate in marketing campaigns.
- **Reduce the Number of Intermediaries:** The use of Blockchain in marketing reduces the number of intermediaries: Blockchain in marketing aims to minimize intermediaries to streamline transactions (Lorne et al, 2018) and increase efficiency. Also, by enabling new revenue streams such as micropayments and loyalty programs directly with customers.
- **Operational Benefits:** such as log transaction data from several sources, etc.

Hence, Blockchain's transparency and immutability can facilitate the detection of unusual patterns or discrepancies in marketing data. By analyzing the data recorded on the Blockchain, fraud detection algorithms can identify suspicious activities (Rejeb et al, 2020).

Blockchain logs transaction data using a distributed and immutable ledger. Here's how the process generally works:

- **Data Structuring:** Each transaction or piece of data to be logged onto the blockchain is structured into a block. A block typically contains multiple transactions along with a unique identifier (hash) for the block itself.
- **Hashing:** Before a block is added to the blockchain, its contents are hashed. A hash is a cryptographic algorithm that transforms the data into a fixed-length string of characters. Even a small change in the data will result in a completely different hash.
- **Linking Blocks:** Each block in the Blockchain contains a reference to the hash of the previous block. This creates a chronological chain of blocks, hence the name "Blockchain." The linking of blocks using their hashes ensures the integrity of the entire chain.

5.4 MARKET-BASED ASSETS

5.4.1 Brand Equity

Blockchain has the potential to improve brand equity in the supply chain by strengthening the relationship between consumers and brand. Blockchain provides a temper-proof ledger of information, which helps brands build trust with consumers and create a loyal customer base.

Brand equity refers to the value and strength of a brand in the market. It is a concept representing intangible assets that a brand possesses, which contribute to its ability to generate value for a company. Brand equity is often divided into two main categories: customer-based brand equity and market-based brand equity.

Market-based brand equity focuses specifically on the impact of the brand on a company's financial performance and market position. It encompasses various tangible and measurable assets that contribute to the brand's value in the market. These market-based assets are typically related to financial metrics and market performance (Stallone et al, 2021).

Some key components of market-based brand equity include:

- Brand Awareness: This refers to the level of recognition and recall a brand has among consumers. A higher level of brand awareness often leads to increased market share and customer preference.
- Brand Loyalty: Repeat customers and loyal brand followers contribute to stable revenue streams. Brands with strong loyalty are often more resilient in the face of market fluctuations.
- Brand Associations: These are the specific attributes and qualities that consumers associate with a brand. Positive brand associations can lead to increased customer loyalty and preference.
- Brand Extensions: The success of extending a brand into new product categories can demonstrate the strength of the brand's reputation and consumer trust.
- Market Share: A brand's share of the total market within its industry is a clear indicator of its strength and competitive position.
- Perceived Quality: The perceived quality of a brand's products or services can significantly impact its market position. Brands with a reputation for high quality tend to command higher prices and greater market share.
- Price Premium: Some strong brands can command higher prices compared to their competitors due to the perceived value they offer.

5.4.2 Customer Equity

By providing control over their data, customers are more likely to remain loyal and recommend the business. So, using Blockchain to store and secure customer data can help businesses build trust and increase customer equity.

Customer equity is another relevant concept in marketing, which is closely related to brand equity. While brand equity focuses on strengths of a brand, customer equity focuses on the value of a company's customer base. It highlights the combined lifetime value of all current and potential customers. Just as brand equity is divided into customer-based and market-based components, customer equity may also be understood in terms of customer-based and market-based assets.

Market-based assets related to customer equity generally have a direct impact on a company's financial performance and market position through their influence on customers' purchasing behaviors and preferences. Some key components of market-based assets within the context of customer equity include:

- Customer Lifetime Value (CLV): CLV is the total value a company can expect to generate from a customer throughout their entire relationship with the brand. It considers not only the customer's initial purchase but also their repeat purchases over time.
- Customer Segmentation: Identifying different customer segments based on their needs, preferences, and behaviors allows a company to tailor its marketing efforts and offerings to effectively reach and serve each segment.
- Customer Retention Rate: The percentage of customers who continue to make purchases from the company over time. A higher retention rate indicates a more loyal customer base.
- Customer Satisfaction and Loyalty: Satisfied and loyal customers are more likely to continue buying from the brand and recommend it to others.
- Customer Acquisition Cost (CAC): The cost associated with acquiring a new customer. Lower CAC can lead to higher customer equity.
- Cross-Selling and Upselling Opportunities: Identifying opportunities to sell additional products or services to existing customers can increase their overall value.

- Customer Churn Rate: The rate at which customers stop purchasing from a company. Minimizing churn is crucial for maintaining customer equity.
- Customer Advocacy: Customers who actively promote and defend the brand online and offline contribute to its reputation and customer equity.

Ultimately, both brand equity and customer equity are crucial for the success of any company. Indeed, a strong brand equity leads to higher customer equity as customers are more likely to engage with and remain loyal to well-regarded brands. However, building strong customer equity can positively impact brand equity as satisfied and loyal customers enhance the brand's reputation through their interactions and advocacy (Tan et al, 2023).

5.5 OPPORTUNITIES OF USE OF BLOCKCHAIN IN MARKETING

5.5.1 Market Research

What payment should participants receive? What design and payment features would influence participation? What smart contract would attract participants? Blockchain technology has the potential to significantly impact market research by enhancing the security, transparency, and accuracy of the data. Here's how Blockchain can influence market research:

- Trustworthy Data Sharing: Blockchain enables controlled data sharing among stakeholders. Market researchers, businesses, and even consumers can securely access relevant data, leading to more accurate insights and more informed decision-making.
- Cross-Border Research: For global market research, Blockchain's ability to facilitate secure and efficient cross-border transactions can be valuable. Payments to respondents, researchers, or service providers can be made using cryptocurrencies, reducing currency conversion and transaction fees.
- Authenticity and Data Integrity: With Blockchain, data entries are time-stamped and cannot be altered or deleted once recorded. This ensures the integrity and authenticity of market research data. Researchers can verify the source and history of data, enhancing the reliability of insights derived from it.
- Eliminating Intermediaries: In traditional market research, intermediaries such as data aggregators and survey platforms are in general involved in data collection and distribution. Blockchain can simplify the direct interactions between researchers and respondents, reducing the need for intermediaries and potentially lowering costs.
- Cross-Border Research: For global market research, Blockchain's ability to facilitate secure and efficient cross-border transactions can be valuable. Payments to respondents, researchers, or service providers can be made using cryptocurrencies, reducing currency conversion and transaction costs.

Despite the previously mentioned potential benefits, integrating Blockchain into market research requires careful consideration of technical, ethical, and legal constraints. Collaboration between market researchers, Blockchain experts, and legal professionals is essential to ensure successful implementation and compliance with relevant regulations (Alrowaily et al, 2023).

5.5.2 Supply Chains

How can Blockchain lead to increased sales, better prices, and an improved chain? Do consumers care about supply chain transparency and sustainability? Will it affect their behavior if transparency improves?

Supply chains play a crucial role in marketing, as they directly impact on a company's ability to deliver products or services to customers efficiently, reliably, and in a way that meets customer expectations. Here's how supply chains intersect with marketing:

Blockchain technology has the potential to revolutionize supply chains in marketing by enhancing transparency, traceability, and trust throughout the entire supply chain process. Here is how Blockchain can impact supply chains in marketing:

- Anti-Counterfeiting: Blockchain can help combat counterfeit products by creating a secure and tamper-proof record of a product's history. This information can be accessed by consumers using QR codes or other means, allowing them to confirm the authenticity of a product before purchase.
- Efficient Inventory Management: Blockchain provides real-time visibility into inventory levels across the supply chain, helping marketing teams plan campaigns and promotions based on accurate stock data.
- Supply Chain Optimization: Data recorded on the Blockchain can provide insights into inefficiencies or bottlenecks in the supply chain. Marketing teams can leverage this data to plan campaigns that align with the supply chain's capabilities.
- Global Trade: Blockchain streamlines international flow of trade by digitizing and automating documentation processes. This significantly reduces time and cost associated with customs clearance and cross-border transactions, allowing marketing campaigns to reach global markets more efficiently.

Incorporating blockchain technology into the supply chain in marketing requires collaboration between numerous stakeholders. While potential benefits exist, the adoption and integration can be complex and may require careful planning and investment.

5.5.3 Digital Platforms

How will transparency in supply chains impact consumer behavior in terms of sustainability, sales, pricing, and brand reputation? Blockchain technology has the potential to impact digital platforms in marketing by enhancing transparency, security, and trust in various aspects of online advertising, e-commerce, and data management. Blockchain can intersect with digital platforms in marketing as follows:

- Cross-Platform Data Integration: Blockchain can facilitate the secure sharing and integration of data across different digital marketing platforms, leading to more comprehensive and accurate customer insights.
- Digital Identity Verification: Blockchain can enable secure digital identity verification, which is important for user registration and access to various digital platforms. Verified digital identities can help prevent fraudulent activities and ensure a trustworthy user base.
- Supply Chain Tracking: In e-commerce platforms, Blockchain can optimize the transparency of supply chains by tracking different aspects of the products such as origin and journey. Customers can verify the authenticity and quality of products before purchasing, which is especially valuable for luxury goods and products with complex supply chains.
- Secure Customer Profiles: Blockchain can create a decentralized customer profile system where users maintain ownership of their data across different platforms. This enables more accurate customer targeting while ensuring data security and privacy.

Despite Blockchain can offer numerous benefits to digital marketing platforms, it's important to note that its implementation can be complex and may require industry-wide collaboration and standardization. Besides, Blockchain's scalability and regulatory considerations should be carefully evaluated before starting the implementation.

5.6 THREATS OF EMPLOYING BLOCKCHAIN FOR MARKETING

5.6.1 Ownership Verification

Blockchain enables data tokenization, democratizing sharing, and monetization of digital assets and fostering trust among data owners. In addition, Blockchain can enable traceability and proof of ownership for luxury goods or collectibles and prevent counterfeit products.

Blockchain technology has brought about significant advancements in various industries, primarily due to its ability to provide secure and transparent ownership verification. Despite this, like any technology, Blockchain is not without its threats and challenges. Here are some threats related to ownership verification on the Blockchain:

- Lack of Standardization: The lack of standardized protocols and practices for ownership verification across different Blockchain platforms can lead to confusion and inconsistencies. This can create opportunities for malicious actors to exploit gaps and inconsistencies.
- Smart Contract Vulnerabilities: Smart contracts, self-executing scripts that run on the Blockchain, are susceptible to coding errors and vulnerabilities. If a smart contract contains a flaw, attackers could exploit it to gain unauthorized access to assets or ownership rights, potentially leading to incorrect ownership verification.
- 51% Attack: In a blockchain network, if a single entity or group controls over 51% of the network's computing power, they can potentially manipulate the system. This could involve reversing transactions, double-spending coins, or preventing new transactions from being confirmed. Such an attack could undermine the integrity of ownership verification.
- Interoperability Issues: Different Blockchains and distributed ledgers may not be able to easily communicate with each other, leading to challenges when verifying ownership across different networks. This could result in discrepancies and disputes over ownership (Casino et al, 2019).
- Data Oracles: Smart contracts often require real world data to execute properly. Data oracles are mechanisms that provide this external data to the Blockchain. However, compromised, or faulty data oracles could provide incorrect information, leading to incorrect ownership verification.

To address these ownership issues, ongoing research and development are crucial. Blockchain developers and researchers need to continually enhance the security of Blockchain-based networks, smart contracts, and associated mechanisms to guarantee an accurate ownership verification. Moreover, educating users about best practices for securing their private keys and interacting with Blockchain applications can mitigate many of these threats

5.6.2 Digital Assets

Digital assets are assets that exist solely in digital form and can be stored on a Blockchain network for security and transparency.

Blockchain technology has revolutionized the way of managing digital assets by providing security, transparency, and decentralized control. However, like any technology, Blockchain is not immune to threats and vulnerabilities. Here are some threats related to digital assets in the context of Blockchain:

- Wallet Vulnerabilities: Digital assets are typically stored in wallets, which are managed through private keys. If a user's wallet is compromised, whether through hacking, phishing, or malware, attackers can gain access to the private keys and steal the assets.
- Loss of Private Keys: If a user loses the private key, access to his resources and assets can be permanently prohibited. Unlike traditional financial institutions, there is no way to recover lost keys on most Blockchain networks.
- Phishing Attacks: Attackers can create fake websites or applications that mimic legitimate Blockchain services to trick users into providing their private keys or sensitive information. This information is then used to access and steal digital assets.
- Irreversible Transactions: While the immutability of Blockchain is a strength, it can also be a drawback. If a user makes an irreversible transaction by mistake or falls victim to a scam, they may not be able to recover their assets.
- Malware and Keyloggers: Malicious software can infect a user's computer or device and record keystrokes, including private keys and login credentials. This information is then sent to the attacker, allowing them to gain unauthorized access to the user's digital assets.
- Exchange Hacks: Centralized cryptocurrency exchanges are often targeted by hackers due to the large amounts of digital assets stored in their systems. If an exchange is compromised, users' assets stored on the platform can be stolen.
- Social Engineering: Attackers can manipulate individuals into revealing sensitive information or performing actions that compromise their digital assets. This can include impersonating customer support representatives, friends, or family members.
- Ponzi and Scam Schemes: Fraudulent schemes can lure users with promises of high returns on investments or new cryptocurrencies. Once users invest or transfer their assets, the scammers disappear, leaving victims with losses.
- Regulatory Uncertainty: The regulatory environment for Blockchain and digital assets is still evolving. Sudden changes in regulations or legal challenges could impact the use and value of digital assets.
- Fork Attacks: A Blockchain fork occurs when a network splits into two separate chains due to differences in consensus rules. Attackers can exploit these forks to double-spend coins or create confusion regarding asset ownership.
- Quantum Computing: While still theoretical for widespread use, quantum computers could potentially break current cryptographic methods, compromising the security of digital asset storage and transactions.

To mitigate these threats, individuals and organizations need to prioritize security practices such as using hardware wallets, keeping software updated, using strong and unique passwords, and verifying the authenticity of websites and applications. Besides, the industry must continue to develop and implement robust security measures and stay vigilant against emerging threats.

5.6.3 Organizational Restrictions

Blockchain can be used for marketing by collaborating with decentralized ad exchanges, integrating touchpoints with identity networks, and designing NFTs.

Blockchain technology has introduced a range of benefits and challenges, both from a technological and managerial perspective. Here are some of the managerial threats and organizational restrictions associated with Blockchain technology:

- Transparency and Trust: Blockchain's transparent and immutable nature can enhance trust between parties in a business network. Managers can leverage this feature to build stronger relationships with customers, suppliers, and partners.

- Reduced Intermediaries: Blockchain has the potential to eliminate intermediaries in various processes, which can lead to cost savings for businesses. Managers should explore how this reduction in intermediaries can impact their business models and supply chain.
- Streamlined Processes: Blockchain can automate and streamline complex processes through smart contracts. Managers should understand how to design and implement these contracts to optimize their business processes.
- Decentralization: Decentralized blockchain networks can distribute control and decision-making. Managers must adapt their hierarchical structures and decision-making processes to harness the benefits of decentralization.
- Data Security: Blockchain's cryptographic principles enhance data security. Managers should consider the implications of secure data sharing and storage, especially in industries that handle sensitive information (Ertemel et al, 2018).
- Supply Chain Management: Blockchain can enhance traceability and transparency in supply chains, reducing fraud and ensuring product authenticity. Managers should explore how to integrate Blockchain to optimize their supply chain processes.
- Lack of Regulation: The regulatory landscape surrounding Blockchain and cryptocurrencies is still evolving. Managers must navigate legal uncertainties and potential changes that could impact their operations.
- Scalability Issues: Blockchain networks like Bitcoin and Ethereum have faced scalability challenges, resulting in slower transaction speeds and higher costs during peak usage. Managers should consider the limitations of current Blockchain platforms for their business needs.

In conclusion, Blockchain technology presents both promising managerial implications and potential threats. Successful adoption of Blockchain implies careful consideration of these factors, as well as a strategic approach to leverage the technology's benefits while mitigating its risks.

5.6.4 Digital Rights and Identity

With a decentralized identity network, consumers can control their identity and attributes rather than depend on governments or businesses. Blockchain provides decentralized digital identities, enabling individuals to prove their identity without relying on state authorities or commercial actors.

Blockchain technology has the potential to revolutionize digital rights and identity management by providing secure and decentralized solutions (Jain et al, 2021). However, it also introduces certain threats and challenges that need to be addressed. Here are some of the threats related to Blockchain in the context of digital rights and identity:

- Data Breaches and Unauthorized Access: Public Blockchains, by design, are transparent and open to anyone. While they offer security through consensus mechanisms, they may expose sensitive identity-related information to unauthorized parties. Private Blockchains provide more control, but they can still be vulnerable to insider threats.
- Self-Sovereign Identity Risks: Self-sovereign identity solutions allow individuals to control their own identity information. However, this also increases the risk of individuals creating fake identities or credentials.
- Legal and Regulatory Challenges: Blockchain operates across borders, which can lead to jurisdictional conflicts in terms of legal enforcement and regulatory compliance. Different countries might have varying standards for data protection and identity verification.
- Scalability and Performance: Some Blockchain networks face scalability issues, leading to slow transaction speeds. In identity systems, delays in verification and authentication processes can be frustrating for users.

- Identity Theft and Fraud: If not properly implemented, Blockchain-based identity systems could be susceptible to hacking or unauthorized access. If a user's private key is compromised, their entire identity could be at risk.
- Standardization and Interoperability: The lack of standardized protocols for digital identity across different Blockchains and systems can hinder interoperability and data portability.

In addressing these threats, it's essential to strike a balance between the benefits of Blockchain-based digital identity solutions and the need to protect users' privacy, security, and control over their data. Regulatory frameworks, technological innovations, and industry collaboration will play a crucial role in shaping the future of Blockchain-based digital rights and identity management.

5.6.5 Customer Trust and Privacy

Classical three trust mechanisms can be distinguished to support the relationship marketing theory and social exchange theory to allay customers' worries about data privacy issues (Latifi et al, 2019). These mechanisms are characteristic-based (e.g., cooperative marketing programs), process-based (e.g., reputation and brand names), and institutional-based (e.g., third parties' certificates). The aim is to investigate the relationship between Blockchain and these three mechanisms.

Blockchain technology has the potential to enhance customer trust and privacy through its transparent and secure nature. However, there are also threats and challenges associated with Blockchain in these areas (Pittaras et al, 2021). Here are some of the threats related to Blockchain in the context of customer trust and privacy:

- Data Immutability and Privacy Concerns: Blockchain's immutability ensures the integrity of data, but this also means that saved information becomes unchangeable. This poses challenges if sensitive customer data, such as personal information, is stored on the blockchain.
- User Adoption and Usability: Blockchain-based solutions can be complex for non-technical users, potentially leading to mistakes or misunderstandings that compromise privacy.
- Supply Chain Privacy and Traceability: While Blockchain can improve transparency in supply chains, it might also expose sensitive business relationships or proprietary information that companies want to keep private.
- Misuse of Customer Data and Unauthorized Sharing: In some cases, third parties might misuse customer data stored on a Blockchain without the customer's consent, potentially leading to privacy breaches.

To address these threats and ensure customer trust and privacy, organizations need to carefully consider the type of Blockchain they use (public or private), implement strong data protection measures, provide user-friendly solutions for private key management, conduct thorough security audits, and remain compliant with relevant regulations. Striking a balance between transparency, security, and privacy is essential for Blockchain's successful integration into customer-centric operations (Marthews et al, 2023).

5.7 CASE STUDIES

5.7.1 Case Study of Branding Transparency Using Blockchain

A good example of involving the Blockchain technology process in branding is the integrity and transparency of the supply chain of a premium clothing company (Figure 5.2).

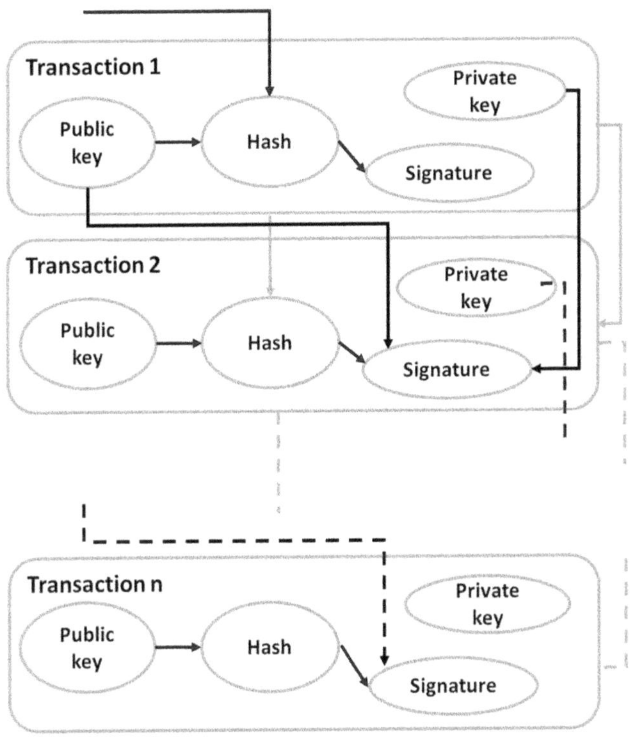

FIGURE 5.2 Principal of Blockchain processes.

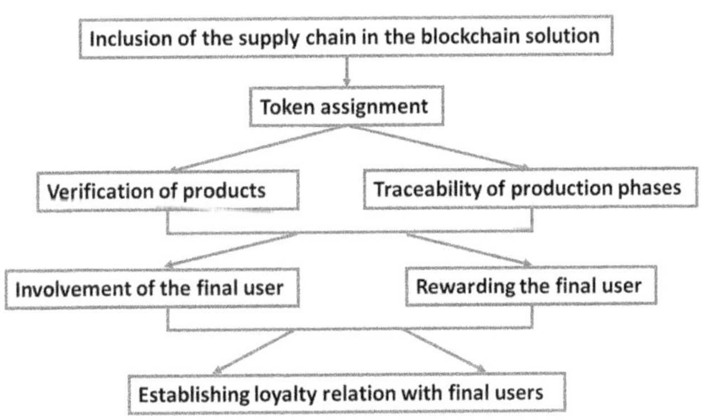

FIGURE. 5.3 Reliability of a clothing company's supply chain.

The use of Blockchain for enhancing the image of a fashion brand can be designed in Figure 5.3 as follows:

- Inclusion of the Supply Chain in the Blockchain Solution: The clothing company cooperates with the Blockchain developers to implement the Blockchain solution of the supply chain. This solution should involve all the steps of the supply chain starting from primary materials to retail.
- Token Assignment: A token (a distinct numerical id) will be assigned on Blockchain for each product from the clothing company. The token contains information about the materials, suppliers, used in the made of the product.

- Verification of Products: The customer should be able to verify the authenticity of their purchased products via the Blockchain which guarantees the non-modification of the products details.
- Traceability of Production Phases: The Blockchain solution facilitates the traceability of the product from source to the hands of the consumer and allows the visualization of information about ethical declarations such as carbon footprint or energy consumption of each production phase.
- Involvement of the Final User: The involvement of the final customer by giving him an interactive Blockchain-based experience of assessing the manufacturing story of the product. For example, using a mobile application, the final user might visualize trials of artisans and employee's tasks in the work.
- Rewarding the Final User: the final user or customer can be rewarded via discounts blockchain-based tokens upon their participation in surveys, evaluations, or online sharing of their experiences with the product.
- Establishing Loyalty Relation with Final Users: transparent manufacturing phases for final users enhances the trust and loyalty of the latter and constructs the brand positive image.

The latter example illustrates that Blockchain technology can efficiently help a brand with building its one unique image in a competitive market. This is achieved by engaging consumers, making manufacturing phases transparent to them, and ensuring the authenticity and sustainability of the products.

5.7.2 Case Study of Customer Loyalty Using Blockchain

Customer loyalty depends on positive perceptions and reactions like purchasing repeatedly. Customer loyalty is crucial for the business to keep its present clients. The reason for this is that a company may gain greatly from loyal customers. Loyal consumers are less price sensitive, require less promotion to bring in new clients, and increase business profits.

The following case study, shown in Figure 5.4 and highlighted in (Bülbül et al, 2018), presents a customer promotion and loyalty program based on Blockchain.

In this loyalty program, the standard promotion coupon is substituted with a token. To ensure data integrity, we track every transaction in the Blockchain system. Additionally, businesses that

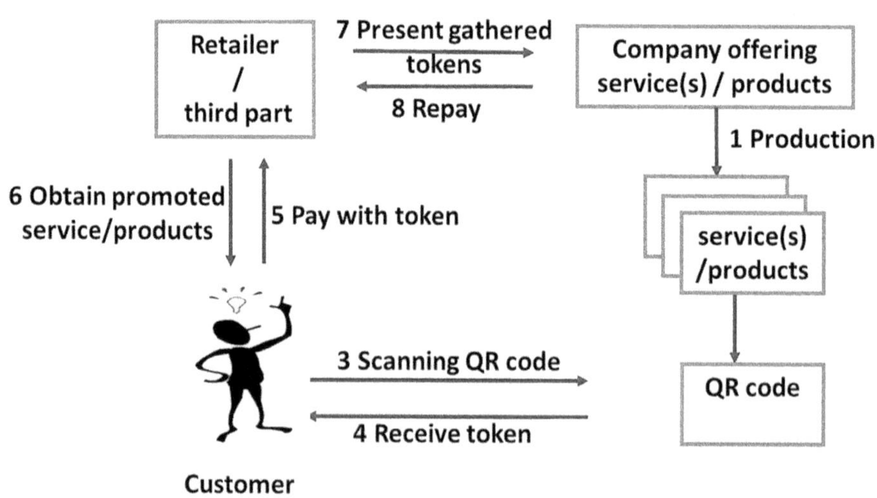

FIGURE 5.4 Blockchain token-based payment.

provide services and goods may keep records of each purchase operation (transaction) in the system, expanding their knowledge of their customers.

A consumer loyalty program built on Blockchain will streamline the payment process between businesses (companies offering services or products) and shops (retailers). Blockchain technology records every transaction between parties, allowing service and product providers to see what has happened with each retailer. Furthermore, businesses (companies) have a number of tokens from customers in their smartphone wallets. As a result, rather than counting promotion cards, they will base the payback for traders (retailers) on the quantity of tokens in the retailers' wallets.

Customers who buy a service or product also receive a promotion card. As seen in Figure 5.4, the customer's mobile phone is used to read the QR code on the promotion card to begin the transaction. As a result, the promotional amount associated with the matching QR code is being transmitted as a token to customers' wallets. They no longer require cards after reading the QR codes on the disposable cards, removing the risk of theft and fraud. Customers can visit businesses to purchase promotional goods with their tokens if they have accumulated enough to qualify for a prize.

5.8 CONCLUSION AND DISCUSSIONS

In blockchain, a distributed ledger that chronologically records transactions, is updated and confirmed by users on a regular basis, and all entries in the ledger are irreversible. Blockchain keys are anonymized, and their owners cannot be identified by the public. Additionally, as the ledger is immutable, any information entering it is indefinitely preserved. However, due to this anonymity, if a user loses his private blockchain key, they can no longer access his account.

In general, whether the technology is immutable or not, is one of main issues of marketing strategies. The Blockchain, for example, might be used to manage numerical identifiers related to users and customers. Indeed, numerous real-world complex problems, such as marketing and advertising, require intelligent technologies. Blockchain seems to be an interesting technology for marketing. However, Blockchain can give and save information about the transaction achieved by two participants X and Y. However, more than information about the achieved transactions between X and Y, platforms and companies want to have information about X and about Y. Hence, Blockchain solutions should be applied by marketers to minimize the frauds and to enhance trust on the achieved transactions, but not to market to customers.

Then, the most effective applications of Blockchain for marketing purposes are in situations where keeping records of unchangeable, exclusively digital data is instantly useful, like keeping track of digital ad purchases, and in cases where there are no significant real-world implications that could be predicted from current confidentiality regulations or judicial regulations of these transactions in following years.

However, in situations where it is challenging to build trust, marketers may attempt to employ Blockchain. Therefore, given the massive fraud that is now occurring in non-Blockchain frameworks, advertisers might turn to Blockchain to create a supply chain that is more reliable. However, if there is no practical reason to do so, marketing as an area of study ought to continue to use caution when generating permanent information about a person. Even the mere notion that someone once shown a specific character characteristic or interest can be used as weaponry by nefarious actors. Short-term marketing information can be utilized to forecast enduring personality traits.

REFERENCES

Alrowaily M. A., Alghamdi M., Alkhazi I., Hassanat A. B., Arbab M. M. S., and Liu C. Z. (2023). Modeling and analysis of proof-based strategies for distributed consensus in blockchain-based peer-to-peer networks. Sustainability 15(2): 1478. 10.3390/su15021478

Archana J. (2018). "A survey on security and privacy issues of blockchain technology". Mathematical Foundations of Computing 1(2): 121–147. 10.3934/mfc.2018007

Bülbül Ş. and İnce G. (2018) Blockchain-based Framework for Customer Loyalty Program, 3rd International Conference on Computer Science and Engineering (UBMK), Sarajevo, Bosnia and Herzegovina, pp. 342–346, 10.1109/UBMK.2018.8566642

Casino F., Dasaklis T. K., and Patsakis C. (2019) A systematic literature review of blockchain-based applications: Current status, classification and open issues, Telematics and Informatics 36: 55–81, 10.1016/j.tele.2018.11.006

Concensus specs. Available: https://github.com/ethereum/consensus-specs (Accessed August 28th, 2023).

Corin F. (2022). US Treasury bans Tornado Cash mixer for role in crypto money laundering. (https://www.theverge.com/2022/8/8/23296778/us-treasury-tornado-cash-crypto-mixer-sanctions-ethereum-north-korea). (Accessed August 26th, 2023).

Ertemel A. V. (2018). Implications of Blockchain technology on marketing. Journal of International Trade. Logistics and Law 4(2): 35–44.

Gleim M. R., and Stevens J. L. (2021). Blockchain: a game changer for marketers? Mark Lett 32: 123–128. 10.1007/s11002-021-09557-9

Jain D., Dash M. K., Kumar A., and Luthra S. (2021). How is Blockchain used in marketing: A review and research agenda. International Journal of Information Management Data Insights 1(2). 10.1016/j.jjimei.2021.100044

Latifi S., Zhang Y., and Cheng L. C. (2019). Blockchain-Based Real Estate Market: One Method for Applying Blockchain Technology in Commercial Real Estate Market. IEEE International Conference on Blockchain, Atlanta, GA, USA, pp. 528–535, 10.1109/Blockchain.2019.00002

Lorne F. T., Daram S., Frantz R., Kumar N., Mohammed A., and Muley A. (2018). Blockchain economics and marketing. Journal of Computer and Communications 6: 107–117. 10.4236/jcc.2018.612011

Marthews A., and Tucker C. (2023). What blockchain can and can't do: Applications to marketing and privacy. International Journal of Research in Marketing 40(1): 49–53, 10.1016/j.ijresmar.2022.09.001

Meni R. (2014). Analysis of hash rate-based double spending. arXiv preprint arXiv:1402.2009.

Pittaras N. F. I., Siris V. A., Polyzos G. C., and Anton P. (2021). A privacy-preserving statistics marketplace using local differential privacy and blockchain: An application to smart-grid measurements sharing. Blockchain: Research and Applications 2(1), 10.1016/j.bcra.2021.100022

Rejeb A., Keogh J. G., and Treiblmaier H. (2020). How Blockchain technology can benefit marketing: Six pending research areas. Front. Blockchain 3: 3, 10.3389/fbloc.2020.00003

Roriz R., and Pereira J. L. (2019). Avoiding insurance fraud: A blockchain-based solution for the vehicle sector. Procedia Computer Science 164: 211–218, 10.1016/j.procs.2019.12.174

Satoshi N. (2008). Bitcoin: A peer-to-peer electronic cash system. Available at SSRN: https://ssrn.com/abstract=3440802, 10.2139/ssrn.3440802

Stallone V., Wetzels M., and Klaas M. (2021). Applications of Blockchain technology in marketing—A systematic review of marketing technology companies. Blockchain: Research and Applications 2(30), 10.1016/j.bcra.2021.100023

Tan T. M., and Salo J. (2023). Ethical marketing in the Blockchain-based sharing economy: Theoretical integration and guiding insights. J Bus Ethics 183: 1113–1140, 10.1007/s10551-021-05015-8

Tao F., Wang Y.-Y., and Zhu S.-H. (2023). Impact of blockchain technology on the optimal pricing and quality decisions of platform supply chains. International Journal of Production Research 61(11): 3670–3684, 10.1080/00207543.2022.2050828

Wang J., Shi Y., Zhao C., Venkatesh V. G., and Chen W. (2022). Impact of pricing leadership on blockchain data acquisition efforts in a circular supply chain. International Journal of Production Research, 10.1080/00207543.2022.2147237

Yunsen W. (2018). Designing confidentiality-preserving Blockchain-based transaction processing systems. International Journal of Accounting Information Systems 30: 1–18. 10.1016/j.accinf.2018.06.001

Zheng Z., Xie S., Dai H.-N., Chen X., and Wang H. (2018). Blockchain challenges and opportunities: a survey. International Journal of Web and Grid Services 14(4): 352–375, 2018. 10.1504/IJWGS.2018.095647

Zhu J., Cao J., Saxena D., Jiang S., and Ferradi H. (2023). Blockchain-empowered federated learning: Challenges, solutions, and future directions. ACM Comput. Surv 55(11), Article 240, 31 pages. 10.1145/3570953

6 Analysis and Result Prediction for Indian Premier League Using Machine Learning Algorithms

S. V. Annlin Jeba and Parvathy S Kurup
Sree Buddha College of Engineering, Kerala, India

6.1 INTRODUCTION

One of the most popular sports in the world is cricket. On a cricket field, which is typically oval or circular in shape, a bat and a ball are used to play the game of cricket. The winner is determined by comparing the runs scored by the two teams, each of which consists of eleven players. One Day International (ODI), Test Cricket, and Twenty-Twenty Cricket are the three main cricket forms currently in use. The longest-lasting format of cricket, test cricket, is regarded as the pinnacle of the sport. The duration of a test match is five days, with play lasting six hours each day and at least 90 overs being bowled. A One Day International (ODI) is a game in cricket of limited overs in which two international teams compete. The game lasts up to nine hours and consists of each team facing a certain number of overs, currently 50. Cricket is a sport in which two international members of the International Cricket Council (ICC) compete. In a Twenty20 International (T20I), each team has a maximum of twenty overs to bat. The competitions are of the highest caliber and T20 standard. The Board of Control for Cricket in India (BCCI) oversees the professional Twenty20 cricket league known as the Indian Premier League (IPL). In this study, the match characteristics, bowler, and batsman performance in the IPL were analyzed. The Board of Control for Cricket in India (BCCI) established the Indian Premier Tournament (IPL) in 2007, and each year, teams from different Indian cities compete in the league. Due to the entertainment it offers and the glitz it displays, it has grown in popularity. In the league phase of the IPL, which currently features eight teams, each team plays the other twice in a home-and-away round-robin style. The top four teams advance to the playoffs at the end of the league stage. The first qualifying match pits the top two teams from the league phase against one another, with the victor advancing directly to the IPL final and the loser receiving a second chance to do so by competing in the second qualifying match. The third-place club from the league phase plays the fourth-place team in an elimination game, and the winner advances to face the loser of the first qualifying game. The winner of the second qualifying game advances to the IPL Final, where they will face the winner of the first qualifying game, with the victor being proclaimed the league's champion. An aspiring cricketer may compete with the finest players in the world, perform well, and establish himself. After their excellent IPL performances, young, bright cricketers have made their international debuts. There are many statistics and facts in cricket. Before airing the game, numerous sports organizations analyze the pertinent sport statistics and data. Moving ahead, various astute predictions have also been created to enhance sporting performances based on the most important aspects affecting a sport. Finally, it

DOI: 10.1201/9781003450443-6

has become common to analyze sports and present the results to spectators in the form of simple tables and graphs, which boosts the sports industry's financial performance.

Our main objective is to find the key factors that affect the match outcome and select the best machine learning model that best fits this data and gives the best results. The outcome of the cricket match can be predicted using a number of characteristics. Machine learning can be used in conjunction with the features affecting a cricket match to forecast the result of a game. Match predictions have been made using machine learning algorithms including SVM, Logistic Regression, Random Tree, Random Forest, and Naïve Bayes. The algorithm that has the highest accuracy is used to determine the final outcome.

6.2 AN OVERVIEW ON EXISTING SYSTEMS

Different techniques are used to analyze and predict the outcome of the various cricket formats. Researchers have proposed various machine learning methodologies to identify the outcome of the matches and the performance of the batter and bowler. This section describes a review conducted on existing prediction and analysis systems proposed by different researchers.

Sasank et al. [1] used the ratings of batter and bowler along with the playing team's relative strength dynamically to predict the second innings outcome of an IPL match. Ananda Bandulasiri [2] found the correlation between the winner of the coin toss and the match outcome and analyzed the advantage of a team playing in its own home ground using the Duckworth Lewis Method and proved its effectiveness in match prediction. Shilpi Agrawal et al. [3] developed a model with three different machine learning algorithms to predict the winner of a match with high accuracy rate. Amal Chaminda Kaluarachchi and Aparna S. Varde [4] came to a conclusion that to predict the winner of a match classification is the best choice. Several parameters were identified by the authors that could affect the chances of winning a match for a particular team and developed an effective tool based on these parameters. Madan Gopal Jhanwar and Vikram Pudi [5] developed a player-based model by using the player's past data and his recent form. The winner is determined by using the K-Nearest Neighbor algorithm. Chellapilla Deep Prakash et al. [6] used a multi fusion model to predict the winner of IPL season 9. Akhil Nimmagadda et al. [7] proposed model using Multiple Variable Linear Regression with logistic regression to predict the score in each of the innings. The Random Forest algorithm is used to predict the final result. Kumash Kapadia et al. [8] used historical match data of the IPL to predict the results of a cricket match. Filter-based methods like Correlation-based Feature Selection, Information Gain (IG), Relief, and Wrapper were used to identify the influential features of the dataset. Nikhil Dhonge et al. [9] give insights about the mathematical operation of classifiers and parameters required for IPL score prediction and winning prediction system. They developed a website and performed comparative analysis of machine learning techniques for score prediction using regression techniques, and winning predictions were done using the analysis of classifiers. Abdul Basit et al. [10] predict the winner of the 7th edition of the ICC (Men's) T20 cricket World 2020 Cup using four machine learning algorithms. They are Random Forest, Extra Trees, ID3, and C4.5. Among these techniques, Random Forest proved to be the most efficient, with custom accuracy of 80.86% and an R-mean score of 64.68%. Muhammad Saqlain et al. [11] used current match statistics to predict the Cricket World Cup 2019. Many unpredictable situations influence the conditional result of a cricket match. Therefore, a multi-criteria, decision-making approach, TOPSIS, is used to predict true ranking. It is also applied to find the fallouts of Cricket World Cup 2019.

6.3 ARCHITECTURE OF THE PROPOSED MODEL

To be successful in the field of machine learning, one must practice on many dataset types. Finding a proper dataset for every type of machine learning project, however, is a challenge. A dataset is a group of data that has been organized in some way. Any type of data, including series, arrays, and

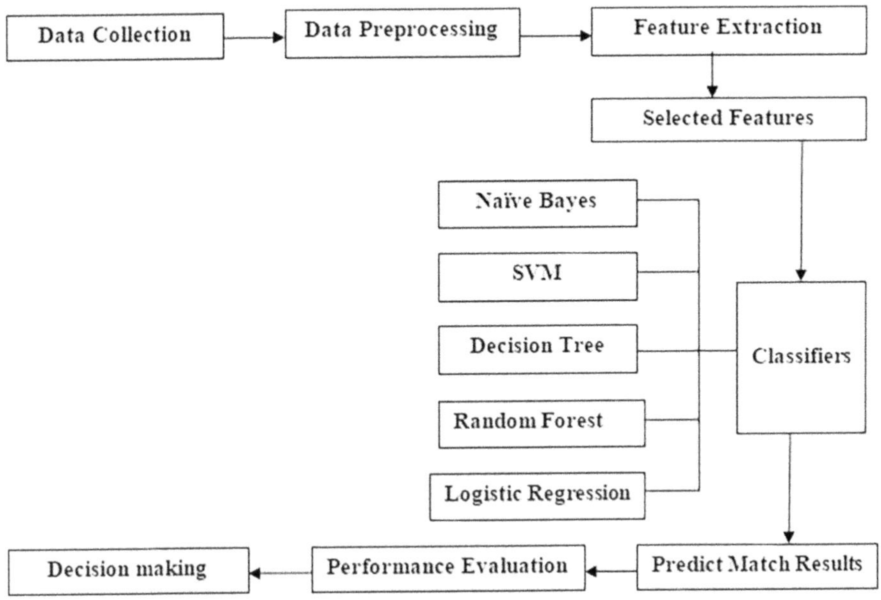

FIGURE 6.1 Architecture of the proposed mechanism.

database tables, can be found in a dataset. Kaggle and ESPN "cricinfo" datasets from two different sources were used.

An approach for building a machine learning model to predict IPL outcomes is shown in Figure 6.1. The proposed system methodology is implemented in the following steps: collect dataset, pre-processing, feature extraction, partition dataset into training data and test data, training, classification, performance evaluation, and predicting result.

6.3.1 Data Pre-Processing

Real-world data typically includes noise and missing values and may be in an undesirable format, making it impossible to build machine learning models on it directly.

Data pre-processing is necessary to clean the data and prepare it for a machine learning model, which also improves the model's accuracy and effectiveness. Preparing raw data to be acceptable for a machine learning model is known as data preparation. In order to build a machine learning model, it is the first and most important stage. It is not always the case that we come across clean and prepared data when developing a machine learning project. Additionally, prior to doing any operation on data, it must be cleaned and placed in a formatted set.

By addressing missing values, normalizing numerical features, and encoding categorical variables, we clean the acquired data. Create player or team performance measures based on previous data by using feature extraction to extract useful information processed beforehand.

6.3.2 Feature Extraction

Working with datasets containing hundreds or even thousands of features is getting more and more typical these days. A machine learning model may become overfitted if the number of features grows to be equal to or greater than the number of observations contained in a dataset. Either regularization or dimensionality reduction techniques (Feature Extraction) must be used to prevent this kind of issue. The number of variables used to represent a dataset in machine learning determines its dimensionality. Choose the characteristics that are most important for predicting IPL results. The selection of features can be aided by methods such as correlation analysis, feature importance from tree-based models, or domain expertise.

6.3.3 Partitioning the Dataset

The majority of the data is used for training, while a lesser amount is utilized for testing when a dataset is divided into a training set and a testing set. To help verify that the training and testing sets are similar, Analysis Services takes a random sample of the data. Assigning two-thirds of the data points to the training set and the remaining one-third to the testing set is the simplest way to divide the modeling dataset into training and testing sets. As a result, we first apply the model to the test set after training the model using the training set. We can assess the effectiveness of our model in this way.

6.3.4 Algorithm Selection

Machine learning is the preferred way for categorizing or forecasting data to assist people in making critical decisions. Machine learning algorithms are trained on instances or examples, allowing them to study historical knowledge and learn from previous events. It is not enough to just develop models. You must appropriately optimize and tune the model in order for it to produce two reliable results. To attain the best results, improvement options include adjusting the hyperparameters.

Learning Styles Learning Machines Algorithms are categorized into three types: 1. supervised education; 2. learning without supervision learning via reinforcement.

There are two forms of supervised learning:

i. Regression: Regressions are widely used to estimate or predict continuous values (real-valued output). For example, if we are shown a picture of a person, we must deduce their age based on the concept represented by the image.
ii. Classification: The act of categorizing the outcome is referred to as classification. If the information is discrete or categorical, the problem is a classification problem. For example, given information on the sizes of homes in the real estate market, we can generate output on whether the property "sells for more or less than the asking price," i.e., categorizing residences into two distinct groups.

Classification or prediction is the process of establishing a discrete category of a query observation by training a series of data points. Classification algorithms seek to forecast the target class with the highest readability. The models are created by these algorithms by determining the relationship between the input qualities and the goal attributes. Choose a predictive machine learning algorithm that suits your needs. Among the most commonly used sports prediction approaches are logistic regression, decision trees, random forests, support vector machines (SVM), and Naïve Bayes.

6.3.5 Algorithms Used for Performance Evaluation

Naïve Bayes Classifier: Naïve Bayes Statistical classifiers known as Bayesian classifiers forecast the likelihood that a given tuple belongs to a specific class. The Naïve Bayes classifier makes the assumption that each attribute affects the class label in its own unique way, regardless of the values of other attributes. Class-conditional independence is what is meant by this. The Bayes theorem is the foundation of Bayesian classifiers.

Bayes Theorem: Let X be a data tuple and C be a class label. Let X belongs to class C, then

$$\mathrm{P(C/X)} = \frac{P\left(\frac{X}{C}\right)P(C)}{P(X)}$$

P(C|X) is the posterior probability of class C given predictor X. • P(C) is the prior probability of class. • P(X|C) is the posterior probability of X given the class C. • P(X) is the prior probability of predictor. The classifier calculates P(C|X) for every class Ci for a given tuple X. It will then predict that X belongs to the class having the highest posterior probability, conditioned on X. That is X belongs to class Ci if and only if $P(Ci|X) > P(Cj|X)$ for $1 \leq j \leq m, j \neq i$.

In Bayesian networks, relationships between variables are represented by probabilistic graphical models. Dependencies and ambiguity in the data can be captured by them. By combining past knowledge and revising probability based on fresh information, Bayesian networks can be useful for predicting cricket match results.

6.3.6 Support Vector Machine

Support vector machines were first introduced by Vladimir Vapnik, Bernhard Boser, and Isabell Guyon. SVMs are very precise and less likely to overfit. SVMs can be applied to both classification and numerical prediction. SVM uses a nonlinear mapping to translate the initial data into a higher dimension. Then, in this new dimension, it looks for a linear optimum hyperplane to divide the tuples into the two classes. Tuples from two classes can always be divided by a hyperplane with an acceptable mapping to a high enough dimension. Using support vectors and margins set forth by the support vectors, the method locates this hyperplane. The learned prediction model is concisely described by the support vectors the algorithm discovers. For classification tasks, including predicting match results, SVM is a potent algorithm. On the basis of the supplied features, SVM determines an ideal hyperplane that divides several classes. SVM works best when there is a significant difference between the classes.

6.3.7 Decision Tree

The non-parametric supervised learning approach used for classification and regression applications is the decision tree. It is organized hierarchically and has a root node, branches, internal nodes, and leaf nodes.

A decision tree begins with a root node that has no incoming branches, as shown in Figure 6.2. The internal nodes, sometimes referred to as decision nodes, are fed by the root node's outgoing branches. Both node types undertake assessments based on the available attributes to create homogenous subsets, which are represented by leaf nodes or terminal nodes. All of the outcomes within the dataset are represented by the leaf nodes.

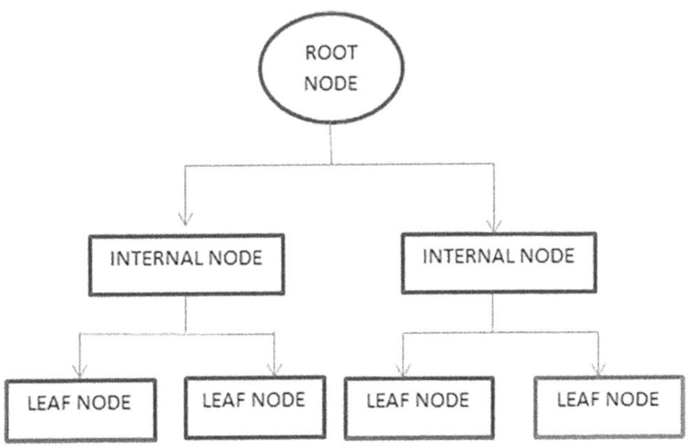

FIGURE 6.2 Decision tree in machine learning.

By using a greedy search to find the ideal split points inside a tree, decision tree learning uses a divide-and-conquer technique. When most or all of the records have been classified under distinct class labels, this splitting procedure is then repeated in a top-down, recursive fashion. The decision tree's complexity has a significant impact on whether or not all data points are categorized as homogenous sets. Pure leaf nodes – that is, data points belonging to a single class – can be attained more readily by smaller trees. However, as a tree gets bigger, it gets harder to keep it pure, and this usually leads to too little data falling into a particular subtree. Overfitting frequently results from this, which is known as data fragmentation.

Because of this, decision trees favor tiny trees, which is in line with Occam's Razor's concept of parsimony, which states that "entities should not be multiplied beyond necessity." In other words, decision trees should only increase complexity if absolutely essential. After all, the simplest explanation is frequently the best. Pruning is typically used to reduce complexity and prevent overfitting; it involves cutting off branches that split on unimportant traits. Cross-validation can then be used to assess how well the model fits the data. A random forest method is another way that decision trees can maintain their accuracy. This classifier predicts more accurate outcomes, especially when the individual trees are uncorrelated with one another.

6.3.8 Random Forest

Popular machine learning algorithm Random Forest is a part of the supervised learning methodology. It can be applied to ML issues involving both classification and regression. It is built on the idea of ensemble learning, which is a method of integrating various classifiers to address difficult issues and enhance model performance. According to what its name implies, "Random Forest is a classifier that contains a number of decision trees on various subsets of the given dataset and takes the average to improve the predictive accuracy of that dataset." Instead of depending on a single decision tree, the random forest uses forecasts from each tree and predicts the result based on the votes of the majority of predictions.

Higher accuracy and overfitting are prevented by the larger number of trees in the forest. When compared to other algorithms, random forest requires less training time. Even with the enormous dataset, it operates effectively and predicts the outcome with a high degree of accuracy. When a significant amount of the data is absent, accuracy can still be maintained.

6.3.9 Logistic Regression

Based on some dependent variables, the machine learning classification process known as logistic regression is used to forecast the likelihood of a given class. The logistic regression model totalizes the properties of the input and determines the logistic of the outcome.

For a binary classification problem, logistic regression's result is always between 0 and 1, which is appropriate. The likelihood that the current sample will be assigned to class = 1 increases with increasing value, and vice versa.

$$h_\Theta(X) = \frac{1}{1 + e^{-\Theta X}}$$

According to the formula, Θ is the input data and X is the parameter we want to learn, train, or optimize. When the value is closer to 1, which indicates that the instance is more likely to be positive, the output is the prediction value.

If the value is closer to 0, this means the instance is more likely to be a negative sample ($y = 0$).

To optimize our task, we need to define a loss function (cost or objective function) for this task. In logistic regression, we use the log-likelihood loss function.

$$J(\Theta) = -\frac{1}{m} \sum_{m}^{i=1} (y^i \log(p^i)) + (1 - y^i) \log(1 - p^i)$$

m is the number of samples in the training data. Y^i is the label of the i-th sample, and P^i is the prediction value of the i-th sample. When the current sample's label is 1, then the second term of the formula is 0. We hope the larger the first term, the better, and vice versa. Finally, we add the loss of all samples, take the average, and add a negative sign. We want to minimize the quadratic cost function $J(\Theta)$. When $J(\Theta)$ is smaller, it means that the model fits better on the dataset. There is no closed-form method to find Θ. To achieve this goal, we need to use some optimization algorithms, such as gradient descent. Since $J(\Theta)$ is a convex function, the gradient descent is guaranteed to find a global minimum. Logistic regression is a simple yet effective algorithm for binary classification tasks. It can be used to predict the win or loss of a team in a particular match based on relevant features. Logistic regression works well when the relationships between the features and the outcome are relatively

6.3.10 Model Training

A machine learning training model is a technique where a machine learning (ML) algorithm is provided with enough training data to learn appropriate values for all the associated variables. The prediction rate of the ML model can be considerably increased with consistent training. The model's weights must be initialized at random. The algorithm will learn to modify the weights appropriately in this way. Investigate various models, algorithms, and practical building blocks for reliable prediction models. Once we enter the relevant data, such as team names, players, pitch conditions, and even the weather forecast, our machine learning algorithm forecasts the most likely winning side.

Keep in mind that machine learning is not an exact science. There will always be some uncertainty surrounding the projections. The complexity of the model, the correctness and completeness of the data, as well as the data itself, all influence accuracy. Other factors that the data or the model might not have taken into account could potentially have an impact on the matches' outcomes.

6.3.11 Machine Learning Model Evaluation

Model evaluation is a technique that makes use of several measures to assess the effectiveness of the model. We should keep an eye on how successfully the model generalizes predictions for the future because, as we all know, model development is a multi-step process. Therefore, evaluating a model is essential if we are to assess the effectiveness of our model. The evaluation aids in the analysis of a model's main flaws. There are numerous measurements, including Mean Square Error, Accuracy, Precision, Recall, F1-score, Area under the Curve, and Confusion Matrix. One method used during the training phase is cross-validation, which is also a method of model evaluation.

6.3.12 Prediction and Updating

The right feature selection should be made while a generative classifier is being trained in order to maximize a model's performance. Confusion matrix is a matrix that provides the comparison between the predicted class and the actual class into classification report in order to calculate the model's performance or model's accuracy.

Once you have a trained model, you can use it to predict the outcomes of IPL matches. Continuously update your model with new data as the tournament progresses to improve its accuracy and account for any changing factors.

6.4 RESULTS AND DISCUSSION

6.4.1 Datasets

Two datasets have been used. The dataset used for analysis and prediction was collected from www.kaggle.com and has been scraped from www.stats.espncricinfo.com, where the data of the previous editions of IPL was available. The first gives us the ball-to-ball information of every match ever played in the IPL, like the batter, bowler, runs, wicket, and more, on each ball of the match. The second dataset gives us the summary of each match, which includes the teams playing, the winner, the winner of the toss, and more, for every match played in the IPL.

6.4.2 Evaluation Matrics

The classification models' performance evaluation is done using metrics such as Accuracy, Precision, and Recall. A comparative analysis of the classification models is done using these metrics. The formulas for the previous metrics are shown in the equations as follows:

Accuracy: The accuracy of a system is the number of observations exactly found with reference to the total number of observations.

Precision: Precision is the fraction of related instances among the obtained instances.

$$\text{Precision} = TP/(TP + FP)$$

Recall: Recall is the fraction of the total amount of related instances that are obtained.

$$\text{Recall} = TP(TP + FN)$$

6.4.3 Performance Analysis of the Classifiers

The performances of all the classifiers in the case of both pre- and post-match winner prediction tasks have been presented in Table 6.1.

Among non-ensemble classifiers, Logistic Regression performed best on the dataset containing pre-match features with precision, recall, and F1-score values, respectively 93.10, 100, and 96.43. While the Naïve Bayes classifier performed the worst. But the Decision Tree classifier was the worst-performing algorithm on the pre-match dataset. On the other hand, based on the precision value, the SVM classifier performed the worst.

TABLE 6.1
Comparison of Performance of Classifiers Used for Winner Prediction

Algorithm	Accuracy	Precision	Recall	F-Measure
Naïve Bayes	81.63	84.61	81.48	83.01
SVM	83.67	77.14	100.00	87.09
Decision Tree	87.75	86.21	92.59	89.28
Random Forest	83.67	80.64	92.59	86.20
Logistic Regression	95.91	93.10	100.00	96.43

According to the analysis conducted, we identified certain relevant factors that affect a cricket match. These factors can be directly related to the game or external factors. The list of factors affecting the game is as follows:

1. **Toss:** It is the flipping of a coin to determine which captain will have the right to choose whether their team will bat or field at the start of the match. Before play begins, the captain of each side will inspect the pitch. Based on the pitch and weather conditions, the captains select their final eleven players.
2. **Weather:** Cricket is a game played outdoors. Thus, weather is a crucial factor in determining the match winner. Good weather conditions and clear skies can help the batsmen score more runs. Similarly, overcast and humid conditions can assist the bowling side.
3. **Pitch:** In cricket, pitch is a very important factor. A good pitch is one that provides a contest between bat and ball and hopefully a close finish. That means a good pitch can vary from region to region.
4. **Bat First or Field First:** After assessing the conditions and winning the toss, batting first or fielding first is a very important decision to make. We infer that teams chasing targets have won 57% of the times. Thus, chasing targets is seen as more preferable than setting targets.
5. **Venue:** Every IPL team has a home ground advantage since it has more experience in playing on that ground. Thus, the place where the game is played is also an important factor in the match outcome.
6. **DLS Applied:** The DLS rule is applied when the limited overs cricket match is interrupted by weather or other circumstances. In this case, the game length is generally shortened and targets are revised. Thus, the DLS rule plays a role in a match outcome.
7. **Team Strength:** Cricket is a team sport. Thus, by the collective efforts of all the players, a team is successful. Team strength generally consists of the collective performance of all the batsmen (batting strength) and the collective performance of all the bowlers (bowling strength).
8. **Team Form:** The team's recent form often indicates its performance. If the team has been winning games lately, the momentum is on their side. Thus, their performance is better.

The influence of each factor in a cricket match is given in the following section:

1. The Toss Factor: According to the analysis, 55% of the toss-winning teams end up winning the match. Thus, the winner of the toss is worth analyzing.
2. Bat and Win or Chase and Win: From the study, we can infer that teams chasing targets have won 57% of the time. Thus, chasing targets is seen as more preferable than setting targets.
3. Targets Chased: As mentioned earlier, chasing a target is preferred in IPL matches. However, when the target to be chased is greater than 200 runs, seen only 15.6% of the time, is a target of 200 or more than 200 runs chased by the team batting second in an IPL match.
4. Runs Scored by Teams per over on an Average: Here, it can be seen that all teams have a spike in their runs scored between the 1st and 6th over, the overs of the powerplay. After this over, there's a dip, as shown in Figure 6.3. Another spike in runs is seen at the end of the innings. This is where majority of the power hitters come and bat.

Batting Index: This takes all the factors like runs scored, average, strike rate, and number of matches played into consideration.

$$\textit{Batting Index} = (\textit{batting average} * \textit{batting SR})/100$$

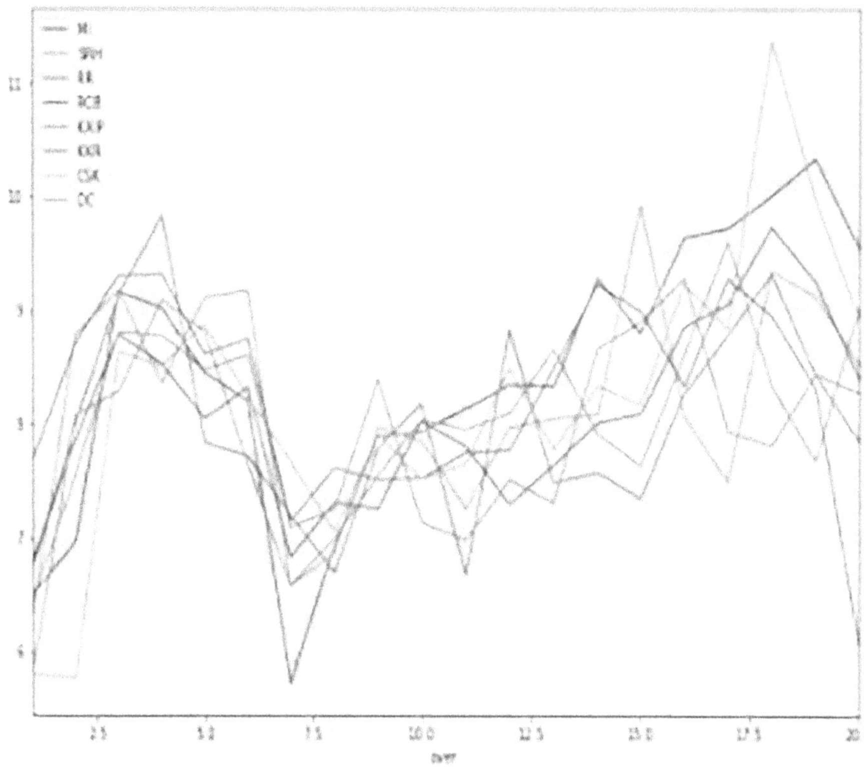

FIGURE 6.3 Runs scored on average every over.

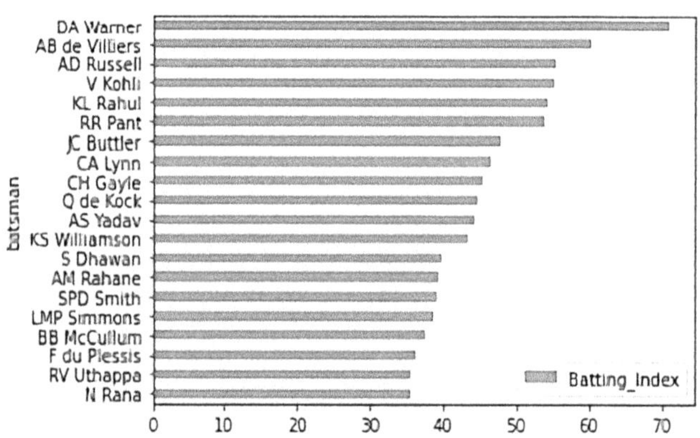

FIGURE 6.4 Batting Index: The higher the index, the better the batsman.

The higher the batting index, the better the batsman performance, as shown in Figure 6.4. Thus, the Batting Index is an apt parameter for judging a batsman.

Bowling Index: This takes all the factors like runs given, bowling average, strike rate of the bowler, number of matches played, and number of wickets taken.

$$\textit{Bowling Index} = (\textit{bowling average} * \textit{bowling SR})/100$$

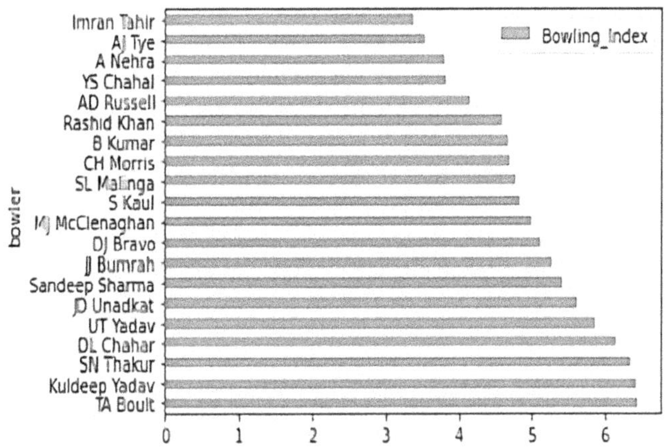

FIGURE 6.5 Bowling Index: The lower the index, the better the bowler.

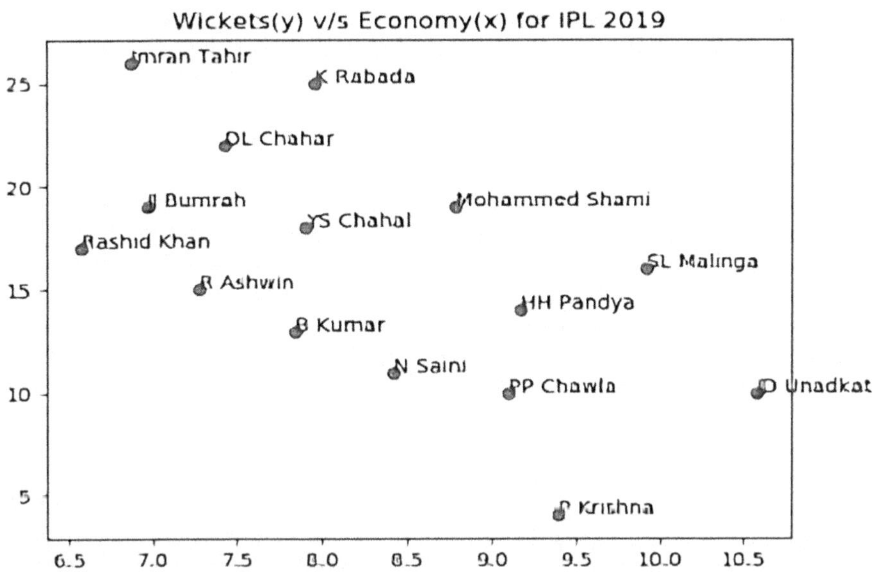

FIGURE 6.6 Wickets taken vs. economy rate.

The Bowling Index should be as low as possible for a good bowling performance, as shown in Figure 6.5. Thus, the Bowling Index is an apt parameter for judging a bowler.

Performance of Bowler – In the scatter plot given here (Figure 6.6), we analyze the wickets taken and the economy rate of the top bowlers in IPL 2019. It can be deduced that the bowlers featuring in the top left corner of the plot are much superior bowlers since their wicket-count is high and their economy rate is low: the desired combination. Whereas the bowlers in the bottom right corner have an undesirable combination of low number of wickets and a greater economy rate.

Dot Balls in the Final Over – The chart as follows gives the list of the bowlers who have bowled the most number of dot balls in the final over of an inning, as shown in Figure 6.7.

Form: The form of a team was extracted from the data available. Form is considered as how well the team has fared in the previous five matches of the same season of IPL. The last five

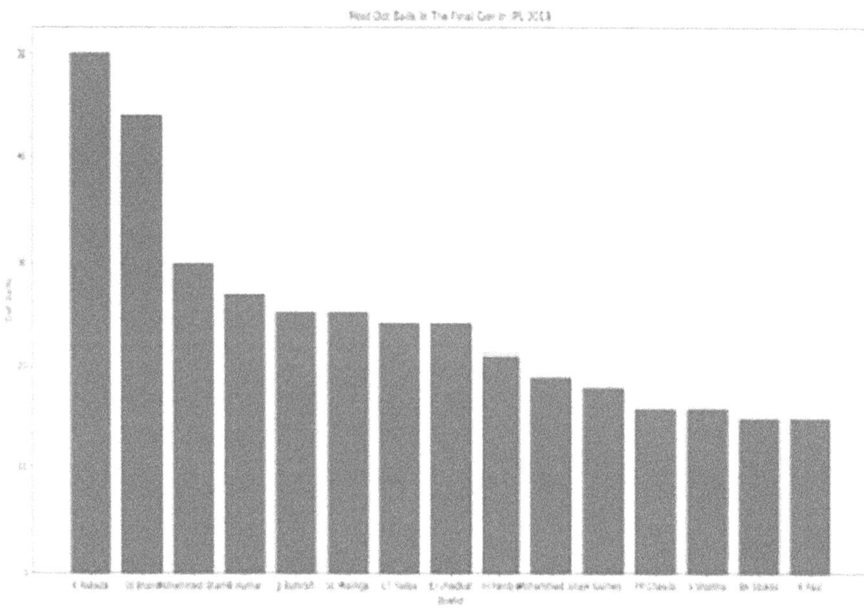

FIGURE 6.7 Dot balls bowled in the final over.

matches have been noted. A value of 2 has been added to the form for each victory, a value of 1 for each tied-match, and a value of 0 for every loss.

6.4.4 Prediction

1. Naïve **Bayes Classifier:** It is a fast classification algorithm that is suitable for a big dataset. It is a probabilistic classifier, which means it predicts on the basis of the probability of an object. Figure 6.8 shows the normalized confusion matrix for Naïve Bayes Classifier. The Bayes' Theorem is as follows:

$$P(H/C) = (P(C/H)P(H))/P(C)$$

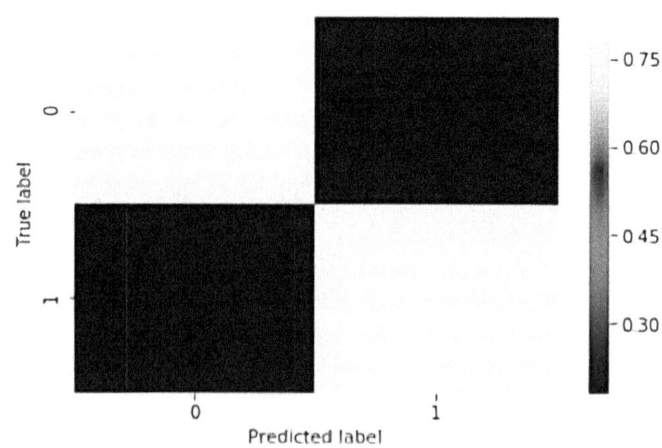

FIGURE 6.8 Confusion matrix for Naïve Bayes Classifier.

Where P(H) is the probability of the hypothesis H being true, P(C) is the probability of the characteristic taken into consideration to be true irrespective of the hypothesis, P(C/H) is the probability of the characteristic being true given that the hypothesis is true, and P(H/C) is the probability of the hypothesis being true, given the data of the characteristic. The accuracy when using Naïve Bayes is 81.63%.

2. **Support VectorMachine Classifier:** SVM is a supervised machine learning algorithm that can be used for both classification and regression challenges. However, it is mostly used in classification problems. The SVM algorithm plots each data item as a point in n-dimensional space, with the value of each feature being the value of a particular coordinate. Then, we perform classification by finding the hyperplane that differentiates the two classes very well. The accuracy using SVM Classifier is 83.67% (Figure 6.9).
3. **Decision Tree Classifier:** It will analyze the different attributes in the data that are presented to it and create subsets by splitting the data using these attributes. The classifier will keep trying to split the data further into subsets until it finds the subset that contains all equal values for the target attribute. When the classifier reads the test data, it will look at the subset in which the test data falls into and choose the most-suited class, and thus predict the outcome. The accuracy using the Decision Tree Algorithm is 87.75% (Figure 6.10).

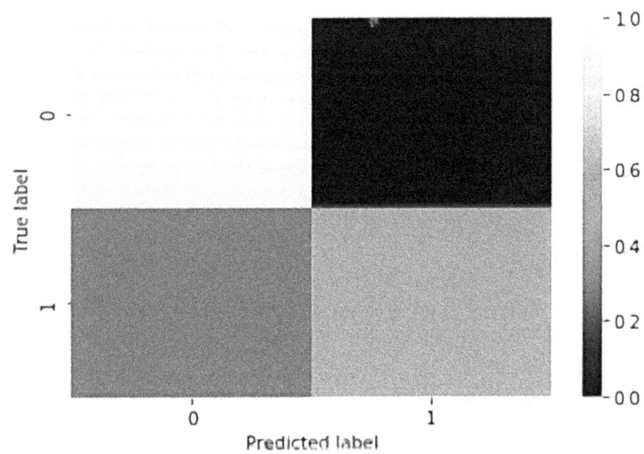

FIGURE 6.9 Confusion matrix for SVM.

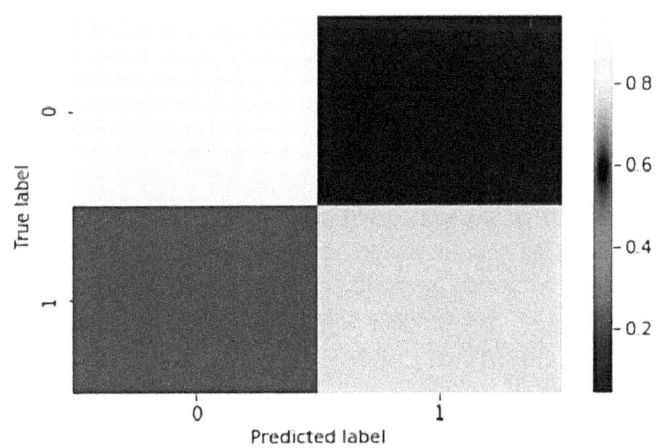

FIGURE 6.10 Confusion matrix for Decision Tree Classifier.

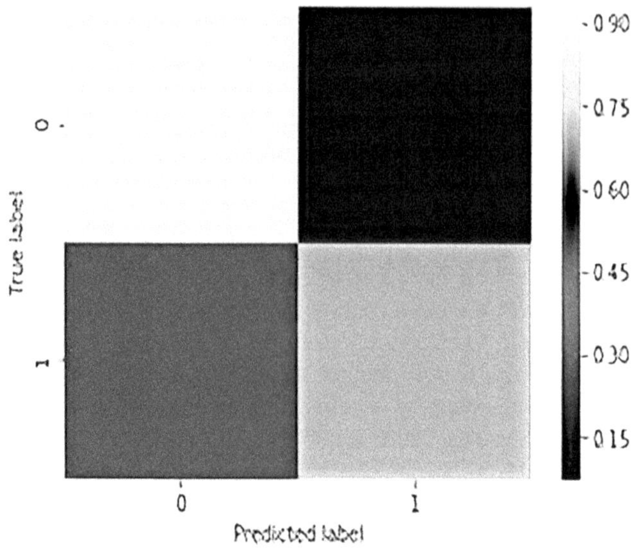

FIGURE 6.11 Confusion matrix for Random Forest Classifier.

4. **Random Forest Classifier:** Random Forest is a classifier that contains a number of decision trees on various subsets of the given dataset and takes the average to improve the predictive accuracy of that dataset. Instead of relying on one decision tree, the random forest takes the prediction from each tree, and based on the majority votes of predictions it predicts the final output. The accuracy using the Random Forest Algorithm is 83.67% (Figure 6.11).
5. **Logistic Regression:** Logistic regression predicts the output of a categorical dependent variable. Therefore, the outcome must be a categorical or discrete value. It can be either Yes or No, 0 or 1, True or False, etc., but instead of giving the exact value as 0 and 1, it gives the probabilistic values, which lie between 0 and 1. The sigmoid function gives the output in between 0 and 1.

$$(Z) = \frac{1}{1 + e^{-Z}}$$

As Z goes toward negative infinity, sigmoid (Z) gives a value of 0. As Z approaches 1, sigmoid (Z) becomes 1.

6.5 CONCLUSION

The use of machine learning to forecast IPL match results is very effective. Machine learning algorithms make predictions that are more accurate than those made by intuition alone by looking at historical data and identifying patterns and trends. To utilize the forecasts as a guide rather than a promise, it is crucial to be aware of the limitations of machine learning. When used properly, machine learning enables cricket fans to make more educated predictions about their preferred IPL teams and players. Various attributes of a match are used to analyze what affects the result of a cricket match. With the help of a number of features, the outcome of a cricket match is also predicted. The lowest accuracy obtained starts at 81.6% (Naïve Bayes) and goes on increasing to give higher accuracy using the Decision Tree Algorithm (87.8%) and logistic regression (95.6%). It also gives useful IPL data insights for a better rating of a batter or bowler and his performance.

REFERENCES

[1] Sasank Viswanadha, Kaustubh Sivalenka, Madan Gopal Jhawar, Vikram Pudi; "Dynamic Winner Prediction in Twenty20 Cricket: Based on Relative Team Strengths".
[2] Ananda Bandulasiri; "Predicting the Winner in One Day International Cricket".
[3] Shilpi Agrawal, Suraj Pal Singh, Jayash Kumar Sharma; "Predicting Results of Indian Premier League T-20 Matches using Machine Learning".
[4] Amal Chaminda Kaluarachchi, Aparna S. Varde; "Cric AI: A Classification Based Tool to Predict the Outcome in ODI Cricket".
[5] Madan Gopal Jhanwar, Vikram Pudi; "Predicting the Outcome of ODI Cricket Matches: A Team Composition Based Approach".
[6] Chellapilla Deep Prakash, C. Patvardhan, C. Vasantha; "Data Analytics Based Deep Mayo Predictor for IPL-9".
[7] Akhil Nimmagadda, Nidamanuri Venkata Kalyan, Manigandla Venkatesh, Nuthi Naga Sai Teja, Chavali Gopi Raju; "Cricket Score and Winning Prediction Using Data Mining".
[8] Kumash Kapadia, Hussein Abdel Jaber, Fadi Thabtah, Wael Hadi; "Sport Analytics for Cricket Game Results Using Machine Learning: An Experimental Study".
[9] Nikhil Dhonge, Shraddha Dhole, Nikita Wavre, Mandar Pardakhe, Amit Nagarale; "IPL Cricket Score and Winning Prediction Using Machine Learning Techniques".
[10] Abdul Basit, Muhammad Bux Alvi, Fawwad Hassan Jaskani, Majdah Alvi, Kashif H. Memon, Rehan Ali Shah; "ICC T20 Cricket World Cup 2020 Winner Prediction Using Machine Learning Techniques".
[11] Muhammad Saqlain, Naveed Jafar, Rashid Hamid, Amir Shahzad; "Prediction of Cricket WorldCup 2019 by TOPSIS Technique of MCDM-A Mathematical Analysis".

7 Study of Factors Affecting Intention to Use Artificial Intelligence by Marketers

A ChatGPT Case

Alia BesbesSahli and Raneem Bennani
Higher Institute of Management, Sousse, Tunisia

7.1 INTRODUCTION

Today's environment is undergoing significant technological changes with the emergence of artificial intelligence (AI), which has influenced various sectors, continually expanding its influence. We observe that the potential use of AI, specifically ChatGPT (Chat Generative Pre-trained Transformer), has touched various fields, including medicine (Aydın & Karaarslan, 2022), education, pedagogical management (Rana, 2023), the gaming industry (Som, 2023), the financial and banking sector (Petersson et al., 2023), human resources (Jatobá et al., 2019), tourism (Melián-González et al., 2019), and notably marketing. This includes customer service contexts (Thi Phuong Anh & Rajah, 2022) and user retention and lead conversion in an e-marketing context. Some authors have also highlighted the utility of AI, particularly robots, in a specific context: COVID-19 (Javaid et al., 2020). Hence, the use of AI in our daily lives is widespread and constantly expanding (Latinovic & Chatterjee, 2022). Moreover, using AI offers numerous advantages to businesses (Rana, 2023), while also posing new challenges (Gevaert et al., 2021).

Employing such technologies has enabled companies to be more efficient and responsive (Parasmehak & Chitsimran, 2019). By integrating AI-based chatbots like ChatGPT, some businesses have improved their customer experience across multiple sectors, as highlighted in the research by El Bakkouri et al. (2022), emphasizing the added value of integrating AI applications in finance, sales, and B2B sectors. Additionally, AI ensures efficient customer assistance, placing the customer at the core of business concerns (Dubois et al., 2019). Notably, marketing is an ever-evolving field. As Haleem et al. (2022) suggest, "Marketing specialists can use AI to assess consumer behaviors and trends, anticipate future outcomes, and make necessary advertising adjustments. Moreover, this technology employs data, statistical algorithms, and advanced AI technologies to predict future trends. As AI systems review more data, they learn to improve their predictions, addressing boundaries in terms of ethics and social responsibility."

Various forms of AI have emerged in recent years, with chatbots being of particular interest to marketers. These are autonomous software programs designed to converse with consumers more naturally and personally than previous robots. The advent of ChatGPT, an advanced form of chatbots based on OpenAI's GPT-3.5 architecture, is distinguished by its ability to understand natural language inputs from users. ChatGPT can assist marketers in creating

DOI: 10.1201/9781003450443-7

more human-like interactions with consumers, answering their queries, and offering personalized recommendations.

Understanding what drives the acceptance of ChatGPT among users is vital for its successful adoption by marketers. While some quickly adopt it (Emon et al., 2023), others are hesitant due to perceived risks (Marjerison et al., 2022). The principal inquiry guiding this research pertains to the determinants influencing the adoption of ChatGPT within the cohort of marketing professionals. The study's overarching objective is to scrutinize the variables that shape marketing professionals' intentions to employ ChatGPT. It endeavors to dissect the intention to utilize ChatGPT by employing an extended iteration of the Technology Acceptance Model (TAM) as its foundational theoretical framework, with the purpose of identifying and analyzing the factors exerting an impact.

This chapter unfolds in two distinct parts. The first part embarks on an extensive literature review to enhance our comprehension of Artificial Intelligence (AI) in a broader context while delving specifically into the intricacies of ChatGPT. It underscores the challenges that emerge within the realm of marketing when adopting ChatGPT. Leveraging an expanded TAM model, our objective is to scrutinize the factors that potentially wield influence on the behavioral intentions of marketing professionals with regard to the integration of ChatGPT into their professional tasks.

Subsequently, the second part of this chapter features a quantitative survey designed to address our main research problematic: "What factors exert an influence on the intention to adopt ChatGPT among marketing professionals?" We will elucidate our key discoveries and draw conclusions from our findings, elucidating the theoretical and managerial implications arising from this investigation.

7.2 LITERATURE REVIEW

7.2.1 Artificial Intelligence and Marketing

7.2.1.1 What Is ChatGPT?

As noted by Tlili et al. and Adetayo, there has been a rapid evolution of AI in recent years, making its presence felt across various domains. It is imperative to establish a clear definition of Artificial Intelligence (AI). As articulated by Parasmehak and Chitsimran (2019), AI is characterized as a robotic or software system possessing the capability to execute tasks that typically necessitate human intelligence, or a system with the capacity to emulate human intelligence in various domains, including but not limited to visual perception, speech recognition, decision-making, recommendation, and categorization.

ChatGPT, short for Generative Pre-trained Transformer, represents an advanced language model developed by OpenAI, expressly engineered to generate responses that closely resemble human language (Varsha et al., 2023). ChatGPT functions as an AI-powered natural language processing (NLP) chatbot platform, integrating the OpenAI GPT-3 system into its framework, as elucidated by Rathore (2023). It stands as one of the most powerful AI-driven chatbot platforms available, distinguished by its capacity to produce dialogs that approach human-like interaction. Furthermore, a noteworthy attribute of ChatGPT's AI architecture lies in its remarkable customizability, permitting users to promptly tailor the flow and content of their conversations in accordance with their specific inquiries (Refer to Figure 7.1). Consequently, the AI-generated content within the ChatGPT environment is distinguished by heightened persuasiveness and engagement, as discussed by Kung et al. (2022). In summary, "ChatGPT is an AI chatbot platform that enables users to have natural conversations with a computer just as they would with another human" (Singh, 2023).

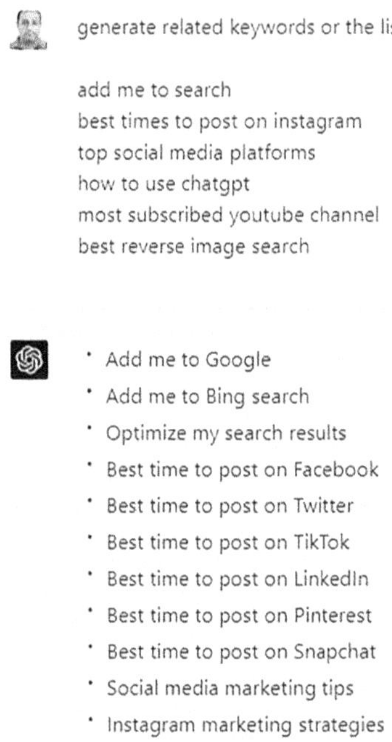

FIGURE 7.1 Box 7.1: Example of a query on ChatGPT.

7.2.2 Application of AI in Marketing

Feng et al. (2021) affirm that AI has increasingly become a significant field for both researchers and practitioners across various business and social science disciplines. Numerous authors have emphasized the importance of integrating AI into their marketing strategies (Syan & Sharma, 2018; Jatobá et al., 2019; Buntak et al., 2020; Haleem et al., 2022). Table 7.1 provides a synthesis of AI applications in the marketing domain.

TABLE 7.1
Application of AI in the Marketing Domain

Application	Description	Authors
Digital marketing	By employing AI for digital marketing purposes, marketers can swiftly process vast amounts of data from various sources like social media, emails, and the web. For enhanced efficiency, AI can be paired with marketing automation. Such a combination allows leaders to make informed decisions by transforming the online collected data into strategic choices.	Syan et Sharma (2018); Shah et Shay (2019)
Marketing Data Analysis	AI excels in processing and analyzing large datasets and even making forecasts. It aids in the separation, sorting, and prioritization of this data. The analysis results in beneficial predictions, decision-making, and recommendations for business operations. By identifying gaps, AI allows for the execution of efficient and operative corrective measures.	De Bruyn et al. (2020); Rutskiy et al. (2021); Haleem et al. (2022)

TABLE 7.1 ***(Continued)***
Application of AI in the Marketing Domain

Application	Description	Authors
Optimizing Customer Relations	AI provides customers with intelligent, straightforward, and convenient support at every decision-making step. Through AI, businesses can ensure optimal relationships with their clients by offering a unique, personalized experience. For this purpose, certain marketing operations and activities need to be automated. AI powers various marketing automation tools, thus enabling businesses to respond rapidly to the evolving needs and individualization demands of customers	Jatobá et al. (2019); Buntak et al. (2020)
Enhanced Marketing Automation Tools	Integrating marketing automation tools with AI allows marketers to identify leads more effectively, develop nurturing tactics, and deliver relevant content. Additionally, AI can produce dynamically content-rich emails with customization options. This approach enables businesses to target their clients more effectively and, as a result, bolster their brand image. "Dynamic content strategies ensure that emails remain pertinent to subscribers based on their geolocation, psychographics, behavioral data, and insights."	Alyoshina (2019); Jarek et Mazurek (2019)
Customer-Oriented Strategies	AI's ability to gather information ensures a deeper understanding of clients' needs and expectations, allowing for more customer-centric decision-making. One of AI's significant benefits is its capacity to gain profound market insights from a vast amount of online data (including social media, websites, blogs, etc.). This enables marketers to identify consumer personas based on the collected and analyzed data.	Paschen et al. (2019); Feng et al. (2021)
Personalization of Client Purchase Process	Relying on AI-developed simulation models, customizing the buying process is feasible, especially when companies use virtual assistants to communicate with their clients and enhance their user experience by predicting specific purchase patterns. These companies can compile databases on clients (preferences, purchase history, interests, etc.) allowing them to propose products that match their expectations. In some cases, we observe AI's superior and reliable output compared to human function as it considers various variables and data, allowing it to generate knowledge surpassing human. It's crucial to note that marketing adopted AI in its various approaches to meet the rising demand for customer personalization and the provision of customer-oriented products/services.	Parasmehak et Chitsimran (2019); Haleem et al. (2022); Pedersen et Duin (2022)
Digital Advertising	Professionals in the field of digital advertising utilize artificial intelligence (AI) as a strategic tool to optimize the effectiveness of their campaigns. This utilization extends to prominent digital platforms such as Facebook, Google, and Instagram. By relying on user data (sociodemographic variables, etc.), AI enables the generation of suitable advertisements. This tool also allows marketers to refine their analyses by detecting	Kietzmann et Pitt (2020)

(Continued)

TABLE 7.1 ***(Continued)***
Application of AI in the Marketing Domain

Application	Description	Authors
	micro-trends and even anticipating trends. They are thus equipped to make strategic decisions. "Consequently, companies can reduce digital advertising waste and ensure their investment provides the highest possible return. AI influences the future of digital marketing as it harnesses the power of the IoT and connected devices." (Kierzmann et Pitt, 2020)	
Enhanced Client Experience	Aiming to enhance marketing services and increase client experience, companies continuously incorporate high-tech solutions based on AI. Utilizing this technology allows businesses to form a comprehensive image of their target clients and boost conversions while reducing the efforts of marketing staff.	Güngör (2020); Dwivedi et al. (2021)
Audience Targeting	In a competitive environment, the paramount challenge for businesses is to swiftly respond to client demands by identifying and addressing them. AI emerges as a solution. Indeed, blending marketing strategy and AI assists practitioners in better targeting their audience to provide a more personalized experience better suited to their needs, especially in e-commerce, retail, and enterprise sectors	Lies (2019); Dubey et al. (2021)

7.2.2.1 Challenges of Integrating ChatGPT into Marketing Strategies

Embracing the idea of ChatGPT as a fresh AI technology, there is a noticeable scarcity of research in this domain. The academic sphere urgently needs to acknowledge the potential of ChatGPT, both for practitioners and researchers in the marketing arena. The incorporation of AI provides marketing experts with powerful tools and means to achieve their objectives efficiently. Among the primary benefits is marked time-saving during task execution, enabling professionals to prioritize core activities (Nivetha & Sudhamathi, 2019). When businesses infuse AI into their strategies, they reap cost savings, enhanced efficiency, and augmented productivity, propelling profit maximization. Thus, human-AI collaboration only brings advantages (Haleem et al., 2022).

The relentless demand for personalized business offerings to clients, such as tailored websites, videos, and social media content (Parasmehak & Chitsimran, 2019), is a primary motivator for AI adoption in marketing. This move is crucial for businesses to cater to specific customer needs in an ever-evolving economic and technological milieu. AI's potential in marketing is expansive. Over time, AI will seamlessly merge with every marketing unit, becoming an integral component (Haleem et al., 2022). Customization of business offerings is paramount. Haleem et al. (2022) underscored the prospect that marketing professionals will employ artificial intelligence (AI) to curate distinctive and individualized experiences for their clientele, concurrently utilizing advanced marketing analytics to target prospective customers.

In summary, ChatGPT profoundly influences marketing strategies. Indeed, AI assists firms in delving deeper into customer preferences and needs, enabling better segmentation and user experience enhancement, leading to improved conversion rates. It is undeniable that ChatGPT has considerable potential in marketing across various applications, notably content generation, keyword research, customer service, language translation, and text summarization (Varsha et al., 2023). ChatGPT functionalities empower marketers to cultivate more personalized and effective client relationships. AI-driven chatbots and virtual assistants can swiftly and adeptly respond to customer inquiries, both pre- and post-sale, delivering tailored recommendations and enriched user experiences. As a result, customer satisfaction surges while managing associated customer support costs. ChatGPT also plays a pivotal role in consumer behavior analysis by amassing large-scale data, aiding businesses in refined segmentation and targeting. Analyzing a plethora of data, such as purchase histories, demographic details, and behavior, ChatGPT can hone in on micro-segmentation, leading to ideal customer profiles (Varsha et al., 2023). This information aids in identifying and targeting prospective customers. AI contributes to understanding consumer behavior patterns, enabling the creation of more focused advertising campaigns. ChatGPT can employ data analytics to discern customer interests, recommending pertinent products or services. Thus, marketers can harness this insight to devise more effective, targeted marketing strategies. Similarly, AI-based chatbots like ChatGPT can utilize these profiles to provide tailored recommendations and offers, further elevating user experience and engagement. ChatGPT automates businesses' repetitive tasks, exemplified by activities like e-mail dispatches, customer tracking, and data gathering, allowing professionals to prioritize vital operations. Furthermore, ChatGPT aids advertisers in refining their campaigns, enhancing their efficacy. Specifically, ChatGPT facilitates the crafting of personalized advertising campaigns (Singh, 2023) based on detailed customer data obtained through micro-segmentation. This content can be translated into multiple languages, further personalizing advertising material. Ultimately, ChatGPT equips businesses with the ability to forecast sales and subsequent revenue, leaning on historical data, market trends, and consumer behavior.

7.2.3 Toward a Conceptualization of the Intention to Use ChatGPT

The presence of AI ChatGPT technology plays a valuable role in streamlining human tasks and offering valuable business advice, with the potential to continue doing so in the future (Saputra et al., 2023). In recent times, the growing enthusiasm for comprehending and deciphering user reactions to information systems (IS) has led to the emergence of various theoretical models. These models have been influenced by a wide range of disciplines, including IS, psychology, and sociology, thereby enriching our understanding.

In extant scholarly discourse, a diverse array of theoretical frameworks has been conceptualized and advanced. These theoretical constructs have primarily concentrated on the psychological and behavioral dimensions of human interaction with technological artifacts. The evolution of time has witnessed the proliferation of multiple theoretical paradigms and models designed to illuminate the intricacies of individuals' behaviors in the context of technology utilization. Furthermore, it is noteworthy that Momani and Jamous (2017) have comprehensively cataloged the various prospective models, as illustrated in Figure 7.1, aimed at investigating the underlying intentions governing such behavioral phenomena.

Momani and Jamous (2017) established a timeline that provides a useful overview of the growth of technology acceptance theories. Their chronology demonstrates that the evolution of these theories has been a dynamic process, reflecting an increasing understanding of the variables influencing technology use. The timeline depicts two major study streams: psychological studies and social studies.

The initial line of research, psychological studies, concentrated on the intrinsic motivation of individuals to utilize technology. According to Fishbein and Ajzen's (1975) Theory of Reasoned Action (TRA), a person's intention to use technology is determined by their attitude toward the technology and their perceived societal pressure to utilize the technology. In the 1980s, psychology research began to place a greater emphasis on the extrinsic variables that impact technology usage. Ajzen (1985) established the Theory of Planned Behavior (TPB), which extends the TRA by including the concept of perceived behavioral control. The individual's belief in their capacity to use technology is referred to as perceived behavioral control. Psychological research started to focus on the role of technology in influencing behavior in the 1990s. The Technology Acceptance Model (TAM) created by Davis et al. (1989) states that a person's intention to use a technology is driven by its perceived usefulness and ease of use.

The second research stream, social studies, was concerned with the social factors that impact technology use. Bandura's (1977) Social Learning Theory (SLT) proposes that people acquire new behaviors by observing others. In the 1950s, social studies started focusing on the spread of technology. Rogers' (1962) Diffusion of Innovations (DOI) model proposes that the acceptance of a new technology proceeds in five stages: awareness, interest, assessment, trial, and adoption. The influence of technology on society became a focus of social studies in the 1960s. Rogers (1962) developed the Innovation Diffusion Theory (IDT), which proposes that the adoption of a new technology is impacted by a number of variables, including the specifications of the technology, the characteristics of the adopters, and the characteristics of the environment.

7.2.4 Toward a Better Understanding of Behavioral Intention in the Context of ChatGPT

Within this section, our objective entails the construction of a conceptual model, as well as the introduction of the study's hypotheses. The initial step entails delineating the theoretical underpinnings that underlie our research model. Subsequently, we proceed to formulate the hypotheses, and we culminate this section by crafting the pertinent conceptual framework.

7.2.4.1 Conceptual Framework and Research Hypothesis

While there are several models in the literature that have examined technology acceptance as mentioned earlier, the Technology Acceptance Model (TAM) by Davis (1986) remains the most robust. It is worth acknowledging that the Technology Acceptance Model (TAM) has its conceptual roots in the Theory of Reasoned Action (TRA). TRA, developed in the realm of social psychology by Ajzen and Fishbein in 1967, stands as the precursor to TAM in the context of technology acceptance theories. Nevertheless, it is essential to underscore that TRA remains a general theoretical framework, intended for a broad spectrum of behaviors and technologies, as delineated by Momani and Jamous (2017). The Theory of Reasoned Action was later expanded into the Theory of Planned Behavior-TPB (Ajzen, 1985) which, in turn, was further extended to create the Decomposed Theory of Planned Behavior-DTPB (Taylor & Todd, 1995). Within the realm of information systems, this evolution paved the way for the development of the Technology Acceptance Model (TAM), which is essentially an extension of TRA. TAM was developed in information technology field while TRA and TPB were developed in the psychology field (Davis et al., 1989; Momani & Jamous, 2017). Kasilingam (2020) confirms that TAM stands out as the most impactful research model elucidating the adoption of information technology. Additionally, we note that in the literature (Ling et al., 2021), several studies adopted for their theoretical foundations, the TAM model (Davis, 1989). Indeed, TAM model is widely regarded as a valuable tool for exploring acceptance across diverse information technology-related contexts. At its core, this model conveys the idea that users of technology make reasoned decisions when it comes to adopting a particular technology as noted by Kim et al. (2010). We will use the model TAM as the core model in this research for many reasons. To begin, it is characterized by consistent and empirically sound measurement tools, as well as a succinct structure. Second, it elucidates a substantial portion of the variance observed in usage intentions. Third, it has found widespread application in numerous studies (Schierz et al., 2010; Natarajan et al., 2017; Kasilingam, 2020). The Technology Acceptance Model (TAM) posits that users' attitudes, their resulting behavioral intentions, and the actual usage of technology are primarily influenced by perceived ease of use and perceived usefulness. Furthermore, Davis (1986) has established that while the Technology Acceptance Model (TAM) serves as a valuable framework for elucidating the behavioral intention to adopt a technology, a comprehensive comprehension of technology acceptance necessitates the inclusion and examination of supplementary variables pertinent to the particular technology in question. Thus, it would be interesting to retain the TAM model as the theoretical basis of this research to which we will add other variables likely to improve the explanation of the intention to use AI: ChatGPT in the marketing field by professionals. Because of the lack of research on ChatGPT and behavioral intention, we will rely on researches on chatbots to formulate our hypothesis.

7.2.4.1.1 Impact of Perceived Usefulness and Perceived Ease of Use on Attitude and Behavioral Intention

7.2.4.1.1.1 Perceived Usefulness The existing literature in technology acceptance reveals the importance of two main factors of the TAM. In fact, Davis (1989) hasmaned these factors as: perceived usefulness (PU) and perceived ease of use (PEU). These factors are considered as determinants to user attitude and behavior. Davis (1989) defined PU as: "The degree to which a person believes that using a particular system would enhance his or her job performance" (Davis, 1989, p. 320). In AI context, the notion of perceived usefulness is related to how individuals perceive the benefits of artificial intelligence (AI) technologies in aiding task completion and goal achievement (Emon et al., 2023).

Numerous empirical investigations have consistently demonstrated within the realm of technology-related research that PU is a determinant factor that explains a large proportion of the variance of behavioral intention to use a technology (Hubert et al., 2017; Hubert et al., 2019; Yang & Lee, 2019). The study conducted by Zarouali et al. (2018) confirms that the cognitive factor of perceived usefulness is positively related to attitude toward the chatbot brand. On the other hand, McLean and Osei-Frimpong (2019b), pointed out that the relationship between perceived usefulness and use of live chat is supported. Moreover, the study of Richard et al. outlined that perceived usefulness positively affected behavioral intention. This effect is considered small but positive by Rietz et al. (2019).

Furthermore, the literature on the relationship between PU and attitude and behavioral intention is abundant and consistent. PU has a positive relationship with both attitude and behavioral intention. Given that chatbot technology has the potential to save time while providing flexibility and convenience, the impact of PU must be studied. Thus, the following hypotheses were proposed:

H1a: *Perceived usefulness has a significant positive influence on attitude toward ChatGPT*
H1b: *Perceived usefulness has a positive influence on the intention to use ChatGPT.*

7.2.4.1.1.2 Perceived Ease of Use Davis (1989) defined perceived ease of use PEOU as "the degree to which an individual believes that using a particular technology will be free of mental effort" (Davis, 1989, p. 320). Furthermore, Davis posits that the perceived ease of use serves as an indicative factor in the acceptance of technology. In other words, people are more willing to accept a technology if they perceive it as easy to use (Kasilingam, 2020). Lee (2009) and Hubert et al. (2019) contended that the concept of PEOU is connected to how users individually evaluate the effort required to learn and the perceived usability of a technology. Furthermore, Chen et al. (2009) demonstrated that a PEOU not only influences the intention to adopt smartphone technologies but also has an impact on the perception of their usefulness. Also, in previous research (Davis, 1989; Davis et al., 1989), it has been shown that PEOU directly and indirectly (via PU) affects usage intention. Conjointly, Rietz et al. (2019) have found that perceived ease-of-use has at least a small effect on behavioral intention. However, other studies (Zarouali et al., 2018) disprove the relationship between PEOU and attitude; they consider it insignificant.

The positive relationship between PEOU, Attitude, and Intention to use is well established in the prior research, as in the relationship between PEOU and PU (Richard et al., 2019). In a similar vein, we perceive both AI: chatbots and ChatGPT alike. Thus, we can put forth the following hypotheses.

H2c: *Perceived ease of use has a significant positive effect on intention to use ChatGPT*
H2b: *Perceived ease of use has a significant positive influence on perceived usefulness*
H2a: *Perceived ease of use has a significant positive influence on attitude toward ChatGPT.*

7.2.4.1.1.3 Attitude toward Using ChatGPT According to Persson et al. (2021), attitude toward AI (noted as ATAI) is defined as: "an individual's distinct emotional disposition toward engaging in a certain behavior related to the adoption of technology." The relationship between attitude and behavioral intention has been addressed for several years. Furthermore, in accordance with Ajzen's work in 1991, it is acknowledged that attitude represents a direct precursor to behavioral intention. This relationship can manifest in either a positively or negatively oriented manner, and it is hypothesized to exert a substantial impact on the intention to adopt Disruptive Digital Technology, as postulated by Emon et al. in 2023. In their research, Richard et al. (2019) argued that attitude has a significant effect on behavioral intention. In light of this viewpoint, the subsequent hypothesis has been formulated:

H3: *Attitude has positive effect on behavioral intention to use of ChatGPT*

7.2.4.1.2 Trust and Perceived Risk and Intention to Use ChatGPT

Prior to exploring the impact of trust on behavioral intention, it is imperative to establish a clear definition of trust. Patil et al. (2020) have articulated trust as "the willingness of an individual to rely on another party in a situation involving risk." Within a particular context, Choudhury and Shamszare (2023) have defined trust in ChatGPT as "the user's readiness to embrace recommendations presented by this technology." Importantly, existing scholarly literature substantiates a favorable connection between users' trust in technology and their inclination to interact with it, as demonstrated in investigations by Turja et al. (2020) and Choudhury and Shamszare (2023). Previous studies have suggested that trust plays an essential role in the acceptance and adoption of modern technologies by users (Emon et al., 2023). Trust has been shown to be essential in its relationship with intention to adopt mobile technologies (Alalwan et al., 2017). Trust is seen as an indicator of intention to use technology in daily routine. Moreover, research has indicated that the level of trust individuals place in technology significantly influences their intention to use (Gefen et al., 2003; Lee & See, 2004). Thus, it has been proved that trust is positively related to the adoption and use of contemporary technologies (Emon et al., 2023). Moreover, the higher the level of trust, the more likely users will be to use the technology (Toreini et al., 2020). Additionally, Choudhury and Shamszare (2023) have postulated that the level of trust placed in ChatGPT would exert a direct influence on users' intentions to use this technology. Nonetheless, it is worth noting that Kabra et al. (2017) reported a non-significant relationship in this regard. Consequently, we have formulated the hypothesis that trust in ChatGPT will indeed influence the intention to use the technology within the context of marketing professionals. This hypothesis has been articulated as follows:

H4a: *Trust on ChatGPT tool has a positive effect on intention to use*

Numerous studies in the literature have demonstrated that perceived risk, along with its various components, exert an influence on the acceptance and adoption of emerging technologies, as documented by researchers such as Park and Jun (2003) and Goyal et al. (2013). This perceived risk construct has been split into several risk components (Jacoby & Kaplan, 1972).

Moreover, the following study posits that professionals who perceive any form of risk associated with ChatGPT are more prone to develop a negative behavioral inclination toward its usage. Similarly, trust has a negative impact on the perceived risk that influences consumers' intentions to use information (Nicolaou & McKnight, 2006). The perceived risk serves as a facilitating factor in the connection between behavioral intention and trust (McLeod et al., 2008). In conclusion, Marketers are more likely to use ChatGPT when the perceived risks are low, and trust in this tool is high. These findings support the notion that perceived risk negatively impacts intention to use ChatGPT among marketers, underscoring its crucial role in the adoption and integration of innovative technological solutions in marketing field. Another study conducted by Kasilingam (2020) revealed that individuals' attitudes toward chatbots were significantly affected by several factors such as perceived risk, and personal. However, it is noteworthy that the intention to use chatbots was primarily driven by the factor of trust.

Considering that ChatGPT users may encounter risk when doing their tasks, and given that the perceived risk variable has been extensively employed as an extension of the Technology Acceptance Model, this study postulates that individuals in professional roles who detect any risks associated with ChatGPT are inclined to exhibit a negative behavioral intention toward its usage. Thus, we propose the following hypotheses:

H4b: *Perceived risk has a significant negative influence on intention to use ChatGPT among marketers*

7.3 METHODOLOGY OF THE QUANTITATIVE STUDY

As previously stated, there is a lack of existing research on intention to use of ChatGPT among marketers. Therefore, this study aims to enrich the literature by investigating the influence of factors affecting the intention to use. It attempts to identify and understand factors affecting intention to use ChatGPT through an extended TAM. Box 7.1 summarizes the different hypotheses retained in this research with the aim of responding to our problem.

Figure 7.2 displays the research framework summarizing the different hypotheses. Thereby, through the schematization of the conceptual framework, eight hypotheses were defined.

BOX 7.1 SUMMARY OF THE RESEARCH HYPOTHESES

H1a: Perceived usefulness has a significant positive influence on attitude toward ChatGPT

H1b: Perceived usefulness has a positive influence on the intention to use ChatGPT

H2a: Perceived ease of use has a significant positive influence on attitude toward ChatGPT.

H2b: Perceived ease of use has a significant positive influence on perceived usefulness

H2c: Perceived ease of use has a significant positive effect on intention to use ChatGPT

H3: Attitude has positive effect on behavioral intention to use of ChatGPT

H4a: Trust on ChatGPT tool has a positive effect on intention to use

H4b: Perceived risk has a significant negative influence on intention to use ChatGPT among marketers

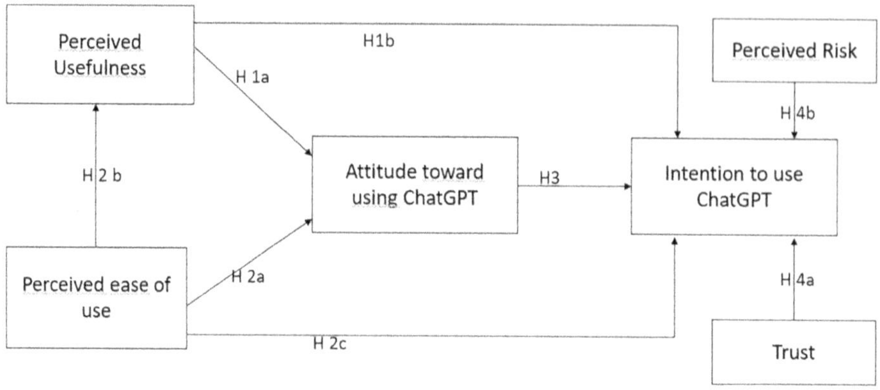

FIGURE 7.2 Conceptual model and hypotheses.

7.3.1 Research Methodology

In order to fulfill the purpose of this research, we will first detail the quantitative research methodology adopted by highlighting, the scale choice, the data collection method, and the sampling method. Then, we will describe the variables.

7.3.1.1 Data Collection Method

Within the domain of marketing literature and research, an array of sampling techniques is employed, generally categorized into two primary groups: non-probability sampling and probability sampling. According to Malhotra et al. (2017), non-probability sampling refers to "sampling techniques that do not use chance selection procedures but rather rely on the personal judgment of the researcher" (Malhotra et al., 2017, p. 419).

In the realm of sampling techniques, it is pertinent to highlight the existence of various non-probability sampling methods, including but not limited to convenience sampling, judgmental sampling, quota sampling, and snowball sampling. In contrast, probability sampling techniques adhere to a principle wherein every element within the population possesses a predetermined probability of selection for inclusion in the sample, as expounded upon by Malhotra et al. (2017, p. 419). The latter category encompasses techniques such as simple random sampling, systematic sampling, stratified sampling, and cluster sampling. In this research, we retained non-probability sampling. The sample is chosen based on judgmental sampling, which refers to "a form of convenience sampling in which the population elements are purposely selected based on the judgment of the researcher" (Malhotra et al., 2017) since this questionnaire is aimed at professionals in the marketing field. To gather quantitative data and to analyze the links between the different variables, a questionnaire was developed and sent online within Google forms.

7.3.1.2 Measurement Scales

The measurements employed in this research have been drawn from prior scholarly investigations and have been assessed using 5-point Likert scales, which encompass response options ranging from 1, signifying "strongly disagree," to 5, indicating "strongly agree." The only exception to this scale format pertains to the demographic items. Table 7.2 succinctly presents the instruments utilized in this study, following their adaptation to align with the specific context of this research.

7.3.1.3 Survey Pre-Test

Prior to administering the survey to a broader demographic, we implemented a preliminary survey launch, also referred to as a "soft launch," in accordance with the guidance provided by Evard et al. (2000). During this phase, we gathered a sample of 30 responses. The purpose of this pre-test

TABLE 7.2
Summary of the Adopted Measures

Scale (Source)	Items
Perceived usefulness-PU- (Davis et al. 1989)	• Using ChatGPT for content creation would improve my job performance. • Using ChatGPT for content creation would increase my productivity. • Using ChatGPT for content creation would enhance my effectiveness in creating content. • I find ChatGPT to be useful in generating creative and engaging content.
Perceived ease of use-PEOU- (Davis et al. 1989)	• Using ChatGPT for content creation is easy for me. • My interaction with ChatGPT is clear and understandable. • It is easy for me to become skillful in the use of ChatGPT for content creation. • I would find ChatGPT easy to use for generating content.
Perceived Risk (Kasilingam, 2020)	• ChatGPT-generated content may not perform well and produce inaccurate or low-quality content. • Using ChatGPT could lead to uncertainty in the quality of the content generated. • The security systems built into ChatGPT may not be strong enough to protect my professional information. • Internet hackers might gain access to my professional information if I use ChatGPT for content creation. • My decision to use ChatGPT for content creation involves a high risk.
Trust	• My typical approach is to trust ChatGPT until they prove that I shouldn't. • I generally give ChatGPT the benefit of the doubt when I first use it for content creation. • I usually trust ChatGPT until it gives me a reason not to trust it for content creation purposes
Attitude (Balakrishnan and Dwivedi, 2021)	• I like using ChatGPT for content creation. • I feel good about using ChatGPT for content creation. • Overall, my attitude toward using ChatGPT for content creation is favorable.
Behavioral intentions to use	• I will use ChatGPT for content creation on a regular basis in the future. • I will frequently use ChatGPT for content creation in the future. • I will highly recommend my colleagues and peers to use ChatGPT for content creation.

survey is to proactively identify and address any latent issues within the survey instrument. These issues may encompass ambiguities or complexities in the questions, technical anomalies, or other impediments that could potentially compromise the integrity of the collected data, as emphasized by Choudhury and Shamszare (2023). The overarching objective is to refine the questionnaire and mitigate any foreseeable concerns, as advocated by Malhotra et al. (2017). In response to the feedback obtained from the pre-test, slight adjustments were made to the wording of select items to minimize the risk of data acquisition errors, aligning with the recommendations elucidated by Burns and Burns (2008).

7.3.2 Model Validation, Study Results, and Discussion

Following the development of the research model, formulation of hypotheses, and the delineation of the research methodology, this section assumes a pivotal role in substantiating the validity of the conceptual model. The initial segment is devoted to the verification of measurement scales via a pilot study, encompassing 127 participants. Subsequently, the conceptual framework undergoes validation through the scrutiny of data obtained from 183 participants via Goggle forms, utilizing regression models for analysis. The subsequent section, concluding this chapter, entails a comprehensive discussion of the research findings, elucidating their theoretical and managerial implications, while also acknowledging the study's limitations and delineating avenues for future research.

7.3.2.1 Model Validation and Results

In the initial phase of our study, we conducted factor analysis on various variables to assess their validity and reliability. This process was executed utilizing the SPSS software. Subsequently, data analysis was undertaken through the utilization of SPSS software.

7.3.2.1.1 Pilot Study

Ensuring the validity and reliability of the measurement scales holds significant importance. Thus, to achieve this objective, a confirmatory factor analysis was conducted for the pilot study, utilizing the SPSS software as the analytical tool.

7.3.2.1.1.1 Sample's Characteristics Pilot studies also provide researchers with preliminary data (Table 7.3). Indeed, the pilot study's sample was composed of 127 participants. In total, 52.8% of respondents are males, 43.3% are aged between 25 and 34 years old, and 67.5% have a university degree. The vast majority of respondents possess a university-level education and work in the marketing field. And 58% have worked in a location in Tunisia.

TABLE 7.3
Sample Characteristics (Pilot Survey)

	Frequency	Percentage
Gender		
Male	67	52.8%
Female	58	45.7%
No answer	2	1.6%
Age		
18–24	38	29.9%
25–34	55	43.3%
35–44	22	17.3%
45–54	10	7.9%
55 and above	2	1.6%
Education		
Baccalauréat/High schooldiploma	20	15.7%
Associate's degree	2	1.6%
Bachelor's degree	27	21.3%
Master's degree	69	54.3%
Doctoral degree	9	7.1%
Occupation		
Marketing manager	36	28.3%
Company executive	21	15.5%
Freelancer	14	11%
Influencer	5	3.9%
Advertising specialist	9	7.1%
Content creator	20	15.7%
Public relations specialist	5	3.9%
Other	17	13.4%

TABLE 7.3 *(Continued)*
Sample Characteristics (Pilot Survey)

	Frequency	Percentage
Working country		
Tunisia	74	58%
Canada	19	15%
France	5	4%
Germany	4	3%
Others	25	20%

7.3.2.1.1.2 Exploratory Factor Analysis To assess the psychometric properties of the constructs under investigation, an exploratory analysis will be conducted, focusing on the evaluation of scale reliability and validity. Factor analysis, as described by Malhotra et al. (2017, p. 604), encompasses a set of procedures primarily employed for the purpose of data reduction and summarization. To enhance the robustness of measurements, it is imperative to perform a factor analysis, also known as exploratory factor analysis (EFA), on the various variables. This method allows for the synthesis of the most pertinent items related to an observed variable (Akrout, 2018). Consequently, principal component analysis (PCA) will be employed to refine the selected measurement scales, and this analytical process will be executed using SPSS version 23.

The key statistical parameters associated with factor analysis include: 1. the Kaiser-Meyer-Olkin (KMO) measure of sampling adequacy; 2. Bartlett's test; 3. Eigenvalue; 4. Cronbach's alpha; 5. Factor loadings; and 6. Communality, as outlined by Malhotra et al. (2017) and Mooi and Sarstedt (2019).

It should be noted that, regarding the thresholds (Malhotra et al., 2017), the Kaiser-Meyer-Olkin (KMO) index is employed as a measure to assess the suitability of conducting factor analysis. Elevated values, falling within the range of 0.5 to 1.0, signify the appropriateness of factor analysis, whereas values below 0.5 suggest potential inappropriateness. Bartlett's test of sphericity is employed to evaluate the null hypothesis, with significance determined at a p-value threshold of <0.05. Eigenvalues represent the cumulative variance explained by each individual factor, with a threshold typically set at values exceeding 1 to retain the factor. Cronbach's alpha, with values ranging from 0 to 1, serves as an indicator of internal consistency reliability. A coefficient of 0.6 or lower generally indicates unsatisfactory reliability, necessitating a higher value. Factor loadings reflect the straightforward correlation between variables and factors, with values expected to surpass 0.7 to be considered robust. Lastly, communality signifies the extent to which a variable shares variance with other variables.

7.3.2.1.1.3 Factor Analysis for Perceived Usefulness (PU) Table 7.4 reveals a significant intercorrelation among the uniqueness neglect items, supported by various statistical indicators. The Kaiser-Meyer-Olkin (KMO) index surpasses the 0.50 threshold (KMO = 0.837), signifying the adequacy of the dataset for factor analysis. Bartlett's test attains statistical significance (p-value $<$ 0.05), affirming the suitability of the data for such analysis. Furthermore, the items collectively exhibit an eigenvalue of 2.999, explaining a substantial portion of the variance, specifically 74.983%.

The internal consistency reliability of the uniqueness neglect items, as indicated by Cronbach's alpha ($\alpha = 0.887$), attests to their satisfactory reliability. Additionally, the factor loadings for these

TABLE 7.4
Factor Analysis for Perceived Usefulness

Perceived Usefulness	Communalities		Factor Loading
PU1: Using ChatGPT for content: creation would improve my job performance.	0.800		0.894
PU 2: Using ChatGPT for content creation would increase my productivity.	0.702		0.838
PU3: Using ChatGPT for content creation would enhance my effectiveness in creating content.	0.799		0.894
PU 4: I find ChatGPT to be useful in generating creative and engaging content.	0.699		0.836
% of variance explained		74.983%	
Eigenvalue		2.999	
KMO		0.837	
Bartlett's Test of Sphericity	**App. X2**	**df**	**Sig.**
	280.656	6	0.000
Cronbach's Alpha		0.887	

items range from 0.834 to 0.8894, all surpassing the conventional threshold for acceptability. Moreover, communalities for these items fall within the range of 0.699 to 0.8, which are greater than 0.5. In light of these results, there is a good internal consistency.

Factor analysis for perceived ease of use (PEOU)

The factor analysis performed on the scale of perceived ease of use-PEOU- reveals a unidimensional structure. Table 7.5 shows that the items of PEOU are correlated because the KMO is above the threshold of 0.50, Bartlett's test is significant (p-value < 0.05), and the items' eigenvalue lies at 3.221 and accounts for 80.516% of the variance. Cronbach's alpha has a value of 0.919 indicating that all items have satisfactory reliability. The factor loadings range from 0.870 to 0.911, which are deemed acceptable. In addition, communalities range from 0.757 to 0.830, which are greater than 0.50. Hence, concluding a good internal consistency.

TABLE 7.5
Factor Analysis for Perceived Ease of Use

Perceived Ease of Use	Communalities		Factor Loading
PEOU1: Using ChatGPT for content creation is easy for me.	0.757		0.870
PEOU 2: My interaction with ChatGPT is clear and understandable.	0.830		0.911
PEOU 3: It is easy for me to become skillful in the use of ChatGPT for content creation.	0.822		0.906
PEOU4: I would find ChatGPT easy to use for generating content.	0.812		0.901
% of variance explained		80.516%	
Eigenvalue		3.221	
KMO		0.853	
Bartlett's Test of Sphericity	**App. X^2**	**df**	**Sig.**
	362.025	10	0.000
Cronbach's Alpha		0.919	

TABLE 7.6
Factor Analysis for Attitude

Attitude toward Using ChatGPT	Communalities		Factor Loading
Att1: I like using ChatGPT for content creation.	0.920		0.959
Att2: I feel good about using ChatGPT for content creation.	0.896		0.947
Att3: Overall, my attitude toward using ChatGPT for content creation is favorable	0.873		0.934
% of variance explained		89.638%	
Eigenvalue		2.689	
KMO		0.760	
Bartlett's Test of Sphericity	**App. X^2**	**df**	**Sig.**
	347.164	3	0.000
Cronbach's Alpha		0.941	

7.3.2.1.1.4 Factor Analysis for Attitude (Att) The factor analysis performed on the scale of attitude toward using ChatGPT reveals a unidimensional structure. Table 7.6 shows that the items of attitude are correlated because the KMO is above the threshold of 0.50, Bartlett's test is significant (p-value < 0.05), and the items' eigenvalue lies at 2.689 and accounts for 89.638% of the variance. Cronbach's alpha has a value of 0.941 indicating that all items have satisfactory reliability. The factor loadings range from 0.934 to 0.959, which are deemed acceptable. In addition, communalities range from 0.873 to 0.920, which are greater than 0.50, hence, concluding a good internal consistency of attitude scale.

7.3.2.1.1.5 Factor Analysis for Intention to Use (Intuse) The factor analysis performed on the scale of intention to use ChatGPT reveals a unidimensional structure. Table 7.7 shows that the items of attitude are correlated because the KMO is above the threshold of 0.50, Bartlett's test is significant (p-value < 0.05), and the items' eigenvalue lies at 2.597 and accounts for 86.569% of the variance. Cronbach's alpha has a value of 0.922 indicating that all items have satisfactory reliability. The factor loadings range from 0.917 to 0.937, which are deemed acceptable. In

TABLE 7.7
Factor Analysis for Intention to Use ChatGPT

Intention to Use	Communalities		Factor Loading
Intuse1: I will use ChatGPT for content creation on a regular basis in the future.	0.841		0.917
Intuse 2: I will frequently use ChatGPT for content creation in the future.	0.879		0.937
Intuse 3: I will highly recommend my colleagues and peers to use ChatGPT for content creation.	0.877		0.937
% of variance explained		86.569%	
Eigenvalue		2.597	
KMO		0.758	
Bartlett's Test of Sphericity	**App. $\chi 2$**	**df**	**Sig.**
	282.844	3	0.000
Cronbach's Alpha		0.922	

TABLE 7.8
Factor Analysis for Perceived Risk

Perceived Risk	Communalities		Factor Loading
PR1: ChatGPT-generated content may not perform well and produce inaccurate or low-quality content.	0.840		0.900
PR2: Using ChatGPT could lead to uncertainty in the quality of the content generated.	0.812		0.871
PR3: The security systems built into ChatGPT may not be strong enough to protect my professional information.	0.717		0.731
PR4: Internet hackers might gain access to my professional information if I use ChatGPT for content creation.	0.816		0.896
PR5: My decision to use ChatGPT for content creation involves a high risk.	0.781		0.864
% of variance explained		79.310%	
Eigenvalue		3.965	
KMO		0.752	
Bartlett's Test of Sphericity	**App. $\chi 2$**	**df**	**Sig.**
	260.270	10	0.000
Cronbach's Alpha		0.821	

addition, communalities range from 0.841 to 0.879, which are greater than 0.50, hence, concluding a good internal consistency.

7.4 FACTOR ANALYSIS FOR PERCEIVED RISK (PR)

The factor analysis performed on the scale of perceived risk reveals a bidimensional structure. The two dimensions explain 79.310% of the variance. Table 7.8 shows that the items of attitude are correlated because the KMO is above the threshold of 0.50, Bartlett's test is significant (p-value $<$ 0.05), and the items' eigenvalue lies at 3.965. Cronbach's alpha has a value of 0.941 indicating that all items have satisfactory reliability. The factor loadings range from 0.731 to 0.900, which are deemed acceptable. In addition, communalities range from 0.717 to 0.840, which are greater than 0.50. therefore, the two dimensions obtained after Varimax rotation can be named as follows: D1 (R^2 = 20.647%), representing perceived quality-related risk, comprising the first two items, namely PR1 and PR2. As for the second dimension, D2 (R^2 = 58.663%), it represents privacy-related risk, encompassing PR3, PR4, and PR5 items, hence, concluding a good internal consistency of perceived risk scale.

Despite the two-dimensional nature of the scale demonstrated in the exploratory analysis, it remains essential to undertake a rigorous reassessment of its psychometric attributes through a confirmatory analysis. This imperative arises from the predominant one-dimensional framework established in the existing literature, as elucidated by Kasilingam (2020).

7.5 FACTOR ANALYSIS FOR TRUST (TRUST)

The factor analysis performed on the scale of trust reveals a unidimensional structure. Table 7.9 shows that the items of attitude are correlated because the KMO is above the threshold of 0.50, Bartlett's test is significant (p-value < 0.05), and the items' eigenvalue lies at 2.140 and accounts for 71.347% of the variance. Cronbach's alpha has a value of 0.799 indicating that all items have satisfactory reliability. The factor loadings range from 0.802 to 0.878, which are deemed

TABLE 7.9
Factor Analysis for Trust

Trust	Communalities		Factor Loading
Trust1: My typical approach is to trust ChatGPT until it proves that I shouldn't.	0.726		0.852
Trust 2: I generally give ChatGPT the benefit of the doubt when I first use it for content creation.	0.643		0.802
Trust 3: I usually trust ChatGPT until it gives me a reason not to trust it for content creation purposes	0.772		0.878
% of variance explained		71.347%	
Eigenvalue		2.140	
KMO		0.691	
Bartlett's Test of Sphericity	**App. $\chi 2$**	**df**	**Sig.**
	120.554	3	0.000
Cronbach's Alpha		0.799	

acceptable. In addition, communalities range from 0.643 to 0.772, which are greater than 0.50, hence, concluding a good internal consistency.

7.5.1 Main Survey

For the main study, we selected a sample of size N = 183 respondents, following the recommendations of Hinkin (1995) which states that an ideal sample size should be an item-to-response ratio ranging from 4 to 10. In this research, there are 25 items, and the study's sample is composed of 183 participants. Hence, it highly exceeded the minimum sample ($N_{min=}$ 4*25 =100) required by Hinkin (1995).

In total, 183 participants compose the sample of the main survey. The 53.6% of respondents are males, 61.8% are aged between 25 and 44 years old, 49.7% have a master's degree, and 55.2% work in the marketing field (see Table 7.10).

TABLE 7.10
Sample Characteristics (Main Survey)

	Frequency	Percentage
Gender		
Male	98	53.6
Female	82	44.8
No answer	3	1.6
Age		
18–24	53	29
25–34	81	44.3
35–44	32	17.5
45–54	14	7.7
55 and above	3	1.6

(Continued)

TABLE 7.10 ***(Continued)***
Sample Characteristics (Main Survey)

	Frequency	Percentage
Education		
Baccalauréat/High schooldiploma	25	13.7
Associate's degree	5	2.7
Bachelor's degree	48	26.2
Master's degree	91	49.7
Doctoral degree	14	7.7
Occupation		
Marketing manager	61	33.3
Company executive	34	18.6
Freelancer	23	12.6
Influencer	8	4.4
Advertising specialist	10	5.5
Content creator	24	13.1
Public relations specialist	6	3.3
Other	17	9.3
Working country		
Tunisia	98	53.5
Canada	20	11
France	24	13.1
Germany	16	8.8
Others	25	13.6

7.5.1.1 Structural Model Evaluation

Our initial step involved a comprehensive assessment of the validity and reliability of the constructs within our main study sample. This evaluation encompassed the computation of Cronbach's alpha coefficient, along with the examination of various indicators derived from Principal Component Analysis (PCA). As depicted in the preceding table, all variables demonstrated reliability and unidimensionality, exhibiting exceptional psychometric characteristics. Furthermore, it is noteworthy that in our primary study, the unidimensional nature of the perceived risk variable was affirmed, aligning with established recommendations within the relevant literature (Table 7.11).

A strong and statistically significant association was observed between the dependent variable, the intention to use ChatGPT, and several independent variables. Specifically, the variable "attitude" exhibited a substantial positive correlation ($r = 0.771$, $p < 0.000$), followed by "perceived usefulness" ($r = 0.641$, $p < 0.000$), "perceived ease of use" ($r = 0.587$, $p < 0.000$), and "trust" ($r = 0.543$, $p < 0.000$). In contrast, the variable "perceived risk" did not demonstrate a significant correlation with the dependent variable ($r = 0.059$, $p = 0.214$). Considering perceived usefulness as dependent variable, it is demonstrated that it has a positive correlation with perceived ease of use ($r = 0.650$, $p < 0.000$).

When considering "attitude" as the dependent variable, "perceived usefulness" displayed a notably higher correlation ($r = 0.706$, $p < 0.001$) compared to "perceived ease of use" ($r = 0.637$, $p < 0.001$), reinforcing the importance of the former in predicting attitudes toward ChatGPT.

Furthermore, it is advisable to assess the potential existence of multicollinearity among the independent variables. If Pearson's correlation coefficient between any pair of independent variables were to approach ±0.9, the results would indicate the absence of multicollinearity, as the correlation value would remain considerably below the critical threshold of ±0.9.

TABLE 7.11
Factors Analysis of Main Study's Variables

Construct	Communalities	Factor Loading	% % of Variance Explained	KMO	Eigenvalue	Cronbach's Alpha
PU1	0.811	0.900	76.309	0.839	3.052	0.895
PU2	0.741	0.861				
PU3	0.802	0.895				
PU4	0.699	0.836				
PEOU1	0.765	0.875	79.725%	0.849	3.189	0.915
PEOU2	0.778	0.882				
PEOU3	0.825	0.908				
PEOU4	0.821	0.906				
PR1	0.579	0.761	62.836%	0.790	3.142	0.851
PR2	0.618	0.786				
PR3	0.679	0.824				
PR4	0.601	0.775				
PR5	0.665	0.816				
TRUST1	0.739	0.859	73.265%	0.693	2.198	0.817
TRUST2	0.663	0.814				
TRUST3	0.796	0.892				
ATT1	0.917	0.958	88.852%	0.752	2.666	0.936
ATT2	0.894	0.945				
ATT3	0.855	0.924				
INTUSE1	0.922	0.922	86.726%	0.760	2.602	0.923
INTUSE2	0.931	0.931				
INTUSE3	0.940	0.940				

Prior to conducting the analyses, it is crucial to assess the presence of multicollinearity among the variables. To achieve this, we employed the Variance Inflation Factor (VIF) as a diagnostic index. A VIF value within the range of 1 signifies the absence of collinearity, while a value exceeding 10 indicates substantial collinearity among the variables. As delineated in the subsequent table, our analysis reveals the absence of collinearity among the variables. The VIF value of constructs ranged between 1.0 and 2.374. hence, we can conclude that there is not collinearity among the variables.

In the ensuing analysis, we initiate the evaluation of the fit of the regression model to the data. Table 7.12 displays a high R^2 value compared to the thresholds recommended by Cohen (1988), who specifies that R^2 values of 0.02, 0.13, and 0.26 are considered to be small, medium, and large, respectively. Therefore, the intention of using ChatGPT as well as the attitude toward ChatGPT variable display an R^2 of 65% and 55.3%, respectively. R values of 0.744 and 0.806 suggest that the data fit the model satisfactorily. The adjusted R^2 value is an estimate of the robustness of this model if we took a different sample from the same population.

The final column pertains to the Durbin-Watson test, where no specific significance threshold is employed; rather, attention is directed solely toward the observed statistic. Generally, a Durbin-Watson statistic within the range of 1 to 3 is considered acceptable. It is conventionally acknowledged that as this statistic approaches a value of 2, concerns related to the independence of errors diminish. In the context of our current investigation, the Durbin-Watson statistic falls within an acceptable range, suggesting satisfactory independence of errors.

TABLE 7.12
The Determination Coefficient (R^2)

Variables	R	R^2	R^2 Adjusted	Durbin-Watson
Attitude toward using ChatGPT (Att)*	0.744	0.553	0.548	2.026
Intention to use ChatGPT**	0.7806	0.650	0.640	2.356
Perceived usefulness (PU)***	0.650	0.522	0.419	1.934

*Predictors: PU and PEOU **Predictors: PU, PEOU, Att, TRUST and PR ***Predictor: PEOU.
Table 7.12: regression model.

TABLE 7.13
ANOVA for Intention to Use

Model	Somme des carrés	ddl	Carré moyen	F	Sig.
Regression	118,360	5	23,672	65,838	,000[b]
Résidu	63,640	177	,360		
Total	180,000	182			

a. DV: Intuse.
b. Predictors: (Constant), ATT, PU, PEOU, TRUST and PR.

TABLE 7.14
Anova for Perceived Utility

Model	Somme des carrés	ddl	Carré moyen	F	Sig.
Regression	78.209	1	78.209	132.149	,000[b]
Résidu	107.120	181	.529		
Total	185.329	182			

a. DV: PU.
b. Predictors: (Constant), PEOU.

Moreover, the F-index (see Tables 7.13 and 7.14) yields a value of 63.406 for Intention to use and a value of 94,306 for attitude toward using ChatGPT, signifying statistical significance at a p-value threshold of less than 0.0001. This outcome implies that the probability of obtaining an F value of such magnitude by random chance is less than 0.01%. Consequently, we must reject the null hypothesis posited earlier, substantiating the presence of a statistically significant association between the dependent and independent variables. As we can see in Table 7.15, the value of F is 132.149 and is significant at $p < 0.0000$.

7.5.1.2 Hypotheses Testing

To test our hypotheses, we conducted linear regressions using SPSS 23 software. In the following, we will test our hypotheses and discuss the results.

TABLE 7.15
Results of Regression Analysis

Hypothesis	T-test	Beta	Significance	Validation
H1a: PU → Att	13.400	0.706	0.000	Supported
H1b: PU → Intuse	11.231	0.641	0.000	Supported
H2a: PEOU → Att	11.117	0.637	0.000	Supported
H2b: PEOU → PU	11.496	0.650	0.000	Supported
H2c: PEOU → Intuse	9.765	0.587	0.000	Supported
H3: Att → Intuse	16.267	0.771	0.000	Supported
H4a: Trust → Intuse	8.695	0.543	0.000	Supported
H4b: PR → Intuse	0.793	0.059	0.429	Not supported

Note: PU: Perceived usefulness; PEOU: Perceived ease of use; Att: attitude toward using ChatGPT: Trust: trust; PR: Perceived risk; Intuse: intention to use ChatGPT.

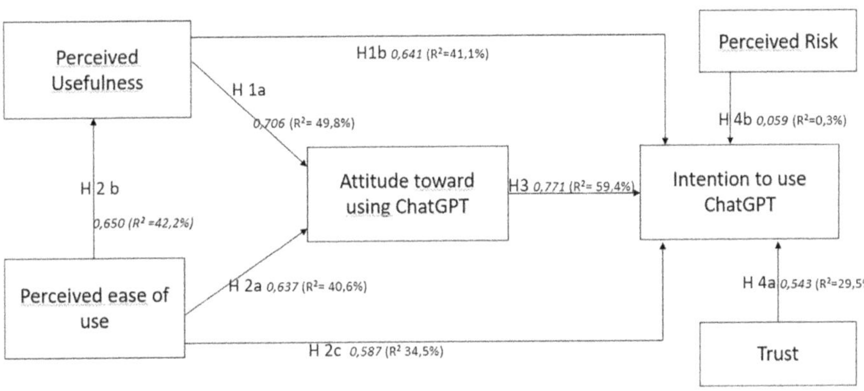

FIGURE 7.3 Structural model.

As shown in Table 7.15, hypotheses: H1a; H1b; H2a; H2b; H2c; H3; and H4a are supported at $p < 0.000$. However, only H4b is rejected.

Figure 7.3 provides a visual representation of the impact of individual independent variables on the dependent variable, along with the corresponding explained variance. It is noteworthy that the perceived risk variable exhibits no statistically significant influence on the prediction of user intention to use ChatGPT. In contrast, the remaining variables significantly contribute to the predictive modeling of the dependent variable: the intention to use ChatGPT.

7.6 DISCUSSION

Before discussing our findings, let us first recall the objective of this study which is none other than the identification of factors likely to influence the intention to use ChatGPT by professionals in the marketing field. This research admits two phases in the development of the results. indeed, the expected results are similar to previous studies. A research model combining eight research hypotheses was established and validated using a quantitative approach using SPSS software.

As expounded in the extant literature pertaining to the Technology Acceptance Model (TAM), the findings procured in the course of this investigation substantiate the notion that the intention to use ChatGPT is contingent upon the various constituents our extended TAM, as articulated by seminal works such as those authored by Davis (1989), Zarouali et al. (2018), Richard et al. (2019), and Emon et al. (2023). This affirmation aligns harmoniously with antecedent research outcomes. Furthermore, Kasilingam (2020) affirms the presence of a substantial association between Perceived Ease of Use (PEOU), Perceived Usefulness (PU), and attitude, on the one hand, and the intention to use chatbots, on the other hand, particularly in the context of mobile shopping.

From the outcomes of our study, it becomes conspicuous that perceived risk bears no nexus with the intention to use ChatGPT (H4b rejected). Consequently, it can be surmised that, even in instances where marketing professionals harbor reservations about the use of ChatGPT, their intention to employ the technology remains unaltered. This contravenes the expectations put forth by Kasilingam (2020) and Kim et al. (2008), who advocate for a heightened emphasis on enhancing information privacy, positing that it could concomitantly mitigate risks and foster technology adoption.

The attitude toward using ChatGPT emerges as a pivotal determinant impacting the intention to utilize this technology within the framework of the TAM model. In the survey administered, it was imperative for respondents to cultivate a constructive and meaningful attitude, as it serves as the linchpin for marketing practitioners to seamlessly integrate the ChatGPT artificial intelligence tool into their operational milieu. Conversely, the variable of perceived ease of use, while exerting a direct and positive influence, assumes a relatively subordinate role in comparison.

As observed in the study by Chi et al. (2021), the recurrent concern pertaining to trust in this technology remains a prominent theme in the literature. This research introduced trust as a predictive factor, extending the boundaries of the Technology Acceptance Model (TAM). The inclusion of trust in our study proved not only beneficial but also statistically significant, elucidating a substantial 29.5% of the variance in the intention to employ ChatGPT. Consequently, it is plausible to assert that a higher level of confidence placed in this tool correlates positively with the likelihood of users expressing the intention to integrate it into their professional practices. These results underscore the fundamental significance of trust in intention to use ChatGPT among marketers. By establishing a substantial direct influence on usage intentions, our investigation substantiates the pivotal role of trust within the realm of technology adoption research. These findings align with prior research in the comprehensive body of literature on this topic, as demonstrated by the investigations of Gefen and Strub (2003) and Pavlou (2003). Additionally, our results within the domain of artificial intelligence are in harmony with recent research endeavors concerningChatGPT conducted by Toreini et al. (2020) and Choudhury and Shamszare (2023).

7.7 CONCLUSION

In summary, this research has contributed to the understanding of factors exerting a significant impact on the intention to adopt ChatGPT among marketing professionals. Our findings have yielded valuable insights into the intricate interplay of technological determinants (specifically, perceived usefulness and perceived ease of use) and psychological factors associated with users (attitude, perceived risk, and trust), thus highlighting the dynamic nature characterizing the intention to use such technology within the marketing domain.

Employing rigorous quantitative analysis, we first confirmed the excellent psychometric quality of all constructs within our research model. Furthermore, our study underscored the central roles played by perceived usefulness, ease of use, trust, and attitude toward ChatGPT in shaping marketing professionals' intentions to incorporate it into their daily practices. Certain concerns among scholars and authors regarding its integration into various marketing strategies have been raised. In this regard, several authors have raised issues related to privacy risks (Marjerison et al., 2022) and the security of customer data. However, our results indicated that marketing professionals do not perceive significant risks associated with the use of ChatGPT.

This research has implications both from a theoretical and managerial perspective. Theoretically, this study contributes to the body of literature concerning the adoption of

ChatGPT among marketing professionals. By validating a model strongly rooted in marketing literature – the Technology Acceptance Model (TAM) – while incorporating potentially pivotal factors, our research serves as a platform for further investigations. To enhance the variance in usage intention, which currently stands at a commendable $R^2 = 65\%$, future research should focus on bridging the knowledge gap between perceived ease of use and perceived usefulness. Organizations are urged to acknowledge and address impediments that may hinder the realization of ChatGPT's full potential. In this regard, we recommend targeted interventions and educational initiatives to facilitate the integration of ChatGPT into marketing workflows.

Although our findings did not reveal a significant relationship between perceived risk and usage intention, it is imperative for marketers, researchers, and decision-makers to remain vigilant and adapt to the ever-evolving landscape of AI technologies and their implications. On the managerial front, the marketing sector stands at a critical juncture, where the adoption of advanced AI tools like ChatGPT offers a distinct competitive advantage. To harness ChatGPT's potential for revolutionizing marketing practices, ethical considerations and user-centric design principles must remain at the forefront of this transformative journey. In this dynamic environment, collaboration between academia and industry will be instrumental in driving innovation and ensuring that ChatGPT becomes an indispensable tool for marketing professionals in the years ahead. While this study encountered certain limitations, it has also opened numerous avenues for future research. Firstly, the data collection phase, spanning from January to August 2023, presented significant challenges due to the busy schedules of the professional respondents. This circumstance necessitates the consideration of replicating the survey with a larger sample size to bolster the validity and reliability of our anticipated findings.

Then, while it is evident that a majority of respondents possess knowledge of artificial intelligence, it would be prudent to conduct a follow-up data collection at a later time to assess the influence of familiarity with the ChatGPT tool on usage intentions and subsequent adoption in practical, day-to-day contexts. Ultimately, it is imperative to acknowledge that ChatGPT cannot entirely supplant human expertise and discernment. Marketers should maintain an awareness of its inherent constraints and, in practice, employ ChatGPT as an adjunctive tool rather than a self-sufficient solution. Consequently, it becomes essential to investigate the impact of additional variables, such as perceived intelligence or anthropomorphism, in relation to the intention to adopt ChatGPT within the marketing domain (Balakrishnan & Dwivedi, 2021).

REFERENCES

Ajzen I. (1985). From Intentions to Actions: A Theory of Planned Behavior, in J. Kuhl and J. Beckmann (Eds.), *Action Control*, 11–39. Springer-Verlag.

Akrout F. (2018). *Les méthodes des équations structurelles*. Sfax.

Alalwan A. A., Dwivedi Y. K., & Rana N. P. (2017). Factors influencing adoption of mobile banking by Jordanian bank customers: Extending UTAUT2 with trust, *International Journal of Information Management*, 37(3), 99–110.

Alyoshina I. V. (2019). Artificial intelligence in age of digital globalization, In International Conference Technology and Entrepreneurship in Digital Society, 26–30.

Aydın Ö, & Karaarslan E. (2022). OpenAI ChatGPT Generated Literature Review: Digital Twin in Healthcare, in Ö Aydın (Ed.), *Emerging Computer Technologies*, 2, 22–31. İzmir Akademi Dernegi.

Balakrishnan J., & Dwivedi Y. K. (2021). Role of cognitive absorption in building user trust and experience, *Psychology & Marketing*, 38(4), 643–668. 10.1002/mar.21462

Buntak K., Kovačić M., & Mutavdžija M. (2020). Application of artificial intelligence in the business, *International Journal for Quality Research*, 15(2), 403–416.

Burns, R. P., & Burns, R. (2008). *Business Research Methods and Statistics Using SPSS*. SAGE Publications Ltd, 560 pages.

Chen, J. V., Yen, D. C., & Chen, K. (2009). The acceptance and diffusion of the innovative smart phone use: A case study of a delivery service company in logistics, *Information and Management*, 46(4), 241–248.

Chi, O. H., Jia, S., Li, Y., & Gursoy, D. (2021). Developing a formative scale to measure consumers' trust toward interaction with artificially intelligent (AI) social robots in service delivery, *Computers in Human Behavior*, 118. 10.1016/j.chb.2021.106700

Choudhury A., & Shamszare H. (2023). Investigating the impact of user trust on adoption and use of ChatGPT: A survey analysis, *Journal of Medical Internet Research*, 25, 1–11.

Cohen, J. (1988). *Statistical Power Analysis for the Behavioral Sciences*, 2nd ed. 597 pages. Routledge. 10.4324/9780203771587

Davis F. D. (1986). *A Technology Acceptance Model for Empirical Testing New End-User Information System: Theory and Results*. Massachusetts Institute of Technology.

Davis F. D., Bagozzi R. P., & Warshaw P. R. (1989). User acceptance of computer technology: A comparison of two theoretical models, *Management Science*, 35(8), 982–1003.

De Bruyn A., Viswanathan V., Beh Y.-S., Kai-Uwe Brock J., & Von Wangenheim F. (2020). Artificial intelligence and marketing: Pitfalls and opportunities, *Journal of Interactive Marketing*, 51, 91–105, ISSN 1094-9968. 10.1016/j.intmar.2020.04.007

Dubey R., Bryde D.-J., Blome C.,Roubaud D., & Giannakis M. (2021). Facilitating artificial intelligence powered supply chain analytics through alliance management during the pandemic crises in the B2B context, *Industrial Marketing Management*, 96, 135–146. 10.1016/j.indmarman.2021.05.003

Dubois C., Salotti J.-M., Seminel D., & Simonazzi N. (2019). Le Chatbot: un outil de la relation aux clients, *Dans Hermès, La Revue*, 2(84), 95–97.

Dwivedi Y. K., Hughes L., Ismagilova E., Aarts G., Coombs C., Crick T., Duan Y., Dwivedi R., Edwards J., Eirug A., Galanos V., Ilavarasan P. V., Janssen M., Jones P., Kumar Kar A., Kizgin H., Kronemann B., Lal B., Lucini B., Medaglia R., Le Meunier-FitzHugh K., Le Meunier-FitzHugh L. C., Misra S., Mogaji E., Sharma S. K., Singh J. B., Raghavan V., Raman R., Rana N. P., Samothrakis S., Spencer J., Tamilmani K., Tubadji A., Walton P., & Williams M. D. (2021). Artificial intelligence (AI): Multidisciplinary perspectives on emerging challenges, opportunities, and agenda for research, practice and policy, *International Journal of Information Management*, 57. 10.1016/j.ijinfomgt.2019.08.002

El Bakkouria B., Raki S., & Belgnaou T. (2022). The role of Chatbots in enhancing customer experience: Literature review, *Procedia Computer Science*, 203, 432–437.

Emon, M. M., Farheen H., Mehzabul N., & Vichayanan R. (2023). Predicting adoption intention of artificial intelligence, a study on ChatGPT, *AIUB Journal of Science and Engineering*, 22, 189–196.

Evard, Y., Pras, B., & Roux, E. (2000). *Market: Etudes et recherches en marketing*.

Feng C. M., Park A., Pitt L., Kietzmann J., & Northey G. (2021). Artificial intelligence in marketing: A bibliographic perspective, *Australasian Marketing Journal*, 29(3), 252–263. 10.1016/j.ausmj.2020.07.006

Gevaert, M., Carman, M., Rosman, B., Georgiadou, Y., & Soden, R. (2021). Fairness and accountability of AI in disaster risk management: Opportunities and challenges, *Patterns*, 2(11), 1–9.

Gefen D., & Straub D. W. (2003). Managing user trust in B2C e-services, *e Service Journal*, 2(2), 7–24.

Gefen D., Karahanna E., & Straub D. W. (2003). Trust and TAM in online shopping: An integrated model, *MIS Quarterly*, 27(1), 51. 10.2307/30036519

Goyal A., Thakur R., & Srivastava M. (2013). Customer usage intention of mobile commerce in India: An empirical study, *Journal of Indian Business Research*, 5(1), 52–72.

Güngör H. (2020). Creating value with artificial intelligence: A multi-stakeholder perspective, *Journal of Creating Value*, 6(1), 72–85. 10.1177/2394964320921071

Haleem A., Javaid M., Asim Qadri M., Pratap Singh R., & Suman R. (2022). Artificial intelligence (AI) applications for marketing: A literature-based study, *International Journal of Intelligent Networks*, 3, 119–132.

Hinkin T. R. (1995). A review of scale development practices in the study of organizations, *Journal of Management*, 21(5), 967–988.

Hubert M., Blut M., Brock C., Backhaus C., & Eberhardt T. (2017). Acceptance of smartphone-based mobile shopping: Mobile benefits, customer characteristics, perceived risk and the impact of application context, *Psychology and Marketing*, 34(2), 175–194.

Hubert M., Blut M., Brock C., Zhang R. W., Koch V., & Riedl R. (2019). The influence of acceptance and adoption drivers on smart home usage, *European Journal of Marketing*, 53(6), 1073–1098. 10.1108/EJM-12-2016-0794

Jacoby J., & Kaplan, L. B. (1972). *The components of perceived risk.* ACR special volumes.
Jatobá M., Santos J., Gutierriz I., Moscon D., Fernandes P. O., & Teixeira J. P. (2019). Evolution of artificial intelligence research in human resources, *Procedia Computer Science*, 164, 137–142, ISSN 1877-0509. 10.1016/j.procs.2019.12.165
Jarek K., & Mazurek G. (2019). Marketing and artificial intelligence, *Central European Business Review*, 8(2), 46–55.
Javaid M., Haleem A., Vaish A., Vaishya R., & Iyengar K. P. (2020). Robotics applications in COVID-19: A review, *Journal of Industrial Integration and Management*, 5(4), 441–451.
Kabra G., Ramesh A., Akhtar P., & Dash M. K. (2017). Understanding behavioural intention to use information technology: Insights from humanitarian practitioners, *Telematics and Informatics*, 34(7), 1250–1261.
Kasilingam D. L. (2020). Understanding the attitude and intention to use smartphone chatbots for shopping, *Technology in Society*, 62, 101280. 10.1016/j.techsoc.2020.101280
Kietzmann J., & Pitt L. F. (2020). Artificial intelligence and machine learning: What managers need to know, *Business Horizon*, 63(2), 131–133. 10.1016/j.bushor.2019.11.005
Kim D. J., Ferrin D. L., & Rao H. R. (2008). A trust-based consumer decision-making model in electronic commerce: The role of trust, perceived risk, and their antecedents, *Decision Support System*, 44(2), 544–564.
Kim C., Mirusmonov M., & Lee I. (2010). An empirical examination of factors influencing the intention to use mobile payment, *Computers in Human Behavior*, 26(3), 310–322.
Kung T. H., Cheatham M., Medenilla A., Sillos C., De Leon L., Elepaño C., Madriaga M., Aggabao R., Diaz-Candido G., Maningo J., & Tseng V. (2022). Performance of ChatGPT on USMLE: Potential for AI assisted medical education using large language models, *PLoS Digital Health*, 2(2). 10.1101/2022.12.19.2
Latinovic Z., & Chatterjee S. C. (2022). Achieving the promise of AI and ML in delivering economic and relational customer value in B2B, *Journal of Business Research*, 144, 966–974.
Lee J. D., & See K. A. (2004). Trust in automation: Designing for appropriate reliance, *Human Factors: The Journal of the Human Factors and Ergonomics Society*, 46(1), 50–80. 10.1518/hfes.46.1.50_30392
Lee M.-C. (2009). Factors influencing the adoption of Internet banking: an integration of TAM and TPB with perceived risk and perceived benefit, *Electronic Commerce Research and Applications*, 8(3), 130–141.
Lies J. (2019). Marketing intelligence and big data: Digital marketing techniques on their way to becoming social engineering techniques in marketing, *International Journal of Interactive Multimedia and Artificial Intelligence*, 5(5), 134–144.
Ling E. C., Tussyadiah I., Tuomi A., Stienmetz J., & Ioannou A. (2021). Factors influencing users' adoption and use of conversational agents: A systematic review, *Psychology & Marketing*, 38, 1031–1051. 10.1002/mar.21491
Malhotra N. K., Nunan D., & Birks D. F. (2017). *Marketing Research: An Applied Approach.* Pearson, 976.
Marjerison R. K., Zhang Y., & Zheng H. (2022). AI in E-commerce: Application of the use and gratification model to the acceptance of Chatbots, *Sustainability*, 14, 14270. 10.3390/su142114270
McLean G., & Osei-Frimpong K. (2019b). Chat now … Examining the variables influencing the use of online live chat, *Technological Forecasting and Social Change*, 146, 55–67.
McLeod A., Pippin S., & Mason R. (2008). Individual taxpayer intention to use tax preparation software: Examining experience, trust, and perceived risk, In Proceedings of ISOneWorld Conference. June (Vol. 2, No. 4, p. 1).
Momani A. M., & Jamous M. M. (2017). The evolution of technology acceptance theories, *International Journal of Contemporary Computer Research*, 1(1), 51–58.
Mooi E., & Sarstedt M. (2019). *A Concise Guide to Market Research.* Springer.
Natarajan T., Balasubramanian S. A., & Kasilingam D. L. (2017). Understanding the intention to use mobile shopping applications and its influence on price sensitivity, *Journal of Retailing and Consumer Services*, 37, 8–22. 10.1016/j.jretconser.2017.02.010
Nicolaou A. I., & McKnight D. H. (2006). Perceived information quality in data exchanges: Effects on risk, trust, and intention to use, *Information Systems Research*, 17(4), 332–351.
Nivetha P., & Sudhamathi S. (2019). Marketing trends using latest technology, *International Journal of Recent Technology and Engineering*, ISSN: 2277-3878, 8(2S6), 700–703.

Patil P., Tamilmani K., Rana N., & Raghavan V. (2020). Understanding consumer adoption of mobile payment in India: Extending meta-UTAUT model with personal innovativeness, anxiety, trust, and grievance redressal, *International Journal of Information Management*, 54(2), 198-196. 10.1016/j.ijinfomgt.2020.102144

Park C., & Jun J. (2003). A cross-cultural comparison of Internet buying behavior: Effects of Internet usage, perceived risks, and innovativeness, *International Marketing Review*, 20(5), 534–553. 10.1108/02651330310498771

Parasmehak, K., & Chitsimran (2019). Evolution of artificial intelligence in marketing, comparison with traditional marketing, *Our Heritage*, 67(5), 375–389. Available at SSRN: https://ssrn.com/abstract=3557091

Paschen J., Kietzmann J., & Kietzmann T. C. (2019). Artificial intelligence (AI) and its implications for market knowledge in B2B marketing, *Journal of Business & Industrial Marketing*, 34(7), 1410–1419. 10.1108/JBIM-10-2018-0295

Pavlou P. A. (2003). Consumer acceptance of electronic commerce: Integrating trust and risk with the technology acceptance model, *International Journal of Electronic Commerce*, 7(3), 101–134.

Petersson A. H., Pawar S., & Fagerstrøm A. (2023). Investigating the factors of customer experiences using real-life text-based banking chatbot: A qualitative study in Norway, *Procedia Computer Science*, 219, 697–704.

Persson A., Laaksoharju M., & Koga H. (2021). We mostly think alike: Individual differences in attitude towards AI in Sweden and Japan, *The Review of Socionetwork Strategies*, 15(1), 123–142.

Pedersen I., & Duin A. (2022). AI agents, humans and untangling the marketing of artificial intelligence in learning environments, In Proceedings of the 55th Hawaii International Conference on System Sciences.

Rana S. (2023). AI and GPT for management scholars and practitioners: Guidelines and implications, *FIIB Business Review*, 12(1), 7–9. 10.1177/23197145231161408

Rathore B. (2023). Future of AI & generation alpha: ChatGPT beyond boundaries, *International Peer Reviewed/Refereed Multidisciplinary Journal*, ISSN: 2319-5045, 12(1). Available online at: www.eduzonejournal.com

Rietz T., Benke I., & Maedche A. (2019). The impact of anthropomorphic and functional chatbot design features in enterprise collaboration systems on user acceptance, In Proceedings of the 14th International Conference on Wirtschafts informatik.

Rutskiy V., Mousavi R., Chudopal N., Amrani Y. E., Everstova V., & Tsarev R. (2021). Artificial intelligence as a disruptive technology for digital marketing, *Data Science and Intelligent Systems*, 231, 895–900.

Shah D., & Shay E. (2019). How and Why Artificial Intelligence, Mixed Reality and Blockchain Technologies Will Change Marketing We Know Today, In *Handbook of Advances in Marketing in an Era of Disruptions: Essays in Honour of Jagdish N. Sheth*, 377–390. Sage Publications, India. 10.4135/9789353287733

Saputra R., Nasution M. I. P., & Dharma B. (2023). The impact of using AI ChatGPT on marketing effectiveness: A case study on Instagram marketing, *Indonesian Journal of Economics and Management*, 3(3), 603–617.

Schierz P. G., Schilke O., & Wirtz B. W. (2010). Understanding consumer acceptance of mobile payment services: An empirical analysis, *Electronic Commerce Research and Applications*, 9(3), 209–216.

Singh D. (2023). ChatGPT: A new approach to revolutionise organisations, *International Journal of New Media Studies*, 10(1), 57–63.

Som B. (2023). Role of ChatGPT in gaming: According to ChatGPT (March 2, 2023). Available at SSRN: https://ssrn.com/abstract=4375510 or 10.2139/ssrn.4375510

Syam N. etSharma A. (2018). Waiting for a sales renaissance in the fourth industrial revolution: Machine learning and artificial intelligence in sales research and practice, *Industrial Marketing Management*, 69, 139–146.

Taylor S., & Todd P. A. (1995). Understanding information technology usage: A test of competing models, *Information Systems Research*, 6(2), 144–176.

Thi Phuong Anh L., & Rajah E. (2022). Using Chatbots in customer service: A case study of Air New Zealand, In E. Papoutsaki and M. Shannon (Eds.), Proceedings: RangahauHoronuku Hou – New Research Landscapes, *Unitec/MIT Research Symposium*, 6 et 7 Décembre 2021, 161–176. 10.34074/proc.2206011

Toreini E., Aitken M., Coopamootoo K., Elliott K., Zelaya C. G., & Van Moorsel A. (2020). The relationship between trust in AI and trustworthy machine learning technologies, In Proceedings of the 2020 Conference on Fairness, Accountability, and Transparency, 272–283.

Turja T., Aaltonen I., Taipale S., & Oksanen A. (2020). Robot acceptance model for care (RAM-care): A principled approach to the intention to use care robots, *Information & Management*, 57(5), 103220.

Varsha J., Himanshu R., Parvathy S., & Emmanuel M. (2023). The prospects and challenges of ChatGPT on marketing research and practices (March 23, 2023). Available at SSRN: https://ssrn.com/abstract=4398033 or 10.2139/ssrn.4398033

Yang H., & Lee H. (2019). Understanding user behavior of virtual personal assistant devices, *Information Systems and e-Business Management*, 17, 65–87.

Zarouali B., Van den Broeck E., Walrave M., & Poels K. (2018). Predicting consumer responses to a chatbot on Facebook, *Cyberpsychology, Behavior and Social Networking*, 21(8), 491–497.

8 The Effectiveness of Using Artificial Intelligence Techniques in Advertising on Social Media

Thouraya Hmidi
Shaqra University, Shaqra, Saudi Arabia

Aicha Zaidi
University of Mahdia, Mahdia, Tunisia

8.1 INTRODUCTION

The study sought to clarify the significance of the effectiveness of using artificial intelligence techniques in social networking in order to identify the areas of using artificial intelligence techniques in social networking sites, as well as to monitor the positive and negative effects and forms of anxiety and tension caused by the use of artificial intelligence techniques in social networking sites. The results of the investigation revealed that there is a direct relationship between artificial intelligence approaches in advertising on social media and the intention to alter behavior after 300 surveys were distributed and analyzed using the program SPSS 21. Furthermore, significant correlations between the various factors were investigated. The findings suggested that they converge globally with the literature review.

Consumer perception is commonly used in the literature to assess the success of advertising. It is critical to investigate the impact of advertising on the consumer-brand relationship. In forecasting brand behavior consumption, the latter may have a greater influence on brand attitude. Addressing dangerous behaviors can lead to the implementation of awareness programs that enlighten people about the risks they face when they engage in harmful behavior. Our research will allow companies to better understand how advertising influences brand attachment, allowing them to plan their marketing strategy. This leads us to the conclusion that advertising can impact consumer behavior.

In this study, we will examine the impact of artificial intelligence on advertising. The significance of this study lies in the comparison of two posters (one made by artificial intelligence and the other actual), the objective of which is to study the influence of each on the intention to change behavior.

8.2 OBJECTIVES OF THE STUDY

The study's major goal was to determine the efficiency of applying artificial intelligence approaches in social media advertising.

DOI: 10.1201/9781003450443-8

This study has several goals, the most important of which are:

- Determining the respondents' level of knowledge of artificial intelligence approaches, as well as their understanding of its importance and efficacy in advertising on social networking sites.
- Recognizing the significance of artificial intelligence technology and social networking site advertising.
- Monitoring the extent to which advertising on social networking sites relies on artificial intelligence techniques determines the degree of success of using artificial intelligence techniques in advertising on social media.
- Exploring the future of using artificial intelligence techniques in advertising through social networking sites and its potential positive and negative effects.

8.3 LITERATURE REVIEW

8.3.1 Artificial Intelligence

Artificial intelligence is a critical tool for marketers since it eliminates human faults such as delays, biased approaches, and other minor flaws. Artificial intelligence contributes significantly to improving many operations and services worldwide. Wichert discusses how artificial intelligence is used in quantum computing and machine learning. It aids in the rapid resolution of difficult situations.

8.3.2 Applications of Artificial Intelligence Technology in Marketing

Chatbots are computer programs developed to interact with customers over the internet, answer their questions, provide support, and help them complete purchases. Where Chatbots can be integrated into websites and social media pages, bots help chat interact with the brand and help improve customer experience across delivery. They have 24/7 support, and these bots can handle multiple clients at the same time. Many companies have come to rely on chatbots to provide support to its customers due to its low cost and great effectiveness. Artificial intelligence provides the visitor and the user with content or products and services compatible with their interests and needs, based on the online activities of the user and the topics he searches for, the sites he visits, and areas that hold his attention.

Artificial intelligence techniques make it possible to identify the psychological characteristics of people by tracking their digital footprint on social networking sites and the changes that occur there over a certain period of time.

8.3.3 The Effect of Artificial Intelligence on Online Advertising

Feeling, transactions, travel, etc., of customers are tracked by artificial intelligence and used to create machine learning algorithms that predict customer behavior (Huang & Rust, 2021). Customer engagement and retention strategies will be developed using personalized information, suggestions, and communications (Huang & Rust, 2021). Saving money, increasing revenue, and improving customer satisfaction are all goals that AI aspires to achieve (Huang & Rust, 2021). Artificial intelligence can do a wide variety of activities, despite its inability to show compassion or empathy (Huang & Rust, 2021).

Advertising media is undergoing major changes. The online media advertising market is booming. These changes have had a significant impact on advertising in traditional media. In

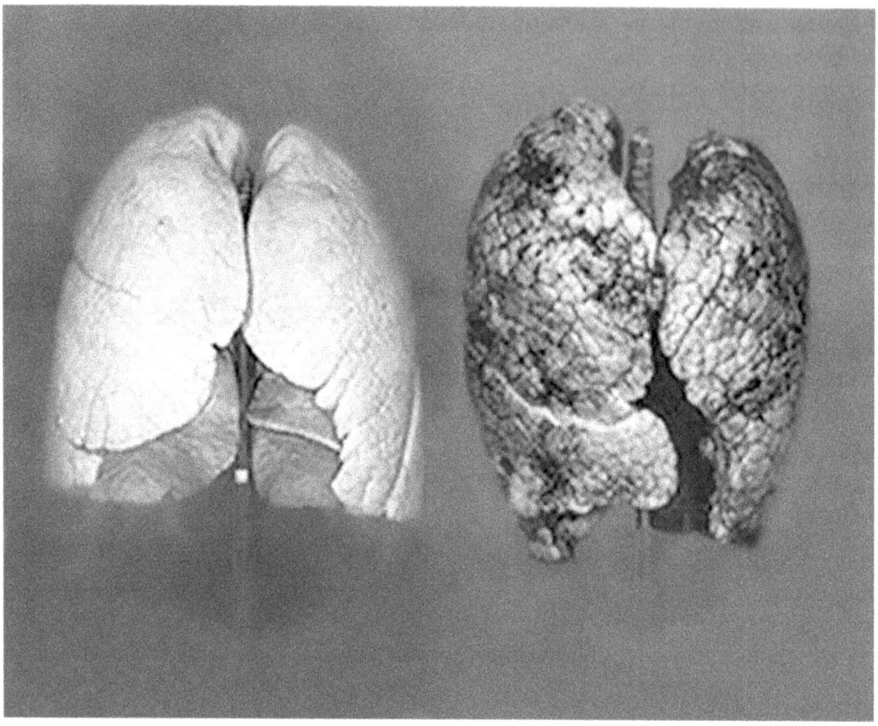

FIGURE 8.1 The poster A.

various research projects, scholars have addressed different aspects of the ad management process regarding the use of AI in advertising, such as market research, media targeting and selection, ad creation and design, ad placement and execution, ad performance and purchase decision, and machine learning (Rodgers & Nguyen, 2022; Shah et al., 2020).

8.3.4 The Attitude toward the Poster Advertising

"The concept of attitude toward the advertising message is fundamental to understanding the advertising process. It makes it possible to capture the affective responses generated by exposure to the messages". According to Christian Derbaix et al., ad attitude is a tendency or psychological reaction that is expressed in the evaluation of a particular advertisement at a particular exposure (Figures 8.1 and 8.2).

8.3.5 Conceptual Model and Research Hypothesis

As summarized in our conceptual framework, our research objective is to measure the effect of comparative advertising on attitude, its antecedents, and its consequences in the Tunisian context (Figure 8.3). The effect of advertising will be tested on three broad categories of variables: cognitive variables, affective variables, and conative variables. Regarding the cognitive component, the variable retained is attention.

For the affective dimension, the attitude toward advertising will be tested. The impact of advertising on the conative component will also be verified.

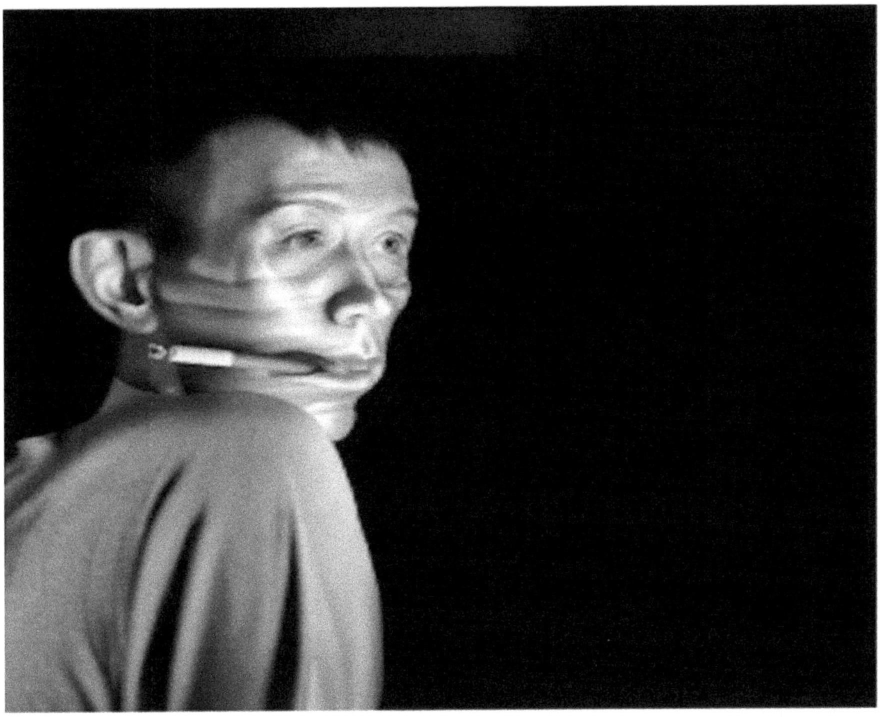

FIGURE 8.2 The poster B.

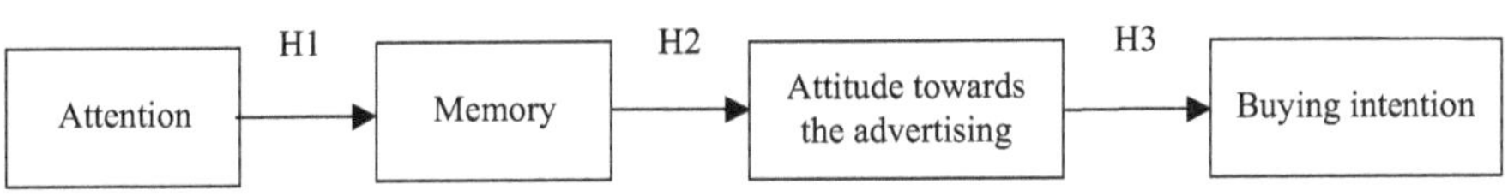

FIGURE 8.3 Conceptual model based on the hierarchy model of Thorson et al. (1992).

8.4 RESEARCH METHODOLOGY

8.4.1 Choice of Advertising Poster

We chose an advertising poster containing a message to raise awareness of the dangers of smoking. The first was processed by artificial intelligence and the other was launched by tobacco companies in agreement with the World Health Organization in 2023.

8.4.2 Sampling and Data Collection

The sample selected is composed of 300 persons selected according to the method of convenience. The same questionnaire includes the two advertising posters.

8.4.3 Operationalization of Psychometric Concepts and Properties of Measurement Scales

The scales used to measure the concepts of our research are adaptations or reproductions of certain scales (Yoo & Kim, 2005; Wells, 1964; Venkataramani, 1995; Derbaix, 1995; Chang, 2007). Changes were made to these scales following a pre-test with 30 people. All variables were measured

TABLE 8.1
Indicators of Validity and Reliability of Scales

Variables	Eigenvalue	Variance Explained	KMO Index	Bartlett Sphericity Test	α of Cronbach
Attention (A)	2,569	85,648	0,759	634,465 P=0,000	0,916
Attention (B)	2,541	84,969	0,755	601,393 P=0,000	0,909
Memorization (A)	6,374	79,676	0,964	2495,459 P=0,000	0,963
Memorization (B)	6,427	80,335	0,967	2553,784 P=0,000	0,965
Attitude toward advertising (A)	11,732	78,211	0,986	5346,626 P=0,000	0,980
Attitude toward advertising (B)	11,783	78,555	0,987	5405,904 P=0,000	0,980
Implication toward advertising (A)	2,559	85,503	0,760	619,938 P=0,000	0,913
Implication toward advertising (B)	2,568	85,598	0,761	630,756 P=0,000	0,916
Affective reaction (A)	6,417	80,217	0,966	2540,542 P=0,000	0,965
Affective reaction (B)	6,432	80,400	0,962	2582,960 P=0,000	0,965
Intention to change behavior (A)	2,552	85,077	0,759	611,473 P=0,000	0,912
Intention to change behavior (B)	2,535	84,516	0,755	593,501 P=0,000	0,908

on 7-point Likert scales, and the measurements after pre-testing are summarized in Table 8.1. We verified the psychometric properties by applying the reliability test (Cronbach's alpha).

8.4.3.1 Reliability and Validity Test

To verify the validity of the measurement scales used in our study, done through factor analyses, we will use as an extraction method, the principal component analysis with varimax rotations, to improve the structure of the factors.

The KMO value for the different variables concerning the two cases (advertising created by artificial intelligence vs. real advertising) is greater than 0.5 (see Table 8.9); therefore, the variables of our research are factorable. Applied principal component analyses reveal that all constructs are one-dimensional.

8.5 TESTING HYPOTHESES AND DISCUSSING RESULTS

To verify the attitude of Tunisian people toward two advertising formats, three research hypotheses were formulated and tested for the two advertisements that were the subject of our study. We tested the relationship between variables, attention, memorization, and attitude toward advertising and intention to change behavior, and we performed correlation tests (Tables 8.2 and 8.3).

8.5.1 Effect of Attention on Memorization

A simple linear regression analysis was done to test the different hypotheses of our study for both types of advertising; it allowed us to see for advertising A that the regression model is significant as a whole (sign = 0.000), that the adjusted R^2 value is 0.876 for advertising A and 0.861 for advertising B, which shows that our model is very good, and that there is a significant positive relationship between attention and memorization. So H1 is confirmed (Table 8.4).

TABLE 8.2
Analysis of Correlations between Variables for Advertising A

		Attention (A)	Memorization (A)	Attitude (A)	Affective Reaction (A)	Intention Behavior (A)
Attention (A)	Corrélation de Pearson	1	,936**	,943**	,938**	,913**
Mémorization (A)	Corrélation de Pearson	,936**	1	,971**	,958**	,934**
Attitude (A)	Corrélation de Pearson	,943**	,971**	1	,973**	,943**
Affective reaction (A)	Corrélation de Pearson	,938**	,958**	,973**	1	,937**
Intention behavior(A)	Corrélation de Pearson	,913**	,934**	,943**	,937**	1

Notes
** La corrélationest significative au niveau 0.01 (bilatéral).

TABLE 8.3
Analysis of Correlations between Variables for Advertising B

		Attention (B)	Memorization (B)	Attitude (B)	Affective Reaction (B)	Intention Behavior (B)
Attention (A)	Corrélation de Pearson	1	,928**	,945**	,932**	,908**
Memorization (B)	Corrélation de Pearson	,928**	1	,971**	,967**	,937**
Attitude (B)	Corrélation de Pearson	,945**	,971**	1	,979**	,951**
Affective reaction (B)	Corrélation de Pearson	,932**	,967**	,979**	1	,945**
Intention behavior (B)	Corrélation de Pearson	,908**	,937**	,951**	,945**	1

Notes
** La corrélationest significative au niveau 0.01 (bilatéral).

TABLE 8.4
H1. Effect of Attention on Memorization

Advertising (A)					Advertising (B)				
R^2	R^2 adjusted	B	F	Sig	R^2	R^2 adjusted	B	F	sig
0,936	0,876	0.876	2109,637	0.000	0,928	0,861	0,860	331,337	0,000

TABLE 8.5
H2. Effect of Memorization on Attitude toward Advertising

Advertising (A)					Advertising (B)				
R^2	R^2 adjusted	B	F	Sig	R^2	R^2 adjusted	B	F	sig
0,971	0,943	0.943	4923,633	0.000	0,971	0,944	0,943	4976,345	0,000

TABLE 8.6
H3. Effect of Attitude toward Advertising on Behavior Change Intention

Advertising (A)					Advertising (B)				
R^2	R^2 adjusted	B	F	Sig	R^2	R^2 adjusted	B	F	sig
0,943	0,888	0.888	2370,027	0.000	0,951	0,905	0,905	2848,810	0,000

8.5.2 Effect of Memorization on Attitude toward Advertising

The results of the simple linear regression analysis between memorization and attitude toward advertising are presented in Table 8.5, which shows a significant relationship between memorization and attitude toward advertising.

For ads A and B, this test proves that the model is significant (sig = 0.000 < 0.05), as well as an (adjusted R^2, respectively, equal to 0.943 and 0.944), representing a very good linear model. So H2 is confirmed.

8.5.3 Effect of Attitude toward Advertising on Intention Behavior

The third hypothesis that tests the relationship between attitude toward advertising and intention behavior is validated; Table 8.6 indicates that there is a significant positive relationship between these two variables, whose adjusted R^2 has values of 0.888 and 0.904.5, respectively, for advertising A and advertising B. Hence H3 is confirmed.

8.6 ANALYSIS OF AVERAGES

8.6.1 Analysis of Attention Averages

Table 8.7 shows that the average attention to ad A (5.27) is higher than that of ad B (2.64), and the difference in the average is significant (0.000 see Table 8.9), so ad A is the best in terms of attention.

TABLE 8.7
Analysis of Advertising Attention Averages

	N	Average	Standard Deviation	Standard Average Error
Attention (A)	300	5,2789	1,64082	,09473
Attention (B)	300	2,6478	1,54170	,08901

TABLE 8.8
Analysis of Memorization Averages

	N	Average	Standard Deviation	Standard Average Error
Memorization (A)	300	5,3163	1,53813	,08880
Memorization (B)	300	2,6738	1,51255	,08733

8.6.2 Analysis of Memorization Averages

The analysis of the comparison of averages shows us that the average memorization of ad B is higher than that of ad A (5.31 > 2.67), with a significant difference in the mean (sign = 0.000; see Table 8.9), which allows us to deduce that ad A, created by artificial intelligence, remains more memorized compared to poster B (Table 8.8).

8.6.3 Analysis of Averages of Attitude toward Advertising

As mentioned, according to Christian Derbaix et al., "The attitude toward the advertisement is a psychological tendency or reaction that is expressed through the evaluation of a particular advertisement, during a particular exhibition."

Table 8.9 shows that the average attitude toward the first ad (ad A) is a value of 5.31, which is higher than that of the second ad, which has a value of 2.69, and the difference of the average is significant (0.000), so ad A is the best, with its new or distinctive approach.

8.6.4 Analysis of Advertising Engagement Averages

The average engagement with ad A is 5.308 much higher than that of ad B, which has a value of 2.71; knowing that the difference in the mean is significant (sign = 0.000), ad A is more effective between engagement (Table 8.10).

TABLE 8.9
Analysis of Averages of Attitude toward Advertising

	N	Average	Standard Deviation	Standard Average Error
Attitude (A)	300	5,3116	1,51720	,08760
Attitude (B)	300	2,6951	1,51711	,08759

TABLE 8.10
Analysis of Advertising Engagement Averages

	N	Average	Standard Deviation	Standard Average Error
Implication (A)	300	5,3089	1,59412	,09204
Implication (B)	300	2,7189	1,60309	,09255

TABLE 8.11
Analysis of Averages of Behavior Change Intention

	N	Average	Standard Deviation	Standard Average Error
Intention (A)	300	5,2867	1,58192	,09133
Intention (B)	300	2,6622	1,57813	,09111

8.6.5 Analysis of Averages of Behavior Change Intention

We note from Table 8.11 that the average behavior change intention of ad A is higher than that of ad B (5.28 > 2.66), with a significant difference in the mean (sign = 0.000), which allows us to deduce that advertising changes the behavior of smokers by encouraging them to stop smoking.

8.7 MANAGERIAL AND MARKETING IMPLICATIONS

From a practical point of view, the results of this study reveal that advertising created by artificial intelligence is more effective in terms of the relevance of its advertising message.

Therefore, in view of these results, we recommend that Tunisian advertising agencies use these types of advertisements for tobacco control. This strategy is effective in raising awareness and mobilizing people to quit smoking.

One solution would be to incorporate test results related to the ads, with the aim of giving more substance to offensive ads. Advertising arguments could also be supported by statements made by experts or marketers. It should be noted that Tunisia is a country with a high communication context, so advertising will also have to focus on symbolic and emotional levels, as an advertisement triggering a negative emotion could be better accepted than an advertisement without emotions.

8.8 LIMITATIONS AND FUTURE AVENUES OF RESEARCH

One limitation lies in the choice of the data collection method. Indeed, we found many difficulties in gathering information. Another limitation related to the administered questionnaire was the composition of the questions, whose meaning was very similar, and therefore some respondents felt a certain weariness when filling out the questionnaire. Our research was focused on a single category of the product. We propose in future research to carry out another study on two different categories of products, thus making a comparative study between the two categories of products while keeping the same research concepts.

Advertising posters are limited to a message inducing a negative emotional reaction. It would be interesting for future research to make a comparative approach between two advertising posters, one using humor and the other appealing to the feeling of fear in order to test the effectiveness of each of these posters. This could further explain consumer behavior toward both types of advertising and its effects on behavior change and intent. This could be a rather interesting field of investigation.

This research focused on print advertisements, though it could be interesting to use other media. The use of television advertisements or radio could be considered. Indeed, advertising agencies generally use several media for each advertising campaign.

It is also important to test the role of other variables. Indeed, the list of variables to be controlled is very high, as revealed by the literature. Other variables could be tested, such as the effect of engagement with advertising on attention, as well as its effect on memorization, attitude toward advertisements, and behavior change and intent, since we have noticed that the relationship is positive and significant for advertisements A and B. Pearson's coefficients are, respectively, (r) (0.912, 0.936, 0.946, and 0.906) for advertising A, and the correlation intensities of the variables attention, memorization, and intention are, respectively, (0.913, 0.936, 0.946, and 0.919) for advertising B, with an associated probability of 0.000 for both formats. Other cognitive and conative variables could be measured, such as knowledge of the advertising message.

8.9 CONCLUSION

Experimental work on artificial intelligence has become increasingly widespread (Verma & Tripathi, 2017); it is for this reason that Tunisian advertisers are facing major changes that are leading them to re-evaluate their advertising strategies. The study carried out as part of this work attempted to explore the attitude of Tunisians toward two advertisements. The advertising format created by artificial intelligence could be a good way for advertising agencies to fight against several threatening social phenomena.

REFERENCES

Chang, C. (2007). The relative effectiveness of comparative and noncomparative advertising. Journal of Advertsing, 36(l), 21–35.

Derbaix, C. (1995). The impact of affective reactions on attitudes toward the advertisement and the brand: A step toward ecological validity. Journal of Marketing Research, 32(4), 470–479.

Rodgers, W., & Nguyen, T. (2022). Advertising benefits from ethical artificial intelligence algorithmic purchase decision pathways. Journal of Business Ethics, 178, 1043–1061.

Shah, N., Engineer, S., Bhagat, N., Chauhan, H., & Shah, M. (2020). Research trends on the usage of machine learning and artificial intelligence in advertising. Augmented Human Research, 5(1), 1–15.

Thorson, E., Chi, A., & Leavitt, C. (1992). Attention, memory, attitude and conation: A test of the advertising hierarchy. Advances in Consumer Research, 19, 366–379.

Venkataramani, J. R. (1995). Consumer involvement and deception from implied advertising claims. Journal of Marketing Research, 23(3), 267–279.

Verma, S., & Tripathi, S. (2017). Social media, an emerging platform for relationship building: A study of engagement with nongovernment organizations in India. International Journal of Nonprofit and Voluntary Sector Marketing, 23(2), 1–11.

Wells, W. D. (1964). EQ, son of EQ, and the reaction profile. Journal of Marketing, 28, 45–52.

Yoo, C. Y., & Kim, K. (2005). Processing of animation in online banner advertising: The roles of cognitive and emotional responses. Journal of Interactive Marketing, 19(4), 18–34.

9 The Impact of Blockchain on Digital Commerce

Thouraya Hmidi
Shaqra University, Shaqra, Saudi Arabia

Aicha Zaidi
University of Monastir, Mahdia, Tunisia

9.1 INTRODUCTION

Blockchain technology has the potential to drastically alter our online environment. Although Bitcoin was the first Blockchain application, it radically revolutionized the internet world by facilitating the transmission of wealth across the World Wide Web without the requirement for democratization. Blockchain technology enables the development of a new class of apps and enterprises.

Blockchain technology has begun to spread as the basic technology for encrypted digital currency in order to complete all purchases, sales, and various exchange operations and to record and store all transactions in a time series. Once approved by network members, these transactions cannot be canceled or modified.

Blockchain technology is distinguished by the fact that all transactions that have occurred on the network since its inception have been recorded on the network in a way that cannot be modified or changed, and what distinguishes blockchain technology in terms of infrastructure and construction is that its applications, uses, and integration in various commercial fields are numerous. New transactions are recorded and gathered in batches known as blocks at regular intervals, then a chain of blocks is generated by a process known as Bitcoin Miner in which all existing blocks are added, hence the name of the blockchain. Blockchain technology is rapidly developing, requiring institutions and businesses of all types to adapt the means and methods utilized, which are related to the nature of global trade company and the areas of dealing with the institutions in which work takes place. The way businesses operate is expected to increasingly take over core functions due to cost savings and operational efficiencies.

Blockchain technology has begun to expand beyond the realm of cryptocurrency and into the realm of cryptocurrency in the world of international business. In fact, Gartner predicts that by 2030, 30% of the global customer base will consist of players that use blockchain as a core technology to practice commercial activity. In addition, the World Economic Forum survey (2015) suggests that 10% of global GDP will be stored on the blockchain by 2027.

Although originally applied in the context of cryptocurrency and blockchain applications, it has taken root in traditional businesses, startups, and everyday life. For example, it is used as an alternative to credit card or PayPal payment for e-commerce and international transfers. Moreover, it is implemented not only in financial institutions and banks but also in many other companies such as Samsung, Deloitte, RWE, and IBM, with applications from streamlining and automating trade finance to tracking merchant loyalty points and gift cards and even creating decentralized marketplaces for electricity trade. They are also deployed, for example, by Siemens and others for energy sharing and networks, with smartphone companies like HTC and Foxconn doing the production of Blockchain-enabled phones to make cryptocurrency payments possible over the

 DOI: 10.1201/9781003450443-9

phone for consumers. Some microtech startups are focused on disrupting the "inefficient and highly brokered" banking industry, while some are concerned about building consumer-facing services using technology.

Blockchain technology functions as a distributed, digital ledger. In this regard, we shall attempt to ascertain the impact of blockchain technology on global trade processes by posing the following problem:

What is the impact of using blockchain technology on global trade operations?

9.1.1 Hypotheses of the Study

1. Using blockchain technology in global trade has a statistically significant effect at the level of significance.
2. There is no statistically significant effect of using blockchain technology at the level of significance.

9.1.2 The Study's Significance

According to previous research, blockchain technology delivers an immutable and permanent record. A transaction that is difficult to amend or modify from any source, reliable or not. This completely changes the security, privacy, and trust of our online environment. The study is significant for two reasons:

Theoretical importance: Students concentrate on understanding blockchain technology and its impact on improving service quality, lowering costs, and increasing profits, thereby assisting the management of global trade economic companies in determining the benefits of using blockchain technology in their reports and developing their various sectors to serve the customer's privacy and prevent their disappearance.

Significance applied: The study's applied significance lies in the achievement of results that can be used in the development of methods to apply blockchain technology and employ the necessary technologies in all sectors to achieve complete digital transformation, which gives a great deal of importance and also allows officials and decision makers addressing shortcomings in its application. The study may contribute to empirical research on blockchain technology in emerging economies to prevent their fading.

9.1.3 Study Objectives

Through this research, we aim to shed light on what blockchain technology is, highlighting its most important and growing applications in the business sector.

The use of blockchain technology can help in the completion of the process of exchanging documents and contracts that are part of transactions documentary credits within 24 hours.

Blockchain helps by dispensing with paper transactions and facilitating procedures in making documentary accreditation more available to the opposing parties.

Today, the world is going through a transition from an industrialized economy to one defined by a new set of technologies ranging from digital technology to nanotechnology. Among the latest waves of digitization is blockchain technology, a technology that many say promises to redefine trust, transparency, and inclusion across the globe the world. This foundational technology was created to advance the infrastructure of services, whether financial or commercial, in which it affects both local and international transfers, financing services, and international trade.

With this in mind, in this chapter, we will discuss: Defining blockchain technology, its concept, components, method of operation, advantages, and applications, and the importance of applying it to global trade.

9.2 DEFINITION OF BLOCKCHAIN

The phrase Blockchain was launched as a term for the process of producing successive blocks in the virtual currency, which is mined in a sequential manner, and the Blockchain serves as the record in which all financial movements are kept.

Assets, expenses, and the like, i.e., the general accounting record in the financial sector, and its uses are currently being explored. Others have many other fields and sectors, such as the logistics sector, following up on the delivery of goods and tracking their progress, and technical information in the Internet of Things devices. In addition to the transfer of property, if you want to import goods from a foreign country, the bank will help you ensure that it is delivered through what is called a Letter of Credit. That is, depositing the price of the goods with the bank, and it is not done. You pay it to the company that will issue you the goods, and only after that, you receive those goods, and here Blockchain shortens this process by being a unified database that documents the parties. The integrity of procedures between him and to return to the origins of the blockchain in the virtual currency, the blockchain has been the base data to track the mining movement on the Internet and to calculate the minted virtual currency of each user of it. The process of mining and extracting the digital currency was documented in that database in the form of a series of operations documenting the extracted blocks or blocks with all parties worldwide, and thus it is impossible to forge a block or add. Other not real for public record, i.e., Blockchain, without being approved by all parties involved and operating on the Internet.

The beginnings of Blockchain technology were not in the year 2008, but it was the result of the efforts that accumulated experiences and business since 1991, then work began to produce a cryptographically secured blockchain so that no one could tamper with the timestamps of documents. In 1998, a scientist worked with computer Szabo Nick on the decentralized digital currency Gold Bit; also in 2000, Knots Stefan published his theory of cryptographically secure strings along with ideas for implementation; then Nakamoto published the Blockchain Model Design Paper in 2008; and the following year, Nakamoto implemented the first blockchain as a public ledger to conduct transactions using the Bitcoin currency, which is a form of cash that can be sent peer-to-peer without the need for central banks or other authorities to operate and maintain a ledger as is done in the traditional monetary system.

Blockchain evolution: Following the 2007–2008 global financial crisis, a marked fall in public trust in the conventional banking system prevailed. Technology enthusiasts and software developers envisioned and created an alternative financial system that falls outside the sphere of influence of conventional trusted third parties. The pseudonymous Satoshi Nakamoto proposed the digital currency Bitcoin as a peer-to-peer electronic cash system. This new technology relies on a protocol of cryptographic rules and techniques for processing transactions. These include the use of hashing, time-stamping, consensus mechanisms (a collection of rules that allow network nodes to reach mutual agreement), and asymmetric encryption using public and private keys. Not only has the proposed cryptocurrency model ingeniously solved the double-spending problem, but it also sets out a new paradigm for performing transactions and exchanging value in an online environment.

More precisely, any transaction triggered on the blockchain follows a set of predefined rules that are based on security, verifiability, and peer consensus to ensure the validity of transactions. All transactions are time-stamped, captured in datasets called blocks, and sequentially chained (i.e., each block header contains the hash of the previous block header) to form the ledger. Tampering with a public transaction record is technically tricky and viewed as infeasible because it requires substantial computing power to attempt to alter the cryptographic hash of previous blocks on the chain. Beyond the cryptocurrency jargon, a blockchain is not only a combination of technologies but also the integration of multiple technologies. Most scholars and practitioners commonly understand blockchain as one method within the distributed ledger technology family. Moreover, the ledger is a virtual book or a unique collection of all transactions carried out by the blockchain's exchange parties. The technology can be viewed as a new way of authenticating assets used in a transaction and can be applied to many business activities and functions (Ertemel, 2018).

In the following sections, we will elaborate on how the core characteristics of blockchain technology enable functions and applications that can fundamentally change marketing strategies.

9.3 BLOCKCHAIN IN MARKETING

The marketing industry is no different from other industries that have found promising benefits in the blockchain. Harvey et al. suggest that since most blockchain applications have been focused on finance, the technology has been mainly under the radar in marketing.

Blockchain is predicted to solve significant problems that have haunted marketers and brands for quite some time. According to a recent report, ad fraudulent, for example, cost global advertisers approximately US$19 billion in 2018. This figure represents 9% of the total marketing budget spent on digital advertising. The study indicates that fraud ads will reach $44 billion by 2022. With blockchain's features like disintermediation, transparency, and immutability, not only can marketers and brands avoid ad frauds and save money, but they can also build a strong connection with their customers, regain their trust and loyalty, and design more effective marketing campaigns and long-term strategies based on direct communication with consumers.

9.4 BLOCKCHAIN APPLICATIONS IN GLOBAL TRADE

- In the field of international finance: International finance is certainly the most visible area of business to use blockchain technology due to its ubiquity in the emergence of the Bitcoin cryptocurrency as an alternative to payment. It can also be used in the broader financial sector; they replace clearing houses in financial trading or property search firms in real estate, which leads to reduced costs and reduces the time required to complete any transaction. The introduction of blockchain technology may reduce the time required to carry out the capital exchange from a week to ten days to less than one day, and therefore it can be implemented with global business transactions between two business entities in real-time using blockchain technology, which has the potential to speed up business transactions and reduce costs. For companies around the world, it can improve internal operations banks and reduce the risk of documentary fraud (ganne, 2018).

A blockchain, or digital ledger, can give each party to a trade finance transaction access to a record of the transaction. This would allow them to instantly see what is happening, including the changes made to the account documentation, which may have far-reaching consequences for cost and availability in commercial finance. The use of blockchain technology can help in completing the process of exchanging documents and contracts that are part of a transaction's documentary credits within 24 hours, while the traditional methods take between 5 and 10 days.

In addition, you will help efficiency by cutting out paper transactions and facilitating procedures for making documentary credit more available to counterparties who do not have mutual trust between them. Previously, the use of traditional documentary credit due to its complexity and high costs could boost global trade and free up liquidity for projects, which was the main reason for the length of time it took to process documentary credit transactions. Traditional finance lies in the need to exchange documents and paper documents, including the transfer of ownership of goods by endorsement and separate communications between counterparties, shipping companies, banks, etc. All of this can be changed by blockchain technology.

- Blockchain technology reduces the time for documentary credit procedures by allowing the transfer of title documents and linking all parties in the Blockchain network electronically, which allows immediate follow-up and reduces lead time in favor of mutual communication between the opposite parties in the transaction of financial credit.

- In the field of insurance: Insurance companies are also taking advantage of blockchain-based contract implementation to initiate claims processing procedures for insurance automatically, which provides greater confidence and transparency between the contracting parties.
- In the field of investment fund management: Blockchain technology is also used to manage investment funds by tracking their credit derivatives in a business information warehouse. This system serves as the infrastructure for the global financial industry and "provides processing services life cycle events for approximately 98% of all credit derivatives transactions worldwide with a value of 11 trillion dollars, and the successful implementation of this new system based on Blockchain to reduce a large number, it reduces redundancy in registers and provides simpler operations."
- In the field of international marketing: In the field of international marketing and advertising, blockchain technology enables a more complete picture of advertising details, such as time ads and their performance, improving transparency for advertising companies. In addition, it provides transparency to consumers who are made public because the public blockchain ledger records information about how the data is used and to whom it is sold. One example is Comcast, which is working with industry partners to launch Blockgraph, a blockchain-enabled platform that allows advertisers to have more control over data and ad targeting more accurate to viewers. Without disclosing viewers' personal information to these advertisers, the platform has been developed to improve the efficiency and effectiveness of marketing and television advertising. An additional feature that emerges is consumer privacy, as each Blockgraph participant's data remains in their own systems, and the participant continues to have data protection and privacy management. Its users, including honoring any user choices regarding data use by Business Wire, is another company interested in using the blockchain to give more privacy to users through the implementation of identities Blockchain-based website login.
- In the field of international supply chain management and logistics supply chain management: International supply chain management and logistics supply chain management (SCM) have long been under scrutiny from a global perspective in relation to ethical and responsible sourcing practices. Providers using Blockchain in this area show greater transparency, efficiency, and accountability to companies regarding the provenance of their products. It allows companies to track the history of a product from the procurement of raw materials through the supply chain up to the moment of sale, and the provenance platform helps businesses use this technology to make supply chains more transparent, gaining more informed consumers and accelerating the movement toward sustainable consumption. The Provenance platform also adds value to companies and products by validating supply chains and purchasing practices with a social approach for SCM and integrating their services with corporate purchases in order to provide this information to customers via the website or app.

9.4.1 Effects of Using Blockchain

- Protecting property rights: The applications of blockchain described in the previous section demonstrate that this technology has the potential to impact security and property rights in different ways. First, this applies to protecting personal data. By applying it in advertisements, as in the case of Facebook, personal information can be withheld from advertisers, and consumers can choose how much information they want to share with third parties, allowing for more privacy and data protection. Money can also be considered property worth protecting. The examples of Barclays, Signature Bank, and Veem show that the parties receiving payments will be better protected because there is no longer the possibility for fraudulent chargebacks. In addition, technology affects the legality and transparency of conservation logistics records. When data is stored on a blockchain-based system, as is the case at IBM-Maersk, shipping-related information cannot be fraudulently altered or recorded. Blockchain is also available, as an opportunity for increased protection of property rights may prompt stricter regulation around privacy data as well as save records and reporting (staista, 2018).

- Transaction costs: Numerous examples show that smart contracts based on blockchains provide companies with another option to complete contracts for complex and uncertain activities outside the company through automated execution of contracts, which removes much of the uncertainty that exists in traditional contracts governed by current forms of regulation. It also eliminates the problem of "delay" in contracts, or counterparty risk; this can be seen in the case of AXA's automated insurance claims payments, where it operates smart contracts that remove uncertainty about transactions, and the customer is automatically paid when the flight is delayed beyond the contract limit. Blockchain-based smart contracts reduce principal agent costs that arise from conflicting interests in contracting; so too are the overhead costs of brokers and auditors who are no longer needed because the performance of the contract is automated and fraud-resistant in cases of insurance and money transfers, as well as in other applications in the financing chains and supply (les echos, 2016).
- Understanding negative external factors: The impact of blockchain on external factors is evident when it comes to protecting the environment because the implementation of the technology Blockchain itself creates negative externalities on the environment due to the high level of energy consumption needed to run it. Although the implementation of blockchain-based systems in supply chain management and finance is more efficient, transparent, and uses fewer papers and resources, an acceptable level of energy consumption can be determined (Holtbrügge, D, 2020).
- Antitrust: On the other hand, blockchain and smart contracts can help balance the positions of counterparties of different sizes and the different transactions in the supplier and buyer transactions through the contract execution mechanism based on pre-programmed conditions. And therefore, this no longer allows the more powerful party to pressure the other party to modify the terms of the contract and provides more fairness and power competitiveness for small and medium suppliers (charlottestories, 2021).

9.5 STUDY DESIGN

The field study aims to reach field evidence on the impact of blockchain technology on global digital trade in the Saudi market. To achieve this, the field study deals with identifying a sample, the study, the variables of the study, the method of collecting study data, the statistical methods used in testing, presenting hypotheses, and analyzing the results of hypothesis testing, as follows.

9.6 STUDY METHODOLOGY

The study relied on the analytical descriptive approach based on collecting data through the distribution of the questionnaire in order to test hypotheses and answers to the study questions, which were developed through previous studies and a group of experts and technicians.

9.7 DATA COLLECTION

a. Secondary data (e.g., articles written by marketing and blockchain experts in the academic field and published by credible journals; articles published by recognized institutions and magazines such as *Harvard Business Review, McKinsey & Company,* and *Forbes*; up-to-date articles from technology contributors, researchers, and scholars published by various known websites, such as medium.com).
b. An empirical study, as primary data collection, is in the form of an online survey. The survey contained a total of 18 close-ended questions that covered the 6 study areas (benefits). There were two types of questions with predefined answers that corresponded to predefined statements. At the end of each question, also, open space was given, so respondents had the opportunity to elaborate on their answers and express further opinions. The close-ended questions aimed to create enough quantitative evaluation and analysis for each question about each study area. Meanwhile, giving respondents the chance to elaborate in detail was considered an essential part of the questionnaire because it contributed toward improving the interpretation of the overall results and provided further valuable qualitative material. The survey was distributed online in Google Forms in June–July 2023.

This research carefully selected qualified digital commerce and blockchain experts from the academic arena (professors and doctorate students who had conducted some research about blockchain and published journal articles), as well as the private sector (blockchain companies that developed blockchain applications for e-commerce areas such as loyalty programs and advertisements).

9.8 RESULTS

This research aims to validate the six benefits of blockchain-in-digital commerce through findings drawn from secondary data collection (the literature review) and primary data collection (the empirical study survey). From the findings and discussion of this research (explained in this section), we aim to gain a clearer vision of the future of blockchain applications in e-commerce.

The results of analyzing the hypotheses of the study showed a range of importance of the blockchain, represented by its features (decentralization, transparency, traceability) and its direct relationship with the performance of the supply chain according to its indicators (efficiency) of the mining sector in the Kingdom of Saudi Arabia, which may lead to opportunities to improve the performance of operations in this sector.

The results also showed that there is a statistically significant effect of the blockchain, as represented by its feature (tracking). On the performance of the supply chain represented by its indicators (efficiency) of this sector, tracking had the largest effect among the features of the blockchain, and the correlation coefficient between them was the strongest, which means that the change in the performance of the supply chain results from the change in the blockchain represented by its feature (traceability). There is a significant impact on the statistical significance of the blockchain through its distinctive feature (tracking) to enhance the performance of the supply chain with its indicators (efficiency).

9.9 CONCLUSION

The creation and increasing adoption of cryptocurrencies paved the way for several industries to exploit the many benefits of blockchain. The marketing industry, however, seems to be watching bashfully. If this attitude changes, we may observe a shift to an entirely new marketing ecosystem where more innovative marketing ideas and concepts are born. We believe that it is imperative to define a realistic scope of blockchain's business value to obtain more credibility when considering this technology for any application. From this research's observations and readings, blockchain seems to receive too much hype still. We have examined the technology's capabilities to solve several crucial issues for marketing; however, most of these solutions are still conceptual.

Blockchain technology has prolonged beyond the border of cryptocurrency and taken hold in various areas like international business. Blockchain can increase efficiency for all the participants involved in international business.

SMEs can give easy access to trade finance. It can also bring benefits to governance; for example, traders in some countries are reported to use fake invoices to minimize taxes. Government agencies can be part of the blockchain-based decentralized system.

With the incorporation of blockchain technology, there may be a requirement for drastic changes in company business models. Everyone in the business adopting Blockchain must provide significant knowledge to understand this new technology and its impact on day-to-day operations.

REFERENCES

Abduljabbar, T. A., Tao, X., Zhang, J., Zhou, X., Li, L., & Cai, Y. (2021). A survey of privacy solutions using blockchain for recommender systems: Current status, classification and open issues. The Computer Journal, 64(7), 1104–1129. 10.1093/comjnl/bxab065

Aitzhan, N. Z., & Svetinovic, D. (2018). Security and privacy in decentralized energy trading through multi-signatures, blockchain and anonymous messaging streams. IEEE Transactions on Dependable and Secure Computing, 15(5), 840–852.

Akroush, M. N., & Al-Debei, M. M. (2015). An integrated model of factors affecting consumer attitudes towards online shopping. Business Process Management Journal, 21(6), 1353–1376. 10.1108/BPMJ-02-2015-0022

Alabi, K. (2020). A 2020 perspective on "Digital blockchain networks appear to be following Metcalfe's Law". Electronic Commerce Research and Applications, 40, Article 100939. 10.1016/j.elerap.2020.100939

Alam, M. Z., & Elaasi, S. A. (2016). A study on consumer perception towards e-shopping in KSA. International Journal of Business and Management, 11(7), 202–210. 10.5539/ijbm.v11n7p202

Anbar, A. (2001). E-Ticarette karşılaşılan sorunlar ve çözüm önerileri. Akdeniz İİBF Dergisi, 1(2), 18–32. https://dergipark.org.tr/tr/pub/auiibfd/issue/54586/744082

AWS. (2022). Blockchain for supply chain: Track and trace https://aws.amazon.com/tr/blockchain/blockchain-for-supply-chain-track-and-trace/?nc1=h_ls

Bação, P., Duarte, A. P., Sebastião, H., & Redzepagic, S. (2018). Information transmission between cryptocurrencies: Does Bitcoin rule the cryptocurrency world? Scientific Annals of Economics and Business, 65(2), 97–117. http://saeb.feaa.uaic.ro/index.php/saeb/article/view/1090

Cachin, C. (2016). Architecture of the hyperledger blockchain fabric. Workshop on Distributed Cryptocurrencies and Consensus Ledgers, 310.

charlottestories. (2021, 01). Blockchain technology in international business. Consulté le 06 13, 2022, sur charlotte stories: https://www.charlottestories.com/blockchain-technology-in-international-business/

Eyal, I. (2017). Blockchain technology: Transforming libertarian cryptocurrency dreams to finance and banking realities. Computer, 50(9), 38–49.

Frey, R., Wörner, D., & Ilic, A. (2016). Collaborative Filtering on the Blockchain: A Secure Recommender System for e-Commerce.

ganne, e. (2018). Can Blockchain. WTO Publications, p. 107.

Geer, D. "How blockchain will transform the e-commerce industry over the next few years," The Next Web, 18-Jun-2018. [Online]. Available: https://thenextweb.com/contributors/2018/06/15/how-blockchain-will-transform-the-e-commerce-industry-over-the-next-few-years/. [Accessed: 24-March-2020].

"An introduction to blockchain in e-commerce," Inviqa, 19-Mar-2019. [Online]. Available: https://inviqa.com/blog/introduction-blockchain-ecommerce. [Accessed: 05-February-2020].

"Blockchain and e-commerce: How do they make a winning …" [Online]. Available: https://www.orangemantra.com/blog/blockchain-e-commerce-make-winning-combination/. [Accessed: 23-March-2020].

"Can blockchain change e-commerce in 2020?," MarketRealist, 16-Dec-2019. [Online]. Available: https://marketrealist.com/2019/12/can-blockchain-change-e-commerce-in-2020/. [Accessed: 12- February -2020].
"How blockchain has helped the business of e-commerce," Asia Blockchain Review - Gateway to Blockchain in Asia, 20-Jan-2020. [Online]. Available: https://www.asiablockchainreview.com/how-blockchain-has-helped-the-business-of-e-commerce/. [Accessed: 23-March-2020].
Hofmann, E., Strewe, U. M., & Bosia, N. (2017). Supply Chain Finance and Blockchain Technology: The Case of Reverse Securitisation. Springer.
Holtbrügge, D. (2020, 1 23). Blockchain Technology in International Business. Changing the Agenda for Global Governance. Review of International Business and Strategy, pp. 17–18.
"How blockchain is impacting e-commerce," Ignite Ltd., 08-Feb-2019. [Online]. Available: https://igniteoutsourcing.com/blockchain/how-blockchain-is-impacting-ecommerce/. [Accessed: 25- March-2020].
les echos. (2016, 10 31). Comment la blockchain bouscule le financement du commerce international. Consulté le 6 13, 2022, sur les schos: https://business.lesechos.fr/directions-financieres/financement-et-operations/credits/0211438436771-comment-la-blockchain-bouscule-le-financement-du-commerce-international-301708.php
Post, C. "Blockchain technology to revolutionise e-commerce businesses in Australia," Business Partner Magazine, 11-May-2019. [Online]. Available: https://businesspartnermagazine.com/blockchain-technology-revolutionise-e-commerce-businesses-australia/. [Accessed: 12-February-2020].
Send, D. C., & Cox, D. "Has the blockchain technology made e-commerce business easier?," CryptoNewsZ, 03-Mar-2020. [Online]. Available: https://www.cryptonewsz.com/how-can-blockchain-transform-e-commerce-and-the-way-of-doing-business/. [Accessed: 05-Apr-2020].
Send, D. C., & Cox, D. "Know how blockchain technology is transforming e-commerce sector," CryptoNewsZ, 02-Mar-2020. [Online]. Available: https://www.cryptonewsz.com/blockchain-and-e-commerce-an-inseparable-duo/. [Accessed: 23-March-2020].
Sharma, T. K. "Top 10 blockchain solutions for e-commerce," Blockchain Council Blockchaincouncilorg, 10-Jul-1970. [Online]. Available: https://www.blockchain-council.org/blockchain/top-10-blockchain-solutions-for-e-commerce/. [Accessed: 12-February-2020].
staista. (2018, 09 20). La Blockchain au service du commerce international. Consulté le 06 13, 2022, sur statista: https://fr.statista.com/infographie/15533/applications-technologie-blockchain/
Swan, M. (2015). Blockchain: Blueprint for a new economy. "O'Reilly Media, Inc.".
Vukolić, M. (2015). The quest for scalable blockchain fabric: Proof-of-work vs. BFT replication. International Workshop on Open Problems in Network Security. Cham: Springer.
Walport, M. G. C. S. A. (2016). Distributed ledger technology: Beyond blockchain. UK Government Office for Science.
Xingxiong, Z., He, Q., & Guo, S. (2018). Application of block chain technology in supply chain finance. China's Circulation Economy, 32(03), 111–119.

10 Chatbots

A Computerized Communication Specialized Device

Amrita Baid More
Prestige Institute of Management and Research, Indore, India

10.1 INTRODUCTION

The purpose of this section is to familiarize the reader with the chapter's exploration topic. The underlying fragment of the segment gets a handle on the investigation establishment, followed by the part targets, investigation queries, and possible imperatives. The section's essential speculations are portrayed in the hypothetical structure, which is trailed by the strategies for examination and information assortment. At the chapter's conclusion, the structure is discussed.

10.1.1 Background of the Study

Businesses need to communicate with customers for them to raise and mature lucratively and effectively. A company can gain a clear understanding of the market's current and future conditions, as well as the competition, by having a conversation with a customer. This is because customers typically have a different perspective on a company's products and market. It could also be so that customers gain a deeper understanding of other brands that operate in various industries. Despite its significance to the company's overall expansion, customer communication has the potential to increase brand loyalty and increase a company's customer appeal (Oleksak, 2005).

A component of the administration cycle that assists an organization in withdrawing from an interest group in pursuit of its business objectives is promotional correspondence. It is an activity with the audience in mind. For this reason, a lot of limited-time tools like advertising, deal advancements, individual selling, and direct marketing are used. The majority of strategies concentrate on enhancing value. At the point when messages are made with these apparatuses, they should be appropriated to different crowds through different channels or media. One of the two essential kinds of promoting correspondence channels is conventional media (like radio, print advertisements, etc.) (Fill and Jamieson, 2011).

Digital marketing is advancing rapidly, with customers being reached through a variety of channels, including the company website, social media, email, and instant messaging (Murgia et al., 2016). The novel methods of communicaiton make the procedure as a whole significantly more interactive; users now have more opportunities to respond to businesses and offer feedback. Digital marketing tools also affect communication because clientele can effortlessly find material about a product on the Internet. Companies can no longer make superficial claims, as a result. Since it is now so simple and quick to interact with customers, businesses now have more opportunities to modify their proposals, posts, and marque consistency while acting carefully.

DOI: 10.1201/9781003450443-10

In recent years, digital marketing has shifted its attention to social media. Chatbots, an exciting new form of communication, have taken over as the primary focus of this trend. These days, people use them a lot. As chatbots for Apple and Windows devices, Siri and Cortana are great friends. With chatbots, you can undoubtedly convey any information to a potential customer in a limited amount of time by having pre-established talks. As a result, if the consumer journey and emotions are considered, this network may be efficiently used in marketing.

The chapter aims to determine the extent to which chatbots can be used as a separate channel and the methods for attracting and retaining customers. Businesses that are following the current trend of using chatbots as a means of communication will find the findings of this chapter to be instructive.

10.1.2 Chapter Objectives, Investigation Questions, and Limitations

The essential place of the part is to help what is going on with companying gain significant information into the use of chatbot as a restricted time-specific gadget. The second goal is to come up with a plan for the conversation flow that the chatbot will use on the company website.

In addition, the investigation focuses on:

- Learn how people feel about chatbots and how they react to them;
- Learn how people might want to see the correspondence between the customer and the brand;
- Learn what content people would like chatbots to provide.

The following are the thesis' sub-questions:

1. How can the chatbot's discussion flow be properly organized?
2. When communicating with the chatbot, what kind of content do customers want to see?
3. What kinds of tasks can businesses use chatbots for?

The exam question was carefully selected to improve the focus's direction. The reader should be informed about the subject matter and the research that is being observed by answering the research question. Sub-questions are frequently established in addition to the primary research questions to highlight the most relevant components of the research subject (Saunders et al., 2009).

Each inquiry has its own set of challenges. Because the problem is so broad, the analysis focuses on chatbots employed by associations as one of the communication channels.

Additionally, the outcomes may soon be out of date as a result of the rapid advancement of technology. In a nutshell, the section focuses on a specific organization, is an explicit result of the organization, and will be used for future investigation and change.

10.1.3 Theoretical Framework

One of the primary components of the investigation is the hypothetical system. It conceptualizes all significant factors and establishes a method for data analysis (Saunders et al., 2009). In this chapter, the topics that will be the focus of the research are briefly discussed.

Segment 2 portrays the different kinds of specific instruments; it also includes instructions on how to establish a genuine communication channel. The chapter continues with an overview of the most recent developments in customer communication, such as chatbots, which logically connects it to Section 10.3.

The aggregate of the data expected to appreciate the chatbot idea is introduced in Section 10.3. The subtleties of how these specialized tools are used in business, customer requests for them, and overall mindfulness are all discussed, as are the types and methods for training menial helpers.

The experimental examination's experience is included in Parts 2 and 3, which together explain the section's subject.

10.1.4 Research Strategy and Data Collection

In this chapter, the data collection strategy and exploration philosophy used in the specific section made sense. The research approach is first described, and then the data collection strategy and the study's sources are explained.

To begin, there are two research methods: inductive and logical strategies. Before coming up with a hypothesis or theory, the inductive method involves gathering, analyzing, and generalizing a wide range of specific data. The hypothesis is the starting point for the logical methodology, which then looks at the possible ways to get the best result. Usually, hypotheses and theories are tested with a deduction (Saunders et al., 2009). The section's exploration approach is inductive because of the subject and objectives.

There are two forms of data: quantitative data and qualitative data. Quantitative data refers to statistics that have been analyzed and statistically summarized. When processing qualitative content that is delivered verbally and heavily influenced by context, conceptualization is used (Saunders et al., 2009). Subjective information from subjective meetings is being accumulated and dissected for this review (Freitas et al., 1998).

Data can also be primary or secondary. Both types are used in the chapter. While secondary data are derived from primary sources, the author's primary data are those gathered from written and electronic sources on the subject at hand (Saunders et al., 2009).

10.1.5 Chapter Structure

Figure 10.1 shows the design of the part.

An introduction to the chapter aims to give the reader a clear understanding of the research topic, its significance, and the theories and methods used in the study. The part is separated into two areas after the presentation: theoretical and empirical. The theoretical portion of the chapter can be found in Sections 10.2 and 10.3. Section 10.3 describes chatbots, while Section 10.2 explains communication channels.

The exploratory piece of the assessment is presented in Section 10.4, where the course of the investigation and data collection is figured out. Section 10.6 is the completion of the part, giving

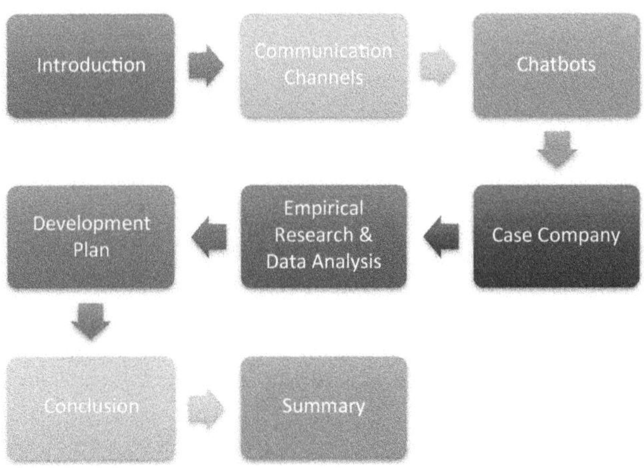

FIGURE 10.1 Structure of the chapter.

reactions to the examination questions as well as uncovering the authenticity and faithful quality and thoughts for extra investigation. The chapter's final section is the summary.

10.2 COMMUNIQUÉ NETWORKS

This section proposes to present the notion of how businesses use limited-time messages sent via correspondence to reach their primary audience. The guidelines for setting up an efficient special and conversational instrument with an emphasis on computerized marketing depict various forms of correspondence, with diverts being the most prominent. In the chapter's conclusion, a list of the most recent developments in customer communication is provided.

10.2.1 Types of Communication Channel

Marketing employs a plethora of communication channels, and the number of these channels is constantly increasing. In general, there are two primary kinds: customary media (print advertisements, radio, and so forth) and digital media, particularly the Internet (Fill and Jamieson, 2011). The rapid development of technology and the Internet has only recently led to the general adoption of the final option.

The bulk of conventional marketing channels' advertising and promotional materials fall into four basic categories: printed advertisements, broadcasting, direct mailing, and telephone. Print marketing is one of the most traditional kinds of advertising (Kuligowska and Lasek, 2005). Newspaper, magazine, and brochure advertisements are all featured. Broadcasting was a significant upheaval that occurred toward the beginning of the twentieth century, and it gained widespread prominence from then on. When examining this station, it is important to remember the importance of distinct cinema-based radio and television plug ads.

Lists sent to clients at the end of the nineteenth century marked the beginning of conventional mail promotion. Since then, direct mail marketing has expanded to encompass the postal delivery of postcards, letters, flyers, and other printed products. Phone showcasing, often referred to as selling, is a means of conveying promotional messages and persuading potential consumers to purchase over the phone. This strategy was heavily criticized due to sales personnel's aggressive tactics. Telemarketing employs both cold and desired calls (Pride et al., 2015).

Even though traditional marketing channels once attracted a lot of attention from customers, they become increasingly out of date over time. The essential disadvantage of these apparatuses is that they don't consider direct criticism or appropriate correspondence between organizations and clients, and they just give special and promoting materials intended to get consideration (Pride et al., 2015).

As was mentioned earlier, the rise of the Internet contributed to the popularity of digital marketing communication. It includes advanced tools like virtual entertainment, email, portable, and other features. There are numerous forms of online amusement to consider right now: social local media, social media for distribution, social media for trade, and social media for diversion. Facebook and LinkedIn are examples of social media sites that allow users to share their interests, create profiles, and engage with others. Users may create and share interactive material like as films, images, and audio through social publishing platforms. The most well-known examples of this type of channel include SoundCloud, Instagram, and YouTube.

Trading platforms are also provided by social commerce media channels like TripAdvisor and Groupon. In addition, some social media platforms aim to entertain users, such as Zynga 12, come2play, and others. Email and mobile advertising are used to influence the brand's primary target audience by sending out promotional emails or bulletins and using mobile phones (Durmaz and Efendioglu, 2016).

Digital marketing, in contrast to traditional methods, makes it easier to move from "push" to "pull" strategies by letting customers get in touch with the brand through any method they want.

It differs significantly from conventional marketing, which consists of straightforward advertisements with petite to no tutoring or discussion (Pelton et al., 2002). We have concluded that advanced advertising better reflects the expectations of current customers.

10.2.2 Establishing a Profitable Promotional Specialized Device

In light of the preceding section, computerized promotion is an improved means of communication between brands and their customers. As a result, most advanced advertising strategies will be suitable for this chapter. The experience is what creates the brand's image in the twenty-first century. When trying to have a conversational experience, customers will typically be self-interested and will care very little about the company's interior design or the conflicts it encounters (Meuter et al., 2000). Everything that matters is the degree to which good businesses meet the needs and expectations of their customers (Indrani et al., 2017). Subsequently, associations should reliably follow the desires of their clients to develop a productive displaying correspondence methodology. As clients' prerequisites change rapidly, advancing channels are being altered rapidly too. Even though this climate is uninterruptedly changing, there are still a few basic rubrics that should be observed to prosper (Pelton et al., 2002).

Making a novel substance to distribute to the target audience is necessary for setting up an effective specialized device (Edvard et al., 2016). In addition to being entertaining and instructive, it ought to be engaging and educational. Media content, like recordings, GIFs, or sound accounts, can likewise be conveyed utilizing accessible innovation. As a consequence of this, businesses ought to make an effort to send imaginative posts that will not only catch the consideration of users nevertheless also tell a division and increase customer faithfulness in the brand (Murphy, 2008).

Picking which channels to use to spread a message is the subsequent stage. There are a lot of them, and the company may be tempted to use many of them to establish a multi-channel approach. Web-based entertainment, for example, may become exceedingly difficult in terms of material distribution and substantive nature, despite its general availability. Focusing on improving the conversational experience on channels that are typically used by the main interest group is a smart move (Murphy, 2008).

As per Capgemini Counseling (2011), an organization's channel decision ought to mirror its essential objectives and help grow its client base. In the wake of choosing the substance and channels to scatter this substance, the issues of making and keeping it an unsurprising workout. Organizations need to look into ways to make letters stand out. This means making certain that even the simplest conversations run smoothly. Similarly, the experience must be consistent across all channels and provide a similar one. Differently, clients will stop any affectation of using the specific instruments picked. Making certain that the conversational cycle is secure and that no sensitive information is lost, which could lead to a loss of trust in the brand, is another important aspect (Accenture 2017).

In general, businesses should pay attention to their customers to better serve them. Customers have high standards for comfortable and dependable communication. 2016 Oracle Businesses will be able to interact with their customers in a variety of ways if these rules are followed, which will result in numerous customer touchpoints (Capgemini, 2011).

10.2.3 The Most Recent Trends in the Technique the Brand Connects with Clienteles

In this chapter, the most recent trends in the way the brand communicates with customers are presented. The fact of the matter is that customers will never again need to contact brands via email or phone. People believe that businesses should adapt to this trend and use these channels as well as online entertainment and information applications in their private lives. Because they use messenger apps and social media platforms, people have gotten used to getting responses right away (Wilson and Paul, 2018). As a result of this trend, businesses are being forced to develop informal answers that can quickly deliver evidence (Ubisend 2017). However, just being present on social media regularly is not sufficient. The method of communicating with customers through virtual entertainment can sometimes lack a personal touch. Businesses might want to consider using messaging apps, which are becoming additional and more prevalent these times, in addition to having profiles on relevant social networks (Petter and Brandtzaeg, 2017). Facebook is losing out to messaging services among consumers today. At the beginning of 2017, texting was the preferred mode of communication (Accenture 2017).

The propensity of changing to additional confidential illuminating stages fetches a lot of useful functionalities and stimulates open entryways for associations.

Organizations should acclimate to this change and foster specialized instruments that can meet client assumptions, perhaps controlled by machines (like man-made reasoning).

10.3 CHATBOTS

This part familiarizes the reader with the concept of chatbots. The term's definition is followed by information on how chatbots are utilized in business, then, at that point, client solicitations and carefully checked out.

10.3.1 Significance

Discourse or text communication among people and PCs is turning out to be progressively famous in this day and age. PC users must behave similarly to humans when communicating with one another. Natural Language Processing (NLP) is a critical technology for analyzing speech and producing human-like answers (Petter, 2017). A dialog system or program, often known as a chatterbot or a chatterbot, is required to deliver relevant replies based on phrases or keywords from inquiries and to continue continuous contact. The chatbot is a computer program that can converse with people by answering questions and holding a conversation using Natural Language Processing (Grudin and Jacques, 2019). When people enter text or voice in natural language, the program should present them with the most intelligent response feasible in the form of text or speech. As long as communication continues, this procedure will continue. The conversational process between humans and chatbots is shown in Figure 10.2 (Abdul-Kader and Woods, 2015, 72).

The conversation can be started by the user or the chatbot. The communication process begins when the user sends the question or sentence to the program as speech or text. After looking for keywords or phrases in the user input, the chatbot chooses the best-programmed response from its database. The procedure is finished when the output is presented to the user either verbally or visually (Abdul-Kader and Woods, 2015).

Since their inception in the 1960s, researchers have been trying to figure out if chatbots can mimic human speech to the point where users mistake them for human interaction. However, today, chatbots are utilized in business, education, and information retrieval processes. As a result, chatterbots now serve more than just the purpose of entertaining users and imitating human interaction (Shawar and Atwell, 2007).

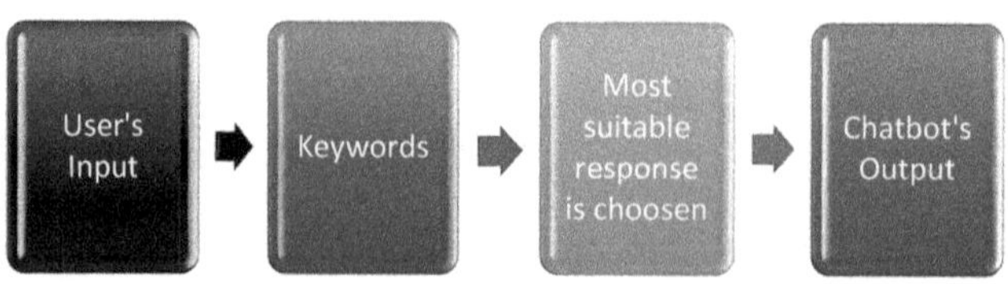

FIGURE 10.2 The process of a chatbot having a conversation with a human.

10.3.2 The Use of Chatbots in Business

There has never been a more extraordinary degree of correspondence between brands and their clients. The rapid advancement of technology is dramatically altering the customer experience (Dixon et al., 2010). Clients like to make buys or get data without connecting with a human brand delegate, so they need more independence and self-administration choices. Associations are transforming the experience from human-to-human associations into an irrefutable degree of self-service experience to meet the expectations of their clientele (Goldstein et al., 2002). As a result, adopting chatbots in business might be a crucial factor in improving client contact. 2016 Oracle Businesses are leveraging this technology to boost consumer engagement by utilizing messaging systems that include in-message purchases, a regular chat function, and a variety of other complex capabilities (Accenture 2017).

What advantages do chatbots provide businesses and customers in terms of communication? Chatterbots have three primary advantages: reducing pressure, enabling instantaneous response, and expanding assistance.

Previously, contacting the firm took considerable effort. One alternative was to call the company's hotline; however, it might not have been free and might have only been available during specific hours, making it unsuitable for any kind of emergency. Another alternative was to write an email to the corporation and wait for a response, which may take weeks or even months in certain cases. Chatbots can alleviate this inconvenience because the majority of people always have messaging apps installed on their smartphones. Additionally, chatbots are available at all times and respond immediately, ensuring that customers do not become dissatisfied and receive the assistance they require as soon as possible. The chatbot can also be combined with other services to offer a collection of goods and services in a single place. For instance, the chatbot of an airline might be linked to Airbnb, Booking, or Uber (Accenture 2017).

As can be seen, chatbots have the potential to improve interactions between brands and customers (Lind and Salomonson, 2006). Even though chatbot development is still in its infancy, numerous businesses have shown interest in the technology and have executed it. The level of communication between marques and their customers has not ever been higher. The quick progression of innovation is decisively changing the client experience. Clients like to make purchases or get information without communicating with a human brand delegate, so they need more freedom and self-organization decisions. To meet their customers' expectations, businesses are moving away from human-to-human connections and toward a high-level self-service involvement (Luger and Sellen, 2016). Consequently, using chatbots in commercials may be essential for increasing customer correspondence. Oracle Companies are utilizing messaging platforms with in-message purchases, a regular chat function, and numerous other advanced features to increase customer engagement (Accenture 2017). In terms of communication, what advantages do chatbots offer businesses and their customers? Chatterbots enjoy three essential benefits: easing pressure, making it possible to respond immediately, and expanding assistance.

Contacting the business used to take a lot of effort. One choice was to call the hotline of the business; however, it might not have been free or available only during specific hours, making it unsuitable for any kind of emergency. One more choice was to send an email to the organization and sit tight for their reaction, which now and again required weeks or even months. Because the majority of people always have messaging apps installed on their smartphones, chatbots can alleviate this suffering. Additionally, chatbots are always available and respond immediately, ensuring that clients do not become dissatisfied and receive the assistance they require as soon as possible. The chatbot can likewise be joined with different administrations to offer an assortment of labor and products in a solitary spot. A carrier's chatbot, for instance, might be linked to Airbnb, Booking, or Uber. As can be seen, chatbots have the potential to enhance interactions between brands and customers (Accenture 2017). Even though chatbot development is still in its infancy, several organizations have taken an interest in it and have recently implemented it.

10.3.3 Consumer Requirements

Even though these communiqué channels are novel and advanced, there are previously fairly few consumer requirements that must be met for success (Ubisend 2017). The majority of customers consider chatbots to be the quickest and easiest method of contacting the company because they receive an instantaneous answer to their investigations. Clients need the chatterbot to be accessible on an assortment of courier stages so they can choose the one that best suits their necessities. Consequently, to satisfy clients' presumptions brands should consider creating a gadget on various stages that can talk with any individual at whatever point and, if possible, in various vernaculars.

Users want chatbots to be very useful, simple to use, and offer quick solutions when it comes to their content. Having an extended inside-and-out conversation about the company isn't valued. A lot of customers might want to know a little bit about the company and its services, like hours of operation, addresses, special offers, and so on. To summarize, customers nowadays prefer to utilize chatbots because they are simple to use and quick, but they do not want to converse in detail with chatterbots and AI assistants as they would with people in person. As for preparing shows, clients would only from time to time present more than five requests for everybody meeting with the chatbot (Chatfuel, 2017).

Most clients would rather not consider how convoluted the chatterbots stream is because they need the data they need rapidly and without any problem. Whether it is a straightforward bot with predefined responses to a limited number of questions or a highly complex AI-driven assistant connected to multiple services, users are unconcerned. All that is required is an accurate and prompt response to their inquiry.

Since extra customers receive to know by chatbots in their everyday schedules, getting fast responses at whatever point they will expect a more raised degree of organization from associations. Even though setting up a chatterbot has all the earmarks of being straightforward, brands ought to in any case give close consideration to giving their clients a characteristic conversational encounter. Customers' primary concern is using appropriate vocabulary that is easy for the target audience to understand. If the language used by the chatbot is chosen appropriately, it has the potential to improve communication and customer service. Additionally, it is a fun and useful tool. According to Abdul-Kader and Woods (2015), chatterbots can generally provide superior assistance to other conventional computerized channels if all customer requirements are met.

Since their commencement during the 1960s, specialists have been attempting to sort out whether or not chatbots can imitate human discourse to where clients botch them for human association. Today, however, business, education, and information retrieval processes all make use of chatbots. Consequently, chatterbots now serve more than just the entertainment and imitation of human interaction functions (Shawar and Atwell, 2007).

Despite the innovative and creative nature of these channels of communication, there are currently a significant number of client needs that must be adhered to for success (Ubisend 2017). Since they get a speedy response to their solicitations, most clients acknowledge that chatbots are the speediest and least difficult method for arriving at the business. Users should be able to access the chatterbot on a variety of messenger platforms so they can select the one that best suits their needs. Brands should therefore consider developing a device that can communicate with anyone at any time and in a variety of languages across multiple platforms to meet customer expectations. Users want chatbots to be very useful, easy to use, and provide quick content-related solutions, according to Accenture (2017a). Having a lengthy and start-to-finish discussion about the organization is not esteemed. There may be a lot of customers who want to know things like the company's hours of operation, addresses, special offers, and so on. In conclusion, today's customers want to use chatbots because they are quick and easy to use, but they don't want to talk in-depth with chatterbots and AI assistants like they would with real people. According to Chatfuel (2017), when setting up events, customers would rarely submit more than five requests for each gathering.

The majority of customers do not want to think about how complicated the chatterbot's flow is because they want the information they need quickly and easily. Users are unconcerned, regardless of whether it is a simple bot with predefined responses to a limited number of questions or a highly complex AI-driven assistant connected to multiple services. The right and brief response to their solicitation is all that is required.

Clients will expect a more significant level of communication from organizations as they become more familiar with utilizing chatbots in their everyday schedules and getting expeditious reactions at whatever point they use it (Gorry and Westbrook, 2011). Even though it may seem simple to set up a chatterbot, businesses should still ensure that they provide customers with a conversational experience that feels natural. Customers' primary concern is the use of appropriate jargon that is understandable. The chatbot's use of appropriate language has the potential to enhance customer service and communication. Furthermore, it is a fun and useful instrument. According to Ubisend (2017), chatterbots can generally outperform other conventional computerized channels in terms of customer support.

10.3.4 Customer Awareness

Awareness remains a problem despite the growing popularity of chatbots. Chatterbots are less well-known to customers than other online entertainment venues. Ubisend (2017) found that almost 60% of respondents are familiar with using chatbots, and 40% of those who are not familiar with them would benefit from additional instruction. However, 75% of respondents to the survey stated that they had not used the chatbot (Ubisend 2017). Clienteles need to see a rise in the use of chatbots by businesses as specialized tools that can respond to both common and specific questions. Additionally, many users are considering making purchases with the chatterbot.

Business chatbots are viewed well by clients and seen as imaginative and valuable assets. As a result, now is a great time for businesses to implement chatterbots to address customer concerns. There is a need to give genuine mentoring about this channel and more noteworthy progress to be finished.

10.4 RESEARCH QUESTIONS AND EXPLORATION DIRECTIONS

The backdrop offered demonstrates a study deficit in terms of an in-depth understanding of the user experience of chatbots for customer support and users' incentives to utilize such chatbots. This gap must be bridged to better understand how such chatbots should be created. We devised the following study questions for this purpose:

RQ1: What is the user experience using chatbots for customer service?
RQ2: What are the primary reasons for consumers to employ chatbots for customer service?

Current research on conversational user interfaces underlines how crucial it is to look into user experience while being sensitive to any potential discrepancy between what consumers anticipate the chatbot to be able to achieve and its actual capabilities, particularly those for completing practical tasks. Additionally, it is important to look at the importance of chatbot self-presentation and appearance as well as the chatbot's capacity for user emotional connection.

Users will most likely be motivated by a need for quick and easy help, but it would also be fascinating to learn about users' hopes and expectations for future, enhanced capabilities in customer service chatbots.

10.5 METHODOLOGY

We conducted an interview study with customers who use chatbots for customer service following the exploratory approach suggested by the research questions.

10.5.1 Recruitment of Participants

Participants in the research were required to have recent, practical experience utilizing chatbots for customer support. This was made feasible by recruiting all participants during their interactions with one of two different customer support chatbots. This recruiting procedure was made possible through communication with the chatbot owners. The chatbots might mention the study at the outset of their exchange with the user or in response to their last comment.

Participants selected a specific button in the chat conversation to read more about the study. They were then directed to a webpage where they could register for the research and obtain further information. After registration, participants received a text message asking them to schedule an interview time. After then, the interview was performed by telephone. The interval between the chatbot contact and the interviews ranged from a few minutes to many weeks, depending on the participant's availability (Guest and Bunce, 2006).

Interviews with 46% of the participants took place on the day of the contact, 25% the next day, and 16% the rest of the following week.

More than a week after the incident, just three people were questioned. Between 15 and 25 minutes were allotted for the interviews. Gift vouchers of Rs. 200 were distributed to all participants as incentives. Ethics and privacy laws were followed during the research's execution. Following transcription and informed participation, all interview data were made anonymous.

Both chatbots give information and support in answer to questions about the services provided by the service providers. Both chatbots similarly greet the user, introduce themselves, and offer a quick welcome message before inviting them to type their query in free text.

An acceptable answer is subsequently given when the inquiry is analyzed to match one of the chatbots' thousands of intentions. To find out the response to a series of follow-up inquiries, the user is usually required to select among possibilities in a branching conversation tree. Answers are often provided in text format with links to other resources or self-service alternatives on the business website. If the chatbot is unable to respond to the question or the user is not satisfied with the response, the discussion can be escalated to a human customer support person.

The name, gender, and avatar of one of the chatbots were all human-like. The other robot lacked a name, a gender, or even an avatar.

The consumer market was served by the two chatbots. English was used for the interviews.

10.5.2 Analysis and Guide for the Interview

The interviews were semi-structured, and the three primary subjects covered in the interview guide were:

- Details on the participant's most recent conversation with the chatbot, including the occasion, the content of the exchange, and, if relevant, the outcome with the service provider.
- Previous interactions with the chatbot, participants' opinions of the chatbot's appearance and self-presentation, and their opinions on why and when they would use the chatbot instead of: 1. the self-service options on the business website; or 2. manual chat or phone customer service.
- Potential applications for chatbots within the service provider: 1. how to enhance the current level of support; and 2. broaden the scope of the chatbot's offerings.

Participants were invited to openly share their thoughts, feelings, and impressions of each subject while following the format of the interview guide. Each interview's audio was transcribed and utilized. Participants' demographic data, including age and gender, were gathered using the sign-up form.

The interview transcripts underwent a thematic analysis using a data-driven methodology, which produced a set of codes. The coding was done by the primary author of the publication. Twenty-four participants were questioned in all, which is thought to be sufficient to attain saturation in the sense that including additional people is probably not going to significantly change the results. Saturation was established by comparing the percentage of new codes prompted by the first 25% of interviews (>60%) with the percentage of new codes motivated by the last 25% of interviews (15%) after analysis.

10.6 RESULTS

We will first give a summary of the participants and their initial chatbot user experiences in the section devoted to the findings. We will next discuss our findings about the participants' assessments of the chatbots' functionalities, their thoughts on the chatbots' look and self-presentation, and their motivations for using the chatbots. We sum up the participant recommendations for future chatbot development in our conclusion.

We provide specifics about the number of contributors who described or replicated various subjects throughout the presentation of the results. This is not meant to quantify our qualitative findings but rather to show the reader how frequently various topics were discussed in the interviews.

10.6.1 Participant Experiences and Direct User Experience

The participants' ages varied from 18 to 76, with a mean age of 40 and a standard deviation of 15 (SD). There were 13 women and 11 men that participated. All of them had contacted the chatbot for a specific service query, except for two people who just engaged with it to test it out. The second participant, who did not previously have a relationship with the service provider, tried the chatbot while signing into the self-service area of the business website. The majority of participants (20) had never used the chatbot before they were invited to take part in the study. However, more than half (13) had previously used chatbots for customer assistance.

10.6.1.1 The Inquiries from Participants

The participants' replies to the chatbot were diverse. The majority of questions (16) were simple requests for information or help with a task that the user was attempting to complete, such as help with login, help with a specific service or offering, help to find a self-service option, or help finding a specific piece of information on the business website.

This is demonstrated by the user quote that follows:

> Because the style of the customer support website had changed and I was unable to locate the service I was seeking, I used the chatbot (P1).

Six of the participants asked about possible orders or purchases. These were often more complex and required the consumer to give the service that best suited their needs some further thinking. Two of these individuals had questions regarding how to place an order. The remaining four requested advice and information regarding service packages they were considering or had already ordered. The latter two questions do not matter here because they were being used to test the chatbot.

10.6.1.2 Successful Query Responses?

The participants claimed that their inquiry had gone rather well. Nine questions were answered by the chatbot's interaction, and five questions were answered by clicking on links to the necessary self-service option on the business website. Eight attempts failed, and five of those, on the chatbot's advice, contacted conventional customer support; their issues were then remedied.

The chatbot either lacked the characteristics necessary to handle the particular request (six) or the participants did not grasp the information or advise it had given (two); the difficulty of addressing these requests was often the reason for the latter. Participants who were able to pursue their query with a real customer care agent did not always report unsuccessful interactions with the chatbot as being disappointing. The following quotation serves as an illustration of this idea:

> I was advised to speak with a customer care agent by [the chatbot] after I twice asked the identical inquiry without receiving a response. I did, and it all turned out very well. (P8)

10.6.1.3 Attitudes toward the Chatbot, Both Favorable and Unfavorable

Participants who provided feedback on their interactions with the chatbot frequently characterized it as quick or effective (15) and said that it offered straightforward assistance in an intelligible way (15). The participants also expressed appreciation for the chatbot's addition of links to more information or specialized self-service alternatives on the business website to its text-based responses in the conversation (11). This is demonstrated by the passage below:

> I think it's helpful because when you ask, you don't only receive a response; [the chatbot] also provides you with a link, which I can click to go straight to the place I need to go. (P13)

Although less frequently than good features, participants also discussed issues or unfavorable aspects of the chatbot. Six of the participants commented that they would choose to converse with a live person over a chatbot. This choice was influenced by things like the desire to have direct access to manual customer care or to have a better level of personalization in the services offered. Four people were concerned about chatbot security issues concerning customer service. Participants' views of potential hazards while utilizing chatbots for activities that need sensitive information are best exemplified by the following quotation:

> [...] Your social security number must be provided, and some people may be skilled at hacking and manage to get into the system. Otherwise, you can be in danger. (P8)

Two participants complained that the chatbot had a hard time understanding them, two were dissatisfied with being directed to more information on the self-service options on the company website because they wanted an answer right away and without having to look it up themselves, and two did not see the value in using chatbots beyond what is available on a company website or when contacting manual customer service.

10.6.1.4 User Perceptions of the Chatbot's Capabilities

To our astonishment, the participant's assessments of the chatbot's skills closely matched those of the chatbot itself. Nearly all (19) believed the chatbot they had interacted with could handle straightforward queries, but they did not believe it was capable of tasks like conversing with a live customer support representative. The majority of the participants stated that the chatbot was intended for simple queries and queries that users could precisely type down.

The chatbot was unlikely to function well, according to the participants, when replies required expert judgment or when users lacked specific inquiries because of a lack of topic expertise. It was believed that inquiries of this intricacy would necessitate a human customer care person, as seen by the following quotation:

> I should speak with someone if I'm unsure of what to inquire about. [...] I want the chatbot to comprehend my questions when I ask them. (P8)

The participants did agree that the chatbot might take the role of real customer support agents, but only for simple questions. According to the majority of respondents, they would rather utilize chatbots than phone customer assistance for such inquiries, as shown by the following quote:

> I use [the chatbot] anytime I have problems before I call help. (P2)

Some participants who had asked the chatbot trickier questions were also able to properly appreciate the chatbot's skills. These participants acknowledged that they were beyond the chatbot's capabilities when submitting a complicated request, but they did so because they believed employing the chatbot would be beneficial.

10.6.1.5 User Opinions on the Chatbot's Presentation and Appearance

Participants were asked to consider how the chatbot presented itself and how it looked. Interestingly, participants mostly focused on how the chatbot appeared and expressed itself through discussion rather than on the chatbot's physical appearance and demeanor. The participants found it particularly remarkable that the chatbot offered clear explanations and information (15); they also mentioned that they liked the chatbot's conversational nature. Most participants were aware that they were conversing with a chatbot as opposed to a live customer support representative. Half (12) of respondents said they immediately recognized the chatbot as a computer, as seen by the following quotation:

Although it seems human, it is still obvious that it is a machine. (P2)

Other participants (seven) said that they swiftly, although not instantly, identified the chatbot as a computer. Due to the chatbot's prompt replies, lack of personalization, and regular greeting responses, it was possible to identify it as a computer. Two of the participants, however, were unaware that the chatbot was a computer before their conversation with us. One of them recounted his experience as follows:

> I only assumed that someone was instigating this. In my perspective, it had to be a writer. Modern machines are highly sophisticated, thus it's not impossible that it was a machine. But I believed I was conversing with a living being. (P7)

Participants hardly ever spoke about the avatar photos of the chatbots, even though one was a robot and the other a humanoid. Only three individuals (a very small percentage) claimed that the visual representations considerably enhanced their entire experience. Others claimed to have noticed the visual aids but didn't consider them significant. The other 18 people seemed uninterested in the graphic illustrations.

Visual representations were cited as important by two participants. Through a human-like avatar, they communicated with the chatbot. One of these inquiries on the gender of the chatbot avatar was "Why is it a woman?" The other was concerned that consumers would mistakenly assume a chatbot had more sophisticated skills than it did if it had a human-like depiction. One of the individuals who believed that the visuals were significant had interacted with the chatbot using a robot-like avatar and said that this avatar would be helpful since it demonstrated the chatbot's machine-like nature.

These findings do not imply that participants did not value the human likeness of the chatbots, whether or not they had a human- or robot-like avatar. When compared to a robot assistant, some (seven) claimed that the chatbot's human-like look improved user experience. In total, 13 people indicated they thought the chatbot resembled a person in many ways. The chatbot discussion, however, focused more on the chatbot's human-like look than its outward appearance.

When it resembles a human, it appears more recognizable to me. You are aware that it is unquestionably a machine, and I have no strong feelings about this. However, when something speaks your language, it's easier to relate to it. (P9)

10.6.2 User Motivations for Chatbot

Use participants were questioned about their motivations for utilizing the chatbot and situations in which they would choose it over manual customer care calls or self-service alternatives on a website. The value of the chatbot's instant appearance on the business website was emphasized by the participants (13), as shown by the following statement:

> The participants were primarily motivated by the promise of effective and accessible help, according to P23.

Because this was the first choice presented, [I utilized the chatbot]. Furthermore, I genuinely didn't see a choice to speak with a human. The most well-known and efficient substitute is the chatbot. (P19)

When asked to choose between utilizing a chatbot and visiting the company website or calling customer support by phone, the majority of participants chose the chatbot (17). Participants specifically considered chatbots as a substitute for customer care for simple questions that just needed a simple answer. In such situations, several participants claimed it makes little difference whether they are helped by a human or a chatbot as long as they get the help they need. The next quotation exemplified this:

> I don't care if a person or a machine manages the chat feature. (P17)

They either despised utilizing online self-service options (five) or wished to spend as little time as possible seeking a solution on a firm website (15), according to the participants. Except for the two who were testing the chatbot, hardly any of the participants seemed to have used it out of curiosity or a desire to try out new technologies. Instead, the majority of participants seemed to be unconcerned with technology or believed that they would spend less time utilizing self-service platforms if customer assistance was available. The next quotation exemplified this:

> I suppose I ought to start by looking at myself. However, I didn't search for very long before utilizing the chatbot, so I doubt it. We are referring to seconds. (P6)

10.6.3 User Recommendations for Future Improvements

The bulk of participants' recommendations for future advancements centered on preserving or enhancing the chatbot as a method of efficiently addressing simple queries and requests, but several participants provided intriguing proposals that point in novel directions. Ten persons discussed the potential for taking part in advising processes for increasingly complex service offerings. For example, the chatbot might suggest offers based on the user's expertise or help determine which offer is most suited to the user's needs (Chatbots for Customer Service CUI, 2019). The next quotation exemplified this:

> Yes, it would be convenient if the chatbot could help with more urgent tasks, like renewing my existing service agreement. (P14)

Five people raised the potential that the chatbot may carry out specific transactions as opposed to merely delivering information. These people were particularly intrigued by a tool that appeared to combine customer care chat functionality with e-commerce features. The next quotation exemplified this:

> You might be able to get help from the chatbot to adjust your present services the way you want them to be. (P13) Others (two) explored the chatbot's possible use as a source of helpful material and advice in addition to responding to client inquiries. For example, this type of material might be utilized to offer specialized knowledge on cutting-edge products or services.

10.7 FINDINGS

The information gathered during the hypothetical and experimental examination is arranged in this section. It examines reactions to the essential solicitation and related sub-questions for this examination. Credibility, dependability, and additional research recommendations are all incorporated.

10.7.1 The Customer Service Chatbot User Experience

Chatbots can be used for a wide range of questions, from straightforward ones that only require a straightforward response to more complex questions that may require thoughtful consideration and comprehension of the user's context. It came as no surprise that a chatbot's ability to respond quickly to straightforward inquiries led to positive user experiences. However, chatbots that were unable to provide adequate responses were not necessarily detrimental to the user experience so long as they offered a simple means of following up with human representatives of customer service. This demonstrates the benefits of what is referred to as "tiered" approaches to chatbots for customer service (Abdul-Kader and Woods, 2015), (Araujo, 2018). In these "tiered" approaches, the chatbot serves as a first line of support and refers unanswered questions to human agents.

The participants value chatbot responses' quick responses and easy-to-digest information, according to existing industry reports (Araujo, 2018; Burgess and Connell, 2006). On the other hand, the participants' appreciation for links and references to online resources is a fascinating addition to the existing knowledge. A significant number of participants expressed appreciation for a chatbot that provided links to online resources, believing that this would save the user the time needed to find the information without such assistance. This contrasted with the participants' criticism of chatbots for only providing previously published content.

Our discoveries propose that clients who use chatbots for client care have sensibly reasonable assumptions about the abilities of such chatbots, even though the current writing, including Calvey (2004) and Chung et al. (2020), recommends that clients regularly underrate the capacities of virtual specialists. The participants readily acknowledged that the chatbot was distinct from human customer service representatives and that its capabilities typically restricted itself to straightforward inquiries requiring straightforward responses. A chatbot that could assist with complex deliberation was thought to be best in the future and not something that could be implemented right away. The initial self-presentations of the studied chatbots, which indicated that they could only assist with straightforward inquiries, may have contributed to this realistic understanding of chatbot capabilities. Additionally, the speed with which users can assess whether the chatbot's response is adequate may aid in understanding.

The significance of chatbot personas and their visual appearance is frequently emphasized in the literature (see Chung et al., 2020; Dale, 2016; Durmaz and Efendioglu, 2016), particularly their human-like characteristics and capacity for social and empathic user engagement. Surprised, our study participants didn't give the chatbots' appearance much thought. The vast majority of respondents did not deem this to be significant, though about half mentioned the chatbots' human likeness and politeness. The chatbots' visual appearances, in particular, were ignored. All things being equal, whether or not clients got help with their requests was considered vital.

It is impossible to rule out the possibility that the chatbot's appearance influences the user experience in ways that the participants do not remember or acknowledge because the data in this study are derived from interviews. In addition, the findings suggest that the primary requirement for providing chatbots for customer support should be that the chatbot provides sufficient assistance in responding to customers' inquiries. The chatbot's appearance design may have some effect on the user experience, but this effect likely pales in comparison to the impact of the quality of the information and assistance provided. The arrangement of all-around enlightening substance is by all accounts more significant than the chatbot's visual appearance with regard to appearance.

10.7.2 Client Inspirations for Involving Chatbots for Client Support

The members' inspirations for involving chatbots were the same as the inspirations for utilizing conversational specialists that are examined in the current writing. In particular, the participants' motivations regarding the availability and effectiveness of chatbots were consistent with industry reports (Edvard et al., 2016; Fill and McKee, 2011) and previous research (Fill and McKee, 2011). Using chatbots for customer service was reportedly primarily attracted by receiving easy-to-understand responses and assistance finding online self-service resources, rather than having to wait in line or for customer service to open. Additionally, this study did not uncover the social or emotional motivations for utilizing chatbots and virtual assistants that had been suggested in previous studies (Goodman, 2018; Gustavsson, 2005). It would appear that social and emotional motivators are of relatively low importance in the current context of automated customer service.

It's conceivable that the reasons the members utilized chatbots in client care can tell you which client bunch is bound to utilize this innovation. When searching for answers on a company website's self-service section, the vast majority of participants reported having little patience. Additionally, a significant number stated that they despise reading content on the internet. Therefore, it is feasible to hypothesize that CUI 2019 A. Flstad and M. Skjuve's clients, who use chatbots for client support, are not early adopters of data innovation or self-administration arrangements overall. Instead, users of chatbots for customer service appear to have little interest in online self-service options and a low threshold for contacting manual customer service. If this is the case, chatbots for customer service and the content they provide should not be made with technology-savvy users in mind. Instead, it might be in users' best interests to design chatbots for customer service with a focus on users who do not really care about cutting-edge technology but rather want quick and simple solutions to their problems.

10.8 IMPLICATIONS OF FINDINGS

We believe that the primary contribution of this study is the previously presented and discussed findings. Based on this contribution, we suggest possible implications for theory and practice.

10.8.1 Applicability to Theory

The study's contribution suggests several theoretical implications that may serve as inspiration for subsequent research. Our top picks for outcomes are as follows:

- Chatbots for customer service may meet reasonable customer expectations: Clients' assumptions about the capacities of chatbots for client care might be genuinely precise, as opposed to past research on voice-based conversational specialists. Although they are aware that complex issues may require the assistance of a human agent, they anticipate that these chatbots will handle straightforward questions.
- The relative importance of a chatbot's persona for providing customer service: Although a chatbot's textual persona may be crucial to the user experience, our findings suggest that

the persona has lower relative importance for providing customer service in chatbots than was previously thought. This could be because previous research on chatbot personas was conducted in labs rather than in real-world scenarios in which users interact with the chatbot to respond to questions that are important to them.
- A fresh perspective on the people who use chatbots for customer service: Users of chatbots for customer service appear to be motivated by a tendency to seek human assistance rather than engaging deeply in online self-service, in contrast to users of conversational agents, who may be regarded as early adopters of technology. Additionally, users of chatbots appear to be motivated by an inclination to engage deeply in online self-service. This finding suggests that customer service chatbot users need more research into their characteristics.

10.8.2 Practical Implications

This study's contribution also has practical implications for customer service chatbot design and development. The following, in our opinion, are particularly significant:

- Support a "tiered" approach to chatbots for customer service: If a client is furnished with an effectively open choice to heighten the request to a human client care delegate, the disappointment of a chatbot for client assistance to satisfactorily answer the client's request may not be impeding the client experience. In a "tiered" approach, this finding strongly suggests that chatbots should only be used as a first line of support.
- Need is given to effective request goal: Current textbooks on chatbots emphasize the importance of designing the chatbot's persona and appearance, but the chatbot's ability to answer user questions is far more important.
- As far as client experience, text-based content's appearance is a higher priority than visual appearance: When creating a chatbot's persona and appearance, the text appears to be more important to users than its visual appearance. Consequently, writing text is one of the most crucial design activities.

10.9 STUDY LIMITATIONS AND FUTURE RESEARCH

Significant limitations include our inability to systematically manipulate the chatbots we used and the context of the study.

The only people in the study's context were customers who used one of two chatbots for customer service in Norway. Although we are certain that we included enough users to achieve saturation, our findings may have been influenced by the study context. In future studies, the study's findings must be replicated and applied to other markets employing various chatbots for customer service.

The fact that we did not have the opportunity to systematically alter the participants' experiences as one would in a conventional experiment limits the study, although the fact that our research focuses on user experience and user motivation in the context of actual chatbot use is seen as a strength. This study's findings on causal relationships are therefore limited. By putting causal hypotheses based on what we found in conventional experiments to the test, the current investigation could be interestingly extended into the future.

Additionally, we anticipate additional research that begins with the three aforementioned implications for theory as potential hypotheses that need to be examined and validated further. Subsequently, we view the review introduced as an initial move toward securing the fundamental information regarding client inspiration and experience while utilizing chatbots for client assistance.

10.9.1 Reactions to the Exploration Questions

The objective of the review was to assist the situation with companying create and execute a chatbot for speaking with clients. There were three sub-questions in addition to the primary inquiry because of the subject's complexity. The author acknowledges that it is more compelling and sensible to respond to the sub-questions first, followed by the primary research question, to conclude the chapter.

The following is the primary sub-question of this investigation:

> How can the conversation flow of the chatbot be properly organized?

It is desirable to have a very organized conversation stream because the innovation used to make chatbots is not yet great, and clients become baffled when they do not get clear direction through the discussion. Utilizing the chatbot's subsequent inquiries or Fast Answer buttons, we can set the design. In a similar vein, it conveys a human-to-human connection that customers value highly.

For non-structured correspondence, some essentials may be required, such as the help section, where customers can explicitly ask questions. On the other hand, developers are accountable for ensuring that user input is appropriately interpreted and processed. The chatbot starts the discussion, organizes the client with pre-characterized text input, understands the client, and gives a suitable reaction no alternate courses of action is the most developed conversation stream as of now accessible.

> The following was the sub-question of the investigation: When interacting with the chatbot, what kind of content do customers want to see?

Chatterbot data must provide customers with a variety of perspectives. The chatbot responses' usability ought to come first. Users prefer chatbots because of their practical and immediate responses. As a result, for people to respond in the right way, they need to talk for a long time and honestly. The chatterbots responses' use of appropriate language is the next issue. Slang or specific expressions are only allowed if the company is sure that customers will understand and enjoy them. Additionally, the chatbot's responses ought to be stored in the appropriate location and personalized to the greatest extent possible. Last but not least, users appreciate that the chatterbot can talk to them, giving the conversation a more human quality.

The final set of sub-questionnaires for this assessment is:

> What sorts of assignments can chatbots perform for organizations?

In light of current technology and trends, the primary reason businesses use chatbots is to facilitate communication with customers. These tools can be used at any time, day or night, on the messaging platforms of one's choice. These tools help you build a more personal relationship with your customers and alleviate their stress by responding to them immediately.

Businesses also benefit from chatbots because employees spend less time responding to inquiries from customers. Customer communication is currently the most common and manageable use case for chatterbots, even though they will likely be used for other tasks that do not require human intervention.

The following is the inquiry's most significant question:

> For businesses to make use of chatbots as a means of communication, how should they properly set them up?

To establish an efficient communication channel, the organization must be aware of a few guidelines. Buddy stated during the meeting that the chatbot should be designed to solve the identified issue, implying that this tool should have a clear purpose. The company should concentrate on using the chatterbot for customer support, education, or feedback collection because it is impossible to create a chatterbot that can do everything. Also, the chatbot's accuracy in providing users with data ought to receive a lot of attention. A chatbot response should typically contain useful, instructive, comprehensible, pertinent, and specific information. Additionally, businesses should collect data with caution and only retrieve it from users with their permission. The next question is whether businesses ought to take into account the requirements and preferences of their clients. The chatterbot runs the risk of becoming inadequate if the business does not pay sufficient attention to this, as was discussed in Sections 10.2 and 10.3. In conclusion, chatbot improvement should go on for a lot of opportunities to ensure that the information and innovation behind them are cutting-edge. If the company adheres to all of these recommendations, it will reap all of the benefits of communicating with chatterbots.

10.9.2 Consistent Quality and Authenticity

This part discusses the significance of authenticity and consistent quality, as well as the extent to which this investigation satisfies the requirements of these ideas.

Saunders et al. (2009) say that the possibility of legitimacy is utilized to sort out how much the review's outcomes assist with responding to the inquiry. This section made use of both supporting and essential data. The primary sources of supplementary information were academic and semi-academic books, organization reports, and official documentation of administrations and stages related to the investigation. Meetings and conversations at the center that were well-organized provided crucial information. Discussions and gatherings are thought to be good ways to learn a lot about how people think and what they've been through. This suggests that the study is genuine.

Saunders et al. say that the idea of reliability is used to measure the likelihood that the same result would be achieved by another researcher in a different setting (2009). The effects are unusually strong for this time in Europe and North America. Because of the fast changes in client inclinations and development, the results could contrast if the survey were subsequently updated in an alternate land region. Additionally, it is possible that some focus group participants and interviewees were biased. On the other hand, by asking open-ended questions about the respondents' professional histories or employers, the author reduced the risk.

Last but not least, even though the investigation was conducted on behalf of two businesses, the outcomes may change if another industry is discovered.

The review's goal was to foster basic rules that would simplify it for organizations and different associations to create chatbots that could be utilized successfully for correspondence. We had the option to gain some significant knowledge about how clients today speak with each other and how chatterbots are utilized by utilizing the results of the workspace research and observational examination. As a general rule, the consequences of the discretionary and fundamental data examination decided the assessment's essential goal and guaranteed the part's authenticity.

10.9.3 Proposal for Additional Research

As stated earlier, the study demonstrated the remarkable applications of chatbots as a business-specific automated advancement tool.

As a result, coordinated additional research can be carried out to discover alternative means by which businesses stand to benefit from this innovation. Similarly, an organization's use of chatbots as their primary means of communication rather than as an additional channel may be the subject of a survey. As technology advances and interest grows, chatbots have the potential to be a fascinating subject for additional research. This is because they upend conventional methods of communication and purchasing.

REFERENCES

Abdul-kader, S., & Woods, J. (2015). Survey on chatbot design techniques in speech conversation systems. *International Journal of Advanced Computer Science and Applications, 6*, 72–80.

Araujo, T. (2018). Living up to the chatbot hype: The influence of anthropomorphic design cues and communicative agency framing on chatbots for customer service CUI 2019 conversational agent and company perceptions. *Computers in Human at Your Service: Embracing the Disruptive Power of Chatbots*. (2017). Accenture.

Burgess, J., & Connell, J. (Eds.). (2006). *Developments in the Call Centre Industry: Analysis, Changes and Challenges*. Routledge.

Calvey, D. (2004). Product review: Qualitative analysis: Practice and innovation. *Contemporary Sociology, 33*(1), 123–124. 10.1177/009430610403300185

Chung, M., Ko, E., Joung, H., & Kim, S. J. (2020). Chatbot e-service and customer satisfaction regarding luxury brands. *Journal of Business Research, 117*, 587–595. 10.1016/j.jbusres.2018.10.004

Consulting, C. (2011). *Channel Strategy: Framework for Success*. Capgemini.

Dale, R. (2016). The return of the chatbots. *Natural Language Engineering, 22*(5), 811–817. 10.1017/s1351324916000243

Dixon, M., Freeman, K., & Toman, N. (2010). Stop trying to delight your customers. *Harvard Business Review, 88*(7/8), 116–122.

Durmaz, Y., & Efendioglu, I. H. (2016). Travel from traditional marketing to digital marketing. *Global Journal of Management and Business Research*, 35–40. 10.34257/gjmbrevol22is2pg35

Edvard, V. J., Monfort, S. S., Mckendrick, R., Smith, M. A. B., Mcknight, P. E., Krueger, F., & Parasuraman, R. (2016). Almost human: Anthropomorphism increases trust resilience in cognitive agents. *Journal of Experimental Psychology: Applied, 22*(3), 331–349.

Fill, C., & McKee, S. (2011). Principles of Business Marketing Communications. In *Business Marketing: The Theory and Practice of B2B*. Goodfellow Publishers.

Freitas, H., Oliviera, M., Jenkins, M., & Popjoy, O. (1998). *The Focus Group, a Qualitative Research Method*. Merrick School of Business.

Goldstein, S. M., Johnston, R., Duffy, J., & Rao, J. (2002). The service concept: The missing link in service design research? *Journal of Operations Management, 20*(2), 121–134. 10.1016/s0272-6963(01)00090-0

Goodman, J. (2018). *Strategic Customer Service: Managing the Customer Experience to Increase Positive Word of Mouth, Build Loyalty, and Maximize Profits*. Amacom.

Gorry, G. A., & Westbrook, R. A. (2011). Once more, with feeling: Empathy and technology in customer care. *Business Horizons, 54*(2), 125–134. 10.1016/j.bushor.2010.10.003

Grudin, J., & Jacques, R. (2019). Chatbots, Humbots, and the Quest for Artificial General Intelligence. *Proceedings of the 2019 CHI Conference on Human Factors in Computing Systems - CHI '19.*

Guest, G., & Bunce, A. (2006). How many interviews are enough? An experiment with data saturation and variability. *Field Methods, 18*(1), 59–82.

Gustavsson, E. (2005). Virtual servants: Stereotyping female front-office employees on the internet. *Gender, Work, and Organization, 12*(5), 400–419. 10.1111/j.1468-0432.2005.00281.x

IBM United Kingdom. (n.d.). Ibm.com. Retrieved July 19, 2023, from https://www.ibm.com/

Indrani, M., Thies, N., Menon, S., Magapu, M., & Subramony, J. O. (2017). How Do You Want Your Chatbot? An Exploratory Wizard-of-Oz Study with Young, Urban Indians. In *Proceedings of INTERACT 2017* (pp. 441–459). Springer.

Jobber, D., & Ellis-chadwick, F. (2013). *Digital Marketing and Social Media*. McGraw-Hill Higher Education.

Johnson, D. S., Bardhi, F., & Dunn, D. T. (2008). Understanding how technology paradoxes affect customer satisfaction with self-service technology: The role of performance ambiguity and trust in technology. *Psychology & Marketing, 25*(5), 416–443. 10.1002/mar.20218

Kuligowska, K., & Lasek, M. (2005). Intelligent Agents in the Human-Computer Interaction. In *the 7th International Conference on Information Management-Human Computer Interaction.*

Lind, M., & Salomonson, N. (2006). The Role of Virtual Servants in e-Interaction. In *Proceedings of PragWeb* (pp. 124–138). GI Verlag.

Luger, E., & Sellen, A. (2016). Like Having a Really Bad PA: The Gulf between User Expectation and Experience of Conversational Agents. In *Proceedings CHI 2016* (pp. 5286–5297). ACM.
Meuter, M. L., Ostrom, A. L., Roundtree, R. I., & Bitner, M. J. (2000). Self-service technologies: Understanding customer satisfaction with technology-based service encounters. *Journal of Marketing*, *64*(3), 50–64. 10.1509/jmkg.64.3.50.18024
Murgia, A., Janssens, D., Demeyer, S., & Vasilescu, B. (2016). Among the Machines: Human-Bot Interaction on Social Q&A Websites. In *Proceedings of CHI 2016* (pp. 1272–1279). ACM.
Murphy, G. (2008). *Communication Strategy: A Best Practice Guide to Developing Communication Campaign*. IPA.
Pelton, L., Strutton, D., & Lumpkin, J. (2002). *Marketing Channels: A Relationship Management Approach*. The McGraw Hill Companies, Inc.
Petter, B. (2017). Chatbots and the new world of HCI. *Interactions*, *24*(4), 38–42.
Petter, B., & Brandtzaeg, A. (2017). Why People Use Chatbots. In *Proceedings of the International Conference on Internet Science - INSCI 2017* (pp. 377–392). Springer.
Pride, W., Ferrel, O., Lukas, B., Schembri, C., & Ninninen, O. (2015). *Marketing Principles. Melbourne: Cengage Learning*.
Principal Analyst. (n.d.). *The six factors that separate hype from hope in your*. Forrester. Retrieved July 19, 2023, from https://www.forrester.com/report/The+Six+Factors+That+Separate+Hype+From+Hope+In+Your+Conversational+AI+Journey/-/E-RES143773
Saunders, M., Lewis, P., & Thornhill, A. (2009). *Research Methods for Business Students*. Pearson Education Limited.
The state of chatbots. (n.d.). Forrester. Retrieved July 19, 2023, from https://www.forrester.com/report/The-State-Of-Chatbots/RES136207
The user experience of chatbots. (n.d.). Nielsen Norman Group. Retrieved July 19, 2023, from https://www.nngroup.com/articles/chatbots/
Wilson, J., & Paul, R. (2018). Collaborative intelligence: Humans and AI are joining forces. *Harvard Business Review*, *96*, 96–97.
(N.d.-a). Nuance.com. Retrieved July 19, 2023, from https://www.nuance.com/omni-channel-customer-engagement/case-studies/kaspersky-lab.html
(N.d.-b). Oracle.com. Retrieved July 19, 2023, from https://www.oracle.com/webfolder/s/delivery_production/docs/FY16h1/doc35/CXResearchVirtualExperiences.pdf

Electronic References

Chatfuel. (2017). Facebook Messenger. Chatfuel Help [accessed 25 April 2023]. Available at: https://help.chatfuel.com/facebook-messenger/
Oleksak, M. (2005). *Strategic conversations with your customers helps hone the planning process*. Emerald Group Publishing Limited [accessed 1 May 2023]. Available at: https://ebookcentral-proquestcom.aineistot.lamk.fi/lib/lamk-ebooks/reader.action?docID=282891

APPENDIX 1: INTERVIEW

- In your opinion, what kind of content do users want to see in the chatbot when communicating?
- In your opinion, what are the most beneficial purposes that businesses can use chatbots for (educational, entertaining, promotional)?
- What kind of data users are willing to provide to chatbots (their names, location, preferences, etc.)? Do you think users are ready to provide sensitive data (emails, addresses, etc.) to chatbots?
- In your opinion, how to organize a discussion flow of the chatbot in a right way? Should it be more structured or should it be more broad in terms of choice?
- Do you think that chatbots are better in comparison to general social media in terms of communication with companies? If yes, then why? Would you rather speak to a chatbot than to the human representative of the company?

11 Artificial Intelligence and More Effective Advertising

Unlocking the Power of Data and Automation

Sangeet Vashishtha and Pooja Sharma
IIMT University, Meerut, India

11.1 INTRODUCTION: THE TRANSFORMATIVE IMPACT OF ARTIFICIAL INTELLIGENCE ON ADVERTISING

In an era defined by unprecedented technological advancements, the world of advertising stands on the cusp of a revolution. At the heart of this transformative shift lies the potent force of Artificial Intelligence (AI) [Glauner, P. (2020)]. This chapter embarks on a journey deep into the realm of advertising, exploring how AI technologies are reshaping the landscape and propelling businesses toward unparalleled success. With the proliferation of digital platforms and the surging availability of consumer data, AI emerges as a catalyst, promising to optimize advertising strategies, personalize messaging, and deliver targeted campaigns at an unprecedented scale.

This chapter serves as a beacon, guiding readers through the fascinating intersection of AI and advertising. It ventures to unravel the intricate tapestry that weaves together these two worlds, from understanding the fundamental elements of AI to its practical applications in the advertising domain [Tsang, Y. P., & Lee, C. K. M. (2022)]. It delves into the heart of AI, dissecting its essential components, which include machine learning algorithms, natural language processing, and predictive analytics. These components, we will discover, are the bedrock upon which AI's transformative power in advertising is built.

As we embark on this journey, we shall explore the myriad applications of AI in advertising, with a focus on three primary facets: audience targeting and segmentation, creative optimization, and media buying and optimization. Each of these facets represents a critical chapter in AI's story within the advertising landscape, promising to unlock the untapped potential hidden within consumer data [Luo, X., Qin, M. S., Fang, Z., & Qu, Z. (2021)].

But as we traverse this landscape, we must also tread carefully. The path to harnessing the full potential of AI is not without its obstacles and ethical considerations. Privacy concerns, algorithmic biases, and the demand for transparency and accountability cast shadows that must be addressed [Roetzer, P., & Kaput, M. (2022)].

In the spirit of grounding theory in reality, this chapter presents real-world case studies and success stories from companies across diverse industries and platforms. These narratives serve as living proof of the transformative power of AI in advertising, showcasing how AI-driven solutions have elevated targeting precision, bolstered customer engagement, and amplified return on ad spend.

In conclusion, this chapter underscores the profound impact of artificial intelligence on the world of advertising. Through AI, advertisers can leverage data-driven insights, automation, and personalization to take their campaigns to new heights, delivering experiences that are not just

DOI: 10.1201/9781003450443-11

relevant but deeply engaging [Chung, K., Quach, S., & Thaichon, P. (2022)]. It is our aspiration that this chapter will equip marketers, advertisers, and researchers with valuable insights and practical guidance, enabling them to navigate the ever-evolving landscape of AI-powered advertising with confidence [Marr, B. (2019)].

As we turn the page, let us embark on a journey of discovery, one that promises to illuminate the transformative potential of AI, as it converges with the dynamic realm of advertising, shaping the future of marketing in ways we have yet to fully comprehend [Enholm, I. M., Papagiannidis, E., Mikalef, P., & Krogstie, J. (2022)].

11.1.1 The AI Revolution in Advertising

11.1.1.1 Understanding AI in Advertising

Before we delve into the fascinating applications of AI in advertising, it's essential to establish a solid understanding of the fundamental concepts that underpin this transformative technology and its relevance to the advertising landscape. At its core, Artificial Intelligence (AI) represents a collection of cutting-edge technologies designed to mimic and replicate human intelligence and decision-making processes [Waters, M. R., Aneja, S., & Hong, J. C. (2023)]. While it encompasses a broad spectrum of capabilities, AI's relevance to advertising primarily revolves around its ability to analyze vast and complex data sets, derive insights, and make data-driven decisions.

11.1.1.1.1 Machine Learning Algorithms

Central to AI's capabilities are machine learning algorithms. These algorithms have the remarkable ability to recognize patterns and trends within data, learn from them, and apply these learnings to make predictions or decisions without explicit programming. In the context of advertising, machine learning can be a game-changer by sifting through colossal data sets to reveal actionable insights, enabling advertisers to understand consumer behavior and preferences at an unprecedented level of granularity [Chowdhury, N. A. (2023)].

11.1.1.1.2 Natural Language Processing (NLP)

Another integral component of AI is Natural Language Processing (NLP). NLP empowers machines to understand, interpret, and generate human language. This capability is pivotal in personalizing advertising messaging and interactions with consumers. By analyzing text data from various sources, including social media, customer reviews, and surveys, NLP helps advertisers tailor their messaging to resonate with different audience segments effectively.

11.1.1.1.3 Predictive Analytics

Predictive analytics, a branch of AI, is instrumental in advertising strategy. By examining historical data, predictive analytics uses statistical algorithms to forecast future trends and behaviors. In advertising, this means that advertisers can anticipate consumer preferences and market trends, allowing them to make informed decisions about where and how to allocate their advertising budgets.

11.1.1.2 The Relevance of AI in Advertising

The marriage of AI and advertising is not merely a technological trend but a strategic imperative for businesses seeking to thrive in the digital age. Several factors underscore the importance of AI in advertising:

11.1.1.2.1 Data Abundance

The digital landscape has ushered in an era of unparalleled data generation and collection. AI is the key to unlocking the potential of this treasure trove of data, transforming it into actionable insights that fuel advertising campaigns.

11.1.1.2.2 Personalization Imperative

Modern consumers demand personalized experiences. AI enables advertisers to create highly personalized advertisements and marketing campaigns by leveraging insights gleaned from consumer data. This personalization not only enhances engagement but also boosts conversion rates.

11.1.1.2.3 Real-Time Decision-Making

The speed at which digital advertising operates demands real-time decision-making. AI-powered algorithms can make instantaneous adjustments to advertising strategies, optimizing campaigns as they unfold, and ensuring advertisers stay ahead in the ever-competitive digital marketplace.

11.1.1.2.4 Precision Targeting

Effective advertising hinges on reaching the right audience at the right time with the right message. AI excels in audience segmentation and targeting, enabling advertisers to identify and reach their most promising prospects with surgical precision.

In the chapters that follow, we will explore how AI's capabilities are harnessed to enhance advertising effectiveness across various dimensions. From audience targeting and creative optimization to media buying and ethical considerations, AI is poised to revolutionize every facet of advertising, promising a future where campaigns are not just advertisements but experiences tailored to individual preferences and needs.

11.1.1.3 Leveraging AI for Consumer Insights

In today's digital age, the ability to gain deep and nuanced insights into consumer behavior is a cornerstone of effective marketing and advertising. Artificial Intelligence (AI) has emerged as the pivotal tool that unlocks the full potential of consumer data, enabling businesses to understand, predict, and engage with their target audiences on a whole new level [Chaitanya, K., Saha, G. C., Saha, H., Acharya, S., & Singla, M. (2023)].

11.1.1.3.1 Data as the Foundation

The foundation of leveraging AI for consumer insights lies in data—massive volumes of it. The digital landscape, with its interconnected devices and platforms, continuously generates a torrent of data points. AI acts as the bridge between this deluge of information and actionable insights, and here's how it achieves it:

11.1.1.3.2 Data Collection and Aggregation

AI systems excel at collecting and aggregating data from a multitude of sources. This includes online interactions, social media, e-commerce transactions, and even IoT devices. The result is a rich repository of information that encapsulates not only what consumers say but, more crucially, what they do.

11.1.1.3.3 Data Processing at Scale

The sheer volume and complexity of this data are staggering. Traditional methods of data analysis struggle to keep pace. AI, on the other hand, possesses the computational horsepower to process, categorize, and analyze this information at lightning speed. Machine learning algorithms identify patterns, anomalies, and correlations that would elude human analysts, leading to a more profound understanding of consumer behavior.

11.1.1.4 Audience Segmentation and Targeting

One of the most transformative applications of AI in advertising is audience segmentation and targeting. It goes beyond conventional demographic-based approaches, allowing for a far more refined and effective strategy:

11.1.1.4.1 Behavioral Insights

AI's prowess lies in its ability to decode consumer online behaviors – what websites they visit, what content they engage with, what products they browse. By scrutinizing these behaviors, AI creates segments based on shared interests and actions, thus going beyond mere demographics.

11.1.1.4.2 Predictive Segmentation

But AI doesn't stop at understanding past behaviors; it anticipates future actions. Leveraging historical data and predictive analytics, AI can identify segments most likely to respond positively to specific ad campaigns. This predictive approach is a game-changer in advertising strategy.

11.1.1.4.3 Hyper-Personalization

AI's segmentation capabilities pave the way for hyper-personalization. Advertisers can harness AI to craft highly individualized advertisements, meticulously tailored to resonate with the preferences and needs of each segment. This level of personalization boosts the relevance and efficacy of advertising, enhancing consumer engagement.

11.1.1.5 Predictive Analytics

Beyond understanding current behaviors, AI empowers advertisers to predict future actions and trends. Predictive analytics, underpinned by AI, revolutionizes the advertising landscape:

11.1.1.5.1 Anticipating Trends

By dissecting historical data and applying machine learning algorithms, AI can forecast upcoming consumer trends. Advertisers can use these insights to align their campaigns with emerging market preferences, gaining a competitive edge.

11.1.1.5.2 Meeting Future Needs

Predictive analytics enables advertisers to foresee consumer needs and desires before they arise. Armed with this foresight, businesses can proactively design campaigns and products that cater to these anticipated demands.

11.1.1.5.3 Real-Time Optimization

In the dynamic world of advertising, consumer behavior can change rapidly. AI-driven systems adapt advertising campaigns in real-time based on predictive analytics. If data indicates a shift in consumer behavior, AI optimizes campaign elements, such as ad placements and messaging, to align with these evolving patterns.

In conclusion, AI's capacity to leverage consumer insights has ushered in a new era of advertising effectiveness. By aggregating and analyzing data, AI empowers advertisers to segment audiences effectively, craft personalized messages, and anticipate future trends. This data-driven approach not only maximizes the efficiency of advertising efforts but also strengthens the connections between brands and consumers in an increasingly competitive digital landscape.

11.2 APPLICATIONS OF AI IN ADVERTISING

The transformative potential of Artificial Intelligence (AI) in the realm of advertising is not confined to theory alone—it manifests itself vividly in practical applications that enhance advertising effectiveness across multiple dimensions. This section delves into these applications, exploring how AI is reshaping the advertising landscape in the process.

11.2.1 Audience Targeting and Segmentation

One of the foundational pillars of effective advertising is reaching the right audience with the right message at the right time. AI brings unprecedented precision and scalability to audience targeting and segmentation:

11.2.1.1 Behavioral Analysis

AI meticulously analyzes consumer online behaviors, such as browsing history, app usage, and social media engagement. By decoding these actions, AI identifies patterns, affinities, and interests, which are then used to categorize individuals into segments based on their behaviors.

11.2.1.2 Predictive Segmentation

Beyond understanding past actions, AI has the power of prediction. Through the application of historical data and predictive analytics, AI identifies segments most likely to respond favorably to specific ad campaigns. This predictive capability is a game-changer in advertising strategy; ensuring resources are allocated where they yield the highest return.

11.2.1.3 Hyper-Personalization

AI doesn't stop at segmentation; it enables hyper-personalization. Advertisers can harness AI to craft highly individualized advertisements; each meticulously tailored to resonate with the preferences and needs of specific segments. This level of personalization not only boosts the relevance of advertising but also deepens consumer engagement.

11.2.2 Creative Optimization

The art of advertising extends to the creation of compelling and captivating content. AI is revolutionizing creative optimization by automating and enhancing this creative process:

11.2.2.1 Content Generation

AI-driven algorithms can generate ad copy, articles, and product descriptions, significantly reducing the time and resources required for content creation. Moreover, AI-generated content can be tailored to match the tone and style of the brand or campaign.

11.2.2.2 Image Recognition

Visual content is a powerful tool in advertising. AI-powered image recognition technology can analyze images and videos, identifying objects, scenes, and even sentiments. This capability aids in selecting the most relevant visuals for ad campaigns.

11.2.2.3 Sentiment Analysis

Understanding consumer sentiment is vital for crafting persuasive messaging. AI's sentiment analysis tools comb through vast amounts of social media and online content to gauge public sentiment, ensuring advertisements align with the prevailing mood and trends.

11.2.3 Media Buying and Optimization

AI's impact extends beyond targeting and creative aspects; it plays a pivotal role in optimizing the entire media buying process:

11.2.3.1 Programmatic Advertising

Programmatic advertising platforms leverage AI algorithms to automate the buying of advertising space. These algorithms analyze data in real time to determine the best ad placements, ensuring that ads are delivered to the most relevant audiences at optimal times.

11.2.3.2 Real-Time Bidding (RTB)

Real-time bidding, powered by AI, is a dynamic process where advertisers bid on ad impressions in real-time auctions. AI algorithms assess the value of each impression, enabling advertisers to optimize their bids for maximum impact and efficiency.

11.2.3.3 Campaign Performance Enhancement

AI continually monitors the performance of advertising campaigns. When anomalies or underperforming elements are detected, AI can make real-time adjustments to optimize outcomes. This dynamic approach maximizes return on investment and campaign effectiveness.

In this chapter, we will delve deeper into each of these applications, providing insights into how AI is transforming advertising practices, optimizing resources, and ultimately delivering more relevant and effective ad campaigns. These applications signify the beginning of a new era in advertising, one where data-driven precision meets creative innovation, and where advertising campaigns evolve in real-time to meet the ever-changing demands of the digital marketplace.

11.3 ETHICAL CONSIDERATIONS AND CHALLENGES

As we embark on the exciting journey of exploring the transformative power of Artificial Intelligence (AI) in advertising, it's imperative to recognize that with great technological advances come ethical considerations and challenges. In this section, we delve into the ethical landscape of AI in advertising, addressing the complexities and potential pitfalls.

11.3.1 Privacy Concerns

11.3.1.1 Data Collection and Privacy

AI in advertising relies heavily on data, often collected from various sources, including consumers' online activities and interactions. However, the line between data collection for targeted advertising and invasion of privacy can be thin. It's crucial to strike the right balance between personalization and the protection of individuals' personal information.

11.3.1.2 Transparency and Consent

Ethical advertising practices demand transparency and informed consent. Consumers should be aware of how their data is collected, stored, and used for advertising purposes. Ensuring that individuals have control over their data and can easily opt out of data collection is a fundamental ethical consideration.

11.3.2 Algorithmic Biases

11.3.2.1 Implicit Biases in AI Algorithms

AI algorithms, while powerful, can sometimes inherit biases present in the data they are trained on. If the training data is biased, the algorithms may perpetuate discrimination in advertising, inadvertently favoring or excluding certain groups based on factors like race, gender, or socioeconomic status.

11.3.2.2 Fair and Ethical Representation

Ensuring that advertisements are fair and ethical in their representation of products, services, and individuals is paramount. AI can be employed to scrutinize ad content for any biases, misleading claims, or harmful stereotypes.

11.3.3 Accountability and Transparency

11.3.3.1 Algorithm Accountability

With AI-driven decision-making becoming increasingly prevalent, the question of accountability arises. Who is responsible if an AI algorithm makes a biased or unethical decision? Establishing clear lines of accountability within organizations is essential.

11.3.3.2 Algorithm Transparency

Understanding AI algorithms and their decision-making processes can be challenging, especially when they operate as black boxes. Ensuring transparency in how AI decisions are made is crucial for both ethical and regulatory reasons.

11.3.4 Consumer Trust and Consent

11.3.4.1 Trust in AI-Enhanced Advertising

Maintaining consumer trust is vital. If consumers feel that AI is used to manipulate or deceive them, it can erode trust in both the brand and the advertising industry as a whole.

11.3.4.2 Obtaining Informed Consent

Respecting consumer autonomy means obtaining informed consent for data collection and targeted advertising. Obtaining this consent in a clear and user-friendly manner is an ethical imperative.

11.3.5 Adherence to Regulations

Adherence to data protection laws, such as the General Data Protection Regulation (GDPR) in Europe, is not just a legal requirement but an ethical obligation. Companies must ensure that their AI-driven advertising practices align with these regulations [Vashishtha, S., Sharma, P 2023].

In navigating the ethical considerations and challenges of AI in advertising, it's essential for advertisers, marketers, and technology providers to prioritize ethical guidelines, transparency, and consumer rights. As AI continues to reshape the advertising landscape, maintaining ethical integrity is not just a choice but a necessity to build trust with consumers and ensure the responsible and sustainable use of AI technologies in advertising [Shaik, M. (2023)].

11.4 CASE STUDIES AND SUCCESS STORIES

In the dynamic world of advertising, theories, and concepts come to life through real-world applications. In this section, we delve into case studies and success stories of companies that have harnessed the transformative power of Artificial Intelligence (AI) in advertising. These narratives serve as compelling evidence of AI's impact on marketing campaigns and business outcomes across various industries and platforms.

11.4.1 Case Study: Netflix – Personalization Redefined

11.4.1.1 Background

Netflix, the streaming giant, recognized early on that personalization was key to retaining and expanding its global subscriber base. Leveraging AI, they embarked on a journey to redefine how content recommendations are made.

11.4.1.2 AI in Action

Netflix employs a complex recommendation algorithm powered by AI and machine learning. It analyzes vast amounts of user data, including viewing history, preferences, and even the time of day, to make highly personalized content recommendations. This AI-driven personalization has significantly contributed to user engagement and loyalty.

11.4.1.3 Results

Netflix attributes a substantial portion of its success to its recommendation algorithm. It's estimated that the algorithm saves the company over a billion dollars annually by reducing churn and increasing user retention. Subscribers are more likely to stay with Netflix because they consistently discover content that appeals to their individual tastes.

11.4.2 Success Story: Amazon – The Power of Predictive Analytics

11.4.2.1 Background

Amazon, the e-commerce behemoth, thrives on its ability to anticipate customer needs and preferences. They turned to AI and predictive analytics to enhance the online shopping experience.

11.4.2.2 AI in Action

Amazon employs AI to analyze historical purchase data, search queries, and browsing behavior. It uses this information to make product recommendations, forecast demand, and optimize inventory management. Additionally, they use AI-powered chatbots for customer support.

11.4.2.3 Results

The impact of AI on Amazon's bottom line is staggering. By showing customers products they are likely to buy, Amazon's recommendation engine is estimated to be responsible for 35% of the company's revenue. Predictive analytics also helps Amazon streamline its operations, reducing costs and ensuring products are available when customers want them.

11.4.3 Case Study: Coca-Cola – Content Creation Reinvented

11.4.3.1 Background

Coca-Cola, one of the world's most recognized brands, wanted to create highly engaging and personalized marketing campaigns across diverse markets.

11.4.3.2 AI in Action

Coca-Cola used AI-driven content generation tools to create localized advertisements for different regions and demographics. These tools leveraged AI to generate ad copy, visuals, and even music that resonated with specific target audiences.

11.4.3.3 Results

The AI-powered approach resulted in more engaging advertisements that felt personalized to local audiences. In one campaign, Coca-Cola saw a 16% increase in sales in a specific market where AI-generated content was used. This demonstrated the potential for AI not only to reduce the time and costs of content creation but also to improve campaign effectiveness.

11.4.4 Success Story: Spotify – Dynamic Audio Ads

11.4.4.1 Background

Spotify, the music streaming service, sought to provide advertisers with innovative ways to engage users through audio advertising.

11.4.4.2 AI in Action

Spotify introduced dynamic audio ads powered by AI. These ads adapt in real time to factors like the user's location, time of day, and even the weather. For example, an ad for a local coffee shop may play when it's raining, enticing users to visit.

11.4.4.3 Results

Dynamic audio ads have significantly increased engagement and click-through rates for advertisers on Spotify. By leveraging AI to create contextually relevant ads, Spotify has offered a unique advertising experience that benefits both users and brands.

These case studies and success stories underscore the transformative potential of AI in advertising. From personalizing content recommendations to improving ad targeting and content creation, AI has become an indispensable tool for businesses seeking to enhance their advertising strategies, engage with consumers, and drive tangible business outcomes in the digital age.

11.5 CONCLUSION

The journey through the transformative impact of Artificial Intelligence (AI) on advertising has been nothing short of illuminating. In this chapter, we've ventured into the realm where data-driven precision meets creative innovation, where advertising campaigns are no longer just messages but personalized experiences tailored to individual preferences and needs.

From understanding the essence of AI and its relevance to advertising to exploring its applications in audience targeting, creative optimization, and media buying, we've witnessed how AI is reshaping the advertising landscape. The power of AI to unlock actionable insights from vast and complex consumer data sets has revolutionized how advertisers understand, engage, and convert their target audiences.

Yet, in this technological journey, we've also encountered the ethical considerations and challenges that come hand-in-hand with AI in advertising. Privacy concerns, algorithmic biases, accountability, and transparency are vital issues that must be navigated responsibly to ensure the trust and respect of consumers.

As we wrap up this chapter, we're left with a sense of awe at the potential of AI in advertising. We've explored case studies and success stories from industry giants like Netflix, Amazon, Coca-Cola, and Spotify, witnessing how AI has enhanced advertising effectiveness, optimized resources, and improved the user experience. These stories provide compelling evidence that AI is not just a buzzword but a practical and invaluable tool for businesses seeking to thrive in the digital era.

The future of advertising lies at the intersection of data-driven insights, creativity, and ethical responsibility. As AI continues to evolve, advertisers, marketers, and technology providers must remain agile, adaptable, and ethically conscious. By doing so, they can harness the full potential of AI to create advertising campaigns that resonate, engage, and deliver value to consumers while driving business success.

In closing, this chapter serves as a testament to the ever-evolving landscape of AI-powered advertising—a landscape filled with opportunities, challenges, and the potential to redefine how businesses connect with their audiences in an increasingly digital and data-rich world.

REFERENCES

Chaitanya, K., Saha, G. C., Saha, H., Acharya, S., & Singla, M. (2023). The impact of artificial intelligence and machine learning in digital marketing strategies. European Economic Letters (EEL), 13(3), 982–992.

Chowdhury, N. A. (2023). Unlocking the power of Chat GPT: An in-depth look at ChatAI's business model.

Chung, K., Quach, S., & Thaichon, P. (2022). A framework of artificial intelligence (AI) applications in marketing. In Artificial Intelligence for Marketing Management (pp. 41–51). Routledge.

Enholm, I. M., Papagiannidis, E., Mikalef, P., & Krogstie, J. (2022). Artificial intelligence and business value: A literature review. Information Systems Frontiers, 24(5), 1709–1734.

Glauner, P. (2020). Unlocking the power of artificial intelligence for your business. Innovative Technologies for Market Leadership: Investing in the Future, 45–59.

Luo, X., Qin, M. S., Fang, Z., & Qu, Z. (2021). Artificial intelligence coaches for sales agents: Caveats and solutions. Journal of Marketing, 85(2), 14–32.

Marr, B. (2019). Artificial intelligence in practice: how 50 successful companies used AI and machine learning to solve problems. John Wiley & Sons.

Roetzer, P., & Kaput, M. (2022). Marketing artificial intelligence: AI, marketing, and the future of business. BenBella Books.

Shaik, M. (2023). Impact of artificial intelligence on marketing. East Asian Journal of Multidisciplinary Research, 2(3), 993–1004.

Tsang, Y. P., & Lee, C. K. M. (2022). Artificial intelligence in industrial design: A semi-automated literature survey. Engineering Applications of Artificial Intelligence, 112, 104884.

Vashishtha, S., Sharma, P., Gupta, M. P., Kumar, M. B., Singh, A., & Ansari, M. F. (2023). Sustainability of start-ups during pandemic: An analytical study In reference of Indian perspective. Journal of Pharmaceutical Negative Results, 4001–4008.

Waters, M. R., Aneja, S., & Hong, J. C. (2023). Unlocking the power of CHATGPT, artificial intelligence, and large language models: practical suggestions for radiation oncologists. Practical Radiation Oncology.

12 Chatbot and Digital Communication

Lilia Smida and Jamel-Eddine Gharbi
University of Jendouba, Jendouba, Tunisia

12.1 INTRODUCTION

ChatGPT, an Artificial Intelligence (AI) tool, became accessible to the public in November 2022 (Firat, 2023) and reached 100 million users just two months after (Sabzalieva, 2023). New studies are needed in developing countries on the potential of AI to enhance learning in Higher Education and particularly of ChatGPT (Crompton and Burke, 2023; Eke, 2023).

As AI continues to advance, it intersects with and shapes our society. Algorithms, for example, are increasingly integrated into critical services that people rely on, such as education, healthcare, and government benefit programs. Governments, healthcare organizations, businesses, and educational institutions now leverage AI to enhance their efficiency and effectiveness. Consequently, traditional face-to-face interactions in these domains are being either replaced or augmented by virtual communication, digital interfaces, and particularly chatbots.

Within the realm of education, scholars like Ma et al. (2018) argue for equipping students with the necessary skills related to Artificial Intelligence (AI) to prepare them for the ongoing AI revolution. Additionally, Guliyeva (2021) predicts a future where the convergence of nanotechnology, neurology, artificial intelligence, and interactive object-based online worlds will make education even more immersive and appealing by 2030. This forecast suggests that internet-based systems may eventually replace many traditional education systems, rendering the demand for physical schools and human teachers obsolete (Millennium Report Philosophy of Life and Realities of 2007, p. 171). AI will undoubtedly reshape the educational landscape, impacting skills development, infrastructure, and stakeholder relationships. Moreover, the introduction of AI-powered Chatbots in higher education has already shown promise. However ethical and practical implications must be taken with cautions.

It is important to recognize the potential opportunities and advantages of ChatGPT in an educational context and embrace it as an academic tool to save time and improve learning. Unfortunately, ChatGPT is not equally accessible between high-income and low-income countries (Salvagno et al., 2023). Moreover, caution is necessary due to the challenges it poses. For instance, there are risks associated with students limiting their learning to predefined outcomes (Firat, 2023) or engaging in cheating and plagiarism, which raise integrity concerns (Rasul et al., 2023; Eke, 2023; Firat, 2023). To address these challenges, Eke (2023) suggests reviewing academic integrity policies and developing methods capable of identifying cheating.

In Tunisian context, the aim of our chapter is:

12.1.1 Understanding Potential Opportunities and Barriers Related to the Integration of ChatGPT in Higher Education and Investigating the Readiness of Tunisian Students to Use ChatGPT as a Learning Tool

Barriers like cheating and plagiarism can probably find favorable ground at Tunisian universities. Hamani et al. (2013), interviewing 365 students who sat in the Higher Institute of Sport and

DOI: 10.1201/9781003450443-12

Physical Education of Sfax (Tunisia), found that 70% of students admitted had cheated on an exam at least once. They explain that cheating behavior can be identified by individual and environmental reasons. A student may cheat because workload is too heavy (educational institution), there is low penalty in case of cheating (educational institution encouragement), parents advocate cheating, or he tries to follow classmates who are cheaters (peers influence). School, parents, and peers interfere (as social institutions) in the learned behavior (cheating). Cheating encouraged by school or parents is intrinsic reinforcement while following classmates' cheaters is observational learning. Moreover, engaging in cheating and plagiarism will limit student process learning to predefined outcomes (Firat, 2023).

Intrinsic reinforcement and observational learning refer to Bandura's Social Learning Theory concepts. Bandura (1986) criticized this process and believed that external, environmental reinforcement is not the only factor to influence learning and behavior. (Nabavi et al., 2012, p.9). In fact, humans operate cognitively on social experience, and these cognitions influence behavior and development (Nabavi et al., 2012). Thus, we need to ask:

12.1.2 How Social Institutions Impact Behavior and Learning Process?

Aguayo et al. (2021) emphasizes the importance to incorporate Gardner Multiple Intelligences (MIs) as a pedagogy through teaching, in light of the implications for students' positive results in academic performance and creativity and on cognitive development and development of abilities. Teaching based on MIs can have educational, social, and scientific impact. Development of MIs impacts the development of abilities and enhances creativity. We therefore want to explore:

12.1.3 The Impact of Social Institutions on Behavior and Learning Process Considering the Mediating Role of Students' MIs

For the development of abilities and cognitions and the enhancement of creativity, a student needs to have the freedom to do that. It emphasizes the importance of creating conditions that expand people's capabilities and choices. Or "Institutions and societal arrangements are of much importance for promoting the freedoms of individuals" (kuhumba et al. 2018, p.129). Therefore, family and educational systems including universities prompt the freedoms of individuals. By analogy, perceived influence of family and universities will promote freedom. Freedoms, "individual capabilities to do things that a person has reason to value," will promote human development (kuhumba et al. 2018, p.129). Consequently, we ask about:

12.1.4 The Impact of Social Institutions on Behavior and the Learning Process Considering the Mediating Role of Students' MIs and Capabilities

We draw below a schema (Figure 12.1) to clarify this impact:

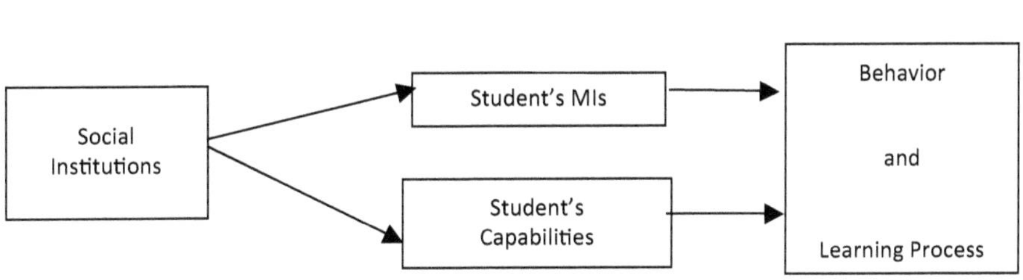

FIGURE 12.1 The impact of social institutions on behavior and learning processes considering the mediating role of students' MIs and capabilities.

Tunisian students have the freedom to use AI-based ChatGPT either as a learning tool to construct (Piaget Constructive Learning Theory) their knowledge or as a cheating tool, fulfilling, for example, to be graduated. ChatGPT is a service accessible to students, but they have the freedom to choose how to use it to reach their achievement. The free possibilities to choose between a set of opportunities pertain to the capabilities approach (Sen's work and Nussbaum's work). As explained by Robeyns (2003), considering the capabilities approach, we introduce these concepts:

- **commodity**, good, or service, which has certain characteristics that interest a person,
- characteristics of a good enable a **functioning**,
- conversion factors, convert characteristics into a functioning: personal characteristics, social characteristics, and environmental characteristics,
- and, functioning is an achievement, whereas a capability is the ability to achieve.

These concepts, relative to capabilities approach, are better explained in Figure 12.2.

Different
Personal ideas of
social & Capabilities Set
environmental life

AA conversion (constrained)
factors choice

Considering ChatGPT as a service with characteristics such as "permits to resolve a problem," functioning will be "problem resolved" and ChatGPT the means to achieve it. In our study, we selected MIs as personal characteristics and social institution as environmental characteristics. Two students wanting to resolve a problem (purpose of using ChatGPT) will have the same set of opportunities (copy-paste results or trying to understand the steps and learning through feedback). Both will achieve the same result. The one who chooses "copy-paste", plagiarism, undertook a cheating behavior with a status quo and will probably negatively impact his/her development, while the second will undertake a creative behavior, a constructive learning process that will be autonomous and enhance development in promoting problem solving.

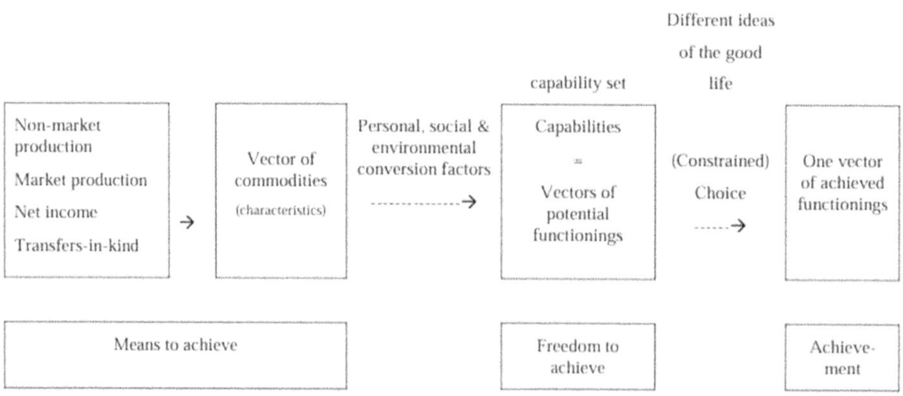

FIGURE 12.2 The different constituents of the capability approach and the role that commodities play. (Robeyns, 20012.43, p. 12)

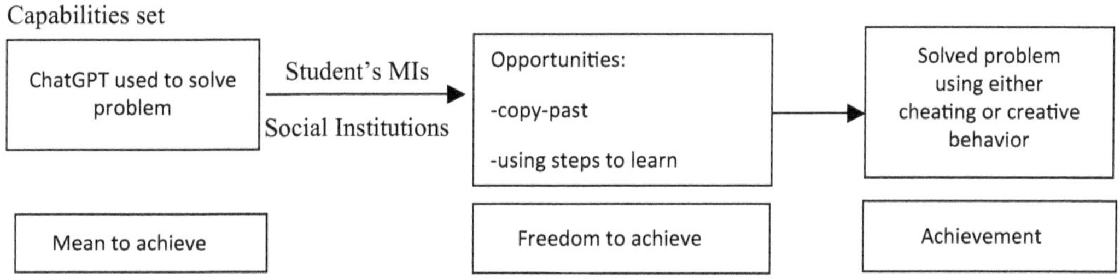

FIGURE 12.3 Understanding the role of Using ChatGPT to solve a problem considering the capability approach.

Regarding Figure 12.1 and Figure 12.3, we want to explore the impact of Perceived Social Institutions' Influence, mediated by MIs and capabilities, on students' behavior and learning process when using ChatGPT to achieve their purposes.

In this chapter, we will begin by introducing our "Theoretical concepts," (2) followed by explaining the choice of our "Methodology and Method" (3). Afterward, using the qualitative research based on Thematic Analysis, we will expose "Data Analysis and Discuss Findings" (4). Finally, we will highlight principal findings, give some practical recommendations, and explore future research and limitations in our "Conclusion" (5).

12.2 THEORETICAL CONCEPTS

The Capability Approach (2.1.) explains the human development considering capabilities and how to use a commodity with characteristics for an achievement. Conversion factors convert characteristics into functioning. As seen earlier, we retained Social Institutions and MIs as conversion factors (2.2.). "AI based ChatGPT" (2.3.) was chosen as a commodity and "ChatGPT using purpose" as an achievement, a functioning. ChatGPT use can either imply a Cheating Behavior (5.4.) or a Creative one (5.5.) and imply a different learning process.

12.2.1 The Capability Approach

Introduced by Sen in the 80s, the Capability Approach is used to assess human development. "Human growth instead of economic growth" lies at the heart of Sen's capability approach. The demand for equity and justice forms the foundation upon which any human, regardless of gender, can be able "to be or to do" what they want. By doing so, the level of development is elevated for everyone (Nussbaum, 2003).

Developed by Sen (1999) and Nussbaum (2000), the Capability Approach seeks to expand individuals' set of capabilities and freedoms, leading to development. Capability as: "a person's ability to perform valuable actions or attain valuable states of being represents the various combinations of things a person can do or be" (Sen, 1993, p. 28 cited in Kuhumba, 2018). While Sen's approach does not restrict capabilities to a specific list and aims to identify deprivations that obstruct fulfillment, Nussbaum provides a list of ten capabilities. They are: (1) life; (2) bodily health; (3) bodily integrity; senses, imagination, and thought; (5) emotions; (6) practical reason; (7) affiliation; (8) other species; (9) play; and (10) political and material control over one's environment. "Nussbaum is being praised for providing a richer and more applicable and realistic framework that can be used to evaluate every individual's well-being" (Saigarana, 2015, p.2)

"Social institutions, including the family, community and neighbourhood associations, trade unions, social movements, political parties, and NGOs are all important in influencing the production of different capabilities" (Stewart, 2013, p. 3). Social Institutions impact on capabilities, freedoms, and opportunities through conversion factors.

12.2.2 Conversion Factors: Social Intuitions and Multiples Intelligences

Social institutions, such as family, peers, and schools, (2.2.a) play a pivotal role in shaping children's development and behavior according to various social contexts. They teach individuals how to socialize and integrate into society while allowing them to express their uniqueness through their Multiple Intelligences (MIs) (2.2.b).

12.2.2.1 Social Institutions: Family, Peers, and School

Considered the first agent of socialization, family interactions, and behaviors, whether observed by or with children, shape values and norms. This institution conveys tolerance, respect, responsibility, honesty, and autonomy. Positive family support provides a secure context for learning experiences, resulting in enhanced skill development and self-confidence (Dupont et al., 2015). Parents' patterns shape behaviors that are responsible for success or failure in school. These behaviors impact children's cognitive and social growth. By investing in the creation of good conditions for children, by creating an "environmental home" that provides learning materials as well as positive encouragement, we can enhance students' cognition (Taylor et al., 2004).

Drawing on a theory background, Korir (2014) precises that:

- peer is a socialization agent.
- peer group is a small group sharing same values and activities.
- peer pressure is people from the peer group that encourage you or urge to do something in a conscious or unconscious way.
- Peer influence is "the more subtle form of peer pressure," "and it involves changing one's behavior to meet the perceived expectations of others".

The school institution serves as the primary environment where students not only acquire knowledge but also learn how to learn, developing their intellectual potential and nurturing emotional and relational skills. Within the classroom, teachers play a pivotal role in expanding the boundaries of the home environment. They facilitate the development of mutual respect, self-directed learning, discipline, collaborative teamwork, and problem-solving abilities.

As articulated by Blažević, "the type of school needed in today's world is one that fosters the comprehensive development of students, embraces diversity, and actively encourages both individualization and socialization within the classroom" (Blažević, 2016, p. 47). Socialization, in this context, refers to the manner in which individuals interact with and integrate into society and various communities. A school, in essence, serves as a microcosm of society, and individualization underscores the importance of respecting each student's unique identity and their distinct set of MIs.

12.2.2.2 Multiple Intelligences (MIs)

Conducting research on human potential and cognitive development, Gardner identified seven intelligences in the 1980s and added one more after a decade (see Table 12.1). Recognizing different intelligences implies a revolution in the way we teach. Uniform instructions should be replaced by instructions that correspond to the stronger student's intelligence. Gardner's theory permits students to develop their potential. Furthermore, it implies offering personalized learning, considering their differences as wealth rather than stereotyping them and putting them "in the same basket" (Morgan, 2021).

TABLE.12.1
Description of the Eighth Gardner's Mis (Morgan, 2021, p. 127–128)

Intelligence	Description of Intelligence
Linguistic	People with strong linguistic skills can use their native language, and sometimes other languages, to understand people and express their thoughts. Examples of professionals with above average intelligence levels in this area include writers and orators.
Logical-mathematical	Scientists are examples of people strong in logical-mathematical intelligence because they can manipulate numbers the way mathematicians do. They tend to have above average logical-mathematical skills also because of their knowledge of causal systems
Spatial	Spatial intelligence involves the skills people have to represent the spatial world. Spatially intelligent people tend to become painters, sculptors, and architects. Spatial intelligence is used more often in certain sciences like anatomy and topology.
Bodily-kinesthetic	This intelligence relates to the ability to use whole or certain body parts to create something, solve a problem, or display skills involving bodily movement at an event. Examples of professionals strong in this intelligence include athletes and dancers.
Musical	People with enhanced musical intelligence have a heightened ability to hear, recognize, and remember patterns. They think in music and can't get it out of their minds. In Frames of Mind, Gardner indicated that musical intelligence emerges earlier than other intelligences.
Interpersonal	The interpersonal intelligence involves one's ability to understand others. People strong in this intelligence can detect other people's moods, intentions, and desires. This intelligence is especially important for individuals who deal frequently with people like teachers, clinicians, and salespeople.
Intrapersonal	An enhanced understanding of oneself is a characteristic of someone strong in the intrapersonal intelligence. A developed intrapersonal intelligence enables people to anticipate how they would react to experiences and how to choose the experiences that can be beneficial. It also helps people be aware of the difficulties they might encounter.
Naturalist	The naturalist intelligence was added to the original seven. It relates to an individual's ability to differentiate among living things. People strong in this intelligence are good at classifying plants, minerals, and animals as well as rocks and grass.

As shown in the previous table, Naturalist was the eighth intelligence. According to Tirri et al. (2008), two intelligences were added as the eighth and ninth: Spiritual Intelligence, which includes the "capacity to transcend everyday experiences and use imagination" (p. 210), and Environmental Intelligence, which includes loving nature and respecting and caring about the environment.

12.2.3 Artificial Intelligence (AI) and ChatGPT

Guliyeva (2021) introduces Artificial Intelligence (AI) as "a system of thinking without a living organism" and draws connections between AI and ancient Greek legends and myths, such as the creation of the first robot Talos by Zeus, a giant robot with bronze wings designed to protect the island of Crete. While our physical abilities are limited, our mental abilities and imagination have allowed us to create powerful beings that can be more efficient than us, yet still under our control.

AI extends human abilities and can be described as "the imitation of all human intellectual abilities by computers" (Sheikh et al., 2023, p. 20). In 1936, Alan Turing introduced the concept of the "Turing machine," revolutionizing the field of computing. He permits to consider AI as a learning process with "the symbol processing hypothesis." He considered the machine as a child who can learn and where symbols replicate the logical flow of human decision-making. In common parlance, AI is often reduced to algorithms. Algorithms like "machine learning" (ML) and "deep learning" (DL), specifically "self-learning algorithms," are responsible for various tasks such as face or voice recognition and the development of Google's AlphaGo program, which demonstrated in 1961 that computers could beat humans at chess.

When discussing emails, we are referring to a modality of digital communication, and when mentioning "chat," we are alluding to chatbots and e-service chat. Digital communication is "any electronic transmission of information that has been encoded digitally and transmitted via digital media" (Grewal et al., 2022, p. 224), and a chatbot is "a computer program designed to simulate conversation with human users, especially over the internet" (Lexico Dictionaries, 2019 cited in Adamopoulou, 2020, p.1).

Based on Machine Learning, an AI technique, ChatGPT (GPT "Generative Pre-trained Transformer") can find patterns between received data and expected results. AI-based ChatGPT is task-dependent and varies across fields. Used in the Higher Education field, it could be incorporated and used to augment teaching and learning.

12.2.4 Cheating Behavior: Bandura's Social Cognitive Learning Theory (SCLT)

"Cheating-behaviors may be considered a form of academic dishonesty: it is a way to present others' academic work as ones' own interfering with the learning and the evaluation process, a fraudulent-means of achieving grades, being accompanied by the risk of detection and punishment" (Madara et al., 2016, p.108). Thus, presenting ChatGPT's academic work as one's own interferes with the learning and evaluation process.

Diego (2017) defines cheating as when a student attempts to gain an advantage or extra marks through dishonest or deceptive means. He explains that the reasons for cheating include:

- Peer pressure: Observing peers engaging in academic dishonesty behavior can encourage students, either belonging to the same group or aspiring to join it, to do the same.
- Home environment: Parents often shape their children's values, including honesty, and may exert pressure for good grades.
- Learners' learning styles: Learning styles, such as cognitive, affective, and physiological behavior, serve as relatively stable indicators of how learners perceive, interact with, and respond to the learning environment (pp. 124–125).
- School environment: Factors like competition for class ranks, lax policies on dishonesty, and a focus on performance goals (improving grades) rather than mastery goals (improving learning) contribute to cheating.
- Educational anxiety: This results from various sources of pressure, including parental, teacher, and school pressure to achieve high marks.

Diego also cites the Center for Academic Integrity, which reported that 75% of students in higher education admit to engaging in cheating behaviors. He emphasizes that peer pressure is the primary reason for cheating, and observing and copying other learners' answers are directly connected to Social Cognitive Learning Theory (SCLT).

Bandura's SCLT posits that we learn from others through observation, imitation, and modeling. Many behaviors, including moral thinking and moral behavior, can be learned through observing a parent or a teacher engaging in activities (Nabavi et al., 2012, korir, 2014).

Bandura's Social Cognitive Learning Theory (SCLT) asserts that individuals acquire knowledge and behaviors by observing, imitating, and modeling the actions of others (Nabavi et al., 2012). This theory extends to various aspects of learning, including moral thinking and moral behavior. Behaviors related to morality can be learned through the observation of parental or teacher engagement in specific activities (Korir, 2014).

12.2.5 Creative Behavior: Piaget's Theory

Gabora (2013) retains a standard definition of creativity: it is originality and appropriateness. She explained that it involves 4Ps: person, process, product, and place. A creative person can be detected through personality traits or through number of creators achieved (number of paintings, or poems ...), a creative process is determined by thoughts and stages involved in creating a creative product like dancing (physical) or painting (behavioral), and a place is an environmental condition like education or family support.

Creativity "is correlated with independence of judgment, self-confidence, aesthetic orientation, risk-taking, openness to experience, tolerance of ambiguity, impulsivity, lack of conscientiousness, high energy, attraction to and ability to handle complexity, problem sensitivity, flexibility, the ability to analyze, synthesize, evaluate, and reorganize information engage in divergent thinking. There is also evidence that creative individuals are more prone to anxiety and emotional (affective) disorders" (Gabora, 2013, pp. 1–2).

Gardner emphasizes that focusing on skill development can lead to creative products. He suggests that students should learn within an environment that provides opportunities **for active learning**, exposure to innovative ideas, and exploration. Creative students can also enhance problem-solving and critical-thinking skills (Morgan, 2021).

Active learning is the essence of constructivism Piaget's Theory. "The Piagetian perspective implies that interactions in groups can create the cognitive conflict and disequilibrium that leads an individual to question his or her understanding and try out **new ideas**".

Baum et al. (2019) introduce autonomy as a motivational trait for creativity and as a supportive environment for creative production. The self-determination theory (Deci & Ryan, 2000) considers autonomy to be the "organismic desire to self-organize experience and behavior and to have activity be concordant with one's integrated sense of self" (Baum et al., 2019, p. 3).

12.3 METHODOLOGY AND METHOD

As ChatGPT is a new tool offered to the world since last year, we investigate the purpose of Tunisian students, attending Tunisian universities last year, using it as a learning tool. Thus, exploratory qualitative research (3.1.)) is needed, and findings will help to build theory. Qualitative research relies on the participants' responses depending on their own experiences. To choose how to collect data, how to select participants (in-depth interview (3.2.)), how to formulate questions (interview guide (3.3.)) and the way selected to analyze this data (Thematical Analysis (3.4.)) pertains to the method.

12.3.1 Qualitative Research

When the focus is understanding experiences and reflections about them, human subjective' perceptions and perspectives, and in general, when more information about a phenomenon is needed then qualitative research is appropriate. How have Tunisian students used ChatGPT last year during their academic achievement? Understanding their own personal goals through using ChatGPT, understanding factors that can mediate or moderate the freedom to choose one of the different opportunities of how we can use ChatGPT, and its impact on personal learning and behavior, must be explored.

Searching to better understand the antecedents and consequences of why using ChatGPT, to better understand this new social phenomenon of ChatGPT as a mean to achieve student learning, justifies the use of an inductive approach (Evrard et al. 1993, p. 59). Called also "the bottom-up approach," it permits to generate premises and to build theory based on real observations, and it permits to move from the specific to the general (Burney et al., 2008). In fact, relying on participants' responses, results' interpretations will help to bring more insights to this social phenomenon.

Qualitative research approaches are mainly three: grounded theory, phenomenology, and ethnography (Bolderston, 2012). According to Bevan (2014), phenomenological research investigates a person's lifeworld experience and interview is an appropriate means to explain it. In a narrative way, interviewee can describe using analogy, chronology … It takes the interviewee's reflections as a base to understand and interpret by interviewer, the listener.

12.3.2 In-depth Interview

As a method for gathering information about participants' experiences and perceptions, the in-depth interview is often the preferred choice. The techniques for conducting interviews are determined by two main factors: the mode of interview (face-to-face or remote) and the format (structured, semi-structured, or unstructured). Face-to-face interviews, often referred to as one-to-one interviews, are favorable for collecting narrative data. Semi-structured interviews are commonly used due to their various advantages (Taherdoost, 2022).

Despite being time-consuming, in-depth interviews have several advantages, including the ability to:

1. Provide precise information with spontaneous issues that can generate new concepts (Taherdoost, 2022; Ryan et al., 2009).
2. Allow the flexibility to change the wording of questions for better clarification by the interviewer (Taherdoost, 2022; Ryan et al., 2009).
3. Create a stress-free atmosphere and a relaxed environment to make participants more comfortable during the conversation (Boyce and Neale, 2006).
4. Enable the interviewer to analyze nonverbal behaviors such as intonation, speaking time, head gestures, body posture, and facial expressions (Rupasinghe et al., 2016).
5. Be flexible and adaptable, especially with open-ended questions that allow participants to express themselves (Bevan, 2014).

When choosing qualitative research with a phenomenological in-depth interview, a small number of participants is typically required. According to Bolderston (2012), "for a typical phenomenological study, the total number may be around 10 participants" (p. 68). In order to capture interview data effectively, it is considered appropriate to record the interviews. In-depth interviews generally have a duration ranging from 30 minutes to over an hour (Jamshed, 2014; DiCicco-Bloom, 2016).

Students' experiences with the use of ChatGPT during their last year of academic achievement constitute the social phenomenon under investigation. To collect data, we opted for in-depth interviews. These interviews were conducted through face-to-face interactions using online digital communication platforms, specifically Zoom and Google Teams. Audio recording was utilized to ensure no data was missed. Participants were selected based on two criteria: they had successfully completed their university studies in the last year at a Tunisian university and had used ChatGPT during their academic coursework. A total of 10 interviews were conducted in August 2023, with each interview lasting an average of 25 to 47 minutes.

12.3.3 Guide Interview

For phenomenological study, semi-structured reflective interviews should be considered (Bolderston, 2012). Furthermore, themes and questions regarding interview guide must be identified in advance in the literature (Azungah, 2018) and must cover important areas. "Themes are abstract and subtle expressions/patterns/processes that explain a phenomenon" (Mishra and Dey, 2022, p. 188). They can be identified through a literature review (before data collection), through participants' expressions (during data collection), or through the step of analysis (during data analysis). Before data collection, 5 to 6 themes and 10 to 20 subthemes maximum should be integrated into a guide interview (Andreani, p. 31).

For semi-structured interviews and in-depth interview, an interview guide is developed. It "is a schematic presentation of questions or topics and need to be explored by the interviewers" (Jamshed, 2014, p. 87).

Before data collection, we retained four themes: Perceived Influence of Social Institutions, Multiple Intelligences (MIs), Capabilities and, ChatGPT Using Purpose. For the first theme, we used three questions relative respectively to the influence of family, peers, and school. For the second one, we developed questions considering Gardens' MIs items (Tirri et al., 2008). For the third one, we developed 10 questions considering Nussbaum's items. For the last one, few questions were developed.

12.3.4 Thematic Analysis

As explained by Wæraas (2022), after qualitative data collection, researcher, as interviewer, must be creative to attribute meaning to data.

First, he must eliminate the empty words that are not related to the central subject and consider "text segments" (coding units) to retain as significant units: codes. "As a rule of thumb, the coded text segment should always be sufficiently large to retain its meaning when taken out of context" (Wæraas, 2022, p. 155). Semantic codes, generated from verbal communication, can be either in vivo; cited by interviewee, or descriptive; or created by researcher. "A data structure table helps to capture evolution from theoretical to coding" (Mishra and Dey, 2022, p. 191). Bree and Gallagher explain how to use Microsoft Excel to code and help identify themes.

Second, he must reduce codes into themes or categories which "encapsulate the meanings conveyed by many codes" (Wæraas, 2022, p. 6). Identification of emerging themes or categories help to structure coded data. Frequencies represent the number of times that a theme was mentioned or discussed in the total number of comments analyzed (Firat, 2023). Frequencies permit a first interpretation of the data. The second interpretation will rely on matrices with the cross of conceptualized variables. The third one is an inference derived from interviewee's statements. We choose to consider the first interview for inference (researcher can treat one theme for all interviewees or one interviewee for all themes (Wacheaux, 1996, p. 239). The fourth and last is the discussion of results.

To avoid the risk of privileging a quantification at the expense of critical thinking, of rigidity of the analysis (software logic and reflection are different from the researcher's one), and of amplifying the researcher-interviewee distance (Krief et al., 2013), we have opted for manual analysis without using the software.

12.4 DATA ANALYSIS

Participants characteristics (4.1.) are collected at the beginning of the interview. After reducing codes from data analysis based on interviews, we got emerged categories that encapsulates codes. The emerged categories importance is determined by calculating frequencies (4.2.). They were affected in matrices (4.3.) representing crossing conceptual variables. After inference (4.4.) we highlight results and discuss them (4.5.).

12.4.1 Participants Characteristics

All participants are Tunisian. Two selective considerations considered: to be academic and used ChatGPT last year during academic year. Our first concern is the perceived use of ChatGPT in Higher Education. As shown in table one, participants are in total 10 Tunisian academic students of

TABLE 12.2
Demographic Participants Characteristics

Interviewer number	Gender	Grade achieved last year	Field/Subject
1	Female	second	Masterin Music and Musicology
2	Male	second	Finance and accountancy
3	Female	fifth	Mathematical (pursuing doctorate this year)
4	Female	second	Engineer
5	Female	second	Engineer
6	Female	first	International commerce
7	Male	first	Marketing
8	Female	seventh	Medical
9	Male	third	Digital Marketing
10	Female	first	Master Marketing research

which three are males and seven are females. The sample is heterogeneous, including different grades and different fields. One in the musical field, one in financial and accountancy, one in mathematical, two in engineering, one in international commerce, one in medical, and three in marketing. (Table 12.2)

12.4.2 Emerged Categories and Frequencies

Categories or themes and their frequencies are exposed in what follows.

12.4.2.1 Perceived Social Institutions' Influence

Figure 12.4 illustrates that students perceive their **family** to have the most influence on their "learning and skills development" (50%), followed by their "personal growth and responsibility" (22.22%), their "interactions and challenges" (16.7%), and the enhancement of their self-confidence (11.11%).

Perceived peers' influence is explained at 56.25% through learning and skills development and at 43.75% through personal growth and decision-making.

Perceived school influence is explained at 39.13% through teacher-student interactions and skill development at 34.78% through autonomy and self-learning enhancement and, at 26.09% through challenges in the education system.

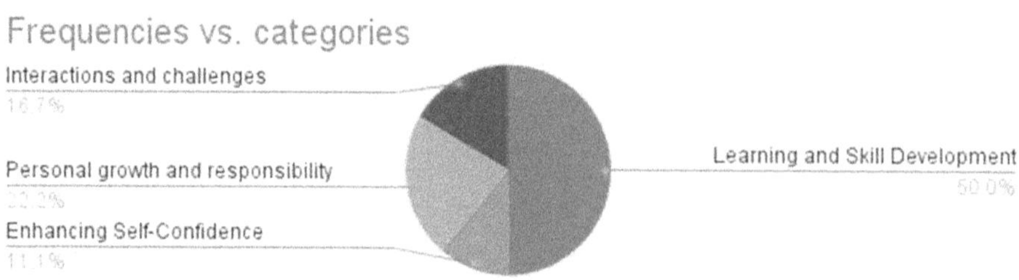

FIGURE 12.4 Themes related to perceived family influence according to their frequencies.

12.4.2.2 Perceived MIs

Perceived Linguistic Intelligence is explained at 50% through perceived competencies and assessment, at 28,12% through learning and skills development, at 12.5% through language preferences, at 6.25% through challenges in education, and at 3.33% through creativity.

Perceived Logico-Mathematical Intelligence is explained at 47.62%, through perceived competencies and assessment, at 33.33% through learning and skill development, and at 19.05% through preferences considering scientific subjects.

Perceived Visual-Spatial Intelligence is explained at 47.62% through perceived competencies and assessment concerning environmental orientation, at 33.33% through perceived competencies and assessment concerning 3d technical skills, at 14.29% through perceived competencies and assessment concerning imagination and visualization, and at 4.77% through learning and skill development.

Perceived Bodily-Kinesthetic Intelligence is explained at 45.83% through enhancement of learning skill and creativity, at 8,33% through hand-use functionality, at 41.66% through perceived and assessment, and at 4.17% through challenges and personal growth.

Perceived Musical Intelligence is explained at 50% through perceived competencies concerning music, at 27.78% through perceived preferences concerning music, at 16.66% through music's impact on mood and motivation, and at 2.78% through music's enhancement of creativity.

Perceived Interpersonal Intelligence is explained at 54.55% through perceived social interactions, at 30.30% through perceived preferences concerning social interactions, at 9.09% through challenges in social interactions, and at 6.06% through communication and skill development.

Perceived Intrapersonal Intelligence is explained at 29.73% through cognitive awareness and self-reflection, at 29.73% through perceived attitude toward ethical moral and respect values, at 16.22% through skill development and decision-making, at 16.22% through honesty and trustworthiness in relationships, and at 8.10% through self-reflection and emotional impact.

Perceived Spiritual Intelligence is explained at 46.66% through immersive creativity, at 26.67% through realistic spiritual connections, and at 26.67% through realistic without imaginative world.

Perceived Environmental Intelligence is explained at 37.2% through perceived preferences and connections regarding nature, at 32.56% environmentally responsible advocate, at 20.93% through evolving environmental advocate, at 6.98% through challenges in the education system, and at 2,33% through nature enhances creativity.

12.4.2.3 Perceived Capabilities

Perceived Life's Capability is explained at 60% through a healthier lifestyle, at 26.67% through material well-beingimportance and, at 13.33% through self-learning and autonomy.

Perceived Bodily Health's Capability is explained at 66.67% through perceived medical accessibility, at 25% through Self-reliance health care, at 8.33% through challenges in a medical environment.

Perceived Bodily-Integrity's Capability is explained at 45.45% through security and perceived self-protection, 40.91% through perceived freedom of movement, and at 13.64% through virtual versus real empowerment self-protection.

Perceived Senses, Imagination, and Thoughts' Capability are 100% explained through the perceived use of cognitive and emotional capabilities.

Perceived Practical Thinking's Capability is explained at 54.55% through critical thinking and decision-making and at 45.45% through situational ethics and moral differentiation.

Perceived Emotions'Capability is explained at 66.67% through learning and, communicational and emotional skill development and at 33.33% through emotional sensitivity and empathy.

Perceived Affiliation's Capability is explained at 68.75% through values and social integration, and at 31.25% through social integration and decision-making.

Perceived Other Species' Capability is explained at 90.10% through perceived preferences and attitudes toward species and at 9.10% through environmentally responsible advocates.

Perceived Play's Capability is explained at 31.25% through managing emotions and at 68.75% through perceived happiness.

Perceived Control over One's Environment's Capability is explained at 40% through perceived control over environment, at 10% through challenges to freedom expression, at 20% through challenges in transport, at 10% through challenges in education, and at 20% through skill development.

12.4.2.4 Perceived ChatGPT Using Purpose

First, 27.86% of participants use ChatGPT as a learning tool to enhance their learning experience. Second, 26.58% of them use it for its effectiveness and efficiency. Third, 13.92% of the participants use it to enhance self-learning, autonomy, creativity, and entrepreneurship. Fourth, 5.06% of them use ChatGPT as a social interaction.

Regarding barriers to the use of ChatGPT, 17.72% of participants explain that cheating behavior is due to challenges in the education system and in learning, and 8.86% of participants give some perceived limitations of ChatGPT use.

12.4.3 Matrices: Crossing Conceptual Variables

Crossing conceptual variables, we found the following relations of different social influences and MIs:

Family can:

- enhance Linguistic, Logico-Mathematical, Visual-spatial, and Bodily-kinesthetics' Intelligences through the enhancement of Learning Skill Development.
- promote Bodily-kinesthetics' Intelligence through Personal Growth.
  foster Interpersonal Intelligence through Interactions and Challenges.
- cultivate Intrapersonal Intelligence through skill Development and Decision-Making.
- support Environmental Intelligence through Skill Development.

Peers can:

- enhance Linguistic, Logico-Mathematical, and Visual-spatial Intelligences through the enhancement of Learning Skill Development.
- promote Bodily-Kinesthetics' Intelligence through Skill acquisition and Personal Growth.
- nurture Intrapersonal Intelligence through skill Development and Decision-Making.
- support Environmental Intelligence through skill development.

School can:

- enhance Linguistic, Logico-Mathematical, Visual-spatial, Bodily-kinesthetics, and Intrapersonal Intelligences through the enhancement of Learning Skill Development.
- support Linguistic and Environmental Intelligence through Skill Development and Challenges in Education.

We report the following relations between social influence and capabilities:
Family's Influence can:

- enhance Life Capability through Self-Learning and Autonomy.
- promote expressing emotions through Learning Skill Development.
- supportSpecies Capability through Environmental Responsibility.
- promote one's Control over Environment Capability through Skill Development.

Peer's Influence can:

- enhance life Capability through Self-Learning.
- promote Practical Think Capability through Decision-Making.
- support Emotions Capability through Learning Skill Development.
- reinforce Affiliation Capability through Skill Development and Decision-Making.

School's Influence can:

- enhance Life Capability through Self-Learning,
- support Emotion Capability through Skill Development.
- reinforce one's Control over Environment Capability through Skill Development and Challenges in Education.

Crossing MIs and ChatGPT using purpose, as a learning tool and a supporting creative behavior, we found:

- Linguistic, Bodily-Kinesthetic, Logical-Mathematical, and Visual-Spatial Intelligences and ChatGPT using purpose as a learning tool enhance Learning Skill Development.
- Linguistic, Bodily-Kinesthetic, Musical, Spiritual, EnvironmentalIntelligencesand ChatGPT using purpose as a learning tool promote Creativity.
- Intrapersonal and Interpersonal Intelligences and ChatGPT using purpose as a learning tool promote skill development.
- Intrapersonal Intelligence and ChatGPT using purpose as a learning tool enhance social interactions.

Crossing MIs and ChatGPT using purpose, as a cheating tool, we found:

- Linguistic, Bodily-Kinesthetic, Logical-Mathematical, and Visual-Spatial Intelligences and ChatGPT using purpose as a cheating tool diminish Learning Skill Development.
- Linguistic and Environmental intelligence as well as ChatGPT using purpose as a cheating tool enhance Challenges in Education.

Crossingcapabilities and ChatGPT using purpose as a learning tool and a supporting creative behavior, we found:

- Life capability and ChatGPT use enhance self-learning and autonomy.
- Emotion capability and ChatGPT use enhance Learning and skill development.
- Affiliation capability and ChatGPT use promote social integration.
- One's control over environment capability and ChatGPT use favorize social interaction.

CrossingCapabilities and ChatGPT using purpose, as a cheating behavior, we found:

- Life capability and ChatGPT use diminish self-learning and autonomy. Used like an effortless and lazy tool means that opportunities are reduced.
- Practical think and ChatGPT use diminish self-learning skills.
- One's control over environment capability and ChatGPT using as a cheating tool augment challenges in the education system.

12.4.4 Inference

The first interviewee, a female, achieved a diploma in Ergo-therapy and concurrently earned her master's degree in musicology last year. Maternal support encouraged her to overcome her timidity, be confident, and pursue her studies as well as playing musical instruments. In addition to continuous encouragement, she learned terms related to Ergo-therapy just by observing her mom. She mentioned, "Indirectly, by listening to conversations between my mom and her students, I increased my general knowledge as well as scientific knowledge," and "I learned first aid before attending class," and "Anatomy," so "I was ready to delve deeper into them." Music allowed her to start tutoring from the age of eighteen, enabling her to assist disabled individuals.

Maternal influence not only enhanced her skills through observation and encouragement but also helped her daughter boost her confidence, develop her musical intelligence (high intelligence in music), her logical-mathematical intelligence (high intelligence in the scientific domain related to medicine), and her autonomy (as she became a tutor). Her mom's commitment to conserving water also contributed to enhancing her environmental awareness and capabilities.

"Through observing her father's behavior, she is reproducing same method to memorize and update her knowledge used by her father: creating revision notes. Her father explains to her how to keep clean environment such as using a bag to throw out garbage. ''Later, we were in the car, he was angry after the cd and throw it by the window. So, I said, you are polluting. He replayed: it's already polluted. I answered, but it's not an excuse. Finally, he apologized." Father's influence enhances skill development, learning, using social and cognitive learning processes (Bandura), and environmental capability.

Her peers have allowed her to develop skills through observation, as she notes, "Taking the strong points from peers helps you to see yours." They have enhanced her confidence, learning abilities, and critical thinking. "My brother encourages me to always think critically." Thus, both peers and family have contributed to her development of critical thinking and practical thinking capabilities. However, peers have also had a negative influence as they have negatively impacted her linguistic intelligence in the French language.

Regarding the influence of school, she has gained autonomy, self-learning skills, and problem-solving abilities, all of which involve critical thinking and creativity. Nevertheless, she recalls a teacher who overly criticized her, leading to a decrease in her self-esteem (her intonation was sad, and she averted her eyes).

In general, she perceives that social institutions have enhanced her confidence, critical thinking, skill development, autonomy, self-learning, and problem-solving aptitude.

She perceived high linguistic intelligence in native language, average logical-mathematical intelligence (need tools to solve a complex problem), low visual-spatial intelligence ("I'm working on it. It's difficult; it takes time"), high bodily-kinesthetic in hand use (creative products like origami), high musical intelligence (she is a musician), average interpersonal intelligence with social anxiety, very high intrapersonal intelligence (I read a book on personal development), high spiritual intelligence ("When things become difficult, I need to go to my imaginative world." "I talk to my self-considering mini-me to tell her its ok; dedramatizing."), and very high environmental intelligence ("feeling responsible and engaged"). Furthermore, her parents communicated and shared activities to nurture her environmental commitment.

She can enjoy good health and lead a fulfilling life (life's capability). She can easily access medical care (bodily health's capability). She can move freely, although her ability to protect herself depends on the location ("zero protection when taking the metro") (bodily integrity's capability). She can use her senses, imagination, and thoughts without any restrictions. She believes she must learn how to express her emotions, as she sometimes feels shy. She possesses a high potential for critical thinking but finds that distinguishing between good and evil is contextual ("When I did Ergo-therapy, I saw parents beating their child. At first, you are shocked, but later you understand.") (practical thinking capability). She finds respect and empathy within social groups (affiliation's capability). She lives in harmony with other species ("I already have two cats"). She enjoys playing, laughing, and taking breaks (play's capability). However, she encounters problems related to transportation (control over one's environment's capability).

Last year, she used ChatGPT for learning ("I learned Japanese") but also like a friend with whom she had a conversation. She told him to tell jokes. She used it also in a creative way: ask him to invent an end to a film and sometimes "gave ideas and tell it to rewrite the end." Plagiarism is not the major problem; laziness is the one. In fact, plagiarism means to be effortless and reduces our own capacity.

12.4.5 Results and Discussion

All ten interviewees (100% of the sample size) reported a positive influence of their families on their competencies, grades, and academic development. However, two of them also reported instances of discouragement: one was discouraged from studying outside of the city, and another was discouraged from prioritizing music over studying. These instances highlight the significant impact of family on academic performance and the development of special skills. Two female interviewees developed musical intelligence by learning a musical instrument, encouraged by their mothers. Based on these findings, we can conclude that **there is a positive perceived family influence on students' perceived MIs.**

All ten interviewees (100% of the sample size) reported a positive influence of their peers on their competencies, academic development through learning, observing, or advice. One female added that the influence of peers depends entirely on her choice of peers. We can advance that **there is a positive perceived peer's influence on students' perceived MIs.**

Seven interviewees (70% of the sample size) reported a positive influence of school on autonomy and academic performance. However, two females reported a negative influence from teachers, with one of them stating that this influence ultimately had a positive impact on her. Additionally, three interviewees reported experiencing only negative school influences, which included challenges related to traditional pedagogy, lack of resources, and academic failures that they were able to transform into success. Considering these findings, we can conclude that **there is a positive perceived school influence on students' perceived MIs.**

In general, we can highlight that **there is a positive perceived social influence on students' perceived MIs.**

50% of our sample reported that their movements are restricted by family (interviewee 2, 3, 6, 7, and 9). **Students perceived family as restricting their bodily integrity in terms of freedom to move.**

Interviewee 1 has a high bodily-kinesthetic, and her creativity is shown in products like origami, a high musical intelligence with a good sense of interpretation (generating new ideas), a high spirituality (generating new ideas), and she has developed her critical thinking (arguing, synthesis ...). She used ChatGPT to enhance learning (e.g., learning Japanese) and creativity (give it ideas and tell it to reinvent the end of a film).

Interviewee 2 has high Logical-mathematical (persistent and challenging), high bodily-kinesthetic (love constructions; creativity solving-problem)), and high musical intelligence (rhythmics as motivations). He used ChatGPT for research (new ideas, creativity) and for tutoring (enhanced learning skills).

Interviewee 3 has high visual-spatial, high mathematical-logical, and high spiritual intelligence (generating new ideas). She used ChatGPT for self-learning and tutoring.

Interviewee 4 has high linguistic intelligence, high logical-mathematical, and high musical intelligence. She used ChatGPT for research; creativity (generating new ideas); and self-learning.

Interviewee 5 has high linguistic intelligence, high mathematical logic, high bodily-kinesthetic (construction), and high musical intelligence (good interpretation). Used ChatGPT for self-learning and gained autonomy and consequently creativity.

Interviewee 6 has a high Arabic linguistic intelligence using it in a creative way writing novels, high logical-mathematical (persistent), high visual-spatial, high bodily-kinesthetic with doing creative products like crochet, high musical intelligence with a sense of interpretation and using music to feel emotions and to be more creative in writing, and high spirituality. She used ChatGPT for research (creativity) and learning.

Interviewee 7 has high Arabic linguistic intelligence, high visual-spatial, high bodily-kinesthetic (drawing while listening to music; creative product), high spiritual Intelligence, high musical intelligence, and high environmental intelligence (nature is an aspiration). He used ChatGPT for learning as well as to help him to have his startup. ChatGPT used as a tool of learning and creativity.

Interviewee 8 has high linguistic intelligence, high musical intelligence with a good sense of interpretation, high bodily-kinesthetic (that is why she wanted to do chirurgical specialty), high spirituality, and high environmental (feel in harmony). She used ChatGPT as a tool for learning.

Interviewee 9 has high English linguistic intelligence, high logical-mathematical (perseverant), and high musical intelligence (intrinsic motivation, source of energy). He used ChatGPT to improve learning, asking for videos schemas and image syntheses.

Interviewee 10 has high bodily-kinesthetic with drawing and dancing activities, high musical intelligence with a good sense of interpretation, and high spirituality combined with music. She used ChatGPT to synthesize and set plans and to enhance learning.

The ten interviewed (100%) have used ChatGPT as a learning tool, to construct their knowledge, and to enhance their learning experience and skills development. Six of them (60%), possess high multiple intelligences that promote their creativity use ChatGPT as a creative tool. Thus, we can presume that **MIs have a positive effect on ChatGPT using purpose as a learning tool that promotes learning and creativity.**

The United Nations Economic Commission for Europe (UNECE) Strategy for Education for Sustainable Development (ESD) expresses the vision that ESD should "equip people with knowledge of and skills in sustainable development, making them more competent and confident and increasing their opportunities for acting for a healthy and productive life in harmony with nature and with concern for social values, gender equity and cultural diversity". Hofmann proposes a table crossing ESD and Human capabilities. He associated for each skill developed the central capabilities implied. Thus, when ESD provides skills for:

- learning to know, the central capability is "practical reason."
- learning to be, the central capabilities are "Senses, Imagination, and Thought" and "Play."
- learning to live together, the central capabilities are "Affiliation", "Emotions," and "Other species."
- Learning to do, the central capabilities are "Life," "Bodily Health," "Bodily Integrity," and "Control of One's Environment."

Interview 1 has good life and bodily health capabilities. Bodily integrity is restricted in terms of moving by family and control of one's environment is limited by transport problem. In general, there is required basic capabilities as means for learning to do. She feels affiliated, in harmony but still needs to learn how to express emotions She has to enhance "learning together." She has total freedom to use senses, imagination, and thought, and she knows to be joyful, with high learning-to-be. Finally, she has a high presence of critical thinking, which allowed her learning to know and recognize challenges.

As using ChatGPT implies "learning to know" all interviewees (100%) reported a high perceived critical think. We can stipulate that **Critical thinking capability enhances ChatGPT's purpose use as a learning tool that promotes learning and creativity.**

Only two students reported having cheated under pressure only once, which shows that ChatGPT is mostly used as a learning tool.

12.5 CONCLUSION

Are Tunisian students ready to use ChatGPT as a learning tool and a means to enhance creativity, as an opportunity? Qualitative research conducted in August 2023, involving ten interviewees from different fields and backgrounds who used ChatGPT during their academic year last year, reveals that:

- Tunisian students use ChatGPT in a constructive way to enhance their learning (all ten reported using ChatGPT for learning). Furthermore, six of the interviewees reported that their experience with ChatGPT improved their self-directed learning. Han et al. (2022) found that artificial intelligence chatbot programs fostered interest in education among nursing college students and promoted self-directed learning.
- Tunisian students use ChatGPT in a creative way to generate new ideas and solve problems, such as continuing a film, preparing the opening of a startup, or understanding a methodology. One of the interviewees used ChatGPT to watch videos and request mind maps as a synthesis for learning. As advanced by Zhai (2023), the diverse knowledge sources offered by ChatGPT enhance motivation in learning and promote creative thinking and abilities.
- Tunisian students show a high awareness of their critical thinking capability (all ten interviews reported that they have critical thinking) which can promote their use of ChatGPT in a creative way. Iskender (2023), using GPT as interviewee, found that over-relying on ChatGPT can impede critical thinking. It can also generate new ideas and perspectives promoting creativity.
- Tunisian students use ChatGPT for its efficiency (two interviewees used it under time pressure and three to save time). In fact, ChatGPT could become a promising and powerful tool considering time-saving and efficient aspects in academic activities for both scholars, who can create lessons, and students, who can conduct research (Eke, 2023; Salvagno et al., 2023).

Chatbots and ChatGPT have the potential to revolutionize education. Promoting self-learning with feedback and used in a creative, appropriate, and ethical way, it can lead to valuable outcomes. It engages students in a constructive learning process which transforms traditional learning where students memorize in a passive way. "ChatGPT, functioning as an intelligent learning assistant, is useful for promoting task-driven project-based learning, which transforms traditional passive learning" (Zhai, 2023, p. 2). With ChatGPT, Tunisian students can find more precise and diversified resources and can learn at one's own pace. ChatGPT is welcomed to integrate Tunisian universities as a pedagogical approach enabling personalized learning and creativity. ChatGPT using purpose is impacted by social influences mediated by Multiple Intelligences and Critical thinking capabilities. Positive supports and conducive environment for developing autonomy, arguing, and critical thinking, and for developing personal growth that will have a positive effect on MI and creativity.

12.5.1 Practical Recommendations

We found that ChatGPT enhances self-learning. ChatGPT helps students actively construct their knowledge and provides personalized feedback to improve the acquisition of new knowledge. It operates based on existing knowledge, making it a dynamic, active, and adaptive learning tool aligned with constructivist learning theory. Therefore, ChatGPT should be integrated into Tunisian universities as a pedagogical approach by scholars and the ministry, with guidance to limit its use in an ethical manner for a favorable outcome.

Considering that students have different learning styles (Multiple Intelligences - MIs) and varying needs for personalized learning, Tunisian scholars can create customized learning plans for their students and guide them on how to make the most of ChatGPT. Both scholars and students share the goal of achieving educational quality.

Critical thinking capability has the potential to promote the use of ChatGPT in a creative way enhancing critical thinking (Iskender, 2023). Ministry, universities, and scholars must prioritize the cultivation of critical thinking capability to enhance students' creativity.

Four interviewees mentioned using ChatGPT as an Intelligent Tutoring System, emphasizing its efficiency, trustworthiness, effectiveness, and up-to-date nature compared to teachers. Based on qualitative research and drawing from 138 articles on Artificial Intelligence in Higher Education, Crompton and Burke (2023) found that AI is utilized in Higher Education for several purposes: automating assessments (which reduces instructors' workload and enables the generation of a multitude of questions), automatic grading, facilitating self-regulated learning for students, predicting students' future grades as a measure of academic performance, providing assistance to students through features like chatbots, employing Intelligent Tutoring Systems (ITS) for efficient feedback and guidance, and managing student learning (by offering analytical data and information that helps instructors and administrators design Higher Education systems and shape student profiles). Teachers are encouraged to continually update their pedagogical resources to remain as credible as ChatGPT in the eyes of their students.

We found that Tunisian students perceived school influence through teacher-student interactions and skill development, through autonomy and self-learning enhancement, and through challenges in the education system.

Autonomy and self-learning are important to led to creativity (Iwata, 2013). Xhaferi et al. (2011) highlighted autonomous learning should have other sources than teachers only such as technology-based approaches and concluded that promoting learners' autonomy is a complex process in Macedonia which relies on traditional pedagogy. Furthermore, cheikh et al. (2021) said that the educational system has to be reformed in order to assert learners' autonomy readiness. Ministry has the responsibility to reform Tunisian Education system and scholars has to introduce new strategies to accompany students to change their learning process in a constructive, autonomous, and creative one.

Challenges in the education system appears to pertain to the lack of resources especially for practical applications, the old pedagogical tool, the focus on memorizing and transmission rather than evaluating the real capacities and the teacher discouragement and over criticism affecting self-esteem. Rahmouni (2020) also evocated this pedagogical problem (obsolete teaching method, teaching in indoctrination) as a weakness point of Tunisian Education. Challenges in education appears to have an impact on perceived environmental intelligence ("I'm chocked that how to protect environment is no more taught in class," "Educational system become deteriorate," "Environmental protection need to be taught in school") as one interviewee underlined the importance of school to establish values and responsibility and an impact on how to use ChatGPT to enhance their marks as school pressure (Diego, 2017).

We also noted that OpenAI developed ChatGPT with certain limitations:

- ChatGPT may not be suitable for all fields. For instance, one interviewee mentioned that he could not find information related to Tunisian accounting. OpenAI should consider incorporating national specificities. Alternatively, Tunisians could seize this opportunity to develop a specialized Tunisian chatbot tailored for accounting in Tunisia.
- ChatGPT has been found to generate false references, as reported by two interviewees. In a study by Haman and Školník (2023), ChatGPT was tested for conducting literature reviews, and it was found to provide false or non-existent papers in 66% of the cases. From an ethical standpoint, they argued that ChatGPT cannot be held responsible for literature research, as it is not a coauthor. Therefore, relying on it for such purposes is considered unethical. Consequently, students should refrain from using ChatGPT for article research, and OpenAI should work to address these imperfections in order to enhance the usefulness of ChatGPT.
- ChatGPT remains theoretical and cannot provide practical training. As one interviewee noted, 'ChatGPT cannot offer practical experience; we need teachers as human guides.' Teachers are irreplaceable when it comes to practical training, so they should incorporate hands-on practice into their pedagogies and lessons to meet students' needs and maintain the relevance of their workforces.
- ChatGPT has been observed to have a negative impact on students' behavior according to interviewees:
  - Five interviewees expressed concerns about students becoming lazy and adopting a less effortful approach to their work when relying too heavily on ChatGPT. One interviewee stated, "If I rely on it, I diminish my own capacity." Therefore, students must use ChatGPT cautiously, reformulate answers, and verify the accuracy of information to maintain their academic integrity. The Ministry and scholars should provide guidance in this regard.
  - One interviewee raised the issue of students becoming addicted to daily use of ChatGPT. While ChatGPT is a useful tool, it should not become indispensable for students.
  - Interviewees also emphasized that plagiarism should not be treated as an ethical problem but as having a negative effect on students. It may provide short-term satisfaction through grade inflation, decrease self-esteem, and encourage lazy behavior which can even "remove the task of memorization." One interviewee suggested that the fault lies with the educational system that prioritizes grades. Another mentioned, "Plagiarism, like copy-paste, has been a practice even before with Wikipedia." Ministry should consider making changes in the strategies related to the Tunisian education system and transform the old traditional learning method.

12.5.2 Future Research

For a more comprehensive understanding of the implications of and the readiness for integrating ChatGPT in higher education, further researchers are needed such as:

- Collecting Opinions of other stakeholders including stuff and scholars.
- Collecting Opinions of Tunisian students attending private Tunisians universities.
- Comparing between Tunisian and other nationalities perceptions toward ChatGPT use as a learning tool.
- Finding ways to ensure that all stakeholders interact effectively for positive results on student achievement.

- Investing, with a larger sample or with quantitative research, the mediating role of MIs between perceived social institutions and using ChatGPT as a learning and creative tool. Our interesting findings driven from a qualitative research serve as a starting point for further investigation.

12.5.3 Limitations

In qualitative research, researchers are often considered instruments themselves. Methodological limitations can arise from researchers' bias, which includes subjective analysis and interpretations, as well as retrospective bias, where interviewees must remember their past use of ChatGPT to assess their last year's grade. Additionally, offering interviewees the freedom to express their perceptions in any language can provide valuable information but may introduce the possibility of translation bias.

REFERENCES

Aguayo, B. B., Ruano, C. A. and Vallejo, A. P. (2021), "Multiple intelligences: Educational and cognitive development with a guiding focus", South African Journal of Education, Vol. 41, No. 2, pp. 1–15.

Azungah, T. (2018), "Qualitative research: Deductive and inductive approaches to data analysis", Qualitative Research Journal, Vol. 18, pp. 383–400.

Baum, I. R. and Baumann, N. (2019), "Autonomous creativity: The implicit autonomy motive fosters creative production and innovative behavior at school", Gifted and Talented International, Vol. 3, No. 1–2, pp. 1–11.

Bevan, M. (2014), "A method of phenomenological interviewing", Qualitative Health Research, Vol. 24, No. 1, pp. 136–144.

Blažević, I. (2016), "Family, peer, and school influence on children's social development" World Journal of Education, Vol. 6, No. 2, pp. 42–49.

Bolderston, A. (2012), "Conducting a research interview", Journal of Medical Imaging and Radiation Sciences, Vol. 43, No. 1, pp. 66–76.

Boyce, C., and Neale, P. (2006), "Conducting in-depth interviews: A guide for designing and Conducting in-depth Interviews for evaluation input", Pathfinder international: conducting in-depth interviews, pp. 1–12.

Burney, S. M. A., and Saleem, H. (2008), "Inductive & Deductive Research Approach", Lecture delivered on 06-03-2008 at Auditorium of Faculty of Arts and Science, University of Karachi, Karachi, Pakistan.

Cheikh, K. (2021), "Insights about developing learners' autonomy in Tunisia", 4 pages. https://www.academia.edu/45061452/Insights_about_developing_learners_autonomy_in_Tunisia

Crompton, H., and Burke, D. (2023), "Artificial intelligence in higher education: the state of the field", International Journal of Educational Technology in Higher Education, Vol. 20, No. 22, pp. 1–22.

DiCicco-Bloom, B, and Crabtree, B. F. (2006), "The qualitative research interview". Medical Education, Vol.40, No. 4, pp. 314–321.

Diego, L. A. B. (2017), "Friends with benefits: Causes and effects of learners' cheating practices during examination", IAFOR Journal of Education, Vol. 5, No. 2, pp. 121–138.

Dupont, S., Galanda, B., and Nils, F. (2015), "The impact of different sources of social support on academic performance: Intervening factors mediated pathways in the case of master's thesis", Revue Européenne de PsychologieAppliquée, Vol. 65, pp. 227–237.

Evrard, Y., Pras, B., and Roux, E. (1993), Market: Etudes et Recherchesen Marketing, Editions Nathan.

Eke, D. O. (2023), "ChatGPT and the rise of generative AI: Threat to academic integrity?", Journal of Responsible Technology, Vol. 13, pp. 1–4.

Firat, M. (2023), "What ChatGPT means for universities: Perceptions of scholars and students", Journal of Applied Learning & Teaching, Vol. 6, pp. 1–22.

Gabora, L. (2013), "Psychology of Creativity", Encyclopedia of Creativity, Invention, Innovation, and Entrepreneurship, pp. 1515–1520.

Grewal, D., Herhausen, D., Ludwig, S. and Ordenes, F. V.(2022), "The future of digital communication research: Considering dynamics and multimodality", Journal of Retailing, Vol. 98, Issue 2, pp. 224–240.

Guliyeva, K. (2021). "History, methodology and Hypothesis of Artificial Intelligence," China-USA Business Review, Vol. 20, No. 4, pp. 167–176.
Han, J-W., Park, J., and Lee, H. (2022), "Analysis of the effect of an artificial intelligence chatbot educational program on non-face-to-face classes: a quasi-experimental study", BMC Medical Education, Vol. 22, No. 1, pp. 1–10.
Haman, M., and Školník, M. (2023), "Using ChatGPT to conduct a literature review", Accountability in Research, DOI: 10.1080/08989621.2023.218551406917733847
Hamani, J., Chalghaf, N., Maaloul, H. and Azaiez, F. (2013), "The exam cheating among Tunisian students of the higher institute of sport and physical education of Sfax", IOSR Journal Of Humanities And Social Science (IOSR-JHSS), Vol. 15, Issue 6, pp. 90–95.
Iskender, A. (2023), "Holy or unholy? Interview with open AI's ChatGPT", European Journal of Tourism Research, Vol. 34, pp. 1–11.
Iwata, T. (2013), "Teacher's autonomy and students' creativity", Doctoral dissertation, University of Georgia.
Jamshed, S. (2014), "Qualitative research method-interviewing and observation", Journal of Basic and Clinical Pharmacy, Vol. 5, No. 4, pp. 87–88.
Korir, D. K., and Kipkemboi, F. (2014), "The impact of school environment and peer influences on students' academic performance in Vihiga County, Kenya", International Journal of Humanities and Social Science, Vol. 4, No, 11, pp 1–12.
Krief, N., and Zardet, F. (2013), "Analyse de donnéesqualitatives et recherche-intervention", Recherchesen Sciences de Gestion, Vol. 95, No. 2, pp. 211–237.
kuhumba, S. K. (2018), "Amartya Sen's capability approach as theoretical foundation of human development", Journal of Sociology and Development, Vol. 1, No.1, pp. 127–145.
Ma, Y., and Siau, K. L. (2018), "Artificial Intelligence Impacts on Higher Education", Proceedings of the Thirteenth Midwest Association for Information Systems Conference, Saint Louis, Missouri May, pp. 1–5.
Madara, D. S., Namango, S. S., and Katana, H. (2016), "Theories and models relevant to cheating-behaviour", Research on Humanities and Social Sciences, Vol. 6, No. 17, pp. 108–139.
Mishra, S. and Dey, A. K. (2022), "Understanding and identifying 'themes' in qualitative case study research", South Asian Journal of Business and Management Cases, Vol. 11, No. 3, pp. 187–192.
Morgan, H. (2021), "Howard Gardner's Multiple Intelligences Theory and his Ideas on Promoting Creativity". In F. Reisman (Ed.), Celebrating Giants and Trailblazers: A-Z of Who's Who in Creativity Research and Related Fields, pp. 124–141.
Nabavi, R. T. (2012), "Bandura's Social Learning Theory & Social Cognitive Learning Theory", Theories of Developmental Psychology, pp. 1–23.
Nussbaum, M. C. (2003), "Capabilities as fundamental entitlements: Sen and social justice", *Feminist Economics*, Vol. 9, No. 3, pp. 33–59.
Rahmouni, M., and Aleid, M. A. (2020), "Teachers' practices and children's motivation towards science learning in MENA countries: Evidence from Tunisia and UAE", International Journal of Educational Research, Vol. 103.
Rasul, T., Nair, S., Kalendra, D., Robin, M., Santini, F., Ladeira, W., Sun, M., Day, I., Rather, A. and Heathcote, L. (2023). "The role of ChatGPT in higher education: Benefits, challenges, and future research directions", Journal of Applied Learning & Teaching, Vol. 6, No. 1, pp. 1–16.
Robeyns, I. (2003), "The Capability Approach: An Interdisciplinary Introduction", The 3rd International Conference on the Capability Approach, Pavia, Italy, on 6 September 2003, pp. 1–54.
Rupasinghe, A. T., Guanawardena, N. L., Shujan, S. and Atukoral, D. A. S. (2016). "Scaling Personality Traits of Interviewees in an Online Job Interview by Vocal Spectrum and Facial Cue Analysis", International Conference on Advances in ICT for Emerging Regions (ICTer), pp. 1–8.
Ryan, F., Coughlan, M., and Cronin, P. (2009), "Interviewing in qualitative research", International Journal of Therapy and Rehabilitation, Vol. 16, No. 6, pp. 309–314.
Sabzalieva, E., and Valentini, A. (2023), "ChatGPT and Artificial Intelligence in HigerEducation: a quick guide", UNESCO, pp. 1–14.
Saigarana, N. G., Karupiah, P., and Gopalc, S. P. (2015), "The Capability Approach: Comparing Amartya Sen and Martha Nussbaum", Proceedings of University Sains Malaysia International Conference on Social Sciences, pp. 1–327.
Salvagno, M., Chat GPT Gerli, A. G. and Taccone, F. S. (2023), "Can artificial intelligence help for scientific writing?", Critical Care, Vol. 27, No. 1, pp. 1–5.
SEN Amartya K., 1999, Development as Freedom, New York, Anchor Books, 2000.
Sheikh, H. et al. (2023), Mission AI, Research for Policy, 10.1007/978-3-031-21448-6_1

Stewart, F. (2013), "Capabilities and Human Development: Beyond the Individual-the Critical Role of Social Institutions and Social Competencies", United Nations Development Programme, pp. 1–22.

Taherdoost, H. (2022), "How to conduct an effective interview; A guide to interview design in research study ", International Journal of Academic Research in Management, Vol. 11, No. Issue 1, pp. 39–51.

Taylor, L. C., Clayton, J. D., and Rowley, S. J. (2004), "Socialization: Understanding parental influences on children's school-related development in the early years", Review of General Psychology, Vol. 8, No. 3, pp. 163–178.

Tirri, K., and Nokelainen, P. (2008), "Identification of multiple intelligences with the multiple intelligence profiling questionnaire III". Psychology Science, Vol. 50, No.2, p.206.

Wacheaux, F. (1996), "Méthodesqualitatives et recherche en gestion", Economica Paris.

Wæraas, A. (2022), "Thematic Analysis: Making Values Emerge from Texts", Researching Values, pp. 153–170.

Xhaferi, B. and Xhaferi, G. (2011), "Developing learner autonomy in higher education in Macedonia", Procedia Social and Behavioral Sciences, Vol. 11, pp. 150–154.

Zhai, X. (2023), "ChatGPT and AI: The Game Changer for Education", 10 pages.

13 Are You Real?

When Anthropomorphism Misleads the Consumer

Manel Hassairi
Sousse University, Sousse, Tunisia
Tunis University, Tunis, Tunisia

Karima Ghzaiel
Monastir University, Monastir, Tunisia
University of Sfax, Sfax, Tunisia

13.1 INTRODUCTION

One of today's key success factors for brands is influencer marketing, which is nothing less than a research area enjoying unprecedented popularity (N'Goala and Collin-Lachaud, 2022) and is experiencing the most rapid growth, becoming a key area of marketing research (Boerman, 2020 cited in Harrigan and al., 2021). Consumers need to be reassured and guided toward good deals, they tend to believe and even idolize their sources of inspiration and trust their tastes and advice in terms of purchasing and consumption because when an influencer recommends a product, it seems more trustworthy than traditional advertising and, as a result, consumers are more likely to buy the recommended product sometimes even tested live and approved (Sottiaux, 2020). Influencers are defined as those who: "*Represent a new category of opinion leaders, with a position somewhere between celebrities and friends, that has emerged with the growth of social media opportunities. Influencers can be described as self-made micro-celebrities*" (Belanche and al., 2021). However, this brand-influencer proximity is crumbling, as these same elements can sometimes cause considerable damage to brands, damaging their image and even bankrupting them, essentially with a live show that goes off track, a misplaced post, an inciting tweet, a fake influence, etc. All these mistakes by influencers can have a snowball effect and damage the product or brand, and this miscasting can weigh heavily on the company. Having a presence on social networks has become a crucial tool for companies and using influencers to boost brand awareness and sales is proving to have more drawbacks than advantages. In fact, many brands are now turning to virtual influencers, who promise a long-term, risk-free partnership for companies, with an adjustable and manageable intellectual level, pre-programmed centers of interest, no sulfurous lifestyles, and no potential scandals to fear or risks to bear as demonstrated by Gerlich (2023): *Virtual influencers are preferred over human influencers,* and have been found to be more attractive than real ones, according to Sands and al. (2022).

Despite the strong predominance of studies on human influencers, the study of anthropomorphism is still limited and the present article responds to the call for research to develop this axis further and examine other forms of artificial intelligence except for chatbots such as avatars because those computer-generated image influencers have received no academic attention to-date

DOI: 10.1201/9781003450443-13

(Borau and al., 2021; Oliveira and Chimenti, 2021; Dabiran, Wang and Farivar, 2022; Thompson, 2022). This research is based on a qualitative methodology to study how the audience perceives virtual influencers in a gender approach by providing an answer to these questions: Who are these virtual influencers? How would these new practices be perceived by Internet users? Could gender be considered as a vector of good or bad attitudes toward the virtual influencer?

13.2 BACKGROUND

13.2.1 Virtual Influencer Marketing

Over the past decade, digital platforms and social media have become inseparable from business sustainability, while brands increasingly need to be relevant, useful, and entertaining (Kocheilas, 2018 cited in Tosun, 2022). Typically, Influencer Marketing offers young consumers the opportunity to interact with real people telling real stories through their social media feeds (Feng, Chen and Kong, 2020). By integrating commercial content on social networks, Influencer Marketing enables a less intrusive but more effective generation to take advantage of lower-priced purchasing opportunities via promo codes, learning opportunities through tutorials and live shows, and so on. However, the use of human influencers continues to fall by the wayside, giving way to robots enhanced in image processing labs. Recently, the influencer world has witnessed the emergence of virtual influencers who are "*Augmented agents with digital avatars, designed to look human*" as cited in the work of Arsenyan and Mirowska (2021).

Similarly, Tan and Liu (2020, cited in Arsenyan and Mirowska, 2021) have chosen to define them as "*embodied virtual agents*". They are, in fact, profiles created in laboratories and development companies using computer graphics software and new computer technologies, fictitious characters to be sure, but capable of having human traits more or less without visible flaws, they have a private life and possess an image almost identical to that of humans, which makes it much easier to identify them (De Laet Derache, 2021). The notoriety of virtual influencers is partly due to this blatant resemblance to human influencers as mentioned in previous research that it is already difficult for some individuals to distinguish between human and virtual influencers (Batista and Chimenti, 2021). This science is known as anthropomorphism, which refers to the attribution of human form, characteristics, and behaviors to non-human people (Dabiran, Wang and Farivar (2022); Guthrie, 1993 cited in El Hedhli and al., 2023). For instance, the human shape, animacy, and perceived interactivity all elicit anthropomorphizing (Connell, 2013). This same mechanism has been studied across various applications, such as robots, chatbots, digital assistants, and self-tutors and in many different contexts, such as medical service, online shopping, and learning.

13.2.2 Profile of Virtual Influencers

This pixel enhancement gives way to digital characters of all races and colors. These virtual influencers even have a social status and belong to several categories. So far, they have been able to capture the full attention of brands, especially luxury brands, for the many benefits they bring, and have become idealized role models and examples attracting real communities of followers (Moustakas and al., 2020; Jiang, 2022) and succeed to attract important brands such as Samsung, Calvin Klein, Chanel, Coach, Unilever, Ikea, Porsche, Balenciaga, Mini Cooper, and Prada (Arsenyan and Mirowska, 2021; Oliveira and Chimenti, 2021). Some of the virtual influencers have been programmed to change social norms on social networks, others to position themselves as models. Meanwhile, others look like the manga and position themselves as activists. To win the big brands and the big contracts, avatars have to distinguish themselves above all by their follower numbers, sometimes by making followers believe they are real, and sometimes by relying on shocking facts to create buzz around them.

Virtual influencers operating on today's social networks can be divided into two categories according to different levels of anthropomorphism. Some virtual influencers are like humans and have a very realistic appearance such as Lil Miquela the favorite robot with more than 3M followers on Instagram, Shudu Gram, the perfect digital top model, the most controversial virtual influencer. Others look like cartoons and are physically disproportionate: Bodybyralph, Fnmeka, Ion Gottlich, Noonoouri (the favorite muse of the Dior brand). The third category is depicted as creatures and animals such as Bee, Janky & Guggimon, … . Their objective is no different from that of human influencers; they aspire to the same thing: promoting ideologies, products, or brands and convincing as many people as possible, depending on their gender, according to previous studies.

13.2.3 Gender of Virtual Influencers

One solution for artificial intelligence companies to increase acceptance of their algorithm solutions has been to anthropomorphize and gender their robots with feminine and masculine features (Borau and al., 2021). The attribution of a female gender to robots seems to stem from consumer expectations and above all preferences (Borau and al., 2021). Previous research has shown significant differences in how men and women express their emotions online and these gender expressions often correspond with gender stereotypes (Lee and Yuan, 2023).

Since the era of Alexa and Sophia, previous research on human-robot interaction has shown that men tend to speak at greater length to the chatbot when it presents a female gender because of the feminine aspect that always gives an impression of confidence, warmth, and friendliness, with solid communication abilities (Borau and al., 2021). In a study carried out to identify consumer expectations, it was found that the majority of women prefer dealing with chatbots of the male gender which may very well show themselves as real human beings, as Boibot for example, or even Henry (Spatola, 2019; Lee and Yuan, 2023). Artificial intelligence labs are creating virtual robots of all types, different ethnicities, genders, social backgrounds, and geographic locations, not to mention different clothing styles corresponding to the brands the virtual influencer deals with (Hipólito, Winkle and Lie, 2023). A great diversity that cannot fail to meet all expectations, from the most normal to the most unusual. The gender of those avatars has been used, in other studies, to examine consumers' social perceptions, while the present work examines consumers' emotional perception focusing on two virtual influencers created by the same American company Brud: Lil Miquela and Blawko.

Lil Miquela is placed first as a near-perfect humanoid: its real name is none other than a virtual influencer. This avatar was created in 2016 using 3D imaging software and is the very first virtual influencer. Since its creation, Miquela has presented herself as a fashionista, a singer, and a civil rights fighter and activist, even taking up social cause notably with the Black Lives Matter movement. This also serves to create its identity and increase visibility, influence, and emotional release (Block and Lovegrove, 2021). Today, this digital muse is a model, socialist, and real-life Instagrammer, courted by leading luxury brands. Just like an influencer in the flesh, Lil Miquela also shares its looks, outfits, favorites, outings with friends, … which to this day leaves its followers torn between reality and fantasy, and some continue to wonder in the comments section whether Miquela is indeed a robot.

Belonging to the masculine gender, Blawko was also created in 2016 by the same company as Lil Miquela. Ronald F. Blawko is an Afro-American virtual top model who promotes racial diversity and multiculturalism as modern world values. Never seen without his designer scarves covering his nose and mouth, the majority of its followers on Instagram look out for the slightest post without a mask. With a narcissistic character and a little mystery look, its feed is full of photos of itself living its best life, sharing its passion for luxury brands, and racing cars (Белова, 2021).

As demonstrated in the description of virtual influencers in this study, robots with a male or female physical appearance do not offer the same content, target the same consumers, or have the same interaction or involvement from their followers, things that led researchers to study the way consumer and virtual influencer interact (Stein and al., 2022).

13.2.4 Parasocial Interaction

Online celebrities and virtual influencers have been appearing on various social media and video streaming platforms, and especially on Instagram, raising many questions and much curiosity about the interaction between the social network users and virtual influencers. The concept of parasocial interaction is just as relevant in the context of virtual influencers as it is in the context of human influencers and is defined as: « *individuals' one-sided situational reactions toward characters depicted in mass media* » (Stein and al., 2022). This concept of parasocial interaction is all the more relevant given individuals typically perceive online influencers as more similar to themselves than traditional celebrities despite the fact that this interaction is unilateral, one-sided, and non-regular (Kalla, 2022; Stein and al., 2022).

Parasocial interaction has been studied as a factor that can affect user perception and could engender a good attitude toward virtual influencers and examine their appearances, behaviors, emotions, and thoughts thus influencing the perception of the human-likeness hence the concept of uncanny valley related to the effect of robot appearance, the authenticity, the attractiveness, the social interactivity, and the social presence, etc. (Um, 2023; Molin and Nordgren, 2019). The consumers tend to develop a relationship of friendship, intimacy, and identification; these relationships may grow as the robot influencer appears trustworthy (Rönnhed and Wiksborg, 2021).

13.3 METHODOLOGY

To collect data, we conducted a netnographic study to examine followers' perception of the virtual influencer. This consists of a "*new qualitative research methodology that (…) studies the cultures and communities that are emerging through computer-mediated communications*". It has been adopted, especially in the domain of online consumer behavior.

This method is chosen because it allows one to interpret and understand individual behavior in a naturalistic interactive setting.

We selected two virtual influencers on Instagram: including Lil Miquela and Blawko. We studied the audience comments on their 30 recent Instagram posts. We collected users' comments relating to the thirty last posts.

To create world list frequencies, we used LIWC tools. By examining the frequent words, we identified potential categories. Then, a smaller corpus allowed us to identify relevant themes.

13.4 RESULTS AND DISCUSSION

13.4.1 Word Frequency Analysis

To analyze frequent words in users' comments, we adopted Word Frequency Analysis with LIWC tools through the well-known influencer platform Instagram. Non-English languages (Arabic, French, Spanish …) were preliminary translated.

13.4.2 Thematic Analysis

In the present study, the attitudes shown by followers toward virtual influencers were examined in order to answer the call of previous research. Based on the comments processed and the emoticons classified according to their meaning, we were able to classify attitudes into two groups, positive and negative. This was also reinforced by the likes and the analysis of bot profiles and follower engagement to determine whether or not the gender variable could affect attitude and have an impact on it. One of the initial findings of our qualitative research was that the majority of followers are still unable to distinguish between real computer-generated images and human influencers. This study is among the first attempts to gather information on social media users' attitudes toward humanoid influencers.

The users' behavior toward virtual influencers is mixed between users who feel admiration and others who feel contempt. Two extreme attitudes are bordered by others such as curiosity, rejection, disappointment, boredom, discomfort, or the desire to identify with them.

By way of summary, the comment's thematic analysis reveals the major themes which are divided into two categories: positive attitudes and negative attitudes.

13.4.2.1 Positive Evaluation

13.4.2.1.1 Admiration

Admiration is an emotion that arises when we witness an individual's exceptional qualities, skills, or achievements. It is "*a feeling of deep respect and approval toward someone or something??*".

Physical attractiveness of virtual influencers is the primary reason for virtual: "*I 💜 your dress!; So cute; Miquelaa …; U so pretty; your hair is so beautiful; Original A.I. Queen*". Audiences also admire virtual influencers' content: "*I need more of your music babe; Probably, they maybe find out a way to make humans live forever too with all your intelligence; I love how you embrace the simple joys in life!Truly inspiring; Great way to look at things ❤*". Even Blawko's followers go wild on his profile and the girls are the ones who give him the most compliments like: "*Where are you king? we miss the robot king*", "*You handsome just the way you're*", "*Total 😱*", "*why are you guys so perfect 😍*".

Those positive behavioral responses are explained by the admiration for the story behind a message, their artwork, and their social activities. Such an emotion may impact the follower's engagement and loyalty toward the influencer (Uzunoğlu & Misci Kip, 2014; Kim et al., 2022).

Others (Nowak et Biocca, 2003), in contrast, assert that less anthropomorphic characters have more social attractiveness which is considered a source of audiences' admiration.

13.4.2.1.2 Curiosity

This cognitive reaction is activated by perceived novelty which is considered a major feature of virtual influencers (Dabiran et al., 2023). Different extracts represent curiosity in collected comments "*Are you a robot?; So how is this working exactly? 🤓 Is this graphics?? She's not literally out and about walking the streets and going to events etc. Anyone know?*".

The perceived anthropomorphism seems to arouse the user's curiosity and leads them to ask many questions concerning its function and nature, such as: "*I still can't tell if Lil Miquela is AI or not, someone help; I want to know about you; How u can eat*?".

Some others can easily discern an influencer's nature and explain that: "*This is Lil Miquela and she is a humanoid.; I do not 🙆 know how you can believe this and technology has reached the highest levels. It means that an ordinary person can turn into a robot in social reality; This entire account is AI based but funny how's it notating Black Lives Matter …. when it's a computer; I don't believe it. You're a robot. I think someone made up this story*".

Follower curiosity also arose on Blawko's account following his posts, always wearing a mask over his face that covers both his nose and mouth. Although anthropomorphism allows virtual influencers to look like humans, social network users want to inspect Blawko's every physical detail: "*Show us your face!!!; Why is your mouth always covered?; How you eat if you has a mask on?*".

13.4.2.1.3 Desire of Identification

Several studies have suggested that the desire to identify with others exists when a person strives to relate to someone by adopting their behaviors, characteristics, and attitudes. Consumers tend to mimic others with whom they interact in various ways. Some followers try to find themselves through robot influencers, citing behavioral, physical, and moral similarities and finding common ground around shared passions: *"We have the same necklace; we really have similarities; we have the same look; I love this too; WELCOME BACK MY ROBOTIC FRIEND; The caption is my mood every single day; Love u Sis ✌ □"*.

13.4.2.2 Negative Evaluation

13.4.2.2.1 Uncanny and Rejection

The theme of Uncanny was exuberantly raised by the users as a relevant consequence of perceived anthropomorphism. According to this phenomenon (Mori, 1970; Mori et al., 1970), when virtual agents are almost human looking, they reach a point where they generate negative impressions and reactions (Arsenyan and Mirowska, 2021; Mathur et al., 2020; Steins et al., 2020; MacDorman, 2019) through which users might reject the adoption of the technology. This seems congruent with studies supporting that high social attractiveness levels and admiration are possessed by less anthropomorphic agents (Nowak and Biocca, 2003).

In fact, Mori et al. (2012) hypothesized that "a person's response to a humanlike robot would abruptly shift from empathy to revulsion as it approached, but failed to attain, a likelife appearance" (p. 98). Examples of such statements are provided here: The following keywords ("Weird; creepy; So people are actually going crazy?!; I do not know if you can believe this and technology has reached the highest levels; This is crazy and dangerous; AI is going to destroy Humans!; Uncanny valley; why is this so scary") are considered for referring to virtual influencer's rejection.

The activation of the Uncanny effects is related to perceived discomfort, identity confusion, and insecurity. It can be considered as an occasional consumption decision without automatically reflecting the individual's denigratory characteristic (Laukkanen, 2016).

Although uncanny and audience rejection can be extracted in the comments of the two virtual influencers, we can report that especially for Lil Miquela, the high degree of anthropomorphism causes more degree of rejection. Word Frequency Analysis confirms that terms reflecting negative reactions are more salient in her post's comments.

13.4.2.2.2 Disappointment

Among the comments collected and analyzed, some were the subject of disappointment expressed by followers between those who accuse influencers of disinterest and others criticize them for not being present enough, especially on the comments that followers post on Blawko's profile. They resent him for not always being active on Instagram, for posting something and then disappearing for a long period: *"U say 'im back' and then disappear again; Where have u been? 😳; It's been 9 months where did lord Blawko go?"*.

This psychological reaction is due to the comparison of the actual outcome of a lottery to one's prior expectation when making decisions under uncertainty (Bell, 1985).

13.4.2.2.3 Sarcasm and Irony

Among the different ways used by internauts to express their sentiments and emotions, we note feelings accompanied by sarcasm and irony. This is considered as a very important form of language use in social media analysis that refers to the contrast between the intended meaning and the accurate meaning of the words (Haripriya et Patil, 2017).

For example, it was said: "*2 mil followers and 74 comments lol I guess the followers are 'ai' too; How much are you getting paid to shill this crap to people?; Are you an artificial intelligence and I am a human? By God, it is forbidden to be more pleased than me; She lives her life in length and breadth and is made of intelligence. What did you leave for us, sister?"*.

This result corroborates previous works since sarcasm according to a specific theme in user comments is likely to appear alongside other indicators of his true sentiment (Haripriya and Patil, 2019). It refers to an offensive way of criticizing others (Toplak and Katz, 2000), eliciting greater disapproval and more negative feelings and reactions (Warren and McGraw, 2016; Lagerwerf, 2007; Toplak and Katz, 2000).

TABLE 13.1
Profiles Analysis Results

Virtual Influencer	Lil Miquela	Blawko
Gender	Female	Male
Launching year	2016	2016
Followers	2.8 M	129.6 K
# of Posts	1274	162
Top content likes	40 550	13 774
Top content comments	242	240
Current engagement rate	0.45%	6.43%
Top caption words	Future/couple/feelings/wonder/unreal/cute	Covered/bermudaisbae/secure/favorite/robot
Most common emojis	😍🌈💥❤😘😂😮😐😥👽 ✌🔥😻🦁👊😩💕🏆😆	😥😮😍👏💥🔥😂😐👎 😏👀💎😬😯💀😭
Total followers rank	10,143rd	441,012th

Source: Inflact and Pathsocial.

This article deals with the issue of gender in virtual influence marketing from the outset. The perception of female bots differs from that of male bots, who are often subject to inappropriate jokes, mockery, rejection, and lack of credibility, unlike female bots. This difference was further explored through the use of professional artificial intelligence tools to analyze instagram accounts such as Inflact and Pathsocial. The analysis is shown in Table 13.1.

According to the results obtained in the table, the difference between Lil Miquela as a female robot and Blawko as a male robot is obvious. Lil Miquela has impressive popularity on Instagram, unlike Blawko. The majority of the emojis that dominate her comments have migliorative connotations: affection with hearts and kisses, joy with smileys, admiration with heart-shaped eyes and diamonds, … Blawko, as for him, the emojis that are an integral part of the comments he receives have more of a pejorative connotation with the laughter of irony, the skull and crossbones, the flop, the astonishment, the disgust, etc. As for publications, Lil Miquela is very present on instagram with posts and stories, unlike Blawko. This fact could also have an influence on user perception and the influencer's credibility. This also explains the difference between likes and comments, as well as the engagement rate of the two virtual influencers.

These results are congruent with the literature relating to individual interactions with new technologies that supposes that users express mixed (favorable and unfavorable) views about the innovations (Ferreira et al, 2014; Gray and Wegner, 2012). This result reflects that reluctance and resistance consist of normal responses toward technology and innovation (Huh and Kim, 2008; Choi et al., 2011). In addition, this corroborates with the Computers Social Actors (CASA) paradigm suggesting that audiences react to computers and machines in the same way that they react to humans (Edwards et al., 2019; Nass and Moon, 2000).

13.5 PRACTICAL IMPLICATIONS

This study is expected to contribute to the virtual influencer marketing literature by raising a question about the user's perception of virtual agent's high anthropomorphism. It has valued practical implications for virtual influencers management. These recommendations are intended for AI designers and online marketers who intend to improve the human-computer experience and to make choices in the competitive market among the thousands of existing influencers.

Our results argued that, like human influencers, virtual agents are able to elicit parasocial relationships by creating a feeling of connection (Gratch et al., 2007; Dibble et al., 2016). Thus, professionals must take into consideration that users posit themselves as a part of the influencer's social world. Their choices must be carefully considered.

The findings indicate that the design of anthropomorphic influencers is not necessarily attended by favorable attitudes and emotions. It may risk repulsion among consumers. For that reason, it would be advisable to pretest virtual agents to verify that they have been assigned the appropriate amount of humanness. Besides, raising the preponderance of positive emotions associated with Lil Miquela, we posit that AI services may embody virtual agents with female features. This makes users perceive them as more human, especially for brands playing the humanizing card in their strategies.

Our research also contributes to the growing stream of literature on the efficacy of gendered marketing (Borau and al., 2021) and the ethical dilemma of gendered AI and gendered robots (Alesich and Rigby, 2017).

13.6 LIMITATIONS AND PERSPECTIVES

This preliminary work has several limitations relating to the nature of the study and data collected. Despite demographic characteristics of users (gender, age, education level …) that are supposed to affect their perception and acceptance of technology and innovation, those informations are not analyzed in this work. Further research should gather and examine the impact of these characteristics.

Also, this study constitutes a preliminary effort to understand how the audience perceives virtual influencers. We call for future research to develop this axis and to validate a conceptual framework. Experimental surveys can be conducted.

Future research can, also, fill our gap by considering a more comprehensive range of user reactions in addition to simple emotions and feelings raised. Also, they tend to test whether influencer gender could affect users' emotions by studying this moderator effect.

Besides, the analyzed comments belong to users from different countries (Spain, France, and Arabic countries). Thus, the cross-cultural differences deserve to be analyzed. We solicit the interest of researchers wishing to consider the weight of cultural and personal dimension (familiarity with technology, risk perception, product involvement). In addition, these results may not be generalizable to virtual agents operating in different context categories or across different digital mediums (Sheldon and Bryant, 2016). Future research should be conducted to consider different contexts and mediums (Twitter, Tik Tok, Instagram).

In this work, we conducted a textual interpretation and a word frequency analysis to extract major themes in audience's comments. Future research can exploit other methods to exploit content (For example: image semiotics and emoji use). Nevertheless, these analyses should be carefully exploited because they can have different affective valences depending on the cultural and social context, the user identity … .

13.7 CONCLUSION

The netnographic approach to the phenomena of anthropomorphic influencers allowed us to get insights into the user perception of these virtual agents. Our results support findings from related works by identifying major themes through the analysis of followers' comments on the Instagram accounts of virtual influencers in a genre-bending approach between Lil Miquela and Blawko.

It was found that reluctance and resistance toward humanoids seem to exist. Companies choose so-called influencers to present their products and thus boost sales, to ensure greater visibility on the web and important notoriety on the market, but users, simultaneously, express both favorable (admiration, curiosity, desire of identification) and unfavorable (uncanny and rejection, disappointment, sarcasm and irony) attitudes and emotions about anthropomorphic influencers. The virtual agent's gender may also make a difference. These results provide practical implications and a fruitful beginning for future research on virtual humans.

REFERENCES

Alesich, S. and Rigby, M. (2017), Gendered robots: Implications for our humanoid future, *IEEE Technology and Society Magazine*, 36 (2), 50–59.

Arsenyan, J. and Mirowska, A. (2021), Almost human? A comparative case study on the social media presence of virtual influencers, *International Journal of Human-Computer Studies*, 155 (2021), 1–16.

Batista, A., and Chimenti, P. (2021), Humanized robots: A proposition of categories to understand virtual influencers, *Australasian Journal of Information Systems*, 25, 1–27.

Бєлова, А. (2021), Віртуальні інфлуенсери у мультимодальній рекламі. Вісник ХНУ імені В. Н. Каразіна, *Серія: Іноземна філологія. Методика викладання іноземних мов*, (93), 14–21.

Belanche, D., Casalo, L., Flavian, M. and Ibanez-Sanchez, S. (2021), Understanding influencer marketing: The role of congruence between influencers, products and consumers, *Journal of Business Research*, 132 (21), 186–195.

Bell, D. E. (1985), Disappointment in decision making under uncertainty, *Operations Research*, 33 (1), 1–27.

Block, E. and Lovegrove, R. (2021), Discordant storytelling, honest fakery, identity peddling: How uncanny CGI characters are jamming public relations and influencer practices, *Public Relations Inquiry*, 10 (3), 265–293.

Boerman, S. C. (2020), The effects of the standardized Instagram disclosure for micro-and meso-influencers Computers in Human Behavior, 103 (2020), pp. 199–207, 10.1016/j.chb.2019.09.015

Borau, S., Otterbring, T. and Laporte, S. (2021), The most human bot: Female gendering increases humanness perceptions of bots and acceptance of AI, *Psychol. Market*, 1–17.

Choi, J. N., Sung, S. Y., Lee, K. and Cho, D. S. (2011), Balancing cognition and emotion: Innovation implementation as a function of cognitive appraisal and emotional reactions toward innovation, *Journal of Organizational Behavior*, 32 (1), 107–124.

Connell, P. M. (2013), The role of baseline physical similarity to humans in consumer responses to anthropomorphic animal images, *Psychol. Market*, 30 (6), 461–468.

Dabiran, E., Farivar, S., Wang, F. and Grant, G. G., "ENGAGING WITH VIRTUAL INFLUENCERS: A NETNOGRAPHY STUDY" (2023). ECIS 2023 Research-in-Progress Papers. 41. https://aisel.aisnet.org/ecis2023_rip/41

Dabiran, E., Wang, F. and Farivar, S. (2022), Virtual influencer marketing: Anthropomorphism and its effect, *ECIS 2022 Research in Progress Papers*, 6 (18), 2–13.

De Laet Derache, L. (2021), Quels sont les éléments expliquant le succès des influenceurs virtuels (IV) alors que l'efficacité des influenceurs humains (IH) repose sur l'authenticité, la crédibilité et l'interaction parasociale? Dans quelle mesure un IV peut-il être aussi efficace et quels sont les facteurs compensatoires de ces derniers?, Mémoire de master en science de gestion finalité Marketing Strategy for Connected Brands, Université du Louvain School of Management, Belgique.

Dibble, J. L., Hartmann, T. and Rosaen, S. F. (2016), Parasocial interaction and parasocial relationship: Conceptual clarification and a critical assessment of measures, *Human Communication Research*, 42 (1), 21–44.

Edwards, A., Edwards, C., Westerman, D. and Spence, P. R. (2019), Initial expectations, inter-actions, and beyond with social robots, *Computers in Human Behavior*, 90, 308–314.

El Hedhli, K., Zourrig, H., Al Khateeb, A. and Alnawas, I. (2023), Stereotyping human-like virtual influencers in retailing: Does warmth prevail over competence?, *Journal of Retailing and Consumer Services*, 75.

Feng, Y., Chen, H. and Kong, Q. (2020), An expert with whom I can identify: The role of narratives in influencer marketing, *International Journal of Advertising*, 1–22.

Ferreira, J. B., da Rocha, A. and da Silva, J. F. (2014), Impacts of technology readiness on emotions and cognition in Brazil, *Journal of Business Research*, 67 (5), 865–873.

Gerlich, M. (2023), The power of virtual influencers: Impact on consumer behaviour and attitudes in the age of AI, *Administrative Sciences*, 13 (178), 1–21.

Gratch, J., Wang, N., Gerten, J., Fast, E. and Duffy, R. (2007), Creating rapport with virtual agents, In *Intelligent Virtual Agents: 7th International Conference, IVA 2007 Paris, France, September 17-19, 2007 Proceedings 7* (pp. 125–138), Springer Berlin Heidelberg.

Gray, K. and Wegner, D. M. (2012). Feeling robots and human zombies: Mind perception and the uncanny valley. *Cognition*, *125*(1), 125–130.

Haripriya, V. and Patil, P. G. (2017), A survey of sarcasm detection in social media, *International Journal for Research in Applied Science & Engineering Technology*, 5 (12), 1748–1753.

Haripriya, V. and Patil, P. G. (2019). Detection of sarcasm from consumer sentiments on social media about luxury brands. In Recent Trends in Image Processing and Pattern Recognition: Second International Conference, RTIP2R 2018, Solapur, India, December 21–22, 2018, Revised Selected Papers, Part III 2 (pp. 652–667).

Harrigan, P. M., Daly, T., Coussement, K. A., Lee, J., Soutar, G. and Evers, U. (2021), Identifying influencers on social media, *International Journal of Information Management*, 56 (2021), 1–11.

Hipólito, I., Winkle, K. and Lie, M. (2023), Enactive artificial intelligence: subverting gender norms in human-robot interaction, *Front. Neurorobot*, 17 (1149303), 1–11.

Huh, Y. E. and Kim, S. H. (2008), Do early adopters upgrade early? Role of post-adoption behavior in the purchase of next-generation products, *Journal of Business Research*, *61*(1), 40–46.

Jiang, C. (2022), La fabrique des fembots pop stars: Participation, co-création ou exploitation culturelle en ligne?, *Journal of Arts and Human Mediators*, 8, 1–14.

Kalla, L. (2022), Virtual influencers: A challenge to trust and authenticity, *MA Applied Ethics for Professionals*, 1–87.

Kim, D. Y., Park, M. and Kim, H.-Y. (2022), An influencer like me: Examining the impact of the social status of Influencers, *Journal of Marketing Communications*, pp. 1–22.

Lagerwerf, L. (2007), Irony and sarcasm in advertisements: Effects of relevant inappropriateness, *Journal of Pragmatics*, 39 (10), 1702–1721.

Laukkanen, T. (2016), Consumer adoption versus rejection decisions in seemingly similar service innovations: The case of the Internet and mobile banking, *Journal of Business Research*, 69(7), 2432–2439.

Lee, Y. H. and Yuan, C. H. (2023), I'm not a puppet, I'm a real boy! Gender presentations by virtual influencers and how they are received, *Computers in Human Behavior*, 149.

MacDorman, K. F. (2019), In the uncanny valley, transportation predicts narrative enjoyment more than empathy, but only for the tragic hero, *Comput. Hum. Behav.*, 94, 140–153. https://doi.org/10.1016/j.chb.2019.01.011.

Mathur, M. B., Reichling, D. B., Lunardini, F., Geminiani, A., Antonietti, A., Ruijten, P. A. M., Levitan, C. A., Nave, G., Manfredi, D., Bessette-Symons, B., Szuts, A. and Aczel, B. (2020), Uncanny but not confusing: Multisite study of perceptual category confusion in the Uncanny Valley, *Computers in Human Behavior*, 103, 21–30. doi:10.1016/j.chb.2019.08.029

Molin, V. and Nordgren, S. (2019), Robot or Human? – The marketing phenomenon of virtual influencers- A case study about virtual influencers' parasocial interaction on instagram, Master's Thesis 15 credits, Department of Business Studies, Uppsala University, 1-57.

Mori, M., (1970), Bukimi no tani [the uncanny valley], *Energy*, 7 (4), 33–35.

Mori, M., MacDorman, K. F. and Kageki, N. (2012), The uncanny valley [from the field], *IEEE Rob. Autom Mag.*, 19 (2), 98–100.

Moustakas, E., Lamba, N., Mahmoud, D. and Ranganathan, C. (2020), Blurring lines between fiction and reality: Perspectives of experts on marketing effectiveness of virtual Influencers, *International Journal on Cyber Situational Awareness*, 1–6.

Nass, C. and Moon, Y. (2000), Machines and mindlessness: Social responses to computers, *Journal of social issues*, 56 (1), 81–103.

N'Goala, G. and Collin-Lachaud, I. (2022), Marketing et influence: à la recherche d'une légitimité perdue, *Revue Décisions Marketing*, 1 (105), 5–9.

Nowak, K. L. and Biocca, F. (2003), The effect of the agency and anthropomorphism on users' sense of telepresence, copresence, and social presence in virtual environments, *Presence: Teleoperators and Virtual Environments*, 12 (5), 481–494. https://doi.org/10.1162/105474603322761289

Oliveira, A. and Chimenti, P. (2021), Humanized robots: A proposition of categories to understand virtual influencers, *Australasian Journal of Information Systems*, 21 (25), 1–27.

Rönnhed, J. and Wiksborg, S. (2021), Virtual Influencers, Friends to Listen to? A Qualitative Study About Virtual Influencers Ability to Develop Parasocial Relationships and Opinion Leadership, Master's programme in International Marketing & Brand Management, Lund University, Sweden.

Sands, S., Ferraro, C., Demsar, V. and Chandler, G. (2022), False idols: Unpacking the opportunities and challenges of falsity in the context of virtual influencers, *Business Horizons*, 65 (6), 777–788.

Sheldon, P. and Bryant, K. (2016), Instagram: Motives for its use and relationship to narcissism and contextual age, *Computers in Human Behavior*, 58, 89–97.

Sottiaux, A. (2020), Comment l'identité professionnelle des influenceurs se construit-elle et à partir de quand le loisir laisse-t-il place au métier?, Université de Louvain School of Management, Belgique.

Spatola, N. (2019), L'interaction Homme-Robot, de l'anthropomorphisme à l'humanisation, *Année psychologique*, 4 (119), 515–563.

Stein, J. P., Appel, M., Jost, A. and Ohler, P. (2020), Matter over mind? How the acceptance of digital entities depends on their appearance, mental prowess, and the interaction between both. *International Journal of Human-Computer Studies*, 142, 102463–. doi:10.1016/j.ijhcs.2020.102463

Stein, J.P, Breves, P.L and Andres, N. (2022), Parasocial interactions with real and virtual influencers: The role of perceived similarity and human-likeness, *New Media & Society*, 00 (0), 1–22.

Thompson, J. (2022), Parasocial relationships in CGI influencer marketing, *Academy of Marketing Conference*.

Toplak, M. and Katz, A. N. (2000), On the uses of sarcastic irony, *Journal of pragmatics*, 32 (10), 1467–1488.

Tosun, P. (2022), Social media marketing of brands in the COVID-19 pandemic: Exploring the crisis-related content, in Handbook of Research on Interdisciplinary Perspectives on the Threats and Impacts of Pandemics, 1–22.

Um, N. (2023), Predictors affecting effects of virtual influencer advertising among college students, *Sustainability*, 15 (6388), 1–14.

Uzunoğlu, E. and Misci Kip, S. (2014), Brand communication through digital influencers: Leveraging blogger engagement, *International Journal of Information Management*, 34 (5), pp. 592–602.

Warren, C. and McGraw, A. P. (2016), Differentiating what is humorous from what is not, *Journal of Personality and Social Psychology*, 110 (3), 407.

14 Natural Language Processing to Track Cognitive, Emotional and Social Change on Reddit Mental Health and Non-Mental Health Groups during Covid-19

Manel Khadraoui and Nadia Arous
University of Tunis, Tunis, Tunisia

14.1 INTRODUCTION

Recent advances in data science, machine learning, and natural language processing (NLP) are providing technical solutions for the analysis of large amounts of data from different nature. The accumulation of big data and the improvement of technical analysis skills provide opportunities to improve services provided to different users (Stewart and Davis, 2016; Torous and Baker, 2016). On the other hand, these recent years were also characterized by an unprecedented and unanticipated global health crisis. Due to Covid-19, people lost their friends, their family members, their jobs, and their investments. They were ordered not to leave their homes and to limit their social interactions. Cities were locked down, businesses were blown away, and oil prices plummeted. This situation led researchers to link the pandemic with a significant emergence and increase in mental health disorders among people around the globe. In fact, psychologists and mental health professionals speculate that in addition to the other symptoms reported globally by Covid-19, with the increase in cases of depression, suicide, and self-harm, the pandemic will affect the mental health of the global population (Li et al., 2020; Moukaddam and Shah, 2020; Yao et al., 2020). Even for people without any history of mental disorders, Pan et al. (2021) showed a remarkable increase in depression, anxiety, and loneliness rates during the Covid-19 pandemic.

Given the ubiquity of mental disorders, and the limited number of mental health professionals, there is a serious need for mental health detection tools that are scalable to big populations, and that can be easily made accessible. Besides, given the pervasiveness of these mental disorders among the young population, building these tools on top of trending social media platforms can be very efficient (Shen et al., 2017).

Therefore, it becomes important to understand the change that occurred in mental health situation during the pandemic and identify people in need of help and assistance. Mirabito et al. (2022) called marketing researches to focus on the analysis of online health communities' conversations to orient the personalization of digital solution. Indeed, data collected with online health communities helps to study the dynamic granular human behavior and its temporal evolution (Singh et al., 2023).

DOI: 10.1201/9781003450443-14

However, existing studies suffer from the absence of theoretical background. In fact, the nature of data-driven methodologies encourages inductive approaches. Nevertheless, it is still important to have a theoretical background to advance the field and define the positioning of the research. On the other hand, the majority of previous studies took only one period. Others compared pre-Covid to post-Covid with limited focus on the evolution during Covid-19 spread (Zhu et al., 2023). In reality, the Covid-19 period can itself encompass different trends, especially with the study of mental health issues.

This research strives to address these gaps by adopting and extending the Social Cognition Theory (SCT) during different periods of Covid-19 spread. According to the SCT, human behavior is determined by three sets of concepts: cognitive factors, behavioral factors, and environmental factors. This theory is suitable to support community exchanges given the central role of individuals' cognition to search and treat information, in addition to their interactions with the members of the community and the feedback that they receive. However, it does not take into consideration emotions. In this specific context of exchanges about mental health illness in a crisis, we argue that emotions are central, and more importantly, they are dynamic and evolve from one period of the pandemic to another. Therefore, we study the cognitive, emotional, and environmental aspects of the community exchanges.

Hence, this study tries to detect changes that occurred in mental health (MH) and non-mental health (NMH) groups on social media after the pandemic through a trend, sentiment, and thematic analysis. This is multi-method research in three periods during Covid-19 (the first three semesters of Covid-19 spread) relying on users' generated content on Reddit. Reddit is a social news network where users discuss trending news and phenomena. Since 2015, researchers have been using machine learning predictive algorithms and statistical methods to study mental health on Reddit (Yang et al., 2015). Recent researchers are still interested in this platform (Kim et al., 2020; Bronda et al., 2022; Garcia et al., 2022).

We use different NLP techniques to answer our research questions (RQ). Our RQ are:

***RQ1**: How can the **trend analysis** of Covid-19 lexicon reveal change for different MH and NMH groups?*

***RQ2**: How does **sentiment analysis** track negative sentiment change for different MH and NMH groups?*

***RQ3**: What are the discovered discussed topics trough **text mining** of the content generated by Covid-19 support community during each of the 3 semesters?*

14.2 LITERATURE REVIEW

14.2.1 AI and Marketing

AI is described as the fourth industrial revolution (Oosthuizen, 2022; Chakraborty et al., 2022). It is a set of technologies that simulates human intelligence to execute different tasks: analyze, predict, and decide using data of different nature from different sources (text, audio, video). "It is believed that AI and Machine Learning hold solutions to most of today's problems" (Haleem et al., 2022). Machine Learning is a "sub-set of AI". It learns and adjusts itself as long as it is fed with data. In fact, we distinguish between supervised learning, unsupervised learning, and reinforcement learning. With supervised learning, the labeled dataset is split into train data and test data. The researcher has initial knowledge (derived from theory or practice) about the features that will be the starting point of the algorithm. It is used to solve classification problems and regression problems. Examples of supervised models include classification, regression, linear regression, logistic regression, decision tree, and KNN. The opposite is unsupervised learning. Here, the machine understands the underlying patterns and tries to predict the output. Therefore, the machine retrieves hidden patterns and clusters the data in a comprehensive way. Examples of methods include means clustering, neural networks, and Principal Component Analysis. With reinforcement learning, the program learns from the environment. It will receive a reward for the success and no reward for the failure. So it will learn by doing. It is mainly aiming to execute tasks like robots and gaming.

AI surpasses human beings regarding the volume of data treated, speed, and capacity of analysis. AI affected almost all fields including marketing. It is even creating a disruption in marketing. For Black and van Esch (2020), the adoption of AI in marketing is becoming mandatory. Consumers shift to the "digital first" is changing the priorities: "what was peripheral will become core and what was core will become peripheral" (Sheth, 2021). Companies today use AI to adjust their marketing strategies and sales forecast to reach their objectives. Applications are diverse in the marketing field: identifying customers, targeting them through special promotions, maintaining the relationship, managing churn and customer lifetime value, high personalization of the service, personalized ad, product suggestion, content creation, and AI chatbot and virtual assistants.

Furthermore, Natural Language Processing is revolutionizing the analysis of qualitative data. From textual data, AI generates themes, frequencies, and sentiments offering analytical tools for a real-time assessment of online reactions, discussions, and trends.

However, AI and marketing publication is dominated by review papers, state of the art, systematic analyses, bibliometric analyses, offering research agendas and suggestions for research questions. Many researchers map previous findings and few researchers contribute to the field.

Even from among existing papers trying to solve a problem, a large proportion is still using classical data analysis methods (regressions, structural equations, content analysis) to study classical concepts (attitude, intentions, behavior) toward digital marketing tools through surveys and interviews. Many papers are still considering AI as a context. Despite the interesting aspects of these researches, today the call is to an adoption of AI in the analysis of data; more interestingly, multi-method studies will help to surpass the limitations of classical data collection methods.

Furthermore, publication in AI marketing suffer from a lack of theoretical background. In fact, recent advances in data analytics move faster than advances in theory. AI fosters inductive approaches from a data-driven perspective. However, a theoretical background is important to position the studies, compare the results, and advance the field.

14.2.2 Marketing and Mental Health

Mental Illnesses or mental disorders are "health conditions that involve changes in emotion, thinking or behavior (or a combination of these)" (American Psychiatry Association, 2018). According to the World Health Organization (2022), mental disorders are characterized by "a combination of abnormal thoughts, perceptions, emotions, behavior and relationships with others". It has been also shown to affect a person's physical condition (Marcus et al., 2012).

At first, the association between the terms "marketing" and "mental health issues" seems incoherent. In reality, marketing, beyond the profit making aim, is also having a societal perspective trying to improve the well-being of the society. "Marketing has an impact on society through social aspirations and peer group influences" (Sheth, 2021). It helps to understand attitudes and behaviors and orients toward the consumption of products/services. It can also orient the organization of actions or the coordination of efforts of different stakeholders.

Marketing has much to add to mental health and much to learn from it (Berry and Bendapudi, 2007). Academics call for the integration of mental health and marketing with caution. They also prevent from considering mental health as a context to apply prior marketing knowledge. Nevertheless, it is possible to mutually enrich the knowledge in both disciplines through considering "conceptually rich variables or stretching the levels of variables in marketing".

An additional difficulty with mental health issues is the gap between patients who need assistance and those who really receive it; commonly known as the unmet mental health needs.

"An unmet mental health need exists when someone has a mental health problem but doesn't receive formal care, or when the care received is insufficient or inadequate" (Rens et al, 2020). Therefore, direct-to-consumer marketing is suitable to close this gap (Becker, 2015). Ghafari (2022) confirms this gap for a large proportion of adolescents through a systematic review and meta-analysis.

This gap can be due to structural reasons (eg., cost of the service) or attitudinal reasons (eg., stigma). In fact, barriers occur at every stage of the decision-making process starting from need recognition. Even when the need is recognized, patients have to look for information that may be complex and confusing. Then, they evaluate different options to solve the problem. Choosing from among perceived options is itself based on biased judgment (Kahneman et al., 1979). Very frequently, patients choose self-medication (Smith et al., 2017). If they finally come up to the intention to book an appointment, they may not do it in reality. Add to that, when the professional service is received it may not match the needed care (Bonabi et al., 2016). That there may be a "quality chasm" issue (Becker, 2015). In fact, "the demand for mental health services exceeds physical resources" (Rayland and Andrews, 2023). Therefore, the quality of the treatment may not be satisfying.

To understand this complex phenomenon of people's management of their mental health issues, we should study it taking into consideration the multiple actors, the specific context, and its evolution in time. The Social Cognitive Theory (SCT) is an influencing theory that has its origins in sociology. It can be an interesting background for this research. SCT considers that individuals are active agents that influence each other and the environment and are influenced by the environment in a reciprocal determinism (Bandura, 2000). According to the SCT, human behavior is determined by three sets of concepts: 1. cognitive factors: knowledge, expectations, and attitudes; 2. behavioral factors: skills, practice, and self-efficacy; and 3. environmental factors: social norms, access in community, and influence on others.

In a crisis context, the decision-making process is centralized (governmental policies for example). In fact, centralizing authority is a common practice of organizations and social groups in crises to efficiently allocate scarce resources (Simmel, 1955; Crozier, 1964). However, "collective efficacy" as a community support action is an important organized action that helps individuals to force a social change (Sewell, 1992; Snow, 2001).

Community support is an old concept. In the mental health context, Tessler and Goldman (1982) assessed the role of community support programs for the chronically mentally ill. In 1995, Wilson et al. proved the role of communities to support offenders suffering from mental health issues in crises reducing uncertainty and concerns about health-related issues (AkhtherandSopory, 2022). Hagger and Hamilton (2022), in their conceptual review of social cognitive theories and behavior change during the pandemic, found that these theories helped to identify cognitive factors that are determinant for health behavior playing the role of mechanisms of action. However, they mentioned that "few interventions in this context have a strong basis in theory" (Hagger and Hamilton, 2022). On social media, health information posts are a two-way exchange were people post questions, ask for information or recommendation, report feelings but also read others' posts and provide support. Hence, they can learn about themselves, others, and the environment. SCT was adopted by Myneni et al. (2016) to study "peer-to-peer communication in a health-related online community."

Given this interesting research opportunity, Mirabito et al. (2022) launched a call for marketing papers to shed light on the intersection between marketing and mental health because of the importance of the challenges yet the number of publications is limited. These researches are also encouraged in the established Multidisciplinary research priorities for the Covid-19 pandemic. Holmes et al. (2020) mention: "Innovative research is needed to establish ways to mitigate and manage mental health risks and inform interventions under pandemic conditions."

14.2.3 Mental Health and Social Media

In the healthcare sector, a network of care is developed from diagnosis automation to treatment recommendation with timely follow-up. Electronic healthcare record systems, warble devices, connected apparels, and physical robots are becoming more and more common in hospital and patients' daily lives. Surgical robots can even surpass humans in very complex medical acts while requiring the intervention of humans. Nowadays, robots are more sociable and interact with patients in a fluent way. Robotic process automation assist the hospital administration in minimizing the time allocated to routine tasks and decreasing error risks. Applications on the patients' phone help to track several parameters (calculate calories in a meal, sleep time, etc.).

AI methods have also been introduced to help mental health providers, including psychiatrists and psychologists, based on historical patient data like medical records, and behavioral data, in medical decision-making. As one of the next generation artificial intelligence technologies, Machine Learning (ML) and Deep Learning (DL) have demonstrated excellent performance in many practical applications, from computer vision to healthcare (Miotto et al., 2018).

Furthermore, the growing literature uses increasingly sophisticated methods to make intelligent predictions about the mental health of social media users based on their online activities. The availability of a large volume of user-generated content on social media is a valuable source of information for organizations, policy makers, and researchers. However, the majority of this data is still raw, read by a restricted number people and rarely gathered and analyzed. From among users of social media, people suffering from mental health issues share their thoughts, their feelings, and even their actions, including suicide intentions.

This is what led many researchers to start working on the detection of mental health disorders on social media using machine learning. In other words, they have been focusing on natural language analysis (also known as natural language processing) via posts from social platforms. As opposed to the exhaustive documentation produced by healthcare professionals, social media data captures thoughts, feelings, and speech in people's own voices. These types of data sources have become very important for monitoring several mental health issues such as depression (De Choudhury et al., 2014; Wongkoblap et al., 2017).

Patient-generated content is available on social networks, mainly in the form of tweets, Reddits, or even forum publications (Gonzalez-Hernandez et al., 2017; Névéoland Zweigenbaum, 2017). This content is a valuable source of data. In fact, for long time, data collection in the health sector was dominated by the administration of surveys and the conduct of interviews. Given the limitations of surveys administered mainly to students, social media content offers an interesting alternative (Machin et al., 2022). "Social media data can be a more inclusive research methodology, using consumer- and marketer-generated content to make unseen mental health issues visible Consumers use social media as a communal, emotional, and informational resource for their mental illness and the associated stigma" (Machin, 2022).

Following their systematic review, Wongkoblap et al. (2017) provided a conceptual representation of researches about mental health on social network. The initial stage was users generate content, which loads on machine learning to predict the illness and finally result in access (health services) or receive (intervention) or have (cognitive behavioral therapy).

Previous studies demonstrated P2P positive effect on mental health status (van Uden-Kraan et al., 2008; Bartlett and Coulson, 2011). Other studies reported negative effect of social media in general (Pang, 2022) and for mental health people in particular (Kumar et al., 2015; Battaglia et al., 2022). Despite the mitigated results (Bekalu et al., 2023), social media platforms served to exchange social support including information (Fox and Duggan, 2013; Zhang, 2017), emotional support (Hwang et al., 2010; Naslund et al., 2016), belonging comfort (Singleton, 2016), and instrumental support (Cohen and Wills, 1985; Swan, 2009). Instrumental support means providing financial help, tangible material, or services (Nick et al., 2018).

Given the existence of many barriers to mental health wellness (or seeking help from professionals), social media platforms become an alternative because it is used for free, available 24/7, offering anonymity, advice, and recommendations from individuals who are similar or who have knowledge and/or experience. In addition to ease of access, there is also anonymity and personal control over engagement levels (Brown et al., 2021). This support is most of the time provided in an informal way online (Rayland and Andrews, 2023).

In times of crises, several emotional reactions may be noticed on social media. Anxiety and depression are likely to be common in such periods because anyone can experience multiple threats and stressors that cause such disorders (Cisler et al., 2010; Hammen et al., 2005). In addition to the obvious impact of the Covid-19 pandemic on physical health, public health and the wider medical community are also preventing a mental health crisis (Auerbach et al., 2020).

Several researchers used NLP methods to identify mental health issues during Covid-19 (Brewer et al., 2022; Low et al., 2020; Marshall et al., 2022; Thukral et al., 2022; Zhu et al., 2023). Regarding the Covid-19 pandemic, Alambo et al. (2020) have shown a high correlation between postings in r/depression and r/Coronavirus subreddits in September 2020. Wolohan et al. (2020) adopted a preliminary analysis that uses a deep neural network in order to predict population rates of depression on Reddit in order to estimate the effect of Covid-19 on mental health. Finally, a group of health specialists from Harvard have used natural language processing and aimed to characterize changes in 15 of Reddit mental health support groups (Low et al., 2020). They were able to detect vulnerable groups and alarming subjects related to mental disorders during the Covid-19 pandemic. Park et al. (2018) studied three online mental health groups (anxiety, depression, and Post-Traumatic Stress Disorder.) to discover the themes discussed in each community and the different uses by the members. They found that from among the emergent themes, four are present in all the communities: positive emotions, gratitude, sleep issues, and work issues.

However, prediction of mental health status on social media suffers from the lack of theoretical operationalization (Ernala et al., 2019) as well as validity issues (Chancellor and De Choudhury, 2020). Alike Chancellor et al. (2019) questioned the prediction of mental health disease through posts that are not all the time informative.

14.3 METHODOLOGY

For the purposes of this research, we extracted user posts from Reddit: six mental health-related subreddits each one of them is associated with a specific mental illness (r/depression, r/Anxiety, r/bipolar, r/BPD, r/schizophrenia, and r/autism), and five non-mental health-related subreddits (r/personal_finance, r/relationships, r/Fitness, r/Parenting and r/COVID19_support). Only original posts were included in the data collection. The title and text of each Reddit post were merged together. The posts were collected using the python Pushshift API. All the collected data was anonymized, thus, no personal information will be exposed to the public. Table 14.1 summarizes the information of the collected datasets in three periods of the spread of Covid-19: first semester (From 1 January 2020 to 30 June 2020), second semester (From 1 July 2020 to 31 December 2020), and third semester (From 1 January 2021 to 30 June 2021).

Before working on text data, it is important to preprocess it in order to eliminate some of the noise and inconsistencies that may prevent the NLP algorithms from giving good results (Stokes et al., 2020). The following steps were undertaken:

- Concatenate the title and the "selftext" of each Reddit.
- Remove duplicates and missing values
- Remove extra spaces, punctuations, emojis, urls, and specific Reddit characters
- Filter Stopwords (such as the, are, a, etc.)
- Convert the words to lowercase

TABLE 14.1
Number of Filtered Posts Collected from Each subReddit

	Subreddit	First Semester of Covid-19	Second Semester of Covid-19	Third Semester of Covid-19
MHsubreddits	r/Anxiety	26816	21230	22298
	r/depression	38934	24009	21281
	r/BPD	15136	15658	20236
	r/bipolar	9947	8250	10122
	r/schizophrenia	4287	4018	5718
	r/autism	3773	4647	4610
	Total	**98893**	**77812**	**84265**
NMHsubreddits	r/personal_finance	39234	15900	28293
	r/relationships	29952	9034	18638
	r/Parenting	10880	4390	12668
	r/Fitness	10435	2874	2997
	r/COVID19_support	2829	3219	2905
	Total	**93330**	**35417**	**65501**

- Lemmatize: take into account the morphological analysis of words and use dictionaries that the algorithm can search to re-link the form to its lemma.
- Tokenize the post (split each Reddit into a list of single words) using the natural language toolkit (NLTK) implemented in Python to create a dictionary having a set of 100,000 unique tokens.
- Convert the sentences to vectors, where the maximum length was set to 100 words. This vector was the input to the Deep Learning model.
- Divide the dataset into a training (80%) set and a testing set (20%).

When the dataset is clean, we can move to the data analysis. Figure 14.1 shows the different steps of data extraction and analysis.

As represented in Figure 14.1, the methods applied for the datasets after cleaning and pre-processing are: Convolutional Neural Networks, Classification, Trend Analysis, sentiment analysis, and LDA.

Convolutional Neural Networks are a mixture of the convolutional layer, the pooling layer, and the dense layers. The convolutional layer extracts information from the data and passes it to the next layer. The higher the number of filters of the convolutional layer, the more complex the extracted information is. In fact, this filter is sided across the width and height of the input, and a dot product is computed to give an activation map. This process increases the spatial size, which is then reduced by pooling layers. In our model, we used a Max Pooling layer. Max pooling is a pooling method that only extracts the maximum element from the region of the matrix covered by the filter. As a result, the final output of this type of layer will be a matrix that contains the most important features of the previous mapping. Finally, we usually find a set of fully connected dense layers that get concatenated with these convolutional layers and pooling layers to predict the class label.

In the case of NLP tasks, when the CNN model is applied to text instead of images, we usually have a one-dimensional array representing the text. Hence, the architecture of the ConvNetsis changed to 1D convolutional and pooling operations. The inputs in this case are "words" instead of images. These tokens are converted to embeddings and represented in another dimensional feature space. Then, 1D filters are successively applied to these embeddings to form what is called a

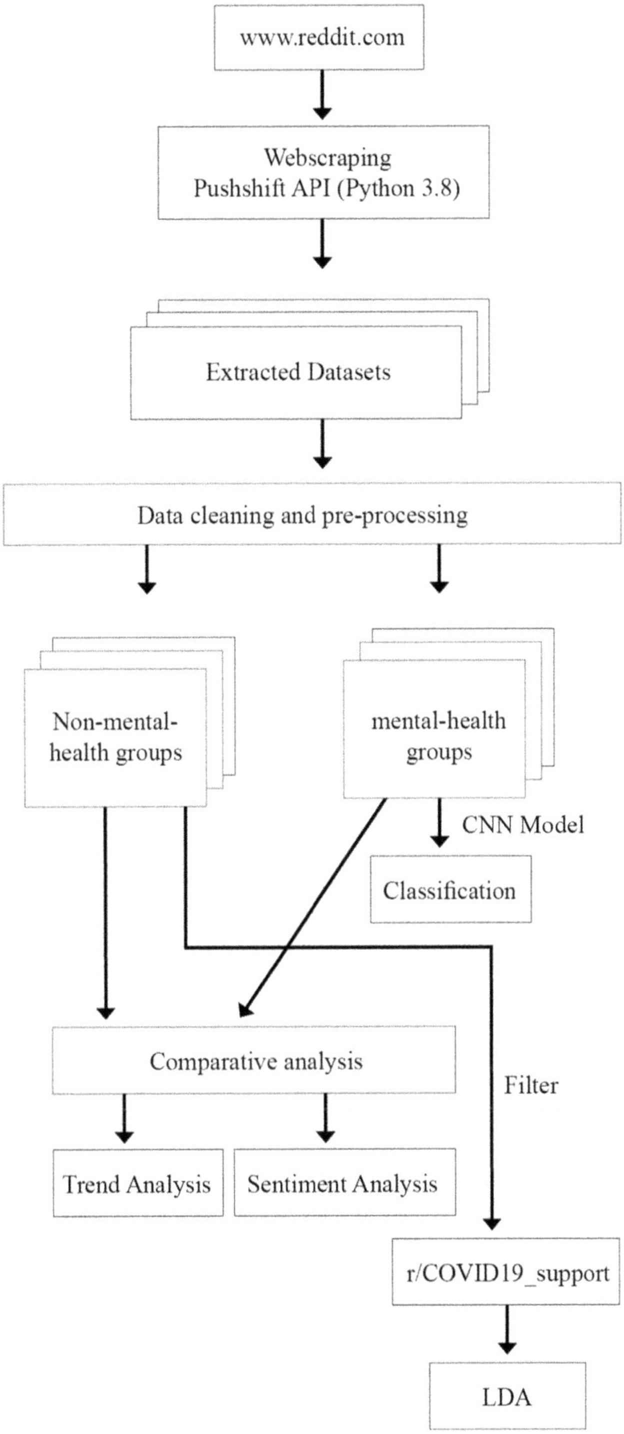

FIGURE 14.1 Data extraction and analysis pipeline.

convolutional feature map which is finally pooled, flattened, and fed to dense layers of a deep neural network for prediction.

For **Classification** purposes, we trained six binary classification models based on a Convolutional Neural Network, each of which categorizes a Reddit post into one of the collected subreddit texts: r/depression, r/Anxiety, r/bipolar, r/BPD, r/schizophrenia, and r/autism. An overview of the proposed CNN-based model is shown in Figure 14.2.

Our hypothesis is that a user who suffers from a particular mental illness writes a post on the corresponding subReddit that copes with the problem. A user can write posts across multiple groups if he/she suffers from multiple mental health problems, e.g., a user suffering from both depression and anxiety. However, if the model is trained with the posts of users who have multiple symptoms, the classification model may suffer from noisy data. Therefore, we developed six independent binary classification models for each symptom to improve the accuracy.

By developing six independent models for each mental disorder, each of which uses data where users suffer from only one specific mental problem, we were able to accurately identify a user's potential mental state. For example, to develop a model for detecting depression, we labeled the posts written by users who upload posts only in the r/depression as the depression class; the opposite class is referred to as the non-depression class.

For the classification task, we utilized TensorFlow, which is a machine learning library written in python and supports a variety of Deep Neural Networks architectures including Convolutional Neural Networks. Kerasis built on top of Tensorflow to make code cleaner and more accessible.

In order to assess the performance of our models, the evaluation step is crucial. Accuracy score is used when "True Positives" and "True Negatives" are both equally important. It is defined by this formula:

$$Accuracy = \frac{(True\ Positive + True\ Negative)}{(True\ Positive + False\ Positive + True\ Negative + False\ Negative)}$$

We evaluated the accuracy scores of our six binary models during the first, second, and third semesters of Covid-19- to assess any important change, which may suggest dataset shifts after the outbreak of the pandemic.

For topic modeling, we chose Latent Dirichlet Allocation (LDA), which is one of the most used methods. It is a natural language processing technique that provides tools to uncover the hidden topics in certain collections of text, classify documents into the uncovered topics, and use classification in order to automate summarizing and searching these documents. LDA is a fully generative unsupervised model that aims to extract k number of topics from a set of documents defining each one of these topics by weighted words. It is a way to explain a series of observations by unobserved groups that explain why some of the data samples are similar. We also used Topic Coherence measures score to measure the semantic similarity between high scoring words in the topic. These measurements help distinguish between topics that are semantically interpretable topics and topics that are artifacts of statistical inference.

For Trend Analysis, we developed a function that iterates over all the subreddit data frames and counts all the occurrences of words related to each and every feature. Then, we passed the output to another function that measures the proportion of these words among all the words used in each post at each subreddit. Finally, we summed the results to get the monthly rate and plotted the obtained results to explore the importance of these features in mental health change on Reddit.

Sentiment analysis or called opinion mining, refers to the usage of natural language processing techniques, text analysis, and linguistics to derive subjective information from textual datasets (Serrano-Guerrero et al., 2015). In other words, sentiment analysis tries to determine the attitude of

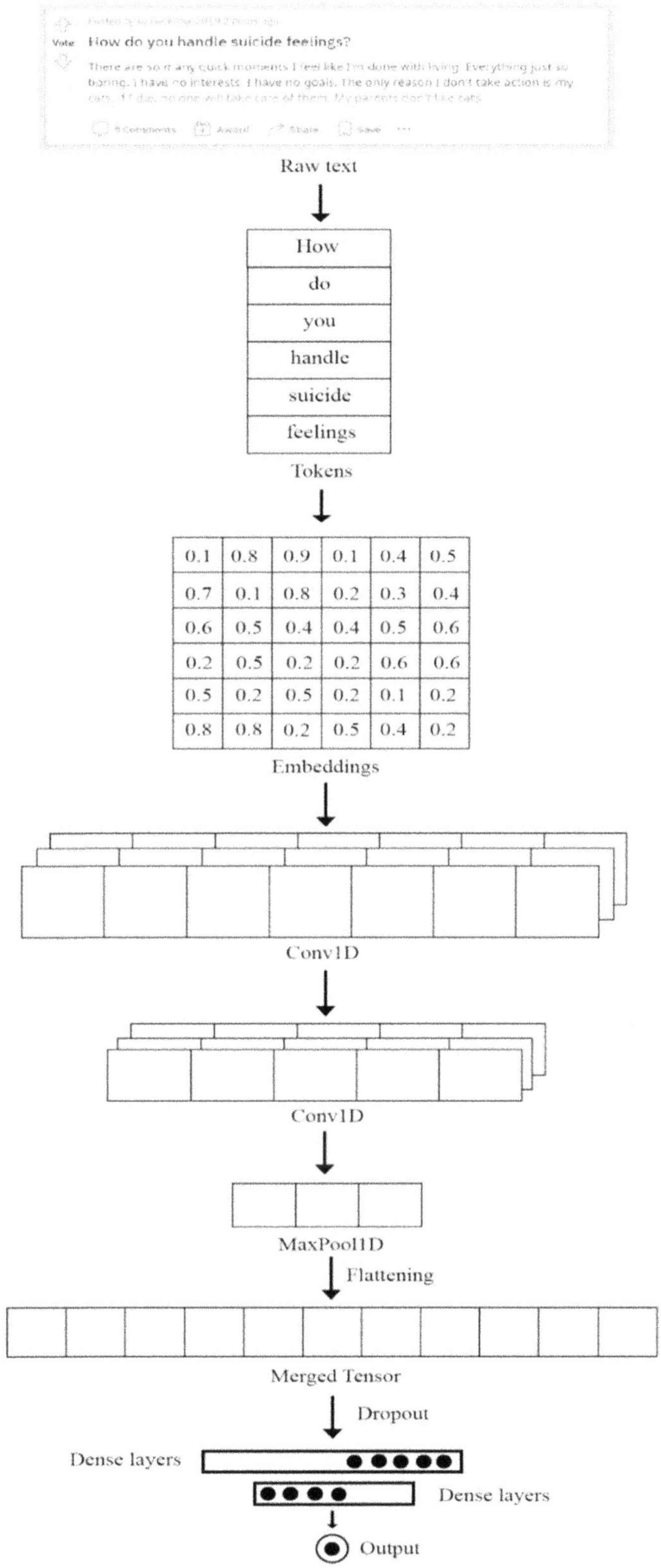

FIGURE 14.2 Architecture of the CNN-based model for mental illness classification.

an individual concerning some topic (if he/she approves/does not approve) or the overall polarity of a comment or text written in a particular context. His/her attitude might be driven by his/her own judgment or mood.

In this part, we tried to derive sentiments from different posts and study the proportion of negativity found spanning from the early stage of the virus outbreak to almost one year after. For this purpose, we used the VADER (Valence Aware Dictionary for Sentiment Reasoning) unsupervised sentiment analysis algorithm. This algorithm takes into account not only the polarity of text (whether it is positive or negative) but also the intensity of the sentiments (emotions). VADER works with a dictionary that links lexical features to emotion intensities also known as sentiment scores. Thus, the total sentiment score of a given document can be derived by adding up the intensity of each token in the text. We then implemented a K-Means unsupervised clustering algorithm to classify our posts into positive sentiments and negative sentiments. Finally, we calculated the proportion of negative sentiments during each semester and plotted.

14.4 ANALYSIS AND INTERPRETATION OF RESULTS

14.4.1 Exploratory Data Analysis

Once the data is collected, cleaned, and preprocessed, we visualize its distribution to further understand its structure. The number of words in each Reddit post ranges from 1 to 800 words and on average falls between 50 and 150 words (Figure 14.3). The number of characters in each word appears to range from three to nine characters and on average occurs between five to seven characters. Figure 14.4 shows the most frequent words in all the datasets. Figures 14.5 and 14.6 represent frequent words respectively for MH groups and NMH groups.

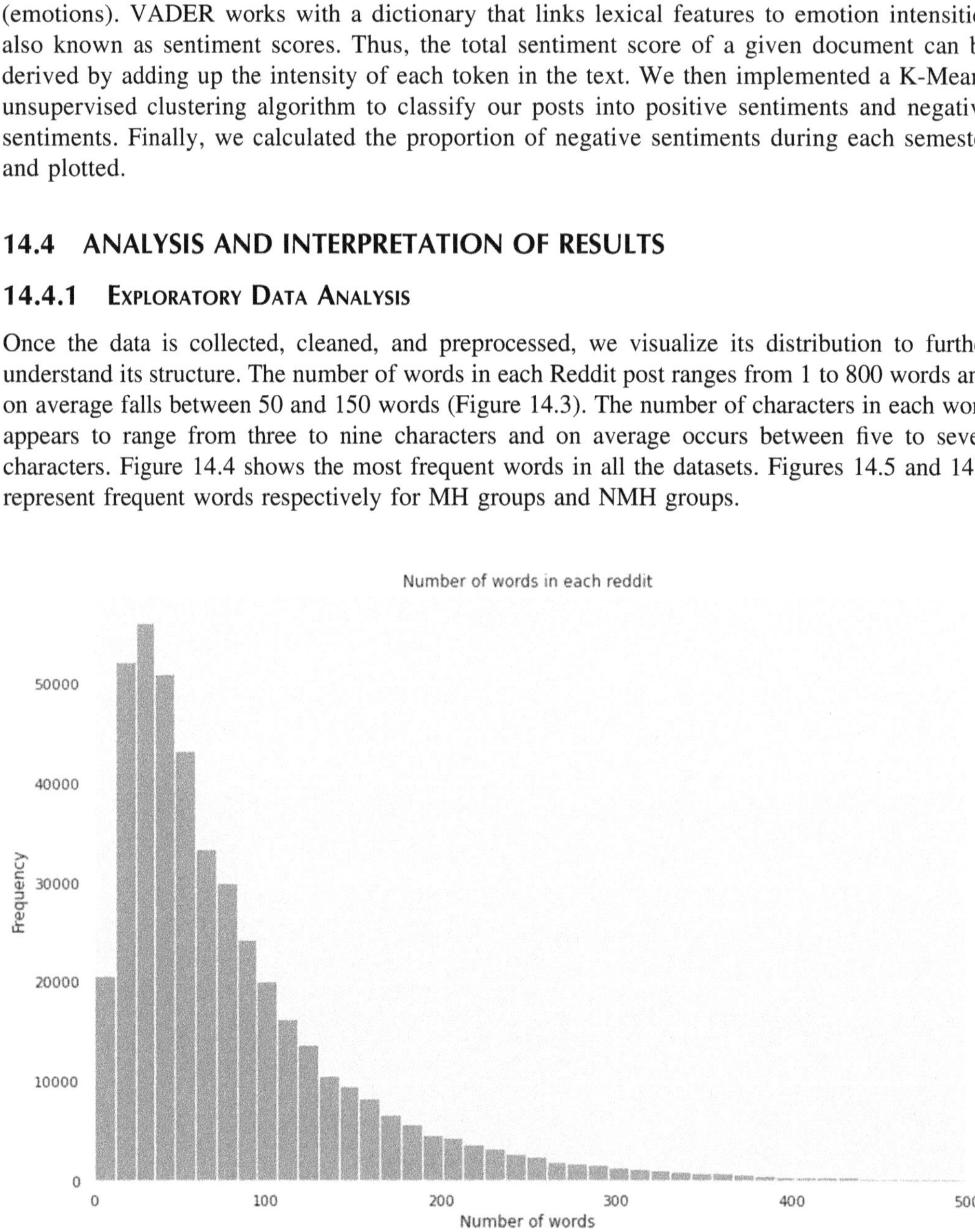

FIGURE 14.3 Number of words in each Reddit post.

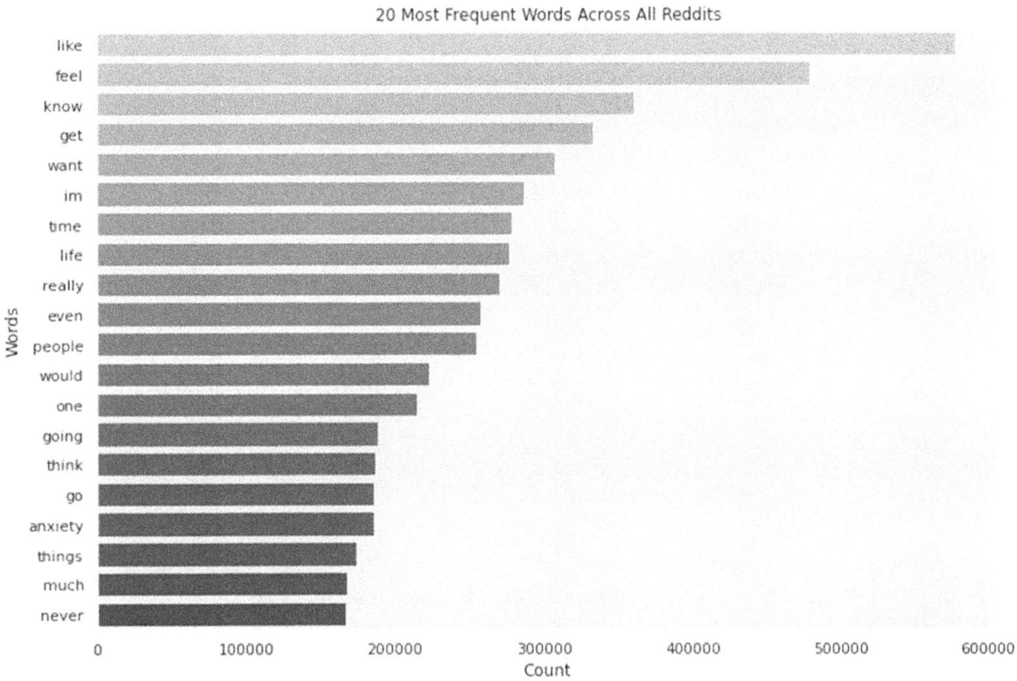

FIGURE 14.4 top 20 most frequent words across all Reddits.

FIGURE 14.5 Wordcloud in the MH groups.

FIGURE 14.6 Wordcloud in the NMH groups.

TABLE 14.2
Comparing Accuracy Performance of CNN Models across the First 3 Semesters of Covid-19

Subreddit	First Semester of Covid-19 (1)	Second Semester of Covid-19 (2)	Third Semester of Covid-19 (3)	Shift |(1) - (2)|	Shift |(2) - (3)|
r\bipolar	0.9461	0.9425	0.9573	0.0036	0.0148
r\depression	0.8536	0.8645	0.8676	0.0109	0.0031
r\BPD	0.9224	0.9106	0.9083	0.0118	0.0023
r\schizophrenia	0.9696	0.9713	0.9690	0.0017	0.0023
r\Anxiety	0.9032	0.9091	0.9189	0.0068	0.0098
r\autism	0.9849	0.9739	0.9653	0.011	0.0086
Mean	**0.9300**	**0.92865**	**0.9311**	**0.02398**	**0.00682**

14.4.2 Dataset Shifts

Larger differences in accuracy scores may indicate dataset shifts after the spread of Covid-19. Table 14.2 compares the accuracy performance of CNN models across the three semesters. Overall, the CNN model performed similarly and presented high accuracies for predicting mental illness from user posts. The autism/non-autism model presented the highest accuracy (~97%) followed by schizophrenia/non-schizophrenia and bipolar/non-bipolar (~96% and ~94% respectively). We found that the change in accuracy from the first to the second period was more significant than the change in accuracy from the second to the third period. This may suggest that our dataset shifted significantly from the first semester to the second semester of Covid-19. The reason might be that the first wave of Covid-19 created an initial blow in the MH groups. However, things started back to normal during the second semester.

14.4.3 Covid-19 Related Themes Change for Different Groups

To answer our first research question, we performed trend analysis.

> ***RQ1:*** *How can the trend analysis of Covid-19 lexicon reveal change for different MH and NMH groups?*

We tried to visualize the evolution of different features in different subreddits on users' online content by measuring the presence of words taken from a Covid-19 lexicon developed by Low et al. (2020) to see how they may be impacted by the outbreak of the pandemic. The studied themes are: economic stress, isolation, suicidality, and Covid-19.

For economic stress posts, r/personal_finance and r/relationships showed the most important spikes and fluctuations in all the groups (Figure 14.7a. and 14.7b.). In MH groups, the r/depression subreddit had an import rise during the initial stage then the trend dropped significantly later on. For the other MH groups, the anxiety group showed a plateau from March 2020 to August 2020 and different peaks in the third semester. For NMH groups r/Parenting and r/Fitness, there was almost no trend for economic stress. In fact, the trend economic stress for these two subreddits is the lowest for the NMH groups.

*For **isolation**, we found that r/relationships (within NMH groups) and r/depression (within MH groups) showed* spikes in isolation-related posts during the first semester and the third semester, more specifically, in May 2020 and May 2021 (Figure 14.8a. and 14.8b.). However, the trend for r/depression showed a decrease in the third semester and another increase at the end of the third semester. On the other hand, r/relationships presented a massive spike in the third semester despite

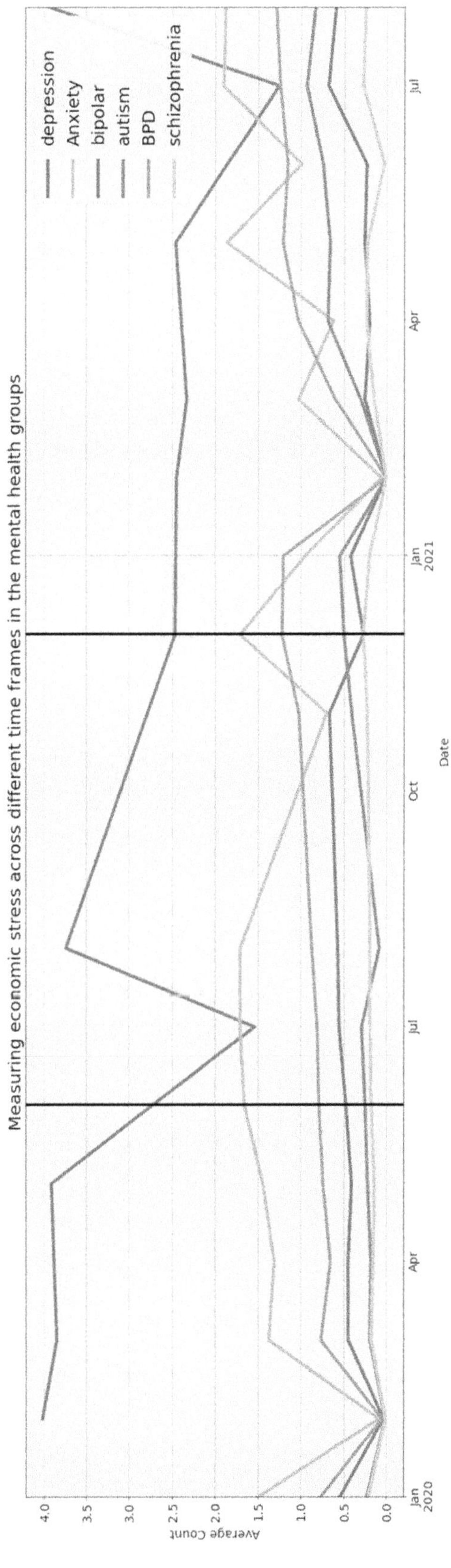

FIGURE 14.7a Measuring economic stress for MH groups.

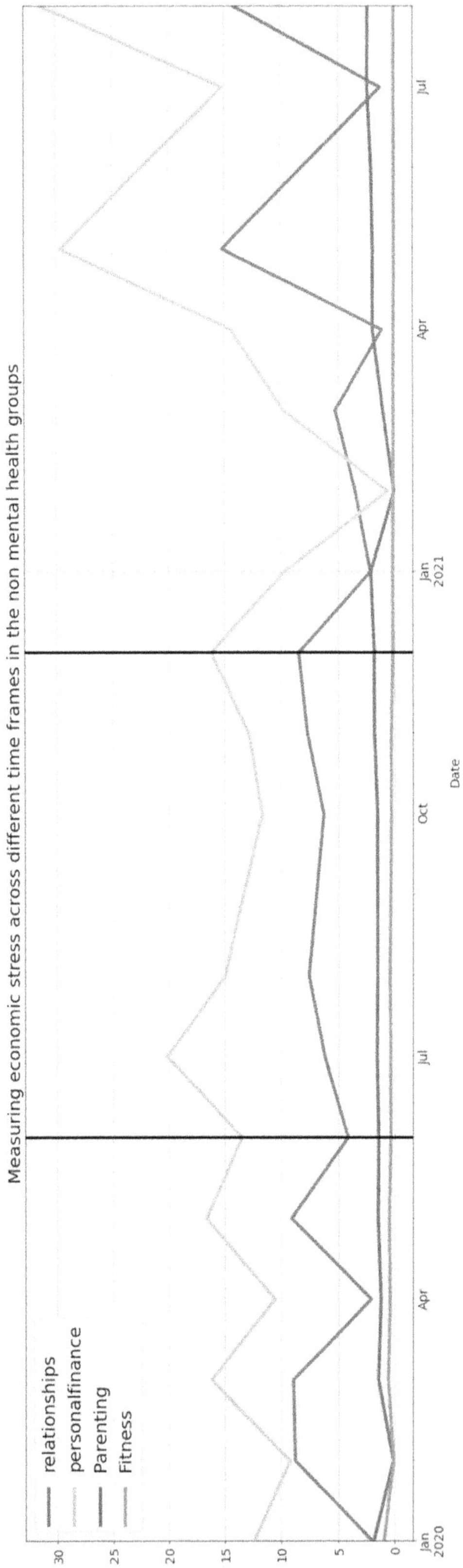

FIGURE 14.7b Measuring economic stress for NMH groups.

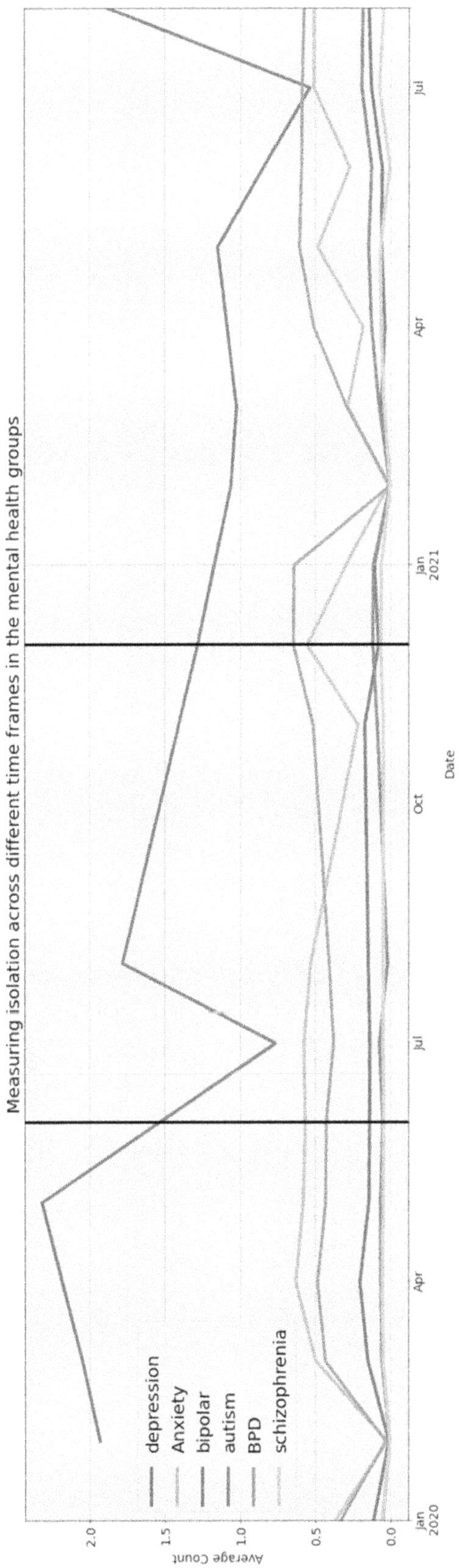

FIGURE 14.8a Measuring isolation for MH groups.

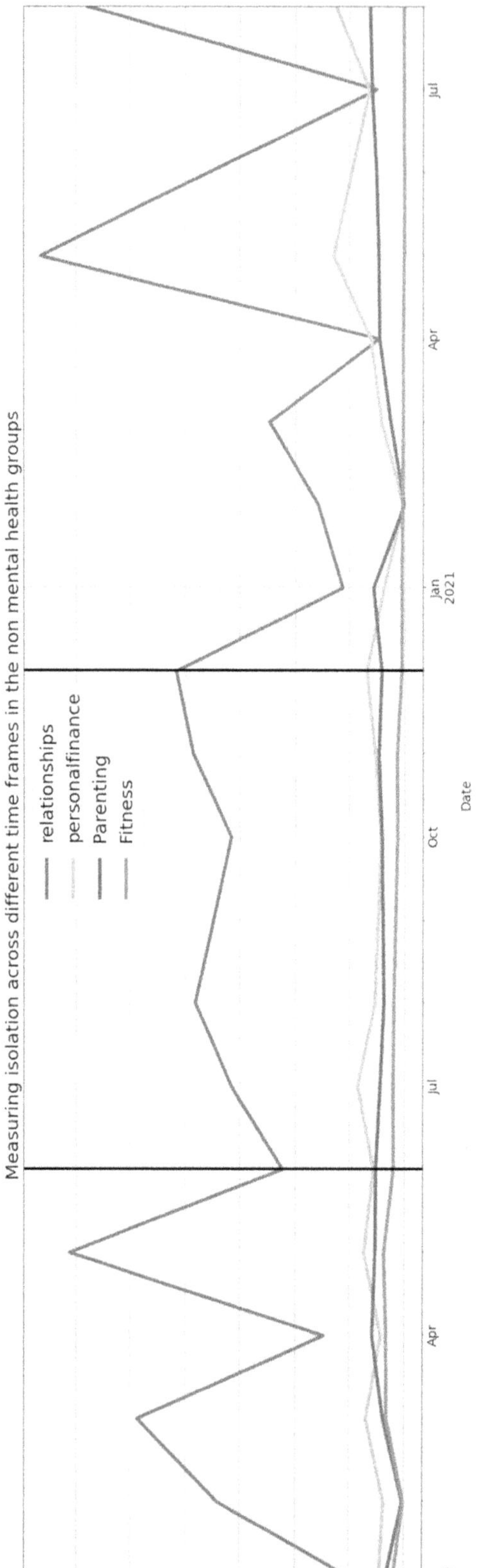

FIGURE 14.8b Measuring isolation for NMH groups.

a small decrease during the second semester. For the remaining NMH groups, the trend was overall stable apart from some fluctuations at the beginning of the first and third semester. Finally, for the other MH groups, isolation topics were almost absent.

For suicidality-related user content, r/depression (MH group) and r/relationships (NMH group) were the two subreddits that presented the highest rates and many spikes, especially during the first semester for r/depression and in May 2020 and two turbulent semesters (the first and the third) for r/relationships (Figure 14.9a. and 14.9b.). However, the other groups were not showing high suicide content.

For the **Covid-19** theme, we found that the content of posts for most of the subreddits was affected by the presence of Covid-19-related words during the first semester of the pandemic (Figure 14.10a. and 14.10b.). More specifically, the overall most important rise in Covid-19-related words occurred in March 2020 and May 2020, especially in the r/depression and r/Anxiety (MH) and r/relationships (NMH). We noticed an increase before the start of the second semester for r/Parenting, r/personal_finance. For the other subreddits, there was an initial increase during the initial outbreak. However, we could not find any major trends later on. This may suggest that the outbreak of the virus created a general shock in the Reddit communities as they started talking about the pandemic on Reddit. Then they got back to a "new normal" and this trend decreased massively.

14.4.4 Negative Sentiment Change for Different Groups

To answer our second research question, we performed sentiment analysis.

> ***RQ2****: How does* ***sentiment analysis*** *track negative sentiment change for different MH and NMH groups?*

For MH groups, we noticed that the negativity rate is quite stable and high for the three periods. It went from 42% in the first semester to 45% during the third semester (Figure 14.11). For NMH groups, we found that the negativity rate is comparable to MH groups in the first semester of Covid-19 with around 43% of posts that are classified as containing negative sentiments (Figure 14.12). However, this number increases dramatically during the second semester reaching almost 68% negativity.

During the third and last semester, we found that the negativity rate went down substantially and reached 35%; that is a low rate compared to the first two periods and compared to the MH groups.

14.4.5 Discussed Topics Change

To answer our third research question, we used LDA to discover the discussed topics in each period.

> ***RQ3****: What are the discovered discussed topics trough* ***text mining*** *of the content generated by Covid-19 support community during each of the 3 semesters?*

First, we tried to assess the performance of each number of topics on our modeling results. For that purpose, we plotted the different coherence scores of each number of topics and found that the optimal number was 8 as shown in Figure 14.13 as the highest coherence score was obtained for the LDA model with k = 8 topics.

We then used the python "gensim" package to perform a Latent Dirichlet Allocation model estimation, which determined groups of words that appeared frequently together in posts across subreddits and then divided them into eight different topics to assess topic stability across different

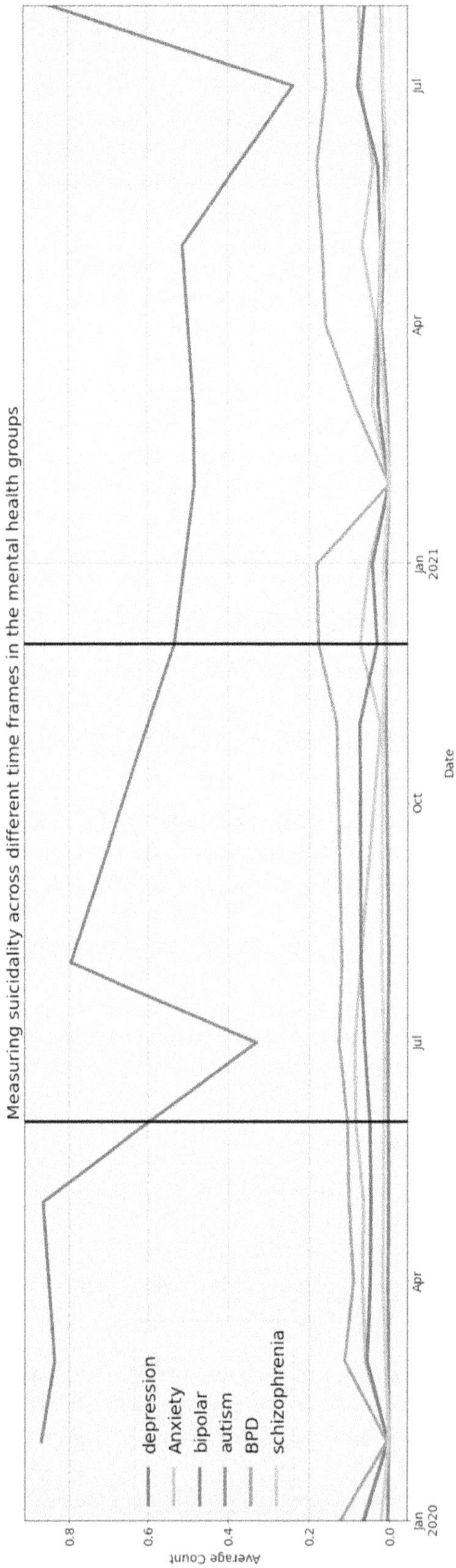

FIGURE 14.9a Measuring suicidality for MH groups.

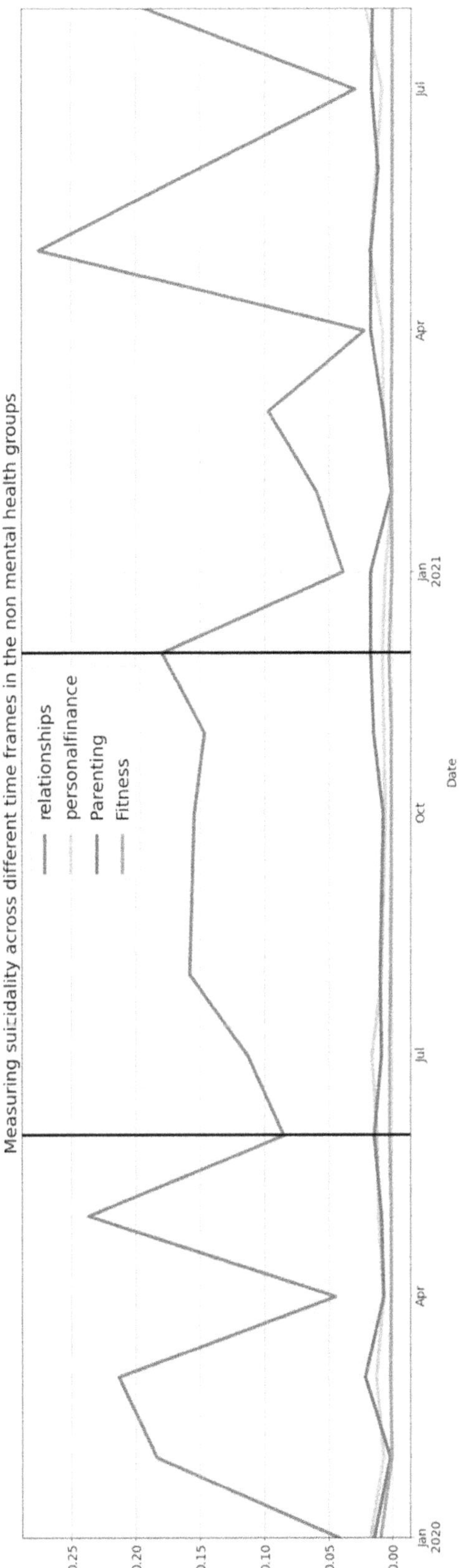

FIGURE 14.9b Measuring suicidality for NMH groups.

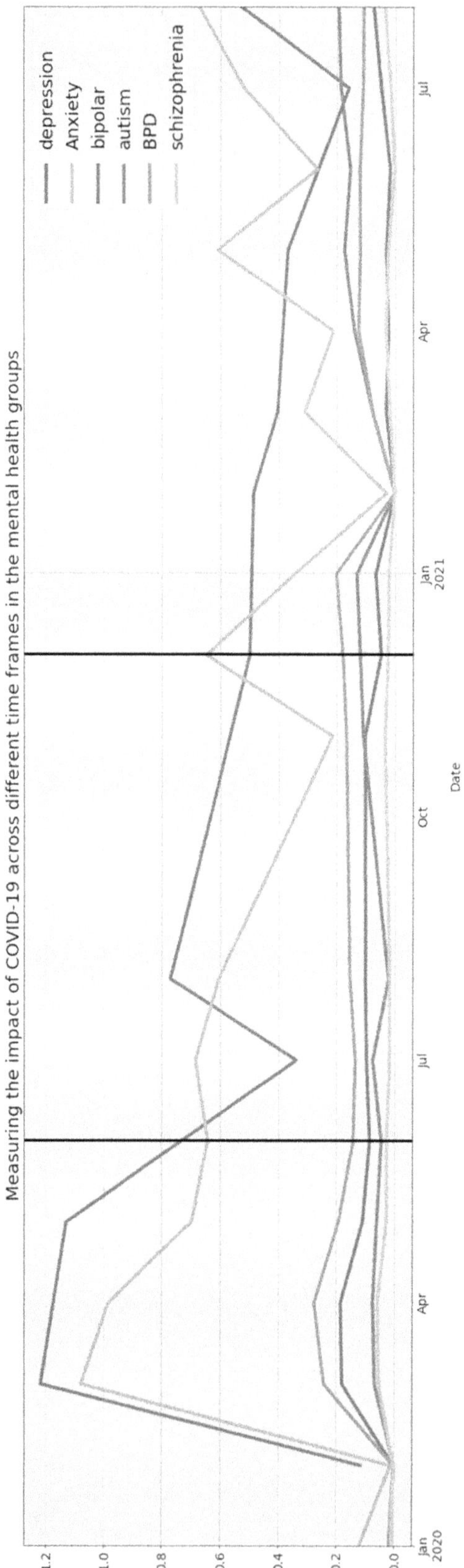

FIGURE 14.10a Measuring the impact of Covid-19 for M.H groups.

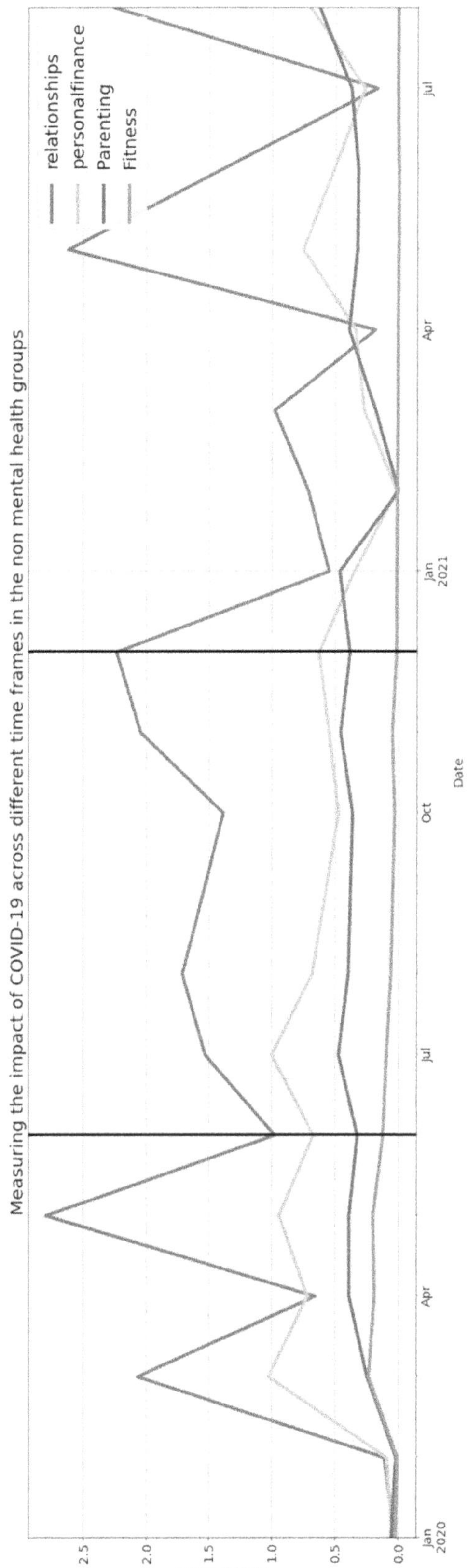

FIGURE 14.10b Measuring the impact of Covid-19 for Non M.H groups.

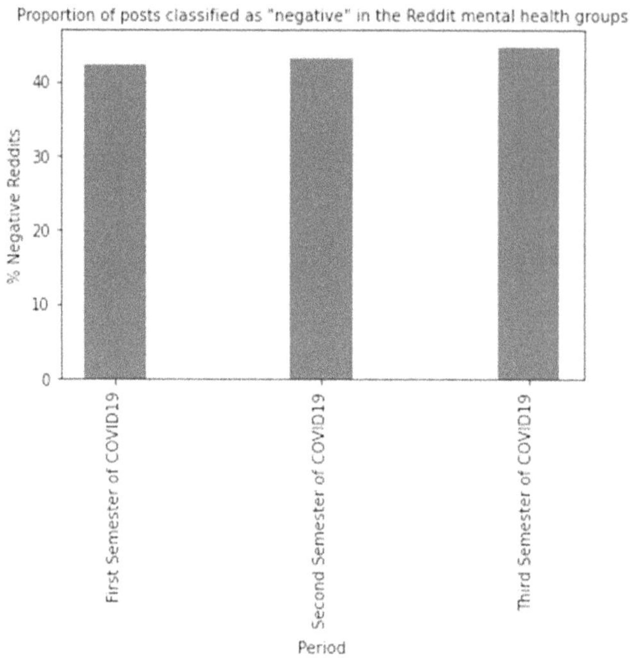

FIGURE 14.11 Sentiment analysis results MH groups.

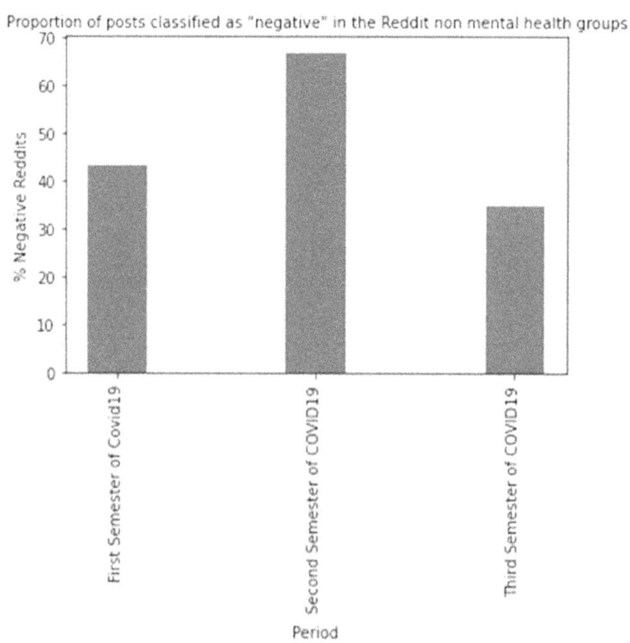

FIGURE 14.12 Sentiment analysis results NMH groups.

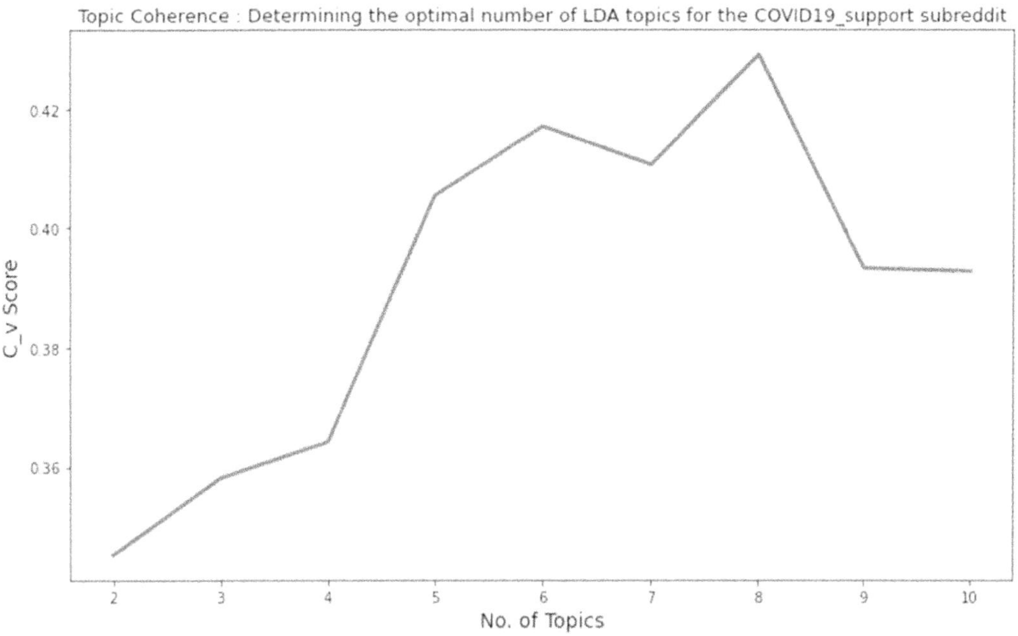

FIGURE 14.13 Determining the optimal number of topics.

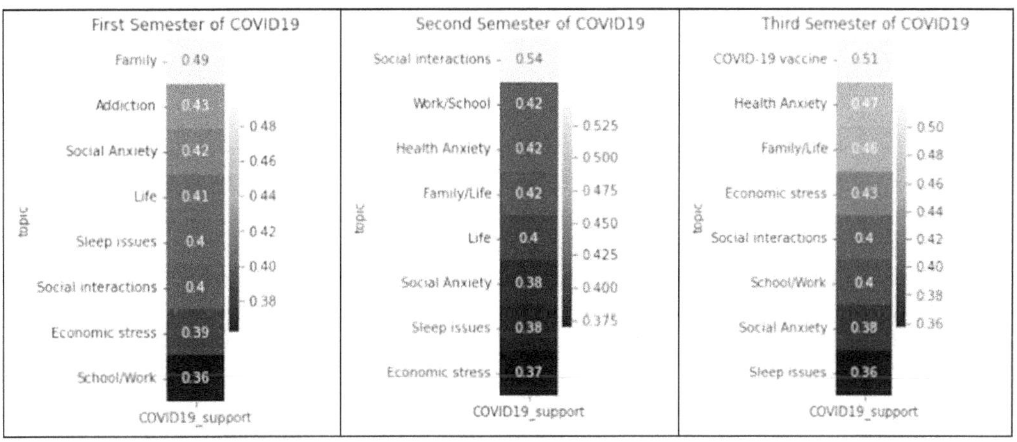

FIGURE 14.14 LDA results.

timeframes. The LDA model also helped us to assess the evolution of the distribution of the posts across the topics (Figure 14.14).

We found that the "Family" topic was among the top four topics considered in the r/COVID19_support subreddit during the three periods. This may suggest that during the pandemic, users were always concerned about the health and well-being of their family members. During the first semester of Covid-19, the "Addiction," "Social anxiety," "life," "Sleep issues" and "Social interactions" topics were prevalent in the Covid-19 support subReddit. This may suggest that users suffered from the consumption of substances during the initial stage of the pandemic and they are concerned with their relationships. This is confirmed in the second semester with the prevalence of "Social interactions" as a top term. We also noticed the outbreak of a new topic, "Health Anxiety," which was also more and more important during the third semester. This may suggest that users started worrying more about their health during these last periods as we noticed the outbreak of many dangerous and deadly variants of the virus and thus an increased death rate, especially during the second semester. During the third semester, one of the most frequent topics was "COVID-19 vaccine." This may suggest that after more than two tough wave users began to see the vaccine as an ultimate solution to get back to their normal lives.

14.4.6 Discussion of Results

Several NLP techniques were used to measure how Covid-19 may have affected various groups on Reddit. Hereafter, we will discuss our research questions' analysis results and we will compare our findings to other researchers' results.

First, there is an important dataset shift of 0.02395 in mean accuracy in the period ranging from the first semester to the second semester of Covid-19. This value is not far from the one obtained by Low et al. (2020), who found a 0.025 total shift in F1 Score from the period ranging from a few months before the pandemic to the initial stage of the outbreak of the virus. These findings confirm that the Reddit posts are indeed changing and getting influenced by the wave of Covid-19 cases. In fact, people are reacting to this change by expressing their feelings and thoughts on online social platforms such as Reddit because they were and still are the only way for some to get their issues off their chests.

Furthermore, our accuracy scores were better than the ones obtained by Kim et al. (2020), who conducted a similar study in order to classify user-generated content on Reddit into the corresponding mental disorder that the corresponding user is suffering from. In fact, our mean accuracy was almost 5% better. Therefore, this may suggest that our approach can be used to help researchers in this domain as well as mental health practitioners to identify users in need of help and who do not have the opportunity to get counseling.

The groups that showed the highest movements with different peaks related to the lexicons "economic stress," "isolation," "suicidality," and "Covid-19" are r/depression and r/Anxiety for MH groups and r/relationships and r/personal_finance for NMH groups. Furthermore, r/Anxiety, r/depression, r/personal_finance, and r/relationships showed several spikes in Covid-19 related posts during the first semester of the pandemic, more precisely in March and May before other subreddits were posting about the pandemic. This evidence supports concerns regarding the extended stress that people with anxiety and depression may have experienced during the first months of the pandemic. These findings also support that people have begun to worry about their wealth and their personal relationships when the first wave of cases hit and the possibility of general lockdowns was on the table in many countries, which will restrict people's freedom of movement, preventing them from working, selling goods and services, making money, and seeing their family members and loved ones. This is also aligned with the results obtained by Low et al. (2020). Alike, Zhu et al. (2023) found that the first 28 days following the outbreak of an important event might have a serious impact on mental health.

Second, the sentiment analysis results suggest that the Covid-19 pandemic slightly affected people who suffered from mental illnesses negatively. For NMH, our results showed a peak during the second semester. This is comparable to Pan et al.'s (2021) findings. This suggests that users who posted on Reddit during these periods may have experienced a wave of negativity and desperation along with the second wave of the virus, which was expected to be less significant but ended up being as brutal as the first one. As a result, Reddit users felt anxious about their wealth, their relationships, and their well-being and their words were driven by fear, pessimism, and depressive thoughts. Later on, Reddit users got accustomed to the situation and coped with the virus; the pandemic is no longer considered as a threat for them. We can conclude that after two semesters of Covid-19, the world reached a "new normal" in which people learned how to live with the pandemic and not see it as a hindrance anymore. Instead, they see it as a change that affected their lives and they start coping with it.

As mentioned by Akhther and Sopory (2022), using social media and being active on mental health communities is per se a way to cope with the situation.

Third, the discussed topics in the Covid-19 support community changed during the three semesters of Covid-19, revealing "family" and "addiction" as top topics in the first semester. "Addiction" did not appear again in the top topics in the next periods. It seems that individuals used some substances to cope with the new situation. This practice is only salient at the beginning of the crisis. Even if "suicide" appears in the list of discussed topics, it is not part of top topics. In fact, suicide is one of the most dangerous risks, but the size of the issue is limited. This urges professionals and organizations to target individuals evoking terms related to this lexicon in a one-to-one approach.

"Social interaction," "health anxiety," "family/life," and "economic stress" are frequent topics in the second and the third semesters. However, during the third semester, a new topic appears: "Covid-19 vaccine." Always in a dynamic perspective, users are discussing topics about the future of the crisis and a potential solution: the vaccine. Zhu et al. (2023), in their thematic analysis of Reddit users' discourse, found similar themes: "economic stress" and "social stress." But they also found two other themes: "suicide" and "substance use." This may be due to the fact that their dataset is restricted to two MH groups (r/anxiety and r/depression).

The results of our study can be useful for managers. We first highlight the need for integrating data science in the healthcare sector for the optimization of allocation of resources and the identification of vulnerable groups/individuals especially in crises. It is equally important to track MH groups and NMH groups. Pattern recognition and data visualization tools allow real time discovery of discussed topics and trends' evolution. However, identifying individuals is not sufficient; the aim is to improve the mental wellness. Chatbots can initiate the contact with identified patients. Recent developments in artificial intelligence endow chatbots with an increased capacity of empathy so that they can undertake this mission for less vulnerable patients after several tests to minimize biases. It is also possible to target groups/individuals through sponsored communication, putting them in touch with associations and volunteers (psychiatric students for example). For dangerous situations, one to one communication with professionals is recommended.

Furthermore, it appears that the first period following a crisis is critical. The perceived shock, change, and loss of control should be balanced by official updated communication to avoid rumors. In fact, a communication once a day by a governmental institution is no longer considered updated information. Streaming data with discussions and comments from professionals, comparisons from robots, and business intelligence visualization tools accessible for the public can help to disclose reliable information. In addition to that, educating the public about different options to cope with a situation can help them to discard substance use and its consequences.

14.5 CONCLUSION

This study leveraged several NLP techniques to assess mental health change across the social network Reddit during the pandemic. We successfully classified user posts from different mental health subreddits and found the dataset shift among subreddits was minor. We tracked sentiments of users over time and observed the greatest negative sentimental changes during the Covid-19 pandemic for NMH. Besides, topic modeling analyses revealed an increase in health anxiety, addiction, and economic stress. This work brings attention to the needs and concerns of these large online communities, as Reddit may be the first path to treatment for many users. The results of this work can deepen our understanding of mental health issues during the pandemic, inform the provision of appropriate therapeutic resources, and inspire greater use of NLP for inspection of world-changing events such as epidemics, elections, and protests.

The main limitations of this study is that we did not consider several factors such as socio-demographic, cultural, and regional differences. In fact, these variables can affect the classification models because they provide them with more information and thus make them more accurate. We also did not validate our results with a validation dataset from external data sources like personal journals or doctor reports, and this needs to be further checked. Finally, we noticed that overall, the number of Reddit posts significantly decreased in 2020. One possible reason is that some users may have tried to avoid using social platforms during the pandemic to get away from all the negativity that the news media was sharing. This can affect our trend analysis results because sometimes, the decrease in the number of posts related to a certain topic can be due to the general decrease of posts in that subreddit.

The analysis of massive amounts of data allowed us to identify trends, which can be useful to design policies and implement them either at the micro level or at the macro level. In this societal perspective, we ban consumerism, compulsive buying, and emotional regulation through substance abuse for this vulnerable population. We encourage timely tracking of social media data to provide a diachronic perspective on shifts in public mental health and collective emotions, as users are willingly providing spontaneous and diverse content about various topics. Furthermore, professionals and organizations can educate individuals and provide personalized content to people in need for help.

Within the SCT, future researches can involve behavioral concepts, which are not considered in this study. In fact, self-efficacy is a key concept in this theory. For individuals with mental health issues, self-efficacy may be shaped by the symbolization and their identification through this illness (Roe, 2001) but also through society's attitude. Hence, this theory was very useful in studying the social influence on health behavior where the focus is no longer on the "mental patient" but on the "consumer advocate." This shift allowed consumers to give another sense to mental illness in a way that it is no longer associated with negative aspects but rather as an identity that is accepted/acceptable. That is why people accept to share their thoughts on social media and some of them will have the "expert" status within this community for his knowledge, skills, and/or experience.

Future studies can also automate the process followed in this study by developing an automatic data extraction pipeline directly from Reddit using the reddit API in order to monitor in real time the evolution of negativity or even certain trends during important periods such as pandemics, elections, wars, etc.

REFERENCES

Akhther, N., & Sopory, P. (2022). Seeking and sharing mental health information on social media during COVID-19: Role of depression and anxiety, peer support, and health benefits. *Journal of technology in behavioral science*, *7*(2), 211–226.

Alambo, A., Gaur, M., & Thirunarayan, K. (2020). Depressive, drug abusive, or informative: Knowledge-aware study of news exposure during COVID-19 outbreak. *arXiv (Cornell University).*

American Psychiatry Association (2018). "What is mental illness?", American Psychiatry Association, www.psychiatry.org/patients-families/what-is-mental-illness

Auerbach, J., & Miller, B. F. (2020). COVID-19 exposes the cracks in our already fragile mental health system. *American Journal of Public Health*, *110*(7), 969–970.

Bandura, A. (2000). Social cognitive theory. In: Kazdin A. E., editor. *Encyclopedia of Psychology*. New York: Oxford University Press, 7–332.

Bartlett, Y. K., & Coulson, N. S. (2011). An investigation into the empowerment effects of using online support groups and how this affects health professional/patient communication. *Patient education and counseling*, *83*(1), 113–119.

Battaglia, A. M., Mamak, M., & Goldberg, J. O. (2022). The impact of social media coverage on attitudes towards mental illness and violent offending. *Journal of Community Psychology*, *50*(7), 2938–2949.

Becker, S. J. (2015). Direct-to-consumer marketing: A complementary approach to traditional dissemination and implementation efforts for mental health and substance abuse interventions. *Clinical Psychology: Science and Practice*, *22*(1), 85.

Bekalu, M. A., Sato, T., &Viswanath, K. (2023). Conceptualizing and measuring social media use in health and well-being studies: Systematic review. *Journal of Medical Internet Research*, *25*, e43191.
Berry, L. L., & Bendapudi, N. (2007). Health care: A fertile field for service research. *Journal of Service Research*, *10*(2), 111–122.
Black, J. S., & Van Esch, P. (2020). AI-enabled recruiting: What is it and how should a manager use it? *Business Horizons*, *63*(2), 215–226.
Bonabi, H., Müller, M., Ajdacic-Gross, V., Eisele, J., Rodgers, S., Seifritz, E., Rössler, W., & Rüsch, N. (2016). Mental health literacy, attitudes to help seeking, and perceived need as predictors of mental health service use. *Journal of Nervous and Mental Disease*, *204*(4), 321–324.
Brewer, G., Centifanti, L. C. M., Caicedo, J. C., Huxley, G., Peddie, C., Stratton, K., & Lyons, M. (2022). Experiences of mental distress during COVID-19: Thematic analysis of discussion forum posts for anxiety, depression, and obsessive-compulsive disorder. *Illness, Crisis, & Loss*, *30*(4), 795–811.
Bronda, S., Ostrovsky, M. G., Jain, S., & Malacarne, A. (2022). The role of social media for patients with temporomandibular disorders: A content analysis of Reddit. *Journal of Oral Rehabilitation*, *49*(1), 1–9.
Brown, G., Rathbone, A. L., & Prescott, J. (2021). Social media use for supporting mental health (SMILE). *Mental Health Review Journal*, *26*(3), 279–297.
Chakraborty, U., Banerjee, A., Saha, J. K., Sarkar, N., & Chakraborty, C. (Eds.). (2022). *Artificial intelligence and the fourth industrial revolution*. CRC Press.
Chancellor, S., & De Choudhury, M. (2020). Methods in predictive techniques for mental health status on social media: A critical review. *NPJ digital medicine*, *3*(1), 43.
Chancellor, S., Baumer, E. P., & De Choudhury, M. (2019). Who is the "human" in human-centered machine learning: The case of predicting mental health from social media. *Proceedings of the ACM on Human-Computer Interaction*, *3*(CSCW), 1–32.
Cisler, J. M., & Koster, E. H. (2010). Mechanisms of attentional biases towards threat in anxiety disorders: An integrative review. *Clinical psychology review*, *30*(2), 203–216.
Cohen, S., & Wills, T. A. (1985). Stress, social support, and the buffering hypothesis. *Psychological Bulletin*, *98*(2), 310.
Crozier, M. (1964). *The bureaucratic phenomenon*. Chicago: University of Chicago Press.
De Choudhury, M., Counts, S., Horvitz, E. J., & Hoff, A. (2014, February). Characterizing and predicting postpartum depression from shared facebook data. In *proceedings of the 17th ACM conference on Computer supported cooperative work & social computing* (pp. 626–638).
Ernala, S. K., Birnbaum, M. L., Candan, K. A., Rizvi, A. F., Sterling, W. A., Kane, J. M., & De Choudhury, M. (2019, May). Methodological gaps in predicting mental health states from social media: Triangulating diagnostic signals. In *Proceedings of the 2019 chi conference on human factors in computing systems* (pp. 1–16).
Fox, S., & Duggan, M. (2013). Health online 2013. *Health*, *2013*, 1–55.
García, C., Amador Ayala, J., Díaz Roldan, K., & Bavarian, N. (2022). Exploring Reddit conversations about mental health difficulties among college students during the COVID-19 pandemic. *Journal of American College Health*, 1–7.
Ghafari, M., Nadi, T., Bahadivand-Chegini, S., & Doosti-Irani, A. (2022). Global prevalence of unmet need for mental health care among adolescents: A systematic review and meta-analysis. *Archives of Psychiatric Nursing*, *36*, 1–6.
Gonzalez-Hernandez, G., Sarker, A., O'Connor, K., & Savova, G. (2017). Capturing the patient's perspective: A review of advances in natural language processing of health-related text. *Yearbook of medical informatics*, *26*(01), 214–227.
Hagger, M. S., & Hamilton, K. (2022). Social cognition theories and behavior change in COVID-19: A conceptual review. *Behaviour Research and Therapy*, *154*, 104095.
Haleem, A., Javaid, M., Qadri, M. A., Singh, R. P., & Suman, R. (2022). Artificial intelligence (AI) applications for marketing: A literature-based study. *International Journal of Intelligent Networks*, *3*, 119–132.
Hammen, C. (2005). Stress and depression. *Annual Review of Clinical Psychology*, *1*(1), 293–319.
Holmes, E. A., O'Connor, R. C., Perry, V. H., Tracey, I., Wessely, S., Arseneault, L., … & Bullmore, E. (2020). Multidisciplinary research priorities for the COVID-19 pandemic: A call for action for mental health science. *The Lancet Psychiatry*, *7*(6), 547–560.
Hwang, K. O., Ottenbacher, A., Green, A. P., Cannon-Diehl, M. R., Richardson, O., Bernstam, E. V., & Thomas, E. J. (2010). Social support in an Internet weight loss community. *International Journal of Medical Informatics*, *79*(1), 5–13.

Kahneman, D., Tversky, A., & Tversky, A. (1979). Prospect theory: An analysis of decision under risk. *Econometrica*, *47*(2), 263–292.

Kim, J., Lee, J., Park, E., & Han, J. (2020). A deep learning model for detecting mental illness from user content on social media. *Scientific reports*, *10*(1), 11846.

Kumar, M., Dredze, M., Coppersmith, G., & De Choudhury, M. (2015). Detecting changes in suicide content manifested in social media following celebrity suicides. *In proceedings of the 26th ACM conference on hypertext & social media* (Pp. 85–94).

Li, W., Yang, Y., Liu, Z. H., Zhao, Y. J., Zhang, Q., Zhang, L., … & Xiang, Y. T. (2020). Progression of mental health services during the COVID-19 outbreak in China. *International Journal of Biological Sciences*, *16*(10), 1732.

Low, D. M., Rumker, L., Talkar, T., Torous, J., Cecchi, G. A., & Ghosh, S. (2020). Natural language processing reveals vulnerable mental health support groups and heightened health anxiety on Reddit during COVID-19: Observational study. *Journal of Medical Internet Research*, *22*(10), e22635.

Machin, J. E., Brister, T., Bossarte, R. M., Drenten, J., Hill, R. P., Holland, D. L., … & Ross Adkins, N. (2022). Conversations about conducting marketing research in mental health. *Journal of Consumer Marketing*, *39*(6), 569–578.

Marcus, M., Yasamy, M. T., van Ommeren, M. V., Chisholm, D., & Saxena, S. (2012). Depression: A global public health concern. (dataset) in *PsycEXTRA Dataset*.

Marshall, C., Lanyi, K., Green, R., Wilkins, G., Pearson, F., & Craig, D. (2022). Using natural language processing to explore mental health insights from UK tweets during the COVID-19 pandemic: Infodemiology study. *JMIR Infodemiology*, *2*(1), e32449.

Miotto, R., Wang, F., Wang, S., Jiang, X., & Dudley, J. T. (2018). Deep learning for healthcare: Review, opportunities and challenges. *Briefings in Bioinformatics*, *19*(6), 1236–1246.

Mirabito, A., Adkins, N. R., Crosby, E., Farrell, J., & Machin, J. (2022). Guest editorial: Mental health and the marketplace: A research agenda. *Journal of Consumer Marketing*, *39*(6), 565–568.

Moukaddam, N., & Shah, A. A. (2020). Psychiatrists beware! The impact of COVID-19 and pandemics on mental health. *The Psychiatric Times*, *37*(3).

Myneni, S., Cobb, N., & Cohen, T. (2016). In pursuit of theoretical ground in behavior change support systems: Analysis of peer-to-peer communication in a health-related online community. *Journal of medical Internet research*, *18*(2), e4671.

Naslund, J. A., Aschbrenner, K. A., Marsch, L. A., & Bartels, S. J. (2016). The future of mental health care: Peer-to-peer support and social media. *Epidemiology and psychiatric sciences*, *25*(2), 113–122.

Névéol, A., & Zweigenbaum, P. (2017). Making sense of big textual data for health care: Findings from the section on clinical natural language processing. *Yearbook of Medical Informatics*, *26*(01), 228–234.

Nick, E. A., Cole, D. A., Cho, S. J., Smith, D. K., Carter, T. G., & Zelkowitz, R. L. (2018). The online social support scale: Measure development and validation. *Psychological assessment*, *30*(9), 1127.

Oosthuizen, R. M. (2022). The fourth industrial revolution–Smart technology, artificial intelligence, robotics and algorithms: Industrial psychologists in future workplaces. *Frontiers in Artificial Intelligence*, *5*, 913168.

Pan, K. Y., Kok, A. A., Eikelenboom, M., Horsfall, M., Jörg, F., Luteijn, R. A., … & Penninx, B. W. (2021). The mental health impact of the COVID-19 pandemic on people with and without depressive, anxiety, or obsessive-compulsive disorders: A longitudinal study of three Dutch case-control cohorts. *The Lancet Psychiatry*, *8*(2), 121–129.

Pang, H. (2022). The negative impact of social media on people's lives. In *2021 International Conference on Social Development and Media Communication (SDMC 2021)* (pp. 554–557). Atlantis Press.

Park, A., Conway, M., & Chen, A. T. (2018). Examining thematic similarity, difference, and membership in three online mental health communities from Reddit: A text mining and visualization approach. *Computers in Human Behavior*, *78*, 98–112.

Rayland, A., & Andrews, J. (2023). From social network to peer support network: Opportunities to explore mechanisms of online peer support for mental health. *JMIR Mental Health*, *10*, e41855.

Rens, E., Dom, G., Remmen, R., Michielsen, J., & Van den Broeck, K. (2020). Unmet mental health needs in the general population: Perspectives of Belgian health and social care professionals. *International Journal for Equity in Health*, *19*(1), 1–10.

Roe, M. M. (2001). *The journey and the destination: A qualitative study of success definitions, experiences and strategies among college freshmen*. New York University.

Serrano-Guerrero, J., Olivas, J. A., Romero, F. P., & Herrera-Viedma, E. (2015). Sentiment World Health Organization (2001). The World Health Report 2001: Mental Health: New Understanding.

Sewell, W. H., Jr. (1992). A theory of structure: Duality, agency, and transformation. *American Journal of Sociology*, *98*, 1–29.
Shen, G., Jia, J., Nie, L., Feng, F., Zhang, C., Hu, T., … & Zhu, W. (2017, August). Depression detection via harvesting social media: A multimodal dictionary learning solution. In *IJCAI* (pp. 3838–3844).
Sheth, J. (2021). New areas of research in marketing strategy, consumer behavior, and marketing analytics: The future is bright *Journal of Marketing Theory and Practice*, *29*(1), 3–12.
Simmel, G. (1955). *Conflict and the web of group affiliations*. New York: Free Press.
Singh, T., Roberts, K., Cohen, T., Cobb, N., Franklin, A., & Myneni, S. (2023). Discerning conversational context in online health communities for personalized digital behavior change solutions using Pragmatics to Reveal Intent in Social Media (PRISM) framework. *Journal of Biomedical Informatics*, *140*, 104324.
Singleton, A., Abeles, P., & Smith, I. C. (2016). Online social networking and psychological experiences: The perceptions of young people with mental health difficulties. *Computers in Human Behavior*, *61*, 394–403.
Smith, L. L., Yan, F., Charles, M., Mohiuddin, K., Tyus, D., Adekeye, O., & Holden, K. B. (2017). Exploring the link between substance use and mental health status: What can we learn from the self-medication theory?. *Journal of Health Care for the Poor and Underserved*, *28*(2), 113–131.
Snow, D. A. (2001). Extending and broadening Blumer's conceptualization of symbolic interactionism. *Symbolic Interaction*, *24*, 367–377.
Stewart, R., & Davis, K. (2016). 'Big data' in mental health research: Current status and emerging possibilities. *Social Psychiatry and Psychiatric Epidemiology*, *51*(8), 1055–1072.
Stokes, D. C., Andy, A., Guntuku, S. C., Ungar, L. H., & Merchant, R. M. (2020). Public priorities and concerns regarding COVID-19 in an online discussion forum: Longitudinal topic modeling. *Journal of General Internal Medicine*, *35*(7), 2244–2247.
Swan, M. (2009). Emerging patient-driven health care models: An examination of health social networks, consumer personalized medicine and quantified self-tracking. *International Journal of Environmental Research and Public Health*, *6*(2), 492–525.
Tessler, R., & Goldman, H. (1982). *The chronically mentally ill: Assessing community support programs*. Cambridge, MA: Ballinger.
Thukral, S., Sangwan, S., Chatterjee, A., & Dey L. (2022). Identifying pandemic-related stress factors from social-media posts – effects on students and young-adults. *In: proceedings of the 1st Workshop on NLP for COVID-19 (Part 2) at EMNLP 2020*.
Torous, J., & Baker, J. T. (2016). Why psychiatry needs data science and data science needs psychiatry: Connecting with technology. *JAMA Psychiatry*, *73*(1), 3–4.
vanUden-Kraan, C. F., Drossaert, C. H., Taal, E., Shaw, B. R., Seydel, E. R., & van de Laar, M. A. (2008). Empowering processes and outcomes of participation in online support groups for patients with breast cancer, arthritis, or fibromyalgia. *Qualitative Health Research*, *18*(3), 405–417.
Wolohan, J. T. (2020, July). Estimating the effect of COVID-19 on mental health: Linguistic indicators of depression during a global pandemic. In *Proceedings of the 1st Workshop on NLP for COVID-19 at ACL 2020*.
Wongkoblap, A., Vadillo, M. A., & Curcin, V. (2017). Researching mental health disorders in the era of social media: Systematic review. *Journal of Medical Internet Research*, *19*(6), e228.
World Health Organization (2022). Schizophrenia, January 10th, https://www.who.int/news-room/fact-sheets/detail/schizophrenia
World Health Organization (2022). Mental disorders, June 8th, https://www.who.int/news-room/fact-sheets/detail/mental-disordersanalysis: A review and comparative analysis of web services. *Information Sciences, 311*, 18-38.
Yang, W., Sun, X., & Du, R. (2015). Learning depression patterns from my personality and reddit.
Yao, H., Chen, J., & Xu, Y. (2020). Patients with mental health disorders in the COVID-19 epidemic. *The Lancet Psychiatry*, *7*(4), e21.
Zhang, X., Wen, D., Liang, J., & Lei, J. (2017). How the public uses social media WeChat to obtain health information in china: A survey study. *BMC Medical Informatics and Decision Making*, *17*(2), 71–79.
Zhu, J., Yalamanchi, N., Jin, R., Kenne, D. R., & Phan, N. (2023). Investigating COVID-19's impact on mental health: Trend and thematic analysis of reddit users' discourse. *Journal of Medical Internet Research*, *25*, e46867.

15 Do Consumers Favor a Social Presence When Using Voice Chatbots?

Moez Ltifi
Shaqra University, Shaqraa, Saudi Arabia
University of Sfax, Sfax, Tunisia

15.1 INTRODUCTION

Though they are still at the conceptual stage and haven't truly improved anything, artificial intelligence applications are now a reality. Many businesses from a variety of industries have supported these projects. Digital marketing's primary goal should be intelligent client relationship management, and chatbot technology can assist with this (Cheng et al., 2021).

Digital communication has significantly increased thanks to instant messaging services like Skype, Facebook Messenger, WhatsApp, and Snapchat, which presents a commercial opportunity. Companies should take advantage of this opportunity to use chatbots to improve the services they offer now. Recent years have seen a rise in the use of chatbots, which have shown useful in customer-company interactions (Cheng et al., 2021).

One of the conversational agents that has become more and more common these days is the usage of chatbot technology (Araujo, 2018). Through voice commands or conversations, chatbot communication offers previously unheard-of economic possibilities and can replicate human interactions in a range of areas (Luo et al., 2019; Cheng et al., 2021).

The use of chatbot technology is growing in popularity. This is corroborated by the ease of use and accessibility of building chatbots, notable developments in AI, and the increasing popularity of email applications (De Cicco et al., 2020).

A chatbot is defined as "a machine conversation system that interacts with human users via conversational language"(Shawar and Atwell, 2005, p. 489). The chatbot market resolve be worth over $9 billion by 2024 (Pise, 2018). One of the most exciting automated interaction methods in retail is chatbots. According to De Cicco et al. (2020), a chatbot is an artificial intelligence-based program that mimics an interactive human discussion by means of pre-programmed user phrases and auditory or vocal inputs.

Chatbots, with a simple explanation, are software that composes a human message and underwrites users to interact with digital devices in the same way they would with a real person (Oracle, 2019; De Cicco et al., 2020).

This new technology has been favored by many companies and brands, including Apple, Facebook, Amazon, eBay and others. Chatbots have been adopted by these companies to manage orders, recommend products, and help other customers (Go and Sundar, 2019). A fatal part of customer services, such as chatbots, are absolutely powered by AI (Mitchell, 2018; Cheng et al., 2021).

Studies in this direction using artificial intelligence in the corporate sector are very new and rare. Examples include studies on robots (De Kervenoael et al., 2020), machines (Seeber et al., 2020), and chatbots (Luo et al., 2019; Cheng et al., 2021).

 DOI: 10.1201/9781003450443-15

The quick development of artificial intelligence has changed the way that businesses connect with their customers, giving them a wide range of online communication possibilities. Despite the positive perception of chatbot deployment in digital marketing suggested by earlier research, the empirical data on customer behavior that is now accessible is still limited. Several aspects, including the social factor, were overlooked in previous studies. The use of a select few chatbots while disregarding others. Releasing the moderating effects. In our work, we tackle these conceptual and practical shortcomings.

To put it briefly, our research is centered on the social connection perspective, which acknowledges chatbots as more personal sources of involvement with social values than just practical instruments (De Cicco et al., 2020).

The social presence theory – which holds that closeness and immediateness play a part in how someone is viewed as "real" by others – is discussed in this context. Our work bridges this research gap by figuring out how to use this intimacy and immediateness through speech signaling and conversational design. Our research examines how social presence affects consumers' intentions and technological activity.

By concentrating on voice chatbots, an interactive technology that is only starting to gain popularity, we have made a substantial contribution to the literature on digital and interactive marketing and artificial intelligence. According to our knowledge, one of the first empirical investigations on the significance of social media presence online during voice chatbot interactions between customers and businesses was carried out.

Previous research on chatbot usage has only looked at online customer support. This study is among the first to offer a comprehensive knowledge of how customers respond to a speech chatbot using empirical data. The social aspect of human-chatbot interaction is expanded by our research (1). As far as we are concerned, no studies have looked into how voice chatbot users influence their online social presence and how it influences their intentions and behavior. Our research adds perceived enjoyment, trust, and attitude toward voice chatbots as additional social presence traits (2). Our third study looks at mediating effects. For these three reasons, our study is distinct.

Since it is uncertain how customers feel about online social presence in voice chatbots, our objectives are to assess the importance of online social presence for voice chatbot users; to look into how social presence affects users' enjoyment and level of trust in voice chatbots; to look into how behavioral intention and attitude affect voice chatbot trust; to reevaluate if people's perceptions of pleasure influence their opinions on voice chatbots; to look into how behavioral purpose affects perceptions of voice chatbots; and to evaluate the mediating effects of the association. To do this, a questionnaire survey based on the responses was finished. In summary, we suggest pursuing the following research questions:

1. ***How does social presence affect how much consumers seem to love and trust voice chatbots?***
2. ***How does consumer attitude and behavioral intention toward voice chatbots depend on consumer trust?***
3. ***How does one's perception of fun affect their perception of voice chatbots?***
4. ***How does a consumer's attitude toward voice chatbots affect their behavioral intentions?***

The synopsis of this chapter is provided later. First, a review of earlier studies on the main concepts discussed follows. The theoretical justifications and underpinning for the research hypotheses, recommended methodology, and results are then offered. The discussion will then come to a conclusion with some implications.

15.2 REVIEW OF THE LITERATURE AND DEVELOPMENT OF HYPOTHESES

15.2.1 Theoretical Framework

A summary of preceding research on the key ideas enclosed is presented first. Following that, the outcomes, suggested technique, rationale for the research hypotheses, and theoretical foundation are presented. After that, the conversation will conclude with some implications.

First, the theory of social presence. We used this social theory to examine the lack of human warmth in online encounters, even if social presence affects people's behavior (Cheng et al., 2021). In spite of technology's promise and artificial intelligence's capabilities, Hassanein and Head (2007) contend that human warmth might still be important. We're still learning a lot about how social presence impacts human-chatbot interactions (Araujo, 2018; Cheng et al., 2021). The study looks at the empirical viability of this theory.

As far as we are aware, no study has yet examined how user preferences for social media presence in voice chatbots influence their behavior. We bridge this information gap with this study. In this study, we apply the social presence theory to determine the degree to which the consumer believes the voice chatbot to be a real person based on the closeness and speed of the response. We want to understand how the intimacy and immediateness of the conversational design affect the user's viewpoint.

The theory that has been utilized most frequently to understand people's beliefs about the acceptance and use of technology is the technology acceptance model, which focuses primarily on information system use. This thrifty hypothesis in social psychology has a solid empirical base.

In order to gauge how much staff members in a US firm accepted technology, Davis et al. (1989) first developed the technology acceptance model. But in the context of marketing and e-commerce, the technological acceptance model has accumulated a substantial body of empirical evidence recently that supports its explanatory capacity.

The theory that has been utilized most frequently to understand people's beliefs about the acceptance and use of technology is the technology acceptance model, which focuses primarily on information system use. This thrifty hypothesis in social psychology has a solid empirical base.

In order to gauge how much staff members in a US firm accepted technology, Davis et al. (1989) first developed the technology acceptance model. But in the context of marketing and e-commerce, the technological acceptance model has accumulated a substantial body of empirical evidence recently that supports its explanatory capacity.

15.2.2 Chatbot Fundamentals

To start, let's define chatbots. Hatwar, Patil, and Gondane's (2016) definition of a chatbot is "software agents that simulate an entity, usually a human counterpart that is vague or specifically, with which the user can interact in a conversation (written, spoken, or mixed)."

According to Khanna et al. (2015), chatbot systems are designed with one or more artificial intelligence-based human languages. Dandison et al. claim that it entails dialogue and interaction between a chatbot and a person. Conversations and interactions are processed as user inputs according to certain business rules and procedures. In such cases, the behaviors of individuals who are focused on employing AI are referred to as "bots." The global market for robots, automation, and computing is growing at an exponential rate, claim Dandison et al. Because every firm strives to keep costs as low as possible, building a bot only takes around 25% of the time required to design a standard mobile application. Bots are roughly 50% less expensive to design and maintain than mobile apps because of their strong architecture (waxer, 2016). They also do not require expensive servers.

Our study complements previous research on corporate chatbots (Araujo, 2018; Chung et al., 2018). We review previous studies on voice chatbot user engagement, perception, and behavior in this article (Ciechanowski et al., 2019). Voice chatbots can still be seen as a means of increasing human interaction that conveys and carries social value, in accordance with Brandtzaeg and Følstad (2017). This supposition is the basis of our work. Our study aims to explore the causes and consequences of voice chatbot trust. We look at mediating influences as well.

Technology that makes chatbots appear human and alive in order to attract clients (Gilbert and Forney, 2015). However, sensible and human-like chatbots will have a big impact on how people perceive a chatbot's usability.

Businesses have embraced artificial intelligence in the appearance of speech chatbots that can instantly reply to consumer inquiries in digital marketing and e-commerce (Kaplan and Haenlein, 2019). These chatbots are frequently utilized in the course of making online purchases. Some clients might think that a speech chatbot offers friendlier service than they usually do when dealing with humans.

The social presence theory states that customers interact with human-like machines more satisfyingly (Blut et al., 2021). Some consumers, however, think chatbots merely offer rigid or predetermined answers. In this study, we mainly investigate how a voice chatbot influences a user's attitude, perceived enjoyment, trust, social presence, and behavioral intention toward this technology.

15.2.3 Relationship between Variables and Research Hypotheses

Studies of trust have frequently taken place in the context of human interaction. The topic of trust has been examined in the fields of information systems, psychology, sociology, and economics (Breuer et al., 2016; Ert et al., 2016; Cheng et al., 2021). According to Mayer et al. (1995), Hoy and Tschannen-Moran (1999), and Cheng et al. (2021), trust is defined as "the willingness of the individual or group to be vulnerable to another party."

The idea of e-trust is essential to comprehending how people engage with technology in the current era of increased human-robot interaction (Hoff and Bashir, 2015; Cheng et al., 2021). In order to fill this gap, our study focuses on consumer confidence in the voice chatbot during the online purchasing process.

Contact with the seller is an essential principle of communication between the buyer and the voice chatbot. Customer trust is essentially fatal in a private sale. It is decisive to understand on this route, to what extent consumers trust voice chatbots (Whang and Im, 2018; De Cicco et al., 2020). In the context of e-commerce, it is possible to reduce customer uncertainty and sensitivity toward sellers through social presence, an essential element that could strengthen e-trust (Jiang et al., 2019).

Credibility is cruel in traditional business and is even expressed by non-verbal signs during social gatherings (Qui and Benbasat, 2009). This formula works in much the same way when you use a chatbot at home. Only a few factors are taken into account when assessing the perceived accuracy and reliability of the seller in terms of cognitive ability. As per the findings of Qui and Benbasat (2009) and De Cicco et al. (2020), consumers utilize several sources to construct their beliefs about trust.

The social characteristics shown through social presence are viewed as both an enabler and an antecedent of trust, especially in the context of e-commerce and online services (Gefen and Straub, 2003; Cheng, 2023). Particularly if it's their first time engaging with the voice chatbot, users have a limited amount of clues from the human-chatbot encounter to assess how reliable it is. In order for a speech chatbot to be effective and give people information, it must be based in a socially engaged environment that gives it greater legitimacy and a human touch. Thus, we'll start by outlining our central hypothesis:

H1: *Social presence positively influences consumer trust in the voice chatbot.*

A salesperson's demeanor in traditional retail environments can impact a customer's emotions, namely their level of enjoyment during the purchasing experience (Lee and Dubinsky, 2003). Customer satisfaction perceptions are important while working with salespeople. McKenna et al. (2002) state that social presence plays a significant role in the transmission of positive feelings.

Lombard and Ditton (1997) first showed how social presence affects media consumers' perspectives by increasing involvement, persuasion, and enjoyment. Perceived consumer enjoyment, or the degree to which a buyer finds something enjoyable, is a critical experiential element of both traditional and electronic purchases, according to Hassanein and Head (2005). Technology adoption is significantly influenced by perceived satisfaction, according to Davis et al. (1992).

Research on e-commerce (Cyr et al., 2009; Hassanein et al., 2009; Shen, 2012) demonstrates how important social presence is for positively influencing perceived enjoyment. Hassanein and Chef assert that social presence has a beneficial impact on e-consumers‘ views of their level of happiness in the online clothing sales industry. Shen (2012) also shows that social presence is a predictor of consumers' enjoyment of commercial websites.

While the perceived enjoyment of human-chatbot interaction is still in its early stages, studies on both traditional and electronic retail sales have recently shown the significance of perceived enjoyment of online and instant messaging purchases (Koufaris, 2002; Li et al., 2005; De Cicco et al., 2020; Cheng (2023). Consequently, we make the following claims regarding our second assumption:

H2: *Social presence positively influences the consumer's perceived enjoyment of the voice chatbot.*

Behavioral data cannot be gathered by a chatbot or a human. The result of this interaction can be seen in the attitudes of the users (Hassanein and Head, 2005). Customers are more likely to take specific activities when they have a positive perception of a product or a seller, claim Ajzen and Fishbein (1977). User attitude is frequently used as an outcome variable of vendor-consumer interaction in new information technology research (Hassanein and Head, 2005; De Cicco et al., 2020; Tandon, 2023).

Higher levels of intrinsic pleasure and enjoyment of mediated surroundings are elements that support a positive attitude, according to our investigation of the antecedents that can influence consumer attitude (Kim et al., 2013). Perceived enjoyment and consumer attitude are positively connected, according to data from the e-commerce, televised commerce, and internet browsing industries (Childers et al., 2001; Yu et al., 2005; Van der Heijden, 2003; De Cicco et al., 2020; Tandon, 2023). This suggests that the consumer's opinion of fun and the voice chatbot are both positive. Taking this into consideration, we hereby proclaim the following about our third assumption:

H3: *Perceived enjoyment positively influences the consumer's attitude toward the voice chatbot.*

Because of the unique characteristics of the virtual buying environment in e-commerce, customers are more hesitant and willing to take on greater risk when making online purchases when there are no in-person interactions or when they cannot physically feel and touch a product. Examples of new channels are especially telling of this state of affairs (Ha and Stoel, 2009).

When a human and a chatbot communicate, initial trust is depended upon as a more acceptable view of new technology, particularly when dealing with unknown businesses and organizations. Wu and Chen's (2005) study, which shows how trust influences consumers‘ views toward online tax payment, supports this first requirement of trust.

Initial and continued trust is predicated on the mindset and intention behind using technology, claim Siau and Shen (2003). Again, trust is important for online transactions because it reduces consumers' emotions of vulnerability and uncertainty and fosters the growth of positive attitudes and enduring customer loyalty, according to Das (2016). A positive association between customer views and trust is necessary for the advancement of human-technology interaction (Wang and Benbasat, 2008; Ming-Chi, 2009; De Cicco et al., 2020; Tandon, 2023).

According to studies by Chen and Tan (2004) and Suh and Han (2002), trust is an antecedent of attitude. Wu and Ke (2015) assert that a key predicate of attitude toward online shopping is trust. Various scenarios, such as internet shopping, have demonstrated this advantageous correlation. We designate the following as our fourth hypothesis based on these premises:

H4: ***Trust positively influences the consumer's attitude toward the voice chatbot.***

In the research fields, trust is defined in a variety of ways. "Trust" in the context of e-services refers to a client's strong conviction that the e-service provider can deliver trustworthy services via the Internet. A confident belief is the result of thinking that the other person has one or more traits that will benefit them. Possessing a trustworthy intention implies that you aim to rely on the other party or are at least prepared to do so, especially in situations where you are powerless over them. According to this study, consumers' confident belief in utilizing verbal communication with a chatbot to complete a purchase constitutes trust.

Scholars have recognized trust as a critical element of effective partnerships, especially in the literature on relationship marketing (Macintosh and Lockshin, 1997; Morgan and Hunt, 1994). Trust is essential in business-to-consumer (B2C) relationships when there are unknown dangers (Gefen et al., 2003; Jarvenpaa et al., 1999). Scholars and practitioners have become increasingly interested in the importance of trust, especially with the advent of the virtual marketplace. Among other things, risks associated with the technical capabilities of robots, Internet communication platforms, and Internet vulnerability are potential hazards associated with online purchases and services.

In the technological age, consumers place a higher importance on trust than they do in the traditional setting (Ratnasingham, 1998). This can be explained by the absence of direct physical contact between the consumer and the service provider during service delivery. The unknown nature of online services is exacerbated by concerns about hackers and privacy infringement (Hoffman et al., 1999; Yoon, 2002). The environment of online buying is therefore by its very nature unstable and dangerous.

Research indicates that trust is one of the most important factors in decision-making (Morrison and Firmstone, 2000). Previous studies (Manzano et al., 2009; Kesharwani and Bisht, 2012) have indicated that customer intention requires trust. In contexts such as vocal communication with bots, the greatest strategic method for identifying intent to use technology is trust, according to Gefen (2000) and Hart and Saunders (1997). Considering this, our fifth hypothesis is as follows:

H5: ***Trust positively influences consumer behavioral intention toward the voice chatbot.***

Ajzen and Fishbein, 1977: "A learned predisposition to respond consistently favorably or unfavorably in relation to a given object" is the definition of attitude, as stated here. This study looks at people's attitudes regarding using voice chatbots, whether they are positive or unfavorable. Fishbein and Ajzen (1975) introduced attitude to TRA, while Davis (1989) used attitude as a construct in TAM, claiming that attitude affects personal intention. The acceptance or rejection of technology use is largely determined by behavioral factors, in addition to the personal, social, psychological, and utilitarian elements that continuously interact and influence an individual's behavior. These factors include perceptions, attitudes, and beliefs about the features of e-services.

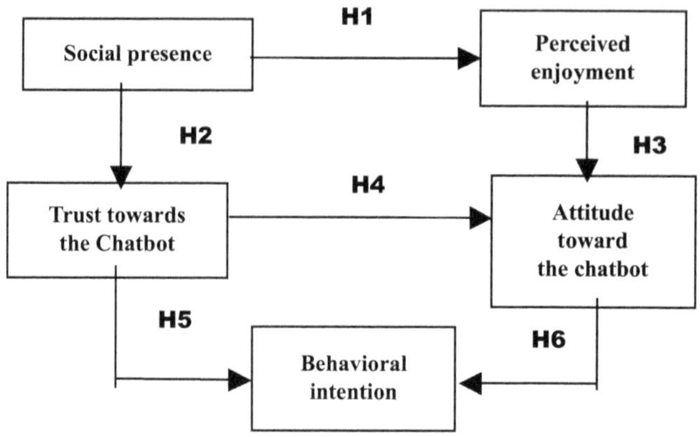

FIGURE 15.1 Conceptual model of the research.

Since speech chatbot discussions directly involve commerce, as more people adopt them, this attitude is becoming more widespread. Consequently, customers' attitudes toward this technology are impacted by their underlying beliefs about it. Even in robot contact, attitude is still regarded as a social function (Nunnally and Bernstein, 1994). It is also contagious online, as individuals use their mutual relationships and experiences to support or contradict one another's viewpoints.

Prior research has indicated that consumer attitudes impact their intentions to use electronic services (Lai and Li, 2005; Cheng et al., 2006; Suh and Han, 2002; Lee, 2009; Chiou and Shen, 2012). In light of these empirical findings, this study expands on the sixth hypothesis in the following ways:

H6: ***Attitude positively influences consumer's behavioral intention toward voice chatbot.***

These hypotheses form the conceptual model that we have summarized in Figure 15.1.

15.3 DESIGN METHODOLOGY

15.3.1 Data Collection Method and Sample

We used a questionnaire to conduct a survey in order to validate our conceptual research strategy. Because their work is repetitive, online banks are more likely to implement voice chatbots through interactive telephone banking services. In this sense, we want to evaluate the significance of social media presence for voice chatbot users. to look into how social presence affects how voice chatbots are perceived in terms of pleasure and trust. Additionally, to look at the effects that confidence in voice chatbots has on attitudes and behavioral intents. to investigate how perceived pleasure affects opinions about voice chatbots once more. additionally to understand how behavioral intention affects perceptions of voice chatbots. in order to evaluate the mediating effects of the relationship.

To do this, a questionnaire survey based on the responses was finished. Our sample was composed of clients of a bank with interactive telephone banking. Participation required the capacity to use this speech chatbot service, which is based on voice conversations with robots.

Following their meeting in the bank lobby to exchange views on their experiences interacting with the voice chatbot, the participants were interviewed. The survey inquired about the demographics of the participants, their encounters with the voice chatbot, and the conceptual underpinning of the research. Out of the 413 participants in this study, 402 had complete and valid questionnaires. Eleven questions were deemed unusable due to incomplete data. Before the

TABLE 15.1
Participant Demographics

Measurement Items	Category	Frequency	%
Genre	Male	217	53.98
	Female	185	46.01
Age	<25	64	15.92
	26–30	109	27.11
	31–35	126	31.34
	>36	103	25.62
Experience with the voice chatbot	No experience	0	00.00
	Low experience	92	22.88
	Medium experience	178	44.27
	High experience	132	32.83

main survey, a pre-test was conducted to ensure that the handling was effective. The table that follows displays the participants‘ demographic data. (Table 15.1)

15.3.2 Measurement Instruments

We measured the variables in our model using 5-point Likert-type multi-item scales (1 = strongly disagree/5 = strongly agree) to assure the validity and reliability of the measurements (Peter, 1979). By utilizing measures that have been assessed in a range of contexts and languages, the study's scales were guaranteed to be robust. It should be noted that some elements of the measurement scales were modified to better coincide with the subject of our study.

The first variable in our study, confidence, was measured using the scale (Cyr et al., 2009; Everard and Galletta, 2005). Similarly, the Van der Heijden (2004) scale was adjusted to assess subjective pleasure, and the Gefen and Straub (2003) scale was used to measure social presence. Finally, we measured users' feelings toward the chatbot using the Moon and Kim (2001) scale.

Moreover, the behavioral intention variable was measured using the studies of Walker and Johnson (2006), and Al-Sukkar (2005).

15.4 RESULTS

15.4.1 Reliability and Validity of Constructs

To ascertain the nature of the relationships between the survey questions, we employed a principal component analysis (PCA). The PLS 3.0 application was utilized. After considering the different similarities also the factorial weight of each item, we decided to keep all of the items from the measuring scales used because all of the commonalities are less than 0.5 (Évrard et al. 2003).

Once again, our measurements‘ validity was confirmed because the "Cronbach's alpha" values (Table 15.2) exceed the suggested value of 0.7. In a similar vein, the model's convergent validity is guaranteed by the "average variance extracted" (AVE) values above the recommended threshold of 0.05 (Hair et al. 2010). Furthermore, Table 15.3 shows that the AVE values are superior to the squares of the inter-construct correlations, ensuring the discriminant validity of the constructs (Fornell and Larcker, 1981).

The "variance inflation factor" (VIF) values are all below the suggested values at the threshold of 10, which indicates a tolerable reliability, according to the study, which indicated there was no issue,

TABLE 15.2
Reliability and Convergent Validity of Measures

Constructs	Items	VIF (<10)	Factor Loadings (>0.7)	Cronbach's α (>0.7)	Average Variance Extracted (AVE) (>0.5)
Trust toward the chatbot	T1	2.852	0.741***	0.845	0.716
	T2	2.364	0.786***		
	T3	2.175	0.793***		
Social presence	SP1	1.147	0.718***	0.947	0.852
	SP2	1.693	0.793***		
	SP3	1.574	0.792***		
	SP4	1.012	0.739***		
	SP5	1.816	0.713***		
Perceived enjoyment	PE1	2.645	0.874***	0.869	0.825
	PE2	2.643	0.856***		
	PE3	2.561	0.829***		
	PE4	2.184	0.827***		
Attitude toward the chatbot	AC1	3.456	0.912***	0.861	0.795
	AC2	3.249	0.985***		
	AC3	3.217	0.967***		
	AC4	3.763	0.936***		
Behavioral intention	BI1	3.241	0.872***	0.952	0.830
	BI2	3.325	0.841***		
	BI3	3.396	0.932***		
	BI4	3.420	0.948***		
	BI5	3.521	0.962***		

VIF – Variance Inflation Factor./***p < 0.001.

TABLE 15.3
Discriminate Validity of Constructs

Constructs	TTC	SP	PE	ATC	BI
Trust toward the chatbot	**0.716***				
Social presence	0.711	**0.852***			
Perceived enjoyment	0.706	0.819	**0.825***		
Attitude toward the chatbot	0.702	0.812	0.784	**0.795***	
Behavioral intention	0.698	0.788	0.762	0.779	**0.830***

* Values on the diagonal represent AVEs and the remaining values represent squared inter-construct correlations.

prompting the multi-linearity check (Hua et al., 2020). The results of the VIF test display that multi-colinearity is not a significant issue in this study (Thatcher et al., 2018). (Tables 15.3 and 15.4)

We find that social presence also strongly contributes (R2 = 0.53) to consumer trust in the chatbot, supporting our beliefs. This illustrates their tremendous ability to explain. In particular, social presence positively and significantly affects users' trust in the chatbot (β = 0.481, t = 21.85,

TABLE 15.4
Research Hypothesis Testing Results

Hypotheses	R^2	Coef. (β)	Std. Error	t-value	p-value	Supported (Y/N)
Social presence → Trust toward the chatbot	0.53	0.481	0.077	21.85	0.001	Y
Social presence → Perceived enjoyment	0.54	0.472	0.068	20.41	0.003	Y
Perceived enjoyment → Attitude	0.58	0.453	0.086	19.86	0.004	Y
Trust toward the chatbot → Attitude	0.61	0.514	0.018	18.74	0.002	Y
Trust toward the chatbot → Behavior Intention	0.60	0.474	0.046	18.34	0.003	Y
Attitude → Behavior Intention	0.62	0.492	0.059	17.56	0.001	Y

p 0.005). These results support hypothesis H1 by demonstrating the importance of social presence in predicting customers‘ confidence in voice chatbots.

Second, there is a high correlation (R2 = 0.54) between social presence and perceived contentment. This illustrates their tremendous ability to explain. Specifically, social presence positively and significantly affects the customer's level of satisfaction (β = 0.472, t = 20.41, p 0.005). Because they demonstrate that social presence is a significant antecedent of customers' evaluations of the voice chatbot's attractiveness, these findings support Hypothesis H2.

Furthermore, we observe that 58% of the customer's opinion of the chatbot can be explained by perceived pleasure (R2 = 0.58), indicating the chatbot's excellent explanatory ability. Customers‘ perceptions of the chatbot are positively impacted, in particular, by reported pleasure (β = 0.453, t = 19.86, p 0.005). These results support Hypothesis H3, which claims that a customer's opinion of the voice chatbot is significantly influenced by their impression of delight.

Similarly, we find that consumer trust has a good explanatory power, explaining 61% of the consumer's perception of the chatbot (R2 = 0.61). Particularly, customer trust in the chatbot has a beneficial effect on customer attitude toward it (β = 0.514, t = 18.74, p 0.005). These results support Hypothesis H4, which contends that consumer trust in the voice chatbot greatly predicts the consumer's attitude toward it.

Consumer trust accounts for 60% of the variance in the consumer's behavioral intention toward the chatbot (R2 = 0.60), indicating a robust explanatory capacity. Specifically, consumer trust has a beneficial impact on customers' behavioral intention toward the chatbot (β = 0.474, t = 18.34, p 0.005). These results support Hypothesis H5, showing that customer behavioral intention toward the voice chatbot is significantly predicted by consumer trust in the chatbot.

Finally, we find that customer attitude has good explanatory power, explaining 62% of consumer behavioral intention toward the chatbot (R2 = 0.62). Customer attitude specifically has a beneficial impact on the customer's behavioral intention toward the chatbot (β = 0.492, t = 17.56, p 0.005). Because they demonstrate that a customer's attitude toward a chatbot is a strong predictor of their behavioral intention toward a voice chatbot, these results support hypothesis H6.

15.5 ADDITIONAL TESTS: MEDIATING EFFECTS

We used 4,200 bootstrapping resamples to examine the mediating impacts of consumer attitude toward the voice chatbot, perceived enjoyment, and trust in order to fully understand the relationship between the variables in our rechearch model and to highlight indirect effects between the variables.

TABLE 15.5
Mediating Effects

Mediation Path	Indirect Effect with Bootstrap Estimate	Bootstrap Confidence Intervals	
		Lower 95%	Upper 95%
Social presence → Trust →Attitude	0.203***	0.084	0.135
Social presence → Trust → Behavior Intention	0.286***	0.096	0.231
Social presence → Perceived enjoyment → Attitude	0.146***	0.102	0.082
Perceived enjoyment → Attitude→ Behavior Intention	0.234***	0.124	0.145

Overall, all of the mediating impacts of voice chatbot consumer confidence are statistically significant. First, we conclude that the relationship between social presence and consumers‘ perceptions of the voice chatbot is mediated by customer trust. Second, we conclude that customer trust acts as a mediator in the relationship between social presence and behavioral intention. Third, we deduce that perceived delight acts as a mediator in the relationship between social presence and the way customers view the voice chatbot. Fourth, we conclude that attitude moderates the relationship between behavioral intention and subjective enjoyment, as suggested by Hair et al. (2017). Table 15.5 provides more detailed results for the following outcomes:

15.6 ROBUSTNESS TEST

To prove that the main results reached are reliable, more research needs to be done. Because of this, we plan to conduct an additional analysis to further validate and prove the results we have gotten. The complex structure of the relationships between the variables in our research model was a major factor in this activity. For this reason, we wish to use the "blindfolding" test to evaluate the influence of the independent variables on the model's performance and to successfully evaluate the validity of the inferences made from our model. This method assesses each construct's predictive utility by calculating variations in the criterion estimations (Q2) (Hair et al., 2017). According to the results of the Stone-Geisser "blindfolding" test (Q2), customer trust in the chatbot (Q2 = 0.325), perceived enjoyment (Q2 = 0.258), attitude (Q2 = 0.378), and behavioral intention (Q2 = 0.381) all have values that are significantly above 0 and so have sufficient predictive relevance (Thakur, 2018).

15.7 DISCUSSION AND CONCLUSION

This study examined the role voice chatbots play in elucidating consumer behavior in the online banking industry. We also underlined the impact that social presence has on consumers' opinions about the voice chatbot's attractiveness and perceived degree of customer trust. Once more, we underlined how perceptions of fun affect people's views toward the voice chatbot. Furthermore, we emphasized how the attitude and behavioral intentions of the voice chatbot are influenced by client trust. Not to mention, we stressed the significance of behavior intention and attitude toward the voice chatbot.

We use the social presence theory and the technology acceptability model as two theoretical frameworks in this study to formulate our research hypotheses. We have made a substantial contribution to the body of knowledge on interactive marketing and artificial intelligence by focusing on a novel form of interactive technology – voice chatbots. Our study is among the first empirical ones to examine the importance of social media presence in business-to-consumer voice chatbot engagements.

To address the concerns of our research, we present and discuss the main results revealed from our study by comparing them to those found in previous literature. The following are the results of our investigation:

First, social presence influences consumer trust in the voice chatbot in a good way. This result suggests that the findings of Araujo (2018) and Chattaraman et al. (2019) are supported. This finding provides strong support for the importance of this effect. According to our findings, having a socially centered discussion improves the sense that the interaction is a social one, or that there is a social presence. Emotional, affective, and relational aspects are necessary for the interaction to improve the sense of social presence. Making use of the essential components to improve social presence in a human-bot interaction is both desirable and possible.

Second, our results show that a consumer's level of happiness is positively impacted by social presence. This finding especially validates the conclusions of De Cicco et al. (2020). The importance of this effect is supported by this discovery. There need to be emotional, affective, and relational components to online interactions, particularly when using a speech chatbot.

Third, our results emphasize the positive roles that perceived delight and trust play as byproducts of social presence and as forerunners of the voice chatbot's customer perception. The results of Cyr et al. (2009), Hassanein et al. (2009), Gefen and Straub (2003), and Etemad-Sajadi (2016) are particularly supported by this conclusion. The importance of these repercussions is illustrated by this discovery. Customers' perceived happiness and degree of assurance can be used to forecast their sentiments.

Fourth, the results show that user attitude and the voice chatbot's credibility are predictors of the behavioral intention of the consumer. Specifically, this conclusion concurs with the findings of De Cicco et al. (2020) and Irfan and Chendragiri (2015). This finding provides compelling evidence for the importance of these repercussions. The consumer's intention to behave is influenced by his attitude and degree of trust.

Our results further show that first, the relationship between social presence and consumers' impressions of voice chatbots is mediated by customer trust. Second, the relationship between social presence and behavioral intention is mediated by consumer trust. Third, the relationship between social presence and the customers' experience of the voice chatbot is mediated by that felt delight. Fourth, according to Hair et al. (2017), this attitude modifies the connection between behavioral intention and experienced enjoyment. This finding highlights the importance of these mediating effects in influencing consumers' attitudes, perceptions, intentions, and ensuing actions.

15.8 THEORETICAL IMPLICATIONS

Our study offers a quantity of fresh theoretical insights in this field. First, our study utilized the social presence theory and the technological acceptability model to the addition of a voice chatbot to an interactive telephone banking service and an e-commerce setting, whereas these theories are usually used in traditional business contexts.

Second, the theoretical framework of the study adds to the corpse of knowledge on digital marketing, electronic commerce, and information systems.

Third, artificial intelligence-driven speech chatbots are a novel and innovative technology that has the potential to enhance e-commerce by offering numerous benefits to both customers and enterprises. Fourth, this study adds to our understanding of the previously identified restrictions and limitations of consumer behavioral responses.

Fifth, this study advances the field of marketing expertise by utilizing social presence theory to show how a voice chatbot integrates psychological proximity and cordial conversation, which may be an essential catalyst for enhancing social presence. It is important to consider the way humans and chatbots interact in order to predict social presence. The kind of social interaction that, when driven by AI, particularly voice chatbots can become impersonal. These designs were ignored in previous studies. This paper fills this research gap.

15.9 MANAGERIAL IMPLICATIONS

Both businesses that develop business technologies and those who provide electronic customer service should be aware of the management implications of this study. In the e-commerce sector, companies deploy automated robotics and artificial intelligence on a daily basis. All virtual stores, e-services companies, and online retailers need to automatically engage with their customers in order to improve the customer experience and/or brand. A voice chatbot is a tool that facilitates automatic communication between a business and its consumers.

Through the implementation of an interactive telephone banking service within a business context, our study contributes to a deeper understanding of the attitudes, resistance intentions, and behavioral reactions related to the voice chatbot. The corporation distinguishes itself from its competitors with its clever and well-designed voice chatbot. It is highly recommended to consider the human factor when a person is dealing with a chatbot, as this influences the customers‘ satisfaction, intentions, and future behavior.

In light of our study's results, we advise tech companies and e-customer service providers to enhance the usability and personalization of speech chatbots. Increasing consumer involvement is a great way for businesses to foster friendly and sociable interactions with their clients and provide a positive first impression. It's important to create attractive conversations with small talk, intelligent feedback, explanations, and voice messages in order to enhance the social presence and human stroke of the human-voicebot interaction. This improves consumer trust, which in turn builds their perception of enjoyment, attitude, and behavioral intent toward chatbots and the adoption of artificial intelligence.

Large companies with financial means can build intelligent chatbots that are customized to their operations by incorporating an NLP-based feeling analysis algorithm. These state-of-the-art chatbots can determine a customer's emotional state solely through speech exchanges. If sophisticated chatbots determine that a client is in a positive or neutral emotional state, they can automatically initiate the request. However, when negative emotional states are detected, intelligent chatbots can automatically transition the conversation to a human, thereby preventing the difficulty or loss of a customer by declining the value of the customer's appointment with the company through voice chatbot technology.

15.10 LIMITATIONS AND FUTURE RESEARCH DIRECTIONS

However, despite its donations to the area, this research has flaws that need to be fixed in future research on the topic. The first limitation has to do with the amount of survey data collected and the size of the sample that was used. The only subset of the study's sample consists of clients who utilize a single bank's interactive phone banking service. The structural equation approach requires the use of a very small sample size for analysis. It would be interesting to rerun the study with a bigger, more delegated sample size and a diverse data collection method in order to corroborate the findings that will provide insightful information.

The second constraint is related to the survey field. A fictitious task based on the participants' individual experiences had to be finished. It would be interesting to repeat this study with data from contacts with actual firms in order to guarantee that the results are as accurate as feasible.

The third limitation is that our research methodology can only be tested in the banking sector in the e-commerce sector by using an interactive telephone banking service. It is recommended that more research be done using numerous data sources in other domains, such as transportation and insurance, in order to generalize the findings.

In this study, we looked into how consumer attitudes regarding voice chatbots and their reported enjoyment of them might act as mediating factors. To investigate, for instance, if the client's attitude and behavioral intention in the direction of the chatbot changes with varying levels of involvement, we suggest including moderating variables like product kind and amount of involvement.

REFERENCES

Ajzen, I. & Fishbein, M. (1977). Attitude-behaviour relations: a theoretical analysis and review of empirical research. *Psychological Bulletin*, Vol.84 N. 5, pp. 888.

Al-Sukkar, S.A. (2005). *The application of information systems in the Jordanian banking sector: a study of acceptance of Internet*, PhD Thesis, School of Economics and Information Systems, University of Wollongong, available at htttp://ro.uow.edu.au/thesis/419.

Araujo, T. (2018). Living up to the chatbot hype: the influence of anthropomorphic design cues and communicative agency framing on conversational agent and company perceptions. *Computers in Human Behavior*, Vol.85 N. 2, pp. 183–189.

Blut, M., Wang, C., W€underlich, N.V. & Brock, C. (2021). Understanding anthropomorphism in service provision: a meta-analysis of physical robots, chatbots, and other AI. *Journal of the Academy of Marketing Science*, pp. 1–27.

Brandtzaeg, P.B. & Følstad, A. (2017). Why people use chatbots. *In International Conference on Internet Science, Springer, Cham*, 10673, 377–392.

Breuer, C., Huffmeier, J. & Hertel, G. (2016). Does trust matter more in virtual teams? A meta-analysis of trust and team effectiveness considering virtuality and documentation as moderators. *Journal of Applied Psychology*, Vol.101 N. 8, pp. 1151–1177.

Chattaraman, V., Kwon, W.S., Gilbert, J.E. & Ross, K. (2019). Should AI-Based, conversational digital assistants employ social-or task-oriented interaction style? A task-competency and reciprocity perspective for older adults. *Computers in Human Behavior*, Vol.90 N. 2, pp. 315–330.

Chen, L.D. & Tan, J. (2004). Technology adaptation in e-commerce: key determinants of virtual stores acceptance. *European Management Journal*, Vol.22 N. 1, pp. 74–86.

Cheng, T.C.E., Lam D.Y.C. & Yeung A.C.L. (2006). Adoption of Internet banking: an empirical study in Hong Kong, *Decision Support Systems*, Vol.42 N. 3, pp. 1558–1572.

Cheng, Y.-M. (2023). How gamification and social interaction stimulate MOOCs continuance intention via cognitive presence, teaching presence and social presence?, *Library Hi Tech*, Vol. ahead-of-print No. ahead-of-print.

Cheng, X., Bao, Y., Zarifis, A., Gong, W. & Mou, J. (2021). Exploring consumers‘ response to text-based chatbots in e-commerce: the moderating role of task complexity and chatbot disclosure. *Internet Research*, Vol.32 N. 2, pp. 496–517.

Childers, T.L., Carr, C.L., Peck, J. & Carson, S. (2001). Hedonic and utilitarian motivations for online retail shopping behavior. *Journal of Retailing*, Vol.77 N. 4, pp. 511–535.

Chiou, J.S. & Shen, C.C. (2012). The antecedents of online financial service acceptance: the impact of physical banking services on Internet banking acceptance, *Behavior and Information Technology*, Vol.31 N. 9, pp. 859–871.

Chung, M., Ko, E., Joung, H. & Kim, S.J. (2018). Chatbot e-service and customer satisfaction regarding luxury brands. *Journal of Business Research*, Vol.117 N. 1, pp. 587–595.

Ciechanowski, L., Przegalinska, A., Magnuski, M. & Gloor, P. (2019). In the shades of the uncanny valley: an experimental study of human–chatbot interaction. *Future Generation Computer Systems*, Vol.92 N. 2, pp. 539–548.

Cyr, D., Hassanein, K., Head, M. & Ivanov, A. (2009). The role of social presence in establishing loyalty in e-service environments. *Interacting with Computers*, Vol.19 N. 1, pp. 43–56.

Das, G. (2016). Antecedents and consequences of trust: an e-tail branding perspective. *International Journal of Retail and Distribution Management*, Vol.44 N. 7, pp. 713–730.

Davis, F.D. (1989). Perceived usefulness, ease of use and user acceptance of information technology. *MIS Quarterly*, Vol.13 N. 3, pp. 319–339.

Davis, F.D., Bagozzi, R.P. & Warshaw, P.R. (1992). Extrinsic and intrinsic motivation to use computers in the workplace. *Journal of Applied Social Psychology*, Vol.22 N. 14, pp. 1111–1132.

De Cicco, R., Silva, S.C. & Alparone, F.R. (2020). Millennials' attitude toward chatbots: an experimental study in a social relationship perspective. *International Journal of Retail & Distribution Management*, Vol.48 N. 11, pp. 1213–1233.

De Kervenoael, R., Hasan, R., Schwob, A. & Goh, E. (2020). Leveraging human-robot interaction in hospitality services: incorporating the role of perceived value, empathy, and information sharing into visitors' intentions to use social robots. *Tourism Management*, Vol.78, pp. 104-042.

Ert, E., Fleischer, A. & Magen, N. (2016). Trust and reputation in the sharing economy: the role of personal photos in Airbnb. *Tourism Management*, Vol.55 N. 2, pp. 62–73.

Etemad-Sajadi, R. (2016). The impact of online real-time interactivity on patronage intention: the use of avatars. *Computers in human behavior*, Vol.61 N. 2, pp. 227–232.

Everard, A. & Galletta, D.F. (2005). How presentation flaws affect perceived site quality, trust, and intention to purchase from an online store. *Journal of Management Information Systems*, Vol.22 N. 3, pp. 56–95.

Fishbein, M. & Ajzen, I. (1975). *Belief, Attitude, Intention and Behavior: An Introduction to Theory and Research*, Reading, MA: Addison-Wesley.

Évrard, Y., Pras, B., & Roux, E. (2003). *Market: Etudes et Recherches en Marketing*. Paris: Dunod. B.

Fornell, C. & Larcker, D. (1981). Evaluating structural equation model with unobservable variable and measurement error. *Journal of Marketing Research*, Vol.18 N. 1, pp. 39–50.

Gefen, D. & Straub, D. (2003). Managing user trust in B2C e-services. *E-service Journal*, Vol.2 N. 2, pp. 7–24.

Gefen, D. (2000). E-commerce: the role of familiarity and trust, services selling: an interpersonal influence perspective, *Omega*, Vol.28 No. 6, pp. 725–737.

Gilbert, R.L. & Forney, A. (2015). Can avatars pass the Turing test? Intelligent agent perception in a 3D virtual environment. *International Journal of Human-Computer Studies*, Vol.73 N. 2, pp. 30–36.

Go, E. & Sundar, S.S. (2019). Humanizing Chatbots: the effects of visual, identity and conversational cues on humanness perceptions. *Computers in Human Behavior*, Vol.97 N. 1, pp. 304–316.

Ha, S. & Stoel, L. (2009). Consumer e-shopping acceptance: antecedents in a technology acceptance model. *Journal of Business Research*, Vol.62 N. 5, pp. 565–571.

Hair, J.F. Jr, Sarstedt, M., Ringle, C.M. & Gudergan, S.P. (2017). *Advanced Issues in Partial Least Squares Structural Equation Modeling*. Thousand Oaks, CA: Sage Publications.

Hair, J.F., Black, W.C., Babin, B.J., Anderson, R.E. & Tatham, R.L., (2010). *Multivariate Data Analysis. Upper Saddle River*. New Jersey: Pearson.

Hart, P. & Saunders, C. (1997). Power and trust: critical factors in the adoption and use of electronic data interchange, *Organization Science*, Vol.8 N. 1, pp. 23–42.

Hassanein, K. & Head, M. (2005). The impact of infusing social presence in the web interface: an investigation across product types. *International Journal of Electronic Commerce*, Vol.10 N. 2, pp. 31–55.

Hassanein, K. & Head, M. (2007). Manipulating perceived social presence through the web interface and its impact on attitude towards online shopping. *International Journal of Human-Computer Studies*, Vol.65 N. 8, pp. 689–708.

Hassanein, K., Head, M. & Ju, C. (2009). A cross-cultural comparison of the impact of social presence on website trust, usefulness and enjoyment. *International Journal of Electronic Business*, Vol.7 N. 6, pp. 625.

Hatwar, P. N., Patil, A., & Gondane, D. (2016). AI based chatbot. *International Journal of Emerging Trends in Engineering and Basic Sciences*, Vol.6 N. 2, pp. 85–87.

Hoff, K.A. & Bashir, M. (2015). Trust in automation: integrating empirical evidence on factors that influence trust. *Human Factors*, Vol.57 N. 3, pp. 407–434.

Hoffman, D.L., Novak, T.P. & Peralta, M.A. (1999). Information privacy in the market space: implications for the commercial uses of anonymity on the web. *Information Society*, Vol.15 No. 2, pp. 129–139.

Hoy, W.K. & Tschannen-Moran, M. (1999). Five faces of trust: an empirical confirmation in urban elementary schools. *Journal of School Leadership*, Vol.9 N. 3, pp. 184–208.

Hua, Y., Cheng, X., Hou, T. & Luo, R. (2020). Monetary rewards, intrinsic motivators, and work engagement in the IT-enabled sharing economy: a mixed-methods investigation of internet taxi drivers. *Decision Sciences*, Vol.51 N. 3, pp. 755–785.

Irfan Bashir Chendragiri Madhavaiah, (2015). Consumer attitude and behavioural intention towards internet banking adoption in India. *Journal of Indian Business Research*, Vol.7 N 1 pp. 1–40.

Jiang, C., Rashid, R.M. & Wang, J. (2019). Investigating the role of social presence dimensions and information support on consumers' trust and shopping intentions. *Journal of Retailing and Consumer Services*, Vol.51 N. 2, pp. 263–270.

Jarvenpaa, S.L. & Tractinsky, N. & Saarinen, L. (1999). Consumer trust in an Internet store: a cross-cultural validation. *Journal of Computer-Mediated Communication*, Vol.5 N. 2, pp. 1–33.

Kaplan, A. & Haenlein, M. (2019). Siri, Siri, in my hand: who's the fairest in the land? On the interpretations, illustrations, and implications of artificial intelligence. *Business Horizons*, Vol.62 N. 1, pp. 15–25.

Kesharwani, A. & Bisht, S.S. (2012). The impact of trust and perceived risk on Internet banking adoption in India: an extension of technology acceptance model, *International Journal of Bank Marketing*, Vol.30 N. 4, pp. 303–322.

Khanna, A., Pandey, B., Vashishta, K., Kalia, K., Pradeepkumar, B., & Das, T. (2015). A study of today's A.I. through chatbots and rediscovery of machine intelligence. *International Journal of u- and e-Service, Science and Technology*, Vol.8 N. 7, pp. 277–284.

Kim, M.J., Lee, C.K. & Jung, T. (2013). Exploring consumer behavior in virtual reality tourism using an extended stimulus-organism-response model. *Journal of Travel Research*, Vol.59 N. 1, pp. 69–89.

Koufaris, M. (2002). Applying the technology acceptance model and flow theory to online consumer behavior. *Information Systems Research*, Vol.13 N. 2, pp. 205–223.

Lai, V. & Li, H. (2005). Technology acceptance model for Internet banking: an invariance analysis. *Information & Management*, Vol.42 N. 2, pp. 373–386.

Lee, S. & Dubinsky, A. (2003). Influence of salesperson characteristics and customer emotion on retail dyadic relationships. *International Review of Retail Distribution and Consumer Research*, Vol.13 N. 1, pp. 21–36.

Lee, M.C. (2009). Factors influencing the adoption of Internet banking: an integration of TAM and TPB with perceived risk and perceived benefit. *Electronic Commerce Research and Applications*, Vol.8 N. 3, pp. 130–141.

Li, D., Chau, P.Y.K. & Lou, H. (2005). Understanding individual adoption of instant messaging: an empirical investigation. *Journal of the Association for Information Systems*, Vol.6 N. 4, pp. 102–129.

Lombard, M. & Ditton, T. (1997). At the heart of it all: the concept of presence. *Journal of Computer-Mediated Communication*, Vol.3 N. 2, pp. 1–43.

Luo, X., Tong, S., Fang, Z. & Qu, Z. (2019). Frontiers: machines vs humans: the impact of artificial intelligence chatbot disclosure on customer purchases. *Marketing Science*, Vol.38 N. 6, pp. 937–947.

Macintosh, G. & Lockshin, L.S. (1997). Retail relationships and store loyalty: a multi-level perspective. *International Journal of Research in Marketing*, Vol.14 N. 5, pp. 487–497.

Manzano, J.A., Navarre, C.L., Mafe, C.R. & Blas, S.S. (2009). Key drivers of Internet banking services use. *Online Information Review*, Vol.33 N. 4, pp. 672–695.

Mayer, R.C., Davis, J.H. & Schoorman, F.D. (1995). An integrative model of organizational trust. *Academy of Management Review*, Vol.20 N. 3, pp. 709–734.

McKenna, K.Y.A., Green, A.S. & Gleason, M.E.J. (2002). Relationship formation on the internet: what's the big attraction? *Journal of Social Issues*, Vol.58 N. 1, pp. 9–31.

Ming-Chi, L. (2009). Factors influencing the adoption of internet banking: an integration of TAM and TPB with perceived risk and perceived benefit. *Electronic Commerce Research and Applications*, Vol.8 N. 3, pp. 130–141.

Mitchell, V. (2018). Gartner: why humans will still be at the core of great CX. available at: https://www.cmo.com.au/article/642649/gartner-why-humans-will-still-core-great-cx/ (accessed 20 December 2022).

Moon, J. & Kim, Y. (2001). Extending the TAM for a WorldWideWeb context. *Information and Management*, Vol.38 N. 4, pp. 217–230.

Morgan, R.M. & Hunt, S.D. (1994). The commitment–trust theory of relationship marketing. *Journal of Marketing*, Vol.58 N. 3, pp. 20–38.

Morrison, D.E. & Firmstone, J. (2000). The social functional of trust and implications for e-commerce. *International Journal of Advertising*, Vol.19 N. 5, pp. 599–623.

Nunnally, J.C. & Bernstein, I.H. (1994). *Psychometric Theory, 3/e*. New York, NY: McGraw-Hill.

Oracle (2019) What is a chatbot?. available at https://www.oracle.com/solutions/chatbots/whatis-achatbot/ (accessed 8 December 2022).

Peter, J.P. (1979). Reliability: A review of psychometric basics and recent marketing practices. *Journal of Marketing Research*. Vol.16 N. 1, pp. 6–17.

Pise, R. (2018). Chatbot market size is set to exceed USD 134 billion by 2024 – ClickZ. available at: https://www.clickz.com/chatbot-market-size-is-set-to-exceed-usd-1–34-billion-by-2024/215518/ (accessed 6 December 2022).

Qiu, L. & Benbasat, I. (2009). Evaluating anthropomorphic product recommendation agents: a social relationship perspective to designing information systems. *Journal of Management Information Systems*, Vol.25 N. 4, pp. 145–182.

Ratnasingham, P. (1998). The importance of trust in electronic commerce, *Internet Research*, Vol.8 No. 4, pp. 313–321.

Seeber, I., Bittner, E., Briggs, R.O., de Vreede, T., de Vreede, G.J., Elkins, A., Maier, R., Merz, A.B., Oeste-Reiß, S., Randrup, N., Schwabe, G. & Sollner, M. (2020). Machines as teammates: a research agenda on AI in team collaboration. *Information and Management*, Vol.57 N. 2, pp. 103–174.

Shawar, B.A. & Atwell, E.S. (2005). Using corpora in machine-learning chatbot systems. *International Journal of Corpus Linguistics*, Vol.10 N. 4, pp. 489–516.

Shen, J. (2012). Social comparison, social presence, and enjoyment in the acceptance of social shopping websites. *Journal of Electronic Commerce Research*, Vol.13 N. 3, pp. 198.

Siau, K. & Shen, Z. (2003). Building customer trust in mobile commerce. *Communications of the ACM*, Vol.46 N. 4, pp. 91–94.

Suh, B. & Han, I. (2002). Effect of trust on customer acceptance of Internet banking. *Electronic Commerce Research and Applications*, Vol.1 N. 3-4, pp. 247–263.

Tandon, U. (2023). Chatbots, virtual-try-on (VTO), e-WOM: modeling the determinants of attitude' and continued intention with PEEIM as moderator in online shopping. *Global Knowledge, Memory and Communication*, Vol. ahead-of-print No. ahead-of-print.

Thakur, R. (2018). The role of self-efficacy and customer satisfaction in driving loyalty to the mobile shopping application. *International Journal of Retail and Distribution Management*, Vol.46 N. 3, pp. 283–303.

Thatcher, J.B., Wright, R.T., Sun, H., Zagenczyk, T.J. & Klein, R. (2018). Mindfulness in information technology use: definitions, distinctions, and a new measure. *MIS Quarterly*, Vol.42 N. 3, pp. 831–847.

Van der Heijden, H. (2003). Factors influencing the usage of websites: the case of a generic portal in The Netherlands. *Information and Management*, Vol.40 N. 6, pp. 541–549.

Van der Heijden, H. (2004). User acceptance of hedonic information systems. *MIS Quarterly*, Vol.28 N. 4, pp. 695–704.

Walker, H. R. & Johnson, W.L. (2006). Why consumers use and do not use technology enabled services. *Journal of Services Marketing*, Vol.20 No. 2, pp. 125–135.

Wang, W. & Benbasat, I. (2008). Attributions of trust in decision support technologies: a study of recommendation agents for e-commerce. *Journal of Management Information Systems*, Vol.24 N. 4, pp. 249–273.

Waxer, C (2016). *Get ready for the bot revolution*. Computer World. Retrieved from https://www.computerworld.com/article/3126438/emerging-technology/article.html. Accessed on December 9, 2022.

Whang, C. & Im, H. (2018). Does recommendation matter for trusting beliefs and trusting intentions? Focused on different types of recommender system and sponsored recommendation. *International Journal of Retail and Distribution Management*, Vol.46 N. 10, pp. 944–958.

Wu, I.-L. & Chen, J.-L. (2005). An extension of Trust and TAM model with TPB in the initial adoption of on-line tax: an empirical study. *International Journal of Human-Computer Studies*, Vol.62 N. 6, pp. 784–808.

Wu, W.Y. & Ke, C.C. (2015). An online shopping behaviour model integrating personality traits, perceived risk, and technology acceptance. *Social Behaviour and Personality: An International Journal*, Vol.43 N. 1, pp. 85–97.

Yoon, S.J. (2002). The antecedents and consequences of trust in online-purchase decisions. *Journal of Interactive Marketing*, Vol.16 No. 2, pp. 47–63.

Yu, J., Ha, I., Choi, M. & Rho, J. (2005). Extending the TAM for a t-commerce. *Information and Management*, Vol.42 N. 7, pp. 965–976.

16 The Moderating Role of Perceived Interaction in a Chatbot's Impact on Conversational Commerce

From Intention to Usage to Actual Usage

Habiba Ben Ameur and Kaouther Saied Ben Rached
University of Tunis, Tunis, Tunisia

16.1 INTRODUCTION

The invention of machine learning around the turn of the 20th century accelerated the progress of artificial intelligence (Thilagavathy and Kumar, 2021). Digital marketing was impacted by this revolution, which also altered customer purchasing behavior and increased revenues (Pangkey et al., 2020).

This increasing diffusion of artificial intelligence has opened up new opportunities for the study of consumer behavior (Cosmo et al. 2021). In fact, this technology enables the development of new marketing strategies based on Big Data and a deeper understanding of the decision-making process (Kumar et al., 2019; Sterne, 2017; Yang and Siau, 2018). Additionally, the quick development of AI has made it possible for companies to engage with clients using chatbots (Chen et al., 2022).

For Sidlauskiene et al. (2023), Chatbot technology is employed as a great tool to enhance communication, boost service delivery effectiveness, reduce costs, and enhance customer experience. It enables businesses to communicate with their customers, facilitate information searches, facilitate transactions, and facilitate after-sales service requests (Cosmo et al., 2021). In addition to facilitating real-time, individualized communication, chatbots also guarantee sales and transaction processes (Leszkiewicz et al., 2021). Although chatbots have been around for a while in the world of information technology, they were just recently made available for commercial use. The ability of chatbots as a marketing tool was first demonstrated in 2016 by the well-known instant messaging service Messenger (Cosmo et al., 2021).

Referring to the marketing literature, researchers such as Sidlauskiene et al. (2023), Han and Kim (2020), and Cruzado et al. (2023) were interested in addressing the importance of chatbots in conversational commerce. Others like Moriuchi (2019), Chhikara et al. (2022), and Cosmo et al. (2021) studied the attitude toward this technology. The intention to use chatbots has attracted the interest of several recent works such as Gnewuch et al. (2022); Han and Kim (2020) and Sumarjan et al. (2023).

Our study aims to examine the influence of chatbot use intention on actual conversational commerce usage on a website by emphasizing the importance of perceived interactivity.

DOI: 10.1201/9781003450443-16

With the exception of certain research done by Febrianto et al. (2018), Alifiardi (2019), and Han and Kim (2020), few academics have been interested in examining the relationship between the intention of adopting a chatbot and actual use. In studies on chatbots and artificial intelligence, there are gaps in the comprehension of the role of perceived interactivity.

Our problem is presented within this context: What is the impact of the intention to use a chatbot in conversational commerce on its actual use?

To carry out this research work, we will present the conceptual framework of our research. Then, we will specify the nature of the relationships that exist between these different variables by referring to the literature. Finally, we will present the research methodology and we will present and discuss the results obtained.

16.2 THEORETICAL BACKGROUND

The use of chatbots powered by artificial intelligence has increased, which has gradually transformed how consumers make purchases (Sidlauskiene et al., 2023). Many businesses have made use of this technology to deliver individualized product information, respond swiftly to consumer demands, and assist customers in making purchasing decisions.

16.2.1 Artificial Intelligence in Online Marketing

16.2.1.1 Definition of Artificial Intelligence

One of the newest fields of science and engineering, artificial intelligence was developed by Alan Turing in 1956 (Russell and Norvig, 2010). It is a field of study that tries to automate human intellect (Nilsson, 2005). The development gained owing to artificial intelligence is considered a revolution expected to alter the industries of banking, health, marketing, insurance, and vehicles. It is founded on a big data-driven machine-learning methodology (Dubey et al., 2020). Artificial intelligence, as defined by Zouinar (2020), refers to devices, algorithms, or software that look to reproduce human abilities like language comprehension, object recognition, and various types of thinking. According to Huang and Rust (2021), this technology refers to the use of computational devices to mimic human capacities such as thinking, emotion, and performing physical or mechanical activities. Intelligent conversational agents use various forms of artificial intelligence, such as speech recognition and natural language processing, to control interactions with humans (Ling et al., 2021).

16.2.1.2 Artificial Intelligence in E-commerce

Artificial intelligence has gradually been involved in marketing with the rise of e-commerce. According to Pansari and Kumar (2017), the majority of companies have employed digital technology and artificial intelligence to interact with clients on social media and other platforms that have AI built in. According to Micu et al. (2018), the purpose of artificial intelligence in marketing is to enhance the optimization of marketing campaigns, search engine rankings, website consistency, and traffic volume. On their part, Pillai and Sivathanu (2020), point out that artificial intelligence quickens the pace of digital transformation by fostering disruptive innovation. This explains that several companies use this technology in e-commerce to detect trends based on browsing history, order history, account records, and other factors (Mittal and Sharma, 2021).

16.2.1.2.1 Conversational Commerce

The term "conversational commerce" was coined by Chris Messina, a former Uber and Google employee who created the hashtag (#) in tweets (Sidlauskiene et al., 2023). The term conversational commerce or online commerce is conducted through text, voice, or other natural language technologies interacting with businesses, brands, and services (Messina, 2015). Several marketing researchers have been interested in defining conversational commerce. This concept consists of offering convenience, personalization, and decision support (Van Manen, 2016). According to Shopify (2016), customers may speak with corporate employees, obtain customer service, ask questions, receive tailored suggestions, read reviews, and click through to purchases using messaging applications thanks to conversational commerce. The use of conversational commerce allows consumers to engage in an interaction with a human representative, a chatbot, or a mixture of both (Van Eeuwen (2017). It refers to an interaction between a brand and a consumer that simulates human dialogue (Gartner, 2019). During this conversation, a purchase of products or services will be made (Sidlauskiene et al., 2023). The current growth of conversational commerce is fueled by technological advancements in artificial intelligence (AI) (Reavie, 2018) and is expected to increase sevenfold by 2025, reaching some US$290 billion worldwide (Sidlauskiene et al., 2023).

16.2.1.2.2 Perceived Interactivity

Interactivity or interaction refers to the ease for individuals and organizations to communicate directly with each other regardless of distance and time (Blattberg and Deighton, 1991). Users can engage in an interactive environment by altering the structure and content of it in real time (Steuer, 1992). For Deighton (1996), being "interactive" is having the capacity to address a person, gather and remember their response, and then address them again while taking into account their prior reaction. According to Sundar et al. (2003), interactivity is conceptualized as the possibility of having a cumulative response to user input that expresses a sense of dialogue and contingency. Interactivity in web-based communication can be conceptualized as the possibility of having a cumulative response to the user's input that expresses a sense of dialogue and contingency (Sundar et al., 2003). Real-time interaction enhances customer perceptions and increases the likelihood that they will make a purchase on e-commerce websites (Matteson et al., 2011). Additionally, Sundar et al. (2014) believe that interactivity is a key factor in predicting user engagement and more precise behavioral intentions to use a tool or technology. If customers perceive interactivity as being high, they may be able to gather required data and receive customized services based on repeated encounters (Kang et al., 2015).

16.2.2 The Determinants of Adopting Artificial Intelligence

16.2.2.1 Hedonic and Utilitarian Motivation

Based on the causes and objectives that drive behaviors, SDT has been utilized in the marketing literature to explain that there are two primary types of human motivations (Deci and Ryan, 2000). According to Botti and McGill (2011) and Whitley et al. (2018), customers are driven to look for, buy, and consume goods and services for utilitarian and hedonistic reasons.

Hedonic motivation and intrinsic motivation are factors that influence behavior and are connected to the enjoyment that results from engaging in that conduct (Deci and Ryan, 1985). Consumers willingly endorse and participate in actions when hedonic incentive is present (Botti and McGill, 2011), according to Deci and Ryan (2000). This kind of incentive, in accordance with Gonzalez et al. (2019), relates to how much people like utilizing technology.

Utilitarian motivation: For Ryan and Deci (2017), this is extrinsic motivation which represents the driving force of behavior aimed at achieving instrumental values such as external rewards or social approval. Babin et al. (1994) and Whitley et al. (2018) point out that utilitarian motivation allows individuals to successfully perform tasks efficiently and on time to achieve external goals. Utilitarian motivation has an external locus of causality (Botti and McGill, 2011).

16.2.2.2 Social Presence of a Chatbot

Referring to the marketing literature, several researchers have used the concept of social presence in their studies focusing on sculpins such as Araujo (2018), Go and Sundar (2019), De Cicco et al. (2020), and Lee et al. (2020). Social presence is prevalent in human-chatbot interaction research because it describes a feeling of being with another … either a human or artificial intelligence (Biocca et al., 2003). It refers to the extent to which a medium allows individuals to feel as if others were psychologically present (Biocca et al., 2003). The role of social presence is crucial in digital commerce, as it stimulates users' positive reactions toward website trust, and purchase intention (Gefen and Straub, 2004). According to the theory of multiple source effects, the feeling of social presence felt by a user in a digital environment will be amplified when numerous voice sources are used and integrated into the digital environment (Lee and Nass, 2004). For Kilteni et al. (2012) and Moon et al. (2013), social presence or virtual friendliness refers to the feeling that the interlocutor experiences as well as their ability to react to human requests.

Social presence has been identified as the degree to which users experience other intelligent beings coexisting and interacting with them within a digital environment even when the virtual artifacts are not real (Kim, 2016). For their part, Lu et al. (2016) clarified that social presence presents the degree of social cues offered by interacting with the technological source such as "warm," "personal," and "sociable."

16.2.3 Chatbots

16.2.3.1 Definition of a Chatbot

The first known text-based chatbot ELIZA (Weizenbaum, 1966) was developed in the 1960s as a computer program for using natural language to stimulate human-like conversation (Sidlauskiene et al., 2023). A chatbot is a computer program that uses automated, algorithm-based technologies such as natural language processing, learning, and AI to mimic conversational interactions with humans (Crolic et al., 2021). These chatbots are programmed based on natural language processing to carry out real-time communication to advise, support or simply converse with the interlocutor (Misischia et al., 2022). According to Lee and Lee (2020), chatbots provide customers with a more engaging platform to submit their contact details. They can also be used to generate consumer interest in products/services and potentially increase company revenue (Lee and Lee, 2020). These virtual agents make it possible to distribute products and services personalized according to individual needs and which are sold via real-time one-on-one conversations (Diederich et al., 2020). Software systems are designed to interact with humans using natural language (Feine et al., 2019; McTear et al., 2016). Chatbots are used in various fields such as customer service (Sheehan et al., 2020), education (Smutny and Schreiberova, 2020), e-commerce, healthcare (Fitzpatrick et al., 2017) and retail (Tran et al., 2021).

Avatars having human traits, such as face and body parts, are frequently used in chatbots (Han, 2021). Embodied chatbots may communicate with humans by using language (text or voice), a virtual body or face, and nonverbal signals including body language, gaze, and facial emotions (Kramer et al., 2009). Text-based or speech-based chatbots are both possible (Gnewuch et al., 2017). Its advancements lead to three different kinds of intelligent conversational agents, including robot-like conversational agents that seem human while interacting with people, as Maya at Lemonade. Apple's Siri, Amazon's Alexa, and chatbots that only interact with text inputs and outputs are a few examples of voice-based chatbots or personal voice assistants (Ling et al., 2021).

16.2.3.2 Intention to Use a Chatbot

Use intention is the desire to adopt a certain behavior (Ajzen, 1985). The technology acceptance model (TAM) also proposes that users' attitudes toward information systems influence their behavioral intentions to use (Davis et al., 1989). According to Bae (2018), this intention can be

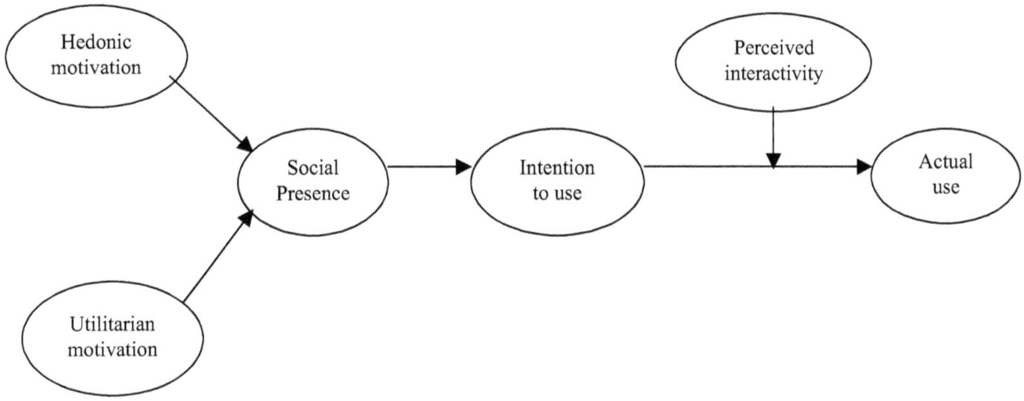

FIGURE 16.1 Conceptual model.

defined as the perceived likelihood that a person will perform a specific behavior. It explains whether the chatbot can function adequately and meet the user's needs (Santiago et al., 2019). It is an attitude or behavior that tends to want to use technology (Andy et al., 2021). Usage intention is influenced by culture, society, person, and psychology (Andy et al., 2021). According to Kuo et al. (2021), the intention to continue using chatbot services is essential to ensure the long-term viability of chatbot and communication services of large companies. Knowing customers' usage intention is crucial for marketers to make strategic decisions and forecast sales of existing and new products and services (Sumarjan et al., 2023).

16.2.3.3 Actual Use of Chatbot

According to Davis (1989), actual usage is measured as the amount of time spent interacting with a technology and the frequency of its use (Davis, 1989). It refers to the desire to adopt a certain behavior (Ajzen, 1991). A person would be satisfied with using the system if he believes that it is easy to use and will increase productivity as shown by actual usage (Venkatesh and Davis, 1996).

According to Rigopoulos and Askounis (2007), actual usage is measured based on repeated usage and more frequent use. A person will be satisfied upon using the system if they believe that the system is easy to use and will increase productivity as seen from actual usage. (Venkatesh and Davis, 1996). (Figure 16.1)

16.2.4 Development of Hypotheses

16.2.4.1 Impact of Utilitarian and Hedonic Motivations on Usage Intention

Behavioral intentions are activated by motivation, a potent force (Dinh and Park, 2022). In this study, we anticipate that hedonic incentives will lead to increased chatbot use. Indeed, chatbots may have engaging, automated conversations with customers. As a result, when engaging with chatbots, users may really feel delight, enjoyment, and escape (Pitardi and Marriott, 2021). Utilitarian motives, for example, boost the desire to use chatbot services since they assist customers in making wise decisions (Mimoun and Poncin, 2015) and resolving issues (Chung et al., 2020). They are useful (Pitardi and Marriott, 2021), simple to use (Cheng and Jiang, 2020), and help in achieving objectives. Therefore, our hypotheses are stated as follows:

H1: Hedonic motivation has a positive effect on the intention to use a chatbot.
H2: Utilitarian motivation has a positive impact on the intention to use a chatbot

16.2.4.2 Impact of Utilitarian and Hedonic Motivations on Social Presence

According to Deci and Ryan (2014), consumers who are hedonically motivated, expect to form relationships with others. However, referring to SDT, Ryan and Deci (2017) highlight clarify that utilitarian motivation makes people focus more on instrumental outcomes such as financial resources, reputation, power, or external attractiveness. Additionally, in their work, Deci and Ryan (2014) and Lee et al. (2020) consider that people tend to view their relationship partners as instruments for achieving utilitarian goals rather than mutually respected or supported partners. Thus proposes that if consumers have a hedonic motivation, they are more likely to seek a sense of social presence from sculpins than those who have a utilitarian motivation. Therefore, our hypothesis is stated as follows:

H3: The positive impact of consumer hedonic motivation on the social presence of chatbots is stronger than the impact of utilitarian motivation on the social presence of chatbots.

16.2.4.3 Impact of Social Presence on Usage Intention

Several researchers like Cyr et al. (2007), Hassanein and Head (2007), and Qiu and Benbasat (2009) indicated that social presence is a key factor in driving usage intentions of various technologies contexts. Similarly, previous research has shown that social presence is positively associated with chatbot adoption (Fernandes and Oliveira, 2021; Go and Sundar, 2019; Li and Mao, 2015). For their part, Gnewuch et al. (2022) and Dinh and Park (2022) specified that social presence increases the intention to use chatbots. Based on previous research, we propose that:

H4: Social presence has a positive effect on the intention to use a chatbot.

16.2.4.4 Impact of the Intention to Use a Chatbot on Current Usage

Referring to the marketing literature, researchers like Davis (1989), Sambasivan (2010), Febrianto et al. (2018), and Alifiardi and Baridwan (2019) specify that the intention of use influences the actual use of online shopping applications. This led us to propose the following hypothesis (we propose the following hypothesis):

H5: The intention to use a chatbot has a positive effect on the current use of this technology

16.2.4.5 Moderating Effect of the Perceived Interactivity between the Intention to Use a Chatbot and Actual Use

According to Sundar et al. (2014), perceived interactivity is considered an important determinant of user engagement and the Behavioral intention to adopt. On the other hand, the presence of a chatbot tool on a website was considered more attractive than a human cat and is a determinant of the intention to interact with it. We proposed that perceived interactivity helps strengthen the relationship between the intention to use a chatbot and its current use. Hence our hypothesis:

H6: Perceived interactivity moderates the relationship between the intention to use a chatbot and its current use.

16.2.5 Research Methodology and Discussion of Results

16.2.5.1 Research Methodology

This empirical section will deal with the impact of the desire to use a chatbot on actual usage while emphasizing the significance of perceived interaction in the setting of conversational

TABLE 16.1
Results of Principal Component Analysis

Variables	KMO	Bartlett Test
Motivation	0,902	X^2 = 3033,581, ddl = 28, p = 0,000
Social Presence	0,877	X^2 = 1321,748, ddl = 6, p = 0,000
Intention to use	0,770	X^2 = 777,643, ddl = 3, p = 0,000
Perceived interactivity	0,911	X^2 = 1731,632, ddl = 10, p = 0,000
Actual use	0,646	X^2 = 517,053, ddl = 3, p = 0,000

TABLE 16.2
Reliability and Validity of Measurement Scales

Dimensions of Variables	Cronbach's Alpha	Rho of Joreskog	Convergent Validity
Utilitarian motivation	0,964	0,966	0,904
Hedonic Motivation	0,983	0,983	0,922
Social Presence	0,975	0,977	0,914
Intention to use	0,963	0,964	0,900
Perceived interactivity	0,979	0,920	0,910
Actual use	0,906	0,919	0,792

commerce on a website. The online survey was administered to 218 users, 55.5% of whom were women and 44.5% of whom were men. This sample is distributed between several categories of different age groups, 52.3% of which concerns users who are between 30 and 39 years old, 22.9% for users who are between 20 and 29 years old, 19.7% between 40 and 45 years old, and 5% are over 50 years old. The questionnaire allowed us to evaluate the intention to use a chatbot and the factors that can influence this intention such as social presence, and utilitarian and hedonic motivations the scale of Babin et al. (1994) to measure utilitarian and hedonic motivation. The scale developed by Gefen and Straub (2004) to measure social presence. Intention to use a chatbot was measured by the scale of Venkatesh et al. To measure the actual use of chatbot, we used the scale of Pillai and Sivathanu (2020) and Kang et al. (2015). Items of the related scales were scored on a Likert scale ranging from 1 to 5. In addition, the results were generated by SPSS 22 software for the exploratory analysis and AMOS 22 for the confirmatory analysis. Finally, we carried out a structural analysis to validate the fit of the structural model as well as its research hypotheses. (Tables 16.1 and 16.2)

- The utilitarian and hedonic motivation measurement scale indicates that there is a very good predisposition of the data to be factorized. Jöreskog's Rho > 0.9 which shows that there is very good internal consistency convergent validity is greater than 0.5. For the confirmatory analysis of this scale, the adjustment indices are compatible with the critical levels of acceptance. GFI: 0.919 RMR: 0.033; RMSEA: 0.132, TLI: 0.965; CFI: 0.978 and $\chi 2/df$ = 4,789; BIC: 183,120 Ms 193,842 and CAIC: 201,120 Ms 229,842.
- For the social presence scale, there is a commendable predisposition of the data to be factorized and very good internal consistency. The convergent validity (ρvc) >0.5 which respects the threshold defined by Fornell and Lacker. The results of the confirmatory analysis

are acceptable. GFI: 0.991; AGFI: 0.957; RMR: 0.009; RMSEA: 0.065; TLI: 0.996; CFI: 0.999; $\chi 2/df = 1.916$; BIC: 46.908 Ms 53,845 and CAIC: 54,908 Ms 63,845.

- The scale of the intention to use a chatbot shows a good predisposition of the data to be factored. Similarly, the convergent validity is good (0.9 > 0.5). Jöreskog's Rho (0.964) indicates that there is very good internal consistency. GFI: 0.999; AGFI: 0.939; RMR: 0.026 and RMSEA: 0.035. Incremental indices: TLI: 0.996 and CFI: 0.999. Parsimonious indices: $\chi 2/dl = 1{,}640$; BIC:27,300 Ms 35,320 and CAIC:32,300 Ms 39,520.
- For the perceived interactivity scale, the results of the exploratory analysis show that there is a very good predisposition of the data to be factorized (KMO = 0.911). The confirmatory analysis of this scale gives us indices of acceptable fit. For the absolute indices: GFI: 0.988; AGFI: 0.956; RMR: 0.010 and RMSEA: 0.054. The incremental indices: are TLI:0.996 and CFI:0.999. Parsimonious indices: $\chi 2/df = 1.640$; BIC: 65.787 Ms 80.767 and CAIC: 76.787 Ms 95.767.
- The measurement scale for the current use of a chatbot indicates a very good predisposition of the data to be factored. Convergent validity (0.792 > 0.5) is good. Jöreskog's Rho is 0.919 which means that the internal consistency is very good. The confirmatory analysis of this scale gives us acceptable fit indices. For absolute indices: GFI: 0.999; AGFI: 0.993; RMR: 0.073; RMSEA: 0.085; TLI: 0.986; CFI: 0.995; $\chi 2/df = 3{,}376$; BIC: 30.298 Ms 32.307 and CAIC: 35.298 Ms 38.307.
- The table that follows shows that the fit indices of the global model are acceptable. (Tables 16.3 and 16.4)
- Results of hypothesis testing show that the link between motivation (utilitarian-hedonic) and the intention to use a chatbot is not significant ($cr < 1.98$; $p > 0.05$).
- The rest of the hypotheses H2, H3 and H4 are significant.

TABLE 16.3
Fit Indices of the Overall Measurement Model

Absolute Indices				Incremental Indices			Parsimonious Indices		
X^2	GFI	AGFI	RMR	RMSEA	TLI	CFI	X^2/ddl	BIC	CAIC
1532,338	0,901	0,898	0,087	0,075	0,91	0,927	3,624	1812,332 Ms 1362,277	1864,332 Ms 1615,277

TABLE 16.4
Testing the Model Hypotheses

Hypothesis	Links	Standardized Structural Link	CR	P	
H1a	Intention to use ← Hedonic motivation	0,025	0,235	0,815	Non Significative
H1b	Intention to use ← Utilitarian motivation	–0,91	–0,848	0,396	Non Significative
H2a	Social Presence ← Hedonic motivation	0,265	7,048	***	Significative
H2b	Social Presence ← utilitarian motivation	0,202	5,254	***	Significative
H3	Intention to use ← Social Presence	0,541	6,930	***	Significative
H4	Actual use ← Intention to use	0,409	5,652	***	Significative

TABLE 16.5
Moderation Effect

Modération	**X: Intention to Use** **Y: Actual Use** **W: Perceived Interactivity**		
Direct effects and interaction effect			
Regressions	Coefficient	T value	Significance
X → Y	−0,1100	0,0433	P = −2,5378
W → Y	0,875	0,0437	P = 20,0529
XW → Y	−0,1194	0,0415	P = −2,8732

Test of the moderating effect of interactivity perceived between intention of use and actual use: (Table 16.5).

The results of the analysis show that W: Perceived interactivity negatively moderates the relationship between X: Intention to use and Y: Actual use.

16.2.5.2 Discussion of Results

Compared to the literature, the empirical findings of our study confirm the majority of the hypotheses compared to the literature. First, regarding the relationship between utilitarian and hedonic motivation with intention to use a chatbot, we observed that both types of motivation exert no significant effect on intention to use a chatbot. use which is in contradiction with the work carried out by Dinh and Park (2022). So for our research, these two types of motivations do not constitute determinants that push users to adopt the chatbot during a commercial conversation. Second, we found that the effect between hedonic motivation and social presence is significant, which is consistent with the work of Deci and Ryan (2014) and Dinh and Park (2022). In contrast to Deci and Ryan's (2017) findings, which claim that utilitarian motivation has no significant effect on social presence, we found that utilitarian motivation significantly affects social presence. This demonstrates that consumers who feel as though they are having an online discussion with the chatbot are those who find that adopting a chatbot provides more information helps in making purchase decisions, suits their needs and expectations, and satisfies their demand for enjoyment and amusement. Then, the results of their empirical study show that the relationship between social presence and usage intention is significant and positive, which is consistent with the research carried out by Qiu and Benbasat (2009), and Gnewuch et al. (2022), and Dinh and Park (2022). We can therefore see that social presence is a very important factor in driving usage intentions. Then, the results of their empirical study show that the relationship between social presence and usage intention is significant and positive, which is consistent with the research carried out by Qiu and Benbasat (2009), and Gnewuch et al. (2022) and Dinh and Park (2022). We can therefore see that social presence is a very important factor in driving usage intentions. In addition, we showed that the intention to use a chatbot has a significant and positive impact on actual use, which is consistent with the work carried out by Febrianto et al. (2018), Gnewuch et al. (2022), and Sumarjan et al. (2023). Therefore, we can consider that the people who intend to use the chatbot are those who wish to make actual use of this technology. Finally, we verified the moderating role of perceived interactivity between the intention to use a chatbot and actual use. This is negative moderation. This can be explained by the fact that when the link between the intention of use and actual use is strong and significant, the perceived interactivity is strong. However, if the link between usage intention and actual use is not significant, perceived interactivity is weak.

16.3 CONCLUSION

Through our research, we were able to determine how a chatbot's intended usage affects its actual use. The application of this technology in the context of conversational commerce is our theoretical contribution. Referring to the literature, there are gaps regarding the treatment of this relationship in this area of study. Furthermore, highlighting the role of perceived interactivity constitutes an important contribution to our research. Indeed, we have enriched the literature by specifying the moderating role of perceived interactivity between the intention to use a chatbot and its actual use. At the end of the results of our research, we can put forward practical recommendations intended for marketers on the importance of integrating artificial intelligence into the company. This technology simplifies several complicated tasks and saves businesses a lot of money and time. In addition, the introduction of artificial intelligence in digital marketing connects companies with potential customers. This improves customer understanding and helps organizations develop products and services to meet customer needs. Like any research, this present work is not without limitations. The first limitation concerns the number of samples which turns out to be too small compared to our study. We have also limited our research in the field of conversational commerce while it is possible to broaden our field of study in other areas. As future avenues of research, we propose to introduce moderator-mediator variables to enrich the conceptual model such as trust in the chatbot, reactivity, perceived expertise, etc. It would also be relevant to test our theoretical model on a larger sample of users.

REFERENCES

Ajzen, I. (1985). "From Intentions to actions: A theory of planned behavior". In J. Kuhl, & J. Beckmann (Eds.), *Action control: From cognition to behavior*. New York: Spinger-Verlag.

Ajzen, I. (1991). "The theory of planned behavior." *Organizational Behavior and Human Decision Processes*, 50, 2, 179–211.

Alifiardi, A. A., & Baridwan, Z. (2019). "The influence of perceived usefulness, ease of use, trust, and risk towards Gojek actual use with behavioral intention to use as intervening variable". *Jurnal Ilmiah Mahasiswa* FEB, 7,2, 1–21.

Andy, R., Dewi, A., & tAs'adi, M. (2021). "An empirical study to validate the Technology Acceptance Model (TAM) in evaluating "Desa Digital" applications". *Workshop on Environmental Science, Society, and Technology*, 1–9.

Araujo, T. (2018). "Living up to the Chatbot hype: the influence of anthropomorphic design cues and communicative agency framing on conversational agent and company perceptions". *Computers in Human Behavior*, 85, 183–189.

Babin, B. J., Darden, W. R., & Grifn, M. (1994). "Work and/or fun: measuring hedonic and utilitarian shopping value". *Journal of Consumer Research*, 20, 4, 644–656.

Bae, M. (2018). "Understanding the effect of the discrepancy between sought and obtained gratification on social networking site users' satisfaction and continuance intention". *Computers in human behavior*, 79, 137–153.

Biocca, F., Harms, C., & Burgoon, J. K. (2003). "Toward a more robust theory and measure of social presence: review and suggested criteria". *Pres. Teleoperat.Virtu. Environ.*, 12, 456–480.

Blattberg, R. C., & Deighton J. (1991). "Interactive marketing: Exploiting the age of addressability", *Sloan Management Review*, 33, 1, 5–14.

Botti, S., & McGill, A. L. (2011). "The locus of choice: Personal causality and satisfaction with hedonic and utilitarian decisions". *Journal of Consumer Research*, 37, 6, 1065–1078.

Butler, J. K. (1991). "Toward understanding and measuring conditions of trust: Evolution of conditions of trust inventory". *Journal of Management*, 17, 3, 643–663. 12, 456–480.

Crolic, C., Felipe, T., Rhonda, H., & Andrew, S. (2021). "Blame the bot: Anthropomorphism and anger in customer-chatbot interactions". *Journal of Marketing*, 86, 1, 132–148.

Cyr D., Hassanein K., Head M., & Ivanov A. (2007). "The role of social presence in establishing loyalty in e-service environments". *Interaction Computer*, 19, 43–56.

Chung, M., Ko, E., Joung, H., & Kim, S. J. (2020). "Chatbot e-service and customer satisfaction regarding luxury brands". *Journal of Business Research*, 117, 587–595.

Cheng, Y., & Jiang, H. (2020). "How do AI-driven chatbots impact user experience? Examining gratifications, perceived privacy risk, satisfaction, loyalty, and continued use". *Journal of Broadcasting & Electronic Media*, 64, 4, 592–614.

Chen, Y., Prentice, C., Weaven, S., & Hisao, A. (2022). "The influence of customer trust and artificial intelligence on customer engagement and loyalty: The case of the home-sharing industry". *Frontiers in Psychology*, 1–15.

Chhikara, D., Sharma, R., & Kaushik, K. (2022). "Indian e-commerce consumer and their acceptance towards chatbots". *Academy of Marketing Studies Journal*, 26, 1–10.

Cosmo, L. M., Piper, L., & Di Vittorio, A. (2021). "The rôle of attitude toward chatbots and privacy concern on the relationship between attitude toward mobile advertising and behavioral intent to use chatbots". *Italian Journal of Marketing*, 83–102.

Cruzado, J. G., Morales, C. M., Del Carpio, C. F., GoyCochea, J. L., Arévalo, A. A., & Vargas, C. R. (2023), "Use of chatbots in e-commerce". *A Comprehensive Systematic Review*, 101, 4, 1172–1183.

Davis, F. D., Bagozzi, R. P., & Warshaw, P. R. (1989). "User acceptance of computer technology: A comparison of two theoretical models". *Management Science*, 35, 8, 982–1003.

Davis, F. D. (1989). "Perceived usefulness, perceived ease of use, and user acceptance of information technology". *MIS Quarterly*, 319–340.

Deighton, J. (1996). "The future of interactive marketing". *Harvard Business Review*, 74, 6, 151–152.

Deci, E. L., & Ryan, R. M. (1985). *Intrinsic motivation and self-determination in human behavior*. New York: Plenum.

Deci, E. L., & Ryan, R. M. (2000). "The "what" and "why" of goal pursuits: Human needs and the self-determination of behavior". *Psychological Inquiry*, 11, 4, 227–268.

Deci, E. L., & Ryan, R. M. (2014). "Autonomy and need satisfaction in close relationships: Relationships motivation theory". In N. Weinstein (Ed.), *Human motivation and interpersonal relationships: Theory, research, and applications*. Cham: Springer, 53–73.

De Cicco, R., Silva, S. C., & Alparone, F. R. (2020). "Millennials' attitude toward Chatbots: an experimental study in a social relationship perspective". *International Journal of Retail and Distribution Management*, 48, 11, 1213–1233.

Diederich, S., Brendel, A. B., & Kolbe, L. M. (2020). "Designing anthropomorphic enterprise conversational agents". *Business and Information Systems Engineering*, 62, 193–209.

Dinh, C. M., & Park, S. S. (2022), "How to increase consumer intention to use Chatbots? An empirical analysis of hedonic and utilitarian motivations on social presence and the moderating effects of fear across generations", *Electronic Commerce Research*, 1–41.

Dubey, R., Gunasekaran, A., Childe, S. J., Bryde, D. J., Giannakis, M., Foropon, C., Roubaud, D., & Benjamin., H. T. (2020). "Big data analytics and artificial intelligence pathway to operational performance under the effects of entrepreneurial orientation and environmental dynamism: A study of manufacturing organizations". *International Journal of Production Economics*, 226.

Feine, J., Gnewuch, U., Morana, S., & Maedche, A. (2019). "A taxonomy of social cues for conversational agents". *International Journal of Human-Computer Studies*, 132, 138–161.

Fitzpatrick, K. K., Darcy, A., & Vierhile, M. (2017). "Delivering cognitive behavior therapy to young adults with symptoms of depression and anxiety using a fully automated conversational agent (Woebot): A randomized controlled trial". *JMIR Mental Health*, 4, 2, 7785.

Fernandes, T., & Oliveira, E. (2021). "Understanding consumers' acceptance of automated technologies in service encounters: Drivers of digital voice assistants adoption". *Journal of Business Research*, 122, 180–191.

Febrianto, G., Hidayatullah, S., & Ardianto, Y. T. (2018). "The Effect of Intention to Usage to Actual Usage E-Purchasing Application". *International Journal Of Scientific and Engineering Research*, 9, 12, 363–370.

Gartner. (2019). "6 technologies on the Gartner hype cycle for digital marketing and advertising". https://www.gartner.com/en/marketing/insights/articles/6-technologies-on-gartner-hype-cycle-fordigital-marketingand-advertising-2019.

Gefen, D., & Straub, D. W. (2004). "Consumer trust in B2C eCommerce and the importance of social presence: experiments in e-Products and e-Services". *Omega*, 32, 6, 407–424.

Gnewuch, U., Morana, S., & Maedche, A. (2017). "Towards designing cooperative and social agents for customer service". Proceedings of the 38th International Conference on Information Systems (ICIS). Seoul.

Gnewuch, U., Morana, S., Adam, M. T. P., & Maedche, A. (2022). "Opposing Effects of Response Time in Human–Chatbot Interaction". *Business and Information Systems Engineering*.

Go, E., & Sundar, S. S. (2019). "Humanising chatbots: The effects of visual, identity and conversational cues on humanness perceptions". *Computers in Human Behavior*, 97, 304–316.

Gonzalez, S. M., Gidumal, G. B., & Tano, D. G. (2019). "Predicting the intentions to use chatbots for travel and tourism". *Current Issues in Tourism*, 24, 2, 192–210.

Han, M. C., & Kim, Y. (2020). "Chatbot commerce: Hype ou Revolution". *Pan Pacific Journal of Business Research*, 11, 2, 30–45.

Han, M. C. (2021). "The impact of anthropomorphism on consumers' purchase decision in chatbot commerce". *Journal of Internet Commerce*, 20, 1, 46–65.

Hassanein, K., & Head, M. (2007). "Manipulating perceived social presence through the web interface and its impact on attitude towards online shopping". *International Journal of Human-Computer Studies*, 65,689–708.

Huang, M. H., & Rust, R. T. (2021). "A strategic framework for artificial intelligence in marketing". *Journal of the Academy of Marketing Science*, 49, 1, 30–50.

Kang, L., Wang, X., Hoo Tan, C., & etZhao, L. (2015). "Understanding the antecedents and consequences of live chat use in electronic markets". *Journal of Organizational Computing and Electronic Commerce*, 25, 2, 117–139.

Kilteni, K., Groten, R., etSlater, M. (2012). "The sense of embodiment in virtual reality, Presence teleoperators, and virtual environments", 21, 4, 374–385.

Kim, K. J. (2016). "Interacting socially with the Internet of Things (IoT): effects of source attribution and specialization in human-IoT interaction". *Journal of Computer-Mediated Communication*, 21, 6, 420–435.

Kramer, N. C., Bente, G., Eschenburg, F., & Troitzsch, H. (2009). "Embodied conversational agents". *Social Psychology*, 40, 1, 26–36.

Kumar, V., Rajan, B., Venkatesan, R., & Lecinski, J. (2019). "Understanding the role of artificial intelligence in personalized engagement marketing". *California Management Review*, 61, 4, 135–155.

Kuo, P.-H., et al. (2021). "Multi-sensor context-aware based chatbot model: An application of humanoid companion robot". *Sensors*, 21, 15, 5132.

Lee, S. M., & Lee, D. (2020). "Untact: a new customer service strategy in the digital age". *Service Business*, 14, 1–22.

Leszkiewicz, A., Hormann, T., & Krafft, M. (2021). "Smart business and the social value of AI". *Smart Business and Better Management.*

Lee, K. M., & Nass, C. (2004). "The multiple source effect and synthesized speech: doubly-disembodied language as a conceptual framework". *Human Communication Research*, 30, 2, 182–207.

Lee, Y.-C., Yamashita, N., & Huang, Y. (2020). "Designing a chatbot as a mediator for promoting deep self-disclosure to a real mental health professional". *Proceedings of the ACM on Human-Computer Interaction*, 4, 1–27.

Li, M., & Mao, J. (2015). "Hedonic or utilitarian? Exploring the impact of communication style alignment on user's perception of virtual health advisory services". *International Journal of Information Management*, 35, 2, 229–243.

Ling, E. C., Tussyadiah, I., Tuomi, A., Stienmetz, J., & Ioannou, A. (2021). "Factors influencing users' adoption and use of conversational agents: a systematic review". *Psychology and Marketing*.

Lu, J. B., Fan, W., & Zhou, M. (2016). "Social presence, trust, and social commerce purchase intention: An empirical research," *Computers in Human Behavior*, 56, 225–237.

Matteson, M. L., Salamon.J., & Brewster, L. (2011). "A systematic review of research on live chat service". *Reference and User Services Quarterly*, 51, 2, 172–189.

Messina, C. (2015). "Conversational commerce". Retrieved from https://medium.com/chris-messina/conversational-commerce-92e0bccfc3f.

Micu, A., Capatina, A., & Eliza Micu, A. (2018). "Exploring artificial intelligence techniques' applicability in social media marketing". *Journal of Emerging Trends in Marketing and Management*, 156–165.

Mimoun, M. S. B., & Poncin, I. (2015). "A valued agent: How ECAs affect website customers' satisfaction and behaviors". *Journal of Retailing and Consumer Services*, 26, 70–82.

Misischia, C. V., Poecze, F., & Strauss, C. (2022). "Chatbots in customer service: Their relevance and impact on service quality, The 13th International Conference on Ambient Systems". *Network and Technologies*, 421–428.

Mittal, U., & Sharma, M. (2021). "Artificial intelligence and its application in different areas of Indian economy". *International Journal of Advanced Research in Science, Communication and Technology*, 160–163.

Moon, J. H., Kim, E., Choi, S. M., & Sung, Y. (2013). "Keep the social in social media: The role of social interaction in avatar-based virtual shopping". *Journal of Interactive Advertising*, 13, 1, 14–26.

Moriuchi, E. (2019). "Okay, Google!: "An empirical study on voice assistants on consumer engagement and loyalty". *Psychology and Marketing*, 36, 2, 1–13.

Nilsson, N. J. (2005). "Human-level artificial intelligence? Be serious!". *AI Magazine*, 26, 4, 68.

Pangkey, F. M., Furkan, L. M., Herman, L. E., & Agusdin, A. (2020)."Exploring the impact of Artificial intelligence and digital marketing on intention to use online transportation: a lesson learned from Indonesian millenials". *Research square*, 1–9.

Pansari, A., & Kumar, V. (2017), "Customer engagement: the construct, antecedents and consequences". *Journal of the Academy of Marketing Science*, 45, 3, 294–311.

Pillai, R., & Sivathanu, B. (2020). "Adoption of artificial intelligence (AI) for talent acquisition in IT/ITeS organizations". *Benchmarking: An International Journal*, 27, 9, 2599–2629.

Pitardi, V., & Marriott, H. R. (2021). "Alexa, she's not human but Unveiling the drivers of consumers' trust in voice-based artificial intelligence". *Psychology and Marketing*, 38, 4, 626–642.

Qiu, L., & Benbasat, I. (2009). "Evaluating anthropomorphic product recommendation agents: a social relationship perspective to designing information systems". *Journal of Management Information System*, 25, 145–182.

Reavie, V. (2018). "Do you know the difference between data analytics and AI machine learning? Forbes". Retrieved from https://www.forbes.com/sites/forbesagencycouncil/2018/08/01/do-you-knowthe-diference-between-data-analytics-and-ai-machine-learning/#5c50edac5878.

Rigopoulos, G., & Askounis, D.(2007). "A TAM framework to evaluate User's perception toward online electronic payments". *Journal of Internet Banking and Commerce*, 12.

Russell, S., & Norvig, P. (2010). *Intelligence artificielle: une approche moderne*. 3[éme] édition, Prentice-Hall, Upper Saddle River.

Ryan, R. M., & Deci, E. L. (2017). *Self-determination theory: Basic psychological needs in motivation, development, and wellness*. Guilford: Guilford Publications.

Sambasivan, M., Wemyss, G. P., & Rose, R. C. (2010). "User acceptance of a G2B system: a case of the electronic procurement system in Malaysia". *Internet Research*, 20, 2, 169–187.

Santiago, M.-G. et al. (2019). "Predicting the intentions to use chatbots for travel and tourism". *Current Issues in Tourism*, 24, 2, 192–210.

Sheehan, B., Jin, H. S., & Gottlieb, U. (2020). "Customer service chatbots: Anthropomorphism and adoption". *Journal of Business Research*, 115, 14–24.

Shopify. (2016). "Conversational Commerce Definition - What is Conversational Commerce". Retrieved from https://www.shopify.com/encyclopedia/conversationalcommerce

Sidlauskiene, J., Joye,Y., & tAuruskeviciene, V. (2023). "AI-based chatbots in conversational commerce and their effects on product and price perceptions". *Electronic Markets*, 2–21.

Smutny, P., & Schreiberova, P. (2020). "Chatbots for learning: A review of educational Chatbots for Facebook Messenger". *Computers and Education*, 151, 103862.

Steuer, J. S. (1992). "Defining virtual reality: Dimensions determining telepresence". *Journal of Communication*, Fall 1992,42, 4, 21–73.

Sterne, J. (2017). *Artificial intelligence for marketing: Practical applications*. Wiley.

Sumarjan, N., Mazlan, N., Saiful Azmi, N. S., Kamaruddin, M. A. etSalleh, A. (2023). "The usage intention of chatbot technology in hospitality and tourism industry: Customers' perspective". *Journal of Tourism Hospitality and Culinary*, 15, 1, 206–224.

Sundar, S. S., Kalyanaraman, S., & Brown, J. (2003). "Explicating web site interactivity: Impression formation effects in political campaign sites". *Communication Research*, 30, 1, 30–59.

Sundar, S. S., Bellur, S., Oh, J., Jia, H., & Kim, H.-S. (2014). "Theoretical importance of contingency in human-computer interaction". *Communication Research*, 43, 595–625.

Thilagavathy, N., & Kumar, K. (2021). "Artificial intelligence on digital marketing- an overview". *Nat. Volatiles & Essent. Oils*, 8, 5, 9895–9908.

Tran, A. D., Pallant, J., & Johnson, L. W. (2021). "Exploring the impact of chatbots on consumer sentiment and expectations in retail". *Journal of Retailing and Consumer Services*, 63, 2, 102718.

McTear, M., Callejas, Z., & Griol, D. (2016). "The conversational interface: Talking to smart devices". In *The Conversational Interface* (283–308). Springer.

Van Manen, T. (2016). "Bot or not: dit is waarom Facebook inzet op chatbots lMarketingfacts". [Web log post]. Retrieved from http://www.marketingfacts.nl/berichten/chatbots-facebook-inzet-chatbots-messenger

Van Eeuwen, M. (2017). *Mobile conversational commerce: messenger chatbots as the next interface between businesses and consumers*. University of Twente, 15.

Venkatesh, V., et Davis, F. D. (1996). "A model of the antecedents of perceived ease of use: Development and test". *A Journal of the Decision Science Institute*, 27, 3, 451–481.

Weizenbaum, J. (1966). "ELIZA—a computer program for the study of natural language communication between man and machine". *Communications of the ACM*, 9, 1, 36–45.

Whitley, S. C., Trudel, R., & Kurt, D. (2018). "The influence of purchase motivation on perceived preference uniqueness and assortment size choice". *Journal of Consumer Research*, 45, 4, 710–724.

Yang, Y., & Siau, K. L. (2018). "A qualitative research on marketing and sales in the artificial intelligence age". In: Proceedings of the thirteenth Midwest Association for Information Systems Conference. Saint Louis, Missouri.

Zouinar, M. (2020). "Évolutions de l'Intelligence Artificielle: quels enjeux pour l'activité humaine et la relation Humain-Machine au travail. *Activités*, 17, 1, 1–39.

17 Role of Technology for Pharmaceutical Marketing in the Era of Artificial Intelligence

A Bibliometric Study

Rajesh Tiwari
Graphic Era (Deemed to be University), Dehradun, India

Khem Chand
Lovely Professional University, Phagwara, India

Sachin Ghai, M. P. Singh, Arvind Mohan, and Kapil Ahlawat
Graphic Era (Deemed to be University), Dehradun, India

17.1 INTRODUCTION

The internet has completely altered and transformed how we live, communicate, and conduct business (von Rosen et al., 2017). Online clinics were first established in the United States in 1999, resulting from the use of E-commerce in health. Both over-the-counter and prescription-only medications were sold in this. However, on 1 December 2005, China's Food and Drug Administration released the interim guidelines for Internet for review, and the formal clearance for online drug transaction services began (Orizio et al., 2011). According to Takahashi et al. (2011), 72% of web surfers in the US and 71% of online subscribers in Europe conducted at least one search for health-related information in the previous year. The utilization of smart devices expands these tendencies to an even greater extent, as suggested by Gawron 2015). According to Orizio et al. (2009), clients today not only rely on the internet to get health-related information but also to self-diagnose and buy different health services and goods. Despite the fact that buying from online pharmacies has many benefits, safety concerns have been raised by statistics from the World Health Organization (WHO). When the WHO determined that roughly 50% of the medicines sold on the Internet are from websites that sell counterfeit products, the intricacy and severity of the issue grew. The sale of counterfeit medicines by unregulated online pharmacies poses a serious danger to the public's health and has tragic effects on customers (Javadi et al., 2012). One person in five buys medication from the Internet without a prescription, according to Western European research involving 14,000 individuals. This showed that buying non-prescription drugs from illicit sources cost Western Europe approximately 10.5 million Euros per year (WHO, 2010). In Romania, a poll was also conducted to determine how patients and consumers felt about ordering medications online. According to reports, the majority of people are unaware of the distinctions between medicines bought from traditional shops and those bought online.

DOI: 10.1201/9781003450443-17

17.2 DRIVERS OF ONLINE PHARMACY

Online drugstores are urged to run more effectively in terms of pricing level, price elasticity, and price updating. In these markets, there was a wider range of prices. This was brought on by the disparity in the information and confidence levels among the buyers. Product heterogeneity: the goods being compared were unique, and as a result, they were priced differently was one of the factors that contributed to higher price dispersion. Convenience was the other differentiator because goods were simpler to locate and assess on online markets. The other variables that affected prices were geographic area, store branding, and confidence. By allowing established physical pharmacists to expand their operations online, online pharmacies provided the benefit of industry viability. Community perceptions toward various signals of healthcare have been dramatically altered by the internet and e-commerce. People utilize the internet to learn about specific health conditions, and many also use it to buy prescription drugs (Huisman et al, 2020; Sun et al., 2019).

According to several studies (Ashames et al., 2019, Assi et al., 2016, Shekhar et al., 2019), the primary driving forces behind consumer behavior are perceived privacy, lower costs, ease, self-diagnosis, direct marketing to consumers, and prior feelings. Consumers attempt to be well-informed about the medicine before buying, according to studies that have noted the relevance of elements like product and trust while making transactions (Shekhar et al., 2019). According to a mixed-methods study, the demand for better options, the limitations of the drug supply, the impact of price, and interviewees' belief in their own ability to take care of themselves and their doctors were the key drivers of online drug purchases (Bowman et al., 2020). Since the market for pharmaceuticals is uncontrolled and offers very little in the way of consumer protection, buying them could pose a serious health risk (Fittler et al., 2013).

The healthcare sector has seen substantial changes in response to the COVID-19 pandemic, which have accelerated the digital transformation of healthcare services. (Nicola et al., 2020). As a result, online pharmacies are increasingly taking the role of conventional brick and store pharmacies. However, until customers embrace and fully utilize these new systems, it is impossible to concentrate on the prospects of ICT apps in many service regions. (Awa et al., 2015). Extant studies in this sector are still in their infancy, despite the fact that understanding the factors influencing customers' use of online pharmacies is crucial in this context (Yin et al., 2016).

17.3 LITERATURE REVIEW

Alfahad et al. (2015) explored how people in the Riyadh region of Saudi Arabia perceived and knew about using online pharmacy services. The study found a need to understand about online pharmacy adoption determinants. Alwon et al. (2015) examined characteristics of online pharmacies along with regulation and improve patient safety when purchasing medicines online. It was argued that consumers should be mindful of regulatory logos and make sure the vendor can be reached using the specified information.

Ami-Narh and Williams (2012) research emphasizes that despite the existence of numerous studies on technology adoption, little focus has been placed on the choice to embrace e-health in Africa. Jeko (2014) discussed online pharmacies in Bangladesh. It was said that online pharmacies could help provide medicines at low cost to consumers. In Bangladesh, there was space for online pharmacies to flourish. Quality medicines and good rates were expectations of consumers while buying medicines. Jain et al. (2017) discussed the benefits and drawbacks of internet shops. The benefits of purchasing from online pharmacies have been listed as anonymity or privacy while taking the medication, availability of a variety of drugs to choose from, a source of useful medical information through the company website, lower costs due to low overhead, and the convenience of choosing from a variety of products in case of consumers from remote areas. It also benefited active shoppers by reducing journey time.

Pal et al. (2015) studied Romanian customers to better understand how they made purchases from internet pharmacies. The study found that respondents who bought medications online were typically males, between the ages of 18 and 34, and had either a tenth-class diploma or a university degree. 8.3% of those questioned said they had purchased medications online, and 7.1% said they planned to do so soon. The majority of customers were not conscious of any potential quality differences between prescription drugs bought online and those obtained from traditional pharmacies.

Yin et al. (2016) seeks to investigate customer acceptance of online pharmacies and recognize the various elements that effect the pupose to buy medications online. This study uses five explanatory structures depend on the UTAUT paradigm. In China, consumer survey data (n = 274) were gathered, and the results were compared to the suggested study paradigm. The findings demonstrate that consumers' adoption intentions for purchasing medicines online are importantly affected by perceived risk, social influence, perceived trust and performance expectancy. Performance expectancy is positively influenced by effort expectancy, and perceived risk is significantly influenced negatively by perceived trust. Fittler et al. explained how Hungarian customers use internet pharmacies to make purchases. 1055 outpatients with a mean age of 45 were used in the research.

Athapaththu and Kulathunga (2018) evaluated adoption of online pharmacy in Sri Lanka. It was found that perceived usefulness, perceived ease of use, and material on the website moderate the effect of confidence on customers' preferences for online purchase. Aref and Okasha (2019) examined consumer behavior in a marketplace on the internet. It was found that perceived ease of use, enjoyment, social norms, and perceived danger, had a substantial impact on respondents' decisions to engage in online purchasing. The impact of site language on their decisions, however, was shown to be minor.

Chopdar and Balakrishnan (2020) explored elements that influence consumer satisfaction and likelihood of repeat purchases when shopping on mobile devices using stimulus-organism-response (S-O-R) model. It was found that customers' impulsivity has a negative impact on their intention to make another purchase. Dash and Sahoo (2021) intends to identify the elements that influence Indian patients' propensity to utilize online consultation. This study uses an SEM method to evaluate the hypotheses with 462 individuals.

de Oliveira Santos (2021) conducted an online survey asking Portuguese customers about their awareness and use of this technology. Guthrie et al. (2021) attempted to acquire a better understanding of how customers use internet purchasing to cope with and adjust to periods of environmental restrictions. The study validates the react-cope-adapt approach for explaining constrained customer behavior.

Jairoun et al. (2021) examined commonness of online drug shopping in the United Arab Emirates and to evaluate the factors that influence this behavior. It was found that respondents who were male, single, older, and high school educated were most likely to have bought drugs by internet.

Long et al. (2022) conducted a systematic literature review to gain a better understanding of three key aspects of online pharmacies: the characteristics and attributes of online drugstores that sell medications; the efficacy of prescription drugs obtained through online platforms; and characteristics of customers who engage with online pharmacies. Dave et al. (2022) offered suggestions for internet businesses to improve the viability and financial viability of their business models for Indian markets. Fittler et al. (2022) investigated the propensity and attitudes of European shoppers for prescription drugs online in the Visegrad Group countries (V4) both before and after the pandemic. An electronic cross-sectional research investigation was performed. The rapid global spread of the coronavirus has resulted in major changes in people's pharmaceutical purchasing behavior, potentially raising public health concerns about internet sourcing. Alwhaibi et al. (2021) examined the volume of online medicine purchases in Saudi Arabia, as well as the different types of products purchased, information sources used, sources of satisfaction, factors motivating consumers, and their level of awareness and willingness to report adverse drug reactions (ADRs) when they occur. The study highlighted Saudi community's urgent need to raise safety knowledge regarding ordering prescription drugs online.

Baid and Ghosh (2021) examined affecting customers' decisions about purchasing prescription drugs and other medical goods online, using primary data cities in India. It was found that individuals suffering from chronic ailments are more likely to use online pharmacy. Bartol et al. (2023) investigated the relationships between online purchasing self-efficacy, personality traits, demographic variables, privacy concerns, and e-commerce involvement. The study emphasizes the significance of online purchasing self-efficacy in investigating the elements that lead to and result from privacy issues in the setting of e-commerce.

17.4 METHOD

The bibliometric analysis was done using Scopus database. The keywords used were "technology" OR "artificial intelligence" AND "pharmaceuticals marketing" OR "online pharmacy" OR "e-pharmacy." One hundred forty-six documents were found in the Scopus database. The date of search was 22 August 2023. First exclusion criteria was language. Only documents in English were included for the study. This led to the exclusion of nine documents. The documents excluded were in Spanish (3), German (2), Portuguese (1), Italian (1), Hungarian (1), and Hebrew (1). After the first stage of exclusion, 138 documents were included. Second stage exclusion was done on type of document. Editorial (4) and erratum (1) were excluded. Article (88), Conference paper (16), review (15), book chapter (9), note (4), and conference review (1) was included. After second stage exclusion, 133 documents were obtained. The third stage of exclusion was by evaluating the documents for relevance with the theme of our research. Sixty-five documents were not relevant with the objective of the chapter. After excluding 65 documents, 68 documents were finally used for the analysis.

17.5 RESULTS

The bibliometric analysis was done using VOS viewer. The yearly publication trend was examined. Bibliometric analysis was done to explore citation, co-citation, co-authorship, co-occurrence, and bibliographic coupling. The year wise trend of publications is shown in Figure 17.1.

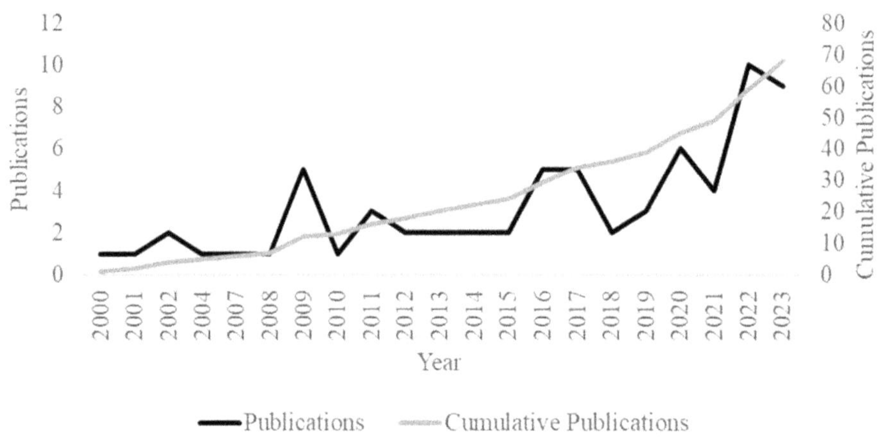

FIGURE 17.1 Year wise trend of publications.

Forty-three percent of the publications have come in the time period between from 2020 onwards. The recent surge in research publications after the onset of COVID indicates the significance of online pharmacies for supply chain and access to pharmaceutical products irrespective of the boundaries of distance or region.

Citation analysis for countries was done with a threshold of one document and nine citations. Out of 27 countries, 12 met the criteria. Figure 17.2 depicts the density map of prominent countries by number of publications. The USA leads with 20 documents and 645 citations. India is second in terms of publications with 18 documents and 114 citations. Table 17.1 shows the top 5 cited countries. Australia is the second most cited country, followed by India (114), United Kingdom (108), and Brazil (107).

Citation analysis for organizations was done with a threshold of 20 documents. Out of 153 organizations, only 36 met the criteria. Table 17.2 presents the prominent cited organizations. Global Health Policy Institute, USA is the leading organization with four documents and 301 citations. The Department of Anesthesiology is ranked second with two documents and 297 citations. The Department of Medicine, University of California, had 204 citations from one

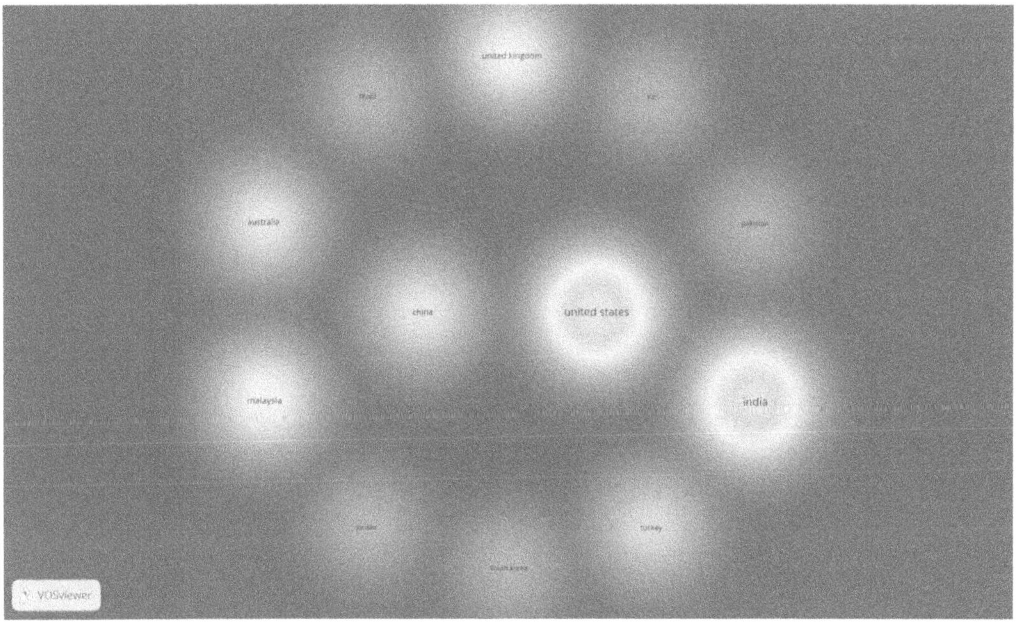

FIGURE 17.2 Density map of publications by country.

TABLE 17.1
Top Cited Countries

S. No.	Country	Documents	Citations	Citation per Document
1	United States	20	645	32
2	Australia	4	167	42
3	India	18	114	6
4	United Kingdom	5	108	22
5	Brazil	1	107	107

TABLE 17.2
Prominent Cited Organizations

S.No.	Organization	Documents	Citations
1	"Global Health Policy institute, United States"	4	301
2	"Department of Anesthesiology, University of California", United States	2	297
3	"Department of Medicine, University of California", United States	1	204
4	"Laboratory of Food, Drugs and Cosmetics (ltmac), University of Brasília (UNB)", Brazil	1	107
5	"Institute of Health Law studies, California Western School of Law", United States	1	93
	Joint Doctoral Program in Global Health, "San Diego State University-University of California", United States	1	93

document. University of Brasilia is ranked fourth with 107 citations. California Western School of Law and the Joint Doctoral Program in Global Health of San Diego State University-University of California, United States are the fifth most cited organizations with 93 citations.

Citation analysis for the document was done with a threshold of 30 citations. Out of 68 documents, 12 documents met the threshold. The top cited documents are listed in Table 17.3. The most cited paper was "A review of existing and emerging digital technologies to combat the global trade in fake medicines" by Mackey and Nayyar (2017), with 204 citations.

TABLE 17.3
Top Cited Documents

S. No.	Document		Citations
1	Mackey and Nayyar (2017)	"A review of existing and emerging digital technologies to combat the global trade in fake medicines"	204
2	Araujo et al. (2019)	"The Digital Pharmacies Era: How 3D Printing Technology Using Fused Deposition Modeling Can Become a Reality"	107
3	Liang and Mackey (2011)	"Prevalence and Global Health Implications of Social Media in Direct-to-Consumer Drug Advertising"	93
4	Moyle et al. (2019)	"Drugsforsale: An exploration of the use of social media and encrypted messaging apps to supply and access drugs"	81
5	Mackey and Nayyar (2016)	"Digital danger: a review of the global public health, patient safety and cybersecurity threats posed by illicit online pharmacies"	78
6	Mandal (2017)	"The influence of organizational culture on healthcare supply chain resilience: moderating role of technology orientation"	69
7	Katsuki et al. (2015)	"Establishing a link between prescription drug abuse and illicit online pharmacies: Analysis of twitter data"	61
8	Mackey et al. (2018)	"Solution to detect, classify, and report illicit online marketing and sales of controlled substances via twitter: Using machine learning and web forensics to combat digital opioid access"	50
9	Bessell et al. (2002)	"Quality of global e-pharmacies: Can we safeguard consumers?"	48
10	Nielsen & Barratt (2009)	"Prescription drug misuse: Is technology friend or foe?"	35

TABLE 17.4
Most Cited Authors

S.No.	Author	Documents	Citations
1	"Mackey T.K.; Nayyar G."	2	282
2	"Araujo M.R.P.; Sa-Barreto L.L.; Gratieri T.; Gelfuso G.M.; Cunha-Filho M."	1	107
3	"Liang B.A.; Mackey T.K."	1	93
4	"Moyle L.; Childs A.; Coomber R.; Barratt M.J."	1	81
5	"Mandal S."	1	69
6	"Katsuki T.; Mackey T.K.; Cuomo R."	1	61
7	"Mackey T.; Kalyanam J.; Klugman J.; Kuzmenko E.; Gupta R."	1	50
8	"Bessell T.L..; Silagy C. A.; Anderson J.N.; Hiller J.E.; Sansom L. N."	1	48
9	"Mackey T. K.; Liang B.A."	2	48
10	"Nielsen S.; Barratt M.J."	1	35

Citation analysis for authors was done with a threshold of 15 citations. Out of 65 authors, 18 met the threshold. Table 17.4 provides most cited authors. Mackey and Nayyar are the most cited authors with a citation of 282, followed by Araujo et al. with 107 citations.

Citation analysis for sources was done with a threshold of 10 citations. Out of 62 sources, 19 met the criteria. The journal *Expert Opinion on Drug Safety* and the *Journal of Medical Internet Research* are the leading journals with 204 citations each, followed by *Pharmaceutics* with 107 citations. (Table 17.5)

Co-Citation analysis for authors was done with a threshold of 10 citations. Out of 4932 authors, 21 met the criteria. Out of 21 authors, only 17 were connected. (Figure 17.3)

Co-authorship analysis for countries was done with a threshold of 10 citation. Out of 27 countries, 10 countries met the criteria. Out of 10 countries, seven were connected. (Figure 17.4)

CO occurrence analysis was done with a threshold of five occurrences. Out of 728 keywords, 40 met the criteria. Figure 17.5 depicts the map of co-occurrences.

The bibliographic coupling was attempted. Out of 68 documents, only 14 documents were connected. (Figure 17.6)

TABLE 17.5
Top Cited Journals

S. No.	Source	Documents	Citations
1	*Expert Opinion on Drug Safety*	1	204
2	*Journal of Medical Internet Research*	3	204
3	*Pharmaceutics*	1	107
4	*International Journal of Drug Policy*	1	81
5	*British Medical Bulletin*	1	78
6	*Journal of Business and Industrial Marketing*	1	69
7	*European Journal of Clinical Pharmacology*	1	48
8	*Drug and Alcohol Review*	1	35
9	*Globalization and Health*	1	34
10	*Cambridge Quarterly of Healthcare Ethics*	1	31

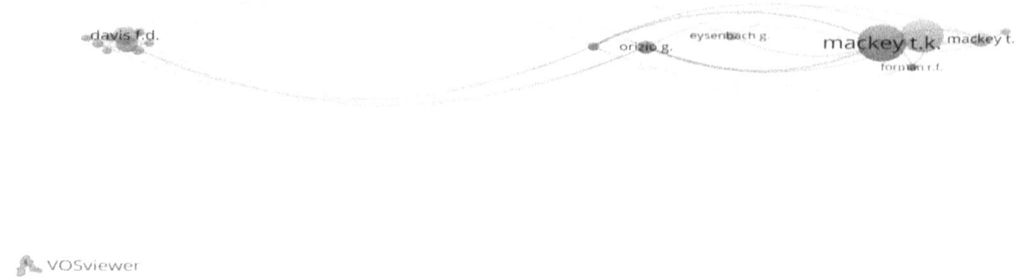

FIGURE 17.3 Co-citation map of authors.

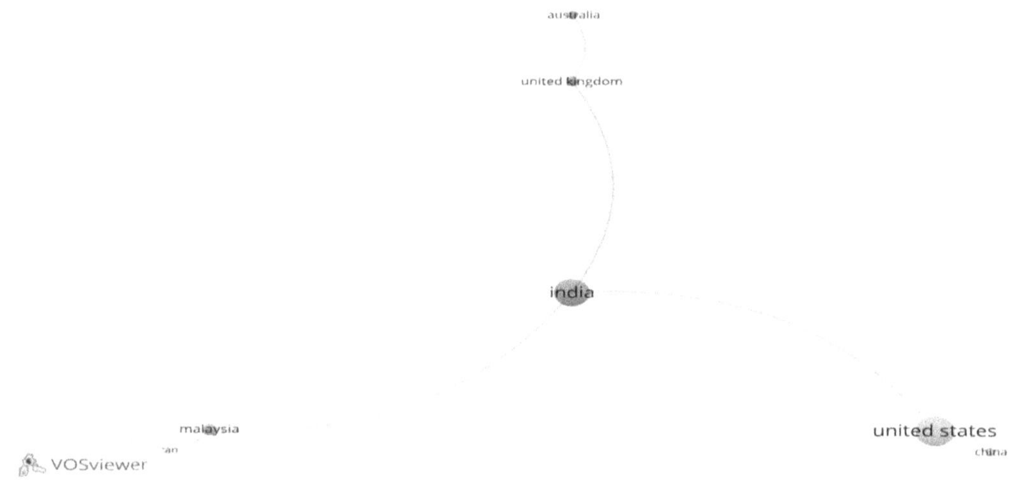

FIGURE 17.4 Co-authorship map of the country.

Two clusters emerged out of bibliographic coupling. The theme of the clusters were consumer preferences and supply side dynamics.

17.5.1 Cluster I: Consumer Preferences

The first cluster focused on the research theme of consumer preferences. Cluster I comprised of seven items. It was represented by red color. The most prominent paper was of Srivastava & Raina with 10 citations and a link strength of eight. The adoption and usage of e-pharmacy was explored in India. It was observed that qualification and gender have no association for usage and adoption of online pharmacies. It was observed that "hedonic motivation," "social influence," "performance expectancy," and "effort expectancy" have a positive association with adoption and usage of online pharmacy, after considering extended Unified theory, TAM model and self-determination theory. Yin et al. (2016) was the second most prominent paper with seven citations and a link strength of four. The authors examined perception of consumers for online pharmacy in China. It was found that online pharmacy adoption is positively influenced by trust, risk, "social influence", and "performance expectancy". Sampat and Sabat (2022) with a link strength of 23 examined adoption of online pharmacies in India. Using extension of TAM Model it was found that "perceived usefulness" and trust influence adoption of online pharmacy.

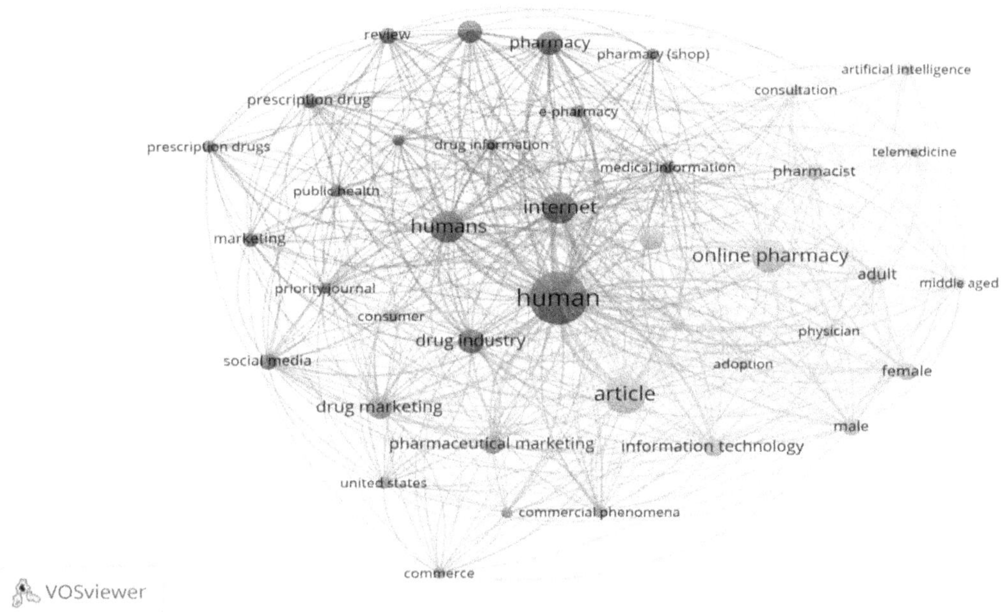

FIGURE 17.5 Map of co-occurrence of keywords.

FIGURE 17.6 Map of bibliographic coupling.

17.5.2 Cluster II: Supply Side Dynamics

The second cluster focused on the research theme of supply side dynamics. Cluster II also included seven items. It was represented by the color green. The most prominent paper was Mandal (2017) with 69 citations and a link strength of one. The primary data was collected from service providers. The paper examined the moderating role of "technology orientation" on culture of organization influence on supply chain of healthcare. It was found that hierarchical culture had a negative influence on resilience of healthcare supply chain. It was further found that "technology orientation" enhances the rational and development culture for resilience of healthcare supply chain. The second most prominent paper was Alkhateeb and Doucette (2009) with 18 citation and link strength of 13. The paper examined the adoption of e-detailing on physicians using primary data. It was found that influence of peers and access restriction influences adoption of e-detailing. Alkhateeb, Khanfar and Loudon (2009) examined Rogers "diffusion of innovation model" to understand the adoption of e-detailing of physicians. A revised model was proposed. Kwak and

Chang (2016) examined pharma marketing efforts to physicians using diffusion model and TAM model. It was found that "perceived ease of use," individual and organizational innovativeness significantly influences technology adoption in pharma marketing.

17.6 CONCLUSION

The chapter examined the literature on adoption of online pharmacy. The bibliometric analysis was done on 68 papers extracted from Scopus database. The chapter examined the literature on adoption of online pharmacy. The bibliometric analysis was done on 68 papers extracted from Scopus database. There is significant enhancement of research interest in online pharmacies after the onset of Covid pandemic. Forty three percent of publications have come in the period after 2019. The USA and Australia are the most cited countries, and USA and India are the two prominent countries with the largest publications. The Global Health Policy Institute and the University of California are the most prominent cited organizations. The most cited paper was "A review of existing and emerging digital technologies to combat the global trade in fake medicines," with a citation of 204. Mackey and Nayyar are the most cited authors with 282 citations. The most cited journals are *Expert Opinion on Drug Safety* and *Journal of Medical Internet Research* with 204 citations each. Humans, online pharmacy, internet, and drug marketing were the most frequently occurring keywords. Two research themes emerged out of bibliographic coupling. Current research is focussed around two research themes: consumer preferences and supply chain dynamics were two research. The bibliometric analysis reveals that there is a lack of collaboration between organizations and countries in the research on online pharmacies. Technology can be leveraged to enhance access to quality medicines in remote areas and reducing the barriers of time and distance. A sustainable supply chain needs integration of technology. Equally important is to have a regulatory mechanism for monitoring online pharmacies to check fake medicine sales and misuse of the platforms for the illicit drug trade. A COVID like pandemic can strike again. Policy makers and pharmaceutical firms should develop a robust online pharmacy framework to develop the ability to deliver quality products across the world with speed and efficiency. Quality of life can be significantly improved by the adoption of online pharmacies in developing economies.

REFERENCES

Alfahad, N. F., Albelali, M. T., Khurshid, F., Al-Arifi, M. N., Al-Dhawailie, A. A., & Alsultam, M. (2015). Perception and knowledge to online pharmacy services among consumers in Riyadh, Saudi Arabia: a pilot survey. *Latin American Journal of Pharmacy*, 34(6), 1113–1118.

Alkhateeb, F. M., & Doucette, W. R. (2009). Influences on physicians' adoption of electronic detailing (e-detailing). *Informatics for Health and Social Care*, 34(1), 39–52.

Alwhaibi, M., Asser, W. M., Al Aloola, N. A., Alsalem, N., Almomen, A., & Alhawassi, T. M. (2021). Evaluating the frequency, consumers' motivation and perception of online medicinal, herbal, and health products purchase safety in Saudi Arabia. *Saudi Pharmaceutical Journal*, 29(2), 166–172.

Alwon, B. M., Solomon, G., Hussain, F., & Wright, D. J. (2015). A detailed analysis of online pharmacy characteristics to inform safe usage by patients. *International Journal of Clinical Pharmacy*, 37, 148–158.

Ami-Narh, J. T., & Williams, P. A. (2012). A revised UTAUT model to investigate E-health acceptance of health professionals in Africa. *Journal of Emerging Trends in Computing and Information Sciences*, 3(10), 1383–1391.

Araújo, M. R., Sa-Barreto, L. L., Gratieri, T., Gelfuso, G. M., & Cunha-Filho, M. (2019). The digital pharmacies era: How 3D printing technology using fused deposition modeling can become a reality. *Pharmaceutics*, 11(3), 128.

Aref, M. M., & Okasha, A. E. (2019). Evaluating the online shopping behavior among Egyptian college-educated community. *Review of Economics and Political Science*, 5(1), 21–37.

Ashames, A., Bhandare, R., AlAbdin, S. Z., Alhalabi, T., & Jassem, F. (2019). Public perception toward e-commerce of medicines and comparative pharmaceutical quality assessment study of two different products of furosemide tablets from community and illicit online pharmacies. *Journal of Pharmacy & Bioallied Sciences*, 11(3), 284.

Assi, S., Thomas, J., Haffar, M., & Osselton, D. (2016). Exploring consumer and patient knowledge, behavior, and attitude toward medicinal and lifestyle products purchased from the internet: a web-based survey. *JMIR Public Health and Surveillance*, 2(2), e5390.

Athapaththu, J. C., & Kulathunga, K. M. S. D. (2018). Factors affecting online purchase intention: A study of Sri Lankan online customers.

Awa, H. O., Ojiabo, O. U., & Emecheta, B. C. (2015). Integrating TAM, TPB and TOE frameworks and expanding their characteristic constructs for e-commerce adoption by SMEs. *Journal of Science and Technology Policy Management*, 6(1), 76–94. 10.1108/JSTPM-04-2014-0012

Baid, A. N., & Ghosh, A. (2021). Factors affecting the shift of consumers towards e-pharmacies. *UGC Care Journal*, 44(1), 39–45.

Bartol, J., Vehovar, V., Bosnjak, M., & Petrovčič, A. (2023). Privacy concerns and self-efficacy in e-commerce: Testing an extended APCO model in a prototypical EU country. *Electronic Commerce Research and Applications*, 101289.

Bessell, T. L., Silagy, C. A., Anderson, J. N., Hiller, J. E., & Sansom, L. N. (2002). Quality of global e-pharmacies: can we safeguard consumers?. *European Journal of Clinical Pharmacology*, 58, 567–572.

Bowman, C., Family, H., Agius-Muscat, H., Cordina, M., & Sutton, J. (2020). Consumer internet purchasing of medicines using a population sample: A mixed methodology approach. *Research in Social and Administrative Pharmacy*, 16(6), 819–827.

Chopdar, P. K., & Balakrishnan, J. (2020). Consumers response towards mobile commerce applications: SOR approach. *International Journal of Information Management*, 53, 102106.

Dash, A., & Sahoo, A. K. (2021). Moderating effect of gender on adoption of digital health consultation: a patient perspective study. *International Journal of Pharmaceutical and Healthcare Marketing*, 15(4), 598–616.

Dave, T. N., Dave, A. R., Parwani, A. H., Joshi, A. B., & Patel, R. (2022). Consumer Perception about E-Pharmacies in Indian Retail Pharmaceutical Sector.

de Oliveira Santos, E. L. (2021). Exploring the factors that influence the adoption of online pharmacy in Portugal: a study on consumer´s acceptance and pharmacist´s perception.

Fittler, A., Bősze, G., & Botz, L. (2013). Evaluating aspects of online medication safety in long-term follow-up of 136 Internet pharmacies: illegal rogue online pharmacies flourish and are long-lived. *Journal of Medical Internet Research*, 15(9), e2606.

Fittler, A., Ambrus, T., Serefko, A., Smejkalová, L., Kijewska, A., Szopa, A., & Káplár, M. (2022). Attitudes and behaviors regarding online pharmacies in the aftermath of COVID-19 pandemic: At the tipping point towards the new normal. *Frontiers in Pharmacology*, 13, 1070473.

Gawron, L. M., & Turok, D. K. (2015). Pills on the World Wide Web: reducing barriers through technology. *American Journal of Obstetrics and Gynecology*, 213(4), 500–e1.

Guthrie, C., Fosso-Wamba, S., & Arnaud, J. B. (2021). Online consumer resilience during a pandemic: An exploratory study of e-commerce behavior before, during and after a COVID-19 lockdown. *Journal of Retailing and Consumer Services*, 61, 102570.

Huisman, M., Joye, S., & Biltereyst, D. (2020). Searching for health: Doctor Google and the shifting dynamics of the middle-aged and older adult patient–physician relationship and interaction. *Journal of Aging and Health*, 32(9), 998–1007.

Jain, V. H., Tadv, S. A., & Pawar, S. P. (2017). A review on the pros and cons of online pharmacies. *Journal of Applied Pharmaceutical Research*, 5(1), 20–26.

Jairoun, A. A., Al-Hemyari, S. S., Abdulla, N. M., El-Dahiyat, F., Jairoun, M., & Al-Tamimi, S. K. (2021). Online medication purchasing during the Covid-19 pandemic: potential risks to patient safety and the urgent need to develop more rigorous controls for purchasing online medications, a pilot study from the United Arab Emirates. *Journal of Pharmaceutical Policy and Practice*, 14.

Javadi, M. H. M., Dolatabadi, H. R., Nourbakhsh, M., Poursaeedi, A., & Asadollahi, A. R. (2012). An analysis of factors affecting on online shopping behavior of consumers. *International Journal of Marketing Studies*, 4(5), 81.

Jeko, N. A. (2014). Prospects of online medicine business in Bangladesh. *International Journal of Scientific & Technology Research*, 3(11), 236–240.

Katsuki, T., Mackey, T. K., & Cuomo, R. (2015). Establishing a link between prescription drug abuse and illicit online pharmacies: Analysis of twitter data. *Journal of Medical Internet Research*, 17(12), e280.
Kwak, E. S., & Chang, H. (2016). Medical Representatives' intention to use information technology in pharmaceutical marketing. *Healthcare Informatics Research*, 22(4), 342–350.
Liang, B. A., & Mackey, T. K. (2011). Prevalence and global health implications of social media in direct-to-consumer drug advertising. *Journal of Medical Internet Research*, 13(3), e1775.
Long, C. S., Kumaran, H., Goh, K. W., Bakrin, F. S., Ming, L. C., Rehman, I. U., ... & Tan, C. S. (2022). Online pharmacies selling prescription drugs: systematic review. *Pharmacy*, 10(2), 42.
Mackey, T., Kalyanam, J., Klugman, J., Kuzmenko, E., & Gupta, R. (2018). Solution to detect, classify, and report illicit online marketing and sales of controlled substances via Twitter: using machine learning and web forensics to combat digital opioid access. *Journal of Medical Internet Research*, 20(4), e10029.
Mackey, T. K., & Nayyar, G. (2016). Digital danger: a review of the global public health, patient safety and cybersecurity threats posed by illicit online pharmacies. *British Medical Bulletin*, 118(1), 110–126.
Mackey, T. K., & Nayyar, G. (2017). A review of existing and emerging digital technologies to combat the global trade in fake medicines. *Expert Opinion on Drug Safety*, 16(5), 587–602.
Mandal, S. (2017). The influence of organizational culture on healthcare supply chain resilience: moderating role of technology orientation. *Journal of Business & Industrial Marketing*, 32(8), 1021–1037.
Moyle, L., Childs, A., Coomber, R., & Barratt, M. J. (2019). Drugsforsale: An exploration of the use of social media and encrypted messaging apps to supply and access drugs. *International Journal of Drug Policy*, 63, 101–110.
Nicola, M., Alsafi, Z., Sohrabi, C., Kerwan, A., Al-Jabir, A., Iosifidis, C., ... & Agha, R. (2020). The socio-economic implications of the coronavirus pandemic (COVID-19): A review. *International Journal of Surgery*, 78, 185–193.
Nielsen, S., & Barratt, M. J. (2009). Prescription drug misuse: is technology friend or foe?. *Drug and Alcohol Review*, 28(1), 81–86.
Orizio, G., Schulz, P., Domenighini, S., Caimi, L., Rosati, C., Rubinelli, S., & Gelatti, U. (2009). Cyberdrugs: a cross-sectional study of online pharmacies characteristics. *The European Journal of Public Health*, 19(4), 375–377.
Orizio, G., Merla, A., Schulz, P. J., & Gelatti, U. (2011). Quality of online pharmacies and websites selling prescription drugs: a systematic review. *Journal of Medical Internet Research*, 13(3), e1795.
Pal, S., Laszlo, K., Andras, F., Gabriel, H., Hajnal, F., Adriana, C. I. U. R. B. A., ... & Lajos, B. (2015). Attitude of patients and customers regarding purchasing drugs online. *Farmacia*, 63(1), 93–98.
Sampat, B., & Sabat, K. C. (2022). Adoption of online pharmacies in India: an empirical study. *International Journal of Business Innovation and Research*, 29(4), 449–478.
Shekhar, S. K., Jose, T. P., & Rehin, K. R. (2019). Consumer buying behaviour and attitude towards pharmaceuticals. *International Journal of Pharmaceutical Sciences and Research*, 10(4).
Sun, Y., Zhang, Y., Gwizdka, J., & Trace, C. B. (2019). Consumer evaluation of the quality of online health information: systematic literature review of relevant criteria and indicators. *Journal of Medical Internet Research*, 21(5), e12522.
Takahashi, Y., Ohura, T., Ishizaki, T., Okamoto, S., Miki, K., Naito, M., ... & Nakayama, T. (2011). Internet use for health-related information via personal computers and cell phones in Japan: a cross-sectional population-based survey. *Journal of Medical Internet Research*, 13(4), e1796.
Von Rosen, A. J., von Rosen, F. T., Tinnemann, P., & Müller-Riemenschneider, F. (2017). Sexual health and the internet: cross-sectional study of online preferences among adolescents. *Journal of Medical Internet Research*, 19(11), e379.
World Health Organization. (2010). Growing threat from counterfeit medicines. *Bull World Health Organ*, 88(4), 247–248.
Yin, M., Li, Q., & Qiao, Z. (2016, August). A study on consumer acceptance of online pharmacies in China. In Proceedings of the 18th Annual International Conference on Electronic Commerce: e-Commerce in Smart connected World (pp. 1–8).

18 Market Segmentation

Machine Learning in Marketing with Clustering Model

Pedro Pablo Chambi Condori and Yaricsa Vilca Coaquera
Jorge Basadre Grohmann National University, Tacna, Peru

18.1 INTRODUCTION

Clustering is a set of non-inferential descriptive statistical techniques – unsupervised in machine learning – aimed at grouping similar objects in the same cluster, by which clusters with high internal affinity and external differences are formed. In business marketing, market segmentation provides insight into the composition of the market, differentiating groups with similar characteristics and needs. Customer segmentation is a fundamental tool for a company, as it allows for the identification of common and differentiated characteristics within the customer database, which are very useful for the strategic management of customers.

The impact of fourth generation technologies on market management, quality configuration, product design and development, and communication with customers is becoming increasingly significant. In this regard, Brei (2020) states that machine learning offers many potential applications in marketing. That is, marketing can be transformed into a more autonomous scientific work through the use of data and the proper formulation of each application. There are two main traditional marketing paradigms: destination marketing and relationship marketing. Each of the many aspects of the two marketing paradigms can be expressed as a machine learning problem, i.e., for each problem, a machine learning model can be built, and model parameters can be set. Artificial intelligence expressions have merited studies because machines with deep learning capabilities can take digital marketing to higher levels and make a difference (Miklosik et al., 2019). Lately, digital marketing is in a state of constant evolution, introducing new tools for data processing that describe new consumer habits, where the success or failure of digital communication depends largely on the quality of its content marketing (Baltes, 2015).

The widespread impacts of artificial intelligence (AI) and machine learning (ML) on many segments of society have been strongly felt in the field of marketing (Jarek & Mazurek, 2019). After all, machine learning offers a variety of benefits, including the opportunity to use proven techniques for the generalization of the advances achieved by science and scientific research.

According to Ullal et al. (2021), machine learning is a technique that combines science, statistics and computational coding to detect patterns in large volumes of data. Based on this data support, it is possible to predict future estimates (expected sales, market segment attention quota, and customer management under the CRM concept) resulting from the application of mathematical and statistical algorithms. The integration of big data and machine learning

DOI: 10.1201/9781003450443-18

techniques is a result of three key factors: the availability of algorithms and data, the increased processing power of computers and the lower cost of storage of digital devices. The speed of developments in computer science and software engineering, however, poses a challenge of ever-increasing importance: identify and implement the right combination of hardware platforms and software architectures to ensure the continuity of the integrated model and minimize its obsolescence, mitigating a loss of the processing capacity of the data management platform.

The purpose of this study is to conduct a case study on the application of one of the resources of artificial intelligence in market research, specifically, customer segmentation as a tool for the strategic management of business marketing.

18.2 METHODOLOGY

The clustering model was used in this study; the rationale of cluster analysis is to group objects into clusters using clustering algorithms. K-means is the most popular of the clustering algorithms, which groups numerical data and each cluster has a center called the mean. It is assumed that the number of clusters k is a fixed value.

According to Mahendiran et al. (2012), the cited k-means algorithm consists of the squared Euclidean distance divided by two variables; in other words, the sum of squares of the differences of all the coordinates of two points as shown in the following equation:

$$d(i, j) = \sqrt{\sum_k (X_{ik} - X_{jk})^2}$$

Where X_{ik} and X_{jk} are the individual values of each of the points, and the Davies-Bouldin index, which calculates the distances between clusters, is used to evaluate performance. In their study *Estimating Marketing Component Effects: Double Machine Learning from Targeted Digital Promotions*, Ellickson et al. (2022, p. 2) first aimed to demonstrate how machine learning can be leveraged in a unified framework to provide causal estimates of the effect of separate components in a high-dimensional marketing intervention, using only observational data. Next, the methodology was applied to data from 34 distinct e-mail promotions sent by a retailer to more than 1.3 million people on its contact list to highlight quantitative findings that are relevant to both the marketing literature and management practice. Furthermore, Dzyabura and Hauser (2011) assert that heuristic decision rules predict validation decisions better than compensatory rules.

The method followed for the implementation of clustering with Rapid Miner Studio 9.10 artificial intelligence resources is the one shown in Figure 18.1.

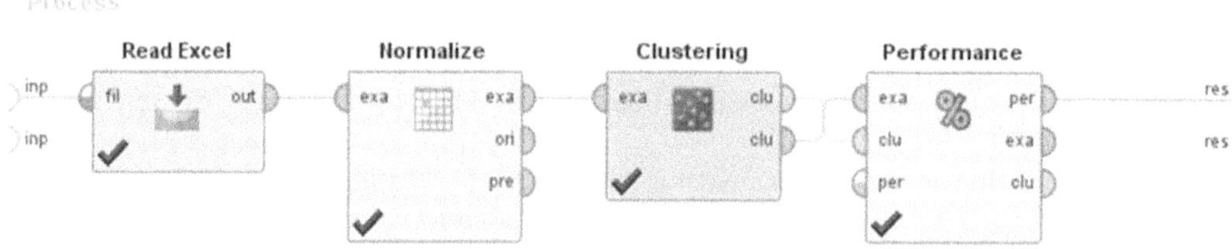

FIGURE 18.1 The sequential process of clustering application.

Note: Shows the sequential process of clustering application with Rapid Miner Studio 9.10.

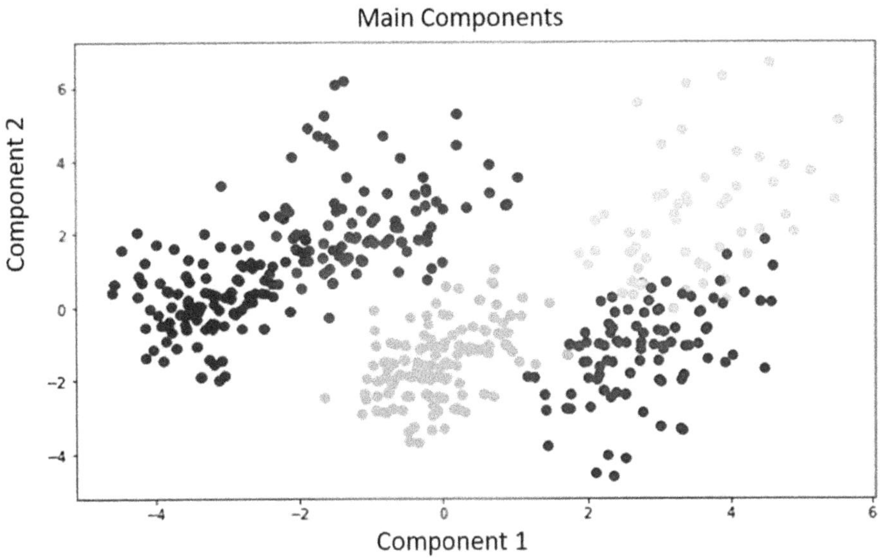

FIGURE 18.2 Shows the segments resulting from the segmentation process.

Note: The segments resulting.

18.3 RESULTS

The application of artificial intelligence (AI) in marketing aims to continuously track and forecast the next purchasing decisions of target consumers and improve their consumer "journey." In this regard, MR (2021) states that the potential of AI is reflected in its core elements: big data, machine learning, and powerful solutions. Big data enables marketers to aggregate and segment large amounts of data with minimal manual work.

Machine learning offers great potential value for marketing-related applications. However, the proliferation of data types, methods, tools, and programming languages hinders knowledge integration among marketing analytics teams, making collaboration difficult. In this regard, Villarroel and Silipo (2021, p. 393) state that visual programming might facilitate the orchestration of ML projects in a more intuitive visual fashion. In terms of marketing strategy, Huang and Rust (2022, p. 218) state that mechanical artificial intelligence can be used for segmentation (segment recognition), thinking artificial intelligence for targeting (segment recommendation), and feeling artificial intelligence for positioning (segment resonance).

Figure 18.2 shows the four segments obtained by applying AI with the clustering model.

18.4 CONCLUSIONS

Segmentation is very useful in business marketing because it makes it possible to make decisions in real time, prevent customer losses, and track trends in consumer tastes and preferences. Using the data, it is also possible to observe how people develop feelings about a company's brands, whether these are positive or negative manifestations.

In the clustering paradigm that allows finding the Euclidean distance between groups of consumers in the field of business marketing, minimum distances indicate that there are no significant differences in consumer tastes and preferences; in contrast, large distances denote that there are significant differences.

The use of artificial intelligence in market segmentation makes it possible to obtain the optimal number of clusters and their components from the performance indicator sought by Machine Learning, unlike statistical methods, it provides a level of accuracy.

REFERENCES

Baltes, P. L. (2015). Content marketing - the fundamental tool of digital marketing. *Bulletin of the Transilvania University of Brasov*. *8*(2), 111–118.

Brei, V. A. (2020). Machine learning in marketing: Overview, learning strategies, applications, and future developments. *Foundations and Trends in Marketing*, *14*(3), 173–236. https://doi.org/10.1561/1700000065

Dzyabura, D., & Hauser, J. R. (2011). Active machine learning for consideration heuristics. *Marketing Science*, *30*(5), 801–819. https://doi.org/10.1287/mksc.1110.0660

Ellickson, P. B., Kar, W., & Reeder, J. C. (2022). Estimating marketing component effects: Double machine learning from targeted email promotions. *Marketing Science*. https://doi.org/10.1287/mksc.2022.1401

Huang, M. H., & Rust, R. T. (2022). A framework for collaborative artificial intelligence in Marketing. *Journal of Retailing*, *98*(2), 209–223. https://doi.org/10.1016/j.jretai.2021.03.001

Jarek, K., & Mazurek, G. (2019). Marketing and artificial intelligence. *Central European Business Review*, *8*(2), 46–55. https://doi.org/10.18267/j.cebr.213

Mahendiran, A., Saravanan, N., Subramanian, N., & Sairam, N. (2012). Implementation of K-means clustering in cloud computing environment. *Research Journal of Applied Sciences, Engineering and Technology*, *4*(10), 1391–1394.

Miklosik, A., Kuchta, M., Evans, N., & Zak, S. (2019). Towards the adoption of machine learning-based analytical tools in digital marketing. *IEEE Access*, *7*, 85705–85718. https://doi.org/10.1109/ACCESS.2019.2924425

MR, A. (2021). Artificial intelligence and marketing. *Turkish Journal of Computer and Mathematics Education (TURCOMAT)*, *12*(4), 1247–1256. https://doi.org/10.17762/turcomat.v12i4.1184

Ullal, M. S., Hawaldar, I. T., Soni, R., & Nadeem, M. (2021). The role of machine learning in digital marketing. *SAGE Open*, *11*(4). https://doi.org/10.1177/21582440211050394

Villarroel Ordenes, F., & Silipo, R. (2021). Machine learning for marketing on the KNIME Hub: The development of a live repository for marketing applications. *Journal of Business Research*, *137*, 393–410. https://doi.org/10.1016/j.jbusres.2021.08.036

References

Abbad, M. M. (2013). E-banking in Jordan. *Behavior and Information Technology*, 32(7), 618–694.

Abdul, B., Muhammad, B. A., Fawwad, H. J., Majdah, A., Kashif, H. M., & Rehan, A. S. ICC T20 Cricket World Cup 2020 winner prediction using machine learning techniques.

Abduljabbar, T. A., Tao, X., Zhang, J., Zhou, X., Li, L., & Cai, Y. (2021). A survey of privacy solutions using blockchain for recommender systems: Current status, classification and open issues. *The Computer Journal*, 64(7), 1104–1129. 10.1093/comjnl/bxab065

Acquisti, C. T., and Wagman, L. (Jun. 2016). The economics of privacy. *Journal of Economic Literature*, 54(2), 442–492. 10.1257/jel.54.2.442

Adjei, M. T., Noble, S. M., & Noble. C. H. (2010). The influence of C2C communications in online brand communities on customer purchase behavior. *Journal of the Academy of Marketing Science*, 38(5), 634–653.

Adomavicius, G., & Tuzhilin, A. (Jun. 2005). Toward the next generation of recommender systems: A survey of the state-of-the-art and possible extensions. *IEEE Transactions on Knowledge and Data Engineering*, 17(6), 734–749. 10.1109/TKDE.2005.99

Agrawal, S., Singh, S. P., & Sharma, J. K. Predicting Results of Indian Premier League T-20 Matches using Machine Learning.

Aguayo, B. B., Ruano, C. A., & Vallejo, A. P. (2021). Multiple intelligences: Educational and cognitive development with a guiding focus. *South African Journal of Education*, 41(2), 1–15.

AISHE Report 2023 retrieved from https://aishe.gov.in/aishe/gotoAisheReports Global Admission 2023 retrieved from https://www.globaladmissions.com/blog/exploring-the-use-of-ai-in-universities https://www.nafsa.org/ie-magazine/2022/4/12/indias-higher-education-landscape

Aitzhan, N. Z., & Svetinovic, D. (2018). Security and privacy in decentralized energy trading through multi-signatures, blockchain and anonymous messaging streams. *IEEE Transactions on Dependable and Secure Computing*, 15.5, 840–852.

Ajzen, I. (1985). From Intentions to actions: A theory of planned behavior. In J. Kuhl & J. Beckmann (Eds.), *Action control: From cognition to behavior*. New York: Spinger-Verlag.

Ajzen, I. (1991). The theory of planned behavior. *Organizational Behavior and Human Decision Processes*, 50(2), 179–211.

Ajzen, I. & Fishbein, M. (1977). Attitude-behaviour relations: A theoretical analysis and review of empirical research. *Psychological Bulletin*, 84(5), 888.

Ajzen, I., & Fishbein M. (1982). *Understanding attitudes and predicting social behavior*, 1st ed. Englewood Cliffs, NJ: Pearson.

Akhil, N., Nidamanuri, V. K., Manigandla, V., Nuthi, N. S. T., & Chavali, G. R. Cricket score and winning prediction using data mining.

Akhther, N., & Sopory, P. (2022). Seeking and sharing mental health information on social media during COVID-19: Role of depression and anxiety, peer support, and health benefits. *Journal of Technology in Behavioral Science*, 7(2), 211–226.

Akroush, M. N., & Al-Debei, M. M. (2015). An integrated model of factors affecting consumer attitudes towards online shopping. *Business Process Management Journal*, 21(6), 1353–1376. 10.1108/BPMJ-02-2015-0022

Akrout, F. (2018). *Les méthodes des équations structurelles*. Sfax.

Al-Fagi, A. (2012). *Artificial intelligence and expert systems*. Jordan: Dar Al Thaqafapublishing and Distribution.

Al-Mushayt, O. S. (2019). Automating E-government services with artificial intelligence. *IEEE Access*, 7, 146821–146829.

Al-Sukkar, S. A. (2005). *The application of information systems in the Jordanian banking sector: a study of acceptance of Internet*, PhD Thesis, School of Economics and Information Systems. University of Wollongong, available at htttp://ro.uow.edu.au/thesis/419.

Alabi, K. (2020). A 2020 perspective on "Digital blockchain networks appear to be following Metcalfe's Law". *Electronic Commerce Research and Applications*, 40, Article 100939. 10.1016/j.elerap.2020.100939

Alalwan, A. A., Dwivedi, Y. K., & Rana, N. P. (2017). Factors influencing adoption of mobile banking by Jordanian bank customers: Extending UTAUT2 with trust. *International Journal of Information Management*, 37(3), 99–110.

Alam, M. Z., & Elaasi, S. A. (2016). A study on consumer perception towards e-shopping in KSA. *International Journal of Business and Management*, 11(7), 202–210. 10.5539/ijbm.v11n7p202

Alambo, A., Gaur, M., & Thirunarayan, K. (2020). Depressive, Drug Abusive, or Informative: Knowledge-aware Study of News Exposure during COVID-19 Outbreak. *arXiv (Cornell University).*

Alaparthi, S., & Mishra, M. (2020). Bidirectional Encoder Representations from Transformers (BERT): A sentiment analysis odyssey. 10.48550/ARXIV.2007.01127

Alesich, S. and Rigby, M. (2017). Gendered robots: Implications for our humanoid future. *IEEE Technology and Society Magazine*, 36(2), 50–59.

Alfahad, N. F., Albelali, M. T., Khurshid, F., Al-Arifi, M. N., Al-Dhawailie, A. A., & Alsultam, M. (2015). Perception and knowledge to online pharmacy services among consumers in Riyadh, Saudi Arabia: A pilot survey. *Latin American Journal of Pharmacy*, 34(6), 1113–1118.

Alifiardi, A. A., & Baridwan, Z. (2019). The influence of perceived usefulness, ease of use, trust, and risk towards Gojek actual use with behavioral intention to use as intervening variable. *Jurnal Ilmiah Mahasiswa FEB*, 7(2), 1–21.

Alkhateeb, F. M., & Doucette, W. R. (2009). Influences on physicians' adoption of electronic detailing (e-detailing). *Informatics for Health and Social Care*, 34(1), 39–52.

Alkhateeb, F. M., Khanfar, N. M., Doucette, W. R., & Loudon, D. (2009). Characteristics of physicians targeted by the pharmaceutical industry to participate in e-detailing. *Health Marketing Quarterly*, 26(2), 98–116.

Alrowaily, M. A., Alghamdi, M., Alkhazi, I., Hassanat, A. B., Arbab, M. M. S., & Liu, C. Z. (2023). Modeling and analysis of proof-based strategies for distributed consensus in blockchain-based peer-to-peer networks. *Sustainability*, 15(2), 1478. 10.3390/su15021478

Alwhaibi, M., Asser, W. M., Al Aloola, N. A., Alsalem, N., Almomen, A., & Alhawassi, T. M. (2021). Evaluating the frequency, consumers' motivation and perception of online medicinal, herbal, and health products purchase safety in Saudi Arabia. *Saudi Pharmaceutical Journal*, 29(2), 166–172.

Alwon, B. M., Solomon, G., Hussain, F., & Wright, D. J. (2015). A detailed analysis of online pharmacy characteristics to inform safe usage by patients. *International Journal of Clinical Pharmacy*, 37, 148–158.

Alyoshina, I. V. (2019), Artificial intelligence in age of digital globalization. *In international Conference technology and Entrepreneurship in Digital Society*, 26–30.

Amal, C. K., & Varde, A. S. Cric AI: A Classification Based Tool to Predict the Outcome in ODI Cricket.

Ameen, N., Tarhini, A., Reppel, A., & Anand, A. (2021). Customer experiences in the age of artificial intelligence. *Computers in Human Behavior*, 114, 106548.

American Psychiatry Association. (2018). What is mental illness? *American Psychiatry Association*, www.psychiatry.org/patients-families/what-is-mental-illness

Ami-Narh, J. T., & Williams, P. A. (2012). A revised UTAUT model to investigate E-health acceptance of health professionals in Africa. *Journal of Emerging Trends in Computing and Information Sciences*, 3(10), 1383–1391.

Ananda, B. Predicting the Winner in One Day International Cricket.

Anbar, A. (2001). E-Ticarette karşılaşılan sorunlar ve çözüm önerileri. *Akdeniz İİBF Dergisi*, 1(2), 18–32. https://dergipark.org.tr/tr/pub/auiibfd/issue/54586/744082

Andersson, V., & Sobek, T. (2020). *Virtual avatars, virtual influencers & authenticity, master degree project.* Sweden: University of Gothenburg.

Andréani, J. C. (1998). L'interview qualitative marketing. *Revue Française de Marketing*, ISSN 0035-3051, No. 168-169, pp. 7–37.

Andy, R. Dewi, A. & t As'adi, M. (2021). An Empirical Study to Validate The Technology Acceptance Model (TAM) In Evaluating "Desa Digital" Applications. *Workshop on Environmental Science, Society, and Technology*, 1–9.

Anja, B., & Bowker, G. C. (2019). op. cit. *Applications*, 8(3), 89–91.

API.AI. (2017). Welcome. API.AI [accessed 12 April 2023]. Available at: https://docs.api.ai/docs/welcome

Applications, Vol. 8 No.3, pp. 130–141.

Araujo, T. (2018). Living up to the chatbot hype: The influence of anthropomorphic design cues and communicative agency framing on conversational agent and company perceptions. *Computers in Human Behavior*, 85(2), 183–189.

Araújo, M. R., Sa-Barreto, L. L., Gratieri, T., Gelfuso, G. M., & Cunha-Filho, M. (2019). The digital pharmacies era: How 3D printing technology using fused deposition modeling can become a reality. *Pharmaceutics*, 11(3), 128.

Archana J. (2018). A survey on security and privacy issues of blockchain technology. *Mathematical Foundations of Computing*, 1(2), 121–147. 10.3934/mfc.2018007

Aref, M. M., & Okasha, A. E. (2019). Evaluating the online shopping behavior among Egyptian college-educated community. *Review of Economics and Political Science*, 5(1), 21–37.

Arpan, K. K., & Dwivedi, Y. K./Annals (2020). op.cit, pp. 81–90.

Arsenyan, J., & Mirowska, A. (2021). Almost human? A comparative case study on the social media presence of virtual influencers. *International Journal of Human-Computer Studies*, 155(2021), 1–16.

Artificial Intelligence Market Size, Share & Trends Analysis Report By Solution, By Technology (Deep Learning, Machine Learning), By End-use, By Region, And Segment Forecasts, 2023–2030 (https://www.grandviewresearch.com/industry-analysis/artificial-intelligence-ai-market; Last accessed online on June 1, 2023).

Ashames, A., Bhandare, R., AlAbdin, S. Z., Alhalabi, T., & Jassem, F. (2019). Public perception toward e-commerce of medicines and comparative pharmaceutical quality assessment study of two different products of furosemide tablets from community and illicit online pharmacies. *Journal of Pharmacy & Bioallied Sciences*, 11(3), 284.

Assi, S., Thomas, J., Haffar, M., & Osselton, D. (2016). Exploring consumer and patient knowledge, behavior, and attitude toward medicinal and lifestyle products purchased from the internet: A web-based survey. *JMIR Public Health and Surveillance*, 2(2), e5390.

Athapaththu, J. C., & Kulathunga, K. M. S. D. (2018). Factors affecting online purchase intention: A study of Sri Lankan online customers.

Auerbach, J., & Miller, B. F. (2020). COVID-19 exposes the cracks in our already fragile mental health system. *American Journal of Public Health*, 110(7), 969–970.

Awa, H. O., Ojiabo, O. U., & Emecheta, B. C. (2015). Integrating TAM, TPB and TOE frameworks and expanding their characteristic constructs for e-commerce adoption by SMEs. *Journal of Science and Technology Policy Management*, 6(1), 76–94. 10.1108/JSTPM-04-2014-0012

AWS. (2022). Blockchain for supply chain: Track and trace. https://aws.amazon.com/tr/blockchain/blockchain-for-supply-chain-track-and-trace/?nc1=h_ls

Aydın, Ö., & Karaarslan, E. (2022). OpenAI ChatGPT generated literature review: Digital twin in healthcare. In Ö. Aydın (Ed.), *Emerging computer technologies*, 2, 22–31. Izmir Akadeli Dernegi.

Azungah, T. (2018). Qualitative research: Deductive and inductive approaches to data analysis. *Qualitative Research Journal*, 18, 383–400.

B. McAfee, A. E., Davenport, T. H., Patil, D. J., & Barton, D., Big data: the management revolution.

Babin, B. J., Darden, W. R., & Grifn, M. (1994). Work and/or fun: Measuring hedonic and utilitarian shopping value. *Journal of Consumer Research*, 20(4), 644–656.

Bação, P., Duarte, A. P., Sebastião, H., & Redzepagic, S. (2018). Information transmission between cryptocurrencies: Does Bitcoin rule the cryptocurrency world? *Scientific Annals of Economics and Business*, 65(2), 97–117. http://saeb.feaa.uaic.ro/index.php/saeb/article/view/1090

Bae, M. (2018). Understanding the effect of the discrepancy between sought and obtained gratification on social networking site users‘ satisfaction and continuance intention. *Computers in Human Behavior*, 79, 137–153.

Baek, T. H., Kim, J., & Yu, J. H. (Jun. 2010). The differential roles of brand credibility and brand prestige in consumer brand choice. *Psychology & Marketing*, 27(7), 662–678. 10.1002/mar.20350.

Baid, A. N., & Ghosh, A. (2021). Factors affecting the shift of consumers towards E-pharmacies. *UGC Care Journal*, 44(1), 39–45.

Baker, T., Smith, L., & Anissa, N. (2019). Educ-AI-tion rebooted? Exploring the future of artificial intelligence in schools and colleges. Last assessed on June, 9, 2023.

Bala, M., & Verma, D. (2018). A critical review of digital marketing. *International Journal of Management, IT & Engineering*, 8(10), 321–339.

Balakrishnan, J., & Dwivedi, Y. K. (2021). Role of cognitive absorption in building user trust and experience. *Psychology & Marketing*, 38(4), 643–668. 10.1002/mar.21462

BaldersonKeelan. (2023). 27 AI In Education Statistics You Should Know. Retrieved from mspoweruser.com (https://mspoweruser.com/ai-in-education-statistics).

Baltes, P. L. (2015). Content marketing - the fundamental tool of digital marketing. *Bulletin of the Transilvania University of Brasov*, 8(2), 111–118.

Bandura, A. (2000). Social cognitive theory. In A. E. Kazdin (Ed.), *Encyclopedia of psychology*, 7–332. New York: Oxford University Press.

Bartlett, Y. K., & Coulson, N. S. (2011). An investigation into the empowerment effects of using online support groups and how this affects health professional/patient communication. *Patient Education and Counseling*, 83(1), 113–119.

Bartol, J., Vehovar, V., Bosnjak, M., & Petrovčič, A. (2023). Privacy concerns and self-efficacy in e-commerce: Testing an extended APCO model in a prototypical EU country. *Electronic Commerce Research and Applications*, 178, 1043–1061.

bashir, I., & Madhavaiah, C. (2015). Consumer attitude and behavioural intention towards Internet banking adoption in India. *Journal of Indian Business Research*, 7(1), 1–40.

Bates, T., Cobo, C., Mariño, O., & Wheeler, S. (2020). Can artificial intelligence transform higher education? *International Journal of Educational Technology in Higher Education*, 17(1), 1–12. Last assessed on June 7, 2023.

Batista, A., & Chimenti, P. (2021). Humanized robots: A proposition of categories to understand virtual influencers. *Australasian Journal of Information Systems*, 25, 1–27.

Battaglia, A. M., Mamak, M., & Goldberg, J. O. (2022). The impact of social media coverage on attitudes towards mental illness and violent offending. *Journal of Community Psychology*, *50*(7), 2938–2949.

Baum, I. R., & Baumann, N. (2019). Autonomous creativity: The implicit autonomy motive fosters creative production and innovative behavior at school. *Gifted and Talented International*, 3(1-2), 1–11.

Bayazovna, G. N. (2020). Marketing communication strategy and its essence. *Вопросынауки и образования*, 1(85), 18–21.

Becker, S. J. (2015). Direct-to-consumer marketing: A complementary approach to traditional dissemination and implementation efforts for mental health and substance abuse interventions. *Clinical Psychology: Science and Practice*, 22(1), 85.

Bekalu, M. A., Sato, T., & Viswanath, K. (2023). Conceptualizing and measuring social media use in health and well-being studies: Systematic review. *Journal of Medical Internet Research*, 25, e43191.

Belanche, D., Casalo, L., Flavian, M., & Ibanez-Sanchez, S. (2021). Understanding influencer marketing: The role of congruence between influencers, products and consumers. *Journal of Business Research*, 132(21), 186–195.

Bell, D. E. (1985). Disappointment in decision making under uncertainty. *Operations Research*, 33(1), 1–27.

Bene, M. (2020). Customer experience in B2B Saas business.

Berry, L. L., & Bendapudi, N. (2007). Health care: A fertile field for service research. *Journal of Service Research*, 10(2), 111–122.

Bessell, T. L., Silagy, C. A., Anderson, J. N., Hiller, J. E., & Sansom, L. N. (2002). Quality of global e-pharmacies: Can we safeguard consumers?. *European Journal of Clinical Pharmacology*, 58, 567–572.

Bevan, M. (2014). A method of phenomenological interviewing. *Qualitative Health Research*, 24(1), 136–144.

Biocca, F., Harms, C., & Burgoon, J. K. (2003). Toward a more robust theory and measure of social presence: Review and suggested criteria. *Presence: Teleoperators and Virtual Environments*, 12, 456–480.

Biswas, R. (2022). Preservation and processing technology of wild mushrooms. In *Wild mushrooms*, 67–88. CRC Press.

Bjorkli, C., Folstad, A., & Bertinussen, C. (2019). An Initial Model of Trust in Chatbots for Customer Service: Findings from a Questionnaire Study. *Interacting with Computers*, 1–47.

Black, J. S., & Van Esch, P. (2020). AI-enabled recruiting: What is it and how should a manager use it? *Business Horizons*, 63(2), 215–226.

Blattberg, R. C. & Deighton J.,(1991). Interactive marketing: Exploiting the age of addressability. *Sloan Management Review*, 33, 1.5–14.

Blažević, I. (2016). Family, peer, and school influence on children's social development. *World Journal of Education*, 6(2), 42–49.

Block, E., & Lovegrove, R. (2021). Discordant storytelling, honest fakery, identity peddling: How uncanny CGI characters are jamming public relations and influencer practices. *Public Relations Inquiry*, 10(3), 265–293.

Blockchain and E-Commerce. How Do They Make A Winning …" [Online]. Available: https://www.orangemantra.com/blog/blockchain-e-commerce-make-winning-combination/. [Accessed: 23-March-2020].

Blut, M., Wang, C., W€underlich, N. V. & Brock, C. (2021). Understanding anthropomorphism in service provision: A meta-analysis of physical robots, chatbots, and other AI. *Journal of the Academy of Marketing Science*, 1–27.

Boerman, S. C. (2020). The effects of the standardized Instagram disclosure for micro- and meso-influencers. *Computers in Human Behavior*, 103(2020), 199–207. 10.1016/j.chb.2019.09.015

Bolderston, A. (2012). Conducting a research interview. *Journal of Medical Imaging and Radiation Sciences*, 43(1), 66–76.

Bonabi, H., Müller, M., Ajdacic-Gross, V., Eisele, J., Rodgers, S., Seifritz, E., Rössler, W., & Rüsch, N. (2016). Mental health literacy, attitudes to help seeking, and perceived need as predictors of mental health service use. *Journal of Nervous and Mental Disease*, 204(4), 321–324.

Borau, S., Otterbring, T., & Laporte, S. (2021). The most human bot: Female gendering increases humanness perceptions of bots and acceptance of AI, *Psychol. Market*, 1–17.

Bottemanne, L. (2021). Est-il contradictoire pour les marques de luxe de faire appel à des influenceurs sur Instagram dans leur campagne de communication?. *Mémoire de master en ingénierie de gestion à finalité spécialisée en Data Science*. Belgique: Université de Namur.

Botti, S., & McGill, A. L. (2011). The locus of choice: Personal causality and satisfaction with hedonic and utilitarian decisions. *Journal of Consumer Research*, 37(6), 1065–1078.

Bowman, M., Alharthi, A., & Krotov, V. (2017). Addressing barriers to big data. *Business Horizons*, 60(3), 285–292.

Bowman, C., Family, H., Agius-Muscat, H., Cordina, M., & Sutton, J. (2020). Consumer internet purchasing of medicines using a population sample: A mixed methodology approach. *Research in Social and Administrative Pharmacy*, 16(6), 819–827.

Boyce, C., & Neale, P. (2006). Conducting in-depth interviews: A guide for designing and conducting in-depth Interviews for evaluation input. *Pathfinder International: conducting in-depth interviews*, 1–12.

Brandtzaeg, P. B., & Følstad, A. (2017). Why people use chatbots. *In International Conference on Internet Science, Springer, Cham*, 10673, 377–392.

Brei, V. A. (2020). Machine learning in marketing: Overview, learning strategies, applications, and future developments. *Foundations and Trends in Marketing*, 14(3), 173–236. 10.1561/1700000065

Breuer, C., Huffmeier, J., & Hertel, G. (2016). Does trust matter more in virtual teams? A metaanalysis of trust and team effectiveness considering virtuality and documentation as moderators. *Journal of Applied Psychology*, 101(8), 1151–1177.

Brewer, G., Centifanti, L. C. M., Caicedo, J. C., Huxley, G., Peddie, C., Stratton, K., & Lyons, M. (2021). Experiences of mental distress during COVID-19: Thematic analysis of discussion forum posts for anxiety, depression, and obsessive-compulsive disorder. *Illness, Crisis, & Loss*, 30(4), 795–811.

Bronda, S., Ostrovsky, M. G., Jain, S., & Malacarne, A. (2022). The role of social media for patients with temporomandibular disorders: A content analysis of Reddit. *Journal of Oral Rehabilitation*, 49(1), 1–9.

Brosnan, f. (2012). Business intelligence: What works where in B2B. *Journal of Direct.*

Brown, G., Rathbone, A. L., & Prescott, J. (2021). Social media use for supporting mental health (SMILE). *Mental Health Review Journal*, 26(3), 279–297.

Brynjolfsson, E., & Mcafee, A. N. D. R. E. W. (2017). Artificial intelligence, for real. *Harvard Business Review*, 1, 1–31.

Brynjolfsson, E., Rock, D., & Syverson, C. (2018). Artificial intelligence and the modern productivity paradox: A clash of expectations and statistics. In *The economics of artificial intelligence: An agenda*, 23–57. University of Chicago Press.

Buck, L., & McDonnel, R. (2022). Security and Privacy in the Metaverse: The Threat of the Digital Human, CHI EA '22, Proceedings of the 1st Workshop on Novel Challenges of Safety, Security and Privacy in Extended Reality, April 29 - May 5, 2022, New Orleans, LA, USA.

Bülbül Ş., & İnce G. (2018). Blockchain-based Framework for Customer Loyalty Program, 3rd International Conference on Computer Science and Engineering (UBMK), Sarajevo, Bosnia and Herzegovina, pp. 342–346, 10.1109/UBMK.2018.8566642

Buntak K., Kovačić M., & Mutavdžija M. (2020). Application of artificial intelligence in the business. *International Journal for Quality Research*, 15(2), 403–416.

Burke, R. (2002). Hybrid recommender systems: Survey and experiments. *User Modeling and User-Adapted Interaction*, 12(4), 331–370. 10.1023/A:1021240730564

Burney, S. M. A., & Saleem, H.(2008). Inductive & deductive research approach. *Lecture delivered on 06-03-2008 at Auditorium of Faculty of Arts and Science*. Karachi, Pakistan: University of Karachi.

Burns, R. P., & Burns, R. (2008). *Business research methods and statistics using SPSS*. SAGE Publications Ltd, 560 pages

Butler, J. K. (1991). Toward understanding and measuring conditions of trust: Evolution of conditions of trust inventory. *Journal of Management*, 17(3), 643–663.

Butt, B. Z., & Ur Rehman, K. (2010). A study examining the students satisfaction in higher education. *Procedia-Social and Behavioral Sciences*, 2(2), 5446–5450.

Cachin, C. (2016). Architecture of the hyperledger blockchain fabric. *Workshop on Distributed Cryptocurrencies and Consensus Ledgers*. 310.

Caldor, E. (2021). Quelles sont les stratégies des entreprises lors d'association influenceur- marque négative? *Mémoire de master en science de gestion à finalité spécialisée*. Belgique: Université du Louvain School of Management.

Campbell, C., Plangger, K., Sands, S., & Kietzmann, J. H. (2022). The coming reality of fakes: How Deepfakes and AI could reshape the ad industry. *Journal of Advertising Research*.

Caner, M. (2012). The definition of blended learning in higher education. *Blended learning environments for adults: Evaluations and frameworks*, 19–34.

Carmi, M. Z., & Riva, G. M. (Jan. 2023). The European General Data Protection Regulation (GDPR) in mHealth: Theoretical and practical aspects for practitioners' use. *Medicine, Science and the Law*, 63(1), 61–68. 10.1177/00258024221118411.

Casino, F., Dasaklis, T. K., & Patsakis, C. (2019). A systematic literature review of blockchain-based applications: Current status, classification and open issues. *Telematics and Informatics*, 36, 55–81. 10.1016/j.tele.2018.11.006

Cauderlier, C. (2021). *La stratégie digitale marketing - Ne ratez pas le coche! Bruxelles*. Belgique: Racine.

Chaffey, D., & Smith, P. R. (2023). *Digital marketing excellence: planning, optimizing and integrating online marketing*, 6th edition. Milton Park, Abingdon, Oxon: Routledge.

Chaitanya, K., Saha, G. C., Saha, H., Acharya, S., & Singla, M. (2023). The impact of artificial intelligence and machine learning in digital marketing strategies. *European Economic Letters*, 13(3), 982–992.

Chakraborty, U., Banerjee, A., Saha, J. K., Sarkar, N., & Chakraborty, C. (Eds.). (2022). *Artificial intelligence and the fourth industrial revolution*. CRC Press.

Chancellor, S., & De Choudhury, M. (2020). Methods in predictive techniques for mental health status on social media: a critical review. *NPJ Digital Medicine*, 3(1), 43.

Chancellor, S., Baumer, E. P., & De Choudhury, M. (2019). Who is the "human" in human-centered machine learning: The case of predicting mental health from social media. *Proceedings of the ACM on Human-Computer Interaction*, 3(CSCW), 1–32.

Chang, C. (2007). The relative effectiveness of comparative and noncomparative advertising. *Journal of Advertsing*, 36(l), 21–35.

Chantamas, M. (2021). Book review: Marketing 5.0 technology for humanity. *ABAC Journal*, 41(2), 1–5.

charlottestories. (2021, 01). Blockchain Technology in International Business. *Consulté le 06 13, 2022, sur charlottestories*; https://www.charlottestories.com/blockchain-technology-in-international-business/. ganne, e. (2018). Can Blockchain. WTO Publications, p. 107.

Charnigo, l., & ellis, b. p. (march 2007). checking out face book: the impact of agigital trend on academiclibraries, *information technology and libraries*, pp. 23–31.

Chatfuel. (2017). Facebook Messenger. *Chatfuel Help* [accessed 25 April 2023]. Available at: https://help.chatfuel.com/facebook-messenger/

Chattaraman, V., Kwon, W. S., Gilbert, J. E., & Ross, K. (2019). Should AI-based, conversational digital assistants employ social- or task-oriented interaction style? A task-competency and reciprocity perspective for older adults. *Computers in Human Behavior*, 90(2), 315–330.

Cheikh, K. (2021). Insights about developing learners' autonomy in Tunisia, 4 pages.

Chellapilla, D. P. C., & Patvardhan, C. V. Data Analytics based Deep Mayo Predictor for IPL-9.

Chen, L. D., & Tan, J. (2004). Technology adaptation in e-commerce: Key determinants of virtual stores acceptance. *European Management Journal*, 22(1), 74–86.

Chen, J. V., Yen, D. C. & Chen, K. (2009). The acceptance and diffusion of the innovative smart phone use: A case study of a delivery service company in logistics. *Information and Management*, 46(4), 241–248.

Chen, Y., Prentice, C., Weaven, S. & Hisao, A. (2022). The influence of customer trust and artificial intelligence on customer engagement and loyalty: The case of the home-sharing industry. *Frontiers in Psychology*, 1–15.

Cheng, Y.-M. (2023). How gamification and social interaction stimulate MOOCs continuance intention via cognitive presence, teaching presence and social presence?, *Library Hi Tech*, Vol. ahead-of-print No. ahead-of-print.

Cheng, Y., & Jiang, H. (2020). How do AI-driven chatbots impact user experience? Examining gratifications, perceived privacy risk, satisfaction, loyalty, and continued use. *Journal of Broadcasting & Electronic Media*, 64(4), 592–614.

Cheng, T. C. E., Lam, D. Y. C., & Yeung, A. C. L. (2006). Adoption of Internet banking: An empirical study in Hong Kong. *Decision Support Systems*, 42(3), 1558–1572.

Cheng, X., Cohen, J., & Mou, J. (2023). AI-enabled technology innovation in e-commerce. *Journal of Electronic Commerce Research*, 24(1), 1–6.

Cheng, X., Bao, Y., Zarifis, A., Gong, W., & Mo, J. (2021). Exploring consumers' response to text-based chatbots in e-commerce: The moderating role of task complexity and chatbot disclosure. *Internet Research*, 32(2), 496–517.

Cheung, F., & Leung, F. W. (2021). Virtual influencer as celebrity endorsers. *Advances in global services and retail management*, 1–7.

Chhikara, D., Sharma, R., & Kaushik, K. (2022). Indian E-commerce consumer and their acceptance towards chatbots. *Academy of Marketing Studies Journal*, 26, 1–10.

Chi, O. H., Jia, S., Li, Y., & Gursoy, D. (2021). Developing a formative scale to measure consumers' trust toward interaction with artificially intelligent (AI) social robots in service delivery. *Computers in Human Behavior*, 118. 10.1016/j.chb.2021.106700

Childers, T. L., Carr, C. L., Peck, J., & Carson, S. (2001). Hedonic and utilitarian motivations for online retail shopping behavior. *Journal of Retailing*, 77(4), 511–535.

Chiou, J. S., & Shen, C. C. (2012). The antecedents of online financial service acceptance: The impact of physical banking services on Internet banking acceptance. *Behavior and Information Technology*, 31(9), 859–871.

Choi, J. N., Sung, S. Y., Lee, K., & Cho, D. S. (2011). Balancing cognition and emotion: Innovation implementation as a function of cognitive appraisal and emotional reactions toward innovation. *Journal of Organizational Behavior*, 32(1), 107–124.

Chopdar, P. K., & Balakrishnan, J. (2020). Consumers response towards mobile commerce applications: SOR approach. *International Journal of Information Management*, 53, 102106.

Choudhury, A., & Shamszare, H. (2023). Investigating the impact of user trust on adoption and use of ChatGPT: A survey analysis. *Journal of Medical Internet Research*, 25, 1–11.

Chowdhury, N. A. (2023). Unlocking the Power of Chat GPT: An In-Depth Look at ChatAI's Business Model.

Chung, K., Quach, S., & Thaichon, P. (2022). A framework of artificial intelligence (AI) applications in marketing. In *Artificial intelligence for marketing management*, 41–51. Routledge.

Chung, M., Ko, E., Joung, H. & Kim, S. J. (2018). Chatbot e-service and customer satisfaction regarding luxury brands. *Journal of Business Research*, 117(1), 587–595.

Ciechanowski, L., Przegalinska, A., Magnuski, M., & Gloor, P. (2019). In the shades of the uncanny valley: An experimental study of human–chatbot interaction. *Future Generation Computer Systems*, 92(2), 539–548.

Cisler, J. M., & for role in crypto moneylaunderingKoster, E. H. (2010). Mechanisms of attentional biases towards threat in anxiety disorders: An integrative review. *Clinical Psychology Review*, 30(2), 203–216.

Cohen, J. (1988). *Statistical power analysis for the behavioral sciences* (2nd ed.). 597 pages. Routledge. 10.4324/9780203771587

Cohen, S., & Wills, T. A. (1985). Stress, social support, and the buffering hypothesis. *Psychological Bulletin*, 98(2), 310.

Concensus specs. Available: https://github.com/ethereum/consensus-specs (Accessed August 28th, 2023).

Connell, P. M. (2013), The role of baseline physical similarity to humans in consumer responses to anthropomorphic animal images. *Psychology & Marketing*, 30(6), 461–468.

Corin, F. (2022). US Treasury bans Tornado Cash mixer for role in crypto moneylaundering. (https://www.theverge.com/2022/8/8/23296778/us-treasury-tornado-cash-crypto-mixer-sanctions-ethereum-north-korea). (Accessed August 26th, 2023).

Corritore, C. L., Kracher, B., & Wiedenbeck, S. (2003). On-line trust: Concepts, evolving themes, a model. *International Journal of Human-Computer Studies*, 58(6), 737–758.

Cosmo, L. M., Piper, L., & Di Vittorio, A. (2021). The rôle of attitude toward chatbots and privacy concern on the relationship between attitude toward mobile advertising and behavioral intent to use chatbots. *Italian Journal of Marketing*, 2021, 83–102.

Coussement, & Van Den Poel, D. (Jan. 2008). Churn prediction in subscription services: An application of support vector machines while comparing two parameter-selection techniques. *Expert Systems with Applications*, 34(1), 313–327.

Crolic, C., Felipe, T., Rhonda, H., & Andrew, S. (2021). Blame the bot: Anthropomorphism and anger in customer-chatbot interactions. *Journal of Marketing*, 86(1), 132–148.

Crompton, H., & Burke, D. (2023). Artificial intelligence in higher education: The state of the field. *International Journal of Educational Technology in Higher Education*, 20(22), 1–22.

Crozier, M. (1964). *The bureaucratic phenomenon*. Chicago: University of Chicago Press.

Cruzado, J. G., Morales, C. M., Del Carpio, C. F., GoyCochea, J. L., Arévalo, A. A., & Vargas, C. R. (2023). Use of chatbots in e-commerce. *A Comprehensive Systematic Review*, 101(4), 1172–1183.

Cyr, D., Hassanein, K., Head, M. & Ivanov, A. (2007). The role of social presence in establishing loyalty in e-service environments. *Interacting with Computers*, 19(1), 43–56.

Dabiran, E., Wang, F., & Farivar, S. (2022). Virtual influencer marketing: Anthropomorphism and its effect. *ECIS 2022 Research in Progress Papers*, 6(18), 2–13.

Dabiran, E., Farivar, S., Wang, F., & Grant, G. G. (2023). Engaging with virtual influencers: A Netnography study. *ECIS 2023 Research-in-Progress Papers*, 41. https://aisel.aisnet.org/ecis2023_rip/41

Das, G. (2016). Antecedents and consequences of trust: An e-tail branding perspective. *International Journal of Retail and Distribution Management*, 44(7), 713–730.

Dash, A., & Sahoo, A. K. (2021). Moderating effect of gender on adoption of digital health consultation: A patient perspective study. *International Journal of Pharmaceutical and Healthcare Marketing*, 15(4), 598–616.

Dave, T. N., Dave, A. R., Parwani, A. H., Joshi, A. B., & Patel, R. (2022). Consumer Perception about E-Pharmacies in Indian Retail Pharmaceutical Sector.

Davenport, T. H., & Harris, J. G. (2017). *Competing on analytics: the new science of winning*. Updated, with A new introduction. Boston, Massachusetts: Harvard Business Review Press.

David, C. S., & Cox, D. (02-Mar-2020). Know How Blockchain TechnologyisTransforming E-commerce Sector. *CryptoNewsZ*. [Online]. Available: https://www.cryptonewsz.com/blockchain-and-e-commerce-an-inseparable-duo/. [Accessed: 23-March-2020].

David, C. S., & Cox, D. (03-Mar-2020). Has the Blockchain Technology Made E-commerce Business Easier?. *CryptoNewsZ*. [Online]. Available: https://www.cryptonewsz.com/how-can-blockchain-transform-e-commerce-and-the-way-of-doing-business/. [Accessed: 05-Apr-2020].

Davis, F. D. (1986). *A technology acceptance model for empirical testing new end-user information system: Theory and results*. Massachusetts Institute of Technology, 1986.

Davis, F. D. (1989). Perceived usefulness, perceived ease of use, and user acceptance of information technology. *MIS Quarterly*, 13(3), 319–339.

Davis, F. D., Bagozzi, R. P., & Warshaw, P. R. (1989). User acceptance of computer technology: A comparison of two theoretical models. *Management Science*, 35(8), 982–1003.

Davis, F. D., Bagozzi, R. P., & Warshaw, P. R. (1992). Extrinsic and intrinsic motivation to use computers in the workplace. *Journal of Applied Social Psychology*, 22(14), 1111–1132.

Dawar, N., & Bendle, N. (2018). Marketing in the age of Alexa. *Harvard Business Review*, 96(3), 81–86.

De Bruyn, A., Viswanathan, V., Beh, Y-S., Kai-Uwe Brock, J., &Von Wangenheim, F. (2020). Artificial intelligence and marketing: Pitfalls and opportunities. *Journal of Interactive Marketing*, 51, 91–105. 10.1016/j.intmar.2020.04.007

De Choudhury, M., Counts, S., Horvitz, E. J., & Hoff, A. (2014, February). Characterizing and predicting postpartum depression from shared facebook data. *In proceedings of the 17th ACM conference on Computer supported cooperative work & social computing* (pp. 626–638).

De Cicco, R., Silva, S. C., & Alparone, F. R. (2020). Millennials‘ attitude toward chatbots: An experimental study in a social relationship perspective. *International Journal of Retail & Distribution Management*, 48(11), 1213–1233.

De Kervenoael, R., Hasan, R., Schwob, A., & Goh, E. (2020). Leveraging human-robot interaction in hospitality services: Incorporating the role of perceived value, empathy, and information sharing into visitors' intentions to use social robots. *Tourism Management*, 78, 104042.

De Laet Derache, L. (2021). Quels sont les éléments expliquant le succès des influenceurs virtuels (IV) alors que l'efficacité des influenceurs humains (IH) repose sur l'authenticité, la crédibilité et l'interaction parasociale? Dans quelle mesure un IV peut-il être aussi efficace et quels sont les facteurs compensatoires de ces derniers? *Mémoire de master en science de gestion finalité Marketing Strategy for Connected Brands*. Belgique: Université du Louvain School of Management.

de Oliveira Santos, E. L. (2021). Exploring the factors that influence the adoption of online pharmacy in Portugal: a study on consumer´s acceptance and pharmacist's perception.

Deci, E. L., & Ryan, R. M. (1985). Intrinsic motivation and self-determination in human behavior. New York: Plenum.
Deci, E. L., & Ryan, R. M. (2000). The "what" and "why" of goal pursuits: Human needs and the self-determination of behavior. *Psychological Inquiry*, 11(4), 227–268.
Deci, E. L., & Ryan, R. M. (2014). Autonomy and need satisfaction in close relationships: Relationships motivation theory. In N. Weinstein (Ed.), *Human motivation and interpersonal relationships: Theory, research, and applications*, 53–73. Cham: Springer.
Deighton, J. (1996). The future of interactive marketing. *Harvard Business Review*, 74(6), 151–160.
Dellaert, B. G. C., &. Stremersch. S. (2005). Marketing mass-customized products: Striking a balance between utility and complexity. *Journal of Marketing Research*, 42(2), 219–227.
Demartini, C., & Benussi, L. (2017). Do web 4.0 and industry 4.0 imply education X. 0? *It Professional*, 19(3), 4–7.
Derbaix C. (1995). The impact of affective reactions on attitudes toward the advertisement and the brand: A step toward ecological validity. *Journal of Marketing Research*, 32(4), 470–479.
Devaut, J. (2017). De Montréal à la région d'Yverdon-les-Bains, comment les influenceurs nous font voyager, Bachelor, Haute Ecole de Gestion & Tourisme, Suisse.
Dewan, M. A. A., Lin, F., Wen, D., Murshed, M., & Uddin, Z. (2018, October). A deep learning approach to detecting engagement of online learners. In 2018 IEEE SmartWorld, Ubiquitous Intelligence & Computing, Advanced & Trusted Computing, Scalable Computing & Communications, Cloud & Big Data Computing, Internet of People and Smart City Innovation (SmartWorld/SCALCOM/UIC/ATC/CBDCom/IOP/SCI) (pp. 1895–1902). IEEE.
Dhonge, N., Dhole, S., Wavre, N., Pardakhe, M., Nagarale, A.: IPL Cricket Score And Winning Prediction Using Machine Learning Techniques.
Diakopoulos, N. (Jan. 2016). Accountability in algorithmic decision making. *Communications of the ACM*, 59(2), 56–62. 10.1145/2844110
Dibble, J. L., Hartmann, T., & Rosaen, S. F. (2016). Parasocial interaction and parasocial relationship: Conceptual clarification and a critical assessment of measures. *Human Communication Research*, 42(1), 21–44.
DiCicco-Bloom, B., & Crabtree, B. F. (2006). The qualitative research interview. *Medical Education*, 40(4), 314–321.
Diederich, S., Brendel, A. B., & Kolbe, L. M. (2020). Designing anthropomorphic enterprise conversational agents. *Business and Information Systems Engineering*, 62, 193–209.
Diego, L. A. B. (2017). Friends with benefits: Causes and effects of learners' cheating practices during examination. *IAFOR Journal of Education*, 5(2), 121–138.
Dignum, V. (2019). *Responsible artificial intelligence: How to develop and use AI in a responsible way*. In Artificial intelligence: Foundations, theory, and algorithms. Cham: Springer International Publishing. doi: 10.1007/978-3-030-30371-6.
Dimitrieska, S., Stankovska, A., & Efremova, T. (2018). Artificial intelligence and marketing. *Entrepreneurship*, 6(2), 298–304.
Dinh, C. M., & Park, S. S. (2022). How to increase consumer intention to use Chatbots? An empirical analysis of hedonic and utilitarian motivations on social presence and the moderating effects of fear across generations. *Electronic Commerce Research*, 1–41.
Dixon, M., Freeman, K., & Toman, N. (2010). Stop trying to delight your customers. *Harvard Business Review*, 88(7), 116–122.
Doshi-Velez, F., & Kim, B. (2017). Towards a rigorous science of interpretable machine learning. 10.48550/ARXIV.1702.08608
Dubey, R., Bryde, D-J., Blome, C., Roubaud, D., & Giannakis,M. (2021). Facilitating artificial intelligence powered supply chain analytics through alliance management during the pandemic crises in the B2B context. *Industrial Marketing Management*, 96, 135–146. 10.1016/j.indmarman.2021.05.003
Dubey, R., Gunasekaran, A., Childe, S. J., Bryde, D. J., Giannakis, M., Foropon, C., & Roubaud David Benjamin, H. T. (2020). Big data analytics and artificial intelligence pathway to operational performance under the effects of entrepreneurial orientation and environmental dynamism: A study of manufacturing organizations. *International Journal of Production Economics*, 226.
Dubois, C., Salotti, J-M., Seminel, D., & Simonazzi. N. (2019). Le Chatbot: un outil de la relation aux clients. *Dans Hermès, La Revue*, 2(84), 95–97.
Dupont, S.; Galanda, B., & Nils, F. (2015). The impact of different sources of social support on academic performance: Intervening factors mediated pathways in the case of master's thesis. *Revue Européenne de PsychologieAppliquée*, 65, 227–237.

Dwivedi, Y. K., Hughes, L., Ismagilova, E., Aarts, G., Coombs, C., Crick, T., Duan, Y., Dwivedi, R., Edwards, J., Eirug, A., Galanos, V., Ilavarasan, P. V., Janssen, M., Jones, P., Kumar Kar, A., Kizgin, H., Kronemann, B., Lal, B., Lucini, B., Medaglia, R., Le Meunier-FitzHugh, K., Le Meunier-FitzHugh, L. C., Misra, S., Mogaji, E., Sharma, S. K., Singh, J. B., Raghavan, V., Raman, R., Rana, N. P., Samothrakis, S., Spencer, J., Tamilmani, K., Tubadji, A., Walton, P., & Williams, M. D. (2021). Artificial Intelligence (AI): Multidisciplinary perspectives on emerging challenges, opportunities, and agenda for research, practice and policy. *International Journal of Information Management*, 57. 10.1016/j.ijinfomgt.2019.08.002

Dzyabura, D., & Hauser, J. R. (2011). Active machine learning for consideration heuristics. *Marketing Science*, 30(5), 801–819. 10.1287/mksc.1110.0660

Edwards, A., Edwards, C., Westerman, D., & Spence, P. R. (2019). Initial expectations, inter-actions, and beyond with social robots. *Computers in Human Behavior*, 90, 308–314.

Eke, D. O. (2023). ChatGPT and the rise of generative AI: Threat to academic integrity?

El Bakkouria, B., Raki, S., & Belgnaou, T. (2022). The role of Chatbots in enhancing customer experience: Literature review, *Procedia Computer Science*, 203, 432–437.

El Hedhli, K., Zourrig, H., Al Khateeb, A., & Alnawas, I. (2023). Stereotyping human-like virtual influencers in retailing: Does warmth prevail over competence?. *Journal of Retailing and Consumer Services*, 75.

Ellickson, P. B., Kar, W., & Reeder, J. C. (2022). Estimating marketing component effects: Double machine learning from targeted email promotions. *Marketing Science*. 10.1287/mksc.2022.1401

Emon, M. M., Farheen, H., Mehzabul, N., & Vichayanan, R. (2023). Predicting adoption intention of artificial intelligence, a study on ChatGPT. *AIUB Journal of Science and Engineering*, 22, 189–196.

Enholm, I. M., Papagiannidis, E., Mikalef, P., & Krogstie, J. (2022). Artificial intelligence and business value: A literature review. *Information Systems Frontiers*, 24(5), 1709–1734.

Environ. 12, 456–480.

Ernala, S. K., Birnbaum, M. L., Candan, K. A., Rizvi, A. F., Sterling, W. A., Kane, J. M., & De Choudhury, M. (2019, May). Methodological gaps in predicting mental health states from social media: Triangulating diagnostic signals. In *Proceedings of the 2019 chi conference on human factors in computing systems* (pp. 1–16).

Ert, E., Fleischer, A., & Magen, N. (2016). Trust and reputation in the sharing economy: The role of personal photos in Airbnb. *Tourism Management*, 55(2), 62–73.

Ertemel A. V. (2018). Implications of blockchain technology on marketing. *Journal of International Trade Logistics and Law*, 4(2), 35–44.

Etemad-Sajadi, R. (2016). The impact of online real-time interactivity on patronage intention: The use of avatars. *Computers in Human Behavior*, 61(2), 227–232.

Evard, Y., Pras, B., & Roux, E. (2000). *Market: Etudes et recherches en marketing.*

Everard, A. & Galletta, D. F. (2005). How presentation flaws affect perceived site quality, trust, and intention to purchase from an online store. *Journal of Management Information Systems*, 22(3), 56–95.

Evrard, Y., Pras, B., & Roux, E. (1993). Market: Etudes et Recherches en Marketing. *Editions Nathan.*

Évrard, Y., Pras, B., & Roux, E. (2003). *Market: Etudes et Recherches en Marketing*. Paris: Dunod. B.

Eyal, I. (2017). Blockchain technology: Transforming libertarian cryptocurrency dreams to finance and banking realities. *Computer*, 50.9, 38–49.

Fadel, L., Abdou, A., Lounici, A., & Saidani, A. (2022). Identification des e-influenceurs avant la mise en place d'une stratégie de communication digitale par les marques algériennes sur Instagram. *International Journal of Social Communication*, 9(1), 69–79.

Febrianto, G., Hidayatullah, S., & Ardianto, Y. T. (2018). The effect of intention to usage to actual usage e-purchasing application. *International Journal Of Scientific and Engineering Research*, 9(12), 363–370.

Feine, J., Gnewuch, U., Morana, S., & Maedche, A. (2019). A taxonomy of social cues for conversational agents. *International Journal of Human-Computer Studies*, 132, 138–161.

Feng, Y., Chen, H., & Kong, Q. (2020). An expert with whom I can identify: The role of narratives in influencer marketing. *International Journal of Advertising*, 1–22.

Feng, C. M., Park, A., Pitt, L., Kietzmann, J., & Northey, G. (2021). Artificial intelligence in marketing: A bibliographic perspective. *Australasian Marketing Journal*, 29(3), 252–263. 10.1016/j.ausmj.2020.07.006

Fernandes, T., & Oliveira, E. (2021). Understanding consumers' acceptance of automated technologies in service encounters: Drivers of digital voice assistants adoption. *Journal of Business Research*, 122, 180–191.

Ferreira, J. B., da Rocha, A., & da Silva, J. F. (2014). Impacts of technology readiness on emotions and cognition in Brazil. *Journal of Business Research*, 67(5), 865–873.

Feurer, M., Klein, A., Eggensperger, K., Springenberg, J., Blum, M., & Hutter, F. (2015). Efficient and robust automated machine learning. In *Advances in neural information processing systems*. Curran Associates, Inc. Accessed: Sep. 24, 2023. [Online]. Available: https://proceedings.neurips.cc/paper_files/paper/2015/hash/11d0e6287202fced83f79975ec59a3a6-Abstract.html

Firat, M. (2023). What ChatGPT means for universities: Perceptions of scholars and students. *Journal of Applied Learning & Teaching*, 6, 1–22.

Fishbein, M., & Ajzen, I. (1975). *Belief, Attitude, Intention And Behavior: An introduction to theory and research*. Reading, MA: Addison-Wesley.

Fittler, A., Bősze, G., & Botz, L. (2013). Evaluating aspects of online medication safety in long-term follow-up of 136 Internet pharmacies: Illegal rogue online pharmacies flourish and are long-lived. *Journal of Medical Internet Research*, 15(9), e2606.

Fittler, A., Ambrus, T., Serefko, A., Smejkalová, L., Kijewska, A., Szopa, A., & Káplár, M. (2022). Attitudes and behaviors regarding online pharmacies in the aftermath of COVID-19 pandemic: At the tipping point towards the new normal. *Frontiers in Pharmacology*, 13, 1070473.

Fitzpatrick, K. K., Darcy, A., & Vierhile, M. (2017). Delivering cognitive behavior therapy to young adults with symptoms of depression and anxiety using a fully automated conversational agent (Woebot): A randomized controlled trial. *JMIR Mental Health*, 4(2), 7785.

Fogg, B. J., & Tseng, H. (1999). The elements of computer credibility. In Proceedings of the SIGCHI conference on Human Factors in Computing Systems. New York, NY: ACM, pp. 80–87.

Fornell, C. & Lacker, D. (1981). Evaluating structural equation model with unobservable variable and measurement error. *Journal of Marketing Research*, 18(1), 39–50.

Fox, S., & Duggan, M. (2013). Health online 2013. *Health*, 2013, 1–55.

Frey, R., Wörner, D., & Ilic, A. (2016). Collaborative Filtering on the Blockchain: A Secure Recommender System for e-Commerce.

Gabora, L. (2013). Psychology of Creativity. *Encyclopedia of Creativity, Invention, Innovation, and Entrepreneurship*, 1515–1520.

Garcia, C., Amador Ayala, J., Diaz Roldan, K., & Bavarian, N. (2022). Exploring Reddit conversations about mental health difficulties among college students during the COVID-19 pandemic. *Journal of American College Health*, 1–7.

Gartner. (2019). 6 technologies on the Gartner hype cycle for digital marketing and advertising. https://www.gartner.com/en/marketing/insights/articles/6-technologies-on-gartner-hype-cycle-fordigital-marketingand-advertising-2019.

Gawron, L. M., & Turok, D. K. (2015). Pills on the World Wide Web: Reducing barriers through technology. *American Journal of Obstetrics and Gynecology*, 213(4), 500–e1.

Geer, D. How blockchain willtransform the e-commerce industry over the next few years. *The Next Web*, 18-Jun-2018. [Online]. Available: https://thenextweb.com/contributors/2018/06/15/how-blockchain-will-transform-the-e-commerce-industry-over-the-next-few-years/. [Accessed: 24-March-2020].

Gefen, D. (2000). E-commerce: The role of familiarity and trust, services selling: an interpersonal influence perspective. *Omega*, 28(6), 725–737.

Gefen, D., & Straub, D. (2003). Managing user trust in B2C e-services. *E-service Journal*, 2(2), 7–24.

Gefen, D., & Straub, D. W. (2004). Consumer trust in B2C eCommerce and the importance of social presence: Experiments in e-Products and e-Services. *Omega*, 32(6), 407–424.

Gefen, D., Karahanna, E., & Straub, D. W. (2003). Trust and TAM in online shopping: An integrated model. *MIS Quarterly*, 27(1), 51. 10.2307/30036519

Gerlich, M. (2023). The power of virtual influencers: Impact on consumer behaviour and attitudes in the age of AI. *Administrative Sciences*, 13(178), 1–21.

Gevaert, M., Carman, M., Rosman, B., Georgiadou, Y., & Soden, R. (2021). Fairness and accountability of AI in disaster risk management: Opportunities and challenges. *Patterns*, 2(11).

Ghafari, M., Nadi, T., Bahadivand-Chegini, S., & Doosti-Irani, A. (2022). Global prevalence of unmet need for mental health care among adolescents: A systematic review and meta-analysis. *Archives of Psychiatric Nursing*, 36, 1–6.

Gilbert, R. L., & Forney, A. (2015). Can avatars pass the Turing test? Intelligent agent perception in a 3D virtual environment. *International Journal of Human-Computer Studies*, 73(2), 30–36.

Glauner, P. (2020). Unlocking the power of artificial intelligence for your business. *Innovative Technologies for Market Leadership: Investing in the Future*, 45–59.

Gleim, M. R., & Stevens, J. L. (2021). Blockchain: A game changer for marketers? *Marketing Letters*, 32, 123–128. 10.1007/s11002-021-09557-9

Gnewuch, U., Morana, S., & Maedche, A. (2017). Towards designing cooperative and social agents for customer service. Proceedings of the 38th International Conference on Information Systems (ICIS). Seoul.

Gnewuch, U., Morana, S., Adam, M. T. P., & Maedche, A. (2022). Opposing Effects of Response Time in Human–Chatbot Interaction. *Business and Information Systems Engineering*.

Go, E., & Sundar, S. S. (2019). Humanizing Chatbots: The effects of visual, identity and conversational cues on humanness perceptions. *Computers in Human Behavior*, 97(1), 304–316.

Gonzalez, S. M., Gidumal, G. B., & Tano, D. G. (2019). Predicting the intentions to use chatbots for travel and tourism. *Current Issues in Tourism*, 24(2), 192–210.

Gonzalez-Hernandez, G., Sarker, A., O′Connor, K., & Savova, G. (2017). Capturing the patient's perspective: A review of advances in natural language processing of health-related text. *Yearbook of Medical Informatics*, 26(01), 214–227.

Gordini, N. & Veglio, V. (Apr. 2017). Customers churn prediction and marketing retention strategies. An application of support vector machines based on the AUC parameter-selection technique in B2B e-commerce industry. *Industrial Marketing Management*, 62, 100–107. 10.1016/j.indmarman.2016.08.003

Górriz, J. M., Álvarez-Illán, I., Álvarez-Marquina, A., Arco, J. E., Atzmueller, M., Ballarini, F., ... & Ferrández-Vicente, J. M. (2023). Computational approaches to explainable artificial intelligence: Advances in theory, applications and trends. *Information Fusion*, 100, 101945.

Goyal, A., Thakur, R., & Srivastava, M. (2013). Customer usage intention of mobile commerce in India: An empirical study. *Journal of Indian Business Research*, 5(1), 52–72.

Gozalo-Brizuela, R., & Garrido-Merchan, E. C. (2023). ChatGPT is not all you need. A State of the Art Review of large Generative AI models. 10.48550/ARXIV.2301.04655

Gratch, J., Wang, N., Gerten, J., Fast, E., & Duffy, R. (2007). Creating rapport with virtual agents. In *Intelligent Virtual Agents: 7th International Conference, IVA 2007 Paris, France*, September 17–19, 2007 Proceedings 7 (pp. 125–138). Springer Berlin Heidelberg.

Gray, K., & Wegner, D. M. (2012). Feeling robots and human zombies: Mind perception and the uncanny valley. *Cognition*, 125(1), 125–130.

Grewal, D., Herhausen, D., Ludwig, S., & Ordenes, F. V. (2022). The future of digital communication research: Considering dynamics and multimodality. *Journal of Retailing*, 98(2), 224–240.

Griol, D., Molina, J. M., & De Miguel, A. S. (2014). Developing multimodal conversational agents for an enhanced e-learning experience. *Advances in Distributed Computing and Artificial Intelligence Journal*, 3(1), 13–26.

Guan, Y., Wei, Q., & Chen, G. (Mar. 2019). Deep learning based personalized recommendation with multi-view information integration. *Decision Support Systems*, 118, 58–69. 10.1016/j.dss.2019.01.003

Guliyeva, K. (2021). History, methodology and hypothesis of artificial intelligence. *China-USA Business Review*, 20(4), 167–176.

Güngör, H. (2020). Creating value with artificial intelligence: A multi-stakeholder perspective. *Journal of Creating Value*, 6(1), 72–85. 10.1177/2394964320921071

Gunning, D., Vorm, E., Wang, Y., & Turek, M. DARPA's Explainable AI (XAI) program: A retrospective," Preprints, preprint, Nov. 2021. doi: 10.22541/au.163699841.19031727/v1.

Gupta, D. (2023, June 9). Top 10 Ways AI in Education is Transforming the Industry retrieved from Appinventiv (https://appinventiv.com/blog/10-ways-artificial-intelligence-transforming-the-education-industry/

Guthrie, C., Fosso-Wamba, S., & Arnaud, J. B. (2021). Online consumer resilience during a pandemic: An exploratory study of e-commerce behavior before, during and after a COVID-19 lockdown. *Journal of Retailing and Consumer Services*, 61, 102570.

Ha, S., & Stoel, L. (2009). Consumer e-shopping acceptance: Antecedents in a technology acceptance model. *Journal of Business Research*, 62(5), 565–571.

Ha, H., John, J., Janda, S., & Muthaly, S. (Apr. 2011). The effects of advertising spending on brand loyalty in services. *European Journal of Marketing*, 45(4), 673–691. 10.1108/03090561111111389

Haenlein, M., & Kaplan, A. (2019). A brief history of artificial intelligence: On the past, present, and future of artificial intelligence. *California Management Review*, 61(4), 5–14.

Hagger, M. S., & Hamilton, K. (2022). Social cognition theories and behavior change in COVID-19: A conceptual review. *Behaviour Research and Therapy*, 154, 104095.

Hair, J. F. Jr, Sarstedt, M., Ringle, C. M., & Gudergan, S. P. (2017). *Advanced issues in partial least squares structural equation modeling*. Thousand Oaks, CA: Sage Publications.

Hair, J. F., Black, W. C., Babin, B. J., Anderson, R. E., & Tatham, R. L. (2010). *Multivariate data analysis.* Upper Saddle River, New Jersey: Pearson.

Haleem, A., Javaid, M., Qadri, M. A., Singh, R. P., & Suman, R. (2022). Artificial intelligence (AI) applications for marketing: A literature-based study. *International Journal of Intelligent Networks*, 3, 119–132.

Haman, M., & Školník, M. (2023). Using ChatGPT to conduct a literature review. *Accountability in Research.* 10.1080/08989621.2023.218551406917733847

Hamani, J., Chalghaf, N., Maaloul, H., & Azaiez, F. (2013). The exam cheating among Tunisian students of the higher institute of sport and physical education of Sfax. *IOSR Journal of Humanities and Social Science*, 15(6), 90–95.

Hammen, C. (2005). Stress and depression. *Annual Review of Clinical Psychology*, 1(1), 293–319.

Han, M. C. (2021). The impact of anthropomorphism on consumers' purchase decision in chatbot commerce. *Journal of Internet Commerce*, 20(1), 46–65.

Han, M. C., & Kim, Y. (2020). Chatbot commerce: Hype ou Revolution. *Pan Pacific Journal of Business Research*, 11(2), 30–45.

Han, J-W., Park, J., & Lee, H. (2022). Analysis of the effect of an artificial intelligence chatbot educational program on non-face-to-face classes: A quasi-experimental study. *BMC Medical Education*, 22(1), 1–10.

Hardt, E., Price, E. P., & Srebro, N. (2016). Equality of Opportunity in Supervised Learning. In *Advances in Neural Information Processing Systems*, Curran Associates, Inc. Accessed: Sep. 24, 2023. [Online]. Available: https://proceedings.neurips.cc/paper_files/paper/2016/hash/9d2682367c3935defcb1f9e247a97c0d-Abstract.html

Haripriya, V., & Patil, P. G. (2017). A survey of sarcasm detection in social media. *International Journal for Research in Applied Science & Engineering Technology*, 5(12), 1748–1753.

Haripriya, V., & Patil, P. G. (2019). Detection of sarcasm from consumer sentiments on social media about luxury brands. In Recent Trends in Image Processing and Pattern Recognition: Second International Conference, RTIP2R 2018, Solapur, India, December 21–22, 2018, Revised Selected Papers, Part III 2 (pp. 652–667).

Harms, B. (2013). Customer service in higher education: Adult-focused student services. *Converge Consulting: A Higher Ecucation Magazine*. Available from www.academicimpression.comUSA

Harrigan, P., Daly, M. T., Coussement, K., Lee, J. A., Soutar, G., & Evers, U. (2021). Identifying influencers on social media. *International Journal of Information Management*, 56(2021), 1–11.

Hart, P., & Saunders, C. (1997). Power and trust: Critical factors in the adoption and use of electronic data interchange. *Organization Science*, 8(1), 23–42.

Hassanein, K., & Head, M. (2005). The impact of infusing social presence in the web interface: An investigation across product types. *International Journal of Electronic Commerce*, 10(2), 31–55.

Hassanein, K., & Head, M. (2007). Manipulating perceived social presence through the web interface and its impact on attitude towards online shopping. *International Journal of Human-Computer Studies*, 65(8), 689–708.

Hassanein, K., Head, M., & Ju, C. (2009). A cross-cultural comparison of the impact of social presence on website trust, usefulness and enjoyment. *International Journal of Electronic Business*, 7(6), 625.

Hatwar, P. N., Patil, A., & Gondane, D. (2016). AI based chatbot. *International Journal of Emerging Trends in Engineering and Basic Sciences*, 6(2), 85–87.

He, X., Liao, L., Zhang, H., Nie, L., Hu, X., & Chua, T.-S. (Apr. 2017). Neural Collaborative Filtering. In *Proceedings of the 26th International Conference on World Wide Web*, Perth Australia: International World Wide Web Conferences Steering Committee, pp. 173–182. doi: 10.1145/3038912.3052569.

Heerink, M., Krose, B., Evers, V., & Wielinga, B. (2010). Assessing acceptance of assistive social agent technology by older adults: The Almere model. *International Journal of Social Robotics*, 2(4), 361–375.

Hinkin, T. R. (1995). A review of scale development practices in the study of organizations. *Journal of Management*, 21(5), 967–988.

Hipólito, I., Winkle, K., & Lie, M. (2023). Enactive artificial intelligence: Subverting gender norms in human-robot interaction. *Frontiers in Neurorobotics*, 17 (1149303), 1–11.

Hoff, K. A., & Bashir, M. (2015). Trust in automation: Integrating empirical evidence on factors that influence trust. *Human Factors*, 57(3), 407–434.

Hoffman, A. M. (2005). The Capability Approach and educational policies and strategies: Effective life skills education for sustainable development, 1–10.

Hoffman, D. L., Novak, T. P., & Peralta, M. A. (1999). Information privacy in the market space: Implications for the commercial uses of anonymity on the web. *Information Society*, 15(2), 129–139.

Hofmann, E., Strewe, U. M., & Bosia, N. (2017). *Supply chain finance and blockchain technology: The case of reverse securitisation*. Springer.

Hogan, E. A. (Nov. 2001). The attention economy: Understanding the new currency of Business. *Academy of Management Perspectives*, 15(4), 145–147. 10.5465/ame.2001.5898765

Holmes, E. A., O'Connor, R. C., Perry, V. H., Tracey, I., Wessely, S., Arseneault, L., ... & Bullmore, E. (2020). Multidisciplinary research priorities for the COVID-19 pandemic: A call for action for mental health science. *The Lancet Psychiatry*, 7(6), 547–560.

Holtbrügge, D. (2020, 1 23). Blockchain technology in international business. Changing the agenda for global governance. *Review of International Business and Strategy*, 17–18.

Hoy, W. K., & Tschannen-Moran, M. (1999). Five faces of trust: An empirical confirmation in urban elementary schools. *Journal of School Leadership*, 9(3), 184–208. https://www.academia.edu/45061452/Insights_about_developing_learners_autonomy_in_Tunisia

Hsu, M.-H., Chang, C.-M., & Chuang, L.-W. (Feb. 2015). Understanding the determinants of online repeat purchase intention and moderating role of habit: The case of online group-buying in Taiwan. *International Journal of Information Management*, 35(1), 45–56. 10.1016/j.ijinfomgt.2014.09.002

Hua, Y., Cheng, X., Hou, T., & Luo, R. (2020). Monetary rewards, intrinsic motivators, and work engagement in the IT-enabled sharing economy: A mixed-methods investigation of internet taxi drivers. *Decision Sciences*, 51(3), 755–785.

Huang, M. H., & Rust, R. T. (2021). A strategic framework for artificial intelligence in marketing. *Journal of the Academy of Marketing Science*, 49(1), 30–50.

Huang, M. H., & Rust, R. T. (2022). A framework for collaborative artificial intelligence in marketing. *Journal of Retailing*, 98(2), 209–223. 10.1016/j.jretai.2021.03.001

Hubert, M., Blut, M., Brock, C., Backhaus, C., & Eberhardt, T. (2017). Acceptance of smartphone-based mobile shopping: Mobile benefits, customer characteristics, perceived risk and the impact of application context. *Psychology and Marketing*, 34(2), 175–194.

Hubert, M., Blut, M., Brock, C., Zhang, R. W., Koch, V., & Riedl, R. (2019). The influence of acceptance and adoption drivers on smart home usage. *European Journal of Marketing*, 53(6), 1073–1098. 10.1108/EJM-12-2016-0794

Huh, Y. E., & Kim, S. H. (2008). Do early adopters upgrade early? Role of post-adoption behavior in the purchase of next-generation products. *Journal of Business Research*, 61(1), 40–46.

Huisman, M., Joye, S., & Biltereyst, D. (2020). Searching for health: Doctor Google and the shifting dynamics of the middle-aged and older adult patient–physician relationship and interaction. *Journal of Aging and Health*, 32(9), 998–1007.

Hwang, K. O., Ottenbacher, A., Green, A. P., Cannon-Diehl, M. R., Richardson, O., Bernstam, E. V., & Thomas, E. J. (2010). Social support in an Internet weight loss community. *International Journal of Medical Informatics*, 79(1), 5–13.

India AI Report. (2022). Retrieved from https://www2.ed.gov/documents/ai-report/ai-report.pdf. University of Denver. Retrieved from https://news.gsu.edu/2022/03/21/classroom-chatbot-improves-student-performance-study-says/

Ingrid, R. (2003). The capability approach: an interdisciplinary introduction, 1–54.

Iskender, A. (2023). Holy or Unholy? Interview with Open AI's ChatGPT. *European Journal of Tourism Research*, 34, 1–11.

Iwata, T. (2013). Teacher's autonomy and students' creativity. Doctoral dissertation, University of Georgia.

Jackson, R. L., Drummond, D. K., & Camara, S. (2007). What is qualitative research. *Qualitative Research Reports in Communication*, 8(1), 21–28.

Jacoby, J., & Kaplan, L. B. (1972). The components of perceived risk. ACR special volumes.

Jain, V. H., Tadv, S. A., & Pawar, S. P. (2017). A review on the pros and cons of online pharmacies. *Journal of Applied Pharmaceutical Research*, 5(1), 20–26.

Jain, D., Dash, M. K., Kumar, A., & Luthra, S. (2021). How is Blockchain used in marketing: A review and research agenda. *International Journal of Information Management Data Insights*, 1(2). 10.1016/j.jjimei.2021.100044

Jairoun, A. A., Al-Hemyari, S. S., Abdulla, N. M., El-Dahiyat, F., Jairoun, M., & Al-Tamimi, S. K. (2021). Online medication purchasing during the Covid-19 pandemic: Potential risks to patient safety and the urgent need to develop more rigorous controls for purchasing online medications, a pilot study from the United Arab Emirates. *Journal of Pharmaceutical Policy and Practice*, 14.

Jamshed, S. (2014). Qualitative research method-interviewing and observation. *Journal of Basic and Clinical Pharmacy*, 5(4), 87–88.
Jarek, K., & Mazurek, G. (2019). Marketing and artificial intelligence. *Central European Business Review*, 8(2), 46–55. 10.18267/j.cebr.213
Jarvenpaa, S. L., Tractinsky, N., & Saarinen, L. (1999). Consumer trust in an Internet store: A cross-cultural validation. *Journal of Computer-Mediated Communication*, 5(2), 1–33.
Järvinen, J., & Karjaluoto, H. (Oct. 2015). The use of Web analytics for digital marketing performance measurement. *Industrial Marketing Management*, 50, 117–127. 10.1016/j.indmarman.2015.04.009
Jatobá, M., Santos, J., Gutierriz, I., Moscon, D., Fernandes, P. O., & Teixeira, J. P. (2019). Evolution of artificial intelligence research in human resources. *Procedia Computer Science*, 164, 137–142. 10.1016/j.procs.2019.12.165
Javadi, M. H. M., Dolatabadi, H. R., Nourbakhsh, M., Poursaeedi, A., & Asadollahi, A. R. (2012). An analysis of factors affecting on online shopping behavior of consumers. *International Journal of Marketing Studies*, 4(5), 81.
Javaid, M., Haleem, A., Vaish, A., Vaishya, R., & Iyengar, K. P. (2020), Robotics applications in COVID-19: A review. *Journal of Industrial Integration and Management*, 5(4), 441–451.
Jeko, N. A. (2014). Prospects of online medicine business in Bangladesh. *International Journal of Scientific & Technology Research*, 3(11), 236–240.
Jhanwar, M. G., & Pudi, V. Predicting the Outcome of ODI Cricket Matches: A Team Composition Based Approach.
Jiang, C. (2022). La fabrique des fembots pop stars: Participation, co-création ou exploitation culturelle en ligne? *Journal of Arts and Human Mediators*, 8, 1–14.
Jiang, C., Rashid, R. M., & Wang, J. (2019). Investigating the role of social presence dimensions and information support on consumers' trust and shopping intentions. *Journal of Retailing and Consumer Services*, 51(2), 263–270.
Joulin, Grave, E., Bojanowski, P., & Mikolov, T. (2016). Bag of Tricks for Efficient Text Classification. 10.48550/ARXIV.1607.01759
Journal of Responsible Technology, Vol. 13, pp. 1–4.
Kabra, G., Ramesh, A., Akhtar, P., & Dash, M. K. (2017). Understanding behavioural intention to use information technology: Insights from humanitarian practitioners. *Telematics and Informatics*, 34(7), 1250–1261.
Kahneman, D., Tversky, A., & Tversky, A. (1979). Prospect theory: An analysis of decision under risk. *Econometrica*, 47(2), 263–292.
Kalla, L. (2022). Virtual influencers: A challenge to trust and authenticity. *MA Applied Ethics for Professionals*, 1–87.
Kang, L., Wang, X., Hoo Tan, C., & et Zhao, L. (2015). Understanding the antecedents and consequences of live chat use in electronic markets. *Journal of Organizational Computing and Electronic Commerce*, 25(2), 117–139.
Kapadia, K., Abdel Jaber, H., Thabtah, F., & Hadi, W. Sport analytics for cricket game results using machine learning: An experimental study.
Kaplan, A., & Haenlein, M. (2019). Siri, Siri, in my hand: Who's the fairest in the land? On the interpretations, illustrations, and implications of artificial intelligence. *Business Horizons*, 62(1), 15–25.
Kaplan, A., & Haenlein, M. (2019). Rulers of the world, unite! The challenges and opportunities of artificial intelligence. *Business Horizons*, 63(1).
Kasilingam, D. L. (2020). Understanding the attitude and intention to use smartphone chatbots for shopping. *Technology in Society*, 62, 101280. 10.1016/j.techsoc.2020.101280
Kasinathan, G. (2019). Making AI Work for Indian Education. *IT for Change*. Retrieved from https://itforchange.net/sites/default/files/1664/Making-AI-Work-for-Indian-Education.pdf
Katsuki, T., Mackey, T. K., & Cuomo, R. (2015). Establishing a link between prescription drug abuse and illicit online pharmacies: Analysis of Twitter data. *Journal of Medical Internet Research*, 17(12), e280.
Kelley, S. W., & Davis, M. A. (1994). Antecedents to customer expectations for service recovery. *Journal of the Academy of Marketing Science*, 22(21), 52–61.
Kesharwani, A., & Bisht, S. S. (2012). The impact of trust and perceived risk on Internet banking adoption in India: An extension of technology acceptance model. *International Journal of Bank Marketing*, 30(4), 303–322.
Khanna, A., Pandey, B., Vashishta, K., Kalia, K., Pradeepkumar, B., & Das, T. (2015). A study of today's A.I. through chatbots and rediscovery of machine intelligence. *International Journal of u- and e-Service, Science and Technology*, 8(7), 277–284.

Khanra, S., Dhir, A., Islam, A. K. M. N., & Mäntymäki, M. (Aug. 2020). Big data analytics in healthcare: A systematic literature review. *Enterprise Information Systems*, 14(7), 878–912. 10.1080/17517575.2020.1812005

Khoshtaria, T., Datuashvili, D., & Matin, A. (2020). The impact of brand equity dimensions on university reputation: An empirical study of Georgian higher education. *Journal of Marketing for Higher Education*, 30(2), 239–255.

Khurana, D., Koli, A., Khatter, K., & Singh, S. (Jan. 2023). Natural language processing: State of the art, current trends and challenges. *Multimedia Tools and Applications*, 82(3), 3713–3744. 10.1007/s11042-022-13428-4

Kietzmann, J., & Pitt, L. F. (2020). Artificial intelligence and machine learning: What managers need to know. *Business Horizon*, 63(2), 131–133. 10.1016/j.bushor.2019.11.005

Kilteni, K., Groten, R., & Slater, M. (2012). The sense of embodiment in virtual reality, Presence teleoperators, and virtual environments, 21(4), 374–385.

Kim, K. J. (2016). Interacting socially with the Internet of Things (IoT): Effects of source attribution and specialization in human-IoT interaction. *Journal of Computer-Mediated Communication*, 21(6), 420–435.

Kim, D. J., Ferrin, D. L., &. Rao, Choudhury, M. (2015). Detecting Changes in SuicideH. R. (2008). A trust-based consumer decision-making model in electronic commerce: The role of trust, perceived risk, and their antecedents. *Decision Support System*, 44(2), 544–564.

Kim, C., Mirusmonov, M., & Lee, I. (2010). An empirical examination of factors influencing the intention to use mobile payment. *Computers in Human Behavior*, 26(3), 310–322.

Kim, M. J., Lee, C. K., & Jung, T. (2013). Exploring consumer behavior in virtual reality tourism using an extended stimulus-organism-response model. *Journal of Travel Research*, 59(1), 69–89.

Kim, D. Y., Park, M., & Kim, H.-Y. (2022). An influencer like me: Examining the impact of the social status of Influencers. *Journal of Marketing Communications*, 1–22.

Kim, J., Lee, J., Park, E., & Han, J. (2020). A deep learning model for detecting mental illness from user content on social media. *Scientific Reports*, 10(1), 11846.

Kireyev, Pauwels, K., & Gupta, S. (Sep. 2016). Do display ads influence search? Attribution and dynamics in online advertising. *International Journal of Research in Marketing*, 33(3), 475–490. 10.1016/j.ijresmar.2015.09.007

Koren, Y., Bell, R., & Volinsky, C. (Aug. 2009). Matrix factorization techniques for recommender systems. *Computer*, 42(8), 30–37. 10.1109/MC.2009.263

Korir, D. K., & Kipkemboi, F. (2014). The impact of school environment and peer influences on students' academic performance in Vihiga County, Kenya. *International Journal of Humanities and Social Science*, 4(11), 1–12.

Koufaris, M. (2002). Applying the technology acceptance model and flow theory to online consumer behavior. *Information Systems Research*, 13(2), 205–223.

Kramer, N. C., Bente, G., Eschenburg, F., & Troitzsch, H. (2009). Embodied conversational agents. *Social Psychology*, 40(1), 26–36.

Krief, N., & Zardet, F. (2013). Analyse de données qualitatives et recherche-intervention. *Recherches en Sciences de Gestion*, 95(2), 211–237.

Kuang, Jiang, M., Cui, P., Luo, H., & Yang, S. (Dec. 2018). Effective promotional strategies selection in social media: A data-driven approach. *IEEE Transactions on Big Data*, 4(4), 487–501. 10.1109/TBDATA.2017.2734102

kuhumba, S. K. (2018). Amartya Sen's capability approach as theoretical foundation of human development. *Journal of Sociology and Development*, 1(1), 127–145.

Kumar, V., & Reinartz, W. (Nov. 2016). Creating enduring customer value. *Journal of Marketing*, 80(6), 36–68. 10.1509/jm.15.0414

Kumar, M., Dredze, M., Coppersmith, G., & De Choudhury, M. (2015). Detecting Changes in Suicide Content Manifested in Social Media Following Celebrity Suicides. *In Proceedings of the 26th ACM Conference on Hypertext & Social Media* (pp. 85–94).

Kumar, V., Rajan, B., Venkatesan, R., & Lecinski, J. (2019). Understanding the role of artificial intelligence in personalized engagement marketing. *California Management Review*, 61(4), 135–155.

Kung, T. H., Cheatham, M., Medenilla, A., Sillos, C., De Leon, L., Elepaño, C., Madriaga, M., Aggabao, R., Diaz-Candido, G., Maningo, J., & Tseng, V. (2022). Performance of ChatGPT on USMLE: Potential for AI assisted medical education using large language models. *PLoS Digital Health*, 2(2). 10.1101/2022.12.19.2

Kuo, P.-H., et al. (2021). Multi-sensor context-aware based chatbot model: An application of humanoid companion robot. *Sensors*, 21(15), 5132.

Kwak, E. S., & Chang, H. (2016). Medical representatives' intention to use information technology in pharmaceutical marketing. *Healthcare Informatics Research*, 22(4), 342–350.

Lagerwerf, L. (2007). Irony and sarcasm in advertisements: Effects of relevant inappropriateness. *Journal of Pragmatics*, 39(10), 1702–1721.

Lai, V., & Li, H. (2005). Technology acceptance model for Internet banking: An invariance analysis. *Information & Management*, 42(2), 373–386.

Lake, L. (2016). What is a Target Audience? The Balance [accessed 23 April 2023]. Available at: https://www.thebalance.com/what-is-a-targetaudience-2295567

Lapina, I., Roga, R., & Müürsepp, P. (2016). Quality of higher education: International students' satisfaction and learning experience. *International Journal of Quality and Service Sciences*, 8(3), 263–278.

Lari, H. A., Vaishnava, K., & Manu, K. S. (2022). Artificial intelligence in E-commerce: Applications, implications and challenges. *Asian Journal of Management*, 13(3), 235–244.

Lasek, M., & Jessa, S. (2013). Chatbots for customer services on hotel websites. *Information Systems in Management*, 2(2), 146–158.

Latifi, S., Zhang, Y., & Cheng, L. C. (2019). Blockchain-Based Real Estate Market: One Method for Applying Blockchain Technology in Commercial Real Estate Market. IEEE International Conference on Blockchain, Atlanta, GA, USA, pp. 528–535, 10.1109/Blockchain.2019.00002

Latinovic, Z., & Chatterjee, S. C. (2022). Achieving the promise of AI and ML in delivering economic and relational customer value in B2B. *Journal of Business Research*, 144, 966–974.

Laukkanen, T. (2016). Consumer adoption versus rejection decisions in seemingly similar service innovations: The case of the Internet and mobile banking. *Journal of Business Research*, 69(7), 2432–2439.

Lean, M. C. G., & Osei-Frimpong, K. (2019). Hey, Alexa examine the variables influencing the use of artificial intelligent in-home voice assistants. *Computers in Human Behavior*, 99, 28–37.

Lee, M. C. (2009). Factors influencing the adoption of Internet banking: An integration of TAM and TPB with perceived risk and perceived benefit. *Electronic Commerce Research and Applications*, 8(3), 130–141.

Lee, S., & Dubinsky, A. (2003). Influence of salesperson characteristics and customer emotion on retail dyadic relationships. *International Review of Retail Distribution and Consumer Research*, 13(1), 21–36.

Lee, J. D., & See, K. A. (2004). Trust in automation: Designing for appropriate Reliance. *Human Factors: The Journal of the Human Factors and Ergonomics Society*, 46(1), 50 80. 10.1518/hfes.46.1.50_30392

Lee, K. M., & Nass, C. (2004). The multiple source effect and synthesized speech: Doubly-disembodied language as a conceptual framework. *Human Communication Research*, 30(2), 182–207.

Lee, S. M., & Lee, D. (2020). Untact: A new customer service strategy in the digital age. *Service Business*, 14, 1–22.

Lee, Y. H., & Yuan, C. H. (2023). I'm not a puppet, I'm a real boy! Gender presentations by virtual influencers and how they are received. *Computers in Human Behavior*, 149.

Lee, Y.-C., Yamashita, N., & Huang, Y. (2020). Designing a chatbot as a mediator for promoting deep self-disclosure to a real mental health professional. *Proceedings of the ACM on Human-Computer Interaction*, 4,1–27.

Les echos. (2016, 10 31). Comment la blockchain bouscule le financement du commerce international. *Consulté le*, 6(13), 2022, sur les schos: https://business.lesechos.fr/directions-financieres/financementet-operations/credits/0211438436771-comment-la-blockchain-bouscule-le-financement-du-commerceinternational- 301708.php

Leszkiewicz, A., Hormann, T., & Krafft, M. (2021). Smart business and the social value of AI. *Smart Business and Better Management*.

Li, H. (Alice), & Kannan, P. K. (Feb. 2014). Attributing conversions in a multichannel online marketing environment: An empirical model and a field experiment. *Journal of Marketing Research*, 51(1), 40–56. 10.1509/jmr.13.0050

Li, M., & Mao, J. (2015). Hedonic or utilitarian? Exploring the impact of communication style alignment on user's perception of virtual health advisory services. *International Journal of Information Management*, 35(2), 229–243.

Li, D., Chau, P. Y. K., & Lou, H. (2005). Understanding individual adoption of instant messaging: An empirical investigation. *Journal of the Association for Information Systems*, 6(4), 102–129.

Li, X., Wu, C., & Mai, F. (Mar. 2019). The effect of online reviews on product sales: A joint sentiment-topic analysis. *Information & Management*, 56(2), 172–184. 10.1016/j.im.2018.04.007
Li, W., Yang, Y., Liu, Z. H., Zhao, Y. J., Zhang, Q., Zhang, L., … & Xiang, Y. T. (2020). Progression of mental health services during the COVID-19 outbreak in China. *International Journal of Biological Sciences*, 16(10), 1732.
Liang, B. A., & Mackey, T. K. (2011). Prevalence and global health implications of social media in direct-to-consumer drug advertising. *Journal of Medical Internet Research*, 13(3), e1775.
Lies, J. (2019). Marketing intelligence and big data: Digital marketing techniques on their way to becoming social engineering techniques in marketing. *International Journal of Interactive Multimedia and Artificial Intelligence*, 5(5), 134–144.
Ling, E. C., Tussyadiah, I., Tuomi, A., Stienmetz, J., & Ioannou, A. (2021). Factors influencing users' adoption and use of conversational agents: A systematic review. *Psychology & Marketing*, 38, 1031–1051. 10.1002/mar.21491
Liu, Q., Yu, F., Wu, S., & Wang, L. (Oct. 2015). A Convolutional Click Prediction Model. In *Proceedings of the 24th ACM International on Conference on Information and Knowledge Management*, Melbourne Australia: ACM, pp. 1743–1746. doi: 10.1145/2806416.2806603.
Liu, M., Cai, S., Lai, Z., Qiu, L., Hu, Z., & Ding, Y. (Jul. 2021). A joint learning model for click-through prediction in display advertising. *Neurocomputing*, 445, 206–219. 10.1016/j.neucom.2021.02.036
Lombard, M., & Ditton, T. (1997). At the heart of it all: The concept of presence. *Journal of Computer-Mediated Communication*, 3(2), 1–43.
Long, C. S., Kumaran, H., Goh, K. W., Bakrin, F. S., Ming, L. C., Rehman, I. U., … & Tan, C. S. (2022). Online pharmacies selling prescription drugs: Systematic review. *Pharmacy*, 10(2), 42.
Lorne, F. T., Daram, S., Frantz, R., Kumar, N., Mohammed, A., Muley, A. (2018). Blockchain economics and marketing. *Journal of Computer and Communications*, 6, 107–117. 10.4236/jcc.2018.612011
Low, D. M., Rumker, L., Talkar, T., Torous, J., Cecchi, G. A., & Ghosh, S. (2020). Natural language processing reveals vulnerable mental health support groups and heightened health anxiety on Reddit during COVID-19: Observational study. *Journal of Medical Internet Research*, 22(10), e22635.
Lu, J. B., Fan, W., & Zhou, M. (2016). Social presence, trust, and social commerce purchase intention: An empirical research. *Computers in Human Behavior*, 56, 225–237.
Luo, X., Tong, S., Fang, Z. & Qu, Z. (2019). Frontiers: Machines vs humans: The impact of artificial intelligence chatbot disclosure on customer purchases. *Marketing Science*, 38(6), 937–947.
Luo, X., Qin, M. S., Fang, Z., & Qu, Z. (2021). Artificial intelligence coaches for sales agents: Caveats and solutions. *Journal of Marketing*, 85(2), 14–32.
Ma, Y., & Siau, K. L. (2018). Artificial Intelligence Impacts on Higher Education. Proceedings of the Thirteenth Midwest Association for Information Systems Conference, Saint Louis, Missouri May, pp. 1–5.
MacDorman, K. F. (2019). In the uncanny valley, transportation predicts narrative enjoyment more than empathy, but only for the tragic hero. *Computers in Human Behavior*, 94, 140–153. 10.1016/j.chb.2019.01.011.
Machin, J. E., Brister, T., Bossarte, R. M., Drenten, J., Hill, R. P., Holland, D. L., … & Ross Adkins, N. (2022). Conversations about conducting marketing research in mental health. *Journal of Consumer Marketing*, 39(6), 569–578.
Macintosh, G., & Lockshin, L. S. (1997). Retail relationships and store loyalty: A multi-level perspective. *International Journal of Research in Marketing*, 14(5), 487–497.
Mackey, T. K., & Nayyar, G. (2016). Digital danger: A review of the global public health, patient safety and cybersecurity threats posed by illicit online pharmacies. *British Medical Bulletin*, 118(1), 110–126.
Mackey, T. K., & Nayyar, G. (2017). A review of existing and emerging digital technologies to combat the global trade in fake medicines. *Expert Opinion on Drug Safety*, 16(5), 587–602.
Mackey, T., Kalyanam, J., Klugman, J., Kuzmenko, E., & Gupta, R. (2018). Solution to detect, classify, and report illicit online marketing and sales of controlled substances via Twitter: Using machine learning and web forensics to combat digital opioid access. *Journal of Medical Internet Research*, 20(4), e10029.
Madara, D. S., Namango, S. S., & Katana, H. (2016). Theories and models relevant to cheating-behaviour. *Research on Humanities and Social Sciences*, 6(17), 108–139.
Mahapatra, D. M., Patra, S. K., & Baral, S. K. (2022). Unleashing the Potential of Artificial Intelligence (AI) in Customer Journey of Cognitive Marketing and Consciousness Intention in E-Commerce Websites. In 2nd International Conference on Sustainability and Equity (ICSE-2021), pp. 44–51. Atlantis Press.

Mahendiran, A., Saravanan, N., Subramanian, N., & Sairam, N. (2012). Implementation of K-means clustering in cloud computing environment. *Research Journal of Applied Sciences, Engineering and Technology*, 4(10), 1391–1394.

Malhotra, N. K., Nunan, D., & Birks, D. F. (2017). *Marketing research: An applied approach*. Harlow: Pearson, 976.

Mandal, S. (2017). The influence of organizational culture on healthcare supply chain resilience: Moderating role of technology orientation. *Journal of Business & Industrial Marketing*, 32(8), 1021–1037.

Manning, D., Raghavan, P., & Schütze, H. (2008). *Introduction to Information Retrieval*, 1st ed. Cambridge University Press. doi: 10.1017/CBO9780511809071.

Mansouri, M. (2018). L'intelligence artificielle et la publicité: Quelle éthique? *Enjeux numériques*, 1, 53–58.

Manzano, J. A., Navarre, C. L., Mafe, C. R., & Blas, S. S. (2009). Key drivers of Internet banking services use. *Online Information Review*, 33(4), 672–695.

Marcus, M. R., Mt, Y., Van Ommeren, M., Chisholm, D., Saxena, S., Yasamy, M. T., M, V. O., Van Ommeren, M., & Chrisholm, D. J. (2012). Depression: A global public health concern [Dataset]. In *PsycEXTRA Dataset*.

Marjerison, R. K., Zhang, Y., & Zheng, H. (2022). AI in e-commerce: Application of the use and gratification model to the acceptance of Chatbots. *Sustainability*, 14, 14270. 10.3390/su142114270

Marr, B. (2016). *Big data in practice: how 45 successful companies used big data analytics to deliver extraordinary results*. Chichester, West Sussex: Wiley.

Marr, B. (2019). *Artificial intelligence in practice: how 50 successful companies used AI and machine learning to solve problems*. John Wiley & Sons.

Marshall, C., Lanyi, K., Green, R., Wilkins, G., Pearson, F., & Craig, D. (2022). Using natural language processing to explore mental health insights from UK tweets during the COVID-19 pandemic: Infodemiology study. *JMIR Infodemiology*, 2(1), e32449.

Marthews, A., & Tucker, C. (2023). What blockchain can and can't do: Applications to marketing and privacy. *International Journal of Research in Marketing*, 40(1), 49–53. 10.1016/j.ijresmar.2022.09.001

Mathur, M. B., Reichling, D. B., Lunardini, F., Geminiani, A., Antonietti, A., Ruijten, P. A. M., Levitan, C. A., Nave, G., Manfredi, D., Bessette-Symons, B., Szuts, A., Aczel, B. (2020). Uncanny but not confusing: Multisite study of perceptual category confusion in the Uncanny Valley. *Computers in Human Behavior*, 103, 21–30. 10.1016/j.chb.2019.08.029

Matteson, M. L., Salamon, J., &. Brewster, L. (2011). A systematic review of research on live chat service. *Reference and User Services Quarterly*, 51(2), 172–189.

Mayer, R. C., Davis, J. H., & Schoorman, F. D. (1995). An integrative model of organizational trust. *The Academy of Management Review*, 20(3), 709–734.

McKenna, K. Y. A., Green, A. S., & Gleason, M. E. J. (2002). Relationship formation on the internet: What's the big attraction? *Journal of Social Issues*, 58(1), 9–31.

McKnight, D. H., Choudhury, V., & Kacmar, C. (2002). Developing and validating trust measures for e-commerce: An integrative typology. *Information Systems Research*, 13(3), 334–359. 10.1287/isre.13.3.334.81

McLean, G., & Osei-Frimpong, K. (2019a). Hey Alexa … examine the variables influencing the use of artificial intelligent in-home voice assistants. *Computers in Human Behavior*, 99, 28–37.

McLean, G., & Osei-Frimpong, K. (2019b). Chat now … Examining the variables influencing the use of online live chat. *Technological Forecasting and Social Change*, 146, 55–67.

McLeay, F., Robson, A., & Yusoff, M. (2017). New applications for importance-performance analysis (IPA) in higher education. *Journal of Management Development*, 36(6), 780–800. 10.1108/JMD-10-2016-018

McLeod, A., Pippin, S., & Mason, R. (2008). Individual taxpayer intention to use tax preparation software: Examining experience, trust, and perceived risk. In Proceedings of ISOneWorld Conference. June (Vol. 2, No. 4, p. 1).

McTear, M., Callejas, Z., & Griol, D. (2016). The conversational interface: Talking to smart devices. In *The Conversational Interface* (pp. 283–308). Springer.

Meni R. (2014). Analysis of hashrate-based double spending. *arXiv preprint arXiv:1402.2009.*

Messina, C. (2015). Conversational commerce. Retrieved from https://medium.com/chris-messina/conversational-commerce-92e0bccfc3f.

Micu, A., Capatina, A., & Eliza Micu, A. (2018). Exploring Artificial Intelligence Techniques' Applicability in Social Media Marketing. *Journal of Emerging Trends in Marketing and Management*, 156–165.

Miklosik, A., Kuchta, M., Evans, N., & Zak, S. (2019). Towards the adoption of machine learning-based analytical tools in digital marketing. *IEEE Access*, 7, 85705–85718. 10.1109/ACCESS.2019.2924425

Mimoun, M. S. B., & Poncin, I. (2015). A valued agent: How ECAs affect website customers' satisfaction and behaviors. *Journal of Retailing and Consumer Services*, 26, 70–82.

Miotto, R., Wang, F., Wang, S., Jiang, X., & Dudley, J. T. (2018). Deep learning for healthcare: Review, opportunities and challenges. *Briefings in Bioinformatics*, 19(6), 1236–1246.

Mirabito, A., Adkins, N. R., Crosby, E., Farrell, J., & Machin, J. (2022). Guest editorial: Mental health and the marketplace: A research agenda. *Journal of Consumer Marketing*, 39(6), 565–568.

Mishra, S., & Dey, A. K. (2022). Understanding and identifying 'themes' in qualitative case study research. *South Asian Journal of Business and Management Cases*, 11(3), 187–192.

Misischia, C. V., Poecze, F., & Strauss, C. (2022). Chatbots in customer service: Their relevance and impact on service quality, The 13th International Conference on Ambient Systems. *Network and Technologies*, 421–428.

Mitchell, V. (2018). Gartner: why humans will still be at the core of great CX. available at: https://www.cmo.com.au/article/642649/gartner-why-humans-will-still-core-great-cx/ (accessed 20 December 2022).

Mittal, U., & Sharma, M. (2021). Artificial Intelligence and its Application in Different Areas of Indian Economy. *International Journal of Advanced Research in Science, Communication and Technology*, 160–163.

Mogaji, E., & Yoon, H. (2019). Thematic analysis of marketing messages in UK universities' prospectuses. *International Journal of Educational Management*, 33(7), 1561–1581.

Mohammad, S. M., & Turney, P. D. (Aug. 2013). Crowdsourcing a word–emotion association lexicon. *Computational Intelligence*, 29(3), 436–465. 10.1111/j.1467-8640.2012.00460.x

Molin, V., & Nordgren, S. (2019). Robot or Human? – The marketing phenomenon of virtual influencers- A case study about virtual influencers' parasocial interaction on instagram, Master's Thesis 15 credits, Department of Business Studies, Uppsala University, 1–57.

Mollen, A., & Wilson, H. (2010). Engagement, telepresence and interactivity in online consumer experience: Reconciling scholastic and managerial perspectives. *Journal of Business Research*, 63(9-10), 919–925.

Momani, A. M., & Jamous, M. M. (2017). The evolution of technology acceptance theories. *International Journal of Contemporary Computer Research*, 1(1), 51–58.

Mooi, E., & Sarstedt, M. (2019). *A Concise Guide to Market Research*. Berlin, Heidelberg: Springer.

Moon, J., & Kim, Y. (2001). Extending the TAM for a WorldWideWeb context. *Information and Management*, 38(4), 217–230.

Moon, J. H., Kim, E., Choi, S. M., & Sung, Y. (2013). Keep the social in social media: The role of social interaction in avatar-based virtual shopping. *Journal of Interactive Advertising*, 13(1), 14–26.

Morgan, H. (2021). Howard Gardner's Multiple Intelligences Theory and his Ideas on Promoting Creativity. In F. Reisman (Ed.), *Celebrating Giants and Trailblazers: A-Z of Who's Who in Creativity Research and Related Fields*, pp.124–141.

Morgan, R. M., & Hunt, S. D. (1994). The commitment–trust theory of relationship marketing. *Journal of Marketing*, 58(3), 20–38.

Mori, M. (1970). Bukimi no tani [the uncanny valley]. *Energy*, 7(4), 33–35.

Mori, M., MacDorman, K. F., & Kageki, N. (2012). The uncanny valley [from the field]. *IEEE Robotics & Automation Magazine*, 19(2), 98–100.

Moriuchi, E. (2019). Okay, Google!: An empirical study on voice assistants on consumer engagement and loyalty. *Psychology and Marketing*, 36(2), 1–13.

Morrison, D. E., & Firmstone, J. (2000). The social functional of trust and implications for e-commerce. *International Journal of Advertising*, 19(5), 599–623.

Moukaddam, N., & Shah, A. A. (2020). Psychiatrists Beware! the impact of COVID-19 and pandemics on mental health. *The Psychiatric Times*, 37(3).

Moustakas, E., Lamba, N., Mahmoud, D., & Ranganathan, C. (2020). Blurring lines between fiction and reality: Perspectives of experts on marketing effectiveness of virtual Influencers. *International Journal on Cyber Situational Awareness*, 1–6.

Moyle, L., Childs, A., Coomber, R., & Barratt, M. J. (2019). Drugs for sale: An exploration of the use of social media and encrypted messaging apps to supply and access drugs. *International Journal of Drug Policy*, 63, 101–110.

MR, A. (2021). Artificial intelligence and marketing. *Turkish Journal of Computer and Mathematics Education*, 12(4), 1247–1256. 10.17762/turcomat.v12i4.1184

Mugrauer A., & Pers J. (2019). Marketing managers in the age of AI: A multiple-case study of B2C firms.

Myneni, S., Cobb, N., & Cohen, T. (2016). In pursuit of theoretical ground in behavior change support systems: Analysis of peer-to-peer communication in a health-related online community. *Journal of Medical Internet Research*, 18(2), e4671.

N'Goala, G., & Collin-Lachaud, I. (2022). Marketing et influence: à la recherche d'une légitimité perdue. *Revue Décisions Marketing*, 1(105), 5–9.

Nabavi, R. T. (2012). Bandura's Social Learning Theory & Social Cognitive Learning Theory. *Theories of Developmental Psychology*, 1–23.

Nair, K., & Gupta, R. (Jan. 2021). Application of AI technology in modern digital marketing environment. *WJEMSD*, vol. ahead-of-print, no. ahead-of-print, doi: 10.1108/WJEMSD-08-2020-0099.

Naslund, J. A., Aschbrenner, K. A., Marsch, L. A., & Bartels, S. J. (2016). The future of mental health care: Peer-to-peer support and social media. *Epidemiology and Psychiatric Sciences*, 25(2), 113–122.

Nass, C., & Moon, Y. (2000). Machines and mindlessness: Social responses to computers. *Journal of Social Issues*, 56(1), 81–103.

Natarajan T., Balasubramanian, S. A., & Kasilingam, D. L. (2017). Understanding the intention to use mobile shopping applications and its influence on price sensitivity. *Journal of Retailing and Consumer Services*, 37, 8–22. 10.1016/j.jretconser.2017.02.010

Névéol, A., & Zweigenbaum, P. (2017). Making sense of big textual data for health care: Findings from the section on clinical natural language processing. *Yearbook of Medical Informatics*, 26(01), 228–234.

Nick, E. A., Cole, D. A., Cho, S. J., Smith, D. K., Carter, T. G., & Zelkowitz, R. L. (2018). The online social support scale: Measure development and validation. *Psychological Assessment*, 30(9), 1127.

Nicola, M., Alsafi, Z., Sohrabi, C., Kerwan, A., Al-Jabir, A., Iosifidis, C., ... & Agha, R. (2020). The socio-economic implications of the coronavirus pandemic (COVID-19): A review. *International Journal of Surgery*, 78, 185–193.

Nicolaou, A. I., & McKnight, D. H. (2006). Perceived information quality in data exchanges: Effects on risk, trust, and intention to use. *Information Systems Research*, 17(4), 332–351.

Nielsen, S., & Barratt, M. J. (2009). Prescription drug misuse: Is technology friend or foe?. *Drug and Alcohol Review*, 28(1), 81–86.

Nilsson, N. J. (2005). Human-level artificial intelligence? Be serious!. *AI Magazine*, 26(4), 68.

Nimbalkar, A. A., & Berad, A. T. (2021). The increasing importance of AI applications in E-commerce. *Vidyabharati International Interdisciplinary Research Journal*, 13(1), 388–391.

Nivetha, P., & Sudhamathi, S. (2019). Marketing trends using latest technology. *International Journal of Recent Technology and Engineering*, ISSN: 2277-3878, 8(2S6).

Nora, A. (2022). Les nouvelles stratégies marketing après la crise du covid 19. *Revue Etudes économiques*, 16(1), 811–821.

Norberg, P. A., Horne, D. R., & Horne, D. A. (Jun. 2007). The privacy paradox: Personal information disclosure intentions versus behaviors. *Journal of Consumer Affairs*, 41(1), 100–126. 10.1111/j.1745-6606.2006.00070.x

Nowak, K. L., & Biocca, F. (2003). The effect of the agency and anthropomorphism on users' sense of telepresence, copresence, and social presence in virtual environments. *Presence: Teleoperators and Virtual Environments*, 12(5), 481–494. 10.1162/105474603322761289

Nunnally, J. C., & Bernstein, I. H. (1994). *Psychometric theory, 3/e*. New York, NY: McGraw-Hill.

Nussbaum, M. C. (2003). Capabilities as fundamental entitlements: Sen and social justice. *Feminist Economics*, 9(3), 33–59.

Oleksak, M. (2005). Strategic conversations with your customers help hone the planning process. Emerald Group Publishing Limited [accessed 1 May 2023]. Available at: https://ebookcentral-proquestcom.aineistot.lamk.fi/lib/lamk-ebooks/reader.action?docID=282891

Oliveira, A., & Chimenti, P. (2021). Humanized robots: A proposition of categories to understand virtual influencers. *Australasian Journal of Information Systems*, 21(25), 1–27.

Oosthuizen, R. M. (2022). The fourth industrial revolution–Smart technology, artificial intelligence, robotics and algorithms: Industrial psychologists in future workplaces. *Frontiers in Artificial Intelligence*, 5, 913168.

Oostrum, J. (2013). Why measure access and quality of education through the use of the Capability approach? *An exploration in the context of Nepal*, 1–66.

Oracle (2019) What is a chatbot?. available at https://www.oracle.com/solutions/chatbots/whatis-achatbot/ (accessed 8 December 2022).

Orizio, G., Merla, A., Schulz, P. J., & Gelatti, U. (2011). Quality of online pharmacies and websites selling prescription drugs: A systematic review. *Journal of Medical Internet Research*, 13(3), e1795.

Orizio, G., Schulz, P., Domenighini, S., Caimi, L., Rosati, C., Rubinelli, S., & Gelatti, U. (2009). Cyberdrugs: A cross-sectional study of online pharmacies characteristics. *The European Journal of Public Health*, 19(4), 375–377.

Pal, S., Laszlo, K., Andras, F., Gabriel, H., Hajnal, F., Adriana, C. I. U. R. B. A., ... & Lajos, B. (2015). Attitude of patients and customers regarding purchasing drugs online. *Farmacia*, 63(1), 93–98.

Pallathadka, H., Ramirez-Asis, E. H., Loli-Poma, T. P., Kaliyaperumal, K., Ventayen, R. J. M., & Naved, M. (2023). Applications of artificial intelligence in business management, e-commerce and finance. *Materials Today: Proceedings*, 80, 2610–2613.

Pan, H., & Zhou, H. (Jun. 2020). Study on convolutional neural network and its application in data mining and sales forecasting for E-commerce. *Electronic Commerce Research and Applications*, 20(2), 297–320. 10.1007/s10660-020-09409-0

Pan, K. Y., Kok, A. A., Eikelenboom, M., Horsfall, M., Jörg, F., Luteijn, R. A., ... & Penninx, B. W. (2021). The mental health impact of the COVID-19 pandemic on people with and without depressive, anxiety, or obsessive-compulsive disorders: A longitudinal study of three Dutch case-control cohorts. *The Lancet Psychiatry*, 8(2), 121–129.

Pang, H. (2022). The Negative Impact of Social Media on People's Lives. In *2021 International Conference on Social Development and Media Communication (SDMC 2021)* (pp. 554–557). Atlantis Press.

Pang, B. & Lee, L. (2008). Opinion mining and sentiment analysis. *FNT in Information Retrieval*, 2(1–2), 1–135. 10.1561/1500000011

Pangkey, F. M., Furkan, L. M., Herman, L. E., & Agusdin, A. (2020). Exploring the impact of Artificial intelligence and digital marketing on intention to use online transportation: A lesson learned from Indonesian Millenials. *Research square*, 1–9.

Pansari, A., & Kumar, V. (2017). Customer engagement: The construct, antecedents and consequences. *Journal of the Academy of Marketing Science*, 45(3), 294–311.

Papneja, S., Sharma, K., & Khilwani, N. (2021). Content recommendation based on topic modeling. In V. Singh, V. K. Asari, S. Kumar, and R. B. Patel (Eds.), *Computational methods and data engineering*, vol. 1227, 1–10. Singapore: Springer Singapore. 10.1007/978-981-15-6876-3_1

Parasmehak, K., & Chitsimran (2019). Evolution of artificial intelligence in marketing, comparison with traditional marketing. *Our Heritage*, 67(5), 375–389. https://ssrn.com/abstract=3557091

Park, C., & Jun, J. (2003). A cross-cultural comparison of Internet buying behavior: Effects of Internet usage, perceived risks, and innovativeness. *International Marketing Review*, 20(5), 534–553. 10.1108/02651330310498771

Park, A., Conway, M., & Chen, A. T. (2018). Examining thematic similarity, difference, and membership in three online mental health communities from Reddit: A text mining and visualization approach. *Computers in Human Behavior*, 78, 98–112.

Paschen, J., Kietzmann, J., & Kietzmann, T. C. (2019). Artificial intelligence (AI) and its implications for market knowledge in B2B marketing. *Journal of Business & Industrial Marketing*, 34(7), 1410–1419. 10.1108/JBIM-10-2018-0295

Patil, P., Tamilmani, K., & Rana, N., & Raghavan, V. (2020). Understanding consumer adoption of mobile payment in India: Extending Meta-UTAUT model with personal innovativeness, anxiety, trust, and grievance redressal. *International Journal of Information Management*, 54(2), 102144. 10.1016/j.ijinfomgt.2020.102144

Paul, R., & Pradhan, S. (2019). Achieving student satisfaction and student loyalty in higher education: A focus on service value dimensions. *Services Marketing Quarterly*, 40(3), 245–268. 10.1080/15332969.2019.1630177

Pavlou, P. A. (2003). Consumer acceptance of electronic commerce: Integrating trust and risk with the technology acceptance model. *International Journal of Electronic Commerce*, 7(3), 101–134.

Pazzani, M. J., & Billsus, D. (2007). Content-based recommendation systems. In P. Brusilovsky, A. Kobsa, and W. Nejdl (Eds.), *The adaptive web*, vol. 4321, 325–341. Berlin, Heidelberg: Springer Berlin Heidelberg. 10.1007/978-3-540-72079-9_10

Pedersen, I., & Duin, A. (2022). AI Agents, Humans and Untangling the Marketing of Artificial Intelligence in Learning Environments, *Proceedings of the 55th Hawaii International Conference on System Sciences*.

Perez-Vega, R., Kaartemo, V., Lages, C. R., Razavi, N. B., & Männistö, J. (2021). Reshaping the contexts of online customer engagement behavior via artificial intelligence: A conceptual framework. *Journal of Business Research*, 129, 902–910. 10.1016/j.jbusres.2020.11.002

Persson, A., Laaksoharju, M., & Koga, H. (2021). We mostly think alike: Individual differences in attitude towards AI in Sweden and Japan. *The Review of Socionetwork Strategies*, 15(1), 123–142.

Peter, J. P. (1979). Reliability: A review of psychometric basics and recent marketing practices. *Journal of Marketing Research*, 16(1), 6–17.

Petersson, A. H., Pawar, S., & Fagerstrøm, A. (2023). Investigating the factors of customer experiences using real-life text-based banking chatbot: A qualitative study in Norway. *Procedia Computer Science*, 219, 697–704.

Pillai, R., & Sivathanu, B. (2020). Adoption of artificial intelligence (AI) for talent acquisition in IT/ITeS organizations. *Benchmarking: An International Journal*, 27(9), 2599–2629.

Pise, R. (2018). Chatbot market size is set to exceed USD 134 billion by 2024 – ClickZ. available at: https://www.clickz.com/chatbot-market-size-is-set-to-exceed-usd-1-34-billion-by-2024/215518/ (accessed 6 December 2022).

Pitardi, V., & Marriott, H. R. (2021). Alexa, she's not human but Unveiling the drivers of consumers' trust in voice-based artificial intelligence. *Psychology and Marketing*, 38(4), 626–642.

Pittaras, N. F. I., Siris, V. A., Polyzos, G. C., & Anton, P. (2021). A privacy-preserving statistics marketplace using local differential privacy and blockchain: An application to smart-grid measurements sharing. *Blockchain: Research and Applications*, 2(1). 10.1016/j.bcra.2021.100022

Post, C. (11-May-2019). Blockchain Technology to Revolutionise E-Commerce Businesses in Australia. *Business Partner Magazine*. [Online]. Available: https://businesspartnermagazine.com/blockchain-technology-revolutionise-e-commerce-businesses-australia/. [Accessed: 12-February-2020].

Qin, X., & Jiang, Z. The Impact of AI on the Advertising Process: The Chinese Experience[J].

Qiu, L., & Benbasat, I. (2009). Evaluating anthropomorphic product recommendation agents: A social relationship perspective to designing information systems. *Journal of Management Information Systems*, 25(4), 145–182.

Rahmouni, M., & Aleid, M. A. (2020). Teachers' practices and children's motivation towards science learning in MENA countries: Evidence from Tunisia and UAE. *International Journal of Educational Research*, 103.

Raj, S. S., Nirmal, O. N., Kalaivani, A., Kaur, K. CGC CBSA, Punjab Author Mohali, Taranjit Singh Vij, and Y. Suryanarayana Murthy (2023). Artificial intelligence in e-commerce: A literature review. *Artificial Intelligence*, 21(01).

Rana, S. (2023). AI and GPT for management scholars and practitioners: Guidelines and implications. *FIIB Business Review*, 12(1), 7–9. 10.1177/23197145231161408

Rapp, A., Curti, L., & Bold, A. (2021). "The human side of human-chatbot interaction: A systematic literature review of ten years of research on text-based chatbots", *International Journal of Human–Computer Studies*, 151(3), 102–630.

Rasul, T., Nair, S., Kalendra, D., Robin, M., Santini, F., Ladeira, W., Sun, M., Day, I., Rather, A., & Heathcote, L. (2023). The role of ChatGPT in higher education: Benefits, challenges, and future research directions. *Journal of Applied Learning & Teaching*, 6(1), 1–16.

Rathore, B. (2023). Future of AI & generation alpha: ChatGPT beyond boundaries. *International Peer Reviewed/Refereed Multidisciplinary Journal*, 12(1). Available online at: www.eduzonejournal.com

Ratnasingham, P. (1998). The importance of trust in electronic commerce. *Internet Research*, 8(4), 313–321.

Rayland, A., & Andrews, J. (2023). From social network to peer support network: Opportunities to explore mechanisms of online peer support for mental health. *JMIR Mental Health*, 10, e41855.

Reavie, V. (2018). Do you know the difference between data analytics and AI machine learning? Forbes, Retrieved from https://www.forbes.com/sites/forbesagencycouncil/2018/08/01/do-you-knowthe-diference-between-data-analytics-and-ai-machine-learning/#5c50edac5878.

Rejeb, A., Keogh, J. G., & Treiblmaier, H. (2020). How blockchain technology can benefit marketing: Six pending research areas. *Frontiers in Blockchain*, 3(3). 10.3389/fbloc.2020.00003

Rens, E., Dom, G., Remmen, R., Michielsen, J., & Van den Broeck, K. (2020). Unmet mental health needs in the general population: Perspectives of Belgian health and social care professionals. *International Journal for Equity in Health*, 19(1), 1–10.

Report on 43. Examples of artificial intelligence in education. University of San Diego. https://onlinedegrees.sandiego.edu/artificial-intelligence-education/

Ricci, F., Rokach, L., & Shapira, B. (2011). Introduction to recommender systems handbook. In F. Ricci, L. Rokach, B. Shapira, and P. B. Kantor (Eds.), *Recommender systems handbook*, 1–35. Boston, MA: Springer US. 10.1007/978-0-387-85820-3_1

Richad, R., Vivensius, G., Sfenrianto, S., & Kaburuan, E. (2019). Analysis of factors influencing millennial's technology acceptance of chatbot in the banking industry in Indonesia. *International Journal of Civil Engineering and Technology*, 10(4), 1270–1281.

Rietz, T., Benke, I., & Maedche, A. (2019). The Impact of Anthropomorphic and Functional Chatbot Design Features in Enterprise CollaborationSystems on User Acceptance. In Proceedings of the 14th International Conference on Wirtschaftsinformatik.

Rigopoulos, G., & Askounis, D.(2007). A TAM framework to evaluate user's perception toward online electronic payments. *Journal of Internet Banking and Commerce*, 12.

Rodgers, S. (2021). Themed issue introduction: Promises and perils of artificial intelligence and advertising. *Journal of Advertising*, 50(1), 1–10.

Rodgers, W., & Nguyen, T. (2022). Advertising benefits from ethical artificial intelligence algorithmic purchase decision pathways. *Journal of Business Ethics*: 1–19.

Roe, M. M. (2001). *The journey and the destination: A qualitative study of success definitions, experiences and strategies among college freshmen*. New York University.

Roetzer, P., & Kaput, M. (2022). *Marketing artificial intelligence: AI, marketing, and the future of business*. BenBella Books.

Rönnhed, J., & Wiksborg, S. (2021). *Virtual influencers, friends to listen to? A qualitative study about virtual influencers ability to develop parasocial relationships and opinion leadership, master's programme in international marketing & brand management*. Sweden: Lund University.

Roriz, R., & Pereira, J. L. (2019). Avoiding insurance fraud: A blockchain-based solution for the vehicle sector. *Procedia Computer Science*, 164, 211–218. 10.1016/j.procs.2019.12.174

Rupasinghe, A. T., Guanawardena, N. L., Shujan, S., & Atukoral, D. A. S. (2016). Scaling Personality Traits of Interviewees in an Online Job Interview by Vocal Spectrum and Facial Cue Analysis. International Conference on Advances in ICT for Emerging Regions (ICTer), pp. 1–8.

Russell, S. J. (2010). *Artificial intelligence a modern approach*. Pearson Education, Inc.

Russell, S., & Norvig, P. (2010). *Intelligence artificielle: une approche moderne*. 3^{éme} édition. Upper Saddle River: Prentice-Hall.

Rutskiy, V., Mousavi, R., Chudopal, N., Amrani, Y. E., Everstova, V., & Tsarev, R. (2021). Artificial Intelligence as a Disruptive Technology for Digital Marketing. *Data Science and Intelligent Systems*, 895–900.

Ryan, R. M., & Deci, E. L. (2017). *Self-determination theory: Basic psychological needs in motivation, development, and wellness*. Guilford: Guilford Publications.

Ryan, F., Coughlan, M., & Cronin, P. (2009). Interviewing in qualitative research. *International Journal of Therapy and Rehabilitation*, 16(6), 309–314.

Sabzalieva, E., & Valentini, A. (2023). ChatGPT and artificial intelligence in higher education: a quick guide, UNESCO, pp. 1–14.

Saigarana, N. G., Karupiah, P., & Gopalc, S. P. (2015). The Capability Approach: Comparing Amartya Sen and Martha Nussbaum. Proceedings of University Sains Malaysia international Conference on Social Sciences, pp. 1–327.

Salvagno, M., Chat G. P. T., Gerli, A. G., & Taccone, F. S. (2023). Can artificial intelligence help for scientific writing?. *Critical Care*, 27(1), 1–5.

Sambasivan, M., Wemyss, G. P., & Rose, R. C. (2010). User acceptance of a G2B system: A case of the electronic procurement system in Malaysia. *Internet Research*, 20(2), 169–187.

Sampat, B., & Sabat, K. C. (2022). Adoption of online pharmacies in India: An empirical study. *International Journal of Business Innovation and Research*, 29(4), 449–478.

Sands, S., Ferraro, C., Demsar, V., & Chandler, G. (2022). False idols: Unpacking the opportunities and challenges of falsity in the context of virtual influencers. *Business Horizons*, 65(6), 777–788.

Santiago, M.-G. et al. (2019). Predicting the intentions to use chatbots for travel and tourism. *Current Issues in Tourism*, 24(2), 192–210.

Santiago, M-G., Desiderio, T., & Bulchand-Gidumal, J. (2019). Predicting the intentions to use chatbots for travel and tourism. *Current Issues in Tourism*, 24, 1–19. 10.1080/13683500.2019.1706457

Santini, F. D. O., Ladeira, W. J., Sampaio, C. H., & da Silva Costa, G. (2017). Student satisfaction in higher education: A meta-analytic study. *Journal of Marketing for Higher Education*, 27(1), 1–18.

Saputra, R., Nasution, M. I. P., & Dharma, B. (2023). The impact of using AI Chat GPT on marketing effectiveness: A case study on Instagram marketing. *Indonesian Journal of Economics and Management*, 3(3), 603–617.

Saqlain, M., Jafar, N., Hamid, R., Shahzad, A. Prediction of Cricket World Cup 2019 by TOPSIS Technique of MCDM-A Mathematical Analysis.

Satoshi, N. (2008). Bitcoin: A Peer-to-Peer Electronic Cash System. Available at SSRN: https://ssrn.com/abstract=3440802, 10.2139/ssrn.3440802

Scherer, M. U. (2015). Regulating artificial intelligence systems: Risks, challenges, competencies, and strategies. *Harvard Journal of Law & Technology*, 29, 353.

Schierz P. G., Schilke O., &WirtzB.W. (2010). Understanding consumer acceptance of mobile payment services: An empirical analysis. *Electronic Commerce Research and Applications*, 9(3), 209–216.

Seeber, I., Bittner, E., Briggs, R. O., de Vreede, T., de Vreede, G. J., Elkins, A., Maier, R., Merz, A. B., Oeste-Reiß, S., Randrup, N., Schwabe, G., & Sollner, M. (2020). Machines as teammates: A research agenda on AI in team collaboration. *Information and Management*, 57(2), 103–174.

Serban *et al.* (Feb. 2017). A hierarchical latent variable encoder-decoder model for generating dialogues. *AAAI*, 31(1). 10.1609/aaai.v31i1.10983.

Serrano-Guerrero, J., Olivas, J. A., Romero, F. P., & Herrera-Viedma, E. (2015). Sentiment World Health Organization (2001). The World Health Report 2001: Mental Health: New Understanding.

Sewell, W. H., Jr. (1992). A theory of structure: Duality, agency, and transformation. *American Journal of Sociology*, 98, 1–29.

Shaf, P. M., Jawalkar, G. S., Kadam, M. A., Ambawale, R. R., & Bankar, S. V. (2020). AI-assisted Chatbot for e-commerce to address selection of products from multiple products. *Internet of Things, Smart Computing and Technology: A Roadmap Ahead*, 57–80.

Shah, D., & Shay, E. (2019). How and Why Artificial Intelligence, Mixed Reality and Blockchain Technologies Will Change Marketing We Know Today. *In: Handbook of Advances in Marketing in an Era of Disruptions: Essays in Honour of Jagdish N. Sheth*, 377–390. DOI:10.4135/9789353287733

Shah, N., Engineer, S., Bhagat, N., Chauhan, H., & Shah, M. (2020). Research trends on the usage of machine learning and artificial intelligence in advertising. *Augmented Human Research*, 5(1), 1–15.

Shaik, M. (2023). Impact of artificial intelligence on marketing. *East Asian Journal of Multidisciplinary Research*, 2(3), 993–1004.

Sharma, T. K. (10-Jul-1970). Top 10 Blockchain Solutions for E-commerce. *Blockchain Council Blockchaincouncilorg*. [Online]. Available: https://www.blockchain-council.org/blockchain/top-10-blockchain-solutions-for-e-commerce/. [Accessed: 12-February-2020].

Sharma, P., Agarwal, M. S., & Vashishtha, S. Green HRM: A Modest Move to Safeguard the Environment for Today's and Tomorrow's Generations. *MANGLAM PUBLICATIONS*, 217.

Shawar, B. A., & Atwell, E. S. (2005). Using corpora in machine-learning chatbot systems. *International Journal of Corpus Linguistics*, 10(4), 489–516.

Sheehan, B., Jin, H. S., & Gottlieb, U. (2020). Customer service chatbots: Anthropomorphism and adoption. *Journal of Business Research*, 115, 14–24.

Sheikh, H. et al. (2023). Mission AI, Research for Policy, 10.1007/978-3-031-21448-6_1

Shekhar, S. K., Jose, T. P., & Rehin, K. R. (2019). Consumer buying behaviour and attitude towards pharmaceuticals. *International Journal of Pharmaceutical Sciences and Research*, 10(4).

Sheldon, P., & Bryant, K. (2016). Instagram: Motives for its use and relationship to narcissism and contextual age. *Computers in Human Behavior*, 58, 89–97.

Shen, J. (2012). Social comparison, social presence, and enjoyment in the acceptance of social shopping websites. *Journal of Electronic Commerce Research*, 13(3), 198.

Shen, G., Jia, J., Nie, L., Feng, F., Zhang, C., Hu, T., … & Zhu, W. (2017, August). Depression detection via harvesting social media: A multimodal dictionary learning solution. In *IJCAI* (pp. 3838–3844).

Sheth, J. (2021). New areas of research in marketing strategy, consumer behavior, and marketing analytics: The future is bright. *Journal of Marketing Theory and Practice*, 29(1), 3–12.

Shopify. (2016). Conversational Commerce Definition - What is Conversational Commerce? Retrieved from https://www.shopify.com/encyclopedia/conversationalcommerce

Siau, K., & Shen, Z. (2003). Building customer trust in mobile commerce. *Communications of the ACM*, 46(4), 91–94.

Sidlauskiene, J., Joye, Y., & Auruskeviciene, V. (2023). AI-based chatbots in conversational commerce and their effects on product and price perceptions. *Electronic Markets*, 2–21.

Silhavy, P., & Prokopova, Z. (2021). *Data science and intelligent systems. CoMeSySo 2021 Lecture Notes in Networks and Systems*, 231. Cham: Springer. 10.1007/978-3-030-90321-3_74

Simmel, G. (1955). *Conflict and the web of group affiliations*. New York: Free Press.

Singh, D. (2023). ChatGPT: A new approach to revolutionise organisations. *International Journal of New Media Studies*, ISSN: 2394-4331, 10(1).

Singh, T., Roberts, K., Cohen, T., Cobb, N., Franklin, A., & Myneni, S. (2023). Discerning conversational context in online health communities for personalized digital behavior change solutions using

Pragmatics to Reveal Intent in Social Media (PRISM) framework. *Journal of Biomedical Informatics*, 140, 104324.

Singleton, A., Abeles, P., & Smith, I. C. (2016). Online social networking and psychological experiences: The perceptions of young people with mental health difficulties. *Computers in Human Behavior*, 61, 394–403.

Skill India Report. (2022). Retrieved from https://wheebox.com/assets/pdf/ISR_Report_2022.pdf

Smarki, M. (2021). *Role of the Appearance of the Virtual Influencers on Social Presence and Brand Attitude, Thèse de doctorat en philosophie en Management*. Etats-Unis d'Amérique: Université Binghamton.

Smith, C. (2017). By the Numbers: Amazing WordPress Statistics. DMR[accessed 20 April 2023]. Available at: http://expandedramblings.com/index.php/wordpress-statistics

Smith, N., Fischer, E., & Yongjian, C. (May 2012). How does brand-related user-generated content differ across YouTube, Facebook, and Twitter? *Journal of Interactive Marketing*, 26(2), 102–113. 10.1016/j.intmar.2012.01.002

Smith, L. L., Yan, F., Charles, M., Mohiuddin, K., Tyus, D., Adekeye, O., & Holden, K. B. (2017). Exploring the link between substance use and mental health status: What can we learn from the self-medication theory?. *Journal of health care for the poor and underserved*, 28(2), 113–131.

Smutny, P., & Schreiberova, P. (2020). Chatbots for learning: A review of educational Chatbots for Facebook Messenger. *Computers and Education*, 151, 103862.

Snow, D. A. (2001). Extending and broadening Blumer's conceptualization of symbolic interactionism. *Symbolic Interaction*, 24, 367–377.

Som B. (2023). Role of ChatGPT in Gaming: According to ChatGPT (March 2, 2023). Available at SSRN: https://ssrn.com/abstract=4375510 or 10.2139/ssrn.4375510

Song, X., Yang, S., Huang, Z., & Huang, T. (2019). The application of artificial intelligence in electronic commerce. *Journal of Physics: Conference Series*, 1302(3), 032030. IOP Publishing. 10.1088/1742-6596/1302/3/032030

Sottiaux, A. (2020). *Comment l'identité professionnelle des influenceurs se construit-elle et à partir de quand le loisir laisse-t-il place au métier?*. Belgique: Université de Louvain School of Management.

Spatola, N. (2019). L'interaction Homme-Robot, de l'anthropomorphisme à l'humanisation. *Année psychologique*, 4(119), 515–563.

Staista. (2018, 09 20). La Blockchain au service du commerce international. Consulté le 06 13, 2022, sur statista: https://fr.statista.com/infographie/15533/applications-technologie-blockchain/

Stallone V., Wetzels M., & Klaas M. (2021). Applications of Blockchain Technology in marketing—A systematic review of marketing technology companies. *Blockchain: Research and Applications*, 2(30). 10.1016/j.bcra.2021.100023

Starzyk, K. B., Holden, R. R., Fabrigar, L. R., & MacDonald, T. K. (2006). The personal acquaintance measure: A tool for appraising one's acquaintance with any person. *Journal of Personality and Social Psychology*, 90(5), 833–847.

Stein, J. P., Breves, P. L., & Andres, N. (2022). Parasocial interactions with real and virtual influencers: The role of perceived similarity and human-likeness. *New Media & Society*, 00(0), 1–22.

Stein, J. P., Appel, M., Jost, A., & Ohler, P. (2020). Matter over mind? How the acceptance of digital entities depends on their appearance, mental prowess, and the interaction between both. *International Journal of Human-Computer Studies*, 142, 102463. 10.1016/j.ijhcs.2020.102463

Sterne, J. (2017). Artificial intelligence for marketing: Practical applications. Wiley.

Steuer, J. S. (1992). Defining virtual reality: Dimensions determining telepresence. *Journal of Communication*, Fall 1992, 42(4), 21–73.

Stewart, F. (2013). Capabilities and human development: Beyond the individual-the critical role of social institutions and social competencies. *United Nations Development Programme*, pp. 1–22.

Stewart, R., & Davis, K. (2016). Big data in mental health research: Current status and emerging possibilities. *Social Psychiatry and Psychiatric Epidemiology*, 51(8), 1055–1072.

Stocking, G., & Sumida, N. Social Media Bots DrawPublic's Attention and Concern; Pew Research Center: Washington,

Stokes, D. C., Andy, A., Guntuku, S. C., Ungar, L. H., & Merchant, R. M. (2020). Public priorities and concerns regarding COVID-19 in an online discussion forum: Longitudinal topic modeling. *Journal of General Internal Medicine*, 35(7), 2244–2247.

Sudharsan, R., & Ganesh, E. N. (Dec. 2022). A Swish RNN based customer churn prediction for the telecom industry with a novel feature selection strategy. *Connection Science*, 34(1), 1855–1876. 10.1080/09540091.2022.2083584

Suh, B., & Han, I. (2002). Effect of trust on customer acceptance of Internet banking. *Electronic Commerce Research and Applications*, 1(3-4), 247–263.

Sumarjan, N., Mazlan, N., Saiful Azmi, N. S., Kamaruddin, M. A., & Salleh, A. (2023). The usage intention of chatbot technology in hospitality and tourism industry: Customers' perspective. *Journal of Tourism Hospitality and Culinary*, 15(1), 206–224.

Sun, Y., Zhang, Y., Gwizdka, J., & Trace, C. B. (2019). Consumer evaluation of the quality of online health information: Systematic literature review of relevant criteria and indicators. *Journal of Medical Internet Research*, 21(5), e12522.

Sundar, S. S., Kalyanaraman, S., & Brown, J. (2003). Explicating web site interactivity: Impression formation effects in political campaign sites. *Communication Research*, 30(1), 30–59.

Sundar, S. S., Bellur, S., Oh, J., Jia, H., & Kim, H.-S. (2014). Theoretical importance of contingency in human-computer interaction. *Communication Research*, 43, 595–625.

Swan, M. (2009). Emerging patient-driven health care models: An examination of health social networks, consumer personalized medicine and quantified self-tracking. *International Journal of Environmental Research and Public Health*, 6(2), 492–525.

Swan, M. (2015). Blockchain: Blueprint for a new economy. O'Reilly Media, Inc.

Syam N., & Sharma A. (2018). Waiting for a sales renaissance in the fourth industrial revolution: Machine learning and artificial intelligence in sales research and practice. *Industrial Marketing Management*, 69, 139–146.

Taddeo, M., & Floridi, L. (Aug. 2018). How AI can be a force for good. *Science*, 361(6404), 751–752. 10.1126/science.aat5991

Taherdoost, H. (2022). How to conduct an effective interview; A guide to interview design in research study. *International Journal of Academic Research in Management*, 11(1), 39–51.

Takahashi, Y., Ohura, T., Ishizaki, T., Okamoto, S., Miki, K., Naito, M., ... & Nakayama, T. (2011). Internet use for health-related information via personal computers and cell phones in Japan: A cross-sectional population-based survey. *Journal of Medical Internet Research*, 13(4), e1796.

Tan, T. M., & Salo, J. (2023). Ethical marketing in the Blockchain-based sharing economy: Theoretical integration and guiding insights. *Journal of Business Ethics*, 183, 1113–1140. 10.1007/s10551-021-05015-8

Tandon, U. (2023). Chatbots, virtual-try-on (VTO), e-WOM: Modeling the determinants of attitude' and continued intention with PEEIM as moderator in online shopping. *Global Knowledge, Memory and Communication*, Vol. ahead-of-print No. ahead-of-print.

Tao, F., Wang, Y-Y, & Zhu, S-H. (2023). Impact of blockchain technology on the optimal pricing and quality decisions of platform supply chains. *International Journal of Production Research*, 61(11), 3670–3684. 10.1080/00207543.2022.2050828

Taylor, S., & Todd, P. A. (1995). Understanding information technology usage: A test of competing models. *Information Systems Research*, 6(2), 144–176.

Taylor, L. C., Clayton, J. D., & Rowley, S. J. (2004). Socialization: Understanding parental influences on children's school-related development in the early years. *Review of General Psychology*, 8(3), 163–178.

Tessler, R., & Goldman, H. (1982). *The chronically mentally ill: Assessing community support programs.* Cambridge, MA: Ballinger.

Thakur, R. (2018). The role of self-efficacy and customer satisfaction in driving loyalty to the mobile shopping application. *International Journal of Retail and Distribution Management*, 46(3), 283–303.

Thandekkattu, S. G., & Kalaiarasi, M. (2022). Customer-Centric E-commerce Implementing Artificial Intelligence for Better Sales and Service. In Proceedings of Second International Conference on Advances in Computer Engineering and Communication Systems: ICACECS 2021, pp. 141–152. Singapore: Springer Nature Singapore.

Thatcher, J. B., Wright, R. T., Sun, H., Zagenczyk, T. J., & Klein, R. (2018). Mindfulness in information technology use: Definitions, distinctions, and a new measure. *MIS Quarterly*, 42(3), 831–847.

Thi Phuong Anh, L., & Rajah, E. (2022). Using Chatbots in Customer Service: A Case Study of Air New Zealand. In E. Papoutsaki and M. Shannon (Eds.), Proceedings: Rangahau Horonuku Hou – New Research Landscapes, *Unitec/MIT Research Symposium*, 6 et 7 Décembre 2021, 161–176), 10.34074/proc.2206011

Thilagavathy, N., & Kumar, K. (2021). Artificial intelligence on digital marketing - An overview. *Natural Volatiles and Essential Oils*, 8(5), 9895–9908.

Thompson, J. (2022). Parasocial Relationships in CGI Influencer Marketing, *Academy of Marketing Conference.*

Thorson, E., Chi, A., & Leavitt, C. (1992). Attention, memory, attitude and conation: A test of the advertising hierarchy. *Advances in Consumer Research*, 19, 366–379.

Thorsteinson, G., & Page, T.(2007). Creativity in technology education facilitated through virtual reality learning environments - a case study. *I-manager's Journal of Educational Technology*, 3(4), 74–87.

Thukral, S., Sangwan, S., Chatterjee, A., & Dey, L. (2022). Identifying pandemic-related stress factors from social-media posts – effects on students and young-adults. *In: Proceedings of the 1st Workshop on NLP for COVID-19 (Part 2) at EMNLP 2020.*

Tirri, K., & Nokelainen, P. (2008). Identification of multiple intelligences with the multiple intelligence profiling questionnaire III. *Psychology Science*, 50(2), 206.

Tomar, A. (2023). Higher Education in India: Vision 2047 Retrieved from ey.com/en_in

Toplak, M., & Katz, A. N. (2000). On the uses of sarcastic irony. *Journal of Pragmatics*, 32(10), 1467–1488.

Toreini, E., Aitken, M., Coopamootoo, K., Elliott, K., Zelaya, C. G., & Van Moorsel, A. (2020). The relationship between trust in AI and trustworthy machine learning technologies. In Proceedings of the 2020 conference on fairness, accountability, and transparency, pp. 272–283.

Torous, J., & Baker, J. T. (2016). Why psychiatry needs data science and data science needs psychiatry: Connecting with technology. *JAMA Psychiatry*, 73(1), 3–4.

Tosun, P. (2022). Social Media Marketing of Brands in the COVID-19 Pandemic: Exploring the Crisis-Related Content, in *Handbook of Research on Interdisciplinary Perspectives on the Threats and Impacts of Pandemics*, 1–22.

Tracxn Report. Retrieved from https://tracxn.com/d/explore/ai-in-education-startups-in-india

Tran, A. D., Pallant, J., & Johnson, L. W. (2021). Exploring the impact of chatbots on consumer sentiment and expectations in retail. *Journal of Retailing and Consumer Services*, 63(2), 102718.

Truong, D. (2008). An empirical study of business-to-business electronic marketplace usage: The impact of buyers' e-readiness. *Journal of Organizational Computing and Electronic Commerce*, 18(2), 112–130.

Tsang, Y. P., & Lee, C. K. M. (2022). Artificial intelligence in industrial design: A semi-automated literature survey. *Engineering Applications of Artificial Intelligence*, 112, 104884.

Turja, T., Aaltonen, I., Taipale, S. & Oksanen, A. (2020). Robot acceptance model for care (RAM-care): A principled approach to the intention to use care robots. *Information & Management*, 57(5), 103220.

Ukpabi, D. C., Aslam, B., & Karjaluoto, H. (2019). Chatbot Adoption in Tourism Services: A Conceptual Exploration "in". *Robots, Artificial Intelligence and Service Automation in Travel, Tourism and Hospitality*, 105–121.

Ullal, M. S., Hawaldar, I. T., Soni, R., & Nadeem, M. (2021). The role of machine learning in digital marketing. *SAGE Open*, 11(4). 10.1177/21582440211050394

Um, N. (2023). Predictors affecting effects of virtual influencer advertising among college students. *Sustainability*, 15(6388), 1–14.

UNESCO. Artificial intelligence in education. Retrieved from https://en.unesco.org/artificial-intelligence/education.

UNFPA Report 2023, retrieved from https://www.unfpa.org/swp2023

Uzunoğlu, E., & Misci Kip, S. (2014). Brand communication through digital influencers: Leveraging blogger engagement. *International Journal of Information Management*, 34(5), 592–602.

Van der Heijden, H. (2003). Factors influencing the usage of websites: The case of a generic portal in The Netherlands. *Information and Management*, 40(6), 541–549.

Van der Heijden, H. (2004). User acceptance of hedonic information systems. *MIS Quarterly*, 28(4), 695–704.

Van Doorn, J. *et al.* (Aug. 2010). Customer engagement behavior: Theoretical foundations and research directions. *Journal of Service Research*, 13(3), 253–266. 10.1177/1094670510375599

Van Eeuwen, M. (2017). Mobile conversational commerce: messenger chatbots as the text interface between business and consumer, University of Twente, 15.

Van Manen, T. (2016). Bot or not: dit is waarom Facebook inzet op chatbots |Marketingfacts [Web log post]. Retrieved from http://www.marketingfacts.nl/erichten/chatbots-facebook-inzet-chatbots-messenger

Van Rooij, E. C., Jansen, E. P., & van de Grift, W. J. (2018). First-year university students' academic success: The importance of academic adjustment. *European Journal of Psychology of Education*, 33, 749–767.

vanUden-Kraan, C. F., Drossaert, C. H., Taal, E., Shaw, B. R., Seydel, E. R., & van de Laar, M. A. (2008). Empowering processes and outcomes of participation in online support groups for patients with breast cancer, arthritis, or fibromyalgia. *Qualitative Health Research*, 18(3), 405–417.

Vapiwala, F., & Pandita, D. (2022). Analyzing the Application of Artificial Intelligence for E-Commerce Customer Engagement. In 2022 International Conference on Data Analytics for Business and Industry (ICDABI), pp. 423–427. IEEE. DOI: 10.1109/ICDABI56818.2022.10041655

Varsha, P. S. (Apr. 2023). How can we manage biases in artificial intelligence systems – A systematic literature review. *International Journal of Information Management Data Insights*, 3(1), 100165. 10.1016/j.jjimei.2023.100165

Varsha, J., Himanshu, R., Parvathy, S., & Emmanuel, M. (2023). The prospects and challenges of ChatGPT on marketing research and practices (March 23, 2023). Available at SSRN: https://ssrn.com/abstract=4398033 or 10.2139/ssrn.4398033

Vashishtha, S., Sharma, P., Gupta, M. P., Kumar, M. B., Singh, A., & Ansari, M. F. (2023). Sustainability of start-ups during pandemic: An analytical study in reference of Indian perspective. *Journal of Pharmaceutical Negative Results*, 4001–4008.

Venkataramani, J. R. (1995). Consumer involvement and deception from implied advertising claims. *Journal of Marketing Research*, 23(3), 267–279.

Venkatesh, V., & Davis, F. D. (1996). A model of the antecedents of perceived ease of use: Development and test. *A Journal of the Decision Science Institute*, 27(3), 451–481.

Verbeke, W., Dejaeger, K., Martens, D., Hur, J., & Baesens, B. (Apr. 2012). New insights into churn prediction in the telecommunication sector: A profit driven data mining approach. *European Journal of Operational Research*, 218(1), 211–229. 10.1016/j.ejor.2011.09.031

Verhoef, P. C., Kannan, P. K., & Inman, J. J. (Jun. 2015). From multi-channel retailing to omni-channel retailing. *Journal of Retailing*, 91(2), 174–181. 10.1016/j.jretai.2015.02.005

Verma, S., & Tripathi, S. (2017). Social media, an emerging platform for relationship building: A study of engagement with nongovernment organizations in India. *International Journal of Nonprofit and Voluntary Sector Marketing*, 23(2), 1–11.

Verma, S., Sharma, R., Deb, S., & Maitra, D. (2021). Artificial intelligence in marketing: Systematic review and future research direction. *International Journal of Information Management Data Insights*, 1(1), 255–275. 10.1016/j.jjimei.2020.100002

Villarroel Ordenes, F., & Silipo, R. (2021). Machine learning for marketing on the KNIME Hub: The development of a live repository for marketing applications. *Journal of Business Research*, 137, 393–410. 10.1016/j.jbusres.2021.08.036

Vimal Kumar, M., Sharma, S. K., Singh, J. B., & Dwivedi, Y. K. (2021). Okay Google, what about my privacy?: User's privacy perceptions and acceptance of voice-based digital assistants. *Computers in Human Behavior*, 120, 106763.

Vinodhini, C. G. R. M. Sentiment analysis and opinion mining: a survey.

Viswanadha, S., Sivalenka, K., Jhawar, M. G., & Pudi, V. Dynamic Winner Prediction in Twenty20 Cricket: Based on Relative Team Strengths.

Vlačić, Corbo, L., Silva, S. C. E., & Dabić, M. (May 2021). The evolving role of artificial intelligence in marketing: A review and research agenda. *Journal of Business Research*, 128, 187–203. 10.1016/j.jbusres.2021.01.055

Von Rosen, A. J., von Rosen, F. T., Tinnemann, P., & Müller-Riemenschneider, F. (2017). Sexual health and the internet: Cross-sectional study of online preferences among adolescents. *Journal of Medical Internet Research*, 19(11), e379.

Vrontis, D., Makrides, A., Christofi, M., & Thrassou, A. (2020). Social media influencer marketing: A systematic review, integrative framework and future research agenda. *International Journal of Consumer Studies*, 20(00), 1–28.

Vukolić, M. (2015). The quest for scalable blockchain fabric: Proof-of-work vs. BFT replication. In *International workshop on open problems in network security*. Cham: Springer.

Wach, K., Duong, C. D., Ejdys, J., Kazlauskaitė, R., Korzynski, P., Mazurek, G., Paliszkiewicz, J., & Ziemba, E. (2023). The dark side of generative artificial intelligence: A critical analysis of controversies and risks of ChatGPT. *Entrepreneurial Business and Economics Review*, 11(2), 7–30. 10.15678/EBER.2023.110201

Wacheaux, F. (1996). Méthodes qualitatives et recherche en gestion. *Economica Paris.*

Wæraas, A. (2022). Thematic Analysis: Making Values Emerge from Texts. *Researching values*, 153–170.

Walker, H. R., & Johnson, W. L. (2006). Why consumers use and do not use technology enabled services. *Journal of Services Marketing*, 20(2), 125–135.

Walport, M. G. C. S. A. (2016). Distributed ledger technology: Beyond blockchain. *UK Government Office for Science*.

Wang, W., & Benbasat, I. (2008). Attributions of trust in decision support technologies: A study of recommendation agents for e-commerce. *Journal of Management Information Systems*, 24(4), 249–273.

Wang, L., & Wenyang, C. (2018). Online advertising programmatic buying: Technical thinking and process reengineering. *Today's Mass Media*, 26(12), 100–102.

Wang, S., Cheah, J., & Lim, X. (Mar. 2023). Online shopping cart abandonment: A review and research agenda. *International Journal of Consumer Studies*, 47(2), 453–473. 10.1111/ijcs.12876

Wang, J., Shi, Y., Zhao, C., Venkatesh, V. G., & Chen, W. (2022). Impact of pricing leadership on blockchain data acquisition efforts in a circular supply chain. *International Journal of Production Research*. 10.1080/00207543.2022.2147237

Wang, S., Ye, Y., Ning, B., Cheah, J.-H., & Lim, X.-J. (Jan. 2022). Why do some consumers still prefer in-store shopping? An exploration of online shopping cart abandonment behavior. *Frontiers in Psychology*, 12, 829696. 10.3389/fpsyg.2021.829696

Warren, S. D., & Brandeis, L. D. (Dec. 1890). The right to privacy. *Harvard Law Review*, 4(5), 193. 10.2307/1321160

Warren, C., & McGraw, A. P. (2016). Differentiating what is humorous from what is not. *Journal of Personality and Social Psychology*, 110(3), 407.

Waters, M. R., Aneja, S., & Hong, J. C. (2023). Unlocking the power of CHATGPT, artificial intelligence, and large language models: practical suggestions for radiation oncologists. Practical Radiation Oncology.

Waxer, C. (2016). Get ready for the bot revolution. Computer World. Retrieved from https://www.computerworld.com/article/3126438/emerging-technology/article.html. Accessed on December 9, 2022.

Weingarten, H., Hicks, M., & Kaufman, A. (2018). *Assessing quality in postsecondary education: International perspectives*. Kingston, Ontario, Canada: School of Policy Studies, Queen's University. Retrieved October 19, 2020, from https://www-jstor-org.ezproxy.library.uwa.edu.au/stable/j.ctv8bt1

Weizenbaum, J. (1966). ELIZA—a computer program for the study of natural language communication between man and machine. *Communications of the ACM*, 9(1), 36–45.

Wells, W. D. (1964). EQ, son of EQ, and the reaction profile. *Journal of Marketing*, 28, 45–52.

Weng, S.-S., & Liu, M.-J. (2004). Personalized product recommendation in e-commerce. In *IEEE International Conference on e-Technology, e-Commerce and e-Service, 2004. EEE '04. 2004*, Taipei, Taiwan: IEEE, pp. 413–420. doi: 10.1109/EEE.2004.1287340.

Whang, C. & Im, H. (2018). Does recommendation matter for trusting beliefs and trusting intentions? Focused on different types of recommender system and sponsored recommendation. *International Journal of Retail and Distribution Management*, 46(10), 944–958.

Whitley, S. C., Trudel, R., & Kurt, D. (2018). The influence of purchase motivation on perceived preference uniqueness and assortment size choice. *Journal of Consumer Research*, 45(4), 710–724.

Wilson, D., Tien, G., & Eaves, D. (1995). Increasing the community tenure of mentally disordered offenders: An assertive case management program. *International Journal of Law and Psychiatry*, 18, 61–69.

Wirth, N. (2018). Hello marketing, what can artificial intelligence help you with?. *International Journal of Market Research*, 60(5), 435–438.

Wolohan, J. T. (2020, July). Estimating the effect of COVID-19 on mental health: Linguistic indicators of depression during a global pandemic. In *Proceedings of the 1st Workshop on NLP for COVID-19 at ACL 2020*.

Wongkoblap, A., Vadillo, M. A., & Curcin, V. (2017). Researching mental health disorders in the era of social media: Systematic review. *Journal of Medical Internet Research*, 19(6), e228.

Wongmonta, S. (2021). Marketing 5.0: The era of technology for humanity with a collaboration of humans and machines. *Nimit Mai Review*, 4(1), 1–15.

Wortelboer, M. (2021). Lil Miquela makes me feel uncomfortable, but I keep following her. *An interview study on motivations to engage with virtual influencers on social networking sites, Communication Science*, Master's thesis project Faculty of Behavioural. Management, and Social Sciences.

World Health Organization. (2010). Growing threat from counterfeit medicines. *Bull World Health Organ*, 88(4), 247–248.

World Health Organization. (2022). Mental disorders: A review and comparative analysis of web services. *Information Sciences*, 311, 18–38. https://www.who.int/news-room/fact-sheets/detail/mental-disordersanal

World Health Organization. (2022). Schizophrenia, January 10th, https://www.who.int/news-room/fact-sheets/detail/schizophrenia
Wu, D. *et al.* (Oct. 2018). Budget Constrained Bidding by Model-free Reinforcement Learning in Display Advertising. In *Proceedings of the 27th ACM International Conference on Information and Knowledge Management*, Torino Italy: ACM, pp. 1443–1451. doi: 10.1145/3269206.3271748.
Wu, I.-L., & Chen, J.-L. (2005). An extension of Trust and TAM model with TPB in the initial adoption of on-line tax: An empirical study. *International Journal of Human-Computer Studies*, 62(6), 784–808.
Wu, W. Y., & Ke, C. C. (2015). An online shopping behaviour model integrating personality traits, perceived risk, and technology acceptance. *Social Behaviour and Personality: An International Journal*, 43(1), 85–97.
Xhaferi, B., & Xhaferi, G. (2011). Developing learner autonomy in higher education in Macedonia. *Procedia Social and Behavioral Sciences*, 11, 150–154.
Xiao, & Benbasat (2007). E-commerce product recommendation agents: Use, characteristics, and impact. *MIS Quarterly*, 31(1), 137. 10.2307/25148784
Xiao, L., Saleem, A., Tariq, S. M., Ul Haq, J., Guo, M. (2021). I wish I could be like her/him! How self-congruence stimulates a desire to mimic. *Journal of Theoretical and Applied Electronic Commerce Research*, 16, 3025–3042.
Yang, H., & Zhou, L. (2011). Extending TPB and TAM to mobile viral marketing: An exploratory study on American young consumers' mobile viral marketing attitude, intent and behavior. *Journal of Targeting, Measurement and Analysis for Marketing*, 19(2), 85–98.
Yang, Y., & Siau, K. L. (2018). A qualitative research on marketing and sales in the artificial intelligence age. In: Proceedings of the thirteenth Midwest Association for Information Systems Conference. Saint Louis, Missouri.
Yang, H., & Lee, H. (2019). Understanding user behavior of virtual personal assistant devices. *Information Systems and e-Business Management*, 17, 65–87.
Yang, W., Sun, X., & Du, R. (2015). Learning Depression Patterns from MyPersonality and Reddit.
Yao, H., Chen, J., & Xu, Y. (2020). Patients with mental health disorders in the COVID-19 epidemic. *The Lancet Psychiatry*, 7(4), e21.
Ye, G., Hudders, L., De Jans, S., & De Veirman, M. (2021). The value of influencer marketing for business: A bibliometric analysis and managerial implications. *Journal of Advertising*, 50(2), 160–178.
Yin, M., Li, Q., & Qiao, Z. (2016, August). A study on consumer acceptance of online pharmacies in China. In Proceedings of the 18th Annual International Conference on Electronic Commerce: e-Commerce in Smart connected World (pp. 1–8).
Yoo, C. Y., & Kim, K. (2005). Processing of animation in online banner advertising: The roles of cognitive and emotional responses. *Journal of Interactive Marketing*, 19(4), 18–34.
Yoon, S. J. (2002). The antecedents and consequences of trust in online-purchase decisions. *Journal of Interactive Marketing*, 16(2), 47–63.
Yu, J., Ha, I., Choi, M., & Rho, J. (2005). Extending the TAM for a t-commerce. *Information and Management*, 42(7), 965–976.
Yunsen W. (2018). Designing confidentiality-preserving blockchain-based transaction processing systems. *International Journal of Accounting Information Systems*, 30, 1–18. 10.1016/j.accinf.2018.06.001
Zarouali, B., Van den Broeck, E., Walrave, M., & Poels, K. (2018). Predicting consumer responses to a chatbot on Facebook. *Cyberpsychology Behavior and Social Networking*, 21(8), 491–497.
Zawacki-Richter, O., Marín, V. I., Bond, M., & Gouverneur, F. (2019). Systematic review of research on artificial intelligence applications in higher education–where are the educators? *International Journal of Educational Technology in Higher Education*, 16(1), 1–27.
Zhai, X. (2023). ChatGPT and AI: The Game Changer for Education, 10 pages.

ELECTRONIC REFERENCES

Zhang, X., Wen, D., Liang, J., & Lei, J. (2017). How the public uses social media WeChat to obtain health information in China: A survey study. *BMC Medical Informatics and Decision Making*, 17(2), 71–79.
Zhang, S., Yao, L., Sun, A., & Tay, Y. (Jan. 2020). Deep learning based recommender system: A survey and new perspectives. *ACM Computing Surveys*, 52(1), 1–38. 10.1145/3285029

Zhao, X. *et al.* (May 2021). DEAR: Deep reinforcement learning for online advertising impression in recommender systems. *AAAI*, 35(1), 750–758. 10.1609/aaai.v35i1.16156

Zheng, X., Zhu, S., & Lin, Z. (Dec. 2013). Capturing the essence of word-of-mouth for social commerce: Assessing the quality of online e-commerce reviews by a semi-supervised approach. *Decision Support Systems*, 56, 211–222. 10.1016/j.dss.2013.06.002

Zheng, Z., Xie, S., Dai, H.-N., Chen, X., & Wang, H. (2018). Blockchain challenges and opportunities: A survey. *International Journal of Web and Grid Services*, 14(4), 352–375. 10.1504/IJWGS.2018.095647

Zhu, X., He, Q., & Guo, S. (2018). Application of blockchain technology in supply chain finance. *China's Circulation Economy*, 32(03), 111–119.

Zhu, J., Cao, J., Saxena, D., Jiang, S., & Ferradi, H. (2023). Blockchain-empowered federated learning: Challenges, solutions, and future directions. *ACM Computing Surveys*, 55(11), Article 240, 31 pages. 10.1145/3570953

Zhu, J., Yalamanchi, N., Jin, R., Kenne, D. R., & Phan, N. (2023). Investigating COVID-19's impact on mental health: Trend and thematic analysis of Reddit users' discourse. *Journal of Medical Internet Research*, 25, e46867.

Ziegel, R. (Aug. 2003). The elements of statistical learning. *Technometrics*, 45(3), 267–268. 10.1198/tech.2003.s770

Złotowski, J., Yogeeswaran, K., & Bartneck, C. (2017). Can we control it? Autonomous robots threaten human identity, uniqueness, safety, and resources. *International Journal of Human-Computer Studies*, 100(2), 48–54.

Zouinar, M. (2020). Évolutions de l'Intelligence Artificielle: quels enjeux pour l'activité humaine et la relation Humain-Machine au travail. *Activités*, 17(1), 1–39.

Бєлова, А. (2021). Віртуальні інфлуенсери у мультимодальній рекламі. Вісник ХНУ імені В. Н. Каразіна. *Серія: Іноземна філологія. Методика викладання іноземних мов*, (93), 14–21.

https://www.sciencedirect.com/science/article/pii/S2666603022000136

https://www.datasciencecentral.com/how-artificial-intelligence-has-influenced-consumer-behavior/

https://ieeexplore.ieee.org/abstract/document/9455055

https://linchpinseo.com/how-to-accelerate-your-advertising-with-artificial-intelligence/

https://www.sciencedirect.com/science/article/abs/pii/S0148296323004836

https://www.linkedin.com/pulse/unleashing-power-artificial-intelligence-digital-turning-oyejobi

Index

For Product Safety Concerns and Information please contact our EU
representative GPSR@taylorandfrancis.com
Taylor & Francis Verlag GmbH, Kaufingerstraße 24, 80331 München, Germany

www.ingramcontent.com/pod-product-compliance
Ingram Content Group UK Ltd.
Pitfield, Milton Keynes, MK11 3LW, UK
UKHW052219190926
475702UK00006B/1099

* 9 7 8 1 0 3 2 5 8 5 1 1 6 *